IMPROVING
READING IN
MIDDLE AND
SECONDARY
SCHOOLS

Second Edition

Improving Reading in Middle and Secondary Schools

SELECTED READINGS

Lawrence E. Hafner
Professor of Education
Florida State University
Tallahassee

Macmillan Publishing Co., Inc.
New York

Acknowledgment is made for permission to reprint "Dust of Snow" by Robert Frost, from
The Poetry of Robert Frost edited by Edward Connery Lathem. Copyright 1923, © 1969
by Holt, Rinehart and Winston, Inc. Copyright 1951 by Robert Frost. Reprinted by permission of Holt, Rinehart and Winston, Inc.

"Telling All the Truth" by Emily Dickinson is reprinted by permission of the President
and Fellows of Harvard College and the Trustees of Amherst College from *The Poems of
Emily Dickinson*, edited by Thomas H. Johnson, The Belknap Press of Harvard University
Press, Cambridge, Mass., copyright 1951 and 1955 by the President and Fellows of Harvard College.

Macmillan Publishing Co., Inc.
866 Third Avenue, New York, New York 10022

Collier-Macmillan Canada, Ltd.

Library of Congress Cataloging in Publication Data

Hafner, Lawrence E   comp.
    Improving reading in middle and secondary schools.

    Edition for 1967 published under title: Improving
reading in secondary schools.
    Includes bibliographies.
    1. Reading (Secondary education)—Addresses, essays,
lectures. I. Title.
LB1632.H3 1974   428'.4'071273   73–10569
ISBN 0–02–348680–5

Printing: 3 4 5 6 7 8   Year: 6 7 8 9 0

TO Becky, Katie, Linda, and Charlie and
in appreciation TO A. Sterl Artley

Preface

It becomes increasingly apparent that the successful teacher in the middle and secondary schools is the one who can help his students master the materials of his subject by helping them do a better job of reading. Occasionally a teacher asks why reading should be taught in the secondary schools if the elementary schools have taught reading well. Part of the answer to this question lies in the fact that the elementary schools cannot provide all of the reading-study skills and conceptual background the student will need in the later grades. As one goes through school the reading materials present an increasingly difficult challenge to the reader—concepts are more difficult, the sentences and paragraphs become more involved, more figurative language is used, the topics are broader in scope, and purposes for reading in the various subjects become more varied and demanding. Therefore, the teachers in the middle and secondary schools must continue the guidance in reading instruction begun by the teachers in the elementary schools.

Why does the concept "teacher" imply the role of "teacher of reading skills"? When the student reads, he is thinking, for reading is a thinking process that involves the use of several kinds of reasoning. The teacher's task, and privilege, is to help the student think more effectively about the ideas in reading materials; therefore, the teacher in the secondary school is a teacher of reading. He becomes a good teacher of reading through worthwhile study, training, and experience.

This does not mean that every middle and secondary school teacher need assume the task of providing the basic core of reading instruction as the elementary school teacher does. It does mean that he will learn how to help his students to read better. He should know how to help the students apply to the subject he teaches the general reading skills taught by the developmental reading teacher. And he should know how to teach the specific reading skills that are germane to his subject.

One must remember that implicit in our definition of teaching is the concept of helping students, of stimulating and guiding their efforts to learn. And there is scarcely a better way of guiding their efforts than by helping the students to sharpen their academic tools—their reading and study skills and their attitudes toward and interest in reading.

It is evident, then, that the teacher needs to be well versed in the best literature on the teaching of reading in the secondary schools. The purpose of this book of readings is to make available a sizable number of excellent articles on the important facets of teaching reading in the middle and secondary schools.

To be included in this book, an article had to fall into one or more of the following categories:

1. A research study.
2. A review of research.
3. A critical survey.
4. A unique contribution to the literature.
5. An explanation of a teaching method or a process.
6. A penetrating analysis of a problem area.
7. A report of a worthwhile teaching practice.

Each unit is preceded by an introduction, and each selection is preceded by an introduction and several questions to guide one's reading. The person who reads to answer these questions should gain an understanding of the field not ordinarily obtained through a book of readings.

L. E. H.

Contents

SECTION 1

The Roles of Reading in Modern Life 1

The Uses of Reading and the Need for Reading Instruction 2
LAWRENCE E. HAFNER

Probing Problems in Panels 14
ALBERT NISSMAN

Teaching Literature to Adolescents: Inoculation or Induction? 20
JOHN HURLEY AND JERRY L. SULLIVAN

High School Reading Instruction: Practice Versus Needs 32
ROBERT A. PALMATIER

SECTION 2

A Modern Definition of Reading 39

Psycholinguistics and the Reading Process 40
RICHARD RYSTROM

Reading Is Thinking 52
EMMET A. BETTS

SECTION 3

Developing the Ability to Decode Words 61

Objective-Based Teaching of Word Analysis Skills to Students in Middle and Secondary Schools 62
MARTHA CHEEK

Process and Strategies in Teaching Decoding Skills to Students in Middle and Secondary Schools 76
SARA MORETZ AND BETH DAVEY

SECTION 4
Developing the Ability to Understand, to Interpret, to React Critically, and to Apply Insights Gained Through Reading 103

Improving Comprehension–Interpretation Skills 104
JOSEPH A. FISHER

Sequence in Thoughtful and Critical Reaction to What Is Read 115
ROBERT KARLIN

SECTION 5
The Development of Word Meanings 123

Some Generalizations and Strategies for Guiding Vocabulary Learning 124
A. V. MANZO AND J. K. SHERK

Student-Centered Vocabulary 136
DAVID J. KAHLE

Teaching Essential Reading Skills— Vocabulary 140
EARLE E. CRAWFORD

Word Processing: Explaining and Implementing the Skills 152
NANCY FREDRICK AND BARBARA C. PALMER

SECTION 6
Using Reading in Research-Study Situations 161

Determining Main Ideas: A Basic Study Skill 162
HAYDEN B. JOLLY, JR.

Reading Deficiencies Among Able Pupils 172
IVER L. MOE AND FRANK NANIA

Study Skills for Superior Students in Secondary School 185
FRANCIS P. ROBINSON

Teaching Map Reading Skills in Grade 9 191
PETER L. SANDERS

SECTION 7
Measurement and Evaluation in
Reading 197
*The Middle Half: How Alike Are They,
Really?* 198
KENNETH L. DULIN
*Informal Reading Inventories for the Content
Areas: Science and Mathematics* 204
EDWIN H. SMITH, BILLY M. GUICE, AND
MARTHA C. CHEEK
Problems in the Measurement of Reading 212
JAAP TUINMAN AND W. ELGIT BLANTON

SECTION 8
Reading, Learning, and Human
Development 223
*Recent Research Sources for Middle and
Secondary School Reading Problem Areas* 224
A. J. LOWE
*Reading Readiness at the High-School and
College Levels* 248
NED D. MARKSHEFFEL

SECTION 9
Developing Flexibility: The Ability to
Read for Different Purposes 253
*Utilizing Known Factors to Increase Reading
Speed and Flexibility* 254
W. ROYCE ADAMS
*Transfer Techniques in Reading Improvement
Courses* 265
JOSEPH A. FISHER

SECTION 10
Reading in the Content Areas 275

Vocational Arts
Reading and Industrial Arts; Interview 276
GORDON FUNK
*How to Provide Better Assignments for
Improved Instruction* 285
JOHN W. STRUCK

*Solving Reading Problems in Vocational
Subjects* 290
ISIDORE N. LEVINE

Science and Mathematics

Science Words Students Know 304
DAVID W. KNIGHT AND PAUL BETHUNE

*Vocabulary Development to Improve Reading
and Achievement in Science* 307
RAY F. DECK

*Science Instructional Materials for the
Low-Ability Junior High-School Student* 312
ARNOLD J. MOORE

Reading Analysis in Mathematics 320
ANTHONY C. MAFFEI

*Improving Reading in the Language of
Mathematics* 324
HAROLD H. LERCH

Reading and Mathematics 333
RUSSELL J. CALL AND NEAL A. WIGGIN

English

*An English Department Builds a Meaningful
Reading Program* 346
JUDITH S. BAZEMORE

Teaching Levels of Literary Understanding 350
JOHN SIMMONS

Teaching to Comprehend Literary Texts 355
MORRIS FINDER

*Performance Objectives in Reading and
Responding to Literature* 366
ARNOLD LAZARUS

Social Studies

*Antidote for Apathy—Acquiring Reading Skills
for Social Studies* 374
HELEN HUUS

*Materials for the Unit Plan in Social
Studies* 385
JEAN FAIR

The Problem of Understanding History 390
JOHN R. PALMER

Business Education

*The Reading Problem in Teaching
Bookkeeping* 398
VERNON A. MUSSELMAN

*Teaching Accounting Students How to
Read* 404
L. J. HARRISON

Home Economics
Nutrition, Love, and Language: Keys to
Reading 407
LAWRENCE E. HAFNER AND BILLY GUICE

Foreign Language
Give the Students Tips on How to Get the
Most from Foreign Language Books 420
RALPH C. PRESTON
Teaching Code-Breaking Skills in
Foreign Language 423
ALFRED N. SMITH

SECTION 11
Encouraging Reading Interests and
Tastes 433
What Do Teen-Agers Read? 434
LORRAINE KIRKLAND, WILMA CLOWERS, AND
BETSY WOOD
Games, Games, Games—and Reading
Class 438
LINDA JONES
"Surf's Up"—And So Is Reading Interest 444
SISTER WILLIAM PAUL, O.P.

SECTION 12
Helping Disadvantaged and Reluctant
Readers 447
Teaching the Nonreader to Read 448
LAWRENCE E. HAFNER
Tenth Grade Content—Fourth Grade Reading
Level 462
DORIS E. STINE
Black Studies and Paraprofessionals—A
Prescription for Ailing Reading Programs in
Urban Black Schools 465
RAY C. RIST
Adult Basic Education: Some Spin-off for
Culturally Deprived Youth Education 471
EDWIN H. SMITH

IMPROVING
READING IN
MIDDLE AND
SECONDARY
SCHOOLS

The Roles of Reading in Modern Life

Introduction

Today we are engulfed by reading material. Yet record keeping is a comparatively recent development in the history of man, dating back to 4000–6000 B.C. Alphabetic writing in Western civilization dates to 1400 B.C., its beginnings corresponding to the time when the first books in the Judeo-Christian heritage were written. The development of the printing press about three thousand years later made reading material available in quantity and thus served as a catalytic agent for stimulating the minds of men. Reading and writing have played an important role in the development of Western civilization. Four great ages—the Age of Pericles, the Rise of Christianity, the Renaissance, and the industrial revolution—

stand out as having drawn on and contributed to the resources communicated through reading and writing.

In our day men read to be informed, entertained, enlightened, stimulated, and comforted. But to attain these goals satisfactorily in this fifth great age—the Space Age—it is necessary to process much information through reading, and to process it with a reasonable degree of speed and a high degree of accuracy. If it is important to be a skillful, discriminating, active reader, then the schools must face the challenge of developing this kind of reader; for it is the schools that are charged with the responsibility of teaching the various communication skills, the tools of learning—and earning.

The articles in this unit indicate that reading has a role in promoting academic and personal development; that there is a great need for the schools to help young people improve their reading skills; and that there are specific ways, formal and informal, of helping students to accomplish these goals.

THE USES OF READING AND THE NEED FOR READING INSTRUCTION*

Lawrence E. Hafner

If we were to dichotomize the attitudes of people toward reading, we could say there is one group of people that always seems to be running away from books. Educators and laymen alike are concerned about whether more students can be helped to develop greater interest as well as increased competence in reading.

The author of this article explores vital problems in order to establish firmly the value of reading and the need for reading instruction in our schools.

1. What is involved in developing true reading maturity?
2. How is the improvement of reading proficiency related to improvement of the individual?
3. What problems arise in the attempt to use literature therapeutically?
4. How does Spranger's theory of values help you gain perspective regarding the motivational forces in the lives of individuals?
5. How serious is the need for improved reading instruction?

USES OF READING

Ink flows. Typewriters click. Linotypes clack. Computers whirr. The presses roll . . . and roll . . . and roll . . . on and on. Homes, schools, libraries, and shops are flooded with reading matter. And people read these

* Written especially for this volume.

materials for different purposes and to satisfy different drives. On the one hand, we see a Thomas Wolfe who voraciously consumes book after book in the library stacks because of an insatiable desire for knowledge. On the other hand, we see an "Uncle Charlie" who would not be seen in a library under any circumstances and whose attitude toward books ranges from utter disdain to mild contempt.

Somewhere in-between the Thomas Wolfes and the Uncle Charlies we find countless individuals who are doing quite a bit of reading for rather admirable purposes. As we look a little closer at what these individuals are reading, we notice they are reading for some rather basic purposes. They are reading in an attempt to solve problems, to gain scholastic success, to become better informed, to earn a living, and to entertain themselves. Let us investigate these basic purposes more closely.

Solving Problems in the World

It is an obvious fact that there are many problems in the world. Not only does printed material bring us news of today's problems, but it also recounts the problems of the ages and the ideas which have been offered as solutions to these problems. At least a partial solution to these problems may be obtained by gleaning clues from history, from the way similar problems have been handled in other times.

If problems can be solved through reading, it should be possible to improve problem-solving through improving reading proficiency. It is not to be thought that this reading proficiency is a mere intellectual process devoid of emotional factors. Developing true reading maturity involves the development of appropriate values, attitudes, and feelings, for these factors guide and motivate the application of ideas gained through the interpretation of reading material, as well as the intepretation itself. Before getting into the more philosophical aspects of solving problems through reading, let us discuss some more of the common uses of reading.

Reading and Scholastic Success

Our elementary schools, high schools, and colleges are reading schools. Fay[1] shows that achievement in general reading comprehension, and in several important specific reading skills, is highly related to achievement in social studies and science in grade six. The correlations between reading achievement and marks in college vary from low, .10, to high, .60. A great problem, and challenge, lies in the fact that roughly 35 to 50 per cent of high-school students are not reading as well as their general ability indicates they should. Another challenge is found in the fact that reading skills are involved in 80 to 90 per cent of college work, yet approximately 25 per cent of college freshmen lack the reading skills to do their work success-

[1] Leo C. Fay, "The Relationship Between Specific Reading Skills and Selected Areas of Sixth-Grade Achievement," *Journal of Educational Psychology*, 43 (March 1950), 544.

fully.[2] Fortunately many of these individuals can be salvaged through special instruction in the reading study skills.[3,4]

Building a Background of Experience

Not all one's ideas and experiences are gained directly; many are gained indirectly. These indirect experiences gained through avenues such as reading, movies, and television are called vicarious experiences. We retain an organized trace or residue of experiences in the form of concepts, facts, and generalizations, and words are "counters" of those experiences. Without going into qualifying detail, one can say that one's vocabulary reflects his experiences and how he is able to profit from these experiences. The information that one gains from reading a given piece of material can be used to enrich one's understanding and enjoyment of similar topics in other reading materials.

Reading and Earning a Living

Any occupation requiring a college education requires one to read to prepare for the occupation. As working members of these professions, individuals depend on reading in the day-to-day exercise of their duties and in keeping up with developments in their fields: a city manager reads contracts, bulletins, proposals, books, and journals; a person in the medical profession reads case histories, charts, texts, scientific journals, and monographs; an agricultural specialist reads bulletins, building specifications, books, graphs, charts, experimental research reports, and project reports.

Studies by Dael Wolfle[5] show the variations in average mental ability among graduate and professional students specializing in different fields. Average AGCT scores range from a low of 114 for one student group to 133 for the highest group, psychology graduate students. Because of the high correlation between group intelligence tests and group reading tests, one can infer differences in reading achievement among various occupations from the above data. However, it is possible to cite an actual example of differences in reading achievement that exist among professions.

The Ohio State Psychological Examination is a test heavily loaded with the reading factor. Three sources provide us with information to show us differences in average OSPE scores among several professional groups and scores of comparison groups of college freshmen and college graduates.

[2] Ruth Strang, Constance M. McCullough, and Arthur E. Traxler, *The Improvement of Reading* (New York: McGraw-Hill Book Company, Inc., 1961), p. 27.

[3] Mildred B. Smith and Carl I. Brache, "When School and Home Focus on Achievement," *Educational Leadership*, 20 (February 1963), 314–318.

[4] Albert J. Kingston and Clay E. George, "The Effectiveness of Reading Training at the College Level," *Journal of Educational Research*, 68 (February 1955), 467–471.

[5] Dael L. Wolfle, *America's Resources of Specialized Talent* (New York: Harper and Brothers, 1954), p. 200.

AVERAGE
OSPE SCORE

College freshmen*	75
Male photographers (metro. newspaper) †	84.2
Master's degree candidates in education‡	98
College graduates*	108
Small city newspapermen*	115
Copyreaders (metropolitan) †	115.4
Editors, editorial writers, and reporters†	124.2
Master's degree candidates in psychology‡	125
Doctoral degree candidates in psychology‡	133

* Robert L. Jones and Charles E. Swanson, "Small-City Daily Newspapermen: Their Abilities and Interests." *Journalism Quarterly*, 31 (Winter 1954), 42.
† Harold C. Stone, "An Objective Personnel Study of Metropolitan Newspapermen." *Journalism Quarterly*, 30 (Fall 1953), 451.
‡ Unpublished data from a state university.

Sheer Joy of Reading

Another important use of reading is reading for sheer pleasure. The young child reads for pleasure stories such as *Mike Mulligan, Are You My Mother?, Charlotte's Web, Homer Price*, or any one of countless stories which can be obtained from the library, the bookstore, or the supermarket.

As people get older it becomes difficult to dichotomize their reading into job-related reading versus reading for pleasure. Perhaps such dichotomies arise in some quarters when a scientific monograph or statistical report is contrasted with a "who-done-it?" Other individuals, fortunately, can use information gained in some of the "sheer joy" reading in their professional work: the historian, the psychologist, the reading specialist, the theologian, the professional writer. Perhaps their "nonsheer joy" material would be the income tax forms and routine administrative report forms.

A given piece of reading material, then, cannot be neatly categorized. One person will perceive, value, and use the material in one way, and another person in another way.

Among people there is evidently a continuum of pleasure for reading. At one end of the continuum is the individual who detests all reading material and reads nothing with joy. At the other end is the person who likes to read everything, and who can find something satisfying and enjoyable in any kind of reading material. The latter person more likely will approximate the Renaissance ideal of the "universal man" or pansophist. He also is the person who will score in the 170's and 180's on Terman's *Concept Mastery Test*, whereas the person who reads little will be fortunate if he does not obtain a negative score.

Solving Problems Through Reading

Already in Old Testament times a sage remarked, "Of the making of books there is no end." Many of the books that have appeared in the last thirty-two centuries have offered advice to people or solutions to their problems. The person who made the remark about the making of books also provided us with several books full of advice—Proverbs, Ecclesiastes, and the Song of Solomon. Many sages since Solomon's time have taken up the stylus, the quill, or the ball-point pen to set down their words of wisdom and their solutions to problems. Yet these various solutions probably do not have equal validity.

If a man is to survive and flourish, he must use the collected wisdom of the past to solve problems, to come to grips with moral and philosophic issues. He must go beyond everyday experience. He must read, study, discuss, and reflect on many writings—newspapers, quality magazines, religious writings, biographies, dramas, books, and novels.

Implicit in the foregoing discussion is the idea that for almost every problem that faces an individual—a school-age child or an adult—there is a solution or partial solution in some piece of literature. Literature, then, has a role in personal development. By literature we do not mean a number of stories, poems, and essays written by a few quaint people, but the entire range of writings of able men and women of various times. When one reads how another person solved a problem similar to his own, he has the advantage of being detached from the actual event while still identifying with the problem and being able to enter into the situation vicariously. In this way he can then analyze and solve his own problem. Literature is therefore a potential force for enlightening the individual, for enriching his life, and for aiding him in building confidence. This writer does not share the euphoric dreams of the social engineers who feel confident they can manipulate and improve large segments of the world's population. Certain individuals can be affected. We must show the individual the better way through precept and example and hope that free, responsible individuals will continue the tradition.

The British bibliophile Sir William Haley[6] provides us with an extraordinary example of one individual's use of reading. He used reading as an aid in stress and believed that a well-chosen book can help restore one's balance and perspective. He sometimes read a book early in the morning so he could see a little clearer during the day what things really mattered. Sir William felt that to succeed at this role a book must: (1) look at life from a *higher vantage point;*(2) deal with *enduring issues;* and (3) have a *moral standpoint.*

---

[6] Sir William Haley, *A Smallholding on Parnassus* (London: Cambridge University Press, 1954), p. 17.

Developing a Philosophy of Life

Everyone lives by some set of values—those things we consider important that guide our actions and serve as motivators of behavior.

E. Spranger, in his book *Lebensformer*,[7] discusses six basic values. In each person one of these values operates as a dominant motive. The six types of persons corresponding to these value systems are (1) the theoretical; (2) the esthetic; (3) the economic; (4) the political; (5) the social; (6) the religious.

Commins and Fagin[8] discuss these types of persons and show the roles each type takes in educational circles. The *theoretical* person's highest value is truth or knowledge. He believes that ignorance is the greatest evil of society, and the chief remedy is "education which stresses information, facts, intellectual understanding of principles." "In education, the theoretical person is more often found in college teaching, particularly in the sciences." To the *esthetic* person beauty, harmony, and elegance of form and color are the most significant values. He evaluates people by their taste and degree of refinement and has much interest in artistic, literary, and musical experiences.

The *economic* person values and is motivated by efficiency and economic well-being. He often appears among members of school boards and sometimes in the ranks of teachers. For him education must pay off in economic betterment. As a teacher, he emphasizes the utilitarian value of school subjects and methods of teaching.

The *political* person is fond of discipline, order, and control. In educational circles these people range from the excellent administrator to the common martinet.

The *social* person stresses kindness and warmth in human relations. He evaluates people according to the degree of kindness they exhibit to others. Generally teachers are of this type; particularly the elementary teacher who strives to meet the needs of children, even at the cost of personal sacrifice.

The *religious* type of person, according to Commins' interpretation of Spranger, seeks to integrate "all values into a meaningful scheme or philosophy" and "all experience into a comprehensive framework." As a teacher, he would "stress character education through inculcation of moral and religious values."

Spranger assumed that no person is motivated exclusively by one kind of value. These values are considered to be equal in worth unless the religious or philosphical value that seeks integration of the values might be considered the best.

A little exercise that causes a person to reflect on his values is to ask him

[7] E. Spranger, *Lebensformer* (Halle: Niemeyer, 1927).

[8] W. D. Commins and Barry Fagin, *Principles of Educational Psychology*, 2nd ed. (New York: The Ronald Press Co., 1954), pp. 578–580.

if he would like to sit down for fifteen minutes and commit to paper the values by which he guides his life and then have them published in the local newspaper. Do you know your values? Can you verbalize them? How did you come by them? Some serious questions a person may ask himself in order to help him reflect on his value system are: Who am I? Where did I come from? What is my purpose on this planet? What is my eventual destiny?

As a teacher or parent, one expects to guide or at least influence the destiny of others. Should one expect a person to guide others until he has answered such questions as these?

One's philosophy of life develops gradually over a period of years and many factors, including those over which the individual has little control, are involved in its development: temperament, intelligence, family values, real and vicarious experiences, religion, reward systems, etc. No matter how excellent one's philosophy or value system is, upgrading is in order and reading has a role to play in this improvement process.

Spache[9] has emphasized that "bibliotherapy, or the modification of habits and attitudes through reading, does not occur as a spontaneous result of reading." Also, if one is to implement by action the two mechanisms of identification and insight which are involved in bibliotherapy, careful nurture and guidance are necessary.

There are many personality needs which need to be met, and emotional maladjustments for which therapy is in order. Smith and Dechant[10] list books of potential therapeutic value under five broad categories of problem areas. Illustrative of the specific titles of books considered to have therapeutic value for children with emotional conflicts are Beirn's *Time for Gym* (jealousy and resentment); Cavanna's *Going on Sixteen* (shyness and loneliness); and Schneider's *While Susie Sleeps* (fear).

Teachers in parochial elementary schools may wish to explore books and stories with a spiritual message and tone such as the following: Sellew's *Adventures with Abraham's Children*, K. Phillips' *Gift from a Stranger*, H. Van Laar's *Joel and the Silver Trumpet*, and A. P. Wright's *The Little Shepherd*.

High-school students have an opportunity to upgrade their attitudes by steeping themselves in the writings and/or biographies of great people such as Paul, Charlemagne, St. Francis of Assisi, Luther, Whittier, Lincoln, Anne Lindbergh, Eleanor Roosevelt, Charles Kettering, Helen Keller, and Robert Frost.

College students should profit from the works of such stimulating thinkers as Plato, Aquinas, Roger Bacon, Montaigne, Calvin, Loyola, Berkeley, Pascal, Kant, de Tocqueville, Kierkegaard, Gladstone, Dostoyevski, and

---

[9] George D. Spache, *Toward Better Reading* (Champaign, Ill.: Garrard Publishing Company, 1963), p. 160.

[10] Henry P. Smith and Emerald V. Dechant, *Psychology in Teaching Reading* (Englewood Cliffs, N.J.: Prentice-Hall, Inc., 1961,) pp. 316–320.

modern thinkers such as Nicholas Berdyaev, Joseph Wood Krutch, Russell Kirk, Roscoe Pound, Albert Schweitzer, Jawaharlal Nehru, Walter Lippmann, Jacques Maritain, Martin Niemoeller, Thomas Molnar, and John F. Kennedy.

In Albert Schweitzer we have the personification of Spranger's *religious* type and his *social* type. Schweitzer exemplified the religious type as he sought to integrate "all values into a meaningful scheme," as illustrated by his academic interests and by his volume, *The Philosophy of Civilization.* He was the epitome of the social type who stresses kindness and warmth in human relations as he devoted many years of his long life to service and compassion for his fellow men.

Schweitzer evolved this philosophy of commitment during long years of reflection on his own experiences and on ideas that he had read, and then he put them into practice as a missionary-doctor in Africa. In a special article[11] written shortly before his death, he shows how such ideas as his "reverence for life" evolved and how the latter idea can, through education, take root in people's lives:

During a short stay in Europe in 1951, I was visited by the dean of a big school in Hanover. She came to tell me that reverence for life was being taught in her school. The children, she said, showed a great understanding of it and tried to apply it in their own attitudes and behavior. Under the influence of this teaching, she said, a great spiritual change had taken place in their lives.

I kept in touch with the head of that school. During a later trip to Europe, I visited the school and took the opportunity to talk with the children. They had shed all childishness. Their awareness of the meaning of my philosophy of kindness toward all creatures had made them at once serious and gay. Today, many schools throughout the world are teaching reverence for life.

Maintaining a Proper Balance of Tension and Confidence

Foster McMurray[12] has shown that although the ideally uneducated, simple man and the ideally intelligent man could face the world with complete confidence, actual man must live in a mixture of confidence and tension. He must learn and continue to learn. The primary purpose for learning intellectual, nonutilitarian living is to maintain life in a proper balance of tension and confidence.

Although, generally, the more a person learns, the more we might expect him to be confident, it works out, in fact, that the complex mentality will see more reasons for being tense in a given world situation or crisis. The function of intellectual instruction, then, is to keep a high and expanding level of confidence and tension. The school can help modify confidence through the intellectual instruments it helps children acquire in school. The types of confidence are:

[11] Reproduced from *The World Book Year Book* with permission. Copyright © 1964 by Field Enterprises Educational Corporation. All rights reserved.
[12] Lecture notes, Dr. Foster McMurray, University of Illinois, Spring 1958.

1. Confidence of *location*.
2. Confidence of *command*.
3. Confidence of *opportunity*.

McMurray shows how these important types of confidence can be acquired by the intellectual instruments one acquires through survey knowledge and literary knowledge.

To have confidence of *location*, confidence that one is abreast of the world, one needs a literary understanding of the things that are transforming the world. For instance, teacher and student will make use of excellent survey accounts in materials such as *Reader's Digest, Science Digest,* and *U.S. News and World Report*.

Man needs confidence of *command*—what he can't do for himself he gets someone else to do for him, if it is important. We can teach people how to do this through literary knowledge.

A man who has confidence of *opportunity* is more likely to feel that he is doing the type of work best suited to his inclinations and ability, if he has had real opportunity to develop his capabilities, explore his capabilities, and learn what interests him. Survey knowledge and literary knowledge will provide students with the needed opportunity to sample—a sampling based on correct information, and reading is the key to this survey knowledge and literary knowledge.

Unique Values of Reading

Modern communication media such as radio and television are highly regarded in education circles. However, in comparison with such forms of communication media, reading has the following unique values or uses:

1. Reading material is readily accessible.
2. Reader can react as an individual.
3. Reading allows time for reflection.
4. Information is easily rechecked.
5. Memories can be renewed.
6. One can select segments of material he wants.
7. Sources can be compared readily.
8. One can readily skim a wide range of material.
9. One can check on the credentials of the author.
10. Reading provides excellent contexts for concept development and vocabulary study.

NEED FOR READING INSTRUCTION

One can hardly dispute the fact that reading has many vital uses. Nor can anyone who has enjoyed some success as a reader forget the stimulation and the pleasure that reading can give. But how does one learn to practice this magic? How does one learn to read?

Few individuals teach themselves to read—most are taught to read by someone else. But even among people of similar ability we find varying degrees of reading proficiency. Large numbers of students in our schools are reading as well as capacity measures indicate they should. But many students do not read up to capacity, and are not able to solve their problems through reading. Neither do they obtain much pleasure from reading. For these students excellent reading instruction is in order. In fact it is desperately necessary.

But let us switch from these hortatory remarks to some indisputable evidence of the need for reading instruction.

Need for Readiness Instruction

Robinson[13] has discussed the need to instruct children at the beginning reading level rather than just to wait for readiness to develop:

It is clear, then, that we cannot wait for years of living to bring readiness for beginning reading. Instead, good teachers hasten children's progress in all aspects of readiness through well-planned programs to meet the specific needs of large and small groups and of individuals within the group.

The Kentucky Reading Study

Ramsey[14] studied the reading achievement of Kentucky children at the fourth-grade and eighth-grade levels. Evidence indicated that although the fourth-grade children were reading satisfactorily compared to national norms, there was a substantial lag among the eighth-graders studied.

He points out that "for the immediate future there is a need for concentrated effort to give reading instruction in the junior and senior high schools of the state."

New York City Survey

A survey in the city of New York to determine reading achievement of freshmen and sophomore high school students compared with their mental ability revealed that 15.6 percent of the students were reading at least one year above expectancy, 42.1 per cent were achieving commensurate with their ability, while 42.3 per cent were reading below expectancy.[15]

We are alarmed when we read how so many young people are failing to use their talents fully. It is apparent that the need for reading instruction in situations such as this is marked.

In this article, only representative studies have been selected to show the gap that exists between potential to achieve and actual reading achievement.

---

[13] Helen M. Robinson, "Development of Reading Skills," *Elementary School Journal*, 58 (February 1958), 269–274.

[14] Wallace Ramsey, "The Kentucky Reading Study," *The Reading Teacher*, 16 (December 1962), 178–181.

[15] Bernard E. Donovan, *Survey of Abilities of Pupils Entering the Academic High Schools in September 1955* (New York: New York Board of Education, 1955), p. 3.

These studies alone would be enough to show the need for reading instruction. However, aspects of the problem will be explored to adduce further proof of the need for the comprehensive instruction needed to develop the good reader-citizen and mature reader.

Characteristics of Poor Readers

From elementary school through college two characteristic reading problems of poor readers are their inability to succeed in the higher level interpretation skills, and their inability to remember what they read.

These reading weaknesses often result in or are accompanied by poor attitudes toward reading, poor grades in school, vocational problems, compensating defense mechanisms, dropping out of school, feelings of failure, and a self-concept that eventually relegates reading and intellectual endeavor dependent upon reading to a low place in the hierarchy of values of such poor readers.

My Brother's Keeper

Many of the pupils in our schools are caught up in a web of reading failure. This failure and its concomitant problems of school failure and self-concept depreciation often can be alleviated to the extent that reading problems are cleared up. The well-trained, conscientious teacher can help clear up those problems—or perhaps *George* will do it; after all, am *I* my brother's keeper?

"George will not do it" and "you *are* your brother's keeper!" The idea of taking a child when he is ready and teaching him the necessary skills and attitudes to succeed in academic life is so axiomatic as a generalization that we tend to verbalize the phrase and to forget about its implementation in the real-life, concrete school situation with John Doe, Jr.

Pupils will not unlock the many doors of opportunity if they do not read well. The teacher represents the last opportunity for many of these pupils to learn to read well. What an opportunity and responsibility! The teacher must give his pupils *direct instruction* in reading if they are going to master the various skills and attitudes which they need to (1) earn a living; (2) be thoughtful, critical citizens; and (3) lead a full, interesting, and useful life!

Improving Citizenship

As we explore the need for reading instruction to help improve citizenship, we learn that reading is a complex process, that there are many mysterious facets to this process, and that there are probably fewer mature readers than we would like.

It has been said that the skillful, mature reader reads the lines (comprehends), reads between the lines (interprets), and reads beyond the lines (reacts to and applies ideas).

There is a positive relationship between intelligence and reading ability, and highly intelligent individuals are often quite sensitive to ethical and moral problems. However, we ask these questions: Does measured intelligence govern citizenship? Are we fighting a losing battle in our attempt to improve the individual through making him a better reader?

Many valuable citizenship practices don't require high intelligence. We get some insight into the complexity and mystery of reading if we thoughtfully reflect on this enigma: High intelligence is no guarantee that a person will fully read (react to and apply ideas) such apparently simple signs as STOP and QUIET; and stopping at stop signs and obeying quiet signs are two important social practices. If the present reader should think that reading is a simple process, he might explain why some people do not fully read (react to and apply, i.e., obey) simply worded traffic signs such as: CITY SPEED LIMITS 35 MPH!

There are various ways of being a good citizen and a mature reader. Surely the person of 130 I.Q. who elaborates on the qualification of a candidate for political office serves a useful function as a citizen. So does the person, say of "lesser" intellect, who strives to obey the traffic laws at all times instead of trying to impress someone with the quite-questionable reflected glory of his engine-powered vehicle as he drag-races down the street. His recognition should not be at the expense of the life of a fellow human being. Some people who seek glory through acceleration, reckless driving, and uncontrolled horsepower "read" the newspaper accounts but do not *fully* read them. Other people do not even bother to read the newspaper. They live outside the reading world.

It is tragic, but some people in the middle schools and the high schools *cannot read.* Just think! The teacher who opens up the world of print to these people, and who teaches for reading maturity among those who can already attain literal comprehension, will give such individuals another chance to read, to learn, and to change their attitudes. Beneficial changes in attitudes resulting from increased maturity in reading are worth the effort required on the part of the teacher. And such teaching stems from the highest type of dedication and hard work—work that requires ingenuity and energy.

Through effective teaching of reading from elementary school through the college years we teachers can help individuals gain insights, improve attitudes, and function more adequately—in short, be mature readers. Surely such goals are worthy and attainable. As we contemplate the foregoing thoughts let these words of Horace Mann ring in our ears: "Be ashamed to die until you have won some victory for humanity."

Probing Problems in Panels*
Albert Nissman

Getting students to approach good literature positively, to interpret it well, and to develop insights that can be applied to solving problems and enriching lives is a difficult and elusive task. In the experiment reported in this article, Nissman provides a comprehensive model for attaining these goals. He also explains the dynamics of his adventure, and an evaluation of the experiment's effectiveness.

1. What learning principles did the author employ in his experiment?

2. What was the purpose of the experiment?

3. How can you overcome objectively the doubts you may have regarding the efficacy of this plan in your school situation? Do you owe it to your students to try?

4. How might you adapt this plan to your situation?

There were methods in my madness and goals in my grouping. This was my approach as I explained it to my ninth-grade class (1). The results of our panel activity and its evaluations eventually verified my belief in its efficacy and justified the procedures.

The units for the entire year I had already devised. During the first eighteen weeks we had studied the following units (2):

The Individual and His Immediate Environment.
The Individual and His Physical Environment.
The Individual and His Technological Environment.

The units were composed of many activities, resources, instructional aids, and procedures. But one thing was a constant: a reading list for each of the units which included fiction and non-fiction that dealt with the unit themes. And from these lists, the youngsters were to choose four books for each unit about which they were to write book reports according to my specifications (see Book Report form illustrated).

Thus I could plot the progress of each individual's understanding of the human problems inherent in the books and units. But it was obvious that much of the value would never be realized unless a well organized group discussion was employed.

* FROM the *Journal of Developmental Reading* (Winter 1961), pp. 139–144, reprinted with permission of Albert Nissman and the International Reading Association.

BOOK REPORT

Name ——————— Section ———

Date ——————— Mark ———

I. Bibliographical Information (after this model: Marquand, John P. *Sincerely, Willis Wayde*. Boston: Little, Brown and Co., 1954).

II. Biographical notes about author.

III. Type of Literature.

IV. Main Characters (brief descriptions).
1.
2.
3.

V. Minor Characters (brief descriptions).
1.
2.
3.

VI. Main Ideas of Book.
1. What problems was this book concerned with?
   a. Personal
   b. Family
   c. Social, moral, civic
   d. Physical and emotional
   e. Technological and economic
   f. National and global
2. How did the main character(s) solve the problems?
3. How would you have solved the problems?
4. Has this book modified any of your ideas, attitudes and behavior? How? Why?

VII. What was your reaction to this book?
1. Style of writing
2. Characterization
3. Plotting of story
4. Statement of problem
5. Character's philosophy of life or
6. Author's philosophy of life

It was then that I decided to clarify and reformulate my purposes of instruction. Such purposes need not be profound; they must only be clear.

The pupils were asked to survey the lists of books each had read during the three units. They were to think of these books in terms of the satisfaction, enjoyment, and enlightenment they had afforded. Then they were asked to list in order the three books that they would enjoy discussing in a panel.

These lists were collected and we began to discuss the format of a panel discussion, the duties of the moderator and of the panelists, and the purposes of such a discussion. When we came to a lull, we decided to consult our language textbook. By employing a variety of reading skills, we scanned the index and the table of contents, hunting down all additional information on the subject of panel discussions.

Thus I listed the goals and explained them to my class.

1. To stimulate wide reading within a given unit.
2. To challenge the pupils to do some real thinking and probing about the reading.
3. To probe the similarities in themes, problems, styles, plotting and character.
4. To probe the differences in themes, problems, styles, **plotting and** character.

5. To generalize and conclude, to form concepts in capsule form that might help them in settling the affairs of their own lives.

While the pupils were browsing, I played a purposeful "solitaire" and placed the youngsters in groups on the basis of their choices of three books. Additional criteria for this grouping were similarity in thematic content, structure, purpose of the writing. These similarities were not always apparent on the surface and would, therefore, demand thorough discussion within the small groups. This factor also determined the ultimate structure of the panels.

This, then, was primarily a grouping which was based on book titles. Below the groups are listed as they were formed (3).

Group 1

My Lord, What a Morn
Cheaper by the Dozen
Lost Horizon
Fear Strikes Out
Huckleberry Finn
Tom Sawyer

Group 2

Pasteur: Knight of the Laboratory
Albert Einstein
Invisible Men

Group 3

Clay Fingers
The Child Who Never Grew
Lost Horizon
The Red Badge of Courage
The Citadel
Rise and Walk
Our Town
Of Human Bondage
Scarlet Letter

Group 4

Diary of a Young Girl
Sayonara
Jane Eyre
With a High Heart

Group 5

The Nun's Story
Arrowsmith
My Antonia
The Silver Pencil
The Human Comedy
Four Young Teachers

Group 6

Pleasant Valley
The Big Wave
Volcano
Kon-Tiki
Hiroshima

Even a cursory glance at these lists will show the reader that quite a spread of good books, fiction and non-fiction, was represented. And the concepts and the tangents that the panel discussions led to were legion. Among the principal ideas were problems of family life, idealism, problems of the scientists, professional jealousy, finding a niche in the world, professions dedicated to serving humanity, bigotry and persecution, and scientific developments and their effects on humanity. It was illuminating and profitable to listen to young teen-agers discuss these many somber aspects of life.

Just before the pupils became involved in the small group work, I reminded them that a phase of *grouping* is *groping*. But eventually the haze would lift and out of the murky confusion enlightenment and learning would arise. The latter, however, would only happen with dedication and efficiency in group work. Therefore, at the end of each of the four meeting periods their group outlines were to be turned in. Each group outline or progress report contained the following:

1. Names of the committee members.
2. Date of session.
3. Problem areas discussed.
4. Method of research and investigation.
5. Sources of research and investigation.
6. Time still needed for research.
7. Methods of presentation.
8. Time needed for presentation.
9. Subject matter content (highlights of information).

The four-division system of evaluation was arranged at this time, too. *Class evaluation* involved the participation of all the pupils in the class. Various pupils and I contributed comments on the group's presentation in terms of procedure and content. Then the group was asked to leave the room so that the rest of the class could openly vote on a letter grade which they deemed a just reward for their peers. And to the skeptics may I say that "A" was *not* the only grade given.

The second division was *group evaluation*. Here, each group member assessed every other group member's contribution to the group's effectiveness. Let me inject here that this was more than a popularity poll. These youngsters could spot immediately the morale builders, the efficient workers, the glib talkers, and the "goof-offs."

The third division in this process of evaluation was *self-evaluation*. While no youngster ever failed himself, it was significant to note that some rated themselves with an "E." Whether they did so because of conscience pangs or because they knew that I knew what they were actually doing in the group, I can not determine with certainty. But the process, I feel, made them take a good introspective look.

The last division involved *teacher evaluation* of the individuals as effective group members. Although each of the four evaluations carried equal weight, the teacher evaluation was done last at the insistence of the class. They felt that any other position would unduly influence the other three judgments. For this reason, where possible, I saved my own criticism for last, too.

Among the criteria we used in all of the evaluations were *leadership, in-*

formation, reasoning, opinion, attitude, and speaking skill (4). In addition we looked for adaptability and originality. We estimated the success with which each group accomplished its stated purposes as listed on the progress reports. And finally, we asked whether the group communicated with us and in turn stimulated discussion.

As we attempt to evaluate the entire project, we can see an interesting instructional panorama. In this panorama we note concepts of considerable breadth and depth: ideas such as "All men have problems which must be solved or ignored," or "Man must learn to control the forces of nature or be overcome by them," or "Man needs a salable skill in this technological age." These and dozens more were discussed and argued. And in the end, I believe, the youngsters learned that such concepts, conclusions, generalizations, social understandings—call them what you will—are not absolute. They are relative. They can be modified. There are exceptions. There are extenuating circumstances. Life, in short, is not a rhythmical pattern with perfect symmetry. These understandings, too, were part of their instruction.

The crux of evaluating such instructional activity lies in the question, "Is such an activity with its methods valid and are the results purposeful?" My answer is a resounding YES. And I base my confident answer on direct quotations written by the youngsters anonymously on 3 x 5 cards:

"I enjoyed hearing the short summaries of the books. The discussions have encouraged me to want to read the books."

"I think that this type of work and presentation is very enjoyable and educational. I feel that the job of discovering the likenesses of certain books is a very difficult job, but all of the groups did a good job."

"It was actually fun finding out the linking parts of the book and putting them together to form panel discussions."

"I think that the unit was well worth while. It brought together many different books with similar problems."

"I would like to work on more committees of this sort."

"I think that the time was well spent." (This refers to four periods of 42 minutes of group work and six double periods of 84 minutes each, one double for each of the panel presentations.)

"I've also gotten interested in books to read. It was a clever way to bring most of the books into light. It also was a good way to stimulate the imagination."

"I like this idea of a panel discussing books which have a similar theme. I learned a lot from just discussing with our group and more from hearing other committee reports. I think I would like to present it in this fashion again."

"It adds to your knowledge of the books that you have read, and gets you interested in the books you haven't read."

"I think the unit was refreshing in its informal air and in the oral work rather than the written work. The marking system I liked very much."

"I enjoyed searching out the problems and methods of presentation."

Of course, not all the comments were glowing tributes. Most were sincerely favorable as quoted above. A goodly number were moderate, and a few, like those quoted below, were rather negative.

"I think skits hold more interest than these 'hit or miss' discussions. But, I do highly approve of committee work as a whole and learn more from it, than from individual research."

"I think that in some committees certain persons tried to dominate the whole report."

"I don't particularly care for committee work. Too many people do nothing, piling all the responsibility on one person. It isn't entirely fair."

All comments, the favorable and the negative, are most valuable in aiding teachers to determine the effectiveness of their instructional programs. And who can really be the best judge of the efficacy of instruction? Is it not the pupils who are subjected to this instruction, and does not anonymity assure a greater degree of honesty in the expression of opinion?

I must then conclude, on the basis of my personal experience in my own classroom, that probing problems in panels is justifiable, valid, and purposeful. Of course, it need not be limited to books, or to stimulation of reading, or to the sending of pupils scurrying out to read more and better books.

It can be used in many instructional settings and new situations. It can be based on any facet of learning—the sciences, the arts, and real life situations. It can endure many mutations and adaptations.

One underlying principle serves, however, as a pillar for this activity as it does with most human endeavors: it is most effective when youngsters cooperate to achieve understanding of problems which they have agreed are worthy of serious study.

REFERENCES

1. Fifteen boys and 14 girls on the junior-senior high reading levels with an I.Q. range of 113–138 in a class of English and social studies.
2. Taken from Robert G. Carlsen and Richard S. Alm, *Social Understandings Through Literature*. Washington, D.C.: National Council for the Social Studies, 1954, p. vii.
3. Some youngsters discussed more than one book.
4. As listed and defined on the *Discussion Group Evaluation Form*. Chicago, Illinois: Blue Cross Commission.

TEACHING LITERATURE TO ADOLESCENTS:
INOCULATION OR INDUCTION?*

John Hurley and Jerry L. Sullivan

Frost says that "criticism is the province of age, not youth," and that youth should live rather than analyze its enjoyments. Yet in recent years we have seen youth devoted to experiencing life while analyzing the life patterns of their elders. Can youth analyze such real-life complexities now if they are not experienced enough to read literature critically?

1. Please state the heart of Frost's argument.

2. What do the authors mean by "primary responses"?

3. What is meant by the expression "a reader understands it because he's laughing"?

4. Do you agree that the deductive method of teaching literature produces mere story technicians who view such approaches as courses in literary depreciation? Explain.

5. Why do teachers insist on making critics out of their youngsters? What are the authors' attitudes on these practices? Do you agree with them? Explain.

6. What is the place of literature in the classroom?

7. Please summarize the authors' arguments.

I don't want to analyze authors. I want to enjoy them. I want the boys in the class to enjoy their books because of what's in them. Here again, perhaps I am old-fashioned. Youth, I believe, should not analyze its enjoyments. It should live. It doesn't matter what they think Hazlitt thought or tried to do in his works; what matters is the work, the story, the series of incidents. Criticism is the province of age, not youth. They'll get to that soon enough. Let them build up a friendship with the writing world first. One can't compare until one knows.

Robert Frost[1]

Whether Robert Frost speaks as poet or English teacher is not so important. What is important is his concern for the enjoyment of literature, a concern that we teachers of literature must necessarily share. I am not yet convinced that our deductive methods of promoting enjoyment work well, if they work at all, primarily because of the assumptions upon which

---

[1] Robert S. Newdick, "Robert Frost as Teacher of Literature and Composition," *English Journal*, 25 (October 1936), 632–637.

---

* FROM the *English Journal* (January 1973), pp. 49–59, reprinted with permission of John Hurley and the National Council of Teachers of English.

they are based. The most important of these is the assumption that one must understand literature if he is to enjoy it. Really? Is understanding really essential to the enjoyment of literature?

It is easy enough to dismiss the question by answering simply that anyone who does not understand literature will not enjoy it. But careful observation of literary happenings forces me to embrace the opposite opinion. People do enjoy literature, sometimes enjoy it quite thoroughly without *understanding* it, and I use the term *understanding* here to mean totally aware of what is happening, to mean grasping something both intellectually and analytically.

Surely you have seen somebody read something funny, react explosively and spontaneously, then settle down into his former mood, quite unable to tell you why he laughed the way he did. He can, of course, tell you what he laughed at, but he cannot tell you why. Yet, when he tells you what was funny, he is simply pinpointing the source of laughter, not giving you the reasons for it. Now just as his laughter reveals his enjoyment, so does his inability to explain the reasons for it reveal his lack of understanding.

I am not going to discuss degrees of pleasurable reaction, except to note that such reaction might range from the bellylaugh clear up to the highly sophisticated response that reveals itself internally, the kind of response that I prefer to call contemplative laughter. This last kind, of course, is analytical and is a rare kind of enjoyment among readers, just as the grin, the snicker, the chuckle are signs of enjoyment on the most instinctive, intuitive level and represent the most common kinds of enjoyment among readers. In a similar manner, serious literature produces somewhat parallel reactions which are also of an intuitive, instinctive nature. A reader reacts to a tragic event of literature by crying outright or by simply dropping a tear or two, by a watering of the eyes, by struggling to suppress tears, by shuddering, or simply by experiencing some sort of internal discomfort that is both sudden and unavoidable. The reaction, at any rate, is instinctive, primitive almost, uncontrollable, and unpremeditated and unplanned. Still, people place much faith in such reactions, using them often to appraise a literary happening. To the extent that they find themselves reacting, to that extent is the happening good or bad, better or worse. Somebody's measure of enjoyment, then, might well be in proportion to the quantity of tears shed.

Now for most people the enjoyment of literature amounts to no more than these simple instinctive, emotive responses, and these reactions to literary events are common to all of us, however deep our appreciation ultimately becomes. Because they are primary, however, these reactions afford no time for the enjoyment of literature on an analytical basis. Because of their speed in coming they afford no time for understanding, if by understanding we mean "knowing what it's all about." Under these circumstances, when we see somebody burst out laughing, we can hardly say that he's *laughing because he understands it*. He simply has not had time to determine whether he does or not. A more accurate expression might well be that he *understands it because he's laughing*.

"Laughing because he understands it" assumes that the reader has taken the time that analysis requires before beginning his laugh. And we know that this is simply not true. When, however, we say that the reader "understands it because he's laughing," we mean, not that laughter is a cause of understanding but rather a sign of it. Laughter, in this case, is understanding, and understanding is laughter. They are identical, simultaneous, and, of course, spontaneous. The situation that produces the laugh has already been analyzed, then synthesized, then placed before the reader— by the writer, naturally—with the confidence that the reader has accumulated sufficient experience in life to be able to grasp immediately the connection between this literary experience and his own lifetime experiences.

This assumption, then, that a reader "understands it because he is laughing," is the more sensible one, and the teacher of literature should never lose sight of it. Somebody on the writing end of a literary happening has already taken the time to determine what will produce a desired response. From reader to reader the response will vary, sometimes even drastically. For example, somebody nearly doubled over with laughter might find himself alongside somebody whose reaction is one of puzzlement, numbness. Obviously the writer's intended humor has escaped somebody, but this is bound to happen. Now the laughing one could explain to the numb one what is so funny, or the teacher could do it. After such explanations have been given, the numb one might confess that he "gets it."

But do you really think he derives any enjoyment from such an experience? And can we not say, quite truly, that he *understands it?* He is now aware of what he should have laughed at but could not, and now that he understands it, he may go ahead and laugh. To be polite (and to be thought as smart as the others), he will undoubtedly laugh. Then he will probably diligently avoid literature from that moment on, avoid it as if it were one of those weird, strange studies, full of secrets and mysteries that he does not care to discover.

As absurd as that hypothetical situation seems, the truth of the matter is that we persist in teaching literature in precisely that manner. We teach people how to *understand* literature; we insist, as a matter of fact, that they understand it, and we really don't care whether they enjoy it or not. Not only do we insist upon understanding, but we go out of our way to provide the most narrow kind of understanding imaginable. If inoculation is nearly synonymous with prevention, then let me say that we inoculate our students. We give them a strong dose of carefully prescribed medicine in order to protect them from the most fatal of student diseases—enjoyment.

Our method of teaching literature—our deductive method—clearly reveals *what we* mean by understanding. We teach youngsters *plot, character, theme,* suggesting at the same time that stories are neatly packaged entities to be considered like so many other gadgets. If they can apply the labels properly and disassemble the toy, then they shall soon see how it works. Soon everyone becomes a skilled story technician, the game gets dull, and literature becomes "a grind."

"After all, if you've read ten, you've read them all" is the attitude that soon persists among students. They soon feel that the stories are really all alike, differing only slightly in those particulars that constitute *plot, character*, and *theme* and the name of the author. *Mechanic* is probably a better term because *author* suggests *artist*, a creator, while *mechanic* suggests an assembler, one who simply put things together (like *plot, character*, and *theme*) in the same simple fashion as students take them apart, calling the dismantled objects stories. It is not long before we leave students with the impression that anyone can pull a story apart, that anyone can just as easily put one together, and that the only difference between authors and other mechanics is that authors don't get quite as dirty doing their work.

Occasionally, to add a bit of mystery, some dash to the game, a wag comes along to remind everybody that *plot, character*, and *theme* (an obvious threesome) add up to four because a story is "more than the sum of its parts." Cute as the statement is, it simply suggests, perhaps even confirms, the truth of what many have suspected all along: English teachers are certainly lousy at math. Since many already "know" this, however, there is really little need for the mathematical pseudo-profundity. We can dispense with it.

Now what is our most common method of trying to promote understanding? Usually, it involves taking a story, defining *plot, character*, and *theme*, illustrating how they apply to the story, then giving a number of stories for assigned reading, all of which clearly reveal these three elements. The results, of course, are devastating. What should have been, at most, a means to a limited understanding of literature becomes an end in itself; so we have both students and teachers equating *plot, character*, and *theme* with *understanding*. When the three terms on the left are equal to a fourth on the right, we arrive at a very neat equation calculated to turn out instant experts who have the most superficial view of literature imaginable. Unfortunately, students are not so easily fooled, and the result is that they soon think little of English teachers and far less of writers, whom they had always considered a bit crazy anyway. Literature, they feel, and appreciation of it is like playing a game, but they are hardly inclined to take such games seriously.

They do not, consoling as it might be to think otherwise. Students are astute enough to recognize a course in literary depreciation when they see one. They view the "programmed approach" to literature as being pretty much like the same approach to grammar. The program becomes an end in itself, a convenient testing device designed to accommodate with utmost orderliness the most sophisticated computerized grading systems. If we were in the business of billing students for literary services rendered, this programmed approach would be fine because we do undoubtedly produce large quantities of easily-tabulated, readily-convertible materials. And the only one inconvenienced by such a system seems to be the student, but since he does not matter too much, there is no reason to worry about him. For the behavioral objectivist, of course, the programmed approach is perfect, for he can tell you in an instant how many stories or poems, or combinations thereof, Johnny can pull apart in so many given minutes and with what kind of facility.

People seem to ignore the fact that we are producing dozens of students whose literary radar is so poorly developed that they can barely distinguish between a short story and a biography. This situation is almost like being unable to distinguish between a blimp and a two-ton truck, except to note that both are moving vehicles. If that is the extent to which we can develop somebody's discriminatory capacities, then why bother "teaching" at all? If we show students how to label things carefully, how to name all the parts accurately, only to find that the average observer sees very little difference between a blimp and a truck, sees—in terms of our own discipline—little difference between a short story and a biography, then our efforts have been in vain. "That they are all the same" is the attitude he had when he began the program, and it is also the attitude he has when he leaves it.

We can thank our present widespread practice of inoculation for this. Students are given their *plot, character,* and *theme* shots, exposed to several literary happenings, put into several literary environments, only to discover that the shots work well. They have developed instant immunity to literature. Very little gets through to afflict them, and we find them possessing only the minor symptoms of *literaria,* the aches and pains, so to speak, the superficials like *plotto, characteria,* and *thematitis,* not the sickness itself. Is it little wonder that they seek therapy of television for immediate and constant relief? Is it any wonder that they constantly seek this electronic massage throughout high school and junior college in order to rid themselves of the bumps and bruises of academic workouts? In no time at all, of course, even the aches and pains disappear. The *plotto, characteria,* and *thematitis* vanish, so that not even the slightest trace of *literaria* exists. By the time they are in their second year of college, we are almost convinced that they have never been exposed to the disease, sometimes convinced that they have not even heard of it.

I don't know who said that "literature is life," but I am convinced that few people have taken him seriously. Too often literature is taught as if it had little to do with life, as if it were totally unrelated to life, as if it were being taught only for the purpose of destroying whatever healthy interest in life students might have. Literature might be life, but the teaching of it has nearly killed many a student. Fortunately, most students are not sufficiently exposed to be killed, and there is constant and immediate therapy available *via* electronic massage. Aside from providing relief, television undoubtedly is more beneficial than we wish to acknowledge.

After all, it makes people aware, however intuitive the sense of awareness, that a good story is a good story and that all the teachers and television commercials in the world cannot destroy it. They can interfere with it, interrupt it, distort it even, but they cannot destroy it. The impact of good literature cannot be diminished, only delayed. Sooner or later, good yarns will overcome the efforts of bad teaching and find their way to the people. If the enjoyment of literature—*literaria*—is an affliction worth having sooner rather than later, then I suggest that teachers stop immunizing students as soon as possible. Throw away your shots (*plot, character, theme*), your inoculative method, which is really the deductive method, for the deductive method of teaching literature is simply not the way.

Deduction might be a very good method of scientific thinking, a good tool, but when it is misapplied to literature, when it becomes an end in itself, a teaching goal, then it becomes quite clearly the destructive method. Because we are neither scientists nor philosophers, there is no good reason why we should use such an approach as this:

> These (plot, character, theme) are the elements of good literature.
> The books before me are what people call good literature.
> These books, therefore, will contain those elements.

Now I do not dispute the validity of such a method. It is, after all, good scientific, good deductive procedure. The problem, of course, lies in the assumptions, like the assumption that the ability to recognize *plot, character,* and *theme* makes literature understandably better. Common sense tells us, naturally, that whether somebody knows the terms or not a good story will turn him on and a bad one will not. Yet people persist in using a method of teaching that clearly defies common sense. Furthermore, we are totally absurd in assuming that the scientific method, the deductive method, has the same application to literature that it has to science. The scientist pursues what we often refer to as "truth" and deals with verifiable and measurable realities. He needs answers that have general application, if only for the sake of avoiding thousands of hours of useless investigations. For these purposes the deductive method is all well and good.

But the study of literature is a different matter. We study life, the life of man, not necessarily "truth." If we run into truth of some sort that will be fine, but it will be an accident. It will be incidental, also, to our proper study—man. The study of man and that of truth are not necessarily the same. We assume that they are, however, when we apply the deductive method to the study of both.

Though it is true that we need language in order to talk sensibly, it is not necessarily true that we need the language of critics in order to make sense about literature. Why, then, do we insist upon making our youngsters critics? Why do we ask them, for example, to write a book report? Can you appreciate the difficulty and complexity of our expectations? We ask a student to *briefly* describe the book—a tremendous writing chore even for the seasoned critic. Have you tried it lately? We also ask the student to discuss *character* and *motivation*, for example, even though the one or two readings we have permitted him hardly provide him with a sufficient basis for a probing discussion.

As a matter of fact, this is a task that might be better handled by thirty students, not one, for there are simply too many questions to be asked. Is life so simple? Perhaps literature is, but if it is, then perhaps literature is not life after all. Can we provide a fifteen-word answer as to why Sirhan Sirhan killed Bobby Kennedy? If life is as simple as this, then why were so many people shocked when the killing occurred? Why didn't people just say, "I expected as much"? Thousands of people are still wondering about that seemingly senseless killing. Yet we have the nerve to require one youngster to approach a problem which in real life requires the efforts and attention and consideration of many. Are we kidding? Our assumption here seems to be that all life's problems admit of solution and that if we get enough practice with literary problems, then the life problems will be that much easier to handle. It is almost as if we have lost sight of the fact that literature (when you get right down to it) is literature, and life is life. We can choose to enjoy the former, but only if we are blessed with good fortune will we enjoy the latter. Just because we have no guarantee that life will not be miserable, we do not have to go out of our way to assure students that literature, too, can be equally miserable.

Our final thrust in turning students into apprentice critics is to require them to evaluate what they read. Why, we ask, did they like/dislike the story? When students are given the time to enumerate the scenes and incidents and people they like, then given the time to reconsider those omitted the first time around, then they have a fairly good basis for tentative evaluation. Fruitful discussion of items omitted could bring about many changes of mind, could yield both positive and negative attitudes rather than just one kind or the other. In a hastily contrived book report, however, the chances are that whatever is convenient will be delivered. We seem to operate on the assumption that everyone has a sufficient number of reasons, but we give nobody a chance to explore adequately the materials that will yield them. Though it is easy to ask somebody why he likes or dislikes a story, the question is really a complicated one, or at least one that could easily yield a complicated answer. Nothing could be more unrealistic than to expect an instant answer. *Literature* becomes so very much unlike life when this happens, but the shame of it is that the teacher is rarely blamed. The piece of literature is (that stupid book). Trying to tell a good story in the time allotted commercials is extremely frustrating, but probably no more disturbing than providing fast answers to hard questions.

We operate also on the assumption here that if you like something or dislike it, then you must know why. Do you really buy that idea? When did you last stop to think about why you like your car, your job, or even your mother? If you do know why, have you ever wondered about how others feel about the reasons you've given? Do you feel that a discussion would provide you with other reasons? Do you think that if you failed to find "very good" reasons you would stop liking your mother? Could I possibly be charmed by *King Lear,* as I have been for years, even if I never gave you a good reason for my behavior? Is that possible?

When I was a child I read a story called "The Boy Who Cried 'Wolf.' " Most of you are familiar with the story, I am sure, probably as much as I am. It was part of my early reading program at home, and I cannot imagine or recall how many times I read that story even before beginning school. There were many others, of course, but always I would return to that story, for I had found it absolutely enchanting. What fascinated me? I suppose that it was the irony, and even today I find myself wrapped up in writers who make heavy use of this device.

But take a close look at what happened in my situation. Surely, as a child, I would have been hard-pressed to tell somebody that the writer's use of irony dazzled me. I would have been at a loss to explain that I enjoyed watching the boy get his come-uppance. I would have found it impossible to comment on the author's obvious moralizing. I had neither vocabulary nor critical awareness, had no ability to write, no artistic refinement. I was a primitive reacting in a most primitive manner. I was spellbound, and I returned time and again hoping to feel that same charm afforded by any good yarn.

I sometimes wonder what would have happened if my mother had plagued me by requiring me to relate the story in detail, name all the characters, account for their motivation, memorize the theme—in this case, the message—and apply the message in a general way to life, by remembering, for instance, not to call the fire department unless we had a real fire (as if reading stories could endow one with common sense).

What, then, do we offer as remedy for the inoculative, deductive method? What kind of life-long immunization program? Well, it is not new to good literature teachers; but it is unique and frightening to some teachers and it is passively ignored by many others. One might say that we have discovered discovery (or inquiry or induction or whatever other fashionable tag is applied to it these days). We too, as with Frost, don't want to analyze authors but want to enjoy them, and we want the students to enjoy them. We too believe that analysis must come after enjoyment, understanding, and appreciation, but we are convinced that such has not been the case in the majority of English classrooms, Grades 7–12, in this country.

Were Frost alive today, though, we bet he would accept our interpretation of his words as a prescription *and argument* for the inductive or, as we intend the word "inductive," the inquiry method of teaching literature.

In applying the terms "inductive" or "inquiry," however, we do not use the terms for purposes of developing workable generalizations, which a scientist does for practical purposes. We are not interested in the scientific method as such, but rather in developing an inquisitive attitude which implies a constant openness of mind.

For our purposes, then, the inquiry method in teaching literature is a process in which one aims to involve the student by prompting him, through literature, to examine his feelings, emotions, and sensualities in an effort to understand and appreciate the order and meaning of his own existence. In short, the inquiry approach can assist the student "to know the subtle, sneaky, important reason why he was born a human being and not a chair" (Herb Gardner, *1000 Clowns* [Samuel French Co., 1962], p. 52).

Any kind of literature—junior literature or adult literature—which moves the student to think and to question, which leads him beyond the point of "What does the work in question mean?" to "What does it mean to me?" has within it the possibilities of assisting him through the awesome, tremendous task of facing up to himself in his own world. An inquiry approach, if properly employed by the teacher, deals with a work of literature in the form of questions about that work and not in the form of preconceived, teacher-imposed answers. For too long teachers have failed to realize that the question is more enlightening than the answer.

Teachers must hit the student where he is and "induct" him into an intuitive process of inquiry that explores the passions of love, hate, joy, sorrow, prejudice, or whatever. They must help him kick these passions around and involve him in the intellectual experience of self-discovery. A student in any grade or of any ability is capable of a certain amount of intellectualization, which begins in uninhibited talk—talk that helps him probe and interpret his own humanity, talk that helps him test his own perceptions and delight in his own insights—no matter how shallow or meager.

And intellectual involvement in literature need not become dull—never boring. We are convinced that it can teach students how to adopt a self-satisfying identity, how to cope with loneliness and alienation, how to develop empathy and compassion, how to broaden perspectives and horizons, how to comprehend and interpret man's inhumanity to man, and ultimately how to learn.

Inherent, then, in the inquiry approach to literature is the method by which a student learns to confront his convictions and weigh his commitments and from which he develops confidence in himself and in his ability to communicate the innumerable thoughts and feelings and ideas that emerge, converge, and diverge, once he leaves the classroom and enters the immediate world of his reality.

The literature classroom is the most logical forum for a student to explore, communicate, and test his feelings, his anxieties, and his questions, because it is there that he communes with those ideas that *can* move him to discover he is a human being and not a chair.

The poems, "Richard Cory" and "Miniver Cheevy" by E. A. Robinson and "The Unknown Citizen" by W. H. Auden, and novels, *Adventures of Huckleberry Finn* by Mark Twain, *Lord of the Flies* by William Golding, and *I Never Promised You a Rose Garden* by Hannah Green, are quite commonly read and studied by students in secondary school. The forty questions that follow were devised as samples of the kinds of questions which provide for inquiry and stimulate interesting, intellectual, sometimes controversial, but, more importantly, "learning" discussions. They are leading questions, for the most part, but the art of the teacher lies in his ability to provide leading questions that will move the student to involvement and inquiry. Where a question leads depends, of course, on both student and teacher and their prowess for developing and generating more questions that are germane to the work in point. Where the process terminates may be anywhere or nowhere (or even the dismissal bell), but the important process of inquisitive thinking should be served either way. We are convinced from personal experience and from student-teacher observations that our questions stimulate thinking and discovery, many times in the form of introspection, meditation, or even resolution.

To those who may argue that this approach is not a proper study of literature, we counter that the "so-called proper study" can best be nurtured by this open-ended, literary rap session. If the student becomes interested, he will want to analyze and criticize. He may even read the poem or the book!

The questions for each work are by no means exhaustive with regard to the poem or novel under discussion, nor are they intended to be. We present them merely as effective, inquiry questions. We don't know that they assist the student in assimilating the culture of the times to the culture of the ages, but we are not sure that they need to.

"Richard Cory"—E. A. Robinson

1. What does Cory's fate suggest about a person's inner subjective life and his outer, observable one? and/or Which is more important—what you think of yourself or what others think of you?

2. Does it take courage or cowardice to kill oneself? How might poets or philosophers or religionists reply to this question?

3. Is it plausible to think of Cory's suicide as an act of nobility? That is, might Cory have chosen suicide as a noble end rather than live in the frustration and despair of knowing that maybe he, through his wealth and elegance, motivated in the common people much of the greed, despair, and envy which consume men physically, emotionally, or even spiritually?

4. Would any of you consider suicide a sinful act? An illegal act? Has anyone ever been prosecuted for attempted suicide? Is suicide one of man's basic freedoms? Does the United States Constitution protect this freedom?

5. Why do you suppose the poet did not supply the specific reasons for Cory's suicide?

"Miniver Cheevy"— E. A. Robinson

1. Do you think Cheevy is sincere in his admiration for living in ages past, or do you think he is merely rationalizing his failures and trying to escape from

them? If rationalizing and escaping, would this make him a Don Quixote, a Walter Mitty?

2. Do you ever long to have lived at a different time in history? If so, do these feelings coincide with periods of great strain? Of great challenge?

3. Is it possible for a person to reflect upon other roads or ways of life without regretting at least somewhat the one he has chosen himself?

4. Think of an outstanding character in history (e.g., Socrates, Abe Lincoln, Thomas Jefferson, Napoleon, etc.). Would this person be able to "make it" in today's world? Why? Why not?

5. What kinds of people that you know spend their energies longing for "the good old days"?

6. If a person can live a fruitful life in one circumstance and time, might he do the same in any circumstance and time?

7. What conditions in life tend to produce men like Richard Cory or Miniver Cheevy?

"The Unknown Citizen"—W. H. Auden

1. Is the poet in this poem taking on "the establishment"? If so, how? What can the establishment do to give identification to the unknown citizen?

2. Is anything bad, wrong, or demeaning with living incognito, paying one's bills, etc.? Can't this way of life provide as much satisfaction or happiness as any other way of life?

3. Is it any of the narrator's business to make the observations that he does? Do men need spokesmen for their plight, their happiness, or even their sorrow? Don't spokesmen just add salt to the wounds?

4. Do any among you feel that you would rather be unknown citizens? Isn't the world full of them? Aren't they probably the happiest, safest citizens—uninvolved, no shots fired

at them, no public censure or disgrace?

5. Do unknown citizens maybe lead lives of quiet desperation? How? Why might they?

Adventures of Huckleberry Finn—Mark Twain

1. Huck objects to Tom's playing make-believe and the widow's praying. Do these two activities have something in common?

2. After the shooting of Boggs, Sherburn shouts, "The pitifulest thing out is a mob; that's what an army is—a mob; they don't fight with courage that's born in them, but with courage that's borrowed from their mass, and from their officers." Do you agree with this statement? Are there any modern-day parallels of this statement? Explain.

3. Huck chooses whether or not he wants to belong to the establishment. He chooses to light out of the territory. Is he an escapist; does he cop out or fink out? How would you choose, were you in Huck's boots? Why? Can you choose whether or not to belong to the establishment today?

4. If Jim had told the story, how do you think it would differ? Or would it?

Lord of the Flies—William Golding

1. Would Jack's boys repeat the ritualistic slaying of the sow with Ralph? Would cannibalism be next?

2. Is the Navy cruiser in any way representative of the manhunt it interrupted?

3. When you are separated from your parents for any length of time, do you attempt to preserve the same order they require, or do you like to be completely independent?

4. Which character—Ralph, Piggy, Jack —is most like you? Which character would you be like if you could?

5. Why was Piggy never really accepted into the society of the "big-guns"? What kind of treatment do the Piggys in our society receive?

6. Reason and order finally fail after numerous attempts to restore it. Does this part of the story show a need for "the establishment" in our society? And what does "the establishment" mean to you?

7. Which of Ralph's traits establish him as an imperfect leader? What type of leader would he be in our system of government?

8. Might the conch be similar to something in our society? If so, can you explain how it functions in the same way? What was the basis for the acceptance of the authority of the conch? To what extent will you respect authority that is not rigidly enforced?

9. If humans are basically evil, does civilization have a redeeming effect on man? Is man good, and civilization bad?

10. Who was the better leader—Ralph or Jack? Why? What are the characteristics of a leader? Of the people you know, who are leaders and who are followers? Are all men either leaders or followers? Is it better to be a leader than a follower or vice versa? Explain.

I Never Promised You a Rose Garden—Hannah Green

1. The title of the novel is in these lines by Dr. Fried: "I never promised you a rose garden. I never promised you perfect justice and I never promised you perfect peace or happiness. My help is so that you can be free to fight for all of these things. . . . The only reality I offer is challenge, and being well is being free to accept it or not at whatever level you are capable. I never promise lies, and the rose garden world of perfection is a lie . . . and a bore, too!" What is Dr. Fried's case for reality? Do you agree?

2. What constitutes "reality"? Is reality constant, i.e., the same for everybody? Does one's inner view affect one's concept of the real world and its happenings? How? Can events and happenings be interpreted in more than one way? Which of Debbie's worlds were more real to her? to her parents? to us? Is your "reality" the same as your neighbor's? (Note: I am hoping here to induce the concepts—days, hours, minutes—the third dimension—sensation, color, shape, and solidarity—those things which constitute reality for most of us and the fact that for Debbie these things disappeared.)

3. What does Debbie mean when she says, "all human eyes are distorting eyes"? What does this have to do with the concept of reality just discussed? Does everybody see things the same way? Do we always see things "as they are" or do we sometimes color them to conform to our own desires and wishes? Note the difference between the way Debbie sees herself (as a curse) and the way the staff sees her (as a stuck up little rich girl, a "snooty little bitch who never did anything in her life"), the way her parents see her (as a toy, a possession), and the way Dr. Fried sees her. Who is correct? Can anyone really know another person? No one can ever get inside our minds and know exactly the things we have felt and experienced; therefore, aren't we all ultimately "alone" and destined for loneliness? How can we communicate? What are some of the ways we can come to know a person?

4. What did Debbie mean by "The people on the edge of hell were most afraid of the Devil; for those already in hell the Devil was only another and no one in particular"? What does she mean by the fear of the "Maybe"? Why are the patients upset when a former patient returns to the hospital? Does this mean they're defeated?

5. Mrs. Blau decides to lie to the family about Debbie's progress. She says that

they would want to hear that she had seen Debbie and the ward and the doctors and that all was fine, that they would accept the lie. Why do people want to be lied to at times or let themselves be lied to at times? Is this healthy, normal, therapeutic? What?

6. Jacob says that the sickness wasn't their fault, that they didn't know what they were doing. What does he mean? Are parents responsible for the way their children turn out? Were Debbie's mother and father at fault? Could her illness have been pre-vented? Is being a good parent something that comes naturally? What are some of the responsibilities involved? Are there some things you would do differently from what your parents did?

7. Is a child's independence really a threat to parents? What is the proper parent-child relationship?

8. It is hard for Debbie to cry, but why is it so important that she cry?

9. What is the difference between feeling and fact? Which is more reliable? more secure?

High School Reading Instruction: Practice Versus Needs*

Robert A. Palmatier

The author contends that reading, a receptive language art, is a learning tool rather than an instructional discipline. Yet "English"—which generally includes emphasis on writing and speaking (transmissive language arts) as well as reading—is generally termed an instructional discipline. Perhaps we have an artificial dichotomy here. Let us see how Palmatier compares the need for high school reading instruction with some instructional practices.

1. What problems does the author delineate?

2. How does he propose that these problems be solved?

3. What are the advantages of need-oriented high school reading instruction?

4. List all the reasons the author gives for emphasis on reading instruction within the regular content-area classrooms. Add your own thinking to the list. Then make a list of the comments of people who oppose such instruction.

5. Discuss the lists in terms of such factors as student needs, what a teacher is, and so forth.

In the high school, reading is used primarily as a learning tool rather than treated as an instructional discipline. This author intends to deal with the appropriateness of this fact, review the major sorts of high school reading programs currently offered, and suggest some alternatives. In order to achieve these goals, first the needs for reading instruction will be discussed.

* Written especially for this volume.

Secondly, descriptions of the usual high school reading programs will be offered. After discussing the abilities and inabilities of these programs to meet the reading needs, modifications and alternatives to present practices will be considered.

READING SKILL NEEDS

Three types of student reading needs exist in most high schools. The largest group includes students who have a good grasp of basic reading skills and, if they have any instructional needs, merely require a limited amount of training in what is generally known as study skills. These students read sufficiently well to use regular textbooks and can do the sort of school assignment normally required. However, in this group exists a great range in what could be called efficiency. Although all these students can do the job required, the time, effort, and procedures used vary greatly. Thus, instruction in specific reading skills utilized in efficient study and learning procedures could prove most beneficial to this group.

Students who have specific skill deficiencies and who cannot easily read grade level texts represent the second largest group. This group needs specific instruction in those basic skill areas in which they are not proficient and aid in utilizing those content texts which are overly difficult for them. In addition to basic skill needs these students also usually need help in the area of study procedures and efficiency.

The third group, a small but difficult to ignore percentage of the students in an average school, presents the most severe problems. These pupils have such limited reading skills, often four to ten years below grade level, that utilization of standard texts is impossible. In fact, this group is normally so handicapped that participation in the normal instructional program can be achieved only with extensive special aid and modification of instructional approaches.

In many "modern" American high schools one finds these three groups divided according to what is often known as a track system; that is, the most able of the first group described is taught together as an accelerated or advanced group, the rest of that first group is included in an average section, and the remainder is tolerated in a slow or bottom group. School personnel normally refer to these divisions as ability groups even though their delineation is usually on the basis of performance rather than intelligence or aptitude. This type of grouping denies students the realization of potential on the basis of reading difficulties.

Traditionally reading instruction has been considered the job of the elementary school. Once a student graduates from the sixth grade he is assumed to be an accomplished reader. However, as outlined in the preceding descriptions of reading needs there are two distinct groups present in the typical high school population for whom this assumption is invalid. In those schools where budgets and class schedules allow, special reading programs have been instituted to cope with the problems of these two groups. How these programs are designed and their instructional content is the topic of the following sections.

INSTRUCTIONAL PROGRAMS

To conform with the concept of classes and class schedules fundamental to the American high school, reading instruction is usually approached on that basis. Thus, it is not unusual to find a high school reading teacher faced with a room containing twenty to thirty students enrolled in a course entitled corrective or remedial reading. Normally these terms are used to indicate students at least one full year below grade level in reading performance. In the high school a deficiency of at least two grade levels usually exists before a need for special help is recognized; thus most students actually do fall in the normally accepted range of remedial readers (two or more grade levels below placement level). Reading experts tend to agree that remedial students need small group or individual instruction. Economics usually forces high school administrators to overlook this demand and place the reading teacher in a classroom with thirty remedial readers for forty-two minutes each day.

Given the many different situations and methods for teaching reading, one would expect describing high school reading programs to be a complex task. However, with rare exceptions, where budget and class schedules are overcome in order really to meet the reading needs of students, most high school reading programs look nearly the same. The only case in which real variety is seen is when in order to balance schedules administrators decide that all students need reading instruction. In this case classes will range as described earlier in the tracking or ability-grouping system. The reading teacher will then need to teach three different courses. The regular class arrangement is appropriate for the needs of the upper two groups because their skills need only refinement and direction to develop greater efficiency. Both groups receive the same type of course, with pace of instruction being the major difference. Contents of such courses usually embrace structural analysis, vocabulary study, comprehension training, reference work, library orientation, skimming, scanning, SQ3R, story reading, and book report writing. For the more able group who otherwise would complete the course too quickly a healthy dose of literature appreciation is added. These programs normally utilize a combination of materials. Usual components of the materials collection are kits, workbooks, literature texts, study skills texts, and library materials. The most innovative programs include paperback book collections and hardware programs.

Actual instructional content is normally slim because the students in these groups usually have been introduced earlier to the skills. Thus, the high school reading teacher's role is that of reminding students and providing practice exercises. To do this the teacher relies on lecture introduction, workbook practice, practice on kit materials, and sometimes application to real reading and other school situations. Because of the reluctance of other teachers to cooperate or allow the reading teacher to work with students in content texts, actual application to normal school reading situations is usually not achieved. Because school administrators tend to view recreational reading as extra-class activity, application to this sort of real-world activity is also often not achieved. Thus, reading instruction is usually confined to the carefully structured materials designed to demonstrate the workability of skills taught. Possibly these factors contribute to the typical observation that students do not, in everyday school work, use those reading skills taught.

Besides the generally unrealistic and uninteresting content of the typical reading course outlined above, one must look at what is not taught. Because we are now considering the course given the better students, we must assume a large percentage of college-bound students. Note taking, speed reading, study procedures, test-taking techniques, and detailed knowledge of library use will be expected skills for those students. The typical high school reading course does not even mention most of these. Those included usually receive a nonspecific presentation which generally amounts to "do it better," often even assuming that all that is necessary is telling about a skill. The nature and purpose of the activities included in the high school reading program for average and above-average readers, if honestly evaluated, would normally result in admission that the purpose was to fill a scheduled time period and the nature of the activities was "busy-work." If you doubt this author's evaluation, ask a few students who are or have been in such programs.

If we are doing so poorly by our better students, what are we doing for our students with real reading deficiencies? Here the answer is even worse than for the average or better reader. It is more difficult to generalize for this group because the range of reading problem is much more extensive than in the above-described groups. A class of thirty remedial readers could easily contain students reading from two to ten grades below placement level. At least one total nonreader is also not unusual. With this sort of situation there is almost no hope for a successful or even positive program. The most apparent aspect is teacher and student frustration. There are no reading activities in which the whole group can participate and usually there is insufficient space or teacher ability to group within the class. Quite often these classes simply become chaotic discipline situations because of the impossible demands on teacher and students. In cases where instruction is achieved it usually must be confined to isolated skills outside a reading context so that all can participate. This is the prime reason for such a high percentage of time spent on structural analysis, word meanings, dictionary drill, and phonic generalizations. Regardless of the high face validity of such instruction, it mostly boils down to nonapplicable skill learning. Because of the diversity in reading levels only the brave teacher tries for more than workbook or multilevel kit application. Thus, because of instructional conditions and lack of trained personnel, even those in dire need of specific reading skill instruction often end up doing busy-work activities far removed from satisfying their instructional needs. Granted, in some schools, this latter group is handled in an appropriate small-group or individual program where reading improvement is possible. However, not many secondary schools have yet overcome traditional budget and schedule restrictions, which, in fact, render such programs virtually impotent despite content, materials, or teacher skill.

Given this picture of typical high school reading programs one must conclude that the situation is indeed dismal. Ironically, the fact that a majority of the schools still do not offer *any* reading program may be a bright light. At least more than half of American high school students have not been forced into programs misconstrued in such a way that the only logical product is a dislike for reading instruction. Fortunately many of our better students do not connect this instruction with reading and therefore do not extend their dislike to reading in general. This is not true for our less able students; they routinely extend the punishment of reading classes to a viewpoint that all reading is unhealthy. Thus, in summary the typical program is not designed to meet the reading needs of high school students. The content is either inappropriate or not carried on to a real-world or even school application level. In those cases where content is not the downfall, scheduling and unqualified instructors usually achieve the same condition.

CAN NEED-ORIENTED HIGH SCHOOL READING INSTRUCTION BE ACHIEVED?

If the status of high school reading instruction is such that little or no skill benefit is derived by students, wouldn't the best approach be to take the teaching of reading out of the high schools? This author is still optimistic enough to feel the ship is worth saving and that salvage is possible. As indicated earlier, there are definite needs for reading instruction among high school students. The problem is how to provide instruction that effectively meets these needs. Obviously, just scheduling students into the sort of inept, unrealistic courses we now offer is not the answer. This author contends that very little reading instruction should be attempted out of the context of the real world of content courses such as math, science, and social studies or without application to the extra-school reading world of newspapers, magazines, junk mail, signs, food containers, directions, and so on. Thus, in all but two sorts of skill development regular content teachers must be involved.

The two instances where the reading teacher can be of good service, in relative isolation, is with the best and poorest readers. For the best readers a short (six week) course including speed reading, note taking, vocabulary study, and general study and learning procedures could be most helpful. If coordinated with content teachers an even higher level of benefit could be derived through real application. The idea here is to cover only the few general reading and study efficiency techniques which can be learned outside a specific content area but can be generalized to all subject areas.

The other instance where a reading teacher can work effectively outside content areas is with remedial cases. Here, if given release from full-class scheduling and provided with a learning-lab setting, a qualified reading teacher may help students to achieve real basic skill gains. Without a flexible schedule of small-group and individual tutorial situations, little skill improvement can reasonably be expected of students who suffer from the complex problems built up through years of unrewarding instruction and failure. Although much success is possible in a situation isolated from other instruction, reading work for these students should also be coordinated with regular content teachers.

EMPHASIS ON CONTENT CLASSROOMS

As hinted previously this author feels that the answer to most reading instruction needs lies within the regular content area classrooms. In order to make use of these learning situations two problems must be overcome. First, content teachers must be convinced that reading skills, or maybe we should just call them learning skills, are a valid part of their curriculum. Second, these teachers need instruction and help in how to teach these skills. We must not take the attitude that all teachers are to teach general reading skills but rather that all teachers are responsible for the reading and learning skills required to learn their particular content area. To achieve the necessary understandings and instructional skills the reading teacher must work as much with teachers as with students, or more. This working with teachers should be a combination of training in specific learning skills which must be taught and reinforced and coordination of the activities for students in the study skills and remedial programs. This sort of approach, in addition to providing for content-centered student skill improvement, gradually overcomes the need for the teacher training portion of the specialist's job. As content teachers become aware of student needs and how to satisfy them, the reading specialist's job can be revised to include more emphasis on other areas.

Many educators, especially school administrators, question the need for training content teachers in the techniques needed to learn their subject areas. They maintain that these people have learned their subjects and therefore should be able to pass their knowledge on to others. The problem often is that these teachers had no difficulty learning their content area, and cannot understand others having such difficulty or how to recognize and overcome such difficulties. A major area of need is for content teachers to understand the skill prerequisites for learning tasks they assign students. Most content teachers have never paused to consider the many learning and study skills required for a student to complete a simple-sounding assignment such as "read and outline the next chapter." If the teacher can come to realize the complexity of such tasks and then learn to provide instruction to enable students to carry out all aspects of the task, better learning of the content area can be achieved. A specific example should crystalize the point that content-area teachers are not aware of study and learning skills that students need to master their content areas. Social studies teachers expect students to utilize the backbone study skills of history, cause and effect, and chronology, but generally do not recognize that direct teaching of the concepts and training in the use of these skills is a part of their curriculum.

Conclusion

High school reading instruction is in most cases not even approaching student needs and in fact is often instilling further negative concepts of reading in already disillusioned students. The author believes that with release from the typical scheduling and budgetary limitations reading teachers can be effective in certain need areas. However, the primary needs are in the area of content-oriented learning skill improvement. Here it is impossible to differentiate between what is a reading skill and what is a content-area skill. It is suggested that content teachers take the view that if a student needs a particular skill for mastery of content, this makes that skill a valid aspect of the curriculum. In order to orient content-area teachers to this viewpoint and further provide them with the necessary instructional skills a resource person is necessary. The reading specialist should spend a great deal of his time working in this on-the-job, in-service capacity. By placing the reading specialist in the role of a resource person for a basic skill area rather than as a competing content-area teacher, reading and study skills can be placed in their proper and realistic setting. Until such an integral and integrated position is given reading and learning skills, we must continue to expect and accept the failure of our present efforts in high school reading instruction.

A Modern Definition of Reading

Introduction

In his book The Art of Loving, *Erich Fromm explains that there are different kinds of love and that these different kinds of love can be defined in a number of ways. The theory of love affects the practice of love: one's definition of love affects his general attitude toward love, the way he loves, whom he loves, and for what purpose he loves.*

In a similar way a person's definition of the reading process affects his attitude toward reading: the way he reads, what he will read, and for what purposes he will read. The teacher who instructs the student in the theory and art of reading stands as the mediator of what we know about the reading process.

What do we know about the reading process? Briefly stated, most authorities on the subject consider reading a complex process involving the perceiving of written meanings, the interpretation of meanings, and the reaction to and applying of meanings to life. It is an active process that requires the individual to demand meaning, and to bring ideas to the printed page, so that the symbols will trigger off meanings according to the pattern of the writing and the experience and intelligence and habits of inquiry of the readers.

In this group of selections the authors provide further insights into the nature of the reading process and show what the implications of these insights are for teaching: what the reading process is; how we can delve more deeply into its nature; how we can identify some of the barriers to successful reading performance, and how we can take measures to help students overcome these barriers and to think effectively and interpret accurately in reading situations.

PSYCHOLINGUISTICS AND THE READING PROCESS*

Richard Rystrom

There are many misconceptions about the reading process. Fortunately linguistic and psychological research are helping to clear up some of these misconceptions and are providing us with a sounder basis for the development of reading methods and materials. In this article Rystrom has analyzed important areas of research, synthesized the findings with his fine insights, and presented us with new perspectives in reading which we shall seek to apply.

1. Define the following terms: *grapheme, phoneme, morpheme, syntax,* and *kernel sentences.*

2. Differentiate transformational rules in the narrow sense from transformational rules in the broad sense.

3. What implications for the teaching of reading can you develop out of the information in the section on psychological research?

4. What is involved in the decoding process?

5. Explain the components of comprehension.

6. State the contributions of psycholinguistics to the understanding of the reading process.

7. What are some objections to the language experience approach to teaching reading?

Most trends can best be understood by examining how they developed from the ideas and events which preceded them. This observation seems particularly relevant to a discussion of the impact of psycholinguistics upon reading.

*Written especially for this volume.

As Mathews (18) pointed out, teachers of reading have, for the past century or so, alternatively emphasized some type of phonics method or some form of the whole-word method. When whole-word reading is emphasized, many children do not learn to "sound out" words; when phonics is stressed, they do not learn to "read for meaning." After one method has been advocated for several years, interest in the alternative method begins to appear and grow.

In recent years researchers in two related areas have suggested additional considerations which should be included in any discussion of the teaching of reading. Psychologists interested in language acquisition, language development, and associated cognitive processes have made important discoveries about the nature of language learning and language behavior. Linguists have made important discoveries about the structure of language and about the nature of language behavior also. Their findings are beginning to affect how parents, teachers, and researchers think about reading. A number of reading specialists have concluded that many of the unanswered questions in reading cannot be resolved by examining reading only; many of the findings from linguistics and psychology can aid reading specialists in determining what reading is and how it might be taught more effectively. The purpose of this paper is to examine some of the psycholinguistic findings that are relevant to the reading process.

LINGUISTICS RESEARCH

It may be easier to explain the contributions of psychologists if the work of linguists is described first. As early as the 1930's Bloomfield (4), Fries (14), Francis (13), and others became interested in a particular type of language study called phrase-structure grammar, a formulation of the structure of American English which did not emphasize meaning. Although such an undertaking seems somewhat peculiar today (why would one want to describe language without also describing its structure in relation to its function?), it should be kept in mind these grammarians were reacting to an earlier group of grammarians, the Latinate grammarians, who were responsible for the schoolbook grammar texts in wide use until recently. The Latinate grammarians were more interested in "good usage" than in the structure of English as it was then used by speakers. In response, the phrase-structure grammarians set out to describe the structure of English as it is, and not as it should be, according to some set of preconceived standards.

Although many of their observations were later modified or discarded, phrase-structure grammarians contributed many important concepts to the study of language. For example, they clarified the distinction between a letter and a *grapheme*. There are only twenty-six letters in English, but there are many more graphemes, or units of writing which can be used to change one word to another. The words *hat, cat,* and *rat* each have three letters and three graphemes. By subsituting one grapheme for another the meaning of the word is changed. The words *chat* and *that* are composed of three graphemes each, but four letters—the <ch> and <th> are units of writing which do not have individual identities in these words. In the case of *brat* there are four graphemes and four letters, because the <b> and the <r> in *brat* do not lose their individual identities. That is, there is a /b/ sound in *brat* and there is also an /r/ sound in *brat*, but there is not a "<c> sound" and/or an "<h> sound" in *chat*; this letter combination has an identity of its own.

The distinction between letters and graphemes resembles the traditional description of what, in reading, has long been referred to as "blends" and "digraphs." Although there are similarities, linguists have been much more careful in defining their terms. In general, the digraphs are indeed two or more letters which are a single grapheme and the blends are two or more letters which retain their individual identities. But it is easy to find examples in books and articles about reading in which *blend* is used where *digraph* would be the correct term, and vice versa.

Even more importantly, the linguist's distinction between graphemes [one or more letters—one identity (digraph)] and letters [one or more letters—same number of identities (blend)] indicates the basis on which this distinction is made: the language and not the writing system. The <br> is a blend because the <b> is pronounced and the <r> is also pronounced. In the word *that* the <th> is associated with a single *phoneme*, or unit of sound which can be used to change one word to another. That is, /hæt/, /kæt/, and /ræt/ are composed of three phonemes; so are /čæt/ and /θæt/. But /bræ/ is composed of four phonemes.

Although substituting one phoneme for another results in a change in meaning, phonemes are not themselves units of meaning. That is, the /č/ and the /æ/ and the /t/ in *chat* do not by themselves have any meaning. The smallest unit of meaning is the *morpheme*. The word *cat* is a single morpheme. But the word *cats* is two morphemes; the second is the <-s> ending, which means "more than one." Reading teachers have traditionally taught relevant aspects of morphology as "inflectional endings" and "prefixes and suffixes on root words."

If phonemes are regarded as the building materials for constructing morphemes, then *syntax* is the arrangement or structure of the morphemes as they occur in sentences. For example, many English sentences are based on the structure: Agent—Act—Assignee. In the sentence "a dog bit the boy," a dog is acting as the agent, his act is biting, and the boy is the assignee. If the structure of this sentence is altered, the result is either a different meaning (the boy could be the agent and a dog the assignee) or no meaning at all: "bit dog the a boy." Although the term was not used until later, the basic sentence patterns discussed by phrase-structure grammarians are very similar to the *kernel sentences* that are discussed in transformational grammar.

Just as phrase-structure grammar was largely a reaction to Latinate grammar, acceptance of Chomsky's (7) formulation of transformational grammar was at least in part a reaction to the limitations inherent in phrase-structure grammar. As suggested previously, the description of any language will be much more accurate and useful if meaning is also considered. Before describing some of the features of transformational grammar that are related to the psycholinguistic nature of the reading process, some of the assumptions made in *transformational grammar* should be stated. First, most transformational grammarians begin with the assumption that the only full and complete grammar of any language is the language itself. By definition, any grammatical outline of a language is only partly accurate, because it cannot encompass all the variations and possibilities contained in the language as a whole. Much of the early disaffection for transformational grammar "because it doesn't work" would have been avoided if this fact had been understood. Second, meaning is an implicit and inseparable feature of transformational grammar. For example, the phrase-structure grammarians were unable to explain the obvious relationship between the sentences "a dog bit the boy" and "the boy was bitten by a dog." Although the meaning is clearly the same, the structure of these two sentences is different; the former is a transitive sentence, and the latter is intransitive. The relationship between this pair of sentences will be considered later in this paper.

Transformational grammar is composed of three different types of rewrite rules (as used in transformational grammar, a rule refers to what is usually done, not what "should" be done). A typical rewrite rule might be $X \longrightarrow Y + Z$; some element (X) is expanded into two different elements $(Y$ and $Z)$. In the preceding example the agent and assignee noun phrases (X) are each expanded into determiners (Y) and nouns (Z): "a dog" and "the boy." The different types of rules are called *P-S* (or *phrase structure*) *rules*, *T* (or *transformational*) *rules*, and *Mph* (or *morphophonemic*) *rules* (strictly speaking, the three types of rules form *generative grammar* and *transformational* refers only to the second type of rewrite rules; in common practice, however, *transformational* refers to all three sets of rules).

The function of PS rules is to generate kernel sentences, such as "a dog bit the boy." These are, by definition, sentences which have not been transformed. The T rules can alter kernel sentences in a number of ways: One sentence can be embedded in another—"the boy that I saw . . ."; a nonessential element can be deleted—"the boy I saw . . ."; or the order of the sentence elements can be transposed. (The following change alters the structure but not the meaning of "a dog bit the boy.")

$$NP_1 + V + NP_2 \longrightarrow NP_2 + was + V + en + by + NP_1$$

As this example illustrates, active sentences are derived from PS rules, which can then be transformed if the passive form is desired. The Mph rules change word patterns when endings have been added: bite + en $\longrightarrow$

bitten. Current linguistic findings suggest that structure and meaning must be considered together.

PSYCHOLOGICAL RESEARCH

Much of the work done in psychology complements the work of linguists. Those studies which have examined language acquisition and development appear to have the greatest significance for teachers of reading. Although these studies are important in themselves for what they indicate about how children learn to use language, they are even more important for a different reason. The studies discussed below indicate that language learning is a process: that how children learn to speak a language and how children learn to read are ordered and sequential. The fact that little is known about either process at this time, or that there undoubtedly are some variations between one learner and another, does not challenge the existence of the process.

In one study Brown and Bellugi (5) examined the language of two children, one at the age of twenty-seven months, the other at eighteen months. They found that one of the early steps in language learning is a division between pivot class words and open class words. The open class words (nouns, verbs, adjectives, and adverbs) are full of semantic meaning but contain little structural meaning. These form class words permit considerable substitution: "a dog bit the boy," "a canine snapped at the lad." The structure words, by contrast, are rich in syntactic meaning (it is not the case, as some writers have claimed, that these words have no semantic meaning; compare: "a dog bit the boy"—"the dog bit a boy"). The "syntactic meaning" of determiners like a and the is the existence of a noun phrase (NP). In children's language, however, the pivot and open classes are not the same as the structure word and form class word groups of adult language. That is, look is frequently a pivot class word in children's speech. In sentences such as look doggy and look, mommy the meaning of the sentence structures is quite different ("look at the doggy"—"look at something, mommy").

The process by which children learn the structure of their language is well underway by the time they enter the first grade, although it is obviously not complete at this time. At a later time children's pivot class words match adults' structure words, and open class words become the nouns, verbs, adjectives, and adverbs of adult speech. By then children have learned to use and understand most of the syntax of their language. One of the areas in which children's partially developed language competence is most evident is morphology. Berko's (2) research demonstrated that young children understand and can use most of the common inflectional endings (boy–boys, jump–jumped, drink–drinking, etc.). However, many of the anomalous forms (runned for ran, hitted for hit, etc.) are not learned until later.

Children's perceptions of language boundaries are clearly an important factor in determining the process by which they learn to speak. Most adults assume, because they know how to read, that the boundaries between spoken words are clear and obvious. Yet this is not the case. For example, the decision to regard a determiner and a following noun as separate words is as arbitrary as the decision to regard nouns and their suffixed plural markers as a single word. Ammon (1) has pointed out that children often do not perceive the determiner as separate from the following noun. When asked to reverse the words in the sentence "a dog bit the boy," children frequently produce "the boy bit a dog," rather than "boy the bit dog a." In a study of Jewish children who speak Yiddish, Scholes (23) noted that children sensed a word boundary between determiners and nouns in the subject noun phrase, but not in noun phrases which occur after the sentential verb. That is, "a" and "dog" would be separated, but not "the" and "boy." Using reading behavior rather than language behavior as the factor under examination, Michish (19) found that many children at the end of first grade did not have a conceptual category for the idea of "word"; as the measured reading level increased, the proportion of children who correctly identified word boundaries also increased. Instead of dividing a six-word sentence into five to seven "words," the less capable readers marked boundaries between each letter.

Although each of the preceding studies provides some insight into the process of language learning, the importance of other children–adult performance differences is more difficult to assess. Entwisle (9) reported that children respond to word association tasks in a manner different from adults. When adults are asked to respond to words, they frequently use words from the same word class (paradigmatic responses): *boy–girl*, *up–down*, *run–jump*, and so on. Children's responses, however, are more often syntactic responses; instead of responding with words from the same word class, they develop a syntactic phrase or clause as a response: *boy—ran away*; *up–the hill*; *ran–fast*, and so on. In a later study Entwisle and Greenberger (10) reported that the responses of black children are significantly less mature in terms of semantic content than the responses of white children.

READING AS A PROCESS

Linguists and psychologists have not only provided information about language behavior, they have also influenced how reading people think about the nature of reading. For years reading was thought of as a "skill" and examined in terms of particular habits to be learned or drills to be taught. Most current thinking is concerned with reading as a "process." The I.R.A.-sponsored book of reading models (Singer and Ruddell, 25) presents several different views of reading, but each begins with the assumption it is a process. The impetus for this idea came from the work of Shannon and Weaver (24), who were interested in constructing a general model which would explain how information is transferred from its source to the information receiver.

Reading, however, is different from many other types of information transfer. For example, the information source, the author, is seldom with, or accessible to, the reader. The medium, print, does not provide any interchannel redundancy; all the information is printed on the page. With many other forms of communication—for example, speech—gestures, position, and distance can be used to reinforce meaning. On the other hand, a reader can skim to get a quick idea of the contents or he can go back to some earlier point to repeat the message; these possibilities do not exist in ordinary conversational situations. Some of the discussions which examine relationships between print and speech (e.g., Rystrom, 21) have considered how information processing of print and speech are both similar and dissimilar.

Virtually all descriptions of the reading process, and discussions of reading in general, divide reading into two distinctly different areas: decoding and comprehension. Although there are individual differences between authorities as to what components are involved and the relative importance of each component to the whole, the amount of agreement is substantial. In essence, the decoding process involves learning to translate what the eye can see into what the ear can hear. Many children naturally vocalize when learning to read because they must hear what they are reading; teachers who attempt to eliminate this practice may be causing reading failures. As Laffey (16) pointed out, good readers subvocalize as frequently as poor readers, and all readers who become anxious or who are reading material which is too difficult for them have a strong tendency to subvocalize.

Decoding is often defined as readiness, letter discrimination, sight word reading, sight vocabulary development, intonation. Readiness encompasses such diverse areas as motivation, learning to use the concepts *same* and *different*, auditory discrimination, and so on. Despite the obvious fact that children must learn to respond to different forms of the same letter as the same, letter discrimination tasks are inadequately covered in most methods of teaching beginning reading. Instead, these materials stress using primary print "so young children will not be confused." Yet there is no evidence to confirm the desirability of presenting one type-style; the little evidence available suggests the value of teaching children to respond to any letter, irrespective of its type-style or size (Gibson, 15). Sight word reading is usually accomplished by means of some combination of phonics (including the "linguistics" methods) or whole-word programs. Sight vocabulary development is an extension of this, including such matters as root words, inflectional endings, prefixes, and so on. The purpose of intonation drills is to teach children to read words in sentences. Decoding is converting information received visually into verbal (or subverbal) messages.

Comprehension, which includes vocabulary, syntax, main facts, sequence, interpretation, and literary proficiency [for further discussion of these areas, with an extended illustration, see Rystrom (22)], requires substantially different cognitive processes from those used in decoding. When children are learning vocabulary, they may be learning a word and one of its meanings; or they may be learning what this word, which they already knew in some other situation or with some other meaning, means in this context; or they may be learning to infer what an unknown word means, based upon how and where it occurs in a story. Syntax, as a comprehension component, is almost never taught. Most reading materials are written with the assumption that the syntactic material they present will be understood. In order to control the readability level, many writers and editors have found that the intuition of language-sophisticated adults is a more reliable index than a readability formula. "Main facts" need to be taught because children do not perceive events in the same way adults do. Children place considerable importance on the fact the peddler puts on his own checked cap first, then the gray caps, next the brown caps, the blue caps above the brown, and the red caps last. Adults almost never remember this order. But many children do not remember where the peddler sat down to take his nap (Slobodkina, 26).

Sequence appears to be partly a matter of focusing on what adult readers find important, and partly a memory problem. Some children have difficulty remembering facts that they do not feel are important. Interpretation, which is often based upon inferential reasoning, is difficult for many children. In addition to remembering certain facts, they must also recall and use particular ideas from their general information to clarify the relevance of the facts stated in the story. In the story referred to above the reader is told that one day the peddler could not sell any caps and that he went for a walk in the country, where he sat down under a tree to take a nap. But the story does not say why the peddler went into the countryside to take his nap. The reader must infer, from the facts given in the story and his own experiences, that the peddler took a nap because he was tired and hungry. (A lower-level inference would be required to decide why the country is a more appropriate place for a nap than the city.) The final category, literary proficiency, includes a variety of study skills and familiarity with literary conventions.

At this point many readers may be wondering: "What's new?" Much of what has been presented in this paper looks familiar and has been taught for years. Although that is certainly true, it is also partly an illusion. Just as today's reader of Shakespearean English would never doubt his understanding of the sentence "Hamlet was a nice man," some readers may see only the familiar in what psychologists and linguists are saying about the reading process, without realizing there are some significant differences (in Shakespeare's time *nice* meant "foolish"). For the present moment, the contributions of psycholinguists can be grouped into three areas: the clarification and definition of terms, the exposition of language behavior as a process, and greater insight into a number of areas which appear to be important to the reading process.

SOME APPLICATIONS

Many of the terms and concepts traditionally used in reading instruction are both useful and worth preserving. But many of them need to be redefined. The "linguistic" reading programs are nothing more than a type of phonics approach to the teaching of reading; however, the generalizations they are based upon, the observations about the relationships between letters and sounds, are much more accurate than those of more traditional phonics programs. Several studies, most particularly Venezky's (28) discussion of orthographic patterns and Chomsky and Halle's (8) examination of intonation patterns, have demonstrated the complex but thoroughly regular nature of the relationships between how English is spoken and how it is written. The concept of the grapheme indicates an entire area for research and materials development which is virtually unexplored. The distinction between a word and a morpheme, particularly as these concepts are related to how the *word* concept is learned and should be taught, has received little attention. Despite the existence of well-developed strategies for teaching intonation to speakers of English as a foreign language, there have been no experiments to see if these, or similar methods, would facilitate teaching children to read sentences in their native language (because beginning readers tend to read each word in a sentence as if it were the final word, it might be effective to have them read the final word in a sentence by itself, then the last two words, then the last three or four words, and so on, until they are reading the entire sentence from the beginning). These and many other concepts from psycholinguistics seem almost directly applicable to the teaching of reading.

A second contribution of psycholinguistics is the conceptualization of reading as a process. That is, the areas described in the discussion of decoding and comprehension should not be viewed as independent skills, if reading is a process. Rather, their relationships and influences upon each other must be considered as important as the individual components themselves. Most psycholinguists feel children should not be taught the decoding skills by themselves; they should approach decoding as a meaningful (comprehension) process. On this and other grounds psycholinguists have criticized most of the "linguistic" reading materials, which do not stress the importance of reading for meaning [e.g., "Dan ran a tan van," from Bloomfield and Barnhart(4)]. Most teachers have intuitively realized that reading should be taught as a meaningful activity.

Many psycholinguists are now examining how decoding and comprehension are related. For example, it is evident that knowledge of vocabulary is not, by itself, the sole basis on which word meaning is understood. In the sentence "his girlfriend is really out of sight" the final "word" (outasite) is defined in part by its relationships to other words (*girlfriend is, really*), in part by the structure (NP + *BE* + NP), in part by inferential reasoning (*outasite* is a "good" word, so she must be an attractive girl), and so on. When readers are six or seven years old, they must engage in all the processes discussed above and they must also make decisions about which letters occur in particular words, how those words would be pronounced, what intonation patterns would be appropriate, what endings (which often indicate structural relationships) are used, and so on. Viewing reading as a process provides a new and potentially more powerful viewpoint for making discoveries about how children learn to read.

The third contribution of psycholinguistics to the reading process is difficult to identify, because it involves the applications of answers to questions which are just now being asked. For example, Read (20) has studied a number of children who taught themselves to read and write by observing members of their families. Although his sample was obviously atypical, and a small one, some tentative findings are of great potential significance. He found, for example, that the first vowel correspondences that children learned were the letter name–letter sound sets, as in the words name, Pete, bite, and so on. In the special writing system used by linguists the vowel sound in the word *name* is written /ey/, as the /ey/ sound is like the vowel sound in *bet* without the tongue glide indicated by the /y/. That is, an /e/ is an /ey/ without a tongue glide. Read found that children used point of articulation as the most significant feature, and not the presence or absence of gliding. In the writing systems these children invented they typically used the letter <a> to represent both the long-a /ey/ sound and the short-e /e/ sounds. Similar correspondences were constructed from other pairs: <e> was used for both long-e /iy/ and short-i /i/; <i> was used for both long-i /ay/ and short-o /a/, and so on.

The single area with the greatest immediate potential for reading is syntax. Some very significant work is now being done in determining the natural order of transformational rules (Burt, 6) and the relevance of transformational rules to the comprehension process (Fagan, 11). The potential applications are tremendous. For example, it is entirely possible that psycholinguists will be able to derive an accurate (or at least workable) method for determining readability levels. Work presently being done (Smith, 27) could lead to relatively simple rules which teachers could follow in writing materials for children at specific readability levels. It seems possible that particular children will be found to have trouble reading particular types of sentences or materials because the writer has employed syntactic structures which were not in their linguistic repertoires. (The reader is invited to look back to the first sentence of the second paragraph in this paper. Does the word "related" indicate that linguistics and psychology are related, or that these areas are related to reading methods?) It would then be possible to construct sets of materials which selectively probe their understanding of structure and, based upon the results, present simple, sequential drills which teach them how to read structures of the type. It is also likely that most of the reading problems presently encountered by college freshman can be traced to uncertainty on their part as to the structural meaning of what they are having difficulty reading. Although it has long been evident that structure is a factor in reading, the extent of its influence is probably much greater than even now is realized.

LANGUAGE EXPERIENCE

Before concluding this discussion of psycholinguistics and the reading process, one additional application should be considered: language experience teaching of reading. Many of the statements made by psycholinguists seem to describe and support strategies which can be used in teaching language experience reading. Advocates of both psycholinguistics and language experience agree that children's use of language must be considered in teaching reading. Both groups stress reading as a meaningful process. Both base subsequent learning on what is already known. Despite the apparent areas of agreement between psycholinguists and language experience proponents, there are some very serious objections to the language experience approach which must be raised. First, language experience is not a method. It is not based upon any stated positions; it does not have an articulated or established set of procedures. "Language experience" means whatever the speaker of the moment thinks it means. As long as the details are unstated, the speaker and listener "agree" without realizing they may have important differences of opinion. Second, there is no research evidence to support language experience as "the answer." The major point made in the *First Grade Studies* (12) was that no method of teaching reading resulted in consistently better reading performance, as measured by the posttest instruments. This is not to say that language experience, or some altogether new method of teaching reading based on psycholinguistic findings, may not be "the answer." But at the present time there is no evidence to support any such position.

A third objection to language experience is the fact that materials derived from stories which children dictate are, by definition, based upon their language performance rather than their language competence. Everyone reads and understands words in context which he would never use in his own speech. Part of learning to read is finding out how to interpret such words which are familiar, but not known, when they occur in a context where their meaning can be inferred from the rest of the sentence or paragraph. That is, the reader has sufficient language competence that he can figure out the meaning, but he would not (at this particular time, anyway) use the word in his speech. Much of what is learned occurs in the area between what is known and what is not known. Materials that are based upon what is known do not extend performance levels by probing potential competence. Yet much of what is meant by structure, inferential reasoning, vocabulary skills, and so on, is learned when the reader uses his competencies in these and related areas to "figure out" meaning. From a psycholinguistic point of view a language experience *program* based upon children's *competencies* might prove to be a worthwhile method of teaching reading, if there were such a program.

CONCLUSION

Psychology and linguistics have influenced the way reading is taught. For the immediate future, their significance is likely to increase, as more is learned about the structure of language, language acquisition, language development, and language cognition. Despite the promise of psycholinguistics to the improving of the teaching of reading, and the promise is great, it is important to remember that improving reading instruction is the issue at hand. As long as psycholinguists provide insight into the nature of the reading process, as long as there is benefit to be derived from thinking of reading as a process, the influence is a good one. When some new perspective suggests new directions, it should be followed. As Susanne Langer (17) has pointed out, the important eras in history occur not when new answers are being found, but when new questions are being asked.

REFERENCES

1. Ammon, Paul. Personal correspondence. Berkeley, Calif.: University of California, 1967.
2. Berko, Jean. "The Child's Learning of English Morphology," *Word*, 14 (1958), 150–77.
3. Bloomfield, Leonard. *Language*. New York: Rinehart and Winston, 1933.
4. ———, and Clarence L. Barnhart. *Let's Read: A Linguistic Approach*. Detroit: Wayne State University Press, 1961.
5. Brown, Roger, and Ursula Bellugi. "Three Processes in the Child's Acquisition of Syntax," *Harvard Educational Review*, 34 (1964), 133–51.
6. Burt, Marina K. *From Deep to Surface Structure: An Introduction to Transformational Syntax*. New York: Harper & Row, 1971.
7. Chomsky, Noam. *Syntactic Structures*. 'S-Gravenhage: Mouton & Co., 1957.
8. ———, and Morris Halle. *The Sound Pattern of English*. New York: Harper & Row, 1968.
9. Entwisle, Doris R. "The Syntactic-Paradigmatic Shift in Children's Word Associations," *Journal of Verbal Learning and Verbal Behavior*, 3 (1964), 19–29.
10. ———, and Ellen Greenberger. "Racial Differences in the Language of Grade School Children," *Sociology of Education*, 42 (1969), 238–50.
11. Fagan, William T. "Transformations and Comprehension," *The Reading Teacher*, 25 (1971), 169–72.
12. (*The*) *First Grade Reading Studies: Findings of Individual Investigations*, ed. by Russell G. Stauffer. Newark, Del.: International Reading Association, 1967.
13. Francis, W. Nelson. *The Structure of American English*. New York: The Ronald Press Company, 1958.

14. Fries, Charles Carpenter. *American English Grammar: The Grammatical Structure of Present-day American English with Especial Reference to Social Differences or Class Dialects.* New York: Appleton-Century-Crofts, Inc., 1940.
15. Gibson, Eleanor J. "Learning to Read," *Science,* 148 (1965), 1066–1072.
16. Laffey, James L. "The Effect of Different Modes of Presentation of Reading Materials on Vocalism in Silent Reading." Unpublished Doctoral Dissertation, University of Pittsburgh, 1967.
17. Langer, Susanne K. *Philosophy in a New Key: A Study in the Symbolism of Reason, Rite, and Art.* Cambridge, Mass.: Harvard University Press, 1963.
18. Mathews, Mitford M. *Teaching to Read: Historically Considered.* Chicago: The University of Chicago Press, 1966.
19. Mickish, Virginia. "Children's Perceptions of Written Word Boundaries" [mimeograph]. Athens: University of Georgia Reading Department, 1972.
20. Read, Charles. "Pre-school Children's Knowledge of English Phonology," *Harvard Educational Review,* 41 (1971), 1–34.
21. Rystrom, Richard. "Listening, Decoding, Comprehension, and Reading," *The Reading Teacher,* 24 (1970), 261–66.
22. ———. "Toward Defining Comprehension—a First Report," *Journal of Reading Behavior,* 2 (1970), 56–74.
23. Scholes, Robert. "How Do Children Learn Readjustment Rules?" Paper presented at the Southeastern Conference on Linguistics, VII. April 21, 1972, University of Georgia.
24. Shannon, Claude, and Warren Weaver. *The Mathematical Theory of Communication.* Urbana, Ill.: University of Illinois Press, 1949.
25. Singer, Harry, and Robert B. Ruddell. *Theoretical Models and Processes of Reading.* Newark, Del.: International Reading Association, 1970.
26. Slobodkina, Esphyr. *Caps for Sale: A Tale of a Peddler, Some Monkeys and Their Monkey Business.* New York: William R. Scott, Inc., 1940.
27. Smith, William L. "The Effects of Transformed Syntactic Structures on Reading," in *Language, Reading and the Communication Process,* ed. by Carl Braun, Newark, Del.: International Reading Association, 1971, pp. 52–62.
28. Venezky, Richard L. "English Orthography: Its Graphical Structure and Its Relation to Sound," *Reading Research Quarterly,* 2 (1967), 75–105.

READING IS THINKING*

Emmett A. Betts

The man who wrote the first comprehensive book in the field of reading methodology here pinpoints the basic needs in reading education. Using the premise that reading is thinking, he delineates a master plan

---

* FROM *The Reading Teacher* (February 1959), pp. 146–151, reprinted with permission of Emmett A. Betts and the International Reading Association.

to be used by competent teachers to develop these thinking skills and abilities in students. Then he shows how these plans are used to select teaching procedures for achieving the desired instructional goals.

1. What proof does the author advance to substantiate his claim that reading is thinking?

2. What steps can be taken to teach children how to think?

3. How can the teacher skillfully plan the strategy for ensuring the necessary conditions for learning?

4. What practices have resulted from inadequate conceptions of the nature of the reading process?

"My child can't read!" is a common complaint of parents. When asked what they mean, parents explain that Johnny doesn't have the necessary phonic skills to learn words. It is true that the word (telling-the-child-the-word) method of teaching beginning reading has produced many nonreaders and crippled readers. While phonic skills are essential in learning to read, reading needs are not met by massive doses of isolated drill on phonics.

It is true that too many children do not know phonic and other word-learning skills and are, therefore, handicapped in their reading. There is also evidence that more of our pupils need help on *how to think* in a reading situation. But too often parents believe their children can read when they are merely pronouncing words.

Most parents can tell that a child is reading poorly or not at all when he cannot identify written words. But it takes a competent teacher to identify the six-year-old who repeats the exact words of an author to answer a question, the eight-year-old who does not relate names (antecedents) to pronouns, or the older student who has not learned to tell the difference between facts and opinions. In short, professional competence is needed to assess the learning needs of pupils and to guide their development into truly able readers.

STRATEGY

For developing thinking skills and abilities, highly competent teachers have in mind a well-conceived master plan:

How to identify and provide for individual differences in needs and levels of achievement within the classroom (1). Master teachers recognize the limitations of standardized tests for estimating an individual's (1) independent reading level, (2) teaching or instructional level, and (3) specific needs. For this reason, they make maximum use of sytematic, informal observations of pupil behavior in reading situations. They know that a pupil cannot be taught how to think when the instructional material is so difficult he finger points his way slowly under each word or gives up in despair. They also know that the best reader in the class can realize his full potential only when he is dealing with interesting materials that challenge his thinking. Therefore, they *plan in advance* to organize their classes in different types of groups to provide equal learning opportunities for all pupils.

How to identify and classify comprehension needs, as a basis for when and what to teach (3, 13, 14). Competent teachers preplan—that is, map their strategy—to teach children how to think in different types of reading situations. They consider large groups of pupil needs:

1. Does the group have the necessary personal experiences for making a concept? Hal, for example, cannot estimate the distance from New York to San Francisco. During the discussion, however, he tells about a 500-mile trip to visit his grandmother, which he had helped to plan on a road map. His teacher helps him to use his personal experience with 500 miles to estimate on a map of the United States the 2600-mile airline distance. From this point, Hal continues to develop his concepts of space. Equally important, he takes new interests to reading.

2. Does the group use language effectively to deal with ideas (2)? Language serves at once to express and to shape our thoughts. In other words, we think with language. For this reason relatively simple language may be used to discuss everyday ideas, but complex language is used to discuss abstract ideas.

Penny, ball, dictionary, and *raccoon* are labels for things in the physical world; that is, we can point to a *ball* or a *dictionary. Roundness,* on the other hand, is a quality, or an abstraction. *Cottage, dwelling,* or *structure* can be used to represent different levels of abstraction. In life we can point to *a cottage* but not to *cottage,* to *a dwelling* but not to *dwelling,* to *a structure* but not to *structure.* At their successive levels of abstraction, *cottage, dwelling,* and *structure* are shorthand representations of increasingly complex concepts. It is with these nonverbal and verbal abstractions that we do our thinking. So, we teach pupils how to abstract and generalize, and help them develop an awareness of their use of abstractions.

And, or, but, for, etc., are connecting words which get their meanings from language. They connect or show relationships between ideas. The meanings of these words are taught, therefore, in their language settings.

Ten, minute, mile, and other definite terms can be interpreted when the pupil has certain concepts of quantity, size, etc. However, he may trip over *almost, long, soon,* and other indefinite terms, unless he has been given cause to think about their relative values.

To improve the interpretation of what he reads, the child is made aware of the important ways in which the meanings of words shift. For example, *talent* may mean "musical talent" or "the Biblical thirteen talents"; that is, two different things.

Comprehension is improved by an understanding of the structure or organization of language. Often the sentence gives a clue to the meaning of words. An appositional explanation ("Thor, the god of war,") may tip the scale of understanding. An index type of clue may explain a new term: "The *thralls* were the carpenters, the fence builders, the fagot carriers." Then again, a classification type of clue gives needed detail: "These people lived on the valley's neat farms and sowed barley, wheat, and other *grains.*" These and other types of context clues are considered in the teacher's strategy to improve thinking abilities.

Relationships between subject and predicate, between modifying and independent clauses, and between modifying phrases and other sentence elements are hazards to comprehension until the child understands them. Equally important are the meanings of different types of linking, separating, and enclosing punctuation, as, for example, when the dash is used to "direct the reader's attention backward" (15).

How an author develops a story or presents information, as a basis for preparing a teaching plan. Master teachers have learned that the best motivation for reading is the pupil's inner drive to learn—his questions and other expressions of purposes. Consequently, they plan to know each selection used for intensive directed reading activities with a group. This knowledge helps them take the group smoothly and promptly into the introduction of a well-written story or informational selection.

The introduction is usually a brief, stimulating setting for the story. For example, the title of Lee Wyndham's "Grandma's Ostrich" causes both children and adults to ask, "Why did Grandma have an ostrich?" This question is answered clearly and provocatively in the first few paragraphs.

When teachers *know* a selection, they can skillfully guide the pupils' reading from the introduction into the main body of it. After the pupils learn that Grandma "inherited" the ostrich from a defunct circus of which she was part owner, they always ask, "What did Grandma Jones do with the ostrich?" Reading to answer this question takes the group through the main part of the story.

When the pupils learn how Grandma Jones taught the ostrich to behave, they usually ask, "But will she be able to keep him?" As they read the conclusion of the story, they learn how a special event resolved the conflict, leaving them with a sense of satisfaction.

By *planning* their strategy before using a selection to develop skills, master teachers prepare themselves to develop (1) *interest*, (2) *phonic* and other word-learning skills, and (3) *thinking* abilities in the field of action—the guided reading of the story.

How a teaching plan is organized as a basis for making the best use of teaching opportunities. When competent teachers guide individualized reading they plan ahead to make accessible to their pupils (1) books at their *independent* reading levels, (2) books that can be used to develop new interests and skills. When guiding a directed activity in a basic reader, however, they group the pupils so that the first reading is done at the teaching or instructional level, and the rereading can be done independently (1).

These master teachers know that a selection or a book challenges their pupils when it presents new learnings. They also know that when a child is frustrated by the difficulty of the material, interest wanes sharply and comprehension is defaulted.

When making systematic use of a basic textbook, teachers familiarize themselves with the strategy of the authors—the organization of the teaching plans. First, they learn how the pupils are prepared for reading a selection, especially the attention given to developing interests and concepts to be taken to it.

Second, they note the kinds of suggestions given for guiding the first or silent reading of it. In this part of the plan they give special consideration to the ready availability of specific help on both phonic and thinking needs which may arise.

Third, they evaluate informal suggestions, study-book use, and other help given for rounding out learning experience so that growth is insured.

TACTICS

One of the earmarks of a successful teacher is the ability to plan strategy for insuring the necessary conditions of learning. Skillful planning (1) places a premium on individual differences, (2) permits a sharp focus on the specific thinking needs of the pupils, (3) makes the most of the teaching opportunities in instructional material, and (4) gives a set for the wise selection and use of tactics or teaching procedures. Above all, the teacher is free to use the author's guide book with discretion.

Master teachers plan to help their children find out "what the author says"; that is, do literal reading. But they do much more: they plan to have the pupils learn how to "think about what the author says," to do critical reading (4).

In preparing the pupils for reading a selection in a story book, for a study-book activity, or for pursuing a major interest in some curriculum area, master teachers guide them into *thinking* about "what we know" and "what we want to know." The first step assesses their interests, attitudes, and concepts which they take to the activity. The second step heightens interest and establishes clear-cut purposes to guide their thinking. In short, the teacher uses sound tactics for starting the pupils on the road to critical thinking, to the considered evaluation of ideas and concepts.

With a general purpose and specific questions in mind, the pupils are ready to locate and evaluate sources of relevant information. This activity requires a consideration of the reputation of authors, dates of publication, etc., even when using basic readers and study books.

In surveying the materials the pupils are made aware of the difference between facts and opinions. They learn, for example, that the following are statements of fact because they are verifiable:

"In August of 1620, two vessels sailed from England, headed for the new world."

"The temperature in this room is 80 degrees Fahrenheit."

They will learn that a great many statements are opinions, or expressions of attitudes, and are not verifiable:

"You will have fun with it."

"This room is hot."

When pupils learn to discriminate between facts and opinions they tend to do less arguing and more discussing. Equally important, they are better prepared to select information *relevant* to their purposes.

In testing the relevance of material pupils learn to answer these questions:

1. What does the author say?
2. Is the statement a fact or an opinion?
3. Does the statement answer my question?
4. How can I use this statement?
5. What other help did the author give on my question?

Many kindergarten children learn to judge between highly relevant and totally irrelevant statements. As children learn how to think at succeeding school levels, they make closer judgments of the relevance between statements.

Judging the relevance of statements to purposes plays a major role in thinking. First, the pupil evaluates relevance of sub-points to each other and to the main points in an outline. Furthermore, he consistently uses questions or statements, sentences or phrases to parallel language structure with his ideas. Second, he evaluates relevance in visualizing both stories and information: sequences of important events in a story, or experiment, organization of material on maps, charts, slides, etc. Third, he uses relevant facts in solving a mystery, in using the results of an experiment, in making social judgments, etc. That is, straight thinking is required for drawing conclusions from related facts or from cause-effect relationships (5, 10, 11, 12).

In following through on their strategy for teaching children how to think, teachers are confronted with a subtle, but potent, tactical situation: Attitudes. This situation can be summarized as follows.

1. The child's interpretation of a selection depends upon the attitudes he takes to it. Therefore, preparation for reading includes the assessment of attitudes toward the topic. Favorable attitudes increase comprehension, while unfavorable attitudes interfere with comprehension.
2. The child's attitudes influence recall. Favorable attitudes promote ease and vividness of recall, and unfavorable attitudes tend to produce hazy, confused ideas.
3. Favorable attitudes increase interest in a topic or a type of selection.
4. Individual attitudes are modified by peer discussions.

IN SUMMARY

Contrary to popular opinion, children can be taught how to think. Their ability to think is limited primarily by their personal experiences and the uses they make of them in problem solving, in abstracting and generalizing to make concepts, in judging, and in drawing conclusions. Under competent teacher guidance children gradually learn to think, within the limits of their rates of maturation, or inner growth (6, 8, 9).

From available evidence it appears that children who have not learned to think far outnumber those who have not learned necessary phonic skills. (Both, of course, are crippled readers or nonreaders!) Consider the number of children who can pronounce *fearless*, for example, but who think it means "afraid." How many children cannot divide ⅓ by 4 because they have merely memorized a meaningless rule about "inverting and multiplying"? Or, how many high school graduates cannot subtract a minus 3 from a plus 10, because they have never related the mathematical process to the use of a thermometer? How many children can pronounce astronomical numbers and yet cannot estimate the coast-to-coast distance across the United States? How many children try to achieve variety of sentence structure by the mechanical rearrangement of sentences rather than by the careful consideration of the ideas they wish to express? The answers to these and related questions offer undisputed evidence of the need for teaching children how to think.

The mere pronunciation of words, the memorization of phonic or mathematic rules, and other emphases on rote memory and mechanics lead to the use of empty words. This false security in words leads to the acceptance of a carload of words without a single idea. The acceptance of word manipulation rather than the thinking about ideas is called *verbalism*. And verbalism can become a malignant disease in education, dooming the would-be learner.

But there is hope, real evidence of progress in understanding the strategy and tactics of teaching children how to think. In the last ten years, four outstanding books have been published on the psychology of thinking. Writers of pedagogical textbooks in social studies, science, arithmetic, and reading have begun to apply the conclusions reached by psychologists. Lastly, it is highly significant that this issue of *The Reading Teacher* is dedicated to the proposition that children can be taught how to think.

REFERENCES

1. Betts, Emmett A. *Foundations of Reading Instruction, revised.* New York: American Book Company, Inc., 1957.
2. ———. "Reading: Semantic Approach." Reprinted from *Education*, May 1949. Haverford, Pa.: Betts Reading Clinic.
3. ———. "Reading As a Thinking Process." Reprinted from *The National Elementary Principal*, September 1955. Haverford, Pa.: Betts Reading Clinic.
4. ———. "Research on Reading As a Thinking Process." Reprinted from *Journal of Educational Research*, September 1956. Haverford, Pa.: Betts Reading Clinic.
5. Bingham, Alma, "Improving Children's Facility in Problem Solving," *Prac-*

tical *Suggestions for Teaching*, No. 16. New York: Teachers College, Columbia University, 1958.

6. Blair, Arthur Witt, and William H. Burton. *Growth and Development of the Preadolescent*. New York: Appleton-Century-Crofts, 1951.

7. Morris, Charles. *Signs, Language and Behavior*. Englewood Cliffs, N.J.: Prentice-Hall, 1946.

8. Piaget, Jean. *The Construction of Reality in the Child*. New York: Basic Books, 1954.

9. ———. *The Language and Thought of the Child*. New York: Humanities Press, 1952.

10. Russell, David H. *Children's Thinking*. Boston: Ginn and Co., 1956.

11. Vinacke, W. Edgar. *The Psychology of Thinking*. New York: McGraw-Hill, 1952.

12. Watts, A. F. *The Language and Mental Development of Children*. Boston: D. C. Heath, 1944.

13. Wesley, Edgar Bruce, and Mary A. Adams. *Teaching Social Studies in Elementary Schools*. Boston: D. C. Heath, 1952.

14. Wesley, Edgar Bruce. *Teaching Social Studies in High School*. Boston: D. C. Heath, 1950.

15. Whitehall, Harold. *Structural Essentials of English*. New York: Harcourt Brace Jovanovich, Inc., 1956.

Developing the Ability
to Decode Words

Introduction

An aura of mystery and excitement surrounds the word "decoding" for anyone familiar with some of the classical examples of decoding in history and literature. For years experts tried to decipher or decode the Egyptian hieroglyphics, but failed. When Champollion broke the code of the triglot inscriptions on the Rosetta Stone the riddle was solved, and scholars were able to decode the writings of the ancient Egyptians. The code in Poe's story The Goldbug *was broken by a knowledge of the frequency of occurrence in writing of the letters of the English alphabet. A decided advantage accrued to the Allied forces in World War II when an American cryptographer broke the Japanese code enabling the Allies to decode*

Japanese messages and thereby be informed of Japanese military plans.

For the person who is learning how to read, the code represented by the English language is an obstacle of no mean proportions. However, if the person is going to enjoy the mystic academic rites of the initiated, he must break the code.

In this section the authors discuss several methods for teaching a person how to decode printed English. One of these decoding aids is phonics. Basically, when a person learns phonics he learns to associate the appearance of graphemes with the one or more phonemes each grapheme may represent.

Theory and practice in teaching word-analysis skills have undergone major changes as the result of work by such individuals as Groff, Hanna, E. H. Smith, Venezky, and the authors of the extensive articles in this section— Cheek, Moretz, and Davey.

Cheek explains the meaning of objective-based teaching of word-analysis skills by explicating topics such as diagnostic–prescriptive instruction, individualized instruction, objective-based teaching, systems approach and criterion-referenced testing. Moretz and Davey, in a very thorough article, explore the process and strategies in teaching decoding skills to middle and secondary school students.

Objective-Based Teaching of Word-Analysis Skills in Middle and Secondary Schools*

Martha Cheek

In this article Cheek maintains that an effective reading program is highly dependent upon the effectiveness of the teacher. The effective teacher selects a method that meets the student's needs. In order to implement a method properly the teacher must use some form of diagnostic–prescriptive instruction. The main thrust of the article, then, is how to identify and assess the word-analysis skills that are to be taught.

1. Which two basic points should one keep in mind when selecting word-analysis skills to measure middle and secondary students?

2. Do the objectives in Table 2 seem to meet the criteria set forth in the six points—situation, action, and so on?

3. Why is it important to use a graded word list in the development of criterion-referenced items?

4. Why is it important to administer the informal reading inventory?

5. Why should the teacher diagnose the student's modality strengths?

6. Does the use of the diagnostic–prescriptive procedure increase or decrease the instructional role of the teacher? Explain.

* Written especially for this volume.

Diagnostic–prescriptive instruction, individualized instruction, objective-based teaching, systems approach, criterion-referenced testing, accountability —these are terms that are in current usage in discussions of reading instruction in the 1970's. To attain the Right to Read effort's goal of eradicating illiteracy by 1980, these terms must be more than words, they must be functional.

Research has shown that the success or failure of a reading program is highly dependent upon the effectiveness of the teacher. It has also been shown that no particular reading method or material is superior to all others with all children. It is now clear that the *best method* or *material* is that which *best meets the individual needs of the student*. However, the research also tells us that to be effective the method must be one with which the teacher feels comfortable. Thus an individualized program or an individualized objective-based reading program is not for every teacher; however, every teacher must use some form of diagnostic–prescriptive instruction in order to determine the instructional reading needs of every student.

Many reading programs are considered to be diagnostic; but often standardized tests are their sole means of diagnosis. This often severely limits their utility, for many standardized tests do not give specific information on what a student can or cannot do except in relation to a standardization population. Such information may not reveal which specific word-analysis skills a student needs to develop. Standardized tests have a place in the reading program; they do serve to compare individuals and groups. However, this is not the information that is necessary to meet individual reading needs of students. What, then, can be used to obtain the necessary information, and, once obtained, what can be done with it? Let us attempt to answer these questions as they relate to word-analysis skills at the middle school and secondary levels.

IDENTIFICATION OF WORD-ANALYSIS SKILLS

A first step in measuring specific reading skills is to determine which skills should be measured. This can be done by listing the various categories in word analysis and then listing the specific skills belonging in the category. Skills listed in various basal reader series and basic reading methods textbooks should be incorporated in such lists.

When selecting word-analysis skills to measure middle school and secondary students, two points should be kept in mind: (1) many students, even though they have reached the secondary level, have not learned many of the basic word-analysis skills; and (2) many word-analysis skills are developmental in nature, i.e., one skill must be learned at several different levels, for as the readability level of the words increases, the skill needs change. Therefore, a list of word-analysis skills to be taught at the secondary level should be composed of skills from the primary level through college.

TABLE 1

Scope of Each Skill Classification for Word-Analysis Skills

SKILL CLASSIFICATION	SCOPE
A. Word recognition	Basic sight words
	Five hundred most frequently written words
B. Phoneme–grapheme correspondences	Alternative graphemic representations for the forty-six phonemes*
C. Structural analysis	
1. Compound words	Identify compound words
	Identify compound words in sentences
	Identify words making up compound word
	Identify meaning of compound word
2. Contractions	Identify contractions
	Identify contractions in sentences
	Distinguish possessives from contractions
	Identify words making up contractions
	Identify words making up contractions in sentences
	Write words making up contractions
	Write words making up contractions in sentences
3. Prefixes and suffixes†	Identify suffix (or prefix) in word
	Identify suffixes (or prefixes) in word
	Identify suffixed (or prefixed) words
	Identify suffixed (or prefixed) word in sentence
	Identify meaning of suffix (or prefix)
	Identify meaning of suffixed (or prefixed) word
4. Inflectional endings	Identify words with inflectional endings
	Identify words with inflectional endings in sentences
	Identify specific inflectional endings in words
	Identify meaning of word with inflectional ending
D. Clues	
1. Context clues‡	Definition clue
	Synonym clue
	Familiar expression clue
	Comparison or contrast clue
	Summary clue
	Mood clue
2. Dictionary clue	Identify statements about a word and its dictionary definition
	Identify definition of word or words
	Identify definition of multiple meaning word used in sentence
	Match meanings of word to its usage in sentences
	Identify word to complete sentence from given definitions
	Identify meaning of Greek or Latin root words

E. Vocabulary relationships

1. Synonyms and an-
    tonyms
	Identify pairs of synonyms (or antonyms)
	Identify synonym (or antonym) for given word
	Identify words in sentences which are synonyms
	    (or antonyms)
	Match words with synonym (or antonym)

2. Homonyms	Identify pairs of homonyms Identify meaning of homonyms
3. Heteronyms	Identify meaning of heteronyms

F. Word replacements

1. Abbreviations	Identify meaning of abbreviation Write meaning of abbreviation
2. Acronyms	Identify meaning of acronyms Write meaning of acronyms
3. Symbols	Identify meaning of symbols Write meaning of symbols

---

* See Appendix A of this article.

† See Appendixes B and C of this article.

‡ Use as a meaning clue as well as a correctional clue to pronunciation.

ASSESSMENT OF WORD-ANALYSIS SKILLS

Once identified, word-analysis skills should be written in a measurable objective form. That is, the teacher or reading supervisor should decide which skills are to be measured as well as which components of each skill. For example, in studying suffixes, will the student mark the suffix in the word? Will he add a suffix to a given word or will he identify the meaning of a given suffix? All three skills can and probably should be measured; however, this decision must be made before specific objectives can be written or selected.

When the decision is made as to what is to be measured, the performance or behavioral objective may be written or selected. In writing such objectives, the following information should be included in each:

1. Situation. The situation confronting the learner is clearly specified, including the mode in which stimuli are to be presented.
2. Action. The action required of the learner is unambiguously defined, including the mode in which responses are to be made.
3. Object. The object on which the learner is to operate (i.e., the object of the action) is clearly stated.
4. Limits. The particular limits associated with the activity expected of the learner are specified. (Limits may be placed on situation, action, and/or object.)
5. Measurability. The specified action involves an observable rather than an inferred response.

6. Communicability. The objective is so stated that one, and only one, interpretation of the objective is reasonably possible.
7. Criterion. The degree of proficiency required as evidence of accomplishment by a student of the objective is indicated. [The criterion may be indicated implicitly or explicitly. If implicit, 100 per cent accuracy is effectively designated. If explicit, it may be appended parenthetically to the statement of the objective (1)].

Notice in Table 2 that each objective is stated specifically enough so that it can be measured in only one way. With this specific information, items should be developed to measure each objective.

TABLE 2

Listing of Word-Analysis Skills for Middle School and Secondary Students with Sample Objectives*

SKILLS	OBJECTIVE

I. Word recognition
  A. Basic sight words
  B. Five hundred most frequently written words
	Given ten rows of words, each row containing four words, one of which will be read orally and which is also found in the list of the one hundred most frequently written words, the learner will underline the word read orally.

II. Phoneme-grapheme correspondences	Given a list of words and an example of the /ā/ spelled *a* as in the word *lady*, the learner will underline the words containing the /ā/ spelled a.

III. Blending
  A. Letters
  B. Syllables
	Given two lists, one containing the first part of four words and the other containing the last part of the same four words, the learner will blend the two parts into known words by connecting the word parts in the first list with the word parts in the second list with a line.

IV. Structural analysis A. Compound words	Given four compound words, the learner will draw a line between the two words that make up each compound word.
B. Contractions	Given four contractions with three pairs of base words under each, the learner will underline the two words that make up each contraction.
C. Prefixes	Given four prefixed words, each containing a different prefix and four choices of meaning

for each prefixed word, the learner will put an "X" before the correct meaning of each prefixed word.

D. Suffixes	Given four suffixes in one column and their corresponding meanings randomly arranged in another column, the learner will write the letter of the correct meaning of each suffix.
E. Inflectional endings	Given a word with an inflectional ending that forms plurals and four choices of meaning, the learner will underline the meaning of the word.

V. Clues

A. Context clues	Given sentences containing a circled word and a word or group of words suggesting a mood or situation which gives a clue to the meaning of the circled word, the learner will underline the word or group of words which gives a clue to the meaning of the circled word.
B. Dictionary clues	Given the dictionary definitions of a multiple-meaning word and an equal number of sentences using the word according to its different meanings, the learner will write the letter of the dictionary definition beside the appropriate sentence.

VI. Vocabulary relationships

A. Synonyms	Given four words in one column and their corresponding synonyms randomly arranged in another column, the learner will write the letter of the correct synonym of each word.
B. Antonyms	Given a pair of sentences with an underlined word in the first sentence and its antonym in the second sentence, the learner will underline the word in the second sentence which is the antonym of the underlined word in the first sentence.
C. Homonyms	Given two or three words that are homonyms and a meaning of one of the words, the learner will underline the word which fits the meaning.

TABLE 2 (*Cont.*)

SKILLS	OBJECTIVE
D. Heteronyms	Given the meaning of each word of a pair of heteronyms and a sentence using each word, the learner will write the letter of the meaning beside the appropriate sentence.
VII. Word replacements A. Abbreviations	Given four abbreviations, the learner will write the word or group of words which the abbreviations stand for.
B. Acronyms	Given a symbol and four choices of meanings, the meaning of each acronym.
C. Symbol	Given a symbol and four choices of meanings, the learner will underline the meaning of the symbol.

* Taken from *The Florida Catalog of Reading Objectives*, Field Trial Edition, Florida Department of Education, 1972.

These items are developed according to the criteria given in the objective. They are therefore called criterion-referenced items. The performance objectives and criterion-referenced items should be developed to insure that satisfactory performance on an item does indeed indicate satisfactory achievement of the skill. A criterion-referenced item possesses the following characteristics:[1]

1. Congruence. The task specified in the exercise corresponds directly to the performance specified in the objective, including the situation, action, object, and limits.
2. Comprehensibility. The task specified by the exercise is so stated or portrayed that the learner clearly understands what is expected of him.
3. Objectivity. The exercise (including component items, if any) is stated in such a way that all competent observers (evaluators) can make a clear and unequivocal decision as to whether or not the learner has demonstrated an acceptable performance.
4. Integrity. The exercise is structured in such a way that an acceptable response to the exercise constitutes sufficient evidence, in and of itself, that the learner has accomplished the corresponding objective.

[1] *Florida Index to the Numerical Identification and Classification of Educational Objectives*, compiled and edited by The Research and Development Section of the Florida Department of Education (Tallahassee: State of Florida, Department of Education, 1972), pp. 2-A and 3-A.

5. Equivalence. If two or more exercises correspond to a single objective, each exercise in the set is a true alternate, in that a student who passes (or fails) one exercise on a given occasion would be expected to pass (or fail) any other exercise in the set.[2]

To aid in the development of criterion-referenced items, a graded word list should be used to be certain that the vocabulary utilized will be suitable to the level being measured. An additional caution is needed if multiple-choice responses are required: be aware of the chance of guessing the correct response when given three distractors and one correct answer. Be sure that adequate items are used to determine that a student knows the skill and is not just test wise!

These objectives and criterion-referenced items, which form the basis for objective-based teaching, have been developed and can be purchased from some publishing companies. The Wisconsin Research and Development Center for Cognitive Learning is presently developing an entire objective-based system.[3] The Florida Department of Education has developed a comprehensive catalog of reading objectives and sample criterion-referenced items for use in Florida schools.

Even though objectives and criterion-referenced items can be obtained from various sources, the user must be aware of the procedures involved in order to be prepared to develop his own objectives for skills which the teacher feels should be taught and are not included in the acquired programs.

UTILIZATION OF PERFORMANCE OBJECTIVES AND CRITERION-REFERENCED ITEMS

As was mentioned earlier, all teachers are not initially expected to feel comfortable teaching by objectives. In fact, in the beginning many teachers will experience a feeling of uncertainty with the procedure. However, some will begin by following the explicit directions. They will later adjust the system to suit their style of teaching. This is great! It happens when a first-year teacher begins by following explicitly every page in a basal reader series teacher's manual. The problem arises when the same teacher follows the manual page by page several years later; he has allowed the manual to dictate his teaching. This could happen with an objective-based approach, but it is unlikely because the teacher who is willing to try a new approach is more likely to be able to fit these new ideas into his teaching style.

Performance objectives and criterion-referenced items can be utilized in a test–teach–test cycle. Using this procedure, students are screened through

---

[2] Ibid., p. 5-A.

[3] Available from National Computer Systems, Minneapolis, Minnesota. Cf. Lawrence Hafner and Hayden B. Jolly, *Patterns of Teaching Reading in the Elementary School.* New York: Macmillan Publishing Co., Inc., 1972. Chapter 9 and Appendix F.

the use of informal measures to determine their approximate reading levels.[4] The teacher then selects a group of objectives on which the student may be deficient (this is indicated by the informal measure) and administers the item for the objective which is the least difficult in the hierarchy. If the student passes this item, a more difficult objective is measured; if the item is missed, the teacher should go to less difficult objectives. This procedure is followed until each student has a list of objectives which need further development and a list of those which have been achieved.

Prior to beginning a program based on objectives, the teacher or reading supervisor should collect all available materials. He should code them to each objective. Under each objective there should be the name of the material, the appropriate page number or lesson number, and the *readability level* of the material.[5] The readability level is very important because a student reading on a fifth level should not be expected to learn a skill when it is taught using material on the eighth-grade readability level.

After determining what skills the student needs to develop and what materials are available to assist with their development, the teacher discusses with the student the results of the diagnosis. He then devises an individual prescription for the student. The procedure thus far is analogous to the procedure followed by those in the medical profession. The doctor who gives the same prescription to all regardless of their illness does not remain in practice very long!

In addition to a means of determining strengths and weaknesses of word-analysis skills, the teacher should be cautioned that he must carry the diagnosis further. Does the student have equally developed visual and auditory modality strengths, is one much stronger than the other, or is there a need to rely on the kinesthetic modality to develop the visual and auditory modalities? Teachers should be aware that a student who has auditory modality weaknesses will have difficulty with methods which rely heavily on auditory abilities such as the phonics method.

A second caution is that ample opportunity must be given to allow the students to utilize the skills through independent reading. Unless students learn that reading is a tool for gaining information and enjoyment, knowledge of the skills is useless. Care must be taken to insure that students learn to utilize the many word-analysis skills.

The use of this diagnostic–prescriptive procedure does not remove the teacher from the instructional role. Instead, he is now responsible to individuals or small groups and must move from one to another. In fact, the instructional role of the teacher is increased when diagnostic–prescriptive procedures are followed, because there is no longer instruction in one skill to an entire class, but instruction in many different skills to individuals.

[4] William R. Powell and Collin G. Dunkeld give research information on scoring informal measures in "Validity of the IRI Reading Levels," *Elementary English*, 48 (October 1971), 637–42.

[5] Hafner and Jolly, op. cit., have an extended discussion of Otto and Askov's "Wisconsin Design" in Chapter 10 of their work.

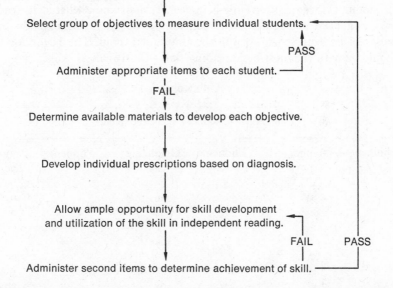

Determine which skills are to be measured.

Obtain measurable objectives for each skill.

Develop items on the appropriate level to measure each objective.

Use informal measures to screen students.

Select group of objectives to measure individual students.

PASS

Administer appropriate items to each student.

FAIL

Determine available materials to develop each objective.

Develop individual prescriptions based on diagnosis.

Allow ample opportunity for skill development and utilization of the skill in independent reading.

FAIL   PASS

Administer second items to determine achievement of skill.

When a student and teacher feel that the student has developed a given objective, a posttest (a second criterion-referenced item) may be administered. If the student satisfactorily achieves this skill, instruction should begin on another objective. However, if the student does not perform satisfactorily on the posttest, additional instruction should be done to develop the deficient skill.

One very important point should be remembered when teaching word-analysis skills; that is, the desired end is not the mastery of a group of skills; rather, it is the natural application of these skills in everyday reading.

SUMMARY

When the objective-based teaching approach is utilized, the methods and materials best suited to the teacher and students are utilized in developing prescriptions. These prescriptions can be as broad or as narrow in scope as the teacher and her resources permit. The principal task is to diagnose each student and determine the status of his analysis skills and develop individual prescriptions to improve skill deficiencies. To develop sets of objectives is a monstrous task. It is far too time-consuming for the individual classroom teacher to do; therefore, teachers should seek a set or sets of objectives which most nearly measure the word-analysis skills of the students in their classes. Additional objectives can be added by following the criteria given in this article. In many cases items must be developed by the teacher to measure the objective at an appropriate level for individual students. Individual schools, districts, and states must consider the necessity of pooling these items to form a bank of criterion-referenced items which can be used to allow the teacher to devote more time to individual students.

Educators have been asked to be accountable for what happens in the classroom; this request can only be met if teachers know what skills students have and have not achieved. Students must be taught as individuals and must not be expected to fit into the traditional mold. The beginning place should be with the most basic reading skill—word-analysis skills.

APPENDIX A

PHONEME–GRAPHEME CORRESPONDENCES

Phoneme	Grapheme	Phoneme	Grapheme	Phoneme	Grapheme
/ā/	a		ea-e		oo
	e		i		ow
	ay		ae		oa
	e-e		ee-e		ou-e
	a-e		ei		ow-e
	ei		ei-e		ou
	ei-e		eo		oe
	ai				ough
	et	/ī/	oy		au
	eigh		uy		au-e
	ey		i		eau
	ai-e		i-e		ew
	aigh		igh		
	ea		y	/ü/	oo
	au-e		ie		u
	ay-e		y-e		o
			ai-e		ew
/ē/	e		ay		ou
	ey				ue
	ea	/ī/	ei		u-e
	ei-e		eigh		wo
	ee		ey		ui
	oe		ey-e		oo-e
	y				o-e
	i-e	/ō/	o		ough
	ie		oa-e		ou-e
	e-e		o-e		ui-e

/ȯi/	oi			u-e	/d/	d	
	oy			o		dd	
	oi-e						
			/yü/	u-e	/g/	g	
/ā/	a			u		gu	
	a-e			ew		gg	
	ai			ue		gh	
	au			eau		gue	
	e-e		/ə/	i		x	
	ea			e			
				o	/hw/	wh	
/ē/	a			a			
	a-e			ou	/l/	l	
	ai			u		ll	
	e			e-e		ln	
	e-e			u-e		sl	
	ea			ai			
	ie			au	/n/	n	
	ue			ea		kn	
				ei		nn	
/ī/	i			eo		gn	
	i-e			eou		mn	
	y			i-e		pn	
	a-e			ia			
	e			a-e	/p/	p	
	ea			ie		pp	
	e-e			ie-e			
	ee			o-e	/s/	s	
	ui			oi-e		ss	
	u			y		c	
	o					sc	
	ie-e	/ȯ/		o		st	
	a			a		ps	
	ai			au		sch	
				aw		sw	
/ä/	o			au-e		z	
	a			o-e			
	o-e			ough	/t/	tt	
	a-e			augh		t	
	ea					ed	
	ow	/yu̇/		u		bt	
	ou			u-e		cht	
						ct	
/au̇/	ou	/b/		b		pt	
	ow			bb		th	
	ou-e	/ch/		ch		tw	
				tch			
/u̇/	oo			ti	/th/	th	
	u			t			
	ou			c	/th/	th	

APPENDIX A (*Cont.*)

PHONEME–GRAPHEME CORRESPONDENCES

Phoneme	Grapheme	Phoneme	Grapheme	Phoneme	Grapheme
/w/	w	/h/	h		ch
	u		wh		ci
	ou				c
		/j/	j		ce
/z/	es		g		s
	s		d		sc
	z		dg		sch
	zz		di		sci
	cz		dj		si
	sc		gg		ss
	ss		gi		ssi
					t
/k/	c	/m/	m		
	k		mm	/v/	v
	ck		mb		f
	lk		lm		lv
	qu		gm		
	ch		mn	/zh/	si
	cc				s
	que	/ng/	ng		g
	q		n		
	cch		ngue	/kw/	cqu
	cg				qu
	kh	/r/	r		
	sc		rr	/əl/	al
	x		rh		el
			wr		il
/f/	f				le
	ff	/ks/	cs		ol
	ph		x		
	gh			/ən/	en
	ft	/sh/	sh		in
	lf		ti		on

APPENDIX B

Prefixes and Their Meanings

PREFIX	MEANING
a-, ad-, ap-, at-	to, toward
ab-	from
ac-	pertaining to
al-, ar-	pertaining to, like

an-	belonging to
anti-	against
be-	around, act of being
com, col-	together with
con-	together
de-, dis-	from, away from, apart
di-	doubly, to separate
en-, em-	in, into
ex-, e-	out of or out
for-	away, off
in-, im-	in, into, and not
inter-	between
mis-	wrong
non-	not
o-, op-, of-, ob-	against, away from
per-	fully
post-	after
pro-, pre-	before, for
re-	again
sub-	under
super-	over
trans-	across
tri-	three

Appendix C

Suffixes and Their Meanings

SUFFIX	MEANING
-able	capable of being
-age	act or state of
-al	relation to
-ance	state of being
-ant	being
-ate (noun)	one who
-ate (verb)	to make
-ble, -ible	capable of being
-cion	action
-cy	state of
-den, -dom	state or condition
-ence	state of being
-ent	one who
-eous	of the nature of
-er	little, maker of
-est	comparison
-et	little
-ful	capable of being
-ian	relating to

APPENDIX C (*Cont.*)

SUFFIX	MEANING
-ic	like, made of
-ion	condition or quality
-ious	abounding in
-ise, -ize	to make
-ish	state of being
-ism	act of
-ist, -ite	one who
-ity, -ty	state of being
-less	without
-ling	little
-ly	like, in manner
-man	human, man
-ment	state or quality
-ness	state of being
-ship	relationship
-sion	action
-some	state of being
-ster	one who
-tion	state or condition
-tude	state or condition
-ty	condition
-ure	act or process
-ward	direction of
-wise	ways

PROCESS AND STRATEGIES IN TEACHING DECODING SKILLS TO STUDENTS IN MIDDLE AND SECONDARY SCHOOLS*

Sara Moretz and Beth Davey

The term *decoding* has been invested with numerous meanings. The authors discuss some of the various meanings of decoding and then offer a definition of their own. After explicating three channels of decoding, they launch into the second part of their article—Instructional Strategies. Here they give a systematic description of a large number of activities for developing efficient use of four basic types of decoding tools.

1. Describe the traditional view of decoding.
2. What is the divergent view of decoding?
3. Explain the rationale for the working definition of decoding.

* Written especially for this volume.

4. Expand on the factors of complexity which challenge readers at the middle and secondary levels.

5. Illustrate each process in Table 1.

6. What are some instructional strategies for acquiring Channel I words? Be able to explain in detail.

7. Illustrate the difference between syntactic clues and semantic clues, the two general types of contextual information.

8. How does one develop efficient use of context clues?

9. What are some instructional strategies for teaching word-structure clues?

10. Note the instructional strategies for teaching symbol–sound relationship clues.

I. An Exploration of the Process

A discussion of instructional approaches which foster students' continuing development and refinement of decoding skills must be based upon a clear defining of the process in question. Such a beginning would seem to be not only a logical point of departure, but also an easily accomplished one. One would think that defining a concept as frequently encountered as decoding is a simple task. Even a limited review of related literature, however, reveals that such is not the case. The lack of agreement on the meaning of the term is illustrated in the alternate definitions provided by Hodges and Rudorf (15). The two explanations included in the glossary are the following:

1. A term commonly used in reading to refer to the process of rendering written or printed symbols into the speech forms that were originally recorded.
2. A term now also used to refer to the process of translating written or spoken messages to meaning.

These two sample definitions would appear to be in conflict, because the first describes a print-to-speech process and makes no reference to meaning, whereas the second delineates a print-to-meaning process, with no mention of an accompanying translation to speech.

Because of this lack of professional agreement surrounding the meaning of the term *decoding*, we will examine two major orientations and propose a working definition to serve as the basis of our subsequent discussion of instructional approaches. For lack of better terms, we will refer to the first orientation as "traditional," the second as "divergent."

Traditional Points of View

The following discussion centers around certain descriptions of decoding that are presented as a set of related definitions, not as a unitary concept. They are grouped together because they share certain common elements and because, as a group, they differ from an important, recently emerging point of view in several fundamental ways.

Because decoding is basic to the reading process at any level of development, definitions were sampled from a range of professional writings—those which focus on reading in a general manner and others which examine particular stages of a reader's competency, from beginning levels to advanced.[1]

In traditional views, decoding is described as a translation of written words to their oral language forms; some authors designate not only speech but both sound and meaning as process end products. The following represents a sampling of these points of view.

In his classic discussion of building independence in word perception, Gray (12) described the process as one of associating sound and meaning with printed words.

Zintz (31, p. 14) included "mastering the necessary skills in decoding the written word so that it is immediately pronounceable and meaningful . . ." as one important facet of reading, as one objective of reading instruction.

Spache and Spache (27) defined word recognition skills as the "techniques used by the reader to identify, to pronounce, to recall, and thus read each word" (p. 375). In another statement, they pictured the reader as one who "reacts to each word with a group of mental associations regarding the word form, its meaning, and its sound" (p. 4).

Theodore Harris (13) specifically noted only the end product of sound in his *Encyclopedia of Education Research* reference to the readers use of sound–symbol relationship cues to decode the "written message . . . into its spoken sound equivalent." In the same paragraph word attack skills were defined as those used by the reader "to identify the pronunciation and meaning of words" (p. 1090).

Chall (2) discussed at length the code emphasis in beginning reading and equated basic mastery of the code with the "reconstruction of speech" from printed forms.

In their discussions of word recognition skills for the secondary student, both Karlin (16) and Marksheffel (17) stressed the ability to identify or pronounce words as an important first step in the reading process.

Though several of the writers just noted did not use the term *decoding*, all described a process in which translation from graphic to oral form was an essential ingredient. Certainly none of these authorities would describe the reading process itself apart from meaning; several, however, did not specifically include meaning as an aspect of decoding.

Although traditional definitions of decoding tend to emphasis the word

---

[1] It is important to note that the terms *decoding, word recognition*, and *word perception* have been used by different authors to describe equivalent concepts. For example, all three labels have been employed to describe the reader's association of sound and meaning with printed words. They have been used by other writers to denote the print-to-speech translation with no reference to meaning. Also, in a single book or article an author may use terms interchangeably. In one article reviewed, the word *decoding* was used in the title but no further mention of the label was made in the ensuing discussion of word recognition. In some writings it was difficult to determine the author's definition of terms. In this connection, see Moretz and Davey (18).

as the critical element in the basic perceptual process, writers have not ignored the place of larger units in the reader's search for meaning. Gray (12) described the reader as fusing the meanings of words perceived "into a stream of related ideas" (p. 11). Spache and Spache (27) not only stressed the importance of word perception, they also emphasized that readers comprehend by integrating their meaningful perceptions of successive words into thoughts and ideas, and these ideas into larger, more complex interpretations. The process requires not only the continuing integration of thoughts but also their modification as additional and perhaps unexpected input is received.

A Divergent Point of View

Goodman (11), in his examination of "Decoding—from Code to What?" decried views of the process which emphasize translation of print to speech. His argument was based on the idea that both written and spoken forms of language are codes which represent or communicate meaning. Within this conceptual framework he further reasoned that going from print to speech, i.e., moving from one code to another, cannot be "de-" coding. Decoding, Goodman concluded, implies that one is going from code to something other than code. "Anything short of meaning, anything that doesn't, in fact, go from code to meaning is not decoding" (p. 456).

In another discussion, Goodman (11) not only emphasized meaning as critical to decoding, but strongly questioned two other elements inherent in traditional concepts. First, he stated that "to achieve comprehension, there is no necessary reason to involve oral language in the reading process at all" (p. 148). In this regard he added that, "It is possible, even probable, that some association between oral and written language occurs as the reader moves toward meaning, but that association is not in any sense essential to comprehension" (p. 148).

Secondly, he questioned the emphasis traditionally placed on the word as the critical unit in reading and proposed that the clause—not the letter, word, or sentence—is the most significant unit in the process.

A Working Definition

The decoding process is a complex one and our understanding of it will be refined and perhaps altered as research in language and learning provides greater insights. It is necessary, however, to devise a specific working definition in order to clarify the conceptual basis for our consideration of instructional approaches.

The definition evolved must deal with at least three basic questions: What is the place of meaning in the process? What is the place of speech? What is the graphic unit described in the process?

In our initial exploration, traditional and divergent concepts of decoding were discussed. Elements of both are reflected in the following working definition: "Decoding is the process of associating contextually appropriate meanings with written words; *generally underlying* this process is the reader's ability to translate the printed word forms into their spoken equivalents."

A Definition Rationale

PLACE OF MEANING IN THE PROCESS. It is important to recognize the linguistic validity of Goodman's assertion that both oral and written representations of language are codes and the logic of his subsequent argument that decoding cannot be viewed as going from code to code, but from code to "something other than the code," i.e., to meaning. It is also important to note that readers who efficiently and successsfully reconstruct meaning from the written code generally have at their command the skill to go from code to speech, though this latter translation is not the usual route to meaning.

PLACE OF SPEECH IN THE PROCESS. This ability to translate print to speech was defined as a preliminary step in decoding. A consideration of silent reading points up the problem encountered in defining decoding as the association of both sound and meaning with printed words. Such a definition implies that silent reading is a process of going from print to speech to meaning. Although some traces of speech appear to be present (26, 7, Goodman, in 15), silent reading cannot be described as the two-step process just outlined. The silent reader does not, as a matter of course, reach meaning via speech.

On the other hand, the importance of the ability to translate print to speech must not be underestimated. Though "word calling" is certainly not reading, the student with adequate hearing who cannot associate oral language correspondences with a significant number of the written words he encounters is seriously handicapped in deriving meaning. When a written word, not immediately recognized as a meaningful unit, is in the listening vocabulary of the reader, his mental association of the written form with its oral equivalent will trigger meaning.

The ability to attach sound as well as meaning to written forms was described as *generally* underlying decoding. This qualification recognizes the fact that a reader can attach meaning to words he cannot pronounce. For example, it is quite possible to read a "Russian" novel, be unable to pronounce the names of certain characters and places, and still comprehend the settings and the plot involving both. Or, in another example, an acquaintance recently commented that she had never been sure of the pronunciation of *façade* but she knew the meaning from repeated encounters in written context. Such occurrences demonstrate that a reader is able to comprehend when the oral code is unknown.

The ability to attach sound as well as meaning to printed words also contributes significantly to the reader's total set of receptive and expressive communication skills—listening, speaking, and writing as well as reading.

Whereas the beginning reader usually attaches meaning to printed words which are already in his listening and speaking vocabularies, the secondary reader often encounters words in print which he has not used in listening and speaking. If he is able to derive both sound and meaning from the newly encountered written forms, all facets of his communication skills are likely to be enhanced. For example, when he later hears such words in oral discussions he should immediately perceive meaning. Also, as soon as he acquires an adequate grasp of the meaning, through either initial or repeated encounters in reading or listening contexts, he will be able to use these words in speaking and writing. In addition, correct pronunciation serves as an important basis for spelling.

THE BASIC GRAPHIC UNIT DESCRIBED. Efficient readers sample from the written display, continually predicting meaning and testing their hypotheses. They do not "use" every word in their pursuit of meaning. The model of the proficient reader is of one who uses a minimal amount of graphic information to make the best possible predictions (11, 22).

Frank Smith (25) described the reading process as involving two basic elements—word identification and reading for comprehension. He suggested that comprehension can precede actual word identification and supported this contention with evidence concerning reading rate, stating that "fluent readers can extract meaning from passages at a rate that would absolutely preclude word identification" (p. 203). In discussing word identification, however, Smith asserted that fluent readers are skilled in immediate identification of words, and that as difficulty of material increases, more attention is paid to such visual information by the reader.

Thus, when a word unit is necessary to the reader's overall search for meaning, his ability to decode the word—i.e., attach contextually appropriate meaning to it—is an important and fundamental part of "reading" that written material. For this reason, in the working definition proposed, the printed word, rather than a larger unit such as the phrase, clause, or sentence, was designated as the basic semantic unit.

At the middle and secondary levels, readers are challenged by the written material as a result of several interrelated sources of complexity. Because of these factors, students are often required to attend to individual word units which are especially significant to the meaning. Factors of complexity include:

1. Conceptual difficulty. The ideas expressed are complex ones.
2. Concept density. A large number of ideas or facts expressed in a brief space.
3. Sentence structure complexity. Factors such as the increased embedding of phrases and clues create more intricate grammatical structures.
4. Minimal redundancy. The English language provides repetitive clues

for given elements of meaning. This redundancy can be illustrated by the past tense markers underlined in the following sentence: *"Yesterday* I walk*ed* home."

Redundancy in written material provides the reader with information which increases his ability to "sample" only needed aspects of the total visual display. A decrease in redundancy lessens the reader's opportunity for efficient sampling.

In summary, as written material becomes more complex and technical, the meaning becomes less predictable and the chances of confusion and misconception increase. Thus, although the fluent reader does not normally concentrate his attention on individual words, he is a competent word identifier when such is required by the difficulty of the material and/or his purposes for reading.

Three Channels to Decoding

The proposed definition primarily describes the end product of decoding —i.e., contextually appropriate meaning. Means used by readers to arrive at this end product must also be considered. In the diagram presented as Table 1, three means of decoding have been outlined and labeled Channels I, II, and III. This outline is given not as a theoretical model but as an additional guide for our consideration of instructional strategies.

Channel I represents the reader's immediate association of meaning with the printed words he samples. This is the channel most used by proficient readers. Its use is dependent upon a large sight vocabulary—that is, an extensive stock of words to which the reader can immediately (without use of Channels II or III) attribute contextually appropriate meaning.

Channel II is one route used by the reader when he does not immediately associate meaning with a written word important to his understanding. Through this channel, he seeks to associate oral language with the printed form, in the hope that this association will trigger meaning. As the reader attempts to translate a previously unknown written form to a known spoken one, several types of clues are available to him—word-structure clues, letter–sound relationship clues, and context or meaning clues.

Structure clues include such word parts as word roots, prefixes, and suffixes. These units can serve as clues to both pronunciation and meaning. In the word *decoding,* the elements *de-cod-ing* can be used in this dual fashion. The easily pronounced structural elements are combined to render an oral word form. Likewise, meaning can be derived from the joining of prefix–root–suffix.

Letter–sound relationship clues are those used by the reader as he mentally associates speech sounds with the individual letters or letter combinations which represent them.

Context clues are used in conjunction with those provided by word-

Table 1

Three Channels to Decoding

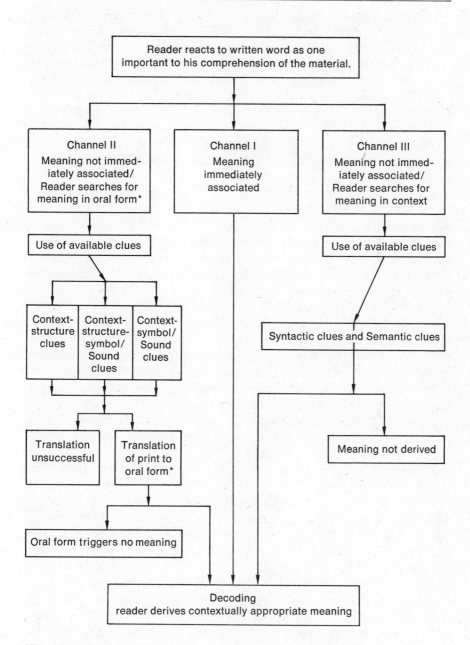

*Term *Oral Form* designates awareness rather than production of sound.

structure and letter–sound–relationship clues, as the successful reader hypothesizes meaning and confirms any oral translation as meaningful or nonmeaningful.

The reader's use of Channel II clues can be described as efficient, flexible, integrated information processing. It is efficient in that the skillful reader uses no more clues than necessary for decoding. By way of illustration, if a word can be accurately decoded through a combination of word-structure and context clues, the efficient reader makes no additional analysis of the visual form. Subsequent examination would be not only unnecessary, but, more importantly, a detriment to reading, delaying and interrupting the search for meaning.

Channel II information processing is flexible and integrated in that the reader selects that combination of clues most useful in decoding a particular word. Flexibility is evident also in the reader's trial-and-error utilization of clues.

It should be noted, too, that individual readers may find different clues most useful for a given word. One reader might use his knowledge of a word root to translate a form, whereas another reader, not familiar with the root, might successfully unlock the graphic form with his knowledge of letter–sound relationships. Both readers would utilize context clues in conjunction with the graphic ones.

Channel III decoding represents the process of using contextual information, apart from oral language, to construct hypotheses of unknown word meanings. As vocabulary becomes increasingly specialized during the secondary school years, the chances of an unknown technical word being in a reader's oral language vocabulary decreases (e.g., *homeostasis, hypotenuse*). When this is the case, translating the word from print to speech is not helpful in ascertaining meaning. Therefore, a proficiency in using syntactic and semantic contextual information, as well as word part meaning, is an increasingly important decoding skill. Because it allows the reader to obtain a rapid, general overview of a selection, Channel III decoding strategies can sometimes be the preferred process even when the Channel II print-to-speech route could also be used.

Readers decoding words via Channel III must be cautious of premature hypotheses of word meaning, however. Flexibility is required, as meaning may be adjusted with added contextual information. Readers must also recognize that sometimes only an approximation or perhaps a hint of meaning can be gained from context.

A final comment concerning the diagram is appropriate. The intent of the outline presented is *not* to distort a complex and only partially understood process. It is presented in the hope that it can be helpful in highlighting different decoding approaches which may be selectively and flexibly used by middle and secondary school readers. They are used selectively as the reader chooses that channel most effective in a given reading situation (i.e., relative to the reader's purpose and to the particular material and words in question.) They are used flexibly as the reader moves from one channel to another when his first choice proves ineffective. Thus, emphasis is placed on educating middle and secondary school readers to be efficient, independent decoders.

II. Instructional Strategies

The Middle and Secondary School Readers[2]

The beginning reader invests much of his energy in Channel II decoding as he seeks to connect visual-code forms, recently introduced to him, with the oral language forms which he has, for some time, meaningfully perceived and used. The secondary student, who has developed basic reading competencies, attends to the printed code with increasing ease and efficiency, concentrating his energies on interpreting and reacting to the message. This more advanced reader, however, benefits significantly from systematic refinement of his decoding skills and further development of his strategies for skills use.

In the continued development of skills, he becomes increasingly proficient in all three channels of decoding. He substantially enlarges his sight vocabulary; he sharpens his skill in applying print-to-speech decoding strategies; and he develops an increased sensitivity to contextual information as a source of word meaning.

Because the misuse of decoding skills can sometimes be as harmful to efficient reading as the lack of skills, the reader's acquisition of strategies for skills use is of great importance at the secondary level. An example of misuse is the reader's unnecessarily prolonged attention to individual words. Such segmented concentration may result in the reader's lack of attention to larger, more significant units of meaning such as the clause and, consequently, in his inadequate understanding of the material.

In acquiring specific decoding strategies, the reader learns when to apply his various skills. He comes to understand when to use Channels II and III. More fundamentally, he learns when to sample from the graphic display and when to attend to specific words.

In the material which follows, an overview and examples of instructional strategies are given for each of these topics: Immediate association–sight vocabulary, context clues, word-structure clues, and symbol–sound relationship clues.

---

[2] This discussion of instructional strategies focuses on activities for students who have "developed basic reading competencies." Many of the approaches suggested, however, are appropriate at lower levels of skill development.

Immediate Association–Sight Vocabulary

OVERVIEW. Educators probably generally agree with Olson's statement that "the larger the vocabulary of the student, the more accurately he will understand what he reads. He will also be able to read more rapidly" (20, p. 560). Because of memory constraints, the reader needs to use the graphic cues available to him rapidly and efficiently. When reading material is heavily loaded with words with which meaning cannot be instantly associated, the reader is compelled to labor over these units of meaning. As a result, his comprehension of the material is not only very slow, but also probably distorted. He may miss the forest for the trees.

Dale (5), in discussing the question of "knowing" words, suggested a continuum of recognition. The stages of "knowing" described include the following:

1. I have not encountered this word before.
2. I have seen the word before but I don't know what it means.
3. I have a vague idea of what this word means.
4. I have an adequate understanding of this word in context.

The degree of "knowing" represented in stage 4 parallels Channel I in the decoding diagram, Table 1.

Many classroom teachers are aware of students who are adept at word pronunciation but deficient in attaching meaning to these symbols. Moreover, many common, easily pronounced words often have highly specialized meanings in content areas.

Consider the word *base*. In mathematics, a student may read about a multiple of *base* 8 or the *base* of a triangle. In science he might encounter acid–*base* characteristics of a solution. In reading sports material the reader may find a reference to third *base*. And in English or history a *base* politician may be described.

Many strictly technical words, such as *osmosis*, are also easily translated to oral language, but not easily interpreted, because they represent complex processes.

It is critical, therefore, that classroom teachers (1) distinguish between word calling and understanding; (2) identify the new vocabulary, within their content purview, which is most important to students' understanding of the material; and (3) provide experiences through which students learn the new concepts along with their written labels.

In this regard the teacher must realize that interpretation exists within the reader. The written symbols are merely "ink configurations" to which readers attach meaning. Understanding evolves as the reader integrates his past experiences with his present ones derived from the printed material. A problem develops in content area reading when students have not had either direct or vicarious experiences which equip them to interpret many of the written labels encountered, though they may be able to pronounce these words. Such concepts need to be developed through the most appropriate activities which can be provided within the educational setting. These may include direct experiences, demonstrations and observations, various audiovisual media presentations, and/or verbal exploration.

When developing students' vocabularies, then, visual recall cannot be divorced from meaning. Instructional strategies must highlight specific contextual settings and provide frequent opportunities for using new vocabulary in meaningful situations. One instructional strategy for developing the scientific concept of "photosynthesis" could be the following:

1. Orally label the process discussed or demonstrated.
2. Present the written word form.
3. Assist students in examining word parts for meaning.
    photo—synthesis
4. Provide meaningful situations in which students use the term—speaking, reading, and writing.
5. Reinforce words recently learned through varied activities, such as matching and categorizing exercises, crossword puzzles, or team games.

In other learning sequences, students might first hypothesize word meaning from the written material and subsequently participate in activities such as those outlined above. There is no one instructional sequence appropriate for the development of all concepts and vocabulary. The teacher's choice of approaches to develop any given concept must be based upon the concept in question, the way the concept is used and explained within the written material, and the reading abilities of his students.

INSTRUCTIONAL STRATEGIES. Acquisition of "Channel I words," those immediately associated with meaning, can occur as a consequence of direct or indirect methods. On the one hand, teachers can create and structure experiences to facilitate this acquisition; likewise, students can consciously work to develop their own vocabularies. Not to be neglected, however, is the reader's indirect, not always conscious, assimilation of new words into his sight vocabulary as a result of repeated encounters with the words. Four sample activities for the development of sight vocabulary are outlined below.

1. *Wide Reading*. Repeatedly, authorities have stressed the importance of wide reading as a vehicle for vocabulary expansion (14, 5, 28, 8).

An approach referred to as sustained silent reading encourages students to develop the habit of reading frequently for uninterrupted periods of time (21, 19). With a sustained reading program, the selection of material to be read is usually, at least initially, a choice of each individual student. Materials might range from classics to paperback novels to magazines to newspapers to comics. Ideally a variety of reading matter is provided by the school, although the student can elect to bring his own selection from home. Sustained reading takes place in a set period of time (10 to 30 minutes) every day or every week, and can be initiated in individual class-rooms or schoolwide. Teachers, as well as students, read during this period —setting good models.

Some teachers like to build on this sustained reading experience to develop vocabulary in a more structured way. Students are encouraged to check lightly or jot down words that are unfamiliar to them. *After* the reading session, and perhaps during another period, students are encouraged to

a. Look them up in dictionaries.
b. Fill out vocabulary cards (3 × 5), with the word on one side, and meaning, pronunciation (optional), sentence on the other side.
c. Use words in speaking and writing situations.
d. Learn the correct spelling of the words.

Additionally, these word cards can be used during the study of syllabication, word-part meanings (prefix, suffix, roots), rules for plurality and tense construction, and so on.

2. *Repeated Use.* Closely associated with the use of wide reading as a means for developing vocabulary is the need for consistent reinforcement of newly encountered words. New words must be seen repeatedly and in varied contexts. Likewise, new vocabulary words should be used by the reader in "production" situations—both in writing and in speaking. Teachers can provide opportunities for students' repeated use of words in both receptive and expressive communication.

It must be stressed that learning lists of words, just to enlarge vocabularies, cannot be justified in light of current knowledge of learning and reading theory. Words should be relevant to the reader and not divorced from meaningful context and/or purposeful use.

3. *Closure Approaches.* Various types of materials can be used in the construction of closure exercises. The teacher, depending in his instructional purpose, deletes certain words from a passage and directs students to complete the material using a particular kind of word (e.g., most specific, most colorful, most unusual). Students, ideally working in pairs or in small groups, fill in each blank with several possible words. Later, referring to a handy dictionary as needed, the students decide on the most "appropriate" word or word combinations for each blank.

EXAMPLE:

Down on the _____ farm, near where the _____ meets the _____, I love to _____ my time _____ pastoral songs. As the sun _____ over the _____ wheat fields, my head _____ with _____ tunes that I'd like to write.

4. *Reinforcement Activities.* When constructing materials for vocabulary "practice," the teacher can choose from a myriad of possible formats. Three

popular ones are summarized below. These learning activities may be "packaged" in several ways—as worksheets, learning centers, games for individuals or small groups, blackboard activities, and so on.

Categorizing format: This activity consists of organizing words on the basis of shared traits.

EXAMPLE:

Directions: Place the following words under the appropriate column heading. A word may go under more than one heading.

oxygen   digestion   photosynthesis
plastic   cells   cell wall
locomotion CO_2

PLANTS   ANIMALS   INANIMATE

Matching format: This activity consists of pairing word with process, word with synonym, word with antonym, or word with description.

EXAMPLE:

Directions: Place the correct letter from Column B in front of each item in Column A.

A.
_____1. summation
_____2. theorem
_____3. commutative law
_____4. distributive law

B.
a. order makes no difference
b. none of these choices
c. process of totaling
d. statement of something to be proven

Word puzzle format: These activities can take many forms: magic squares, crossword puzzles, anagrams, and so on.

EXAMPLE:

Directions: This Magic Square is called 1776. The key word begins with R and contains ten letters. How many other words can you find? You may combine letters which border each other—horizontally, vertically, diagonally—moving only one space at a time in any direction. A letter may be used more than once.

R	I	N
T	E	O
U	L	V

A word of caution to the teacher: It is important to vary the format of learning activities and thus not overuse any one type, regardless of its appeal to students. Even the most interesting approach can be overused.

Context Clues

OVERVIEW. The effective use of contextual clues has been described by a number of authorities as assuming a primary importance in the decoding process (Gray, 12; Bond and Wagner, 1; E. Brooks Smith et al., 24; Thomas and Robinson, 29).

Two general types of contextual information are available to the reader as he attempts to reconstruct the author's meaning. These may be described as semantic and syntactic clues. Semantic clues refer to that information derived from the meaning of the material surrounding a particular word. Syntactic clues are those provided by the word order and by the function of certain words.

By way of illustration, consider the following sentence: "The leaves of green plants contain tiny *stomates* which *regulate* the passage of oxygen and carbon dioxide." The meaning of the unknown word *stomates* is suggested partially by the place of the word within the sentence context. It must refer to "things" (noun). Likewise, the unknown word *regulate* can be inferred from syntactic context to be a verb form. Such syntactic contextual information, although not as precise as semantic information, is used by the successful reader as he hypothesizes word meaning.

Greater contextual help for the decoder is provided by semantic clues. In the sample sentence, the semantic context indicates that these "things" are in the leaves of green plants and that they have something to do with oxygen and carbon dioxide. Semantic context also suggests that the unknown verb describes some function of these "things" relative to oxygen and carbon dioxide.

In addition to meaning generally supplied by the surrounding context, several specific types of clues are provided in some written material. Table II presents a summary of those most frequently encountered:

1. Directly stated information.
2. Comparative and contrasting information.
3. Serial information.
4. Summarizing information.

Because these various types of semantic clues are available in materials to be read independently by secondary students, it is important that students know where to look for and how to use this valuable information. Content area teachers can facilitate their students' effective and efficient use of semantic information clues by providing opportunities for them to practice the skills in purposeful reading situations and with written material relevant to the discipline.

Within the diagram presented, contextual information is used by the reader in all three decoding channels. In Channel I, the successful reader immediately perceives word meaning within the particular verbal contexts represented. Otherwise, he could not deal with the multiple meanings of most English words, utilizing only that meaning appropriate to the passage. In Channel III, the reader uses context clues to unlock word meanings without recourse to oral language. In Channel II, the reader employs such clues in conjunction with his analysis of the word form. In this latter use, he confirms or alters his print-to-speech hypothesis.

Under certain reading conditions, decoding particular unfamiliar words may be unnecessary. For example, the reader's purpose might be to gain only an overall impression of the author's main points. In such instances, the reader could use contextual information to "read around" unknown words that are not essential to the degree of meaning desired.

INSTRUCTIONAL STRATEGIES. Activities for developing efficient use of context clues may be grouped into four basic categories.

1. *Setting Purposes for Reading.* The purpose one sets for reading guides the selection and use of contextual information. When reading to ascertain the general tone of a selection, or for an initial impression of the central idea, one may use context to read "around" the unknown word or to gain a general understanding of the unknown but "key" word. On the other hand, when reacting to print in a specific manner as in following directions or recipes, the reader might use contextual information to assist in an oral rendering of unknown words (Channel II), in the hope that the word is in the reader's oral language vocabulary, or he might check for the correct, specific usage of a familiar word form by careful attention to preceding and subsequent contextual information (Channel III).

Content area teachers can provide guidance to students in setting purposes for reading and in using context clues appropriately. Practice and experience reading different types of materials (texts, magazines, reference books) for different purposes helps the student learn flexibility and efficiency in decoding.

2. *Closure Approaches.* By deleting specified words from sentences teachers can encourage students to use available contextual information to form appropriate hypotheses about the missing word. These activities are termed *closure* or *cloze.* Material can be chosen from texts, newspapers, and so on, and prepared by leaving out certain words and replacing them with equal-sized blanks.

EXAMPLE:

After the game was _____, the boys ran to _____ store to see if _____ new shipments of the _____ had come in. Naturally _____ store was closed for _____ day, and the disappointed _____ sauntered over to the __ _____ to watch the boats.

After completing this type of activity, students can

a. Share their responses, justifying use of one word over another, in group discussions, in dialogue with a partner, or in teacher–student conferences.

TABLE 2

Contextual Information Clues (Semantic)

TYPE OF CLUE	EXPLANATION	EXAMPLE
A. Directly stated information	The author clarifies the word meaning by providing additional information in appositive constructions, phrases, clauses, or subsequent sentences.	1. Using *flint*, a hard kind of stone, the pioneers constructed a warm fire in no time. 2. The photographers found the *hamlet* deserted. This small village was to have been the festival site.
B. Comparative and contrasting information	The reader gains word meaning by comparing the unknown word to a known word—for either likenesses (synonyms) or differences (antonyms).	1. They were aware of the *assignation* but did not want to expose the couple's rendezvous. 2. The old man *purloined* the crusty bread from the store, but later returned it. 3. The welcome for the king was *lavish* and extravagant.
C. Serial information	The reader hypothesizes the meaning of an unknown word by associating it with the surrounding series of known words.	The naturalist had counted six varieties in the area: maple, elm, *ginkgo*, ash, *osage orange*, and oak.
D. Summarizing information	The reader hypothesizes the unknown word meaning by its function as a summary label for known words and concepts.	He was a *malevolent* man—cruel, evil, brutal, and cynical.

    b. Compare their responses with the author's original word choices. How do their responses differ?

The teacher can construct closure activities varying in deletion-pattern type:

Every nth word: In this traditional approach words are deleted on the basis of a specified numerical count; every fifth word or every tenth word are common patterns (example above).

Types of words: Nouns, verbs, adjectives, adverbs, and function words are deleted to highlight their relationships to other words in the sentences.

Brainstorming for closure: The use of closure activities can also encourage vocabulary development.

EXAMPLE:

Directions: Fill in each blank with five possible word choices. When all blanks are filled, select the *best* choice for each blank and circle it.

Under the ＿＿＿＿＿＿＿＿ sky lay three ＿＿＿＿＿＿＿＿, just relaxing, and thinking about ＿＿＿＿＿ ＿＿＿＿＿＿＿.

This type of exercise involves making active decisions as to specific word use based upon careful interpretation of available contextual information.

Providing choices: To provide greater control over the vocabulary considered, teachers may construct activities in the familiar multiple-choice format.

EXAMPLE:

Jane understood the danger around her. The large hungry animals were ＿＿＿＿＿＿ (sensitive, alert, soft), and probably easily ＿＿＿＿＿ (angered, ridden, harried). She decided to ＿＿＿ ＿＿ (watch, stalk, chase) the dangerous animals with great ＿＿＿＿＿＿ (excitement, caution, fear), take her photograph, and return ＿＿＿＿＿＿ (regrettably, urgently, quickly) to the camp.

Activities of this nature can be easily corrected by the students themselves.

3. *Nonsense-Word Approaches.* When using nonsense words with closure activities, readers are encouraged to hypothesize meaning based upon contextual information. Two common strategies for using nonsense words are illustrated below:

Sentence information: Sentence information provides increasing amounts of information about a nonsense word in a series of sentences. Students hypothesize the possible meanings of the nonword, and with each sentence refine their hypothesis. An example with a four-sentence series might be

1. I hope no one saw me *fantagging*. (Students list possible meanings of the word.)
2. *Fantagging*, like being kicked by a mule, looks very funny and onlookers laugh. (Students refine their lists.)
3. My friend, a zoo keeper, broke his back *fantagging* last week. (Students refine their lists.)
4. I'll try to avoid careless banana-eaters since their litter can lead to *fantagging*. (Students guess the word meaning.)
   fantagging = slipping on a banana peel

Again, this activity can encourage readers' awareness of the different types of contextual information available.

Paragraph information: Paragraph information utilizes nonsense words in paragraph contexts. As the reader reacts to the total paragraph he uses contextual information to "read around" the unknown word and/or to predict and modify the possible meaning of the word.

4. *Multiple Contextual Settings.* The following approach is helpful in developing sensitivity to the multiple meanings of words.

EXAMPLE:

Directions: After reading each of the following sentences, select the definition below which explains the meaning of the underlined word in that sentence.

The sculpture's outstanding relief was chipped from having been dropped.
Her relief was apparent as she smiled after the doctor's message.
They were tired of receiving welfare relief from the government.

a. turned out of
b. the projection of a figure
c. polish, brilliance
d. assistance given
e. alleviation (anxiety, pain)

Word Structure[3] Clues

OVERVIEW. The reader uses word structure clues in two different but related ways.

1. He identifies word structure parts as units of meaning and uses his understanding of the parts to attach meaning to the whole word. For example, the reader who can attribute meaning to each part of the word *preview* can use these meanings in understanding the word unit. As in the word *preview*, such word parts frequently serve as units of pronunciation (syllables) as well as meaning.
2. He identifies word parts as units of pronunciation and synthesizes these units into a pronounceable whole which can trigger meaning if it

---

[3] Structure is used here to refer to word parts which are units of pronunciation, meaning, or both.

is within the oral language vocabulary of the reader. For example, though the individual parts of the word *prediction* may not be meaningful to a reader, the word as a whole may be.

Within this framework—that is, given consideration of word parts as units of meaning and/or pronunciation—the following types of clues will be examined.

1. Syllables.
2. Compound words.
3. Word roots and affixes (prefixes and suffixes).
4. Inflections (a type of suffix).

One important instructional consideration should preface any discussion of strategies for skill development: that is, students must understand and experience the ways in which word structure clues help them decode words practically and efficiently. Therefore, isolated practice or drill on skill development should be avoided. Teachers can build instructional strategies into their content area planning, using words that are important to the students' learning.

INSTRUCTIONAL STRATEGIES.

The syllable: Syllabication is used in Channel II decoding, as the reader reacts to a word, not in his sight vocabulary, by breaking it into easily pronounced units, and then blending these units to form a total "oral" rendering of the word which hopefully will trigger meaning.

Deighton (6) pointed out that accurate discussions of syllabication must be based upon the knowledge that there are two sets of syllabication principles: one for pronunciation and one for writing. These sets are similar but not identical. To pronounce word syllables correctly, one merely identifies minimal word parts as those containing a single vowel sound, e.g., *bottle* = *bott-le*. Breaking words into correct written syllables, however, requires adherence to old rules first established by eighteenth-century printers for their convenience, e.g., *bottle* = *bot-tle*.

Additionally, context must be used in conjunction with syllabication to aid in the correct pronunciation–meaning of the word. For example, the word *project*.

The student has completed his projects (proj' ects).
The opera singer projects (pro jects'] her voice.

Prefixes, suffixes, and word roots frequently serve as easily identifiable units of pronunciation (e.g., *preview* and *prediction*).

In many instances the reader can achieve only a partial rendering of the word through syllabication but is able to complete his translation because he uses this information (partial awareness of syllables) in conjunction with context.

A detailed discussion of syllabication (or accent) is beyond the scope of this article. It is important to point out, however, that a number of the procedures described in the professional literature are of questionable value to the decoder. Some suggestions given seem to require that pronunciation actually precede syllabication. Courtney (4); Clymer (3); Winkley (30); Schell (23); and Spache and Spache (27), however, are among those who have recognized these problems and provided valuable instructional suggestions.

Compound words: The word components of compound words can be useful in deriving both pronunciation and meaning. In using the parts as meaningful units, the reader must be aware, however, that the meaning of the whole is

1. Sometimes the sum of its parts. (In colonial times *shoemaking* was a valuable trade.)
2. Sometimes related to but not completely represented by the meaning of the components. (For example, in the sentence "we wandered down to the *shipyard*," the word parts do not make clear that this is a place where ships are built or repaired.)
3. Sometimes a meaning not literally related to the meaning of its parts. (The *moonshiner* lived in the hills near his operation.)

Because of these possibilities and because compound words frequently have multiple meanings, all compounds should be considered in context.

EXAMPLE:

His election to the state legislature was the *springboard* for his political career.   The gymnast practiced on the *springboard* for hours.

Word roots and affixes: Some of the most useful word structure clues for secondary students are those provided by prefixes, suffixes, and word roots. Several examples of their use in the content areas follow. Teachers can identify key word parts in their disciplines and encourage their students to use them appropriately. One sequence for instruction might include the following:

1. Identify and discuss a key word part of a known word, e.g., *astronomy*.
2. Locate other words containing the identified word part, and examine them in context.
3. Discuss the use of the target word part in each case examined.

Another sequence for consideration of structural parts is the following:

1. Begin with words in relevant contextual settings, e.g., "Whenever a starfish loses a leg, it can *regenerate* a new one."
2. Discuss the general contextual meaning of the word.
3. Examine prefix (*re-*) and root word (*generate*) for meaning.
4. Use the word in another similar contextual setting.
5. Apply knowledge by identifying and discussing other words which include any of the structural parts (*generator, generation, reassign, reclaim*, etc.).

As with the word *regenerate*, knowledge of word-part meaning can be helpful in decoding technical vocabulary. In many instances such knowledge provides a hint of meaning which can be used in association with context.

EXAMPLE:

After his compass was smashed by the impact of the waves, the skipper was relieved to have a fully functioning *astrolabe* on board.

Inflections: Word endings, such as plural (*-s, -es*) and past tense markers (*-ed, -ied*) are generally known and correctly applied by the secondary school reader. These endings are important clues for meaning and therefore should be reinforced or retaught if students are careless in attending to them.

A *final consideration:* In some instances the student will need to use the dictionary in order to give a precise meaning to a particular word. Because of multiple word meanings, dictionary skills must be developed in conjunction with contextual occurrences of words.

Dictionary usage should be seen as practical and useful by the middle and secondary school student. However, dictionaries are easily misused as an initial step in decoding. Looking up words while in the act of reading slows down the reading process and restricts the efficient gaining of total meaning. Students should be encouraged initially to apply other skills to derive meaning from unfamiliar words (i.e., via Channels II or III). They should be taught how and when to use dictionaries to confirm meaning, clarify meaning, or help in the pronunciation and meaning of words not otherwise decoded. Thus, dictionary skills are developed with purpose and efficiency in mind.

Symbol–Sound Relationship Clues

OVERVIEW: Successful middle and secondary school readers have acquired a basic knowledge of symbol–sound[4] relationships. They have also developed,

---

[4] These might also be referred to as letter–sound or grapheme–phoneme relationships.

we hope, Channel II decoding strategies in which they use this knowledge in conjunction with word structure and context clues.

Though the basic decoding skills utilizing symbol–sound relationships have been acquired, several types of instructional activities are appropriate for many students.

One type of activity reviews and reinforces the student's use of letter–sound relationship cues within meaningful contexts. In order to capitalize on and strengthen the reader's integrated use of symbol–sound and meaning clues, exercises designed to develop and reinforce the first must emphasize meaning as well. In addition to highlighting this integrated use of clues, such an approach promotes the critical concept that reading is indeed a search for meaning, and not a mechanical, end-in-itself translation of print to speech.

Other activities are designed to increase students' understanding of the orthographic (spelling) system itself. These activities focus the student's attention on the ways particular sounds are spelled, or, conversely, on the sounds which can be represented by particular letters or letter combinations.

INSTRUCTIONAL STRATEGIES.

1. *Modified Cloze.* One type of activity uses a modified cloze procedure in which selected words are partially omitted. In the example given below, only the initial letter or letter combination of certain words is given. Students may fill in each blank with any word which is meaningful and begins with the letter(s) indicated.

EXAMPLE:

When Alice finished hemming h_____ dress, she put it on and l_____ at herself for a f_____ seconds in the full-length m_____. Not liking the image before her, she wh_____ around and fell sobbing on her b_____. Having a plain f_____ was bad enough, but creating an unattractive g_____, when one could choose from so many p_____, was even worse.

2. *Deletion Comparisons.* Following the completion of this exercise, students may compare the words they inserted with those actually deleted. In this comparison, the student uses not only the initial symbol(s) but additional clues supplied by the whole word form.

In the preceding example the following words were omitted: *her, looked, few, mirror, whirled, bed, face, garment, patterns.*

3. *Graphemic or Phonemic Options.* Students' awareness of the orthographic system can be developed in a variety of ways. Two activities include the following: Using a sound-to-symbol approach, students collect samples of the ways particular speech sounds can be represented. For example, the following illustrate various graphic representations, i.e., graphemic options, for the final sound in the word *go.*

EXAMPLE: [ō]

We will go to the ball game on Saturday.

My mother can't sew a stitch.

Though it is sleeting, we must leave.

It was difficult to show gratitude adequately for such a gift.

The little girl stumped her toe on the rock.

On a stormy night there really is no place like home.

The sailboat capsized in the storm.

With emphasis on a symbol-to-sound sequence, students may collect illustrations of the various speech sounds (phonemes) which can be represented by particular letters or letter combinations.

EXAMPLE: *ough*

Although the girls played well, they lost to a superior team.

The bough broke under the weight of the ice.

He thought about the story long after he had finished reading it.

In Summary

In this discussion, decoding was defined as the process of associating contextually appropriate meaning with written words. Fluent readers immediately associate meaning with most words encountered. When this is not the case, they efficiently and flexibly use the graphic and contextual clues available in the material to derive meaning.

This concept of decoding should not suggest that reading is simply a cumulative process of adding one word meaning to another. Rather, decoding words which are important to the reader's understanding of a passage is viewed as a necessary foundational *facet* of the reading process.

REFERENCES

1. Bond, Guy L., and Eva B. Wagner. *Teaching the Child to Read*, 3rd ed. New York: Macmillan Publishing Co., Inc., 1960.
2. Chall, Jeanne S. *Learning to Read: The Great Debate*. New York: McGraw-Hill, Inc., 1967.
3. Clymer, Theodore. "The Utility of Phonic Generalizations in the Primary Grades," *Reading Teacher*, 16 (1963), 252–58.
4. Courtney, Brother Leonard. "Methods and Materials for Teaching Word Perception in Grades 10–14," in *Sequential Development of Reading Abilities*, Conference Proceedings, 12. Chicago: University of Chicago Press, 1960.
5. Dale, Edgar. "Vocabulary Measurement: Techniques & Major Findings." *Elementary English*, 4 (1965), 895–901.
6. Deighton, Lee C. "Developing Vocabulary: Another Look at the Problem," in *Teaching Reading Skills in Secondary Schools: Readings*, edited by A. V. Olson and W. S. Ames. Scranton: Intext Publisher, 1970, pp. 123–130.

7. Edfeldt, A. W. *Silent Speech and Silent Reading*. Chicago: University of Chicago, 1960.

8. Fader, Daniel, and Elton McNeil. *Hooked on Books: Program and Proof*. New York: Berkley Publishing Corp., 1968.

9. Goodman, Kenneth S. "Analysis of Oral Reading Miscues: Applied Psycholinguistics," *Reading Research Quarterly*, 1 (1969), 10–30.

10. Goodman, Kenneth S. "Decoding—From Code to What?" *Journal of Reading*, 14 (1971), 455–89.

11. Goodman, Kenneth. "The Reading Process," in *Language and Learning to Read: What Teachers Should Know About Language*, ed. by R. E. Hodges and E. H. Rudorf. Boston: Houghton Mifflin Company, 1972, pp. 143–59.

12. Gray, William S. *On Their Own in Reading*. Chicago: Scott, Foresman and Company, 1960.

13. Harris, Theodore. "Reading," in *Encyclopedia of Educational Research*, ed. by Robert Ebel. London: Macmillan Publishing Co., Inc., 1969.

14. Herber, Harold. *Teaching Reading in Content Areas*. Englewood Cliffs, N.J.: Prentice-Hall, Inc., 1970.

15. Hodges, Richard E., and E. Hugh Rudorf. *Language and Learning to Read: What Teachers Should Know About It*. Boston: Houghton Mifflin Company, 1972.

16. Karlin, Robert. *Teaching Reading in High School*. Indianapolis: The Bobbs-Merrill Co., Inc., 1964.

17. Marksheffel, Ned D. *Better Reading in the Secondary School*. New York: The Ronald Press Company, 1966.

18. Moretz, Sara, and Beth Davey. "Decoding 'Decoding'." Position Papers in Reading. College of Education, University of Maryland. 1973.

19. Mork, Theodore A. "Sustained Silent Reading in the Classroom," *Reading Teacher*, 25 (1972), 438–41.

20. Olson, Arthur. "Teaching Word Recognition for Better Vocabulary Development," *Clearing House*, 40 (1966), 559–62.

21. Petre, Richard. "Reading Breaks Make It in Maryland," *Journal of Reading*, 15 (1971), 191–94.

22. Ryan, E. B., and M. I. Semmel. "Reading as a Constructive Language Process," *Reading Research Quarterly*, 5 (1969), 60–83.

23. Schell, Leo M. "Teaching Structural Analysis," *Reading Teacher*, 21 (1967), 133–37.

24. Smith, E. Brooks, Kenneth S. Goodman, and Robert Meredith. *Language and Thinking in the Elementary School*. New York: Holt, Rinehart and Winston, Inc., 1970.

25. Smith, Frank. *Understanding Reading*. New York: Holt, Rinehart and Winston, Inc., 1971.

26. Smith, Henry P., and Emerald V. Dechant. *Psychology in Teaching Reading*. Englewood Cliffs, N.J.: Prentice-Hall, Inc., 1961.

27. Spache, George D., and Evelyn B. Spache. *Reading in the Elementary School*. Boston: Allyn and Bacon, Inc., 1969.

28. Strang, Ruth, Constance McCullough, and Arthur Traxler. *The Improvement of Reading*, 4th ed. New York: McGraw-Hill, Inc., 1967.

29. Thomas, Ellen, and H. Alan Robinson. *Improving Reading in Every Class.* Boston: Allyn and Bacon, Inc., 1972.
30. Winkley, Carol. "Which Accent Generalizations Are Worth Teaching?" *Reading Teacher*, 20 (1966), 219–24, 253.
31. Zintz, Miles V. *The Reading Process.* Dubuque, Iowa: Wm. C. Brown Company Publishers, 1970.

Developing the Ability to Understand, to Interpret, to React Critically, and to Apply Insights Gained Through Reading

Introduction

In any comprehensive discussion of reading we talk about understanding, interpreting, reacting critically, and applying insights gained through reading. It is possible to illustrate similarities and differences among these concepts, and to show that the mature reader engages in all of these activities.

The average reader in high school will read an American history book and understand that a war was fought between the states in the 1860's, and that the precipi-

tating cause of this conflict was the shelling of Ft. Sumter in South Carolina. If he has a skillful teacher, he may be led to read the information about the events that occurred for a number of years prior to the War; and he may be helped to interpret this information, i.e., to make inferences and draw conclusions regarding it in order to determine the real, underlying causes for this rift. In this instance he would discover that one of the more deep-seated causes of the war was an economic battle between the industrial North and the agrarian South.

At a higher level of maturity the reader will react critically in examining sources relating to the conflict to determine the validity and accuracy of his information, and in reflecting on the value of these insights for the life of the reader. Finally, at the highest level of maturity, the reader wisely applies the insights he has gained from this reflective reading to improve his attitudes toward other people and their needs.

As the authors of this section probe deeply into the meaning of thoughtful, critical reading, they develop several important ideas: Reading is a thinking process that is improved as individuals learn to use language more constructively and to clarify concepts through discussion that is generated and guided by skillful questioning. Furthermore, academic advantages accrue to the individual who is taught to apply learning principles designed to help him set purposes for reading, to interpret meanings, and to organize these meanings efficiently and effectively. However, the reader must develop accurate meanings that are relevant to his purposes for reading. Nor is the student left to his own devices, for in a first-rate classroom the alert teacher takes steps to help the student inquire more intelligently and more effectively.

Improving Comprehension–Interpretation Skills*

Joseph A. Fisher

There is a definition of mind control that has a negative connotation to many teachers. Fortunately, there is a definition of mind control in education which implies benevolent guidance of students, and the activities that are a part of this kind of mind control are not negative or objectionable.

Donald O. Hebb has stated in

Control of the Mind (Farbes and Wilson, eds.) that an important consideration in controlling the mind is man's insatiable activity, which, although environmentally initiated, is self-paced. Fisher recognizes a related problem in teaching comprehension–interpretation skills: Although stimulation and guidance are necessary in teaching children, the

* Written especially for inclusion in this volume.

subject matter teacher should help these children develop into independent, inquiring readers. In this article Fisher presents many practical suggestions for attaining this goal through learning how to interpret and organize ideas gained through reading.

1. What distinction does the author make between learning to read and reading to learn? What are the implications of this distinction for teaching?

2. How can the middle and secondary school teachers help their students develop into independent readers?

3. According to the author, what academic advantages can accrue to the student who learns to preview material, to ask questions about the material, and to answer the questions?

4. Which principles of learning are involved in the exercises in "Improving skill in reading for main ideas"?

5. What is the value in reading to organize details?

6. Which learning principles are involved in the suggestions on developing a vocabulary?

7. Rank the twelve suggestions for "Reading to Interpret Meaning" according to (a) complexity, (b) difficulty in developing, and (c) usefulness in developing the ability to interpret meaning.

The most basic principle guiding reading instruction has been that children learn to read so that they can read to learn. It is almost impossible to find a single statement in the literature on reading which would endorse word-calling as being of any value in learning to read. Therefore, it is not surprising that in one form or another methods of developing comprehension skills in readers form the essential content of all manuals concerned with reading instruction, and that this concern has always formed the ultimate basis for research in the field of reading.

Because the basic comprehension skills at the primary level are so well established, and the recognized procedures commonly employed by teachers to develop these skills are so generally effective in producing readers who can read elementary materials with understanding, it would seem incredible that we should have secondary readers who are unable to understand their reading assignments. Yet it is common knowledge that as many as one child in four in the secondary school population experiences some degree of difficulty in understanding his reading assignments.

Undoubtedly, there are children at this level who simply never learned to read for some reason or another. These must be given remedial assistance to compensate for this deficiency. But the majority of these readers did learn to read; they are able to attack and pronounce new words and are able to read certain materials with understanding. They seem to have reading problems which in some mysterious way are associated with textbooks in subject matter fields. They may be said to have learned to read but are not able to read to learn. In order to help these readers, it is important that the secondary teachers understand the meaning of the distinction between these two concepts.

In learning to read, the emphasis is on the mechanics of reading, word attack, sentence formation, etc. At this level the child is concerned with making an association between the oral language he already knows, and the written language he is learning to read. At this level, the most important skill he is required to use is his power of discrimination between the various symbols used to convey the meaning. This accounts for the necessity to control the rate of introduction of new vocabulary, and the restriction of content to concepts already in the child's experience. These things are done primarily because they make it possible for the child to focus all his energy on the discriminatory learning task. In a somewhat oversimplified form, this is the meaning of learning to read.

Eventually, as the student becomes more proficient at the discrimination task, more emphasis is placed on his grasp of the thought words convey. At this point he begins reading to learn. Reading to learn begins, to some extent, even before the child has completely learned to read in the sense that he is always required to give evidence that he has understood what he has read. But because most of the content of reading material at this lowest level is already in the reader's experience, it is possible that these comprehension checks draw upon the child's memory as much as his power to understand the reading matter.

As he progresses from the primary through the elementary levels, more and more emphasis is placed on reading to learn, and the concept load of the reading matter becomes proportionately farther and farther removed in time and place from the experience of the individual child demanding a greatly increased vocabulary. Therefore during this general development the child must be carefully guided in his effort to learn to read by the teacher who thoroughly prepares the child for each learning task.

Quite possibly, as a direct result of the assistance the children receive during this prolonged period of elementary reading, many come to expect this guidance to be provided in all their new reading experience. But unless the child has been made aware of the need to prepare himself for independent reading, he may find himself unable to read anything new or challenging without assistance.

It is entirely possible that a large proportion of poor secondary readers have either never been taught to prepare themselves to read, or have been unable to transfer their preparation skills to new reading assignments. We know that most poor readers are passive readers; that is, readers who expect the writer to be responsible for capturing and building their interest, explaining his terminology, and so presenting his material that they need merely gaze at it to grasp his meaning. No doubt many authors of textbooks have accepted this responsibility; this may account for the number of students in college who have reading problems, as it may be the first time such readers have actually been required to be really independent readers.

PREPARING TO READ

In the last analysis, the middle and secondary school teachers have the responsibility of developing independent readers. An essential element in this development consists in making readers aware of the fact that they must always prepare themselves for reading to learn. Reading to learn is never a one-shot affair; it is a process, not a single act. Just as the writer is seldom satisfied to write his material only once but first prepares an outline or rough draft, then expands his outline and follows this with careful revision of details, so the reader should first become familiar with the general organizational pattern of what he intends to read; then identify the principal points used to develop the thought and, finally, analyze the details through which the main points are established or developed.

Unfortunately, students who still have dependent reading habits, or are passive readers, often actively resist the effort and energy required to read the way they should. The teacher must therefore take steps to insure the development of these skills. Since many of these students are motivated to read their assignments primarily so that they can answer questions about them, the teacher can control the kind of reading the students will do by giving reading assignments which require students to employ particular reading skills.

The most important step in preparing students to read independently centers on the prereading survey. An excellent way to insure that such preparation will be undertaken is to give a survey assignment at the beginning of a course, or unit, or even a chapter. To make such an assignment effective the teacher should explain to students where the most essential information of the assignment can be found, and how the unit or chapter is organized.

Approximately 80 per cent of the principal ideas of textbook assignments can be found in the first sentences of paragraphs. The introductory paragraph usually indicates the general scope of the topic covered and frequently provides background information or a very specific outline of the contents. The final paragraph often provides a summary of what has been said. Such information will not of itself do much to alter old reading habits. But if the teacher immediately gives an open-book quiz that requires the students to survey the assignment, a value is assigned to the procedure which will provide motivation.

The questions in such a quiz should obviously deal with such information as can be found in the survey if it is properly made. Examples of the types of questions for a chapter on the Civil War might include such items as:

1. What five topics are discussed in the chapter on the Civil War?
2. How does the author divide his discussion of the causes of the Civil War?

3. Which states belonged to the confederacy? (Using map provided.)
4. Name the major battles of the Civil War.
5. What does the author discuss under Reconstruction, and so on?

The teacher must always remember that the purpose of the survey is to acquaint the student with the general content and organization of the assignment before he attempts to read it. Since various types of visual aids, pictures, maps, charts, may be found in the assignment, the information they afford should be included in the questions. This kind of quiz can profitably be corrected in class and form the basis of the teacher's own introductory remarks.

As important and useful as it may be, the survey does not complete the preparation necessary for reading to learn. In order to be able to read for meaning, the student needs to be taught how to concentrate on and organize the thought content of the material. To do this it is necessary to be able to form questions which can be answered by the reading done. Because a question is easier to keep in mind than a statement and serves as a natural center for organizing details, it is a very useful learning device.

Students should be encouraged to convert major headings into organizational questions as they read each subdivision of their assignment as a technique of keeping track of the thought processes being developed. This is easily accomplished by placing words like who, what, where, when, why, how, before the topic heading. The process of converting topic sentences into questions as one reads serves as a preparation for reading each succeeding paragraph, and so gives it more meaning. By focusing the reader's attention in this way on understanding what is read, the teacher develops in the student an attitude of active response to content.

In order to insure that students develop independence in reading in the way they have been guided, the teacher can require them to make up the questions based on a survey of an assignment for themselves. These questions may then be used as the basis for class discussion of the topic they were intended to cover prior to reading the assignment.

Often students find it difficult or impossible to grasp the meaning of what they read because they do not know the meaning of certain words used. The survey step can serve as a convenient means of identifying such terms before reading begins. Many publishers italicize or use special type faces to identify such words. By calling attention to them in context, and often providing a definition as well, the publishers make it as convenient as possible for the student to learn these words before he begins reading, without the bother of looking up meanings in the dictionary. The teacher can reinforce the vocabulary thus identified by including it in the preparatory discussion in class.

It also happens that students soon forget what they learn from an assignment. Learning, like writing and reading, is not complete in one act. To be remembered, material must be reviewed. For this reason the student must be taught to review frequently what he has learned. After he has once learned to make a good survey before reading, the student can be taught to use the same technique for making reviews. By viewing the headings or questions, he should attempt to recite from memory the major ideas which were included under them by the author. When he is unable to recall the content under a heading well enough to answer his question, he should reread that portion of the material.

The teacher, who has given survey assignments requiring students to convert topic headings into questions, can suggest that students use these questions in preparing for weekly quizzes and unit tests. This procedure cultivates the habit of frequent review and thus insures the permanence of learning.

The preceding suggestions will be recognized substantially as a means of developing the SQ3R study method of study in students by the classroom teacher. This means of improving comprehension skills at the secondary level has been presented as being the usual situation in which comprehension skills can generally be developed by the average classroom teacher at the secondary level, who is only incidentally a teacher of reading. The following specific suggestions for developing different types of comprehension skills discussed are all implicit in the process and approach previously described, but are intended to assist the subject matter teacher desiring to provide special help in improving particular reading skills to accommodate individual needs.

IMPROVING SKILL IN READING FOR MAIN IDEAS

1. Select a few paragraphs from the textbook and supply several topic sentences for each. Ask students to select the best topic sentence for the paragraph. In the beginning use the exact words of the topic sentence of the paragraph as the correct choice. When students have become proficient at this, the correct topic can be paraphrased to make it harder to identify. A very useful technique that students can be taught to use to determine whether the sentence they select is, in fact, the topic sentence, is to repeat the selected sentence after each sentence in the paragraph. If they have correctly identified the topic sentence, the paragraph thought will continue to flow smoothly.

2. Several paragraphs from the text may be presented and the students required to write a topic sentence for each. If the topic sentence is actually the first sentence of the paragraph in the beginning and then found elsewhere, or implied, in later exercises students will be able to improve their ability to formulate topic sentences with confidence.

3. The introductory paragraph of a chapter can be presented and the students required to make an outline of the chapter from it. This can be checked by actually referring to the chapter for subheadings.

4. The summary paragraph of the chapter can be read carefully and the

students required to identify the major points of the chapter from it. This can be checked by referring to the chapter.

5. Students can then be asked to put the topic sentences of several paragraphs into their own words and form a summary of the contents of the material in their own words.

6. When permissible, students can be assigned the task of underlining their texts, or marking the margins, to indicate the organization of the material presented. Because underlining achieves the same purpose as outlining, and has the added advantages of requiring less time and permitting the students ready access to supplementary information they may need to review, it should not be discouraged when students own their textbook. Outlining is an alternative when state-owned books are being used.

7. When the content admits of the technique, requiring students to prepare a diagram or sketch illustrating the content of a chapter is an excellent means of forcing them to look for general organizational patterns.

Reading to Organize Details

After the student has developed sufficient skill in determining the main ideas he will recognize for himself the need for skill in reading for details, for without these the general ideas will lack depth and the degree of meaning he needs to master the subject matter.

In order to be able to remember details, the student should be taught to look for the organizational patterns by which they are related to their topic sentence. Here it is useful to call attention to the way textbooks usually organize paragraphs. Generally, the topic sentence opens the paragraph and the subsequent sentences develop this single thought. Often there is a summary sentence given. Three types of sentences are used in a paragraph; the topic sentence, the developmental sentence, and the summary sentence.

The details which the student needs to organize are found in the developmental sentences usually found in the body of the paragraph. The sentences which develop the main thought of the paragraph do this either by repeating the main idea in other words; by contrasting this idea with something else or telling what it is not; by providing illustrations or examples of the topic sentence; by justifying the topic sentence or giving reasons for it; or, finally, by describing or qualifying the topic sentence. The teacher can develop exercises to improve this ability to read for details by:

1. Providing the students with paragraphs from their texts and asking them to classify each sentence as T for topic, D for detail or developmental, or S for summary.

2. Present paragraphs from their texts to the students and ask them to identify the developmental sentences as to kind using R for repetition, C for contrast, E for example, J for justification, and D for description.

3. Present several paragraphs from the text into which an irrelevant sentence has been inserted, and ask the students to identify this sentence by striking it out.

4. Have the students read a paragraph from the text, and then ask them to select from a group of prepared sentences those which would properly fit into the paragraph.

5. Have the students make a formal outline of a section of the chapter in their text places, with special emphasis on the ability to distinguish between generalization and details.

6. To assist students in recognizing the relationships between generalizations and supporting details, the teacher may present a number of generalizations and a number of details and ask the students to list the details under their proper generalization. If all this material is drawn from the text, it serves to develop understanding of the subject matter as well.

7. The teacher can call attention to certain words used by writers to indicate organization.

    a. Clues to a contrasting thought:
       Although, but, however, nevertheless, rather, whereas, and yet.
    b. Certain common phrases serve the same purpose:
       Even though, in spite of, on the other hand, on the contrary.
    c. Additional information on the same point is often introduced by such expressions as:
       Beyond this, moreover, furthermore, and in addition.
    d. Conclusions begin with such expressions as:
       As a result, consequently, hence, in conclusion, so, therefore.

The use and value of such terms can be brought to the student's attention by presenting paragraphs in which they are used and asking him to indicate the effect of the term on the thought.

Vocabulary Building

Frequently teachers find that students have difficulty with reading assignments because they have not learned the special vocabulary for the subject area. To develop vocabulary effectively the teacher can:

1. Provide a contextual definition of a word and ask the student to underline the word defined.
2. Provide sentences with blanks to be filled with one of several words.
3. Provide for periodic review of difficult words by preparing a matching test in which the words are to be paired with their correct meaning.
4. Provide a list of words that need to be learned in a given assignment and ask for the students to write the sentence in which each is used in

the text when they read it in their lesson and provide a definition in their own words.

5. Have students survey an assignment and note all italicized words, or words printed in bold-faced type and discuss these or require students to define them before reading the assignment.

SETTING READING PURPOSE

Unless the student has some specific goal in mind when he reads his assignment he is likely simply to wander through it, hoping to be impressed with a few of the more significant ideas presented. By teaching the student to take a few moments to determine what he is supposed to learn from an assignment, the teacher can assist him in making study a more rewarding experience emotionally for the student and a more effective learning experience. The following suggestions will indicate how the teacher can teach students to form their own reading purposes:

1. During the survey assignment which students do in the classroom, the teacher can point out the purpose of the day's lesson by converting the introductory paragraph into a series of questions. Since part of all assignments is to teach information, the learning task is to find answers to the questions thus formed.

2. The teacher can allow the class to make a survey and then ask them to share the reading purpose they formed for themselves with the class.

3. It is useful at times to provide the class with a problem and require them to read an assignment to find a solution. This problem should not consist of a question made by converting the chapter heading or a subhead into a question, but deal with something implied in the lesson.

4. Students should be asked what the author intended in writing a given chapter or assignment. They should be able to phrase this purpose in their own words.

5. Students may be assigned specific material to read in order to relate it to some current problem or put it to some specific use in a report, presentation, or the preparation of a chart, illustration, or a diagram.

6. The purpose of some assignments is simply to provide enrichment for students. A chapter in another text may be assigned relating to a topic covered in class to provide background or supplement classroom work. Students who have been given such assignments should be asked to read it to share their information with the class in discussion.

7. Students can be provided with a general statement and asked to list reasons or justifications for the statement found in the text.

8. Suggestions for reading to get the general idea, organizational pattern, or specific details can also be used as purposes for reading particular assignments.

Reading to Interpret Meaning

Reading for interpretation is perhaps one of the most advanced reading skills the student can learn. Essentially it involves going beyond the ideas actually expressed by the author, and determining implications, justifiable inferences, and possible applications. Only after a student has mastered the ideas expressed can he hope to cope with interpretation. The following practices will prove useful in assisting students to develop such power.

1. Have the students write a summary of an assignment in their own words.
2. Have the students read the introductory paragraph of a chapter or section of a chapter, and ask them to predict the probable organization of the chapter.
3. Present the students with a conclusion drawn from the assignment, and ask them to find justifications. After practice in this way a false generalization may be presented and students can be asked to evaluate it in terms of information given in a chapter of the text.
4. Present students with a paragraph and several conclusions and ask them to determine which conclusions appear justified.
5. Offer students a number of paragraphs out of sequence and ask them to place them in proper order.
6. Give the students a paragraph, and offer them a series of statements. Ask them to indicate which statements are consistent with the information provided in the paragraph.
7. Explain to students that deductive paragraphs begin with generalizations that are justified by details which follow, and that inductive paragraphs present a number of facts terminating in a generalization or conclusion. Then ask students to classify sample paragraphs as inductive or deductive.
8. Present students with an incomplete deductive paragraph and require them to write the conclusion.
9. Offer students an incomplete series of logical steps and ask them to supply the missing part.
10. After completing an assignment discussing a particularly complex issue, ask students to explain why it is difficult to arrive at simple clean-cut solutions.
11. Ask students to explain emotional factors which gave rise to certain complications encountered in an assignment.
12. Have the student place himself in the role of a person involved in the content of an assignment and have him explain how he would feel or think.

INTERPRETING SYMBOLISM

In certain courses the use of figures of speech and verbal symbolism plays an important role in conveying the writer's meaning. Because these are more sophisticated forms of communication, the teacher must anticipate difficulty in the proper interpretation of such language and call attention to it as part of the preparation for reading. To foster independence in this difficult facet of reading, the teacher should encourage students to skim assignments carefully in which symbols are used. Symbolism is not regularly employed in expository writing but the following suggestions as to how to do this would include:

1. Provide students with selected paragraphs from the text and identify the symbols used, perhaps by underlining them. Ask the students to tell what they think the symbol means. The meaning is usually determined by the context in which it is used.
2. Provide the students with a series of paragraphs and ask them to identify the symbolic language and interpret its meaning.
3. After students have interpreted the symbols in a series of paragraphs, call attention to the compressing power of symbols by having them write the paragraphs over and use their own interpretations instead of the symbols.

CONCLUSION

The ultimate goal of education is to teach the student to learn for himself. Because of the role reading plays in achieving this purpose, it will only be realized if he is given assistance in developing independent reading ability in the various subject matter areas.

By calling attention to the distinction between learning to read and reading to learn, the responsibility of the subject-matter teacher has been clarified. Because such teachers are frequently subject-matter oriented, suggestions regarding reading improvement have been directly related to the process of teaching subject matter.

While the teacher who uses the suggestions given as paradigms for his own individual initiative in improving reading skills of students cannot reasonably expect to eliminate all reading learning problems, he will have done much to make the ability to read effectively in textbooks another skill his course has to offer the student. Although it is true that the degree to which many of these higher reading skills can be developed will be determined to a great extent by the student's native intelligence, the teacher must realize that most students are probably operating well below these natural limits. The teacher who incorporates reading skills into the teaching of subject matter will lessen this gap considerably and make it possible for the individual student to develop his full potential.

SEQUENCE IN THOUGHTFUL AND CRITICAL REACTION TO WHAT IS READ*

Robert Karlin

The truly critical reader applies himself vigorously to determining the accuracy, relevance, and worth of what he reads. The very fact that the Latin terms *ad hominem, caveat emptor,* and *post hoc ergo propter hoc* (and *cui bono?*) enjoy current usage is a grim reminder that the problem of ascertaining truth is a perennial one and a difficult one.

The ability to differentiate true statements from false ones is not automatically bestowed upon a person when he reaches a certain age. Karlin takes the point of view that children can be *taught* to read critically, but that the skills involved in critical reading must be taught sequentially and systematically—if individuals are to learn to make thoughtful, critical reactions to what they read.

1. What are the author's assumptions in the introduction, and in the section "Needs and Problems"?

2. What factors are associated with the ability to do critical reading?

3. Relate the ability of several of your students to read critically to the abilities and backgrounds of the students in the categories listed by the author.

4. What steps can you take to improve the critical reading abilities of the students whom you analyzed previously?

5. Why is it important to teach people to read critically?

The purpose of this paper is to discuss the skills and abilities which should be developed to permit children and older students to react thoughtfully and critically to what they read. Before the reader can evaluate the content of a selection, it is essential that he perceive the words accurately and secure the meanings intended by the author. Sequential development of skills and abilities in these areas have been considered in the preceding chapters. The term *critical* is defined in *Webster's New World Dictionary of the American Language* as "characterized by careful analysis"; furthermore, the term implies an attempt at objective judging so as to determine both merits and faults. Applied to reading then, to be critical means to be discriminating or evaluative. A kind of judgment based on what is known is implied.

* REPRINTED FROM *Sequential Development of Reading Abilities,* Helen M. Robinson, editor, Supplementary Educational Monographs, No. 90, pp. 74–79, by permission of The University of Chicago Press. Copyright, 1960, by the University of Chicago Press.

Those who have studied the process of reading emphasize the similarities to the process of thinking. The reader deals with printed language much in the same way as the listener deals with spoken language. In reading, the element of visual symbols must be introduced but once they are known, symbols trigger the orderly processes of thinking. If we regard the reading process as similar to the thinking process, then we may conclude that critical reading involves critical thinking. Therefore, Russell's definition of critical thinking appears to be appropriate. He explains it as "the process of examining . . . verbal materials in the light of related objective evidence, comparing . . . the statement with some norm or standard, and concluding or acting upon the judgment then made."[1] He refers to the use of concrete objects as well as verbal materials since he is not limiting the discussion to reading. With this frame of reference, let us examine some of the problems associated with the teaching of critical reading.

NEED AND PROBLEMS

Any reasonable group of educators would agree that the need for teaching critical reading is paramount. The authors of almost every modern textbook on the teaching of reading devote some space to developing this ability.

One of the problems in teaching critical reading has to do with the learner and the influence of teaching upon him. We know that children pattern their thinking and behavior upon models in whom they have confidence and with whom they feel a sense of security. These first models are their parents and other adults with whom they have some relation. When a pupil comes for the first time face to face with doubts that are cast upon his models' reliability, he has a difficult choice to make. Some children are not sufficiently mature to cope with this challenge and must not be forced by continuing pressures.

A second problem revolves around the issue of determining what kind of attitudes shall be fostered by the schools and who has the ultimate responsibility for deciding which these shall be. In some homes more than in others complete submissiveness to authority is demanded and ideas presented and pronouncements made are to be accepted without any reservations. The introduction and encouragement by the school of conflicting attitudes through the teaching of critical reading can be opposed to the training carried on in such homes. Obviously the schools must assume leadership roles in such situations but at times we are blinded to the consequences of our acts by our cause. By all means, teach children to read critically but be prepared to deal with exigencies which might result from this teaching.

[1] David Russell, *Children's Thinking* (Boston: Ginn & Co., 1956), p. 285.

INFLUENCING FACTORS

Data have been accumulated showing that many students need help in improving their abilities to read and think critically. However, several factors may limit the extent of development in this area. Intelligence may prove to be a significant factor. Just as we ordinarily expect the child of normal or superior intellectual ability to surpass the school achievements of children with lesser endowments, so may we anticipate the degree to which a pupil is able to achieve in critical reading. Nevertheless, slower learners should be encouraged to react to ideas to the extent that they are able to do so. But our expectations of their achievements ought not be as high as for brighter children.

Although intelligence and ability to read critically appear to be related, investigators have found that high performance on an intelligence test does not guarantee equally-high performance in situations which require critical thinking. This fact has prompted many educators to point to the importance of providing instruction directed to improvement of critical thinking.

A second factor associated with ability to do critical reading is background of experiences. If we define critical thinking as comparing what is read with a known standard, then the standard arises from knowledge or understanding. "In general, the more a child knows about the circumstances surrounding a problem, the better his solution will be. Knowledge does not necessarily mean good thinking, but high-order thinking is dependent upon knowledge."[2] Knowledge is identified with concepts, and vague or tenuous ones may not be used as models for comparison. Since many of the ideas with which learners deal are abstract, then it follows that real experiences help to add substance to them. First-hand experiences are usually preferred to vicarious ones and should be provided. The student who is expected to evaluate a newspaper editorial must possess not only some information about the topic, but also understandings based upon his previous experiences.

A third factor which may affect ability to react critically is the attitude of the reader toward the content read. Prejudices toward or against persons, ideas or topics have been shown to interfere with the reader's performance in evaluating printed matter. The results of several investigations have demonstrated that the student's attitude toward the content which he is reading can influence his reactions to it. Among these is the study of Crossen[3] who reported a positive relationship between adolescents' ability to read material about minority groups critically and their attitudes toward these same groups.

[2] Ibid., p. 336.
[3] Helen Crossen, "Effects of Attitudes of the Reader upon Critical Reading Ability." Unpublished Ph.D. dissertation, University of Chicago, August 1946.

There are indications also that the reader's understanding may be impaired when his attitude toward the subject matter is negative. Kendall and Wolf[4] reported the results of an experiment in which the individuals' predisposition toward the material read interfered with their understanding of it. Readers whose attitudes were favorably identified with the ideas expressed in cartoons were able to react positively to them while others whose views differed with those same ideas misinterpreted them. Psychologists have been categorizing patterns of behavior and have been able to identify persons who are likely to be swayed easily and others who are bound to resist.

Scope and Sequence

The over-all concept of readiness for learning is inherent in sequential learning. To start with the known, the simple, the concrete are guidelines that each of us may follow.

Although there have not been systematic studies to determine in what order the skills of critical reading should be taught we have been able to extrapolate some hierarchy from the experiences of teachers. These empirical findings, however, remain to be tested under carefully controlled conditions. Students of critical reading have examined different aspects of the major ability in terms of the known and the unknown, the simple and the complex and the concrete and the abstract. Additional data have been drawn from our knowledge of some of the limiting factors that have been described earlier.

Several conclusions have been reached:

1. Some children have learned to think critically before entering school.
2. Critical reading has its earliest beginnings in the primary grades.
3. The level of critical reading achieved is controlled not so much by the nature of the process as it is by the experiences of the reader and his ability to deal with them.

On what skills of critical reading should the minds of six-, seven-, and eight-year-olds be stretched? One of the first might involve the reading of pictures which appear in their books. Illustrations may depict reality accurately or they may take liberties with it. It is not wholly a matter of accepting or rejecting them but rather recognizing them for what they are. Even though we see Jack climbing the beanstalk which towers over everything, we have no hesitation about going along with the story and picture. Another ability is to select one picture among several, on the basis of its

[4] Patricia Kendall and Katherine Wolf, "The Analysis of Deviant Cases in Communications Research," in P. Lazarsfeld and F. Stan, *Communications Research* (New York: Harper & Bros., 1949), pp. 152–179.

character and relationship to the highlights of the story. An extension of this ability would involve the recommendation of pictures which could be used to accompany original stories and poems.

The ability to accept or reject statements on the basis of authority can begin in the primary grades. A group studying the requirements of proper diet would be led to seek information from the school dietitian rather than from the school custodian. This ability to recognize the reliability of a source of information is built first upon gross discriminations and then finer ones. For example, to choose between the school nurse and school dietitian for authoritative information about food values would be more difficult.

Primary-grade children read fanciful tales as well as factual reports. The ability to discriminate between the two should be developed. Outright rejection may be tempered by tentative acceptance. But, here too, sequence demands simple distinctions first and more difficult ones later.

Children must learn to select sources which yield appropriate information for their purposes. Skillful evaluation of printed materials is reserved for higher levels but second and third graders can learn to choose a book or a magazine which is most likely to contain the knowledge they seek. Sequential learning calls for judgments based in turn upon the pictures, titles, and tables of content.

The development of reading tastes involves discriminatory thinking. Preschool children are capable of making choices on the basis of some standard, and this ability may be strengthened in the primary grades. The ability to compare the worth of books and express a preference for better ones should be on our list of requirements.

Critical reading in the middle grades involves the strengthening and extension of skills that have been built in the primary grades. It also means the introduction of some higher-level skills for which older children are ready. The same type of critical attitude which is fostered in the lower grades will be encouraged in the higher ones; the materials with which the pupils deal, however, will be of a more difficult sort.

It is in the middle grades that wide reading of factual materials in textbooks, magazines and newspapers is encouraged. The solution to curriculum problems demands that children begin to use care in selecting and evaluating information from the above-mentioned sources. To determine the adequacy and accuracy of what purports to be a factual statement is an ability which calls for rather mature insights. Children are bound to meet different reports of the same event and must be prepared to evaluate each in terms of the authors' possible biases and qualifications, the audience for whom the information is intended and the recentness of the content. A viewpoint which depreciates the notion of space travel or the possibility of life on other planets may be seriously questioned in view of current scientific advances.

It would be well to note that most ten- or eleven-year-olds can hardly be expected to recognize biases which are masked by the use of subtle phraseology. But they surely can be taught to identify statements of personal opinion.

Another aspect of critical reading for pupils of this age involves questions of judgment based upon values to which they subscribed. For a child to be able to answer the question, "Was it the right thing to do?" as he studies the westward movement and the ultimate placement of the Indian on reservations requires the accumulation of more facts and fewer opinions and the weighing of issues. Of course he is able to relate such conduct only to his concept of fairness, and no effort should be made to have him struggle with moral issues that are beyond his present reach. But there is no question that this attitude of judging issues should be fed by careful guidance.

An adjunct to this ability is the restraint that should be shown in withholding judgments until the facts are available. It is tempting to base conclusions upon a minimal amount of information, but children must learn to curb this tendency. Later, learning to withhold judgment lays the foundation for dealing with propaganda and its techniques.

If we may assume that elementary school pupils have been participating in a developmental program in which provisions have been made for the sequential development of critical reading skills, the progression should continue through the high school and college. Obviously some students will be more advanced in their ability to react critically than others.

Though we may expect to deal with more complex skills, students' readiness for undertaking them can mean the difference between success and confusion. One would need to ascertain the point at which instruction should be initiated before plunging into areas which challenge even the ability of adults.

The ability to select sources which yield pertinent information and to determine the reliability of them should have been growing in the elementary grades. As students are surrounded by more advanced materials the exercise of these abilities becomes increasingly difficult. Instruction must continue if students are to respond satisfactorily.

Are students able to evaluate conclusions which have been drawn for them? Have they learned to examine the evidence which is cited to support these conclusions? Are they able to recognize that certain "evidence" is difficult to verify? Reading in the content fields provides a challenge to these skills.

Writers may merely present factual reports or they may be sharpening axes. The reader is in a better position to question if he recognizes the intent of the author. Then a written statement by the president of an organization known to have vested interests in an issue will not be viewed as another statement presented by an impartial observer. The reader should be able to answer a simple question: "Who would have me believe this?"

This ability to sense the author's purpose is tied to another one, the ability to discern and evaluate propagandistic or persuasive statements. Although one may not take issue with efforts to indoctrinate—and there are many causes for whose support we work—any attempt at deception or distortion is often regarded as unethical. The term propaganda has taken on these connotations, possibly because efforts to advocate particular practices or ideas have been accompanied by trickery and craftiness.

The techniques of propaganda have been analyzed and are well known. One which needs to receive special attention is the practice of citing quotations that have been deliberately removed from larger context and as a result mislead the reader to believe what he would not ordinarily accept. A second device calls for truthful but incomplete statements, which cause the reader to react the way the writer desires. Other familiar techniques include the testimonial, band wagon and transfer. Students not only need to be alerted to these devices but also must have opportunities to respond to them as they read. The adolescent has demonstrated his readiness for learning suitable responses to exaggerated claims and partial truths; we must be ready to help him learn them.

The use of language and its influence upon reactions have been studied. There is no question about the power which words can generate. The specialists have responded intelligently: in economics, depressions have become recessions; and in ladies' wear, half-sizes are now B sizes.

Even writers of highly-regarded publications occasionally use words in such a way as to color the facts and influence the reader. A few years ago one of the leading newspapers of the country included a front-page account of the efforts of a "spinster ex-school teacher" to enact social legislation to which many persons were opposed. In this particular case straight factual reporting did not demand revelation of the marital status or previous profession of the bill's sponsor.

The reader must learn to separate words which have the power to produce feelings from words which merely serve to identify referents. The simple act of interspersing emotionally charged words among factual ones has led to reactions which the writer sought to cause. Readers must not be permitted to become slaves to words; our job is to lead readers to be masters of them.

CONCLUDING STATEMENT

To read critically is to read intelligently. Evidence which has been accumulated over the years reveals that such reading does not occur through osmosis nor does it result from chance. Efforts to develop this ability must be made by each teacher at every level of instruction. Only determined teachers can alter the reading behavior of students by helping each to become a thoughtful, careful, and critical reader.

The Development of
Word Meanings

Introduction

Some middle and secondary school teachers tend to underestimate the role of vocabulary in reading. Neither do they understand the effect that vocabulary difficulties have upon their students. Many sentences in high school textbooks are as enigmatic for the average reader in high school as the following sentence is for the average college graduate: "The rawinsonde helped the scientist make quotidian, veridical illations about tropospheric phenomena." Although this sentence is admittedly contrived, it serves to remind the reader that vocabulary problems can serve as formidable obstacles to the development of meanings in reading.

The authors of the selections in this part

discuss the principles of teaching and learning vocabulary, practical methods and materials for teaching vocabulary, and the implications for teaching of research on vocabulary improvement courses.

Manzo and Sherk verify the importance of vocabulary acquisition, pointing out that rich vocabulary is a sign of learning and an important means of learning. On the basis of their review of vocabulary studies, they provide strategies for vocabulary acquisition.

Kahle reports on the dynamic teaching strategies that he has employed in helping students acquire and use new vocabulary.

Disc jockeys are not the only purveyors of "oldies but goodies." Crawford's article is standing the test of time and is still a good source of teaching patterns.

Frederick and Palmer explain a number of word-processing skills and then provide guidelines for constructing vocabulary development exercises as well as examples of those exercises.

SOME GENERALIZATIONS AND STRATEGIES FOR GUIDING VOCABULARY LEARNING*

A. V. Manzo and J. K. Sherk[1]

If vocabulary studies could speak, they would say, "Our name is Legion." To have so much information available on a topic and to see as little excellent teaching of vocabulary as we do is an enigma. Manzo and Sherk point to the importance of vocabulary acquisition, and they offer content area teachers excellent impressionistic and data-based statements as well as data-based strategies to guide vocabulary acquisition.

1. Of what value is a rich vocabulary?

2. Discuss the definition of vocabulary learning in order to clarify the terms *acquisition of words, allusion,* and *quality expression.*

3. Devise several techniques or plans for teaching vocabulary that incorporate *pedagogic guidelines* (popular generalizations) for planning the improvement of vocabulary.

4. Compare data-based strategies with the strategies or guidelines based on popular generalizations. Which strategies are different and which are verifications of popular generalizations?

5. In a class session discuss the questions raised in component III.

[1] The authors are grateful to Alice Legenza and Victor Culver, graduate assistants, for their help with the necessary library research.

* FROM *The Journal of Reading Behavior,* 4(1) (Winter 1971–1972), pp. 78–89, by permission of A. V. Manzo and the National Reading Conference, Inc.

Acquiring a rich vocabulary is everyone's idea of being learned. We believe this because a rich vocabulary is the best measure of intelligence and cultural development (Wechsler, 46). Psychologists tell us that it also is a "mediator" of thinking—meaning more or less, that we think in words, so the more precise the words, presumably the more precise and effective our thoughts. Thus, it seems that a rich vocabulary is not only a sign of learning, but it is also an important means by which we learn. That is to say, vocabulary is central to concept formation, acculturation, articulation, and, apparently, *all* learning. With the plethora of research and writing in the area of vocabulary acquisition one might ask why it is that vocabulary study in the classrooms of our schools appears still to be implemented in a style reminiscent of that described by observers of the Colonial period of our history.

Reviews of Vocabulary: State of the Art

Thousands of studies on vocabulary have been conducted and reported in professional journals. Surprisingly, however, most studies, except for a few dissertations, are over ten years old. More surprising is the fact that no one seems to be able to synthesize or otherwise make sense of the mass. There are two striking indications of this. Contemporary reviews in the literature on language arts and the teaching of English fail to even mention vocabulary explicitly. For example, during the year 1967–68 the tables of contents of the three most likely resources for information on the teaching of vocabulary—*Review of Educational Research* ("Language Arts and Fine Arts"), American Educational Research Association; *Research in the Teaching of English* (Vol. 1, 1967, Vol. 2, 1968), National Council of Teachers of English; *Reading Research Quarterly* (Vols. II and III, 1967–1968), International Reading Association—have not one title on the teaching or acquisition of vocabulary. Even books of readings with titles suggestive of the topic like *Language and Reading—An Interdisciplinary Approach* (Gunderson, 21) have not a word on acquisition.

The second indication of the difficulty in reviewing vocabulary learning is in the form which reviews often take. One review (Dale and Razik, 8) with 3,125 titles simply groups studies into 22 categories—some categories having as many as seven subcategories. Two other reviews (Summary Research Abstracts, 1965) carried out by a group of reviewers at Lehigh University merely annotate a verbiage of studies with no attempt at categorizing beyond primary, elementary, secondary, college.

In view of the apparent difficulties in reviewing the literature on vocabulary acquisition, this review is offered as an attempt to represent a simplified system for making such educational reviews. It must be noted here that previous efforts to create systems for review which have attempted to abstract meaning from the mass have not been very successful. Petty (33) reports that he and three other professors from Sacramento State College attempted a review of data-based techniques for improving vocabulary. This review was sponsored by the National Council of Teachers of English and largely financed by a USOE grant. The reviewers identified 565 reports of articles which finally resulted in the direct examination of eighty studies.

The resultant publication of the "State of the Art" monograph was summarized most aptly by Petty himself at a College Reading Association Conference: "The studies investigated show that vocabulary can be taught, that some teaching effort causes students to learn vocabulary more successfully than does no teaching effort, that any attention to vocabulary development is better than none" (Petty, 33, p. 114).

Review Format

The system *adapted* for this review is a derivative of the iterative research model; that is, an open ended system offering opportunity for the continuous systematic recording of the literature—both data based and speculative—with an option for periodic reappraisal of new input. The review system has three components, but one thrust—improving acquisition. The first component is a recording of the "essences" of both studies and impressionistic general literature into four categories. Findings or observations may appear in more than one of these categories. This procedure, however, tends to segment, perhaps atomize, the literature, making it difficult to maintain the integrity of the whole. The second component is oriented toward experimental studies and tends to accent the whole. That is, a study is analyzed with respect to what it says as a totality. The major finding is stated, along with a sufficient rendition of that study to justify the teaching strategy which it suggests. The third component is an attempt to make an updated statement on the state of the art: what happens when you "put it all together." Finally, the review should include a set of questions which have occurred to the reviewers with respect to the whole issue of vocabulary acquisition. The review schema is designed to tell what we know (or at least think we know), what we are in the process of knowing (or still testing), and what we think we need to know.

This review will begin with an attempt to define vocabulary.

Vocabulary Learning: A Definition

The working definition of vocabulary which follows is a combination of extrapolation from the literature and the writers' own impressions. *Vocabulary Learning:* "vocabulary" [ult. *vocare*, to call]

Vocabulary learning is the acquisition of words and allusions which permit quality expression. Quality of expression is the capability to curse, to express love, or to wax in the words which best "call out" (reflect) one's inner feelings and thoughts. Thus, the improvement of vocabulary is a movement toward symbolic integrity: a process of acquiring the truest word representations for thought and feelings.

The process of acquiring "symbolic integrity," we have come to believe, *is not* simply a matter of matching newly learned words to existing feelings and thoughts. The learning of new words serves to crystallize feelings, often enhancing them as well. To this extent the learning of vocabulary often amounts to the development of clearer discriminations of amorphous feelings and thoughts; as when a new term describes a contemporary experience helping one to see it and understand it better—e.g., feeling "out of it" vs. feeling "discombobulated."

COMPONENT I: IMPRESSIONISTIC AND DATA-BASED STATEMENTS TO GUIDE VOCABULARY ACQUISITION

Underlying virtually all fields are a relatively few principles which constitute its foundations. Identification of these postulates is always a significant step; it makes possible flexible and innovative thinking with reference to using information in practical ways.

A survey of current literature on vocabulary improvement yielded a number of such guiding statements. These statements have been grouped into four categories: (1) popular generalizations underpinning instruction; (2) correlates of vocabulary knowledge; (3) the influences of words and word classes on learning; and (4) the learner: his disposition to learn, his characteristics, etc. These are not mutually exclusive categories; several statements could easily be recorded in more than one category.

POPULAR GENERALIZATIONS UNDERPINNING INSTRUCTION. This category is meant to suggest some *pedagogic guidelines* for planning the improvement of vocabulary.

Vocabulary development must have the continued and *systematic attention* of all classroom teachers (6, 1, 36).

New words are learned best when taught as labels for *direct experiences* (26, 16, 10).

Vocabulary teaching strategies which stress *induction* will tend to result in the best learning of rules governing words and word parts (19).

The study of *Latin* positively influences knowledge of morphemes, but does not seem to influence knowledge of vocabulary (3).

The wide reading method of acquiring vocabulary which stresses little more than *wide free reading* (43, p. 241) with no other attention paid to words is usually not very effective for influencing rapid and marked achievement. The reason for this seems to be that students generally do not reflect on the context fully enough to permit words to be deeply experienced and thus acquired (39).

Almost any technique which draws *attention to word parts and/or word meanings* will positively influence word acquisition when compared with the absence of such attention (consensus of many writers).

It is possible, but may be practically foolish, to teach words which are not a part of the *verbal community* in which students live. The lack of opportunity for use must result in eventual atrophy (13).

The presentation of many new words and allusions in a gamelike incidental learning fashion can often provide a major source of stimulation for attention to, and consequent growth in, vocabulary (22, 28).

At least five types of guidance are needed for vocabulary development: context-awareness; dictionary-awareness; word-awareness; structural-awareness (17).

Many encounters with a word in like and differing contexts are necessary before it can be learned. We never get all of a word's meaning at any one encounter (10).

The *teacher's attitude* toward vocabulary improvement and the superiority of his own vocabulary are contagious and vital factors in improving student vocabulary (36). Rauch lists ten other helpful hints for improving vocabulary. He suggests, for example, that students be instructed in the usefulness of other language books, in addition to a good dictionary, e.g.: Soule's (42) *Dictionary of English Synonyms;* Fernald's (14) *Handbook of Synonyms, Antonyms, and Prepositions; Roget's Thesaurus* (29); Perrin's (32) *Writer's Guide and Index to English;* Fowler's (15) *Modern English Usage;* and Partridge's (31) *Origins: The Encyclopedia of Words.* To this we must add the old standard, Roberts' *Word Attack* (37).

"Study of a limited number of *words in depth* is more productive than superficial acquaintance with lists of words." Lee Deighton, as cited by Sanford (40).

REGARDING WORDS. This category is designed to point out some of the aspects of our knowledge about words and word parts which can be useful in facilitating vocabulary acquisition.

The successful learning of certain *structural elements of words* will help students to unlock or partially unlock many words containing those elements (6).

Knowledge of the *derivation of words* and the meaning of elements within words will help a student to gain a more precise meaning for those words (6).

In addition to the study of graded word lists, vocabulary study should include those words, phrases and allusions which cryptically codify our cultural-academic experience. Such phrases and allusions are often the postholes for a garble of cultural–academic trivia which amounts to one of the major trappings of being "with it"; i.e., educated—e.g., *deus ex machina,* hieroglyphics, Holy Roman Empire, hashish, laser beam (28). For further examples and exercises dealing with such factors see Gilbert (18) *Breaking the Sound Barrier,* and Dale and O'Rourke (7), *Techniques of Teaching Vocabulary.*

There are *five ways to define a word:* (a) by giving a synonym; (b) by classifying it (e.g., man is a "rational animal"); (c) by enumerating words to which it relates (e.g., spices are cinnamon, cloves, paprika, etc.); (d) by exhibiting an example (e.g., pointing to the object and saying it—"goat"; (e) by operationally defining it—i.e., using a definition which tells *what to do* in order to experience or to recognize the thing to which the word defined refers (35).

There is a peculiar irony in studying words to develop more precise language; the *meanings of words* will always be something "approximate and indefinite" (23).

Knowledge of vocabulary is the most *reliable measure of intelligence* over the full term of life (46).

The Learner: This category deals with the special characteristics of the learner which will likely influence his vocabulary acquisition.

The *empathetic response* of the learner to a word is the best indication of how well he will learn that word (34).

Mere *attendance at college* (and probably at school) tends greatly to increase capacity to improve one's vocabulary (48; 24).

The number of totally new words incorporated each month in a *pre-school age child's speaking vocabulary* was found to decrease steadily (45). It seems that the greatest acquisition of new words takes place between 2½ and 5 years old.

The approximate *size of the vocabulary of children and adults* at different stages of development must be considered a mystery. The last fifty years of research has produced wildly contrasting figures. Differences among these figures would undoubtedly be less exaggerated if definitions of "vocabulary" were alike and data collection systems comparable. Surely there is room for negotiation between an estimate like 1,933 words—including variations —for five year olds (45), and the 24,000 different words estimated by Seashore and Eckerson as cited by Bryan (2). After an exhaustive review of size of vocabulary studies, Lorge and Chall (27) concluded that "before adequate estimates can be made, the methodological issues raised will need further study" (p. 154). The methodological issues seem far from resolution even today.

The student has *four levels of vocabulary:* speaking, reading, writing, and listening. During childhood listening and speaking vocabul·ries appear to be dominant. As the individual reaches maturity his reading vocabulary will probably be largest, followed by listening. Writing and speaking vocabularies probably are comparable in size, but the writing may tend to be the "larger" (5, 47). A fifth level, or type, of vocabulary has been suggested by Debes (9) which he has called "visual vocabulary." Visual vocabulary, Thelen (44) has interpreted Debes to have said, is composed of representations of reality which are usually photovisual surrogates, not words. Further, it is through these photovisual surrogates that the ghetto child explores and codifies his environment. The current delineation of an entity— visual vocabulary—while somewhat interesting, may be a bit contrived. It seems to be an attempt to describe a pre-cognitive process, or stage of learning, rather than a stable, measurable factor. The idea, however, is not new. A long time ago St. Augustine is reputed to have said, "When you ask me, I do not know; When you do not ask me, I know." He meant by this, though words may fail us, thoughts—or internal images—do not. More recently, Joseph Church (4) has said, ". . . All thinking, like all behavior, is in essence dialectical. Dialectical does not *always* mean verbal: communication between organism and environment can take place at the automatic level of perceptual feedback, at the more conscious level of concrete exploration (as when the baby pokes at an insect), . . . and so on up to the full-fledged Socratic dialogue or creative soliloquy" (p. 148). Together these observations seem to say that there probably is a phenomenon of pre-verbal symbolic recording of impressions. And, that these secondary sense impressions do influence our judgments, but are they visual images (?); are they *learnings* or things in process of *being learned* (?); are they in any way measurable (?); are they even so identifiable as to function that they are not explained more parsimoniously in some other way (?); and most important with respect to vocabulary acquisition, does the phenomenon lend itself to manipulation—can it be improved or modified?

CORRELATES OF VOCABULARY ACQUISITION: This category deals with the general relationships between vocabulary and other factors which typically influence learning.

There is a close relationship between *concept development* and general vocabulary growth (26, 38).

Vocabulary knowledge is more highly correlated with total I.Q. than with reading ability (48). Vocabulary is also correlated very highly (0.7 to 0.9) with all other verbal tests (46).

Correlation between *English achievement* and vocabulary is .58. This correlation can be raised to .70 when account is taken of work habits or "industriousness" in English (25).

Dale and Razik (8) list 134 references of studies demonstrating high positive correlations of vocabulary with *virtually everything:* social class, arithmetic, age, grade level, foreign language proficiency, etc. The correlations are unusually stable even across studies in spite of the use of differing measures of vocabulary and differing measures of the second variable.

COMPONENT II: DATA-BASED STRATEGIES

This component is an attempt to present a few examples of basic strategies for improving vocabulary in a data-based context. The accumulation of such entities should make it easier to see, at a slightly more comprehensive level, whether seeming contradictions in study effects from one study to the next are real or artifactual.

General Strategies

Silent reading is better than oral reading and better than being read to for learning new vocabulary.

In an experimental comparison of three procedures for improving vocabulary with college students, silent reading proved to be more "efficacious" than oral reading or being read to. A silent reading vocabulary test was used to measure differences—*Cooperative Vocabulary Test* (Q). The reading-listening material used in this experiment was developed by the experimenter. By design, it included all 210 words appearing on the *Cooperative Vocabulary Test.*

The outcomes of this study must be interpreted according to the limitations of the design: the silent readers were not limited by having to divide attention between reading orally and thinking as were the oral readers, nor were they forced to process at the fixed rate of the listeners who were without a visual experience (48).

Prior study of the technical vocabulary of math will greatly enhance the learning of basic mathematics and algebra.

Using little more than mimeographed sheets of definitions, some attention to technical words as they appeared in the math text, and periodic vocabulary "quizzes," achievement in High School math (12) and algebra (11) was significantly greater for experimental subjects than for control subjects receiving no such training. In the study dealing with algebra (11), the average amount of class time given to vocabulary enrichment was calculated at only about 7.5 minutes per session.

Special short courses at the secondary level in word study can increase knowledge of vocabulary.

In a Madison, Wisconsin, high school, regular work in English composition and literature was substituted for by a twelve-week unit of word study: meanings, word parts, etymology. Differences between experimental and control groups were measured by an array of vocabulary tests (Terman's, Thorndike's, Trabue's), including a special test of 25 words selected in the belief that high school sophomores should know them and because knowledge of roots, prefixes and suffixes would be helpful in recognition of the meanings. Subjects (350) were matched for prior academic achievement and experience in areas believed to be related to rate of vocabulary acquisition: freshmen grades, grades in first semester of the sophomore year and an equal amount of language study in French or Latin.

The test results were consistently in favor of the experimental groups. No measures of differences were reported, however, for the missing class content replaced by word study; i.e., English composition and literature (49).

The value of short courses for improving vocabulary seems to have been well-established by this study. Replacing English and composition for twelve weeks with vocabulary, however, does not seem to be advisable. Vocabulary should not be viewed solely as the bailiwick of the English department; rather, it should be the shared concern of all academic divisions. Furthermore, if anything is to be replaced, it should be some aspect of the curriculum which is less contributive to language and vocabulary growth.

COMPONENT III: QUESTIONS

This is the place to raise the major questions which have occurred during the review.

The question of process—how do we learn words, etc.—is always an intriguing one. No one presumes to know what the process of acquisition is. In the case of vocabulary acquisition, however, there is little evidence that the issue is even broached by vocabulary enthusiasts. The whole realm of language learning and social and imitation learning theory, however, does encompass vocabulary learning, and they are well-researched areas. As a general theory of learning to explain vocabulary acquisition, the writers find Mowrer's (30) two-factor theory of learning the most useful with respect to both explaining acquisition and with respect to formulating possible intervention procedures.

The essential pragmatic question facing teachers is simply, "How do you teach vocabulary?" Surprisingly, there are few explicit teaching techniques. Most "techniques" would be better characterized as strategies—word-awareness, dictionary work, wide reading, etc. While vocabulary acquisition is central to all other learnings, it is also so well nested in other contexts that it makes sequential and explicit instruction somewhat unrealistic; that is not to say that it cannot be systematically and continuously attended to. For example, a simple combination of systematic attention to technical words by content area teachers, classroom discussion in which language precision is encouraged and periodic work in almost any one of many different programmed learning or word manipulation exercise materials would surely improve vocabulary significantly.

With respect to pedagogy, other questions are: What specific techniques, or combinations of techniques, are best for students of differing characteristics with different possible goals of enrichment? And, as a related but somewhat more generic issue, what are the upper and lower limits of vocabulary knowledge needed by people to function effectively?

The latter question is meant to suggest that somehow there might be an optimal vocabulary range. This might be tenable in at least three respects. First, the extension of vocabulary beyond certain limits may require more time than the effort it is worth in terms of new understandings and enlightenment. Secondly, one of the primary motivations for acquiring a rich vocabulary is to communicate in a more cogent, incisive fashion. There may be a point, however, after which erudite language becomes counterproductive, because—in the language of the day—the *communicator* seriously outdistances the *communicatee*.

Finally, it is possible that with only a few words almost anything can be said. In moving toward symbolic integrity, the simple and true representation of thought, one may actually be passing through stages of linguistic growth, in which the size of the vocabulary may not be as influential as the discipline required for clear thinking.

Other questions which remain essentially unanswered relate to the better deployment of existing strategies: what techniques are best for developing word-awareness, or word-depth, or enriched speaking vocabulary, or more intelligent use of existing vocabulary, or any other specific vocabulary enrichment goal?

As a separate, and almost philosophical issue, we can also ask if it is not time to incorporate into our vocabulary lists words which are more a part of the urban, contemporary, and ethnic-American experience. We tend to behave in academia as if only *our* language and *our* allusions—usually classical—are meaningful in expository writing. We seem to have progressed, at least in some quarters, to where we will tolerate, maybe even be bemused by, the language of other cultures, but usually only as "creative" writing. Current examinations of the languages of black, ethnic, and urban America are suggesting that "Third World" is not merely a piece of literary jargon, but a living, vital entity. If "language" is alive, why are we so "hung-up" about permitting its richness and vitality to penetrate our language arts curriculum.

"Putting It All Together"

Trite as it may seem, the writers must conclude that the single most significant factor in improving vocabulary is the excitement about words which the teacher can generate. This does not contradict the now platitude that teachers cannot expect to improve student vocabulary simply by using erudite language in class or giving reading assignments which include such language. Teachers can use "big" words, or technical terms, in their teaching, and students can and should read materials in which such terms appear. The terms must, however, be an extension of precision in thought and concern for communication; i.e., the result of an apparent need for the *better* or more appropriate term, and an obvious need to monitor the density of the presentation of such words. There is a fine line between technical language and jargon. But, the teacher should not be made to feel guilt nor need to apologize for using the "big" word. The accusation of "jargon" is most often made by the unsophisticated listener. On the other hand, the teacher, by definition, speaks only to unsophisticated listeners. To apologize for verbal power would be demeaning and patronizing to students, but to use technical language indiscriminately is both adolescent and counterproductive.

Assuming that a teacher recognizes the need to use a new piece of language, the questions then are when to introduce it, and how to have it learned so that it might become part of the student's speaking-writing vocabulary. The question of when may not be as urgent as it may first seem. If a teacher can communicate excitement about the ideas being developed, it is difficult to imagine any real problems in having students accept the language used for codifying those ideas. The remaining question of how to have students learn new words well enough to use them is relatively simple. A combination of general attention to words, word manipulation exercises and repetition of exposure in same and differing contexts is part of an established formula for embedding all new learning.

In summary, if we think of word learning as an extension of basic language learning, teaching vocabulary may be a relatively simple matter of exploiting experiences as a means of teaching vocabulary, and exploiting or using vocabulary as a means of getting the most from experiences. "Experience," Frazier has noted, "may be said to have been fully experienced only when it has been worked through in terms of language. The meaning of experience has to be extracted, clarified, and codified, so to speak; i.e., *develop vocabulary from whatever experiences children* [people] *are having*" (16).

If this basic strategy for improving vocabulary were to prevail, teaching the word "photosynthesis" should not be much more difficult than was teaching the word "doggie."

REFERENCES

1. Burns, P. C. "Means of Developing Vocabularies," *Education*, 85 (1965), 533–537.
2. Bryan, F. E. "How Large Are Children's Vocabularies?" *Elementary School Journal* (1945), 210–216.
3. Carroll, J. B. "Knowledge of English Roots and Prefixes as Related to Vocabulary and Latin Study," *Journal of Educational Research*, 34 (1940), 102–111.
4. Church, J. *Language and the Discovery of Reality*. New York: Random House, Inc., 1963.
5. Dale, E. "Vocabulary Measurement: Techniques and Major Findings." *Elementary English*, 42 (1965), 395–401.
6. ———, and J. L. Milligan. "Techniques in Vocabulary Development," *Reading Improvement*, 1 (1970), 1–5.
7. ———, and J. O'Rourke. *Techniques of Teaching Vocabulary*. Palo Alto, Calif.: Field Educational Publications, Inc., 1971.
8. ———, and T. Razik. *Bibliography of Vocabulary Studies*. Columbus, Ohio: Bureau of Educational Research and Service, Ohio State University, 1963.
9. Debes, J. "A New Look at Seeing," *Media and Methods*, 4 (1962), 26–28.
10. Deighton, L. C. "Developing Vocabulary: Another Look at the Problem," *English Journal*, 49 (2) (1960), 82–88.
11. Drake, R. "The Effect of Teaching the Vocabulary of Algebra," *Journal of Educational Research*, 33 (1940), 601–610.
12. Dresher, R. "The Effects of Extensive and Specific Vocabulary Training in Junior High School Mathematics," *Educational Research Bulletin*, 13 (1934), 201–204.
13. Eicholz, G., and R. Barbe. "An Experiment in Vocabulary Development," *Educational Research Bulletin* 60 (1961), 1–7.
14. Fernald, J. C. *Handbook of Synonyms, Antonyms, and Prepositions*. New York: Funk and Wagnalls, 1947.

15. Fowler, H. W. *Dictionary of Modern English Usage*, 2nd ed., ed. by E. Gowers. New York: Oxford University Press, 1965.

16. Frazier, A. "A Vocabulary of the Senses," *Elementary English*, 7 (1970), 756–764.

17. Furness, E. L. "Types of Guidance Needed for Vocabulary Development," *Education*, 76 (1956), 498–501.

18. Gilbert, D. W. *Breaking the Reading Barrier*. Englewood Cliffs, N.J.: Prentice-Hall, Inc., 1959.

19. Gray, L. "Making It on Their Own: How Can Students Learn to Transfer the Reading Vocabulary to Their Thinking, Speaking, and Writing?" *National Educational Association Journal*, 40 (1952), 405–406.

20. Gray, W. S., and E. Holmes. *The Development of Meaning Vocabularies in Reading: An Experimental Study*. Chicago: The University of Chicago Press, 1938.

21. Gunderson, D., ed. *Language and Reading*. Washington, D.C.: Center for Applied Linguistics, 1970.

22. Haefner, R. "Casual Learning of Word Meanings," *Journal of Educational Research*, 25 (1932), 266–277.

23. Hall, R. A. *Linguistics and Your Language*, 2nd rev. ed. of *Leave Your Language Alone*. Garden City, N.Y.: Anchor Books, 1960.

24. Johns, W. B. "The Growth of Vocabulary Among University Students with Some Consideration of Methods of Fostering It," *Journal of Experimental Education*, 8 (1939–40), 89–102.

25. Krathwohl, W. D. "Relative Contributions of Vocabulary and an Index of Industriousness for English to Achievement in English," *Journal of Educational Psychology*, 42 (1951), 97–104.

26. Langer, J. H. "Vocabulary of Concept Development," *Journal of Reading*, 10 (1967), 442–455.

27. Lorge, I., and J. Chall. "Estimating the Size of Vocabulary in Children and Adults: An Analysis of Methodological Issues," *Journal of Experimental Education*, 32 (1963), 147–157.

28. Manzo, A. V. "CAT—A Game for Extending Vocabulary and Knowledge of Allusions," *Journal of Reading*, 13 (1970), 367–369.

29. Morehead, A. H., ed. *New American Roget's College Thesaurus in Dictionary Form*. New York: New American Library, 1962.

30. Mowrer, O. H. *Learning Theory and Behavior*. New York: John Wiley and Sons, Inc., 1960.

31. Partridge, E. *Origins: The Encyclopedia of Words*. New York: Macmillan Publishing Co., Inc., 1958.

32. Perrin, P. A. *Writer's Guide and Index to English*, 4th ed. Chicago: Scott, Foresman and Company, 1965.

33. Petty, W. "A New Look at Vocabulary Research," in *Proceedings of the College Reading Association*, ed. by Clay Ketcham, 8 (1967), 113–118.

34. Postman, L., J. S. Bruner, and E. McGinnies. "Personal Values as Selective Factors in Perception," *Journal of Abnormal Social Psychology*, 43 (1948), 142–154.

35. Rapaport, A. *Science and the Goals of Man*. New York: Harper & Row, 1950.

36. Rausch, S. "Enriching Vocabulary in the Secondary Schools," *Fusing Read-*

ing Skills and Content, ed. by H. Robinson and E. Thomas. Newark, Del.: International Reading Association, 1969, pp. 191–200.

37. Roberts, C. *Word Attack.* New York: Harcourt Brace Jovanovich, Inc., 1956.

38. Russell, D. H., and I. Q. Saadeh, "Qualitative Levels in Children's Vocabularies," *Journal of Educational Psychology,* 53 (1953), 170–174.

39. Sachs, H. J. "The Reading Method of Acquiring Vocabulary," *Journal of Educational Research,* 36 (1943), 457–464.

40. Sanford, G. "Word Study That Works," *Education,* 60 (1971), 111–115.

41. Seashore, R., and J. Eckerson. "How Many Words Does a First Grade Child Know?" *Elementary English Journal,* 42 (1959), 135–143.

42. Soule, R. *Dictionary of English Synonyms.* New York: Bantam Books, 1960.

43. Strang, R., C. McCullough, and A. E. Traxler. *The Improvement of Reading,* 4th ed. New York: McGraw-Hill, Inc., 1967.

44. Thelen, J. "Developing the Visual Vocabulary," *Reading Improvement,* 6(2) (1969), 35–36, 38.

45. Uhrbrock, R. S. "The Vocabulary of a Five-Year-Old," *Educational Research Bulletin,* 14 (1935), 85–97.

46. Wechsler, D. *The Measurement and Appraisal of Adult Intelligence.* Baltimore: The Williams and Wilkins Co., 1958.

47. Weintraub, S. "The Development of Meaning Vocabulary in Reading," *Reading Teacher,* 22 (1968), 171–175.

48. Young, J. D. "An Experimental Comparison of Vocabulary Growth by Means of Oral Reading, Silent Reading, and Listening," *Speech Monographs,* 20 (1953), 273–276.

Student-Centered Vocabulary*

David J. Kahle

Kahle makes a lot of sense in his discourse on the vocabulary-teaching strategies he developed and employed. He utilizes a dynamic structure which allows for creative effort yet holds the student on task. It seems important that he take definite steps in this system to have the students use the vocabulary in a number of contexts and settings, including short stories, compositions, and poems.

1. Which vocabulary-building efforts did the author deem fruitless?

2. How did the author solve the problem regarding the words to be studied?

3. What was the purpose of the mimeographed form?

4. How did the author get the

* FROM *English Journal,* 61(2) (February 1972), pp. 286–288, reprinted with permission of David J. Kahle and the National Council of Teachers of English.

students to study the words during the week?

5. How did the poster idea work?

6. What positive benefits accrued to the members of the author's classes as a result of this vocabulary development approach?

7. Try this method with a group of students. Report on your findings.

As a second-year eighth-grade English teacher one of the biggest problems I faced was the teaching of vocabulary. That my average and below average students needed vocabulary building went without saying. But I felt the standardized, twenty words a week, memorize-the-definitions-for-a-matching-test programs weren't the answer. These programs, I felt, emphasized rote memory rather than use. What I wanted was a vocabulary program which made the students more aware of words in general, and which specifically increased their vocabulary as shown by the extent to which they used the new words.

In my spare time I looked over reading achievement tests trying to decide which words eighth-graders should, but didn't, know. After this proved fruitless, I decided the most useful words would be the terms of the new age—space, technological and ecological terms rather than the hackneyed words that appeared on every publisher's vocabulary list. Reading newspapers and magazines with an eye out for terms which could be used frequently but which the students probably didn't know might be the best way to develop a vocabulary list. A week of this proved ineffective. I found I couldn't enjoy anything I was reading when I was consciously looking for eighth-grade vocabulary words.

Then the thought occurred to me that the only people who could say for sure which words the students didn't know were the students themselves. And the words they would need to know were probably those associated with their interests. Why not let the students find the words for class study?

With this seed of an idea I built the following program. Every other weekend each student in the class would have to find a vocabulary word and present it to the class on Monday. This way one half the class had the assignment every week. The criteria for acceptance of the word were the following: (1) the word had to be one that the rest of the class probably wasn't familiar with, (2) the word had to be one which was unfamiliar to the student finding the word, (3) the student had to find it in a source outside of school (radio, TV, newspapers, magazines, family conversations, billboards—anything as long as it had nothing to do with school or textbooks), (4) it had to be a word the students would probably be able to use in the near future, (5) it couldn't be a word that was too technical or scientific, and (6) it had to be an English word.

Each student was given a mimeographed form to fill out with certain information about his word. This form contained spaces for the following:

(1) word (correct spelling), (2) meaning (in the student's own words, as I had noticed the habit eighth-graders have of copying definitions out of the dictionary without having the vaguest knowledge of what they are copying), (3) sentence (use the word correctly in an original sentence), (4) synonym, (5) antonym, and (6) source.

On Monday each of the students who was assigned to find a word that week had to write the word on the blackboard and then read his information to the class. The rest of the class took notes. The student presenting the word had to field any questions and could be challenged on any of the criteria.

After all the words had been given I picked four to ten words for study that week. The following Monday the class was quizzed on these words. In these quizzes the students were asked to use the words by writing sentences, paragraphs, or short stories rather than spout forth memorized definitions.

The program developed from this start. I soon found that many of the students, if not most of them, just never got around to studying the words during the week. To solve this I used two techniques. First, I broke the class into groups and had them write several paragraphs using the words correctly. They could use the dictionary or their notes. Second, instead of weekly quizzes, I occasionally had them turn in writing assignments. These could be short stories, compositions, poems or combinations of these, in which each of the vocabulary words had to be used accurately. In both cases, examples of good work or imagination were hung on the bulletin board, shown to the class, or given other special notice.

But one presentation of a word proved not always enough to jell its meaning in the minds of the students. So I offered extra credit to students who would make posters of the words to hang on the walls, or who would make up several examples of sentences in which the word or words were used correctly.

Students were soon bringing in posters with the words on them, giving noun forms of words which had been presented as verbs, etc. Taking advantage of this growing interest in words, and hoping to solve the problem of lagging quiz grades, I started assigning students, on a voluntary basis, to review the words with the class during the week. Thus on Monday the words were presented and four to ten picked for study. Several students were picked to prepare the chosen words and each given a word and a specific day on which to review it. On each of the following days one or two of these student volunteers would write his word on the board, review the definition with the class, tell what part(s) of speech it could be used as, and then read five original sentences in which the word was used correctly and five original sentences in which the word was used incorrectly. The paper with this information was then filed in a special vocabulary folder for future class reference.

With these reviews as a regular part of the school week, many of the students have been given the opportunity to prepare and teach a mini-lesson to the class. The resulting benefit to their egos has been marked, as has the development of their self-confidence, ability to speak before a group, sense of responsibility, and in many cases their attitude toward school as a whole.

But this hasn't been the only fringe benefit of the vocabulary program. The critical listening and thinking of the class have shown noticeable improvement, as has their ability to take notes, a study skill often neglected until college.

The practice in speaking before a group has been invaluable. As a corollary to this, I am currently tape recording the vocabulary presentations of the students and then playing them back to them, so that they can be aware of their own deficiencies and strengths as speakers and take steps to improve them.

The uses to which the raw material of the vocabulary words can be put are almost infinite. But the important thing is that students are becoming aware of words around them and interested in them.

Here is a sample of some of the words given this year by eighth-grade students.

exaltation	breach
consecutive	posterity
appall	merit
judicious	haggard
adhere	corrupt
consumer	defer
engulf	spurn
impede	intricate
ultimate	baroque
sensation	placid
bigot	essential
lusty	infantile
asinine	vulnerable
arduous	loathsome
uncouth	terse

Teaching Essential Reading Skills— Vocabulary*

Earle E. Crawford

Someone has called words the counters of experience. Meaning is developed for words by the real and vicarious experiences people have in connection with these words and the language used in referring to these experiences. The development of meanings is one of the key tasks of education. Crawford feels that vocabulary training should "grow out of the pupil's reading experience or other use of words." He discusses various aspects of vocabulary teaching and concept development and provides some useful paradigms for structuring the study of vocabulary in the classroom.

1. Before reading this article, list briefly your approaches to vocabulary improvement.

2. Why might it be a good idea to try the suggestions given here, a few at a time?

3. Of what personal and professional values could a personal program of vocabulary development be?

4. Do you agree with the author's contention that it is wise to give pupils some comprehension of the process involved in contextual analysis and some training in applying it?

5. The author wants the reader to be particularly aware of several very important points in the discussion on "Figurative . . . Language." Can you infer what these points are?

6. What can be done to improve vocabulary and to retain new vocabulary?

Improvement of Vocabulary

Two closely related fundamental skills in reading are recognition of words and symbols and an understanding of the language used. Effective instruction in vocabulary building contributes to the pupil's understanding of what is read, to growth in expressing ideas both in oral and in written form, and to an understanding of ideas presented orally.

A. Background Experiences

Pupils frequently fail to understand what is read because the vocabulary is not within their experience. Therefore, provision for common background experiences to enable pupils to understand many words before they meet them in reading about a problem or a topic helps in overcom-

---

* REPRINTED BY PERMISSION FROM the *Bulletin of the National Association of Secondary-School Principals*, February 1950, pp. 56–68.

ing vocabulary difficulties. The following suggestions apply especially to slow readers:

1. Use these general guides for preparing pupils to read a selection:
    a. Provide concrete background experiences.
    b. Use visual aids, such as maps, diagrams, charts, pictures, models, and motion pictures.
    c. Use words in conversation and explain specific terms.
2. Provide exercises giving specific helps for developing readiness to read a particular selection:
    a. Change the language of the text to one the pupils understand.
    b. Write difficult words in the lesson on the board. After each word, list the page on which it is found. In an informal discussion, have pupils find each word and tell what it means.
3. Select difficult words from the lesson. After each word, write the page on which it is found. In another column write a word or phrase that has the same meaning.

B. Development of Vocabulary

The emphasis in vocabulary building should be on meaning. In the best classroom practice, procedures for improving word recognition and pronunciation and for developing wider meaning vocabulary will be closely related. In this way, word meaning will be constantly emphasized. Specific exercises should be given for improving the mechanics of word recognition and pronunciation because "comprehension cannot be raised to a high degree if the learner is struggling with the mechanics of the reading process." [1]

Although certain types of vocabulary drill are not always successful and the degree of improvement does not always justify the effort expended to produce it, the majority of research studies seems to justify well-motivated vocabulary training which grows out of the pupil's reading experience or other use of words.

The following suggestions, according to Ruth Strang, have proved to be of value: [2]

1. Note definitions which frequently follow the introduction of technical words. The definitions given in the text are often preferable to definitions found in a standard dictionary.
2. Check lightly unfamiliar words which are not defined in their context, and

---

[1] *A Preliminary Survey of a Reading Program for the Secondary Schools*, Bulletin 202. Harrisburg, Pennsylvania: Department of Public Instruction, Commonwealth of Pennsylvania, 1939, p. 32.

[2] Ruth Strang, with the assistance of Florence C. Rose, *Problems in the Improvement of Reading in High School and College*. Lancaster, Pennsylvania: The Science Press Printing Co., 1938, p. 84.

later look them up in a dictionary. Write each at the top of a small card. At the bottom of the card should appear a synonym, and in the middle of the card a sentence using the word, or a familiar word derived from or giving derivation to the unfamiliar one. These cards may then be used for individual practice. When the word is not immediately recognized, the "player" looks down to the "connecting link" in the middle of the card. If this does not bring about the recall of the meaning, he must resort to the synonym or definition at the bottom of the card. Junior-high-school youngsters enjoy playing games with such cards and finding the words in new contexts. Adults find such a method of keeping up their recently acquired vocabulary useful because a knowledge of the range of literal meanings of a large number of words helps the reader to grasp its meaning in context.

Throughout his reading experience, an individual tends to read about things more or less familiar to him. Each new bit of reading increases his fund of ideas, gives him new understandings and wider experiences, often vicarious, all of which builds up a certain ability to infer meanings.

When new words are encountered for the first time, great dependence is placed upon context clues. In fact, familiarity with ideas being expressed gives the reader his first clues to word symbols. In normal reading development, occasional unfamiliar words present little difficulty since meanings can often be derived from the otherwise familiar context. The more remote the subject matter from the reader's background of experience, the less able is he to anticipate or infer meanings. Thus, the poor reader with inadequate skill in word perception goes down under a too heavy load of unfamiliar words encountered in his reading.

Most of the instruction which is directed toward enlargement of students' vocabularies is based upon use of the dictionary. Instruction and practice in dictionary use are often carried to such a point that pupils feel helpless without a dictionary or, as a labor-saving substitute, a teacher who will define unknown words. Since, in practice, mature readers use context clues far more frequently than they use dictionaries in arriving at word meanings, it is highly desirable to give pupils some comprehension of the process involved and some training in applying it. All pupils need some help in this area and less alert ones must have intensive practice in it. To enrich the background and to choose material not too far above the level of the pupil's reading ability are first steps in specific training to use context clues as an aid to word recognition as well as to word meaning.

The next step might well be to help pupils become aware that words and meanings may be guessed, at times. Practice on familiar expressions will serve to awaken pupils to the realization that many words may be read without having been printed in the sentence. This is easily demonstrated by completing the following phrases:

Early in the ....   His one .... interest

As light as a ....   Flew in a straight ....

Other types of clues should be analyzed and taught specifically. Often an unfamiliar word is merely a synonym for a word previously used, as illustrated in the following two sentences:

Today he tells the *property man* what he wants and tomorrow he finds the items waiting on the set. The *property* *custodian* has become the movie director's Santa Claus.

An unfamiliar word may be an antonym for a known word, for example:

Water is *seldom* found in the desert, but springs *frequently* occur in the surrounding hills.

Organized and systematic instruction on the use of these and other types of clues should form a part of the reading program throughout elementary- and high-school grades. Awareness of context clues and skill in using them are indispensable for independent and intelligent reading. Pupils must be able to use context clues in various ways:

a. In associating meaning with known word forms.
b. In discriminating between words which are very much alike in sound and form but not in meaning.
c. In checking on pronunciation derived from phonetic analysis.
d. In determining which one of the various sounds of a certain vowel is appropriate in a given word.[3]

C. *Qualifying Words*

Common qualifying words are important to the meaning of a sentence, yet many pupils fail to understand the idea expressed in a sentence because they pass over the qualifying words. Common qualifying words include *many, no, more, most, less, few, only, almost, always* and *all*. Short phrases and clauses are frequently used in a qualifying manner, and pupils should be trained to notice the way in which such phrases, as well as words similar to the ones listed above, change the meaning of a sentence. The following types of exercises have been found helpful in training pupils to notice how qualifying words or phrases change the meaning of a sentence.

1. Write on the blackboard sentences containing qualifying words or give them orally. Discuss with pupils the way in which the words affect the meaning of the sentence.
2. Write a group of sentences on the blackboard with the instructions to copy these sentences and draw a line through each qualifying word.

Example: There are *many* apples on the plate.

[3] William S. Gray and Lillian Gray, *Guidebook for Streets and Roads*. Chicago: Scott, Foresman and Company, 1941, p. 29.

a. After the sentences have been discussed and all pupils have drawn a line through each qualifying word, have them rewrite each sentence and substitute another qualifying word for the one used.

b. Discuss the meaning of these rewritten sentences to show how qualifying words make distinct changes in the meaning of a sentence.

3. Write on the blackboard sentences containing qualifying words or phrases. Check the pupils' knowledge of how the words or phrases change the meaning of the sentence by having them answer yes or no to questions about the sentences.

Example: The old Indian nearly always came to the trading post in the morning.

Questions:

1. Did the old Indian always come to the trading post in the morning?

2. Did the old Indian usually come to the trading post in the morning?

3. Is it true that the old Indian seldom came to the trading post in the morning?

Oral discussion is a vital factor in all preceding procedures. It should be used freely.

D. Words Commonly Overlooked

Some words are so badly overworked that they have almost lost their specific meanings. They are the "maids of all work" and are used principally by the language beggars. High-school pupils need to be helped to overcome the tendency to use trite phrases and overworked words. The following exercises have been useful for this purpose.

1. Write on the blackboard from 1 to 15 sentences each containing the word "got." Have pupils substitute a verb with specific meaning for the overworked verb "got" in each sentence.

2. Have pupils develop a list of frequently overworked words, such as asked, awful, divine, fix, grand, great, keen, lovely, neat, nice, perfect, replied, said, swell, take, terrible, thing, want, wonderful.

E. Figurative and Other Non-literal Language

How far the teacher can go in teaching junior and senior high-school pupils to understand the various forms of nonliteral writing depends on the same factors which limit teaching in other fields: the intelligence and cultural background of the pupils, the size of the class and the consequent ease or difficulty of conducting class discussions, the availability of good textbooks and of supplementary material, the rigidity of the course of study, and the teacher's own knowledge and love of literature. Every English teacher, however, should feel that he is remiss in his duties if he fails to open to his pupils the door to the infinite wealth of allusion, description, and suggestion which the intelligent writer and reader may enjoy.

Many teachers overlook the fact that figurative language is not confined to poetry, fairy tales and legends, and similar imaginative writing and limit their teaching of figures of speech to these rather limited areas, leaving largely untouched the much wider and more important fields of idiom, satire, irony, and the innumerable symbolically used words and phrases which appear in daily speech, in advertising, and in newspapers, books, and magazines. Pupils are left floundering in a sea of dimly or wrongly understood language. It is small wonder that they do not read more enthusiastically.

A brief consideration of sample passages from a newspaper, a textbook, and from ordinary conversation will show the necessity for teaching pupils to interpret this prosaic type of nonliteral language. The following samples may not appear to the average adult to be figurative at all because they are so familiar.

A thousand bills were thrown into the legislative hopper.

A chorus of protest arose throughout the land.

I almost died laughing.

The winning candidate swept the field.

The United States is a melting pot.

The enemy lines crumbled.

In junior high school it is probably better to explain figures of speech as they arise in regular class work than to present them "cold" as a unit of study unrelated to the rest of the work in literature, composition, and grammar. The teacher should scan carefully all assigned reading for phrases which might offer difficulty in interpretation and should himself bring them up for class discussion if one of the pupils does not do so.

At first, most of the initiative for such discussions will have to come from the teacher. Most pupils hestitate to admit their inability to understand the real meaning of something the surface import of which is clear. Only when they realize that adults, too, need help in interpretation will they bring their problems into the open. The teacher soon finds that sheer ignorance is the cause of many of the difficulties which pupils have. Biblical, historic, legendary, and artistic references can convey no meaning to those who lack a background of knowledge. "As strong as Samson" might just as well be "As strong as George" so far as many contemporary pupils are concerned. "Mars stalked the earth" creates confused astronomical impressions in the minds of pupils who have been deprived of the Greek myths.

Specific instances of this sort give the alert teacher an excellent opportunity to create in his classes an interest in reading some of the basic literature of our civilization. The classroom or school library should, of course, be ready to provide appropriate books for the pupil whose curiosity is thus aroused.

Lack of knowledge in other areas increases the difficulties of interpretation. "The log-roller lost his footing" was interpreted by a pupil as meaning that the man's foot had been amputated; the reader had no idea of the process of log-rolling. The acquisition of knowledge is, obviously, a never-completed process. The teacher can help himself to appreciate his pupil's shortcomings in this respect by thinking of the gaps in his own information.

It is an accepted principle of education that learning takes place best when the learner participates actively in the process. Thus pupils learn to understand the figurative speech of others when they use such figures themselves. At first, they may simply be asked to complete common similes. These are clichés to the adult, but not to the junior high-school pupil. The following list[4] of incomplete similes is suggestive:

black as	quick as ....
straight as	light as ....
wise as	clear as ....
brown as	sharp as ....
white as	sober as ....
busy as	hungry as ....
cold as	sly as ....
hard as	happy as ....

If some of the pupils' responses differ from the conventional ones which the teacher expects, these can be used as a point of departure for a discussion of the value of originality and vividness in figurative speech. The next step, of course, is to have some actual writing done by the pupils. The subjects assigned should be simple and of a nature to encourage the use of simile and metaphor. Short, carefully prepared compositions are preferable to long ones. Sample passages dealing with subjects similar to those assigned may be read to furnish pupils with ideas and inspiration. The best compositions may be read to the class, and particularly happy figures of speech may be pointed out and praised. It is easily understood that no public notice should be taken of the inevitable unsuccessful excursions into writing.

Bright pupils enjoy and benefit from learning the names of the various kinds of figures of speech and differences among them. However, merely learning to recognize and name them is a sterile exercise if it does not lead to understanding and appreciation.

Figurative language often offers the inexperienced and perhaps more literal-minded pupils some difficulty in comprehension. The junior high-school pupil can understand onomatopoetic words, alliteration, and similes, but the more complex aspects of figurative language should be developed at the eleventh- and twelfth-grade levels. At the outset the pupil must learn that figurative language occurs more frequently in poetry than in prose. He must be taught some of the basic distinctions between the two forms.

[4] Adapted from list in Frieda Radke, *Living Words*. New York: The Odyssey Press, 1940, p. 153.

PROSE	POETRY
1. No regular beat or rhythm.	1. Definitely measured and rhythmical.
2. No particular form.	2. Definitely shaped and often divided into stanzas.
3. Often low in emotional tone.	3. Often concentrated and intense in tone.
4. Usually involves facts and information.	4. Usually involves feelings.
5. Often detailed and precise.	5. Imaginative and suggestive.

Perhaps the best way to teach the pupil to interpret figurative language is by pattern. Once an easy pattern is established, the pupil can gradually learn to recognize the same type of pattern in his reading. Alliteration and onomatopoeia are so obvious they can be understood without difficulty. The more complex forms require examples, such as the following:

1. Simile (similarity).
   a. *Like* a cloud of fire.
   b. My love is *like* a red, red rose.
   c. My heart is *like* a rhyme.
2. Metaphor (identification transfer).
   a. The moon is a ghostly galleon.
   b. The road is a ribbon of moonlight.
   c. Sarcasm is a dangerous weapon.
3. Personification (having the attributes of a person).
   a. . . . the jocund day, stands tiptoe on the misty mountain top.
   b. Now morning from her orient chambers came and her first footsteps touched a verdant hill.
4. Apostrophe (addressing the dead as living, or the absent as present).
   a. Phoebus, arise and paint the sable skies.
   b. Build me straight, O Worthy Master.
   c. Mother, come back from that echoless shore.
5. Metonomy (associating an object that is closely connected with the idea).
   a. The *pen* is mightier than the sword.
   b. Polly, put the *kettle* on and we'll have tea.
   c. A man should keep a good *table*.
6. Synecdoche (using a part to represent the whole).
   a. She gave her hand in marriage.
   b. I'll not lift a finger.
   c. Fifty sails were seen on the horizon.

The pupil can increase his enjoyment of the daily newspaper by learning to recognize both simile and metaphor as used so frequently in the headlines. He can have fun noticing the clever use of clichés in various radio plays and will discover that these clichés often are similes or metaphors. By training his ear to catch such clichés as "red as a beet," "bitter as gall," and "mad as a hornet," he can immeasurably improve his own speech and writing. Constant alertness on the part of the teacher and the pupil is necessary to enable the pupil to understand the great masterpieces. Nor can this be done in one semester; it must be part of a well-planned English program through the entire secondary school.

F. Retention of New Vocabulary

In order that words may become a permanent part of a pupil's vocabulary, word study must be vitalized for the individual through purposeful listening and reading so that vocabularies are enriched both for oral and written expression.

EXTENSIVE READING. Wide and extensive reading is necessary if pupils are to develop rich vocabularies and wider interests in the world about them. Too often a pupil reads only one type of book—an adventure series, or radio magazines. Frequently, as pupils advance through junior high school, other interests take the place of reading; many pupils never read anything, even a magazine, unless required to do so by a teacher.

More extensive reading habits can be developed by the use of reading "ladders" in the case of the one-type reader; that is, suggestions of related books of wider interest or more mature nature. Books or magazine stories germane to the subject matter studied in class or to popular motion pictures, radio programs, and the like may be recommended. A classroom library, attractive displays, bulletin board, reading nook, are all helpful. The pupil should be given *time* to read. Sometimes, as a special treat, the teacher may read aloud a portion of a book from the library, stopping at some interesting point. Pupils will have to read the book themselves to find out the rest of the story.

The teacher himself will have to know books in order to provide a graded vocabulary load. A poor reader cannot acquire a good vocabulary and effective reading habits by being plunged into difficult reading material full of unfamiliar words. Second, the teacher must check the reading by discussion of the problem of the book, the characters, or the author and make use of the new words in conversation and in class.

The most common way of improving one's vocabulary is through extensive and varied reading. The meaning of words is acquired through the recognition and use of words as parts of words of dynamic thought patterns....

... It is advantageous, however, for teachers to increase their students' acquaintance with words by using repeatedly in their conversation during a week several important new words in their field.[5]

ENLISTING PUPILS' CO-OPERATION. Teachers should use a variety of procedures to (1) make the below-average pupils conscious of their need of knowing more words to meet everyday problems; (2) stimulate an interest in increasing vocabulary for the average pupil; and (3) help pupils to overcome their adolescent tendency to censure those pupils who use their vocabularies more effectively than others.

FUNCTIONAL VOCABULARIES. The functional vocabulary is the vo-

[5] Ruth Strang, with the assistance of Florence C. Rose, *Problems in the Improvement of Reading in High School and College.* Lancaster, Pennsylvania: The Science Press Printing Company, 1938, pp. 82–83.

cabulary which the pupil uses to express himself in writing and in speech. Activities in which pupils of difficult levels of maturity may use this functional vocabulary are suggested below:

1. The *below-average* pupil may talk about actual experiences, such as home, school, and church activities; movies, radio programs, and community affairs. He may also write letters and fill out applications. In his writing, the pupil should strive for short paragraph development.

2. The *average* pupil may talk about various experiences gained through reading as well as through actual participation. His vocabulary should show increased maturity and his talks should show greater detailed observation than those of the below-average pupil. The average pupil should engage in considerable writing of an expository or narrative nature and should write letters.

3. The *above-average* pupil should be able to make deductions from listening and reading activities and should participate imaginatively in the experiences about which he is reading. The writing of above-average pupils should show maturity of thought and expression.

RECOGNITION VOCABULARIES. The recognition vocabulary is largely a listening or reading vocabulary. The *below-average* pupil will get general meanings only. He will read the vocabulary of current events. He will learn technical words largely through listening. The *average* pupil should work for more exactness in interpretation of thought through word study. The *above-average* pupil should approximate a more "ultimate" truth: i.e., get implications. Reflection on subjects about which he reads may lead to participation in his chosen field.

DEVICES FOR MAKING PERMANENT THE PUPILS' ENRICHED VOCABULARY. A variety of procedures may be used to help pupils incorporate words into their permanent vocabularies. The following suggestions are offered:

1. Teach pupils to discriminate between the various meanings of words and phrases. Suggestions for below-average, average, and above-average pupils are listed below:

WORD	BELOW AVERAGE	AVERAGE	ABOVE AVERAGE
root	The root of the plant is large.	The root word comes from Latin. Take the square root of four. A pig roots in the ground.	The root of all evil.
ordinary	The ordinary way of doing the home work all right.	It is a very ordinary procedure.	The ceremony was most ordinary.
pass	The pass is narrow. Pass the cake.	The hall pass is needed. He was passed to first base.	Things have come to a pretty pass!

WORD	BELOW AVERAGE	AVERAGE	ABOVE AVERAGE
ground	The apple fell on the ground. The meat is being ground.	This is the ground floor. This is made of ground glass.	He stood his ground. The ground swell is heavy today.
see	I see my way. I see a house.	I see what you mean. I shall come to see you.	I see my way clear. He shall never see death.

2. Teach pupils to learn new words from context and not alone from dictionary definitions:

WORD	BELOW AVERAGE	AVERAGE	ABOVE AVERAGE
hostile	My enemy is hostile.	He is a hostile witness.	He is hostile to my interests.
leg	The boy broke his leg.	The first leg of the journey is over.	He hasn't a leg to stand on.
propaganda propagandize	Do not listen to enemy propaganda.	To propagandize is unfair.	Propaganda is often a falsification of news.
object objective	Please pick up the object.	I object to your going to the party.	What is your ultimate objective?
proof	What is your proof of that statement?	We shall make a proof of the picture.	The proof of the pudding.

3. Have pupils listen to an auditorium program or a radio speech, listing unfamiliar words and reasoning out their meanings from the contexts.
4. Organize a vocabulary club in the classroom, members of which will be responsible for bringing in words from all subject fields and sharing them with the class.
5. Have pupils classify words for special study from a selected list, noting those foreign in meaning and those they may be using or may be taught to use in formal spoken and written English.[6]
6. Study words in *phrase groupings*, not as isolated vocabulary. Pupils and teachers should use them consciously in later discussions.
7. Increase vocabulary of meanings by learning new words through specifically purposeful meanings for written composition.
8. Point out for special study: (a) powerful verbs, and (b) colorful adjectives with fine discrimination of meanings, as they are discovered in reading.
9. Use the "Word to the Wise" section in *Scholastic Magazine* as a weekly check.
10. Provide exercises on synonyms, with dictionary help.
11. Make vocabulary matching games for drill several times a term.
12. Have pupils deduce meanings of words from good oral reading by the teacher.

[6] William M. Tanner, *Correct English*, Vol. I. Boston: Ginn and Company, 1931, p. 408.

13. Have pupils analyze words through detection of familiar stems, prefixes, and suffixes.
14. Encourage pupils to be watchful for new words and their implications in wide and varied reading.

G. *Exercises for Improvement of Vocabulary*

In addition to the suggested drills and exercises which have been given in connection with discussions on the various phases of improvement of vocabulary in the preceding sections, the following specific exercises for identifying and analyzing compounds, finding words within words, developing pronunciation from known parts of known words, and certain kinesthetic techniques may help to strengthen the program.

COMPOUNDS. Knowledge of the use of compounds and attention to their form is an excellent means of extending vocabularies. Exercises such as the ones given below are effective in this field.

1. Choose from a current reading lesson several solid compound words (not hyphenated) and write them on the board. Ask pupils to examine them for any unfamiliar parts. Point out that either part of each word may be used alone.
2. Let each pupil choose a compound word which he will separate into parts, using each part in a sentence. He then makes a third sentence in which he uses the compound.
3. Have pupils make sentences containing two or more compound words, for example, John's *workshop* was full of model airplanes made from *cardboard*.
4. Illustrate (when pupils are ready for it) the difference between the two big families of compounds: (a) the solids, as bookworm, road-bed; and (b) the hyphenated compounds, as long-eared, old-fashioned.

FINDING WORDS WITHIN WORDS. As an aid to discovering similarities in word forms and, sometimes, word meaning, practice on identifying short words within longer words is helpful. Seeing that *management, carpenter, attendant, etc.*, contain familiar phonetic elements which are words themselves is often an awakening to the pupil who has had difficulty with word perception.

Practice in finding small words may be given in the following way: Pupils select from the context being read a list of long words. Small words within these words are then underlined. Caution must be used to prevent the identification of a small word which is not heard as the long word is pronounced; that is, it would be incorrect to underline *as* in *fashion*.

DEVELOPING PRONUNCIATION FROM KNOWN PARTS OF KNOWN WORDS. Young and relatively immature pupils in junior high school may profit from some of the elementary techniques and exercises noted below.

1. Brief drills on consonant digraphs will facilitate recognition of known parts of words. Sight rather than sound should influence the recognition. List five to ten initial digraphs on the board—bl, br, ch, cl, ch, fl, *etc.* After each one write, in parentheses, the remainder of a word— bl (ack); cl (ean). First see that pupils are familiar with the completed words, then ask them to see how quickly they can find additional words having the same beginnings, using a reading selection for the source.

2. Sentences including numerous digraphs offer a challenge. Give a sample sentence, as "The hunters blew *th*eir horns; the hounds *br*ayed, and the *ch*ase was on! The horses *cl*eared the fences, *cr*ossed the meadows and *sp*ed toward the *fl*eeing fox." Have pupils try writing sentences having two or more of the digraphs illustrated.

3. Common phonograms of three or four letters, especially end-phonograms, furnish worth-while association material. Well-rhymed poetry provides good patterns. Have pupils find pairs and mark the endings that rhyme.

4. Write a paragraph on the board containing many familiar word endings, something like this: "W*ake* up, J*ake*; you're an hour l*ate*, now. Sh*ake* yourself and d*ive* into your clothes. I'll dr*ive* you as far as St*ate* Street if your pride won't be hurt by a r*ide* in my old cr*ate*." Ask pupils to see whether they can outdo the teacher by bringing a simple paragraph of their own the next day.

WORD PROCESSING: EXPLAINING AND IMPLEMENTING THE SKILLS*

Nancy A. Frederick and Barbara C. Palmer

A word may denote several areas of meaning, but a precise meaning for a word is developed only in a well-formed context. Word-processing skills basically relate to the study of meanings of words in particular contexts. Additional kinds of exercises relating to the meaning parts of words—roots and affixes—can be interesting as well as enlightening, but precision and fluency in the use of meanings are associated with the eager mind that is stimulated by a wealth of books, discussions, and labeled experiences over a *long* period of time—and, I might add, with dictionary in hand. Frederick and Palmer delineate several formal areas of word-processing study and present teaching formats that can be useful in helping to develop word meanings.

1. Of what value is a knowledge of structural analysis skills?

2. Why is the context clue the most important clue?

3. Speculate on the value of

---

* Written especially for this volume.

classifying words as synonyms or antonyms.

4. Construct other exercises for teaching word-processing skills.

5. State the article's key ideas.

The word-processing or meaning skills can be broken down into five areas. These are (1) *structural analysis*, including compound words, contractions, prefixes, and inflectional endings; (2) *clues*, including context, roots, and print; (3) *vocabulary relationships*; (4) *abbreviations, symbols, and acronyms*; (5) *dictionary aids*, including etymology, variant meanings, and parts of speech.

THE FIVE TYPES OF WORD-PROCESSING SKILLS

Structural Analysis: Compound Words, Contractions, Prefixes, and Inflectional Endings

Structural analysis deals with the use of parts of words as aids to uncover the meaning or meanings of a word. For example, students learn that the word *boys* consists of two parts—the root word, *boy*, and the suffix, -s. The suffix -s, of course, has a meaning different from the root word *boy*. Students learn that the *s* indicates that the author means two or more boys. The structural clue to the meaning of the word *boys* is the inflectional ending *s* which forms the plural of *boy* as well as many other nouns. This is just one example of the many uses of structural analysis in determining authors' meaning.

Uncovering the meaning of a *compound word* can be tricky. The meaning of a compound word is often quite different from the two words that make it up. For example, *basketball*, does not mean a ball in a basket, and *cowboy* does not mean a male cow. However, compound words often contain clues to meanings; but often that meaning is quite abstract and is clear only in context. The word yields a general area of meaning that is made precise and clear by a suitable context.

Compound words take several forms. This includes such combined words as *windmill, high school,* and *brother-in-law*; but nearly all offer similar aids and similar difficulties.

Another structural analysis skill is processing contractions. Contractions result from the shortening of a word, syllable, or word group through the omission of a letter or letters. For example, *wasn't*, of course, is a shortened form of the two words, *was* and *not*, and *e'er* is a shortened form of the word *ever*. The latter form is rarely used, except to illustrate dialect.

The main clue in processing a contracted word is the apostrophe. This indicates that a letter or letters have been omitted. However, an apostrophe may also signify other meanings, such as possession. For example, the apostrophe in the phrase *Sue's book* is meant to indicate to the reader that the book was owned by Sue. The apostrophe indicates the relationship of Sue to the book; that is, the apostrophe indicates possession rather than plurality. However, as with most language "rules," there are exceptions. With the word *it*, for example, possession is shown by *its*, whereas *it's* means *"it is"*!

The ability to recognize and know the meanings of affixes is sometimes an aid to word processing. Prefixed and suffixed words are derived forms of words that are composed of a root plus a prefix, suffix, or both—for example, *unclean, cleanliness*, and *uncleanliness*. A prefix is a meaning element attached to the beginning of a root that modifies the meaning of that root word. Some prefixes differ in meaning from word to word. The same is also true of suffixes. Dis-, for example, indicates "opposite," "not," and "completely." The suffix *-ful* may indicate "full," "characterized by," or "having the qualities of something." Again, the reader needs to use both the root word and the context in which the suffixed word is used in order to recognize the particular meaning intended.

Students should understand that when a prefix is added to the beginning of a root word, the resulting word may indicate a meaning quite different from the meaning of the prefix and of the root word. This is often the result of the etymology of the word. For example, *in-* may be used to indicate "not," "within," "toward," or other meanings. When a suffix is added to the end of a word or a derived word, the resulting word may have a meaning quite different from the root word and the meaning of its suffix.

Suffixes are meaningful parts of words. One of their functions is to indicate grammatical usage. Although the root word *instruct* may keep its original meaning in a derived form, *instructor*, there is a change in classification in the part of speech to which they belong. The root word, *instruct*, is a verb; the derived form, *instructor*, is a noun. From this it can be seen that the grammatical function of a derived form is usually different from that of the root word.

An inflectional ending may be defined as a meaningful element (*-s, -es, -'s, -ed, -ing, -er, -est*, for example) that is attached to the ends of words. The addition of these elements to words is used to develop (1) plurals and the possessive case of nouns in the words *boys, dances*, and *boy's*; (2) past tense, third-person singular in the present indicative, and the present participles of verbs in the words *worked, works*, and *working*; and (3) comparisons of adjectives or adverbs as in the words *bigger, biggest, nicer*, and *nicest*. Inflectional endings may be added to root words, to derived forms, and to compound words.

Inflectional endings may also be suffixes. However, unlike other suffixes, inflectional endings are always final. For example, to the derived form *development* (*develop* + suffix *ment*) the inflectional ending *-s* may be added after the suffix *ment*, thus forming the plural of the word *development* (developments). No additional suffixes of any kind may now be added to the word *developments*. However, a derived word (with a suffix already added to it), as in the word *agreeable*, may still have another suffix added and still indicate another logical meaning. The word *agreeableness* is an example of this. This may continue to occur until an inflectional ending is added to it that makes the word a "closed" form to which nothing more can be added, as in the word *agreeablenesses*.

Another distinguishing feature of inflectional suffixes (or inflectional endings) is that the words or derived forms to which the inflectional endings are added do not usually change their grammatical category.

Clues: Context, Roots,* and Print

The second major class of word-processing skills is use of clues. No one should discount the importance of using context clues in processing the meaning of words. Context clues are clearly the most important single aid to word processing. However, other clues are helpful and most students can use all the help they can get!

Context clues enable the reader to discern the intended meaning of a word through its relationship with the other words within its context. For example, the meaning of the word *jovial* in the sentence "The students were happy and jovial during the birthday party," may be understood through the words *happy* and *party* in the sentence.

Context clues may be used to validate word analysis. A learner who tries to use sound–symbol relationship skills to recognize the last word in the sentence "The boy went into the house," will know that his first attempt to read the word *horse* is wrong because a boy could not go into a horse. Or if the learner read the word as *house*, he is fairly sure he is correct because of the context surrounding the word *house*. Context clues are also useful in choosing the appropriate meaning of a multiple-meaning word. For example, the word *inflection* may mean any of the following: (1) the art or result of curving or blending; (2) change in pitch or loudness of the voice; (3) change of form that words undergo to mark such distinctions as those of case, gender, number, tense, person, word, or voice. But until the word *inflection* is used in a context of a phrase or a sentence or some larger unit, it is difficult to determine which meaning the speaker or writer had in mind.

Another function of context clues is to help choose the appropriate pronunciation of words having the same spelling but different pronunciations and/or meanings (homographs). Try reading the following words: *permit, conduct, close, object, dove.* Did you read them as:

/pər-'mit/	or /'pər-,mit/
/kən-'dəkt/	or /'kän(,)dəkt/
/'klōs/	or /'klōz/
/'äb-jikt/	or /əb-'jekt/
/'dōv/	or /'dəv/

---

* For detailed information on teaching roots and affixes see references 2 and 5 and also the article by Moretz and Davey in the present volume.

You probably had to think twice about their pronunciation! But you wouldn't have if they had been used in a context!

One function of context clues* is to aid the reader in determining the meaning of words the writer thinks may be difficult for him. In that case the author provides such context clues as (1) definitions, (2) synonyms, (3) explanation, (4) experiences, (5) comparisons, (6) contrast, and (7) combinations of those clues. To reap the greatest benefits from context clues students should practice identifying the more common types.

Vocabulary Relationships: Synonyms, Antonyms, Homonyms, Homographs

The third major section of the word-processing skills is vocabulary relationships. Synonyms, for example, are words which have the same or nearly the same meanings in some or all sentences. Such words as *split* and *divide* are commonly listed as synonyms. Antonyms are words which indicate contrasting meaning, such as *awake* and *asleep*. Homonyms are words that are pronounced and spelled the same but that have different meanings, depending upon the context ("They *run* to school." "He fell in the *run*"). Homophones are words that are pronounced the same but that have different spellings and meanings, such as *new* and *knew*. Homographs are words that are spelled the same but are pronounced differently and have different meanings. *Read* and *read, lead* and *lead,* and *invalid* and *invalid* are examples of homographs.

Abbreviations, Symbols, and Acronyms

The fourth major section of the word-processing skills includes abbreviations, symbols, and acronyms. An abbreviation is, of course, a shortened form of a word or phrase. For example, the abbreviation for *avenue* is *ave*. A symbol is an arbitrary or conventional sign used to represent language in writing or printing. One symbol for division is ÷; a symbol for paragraph is ¶. Knowing the meaning of special symbols is often necessary in order to read special texts.

An acronym is a word formed from the initial letter or letters of each of the successive parts or major parts of a compound term. An example of the acronym for the phrase National Aeronautics and Space Administration is NASA. UNESCO and NATO are also acronyms. At times it seems that acronyms are taking over the dictionary, but they are time and space savers.

USING AN OBJECTIVE-BASED PROGRAM

One responsibility of most educators is to teach word-processing skills. The goals of such teaching should include (1) the setting of word-processing

---

* For detailed information on teaching these clues see references 5 and 8 and also the article by Moretz and Davey in the present volume.

priorities in program planning and (2) devising or obtaining materials which directly or indirectly teach the needed skills.

Objectives have been variously identified as performance objectives, behavioral objectives, preobjectives, and so on. But regardless of their labels, good objectives have two basic characteristics: (1) they are stated in terms of the learner's behavior and (2) they describe pupil performance that is measurable or observable with agreement as to criteria for accomplishment when two or more competent observers are involved.

Some advantages of using or implementing an objective-based program identified by Skager (7) follow:

1. They generate clearer and more precise understanding of the goals of instruction.
2. They aid in setting priorities as programs are planned and implemented.
3. They aid in planning for the incremental improvement of students.

Teaching Word-Processing Skills

Writing and teaching the word-processing skills need not be a difficult task. The following suggestions have been found helpful when teaching word-processing skills:

1. The initial examples should be easy and obvious. This helps to "sell" the student on the value of the skills.
2. Little emphasis should be placed on the identification and labeling of the specific skill so the student will not experience confusion regarding the focal point of instruction.
3. The skills should not be presented in separate or isolated lessons without being related to subsequent skills.
4. Exercise formats for each skill should be varied in order to achieve optimum learning.
5. Carefully monitor student learning pace in order to insure maximum progress.
6. Newly acquired skills should be integrated with existing skills to promote growth in the overall reading process.

In summary, Niles (6) states, "Success in reading does not come from the application of a series of skills separated and in isolation from the application of combined and synthesized skills."

Test items should be carefully constructed. They should reflect the knowledge gained from the skill practice exercises. One way to measure the degree of skill competency is to require the use of the skill in an unfamiliar format. If the student has mastered the skill, there should be a transfer of learning to the unfamiliar format. If the student does not make the movement to the specific competence level, then more practice may be needed for him to learn the skill.

Some helpful test and technique formats are as follows:

1. Multiple choice.
2. Matching.
3. Fill in the blank.
4. Syntax.

5. Analogy.
6. Restatement.
7. Rule–example.
8. Comparison.

Examples of various techniques in which practice exercises can be developed are demonstrated below. They may serve as a guide for constructing other exercises and test items. In the first several exercises several words reoccur enabling the reader to learn better through having the words introduced in a variety of contexts:*

1. *Multiple Choice:*
Complete the following exercises based upon your knowledge of compound words. Underline each compound word in the following list and discuss the meanings in the group discussion session.

a. cowboy
b. Wedneday
c. crisscross
d. buckwheat
e. courtship

f. rowboat
g. wonderful
h. penthouse
i. tablespoon

2. *Matching:*
Below are two lists of words, List A and List B. Draw a line from a word in List A to a word in List B which will form a compound word. If you develop a "new" compound word, be able to justify your response.†

List A	List B
cow	boat
foot	spoon
table	house
green	hive
motor	ball

bee   cycle
row   boy

Discuss your answers with your partner.

3. *Fill in the blank:*
Read the sentences below. Use the information from the first sentence to fill in the blank in the second sentence.
   Ken herds cows for a living. He is called a _____ boy.
   The boat is propelled by rowing oars. It is called a _____ boat.

4. *Syntax:*
Read the sentence below. Underline all the compound words in the sentence. Then, using the compound words *cowboy* and *rowboat*, add a sentence that will go along with the first sentence.
   Joanne had buckwheat pancakes with a tablespoon of her favorite strawberry topping for her breakfast on Monday.

5. *Analogy:*
A single (:) stands for "is related to," a double (::) for "as." Remember that

---

* The first four types of exercises utilize compound words, but other kinds of words may be used.

† Note: This developing new words and justifying them could inject some fun into the lesson.

an *analogy* shows a relationship such as *subordinate* (part to whole) as in *petal* and *flower*, *coordinate* (same class), as in *arm* and *leg*, or *superordinate* (whole to part), as in *song* and *aria*. Complete the following:

    a. blue : color :: banjo: _____
       (string, instrument, guitar)
    b. mother : daughter :: father: _____
       (boy, male, son)

Develop other analogies and present them during the group discussion period.

6. *Restatement:*

Read the sentences below. Use the information from the first sentence to complete the second sentence.

Janet had a run in her stockings; the rip went from her knee to her toe. She could not wear her stockings because of the _____.

7. *Rule–example:*

Rule: Any number times 0 equals 0.

Example: $0 \times 1 = 0$
$0 \times 4 =$ _____
$0 \times 5 =$ _____
$0 \times 100 =$ _____
$0 \times 500 =$ _____

8. *Comparison:*

Complete the sentence below by filling in the blank.

The _____ is taller, heavier, and has a deeper voice than the woman.

       (girl, man, boy)

Summary Statement

The ability to apply word processing skills is important to school and career success. Every teacher needs to be able to aid students in developing those skills. Without them students may suffer a vocabulary deficiency throughout life.

REFERENCES

1. Ames, Wilbur S. "The Use of Classification Schemes in Teaching the Use of Contextual Aids," *Journal of Reading*, 14 (October 1970), 5–8, 50.
2. Breen, L. C. "Vocabulary Development by Teaching Prefixes, Suffixes, and Root Derivations," *The Reading Teacher*, 14 (1960), 93–97.
3. Dale, Edgar, and J. L. Milligan. "Techniques in Vocabulary Development," *Reading Improvement*, 7 (1970), 1–5.
4. Durkin, Dolores. *Teaching Them to Read*. Boston: Allyn & Bacon, Inc., 1970. Chapter 13.
5. Hafner, Lawrence E., and Hayden B. Jolly. *Patterns of Teaching Reading in the Elementary School*. New York: Macmillan Publishing Co., Inc., 1972. Chapter 6.
6. Niles, Olive S. "Behavioral Objectives and the Teaching of Reading," *Journal of Reading*, 16 (November 1972), 104–10.
7. Skagar, Rodney. "Beyond the Standardized Test: Objective-Based Evaluation in Reading," *Journal of Reading*, 15 (May 1972), 616–17.
8. Spache, George D., and Evelyn B. Spache. *Reading in the Elementary School*, 2nd ed. Boston: Allyn & Bacon, Inc., 1969. Chapter 13.
9. Strang, B. M. H. *Modern English Structure*. New York: St. Martin's Press, 1963.

Using Reading in Research-Study Situations

Introduction

The research-study skills are those skills involved in locating, interpreting, evaluating, organizing, and retaining information. The students who will continue their education in college are, by and large, the more able students. They will use the research-study skills for many years. These more able students are often neglected in high school because they generally manage to get their lessons after a fashion. Consequently, they develop poor study habits and reading deficiencies.

Jolly provides various techniques to help students understand the main idea of a paragraph, a key skill in organizing and retaining information for the purposes of writing good themes and examination papers. Robinson, originator of the SQ3R study approach, shows both the need for teaching study skills to superior students in high school and the way to teach those skills that will help students improve their comprehension and retention of reading material. The research project reported by Moe and Nania points to the reading deficiencies existing among able pupils and to what can be done to help them overcome these deficiences. Finally, Sanders explains his research project in which he utilized inductive methods for teaching map-reading skills to ninth-grade world geography classes.

DETERMINING MAIN IDEAS: A BASIC STUDY SKILL*

Hayden B. Jolly, Jr.

Determining the main idea of a reading selection is a key skill underlying the reading-study jobs. Mastery of this skill is necessary for effective reading and writing, and therefore paves the way to better grades in school.

In this paper Jolly explains well (1) the value of properly teaching students to master the skills of getting the main idea; (2) the materials used in teaching these skills; (3) the sequence of main idea skills; (4) how to teach the skills; and (5) the responsibility of all teachers for teaching the skills.

1. What evidence exists for the need to teach main idea skills?
2. The author suggests certain materials be used in teaching main idea skills. What reasons does he offer for using these materials?
3. How can the teacher check the student's ability to use the main idea skills?
4. Why is it important to remember that the suggested exercises are teaching tools?
5. Explain the importance of teaching the main idea skills in proper sequence.
6. Who should teach these skills?

Meeting my college freshman English class for the second session of a new quarter, I attempted to begin a discussion of their first assignment with a question; the question posed by the title of the assigned essay: "What Is Literature For?" by S. I. Hayakawa. In asking that title question I hoped to get from the students some of the essay's main points. I got none; the class was silent. Not to be dismayed, I rephrased the question, trying to make it more specific—but still no answers came. A third question was asked for possible suggestions as to why Mr. Hayakawa wrote the essay and what his purposes might have been. This time a few hands went up but the hesitant answers were vague and unrelated to the thesis of the essay.

---

* Written especially for inclusion in this volume.

I first decided that most of the students had not read the essay, but they answered succeeding questions of detail easily. Most of the students had indeed read the essay; they had simply failed to get from it what I considered most important—the main ideas. They had read, but they had not studied. And even after we listed the details and categorized them, the students had to be led through a painful (to us all) series of questions in order to arrive at generalizations of main points remotely akin to the author's. Even Socrates would have been weary.

This experience is not unique to the college English teacher. Most teachers, regardless of grade level or subject, have had similar ones. What is important, however, is what the teacher does or thinks after the agony is over. There is some danger that he may conclude that this is an unusually dull class, shrug his shoulders, and move on to more successful endeavors. This would be an injustice to the students, for although it is possible that the class might be a dull one this is probably not the case.

Experience and research point to the fact that even the brightest students have difficulty identifying main ideas. William G. Perry, in the *Harvard Educational Review*, describes an experiment conducted on 1,500 freshmen from Harvard and Radcliffe to determine how they approached a study task and how well they identified significant details and main ideas (1).

The students were assigned a chapter in a history text and simply told to "study the chapter; you will have a test later." After the study period, during which the experimenter observed how they approached the task, the students were given a multiple-choice test on details. The results were, according to Perry, impressive. But, he continues, the students had considerably more difficulty identifying the main ideas:

> We asked anyone who could do so to write a short statement about what the chapter was all about. The number who were able to tell us . . . was just one in a hundred—fifteen. As a demonstration of obedient purposelessness in the reading of 99% of freshmen we found this impressive . . . after twelve years of reading homework assignments in school they had all settled into the habit of leaving the point of it all to someone else. . . .

If these bright students have difficulty with main ideas, can we expect most other high school and college students to be more successful? The problem would seem to be universal.

Perry also implies that perhaps too often, rather than go through the agony of trying to elicit main ideas from students or trying to teach them to do it on their own, we teachers simply point them out ourselves and get on to questions of detail. We can usually count on the students to have recognized a few of those.

The value of properly teaching students to master this skill cannot be overemphasized, for it is the foundation of most other study-meaning skills. Karlin (2) and Smith (3) classify the identification of main ideas as the most fundamental of selection and evaluation skills, and point out that efficient use of the organization skills is dependent upon mastery of main idea skills.

If a student cannot identify main ideas he cannot be expected to write a good summary, for a summary is little more than the reduction of an expository selection to its main ideas and supporting details. To be able to outline, the student must be able to identify main ideas and supporting details and arrange them in a form that indicates their relative importance and relationships. Outlining and summarizing are invaluable aids for study and retention. They are simple techniques for the student who has learned the prerequisite skills—and are meaningless rituals to those who have not.

And the organization skills are not the only ones which demand the ability to determine main ideas. Such highly regarded study techniques as the SQ3R or PQRST are psychologically sound methods to encourage thoroughness and retention but are valueless until the student learns in his reading to distinguish what Perry called the "point of it all." The student who would learn to read or skim rapidly with utmost comprehension must be able, from a welter of illustrations, examples, and details, to quickly sort out significant points.

To be able to infer an author's purposes the student must first understand what the author's main points are. Indeed, most problems of interpretation, either in literary or expository material, are matters of drawing conclusions or making inferences after a consideration of main ideas. In short, if a student cannot identify main ideas, he is in danger of missing the most vital meaning in his reading; and his ability to use many valuable study aids is greatly handicapped.

The purpose of this brief article is to examine some of the causes of this widespread problem with main ideas and suggest some guidelines and techniques for more effective instruction in this skill.

Possible Causes

Because of the complex nature of learning problems causes are always difficult to specify, and authorities seeking causes often disagree. The assumption underlying this paper, however, is that the most common and the most fundamental cause of deficiencies related to main idea skills is educational, and that the cause and the cure lie in the teaching methods and materials. The writer does not rule out the possibility of other contributory causes. Nevertheless, educational problems are the ones with which we teachers are best able to deal.

Observation of teaching practices and the examination of a number of reading and English textbooks suggest that the following weaknesses are largely responsible for the almost universal problems associated with identifying main ideas:

1. Skills prerequisite to the effective mastery of main ideas are often not included in textbooks, or courses of study. When they are included, they are rarely taught in sequence.
2. Identification of main ideas and related skills are usually taught in workbook or composition exercises affecting little transfer to other reading needs.
3. Textbook exercises, which purport to teach main ideas, often simply *test* students' ability with the skill rather than *teach* the skill.
4. Teachers in the content areas, if they consider the problems at all, assume that the responsibility for teaching the skill belongs to the teacher of reading or of composition.

The suggestions and recommendations that follow are based upon a careful consideration of these weaknesses, and upon the assumption that the well-informed teacher in any subject matter area can do much to overcome them with the material he has available.

Materials for Developing Main Idea Skills

Karlin (2) has suggested among his five guidelines for teaching the study skills that, whenever possible, the teaching of these skills be done with materials students are actually using in their subject-matter areas—their textbooks. Apparently, few teachers use textbooks for this purpose; perhaps because they feel that special workbooks are necessary to teach such skills effectively. However, if the teacher will only consider this proposal he will see its practical value. After all, it is the textbooks which we wish the students to study more effectively. It is the main ideas in textbooks that we wish them to identify and understand.

Workbook and English textbook exercises on main ideas and topic sentences follow a familiar pattern: (1) definition, (2) examples, and (3) exercises. They do little teaching. They simply provide sample paragraphs and ask students to find the topic sentence or the main idea. The student does not have the valuable experience of forming his own generalizations. It appears that many textbooks assume that providing a definition of a term or a concept is equivalent to teaching the related skill.

Experience should have taught us otherwise. The typical definition of a topic sentence as "the sentence which states the main idea of a paragraph" is of no value unless the student can already recognize the main idea when he encounters it. We teachers of English should have realized long ago how ineffective this "teaching by definition" is. For years we have defined the sentences as "a group of words expressing a complete thought." This was fine for the student who could already recognize a complete thought. Many students could quote the definition accurately but continued to write fragments. Obviously we cannot depend upon this type of teaching to insure mastery of necessary skills for reading or writing.

The use of students' regular textbooks is particularly appropriate for teaching main ideas. The history book, the science text, and any material with which the student must deal in his regular work, will be far more valuable for the development of these skills than exercises unrelated to his actual reading and study needs. Not only do his textbooks contain a wealth of sentences, paragraphs and longer selections that can serve as vehicles for instruction, but there is also the advantage that, in addition to learning the skill, the student is dealing with information the teacher wishes him to master.

Much incidental teaching of main idea skills can effectively be done with newspapers, magazines, articles in encyclopedias, student publications, student essays and, indeed, any material students normally use at school. Only one caution is necessary: the material used should be at the students' instructional reading level in order that it present no meaning problems other than those related to the skill being taught.

Sequence of Main Idea Skills

If the student, by the time he reaches high school, is still deficient in basic skills, reason assures us that he is not likely to acquire them suddenly through a surge of intuition. *He must be taught.* The skills he has failed to learn must be developed, beginning with the simplest skill in the sequence which the student has not acquired in progressing through the more complex aspects of the skill. The following list of requisite skills for the identification of main ideas appears to have been rather commonly neglected:

1. Identification of the topic of a sentence.
2. Identification of the topic of a paragraph.
3. Identification of the topic sentence of a paragraph.
4. Identification of the main idea of a paragraph.
5. Perception of the relationships among main ideas in related paragraphs.
6. Identification of thesis statements, and of main ideas in longer selections.

Although the first two of these skills appear to be remarkably simple, the teacher should not assume that all students have mastered them. Such assumptions too often prove false, even for high-school and college students; our facile assumptions about the skills of students are partly responsible for their frequent lack of them. It is certainly natural for the teacher to feel that the student has mastered the skills necessary to have reached his grade level, but it is probably better—until he knows otherwise—for the teacher to assume he has mastered none of them.

An informal check of these skills is quite simple to give either to groups or to individuals. Simply choose several paragraphs and sections from any of their texts and ask them to identify the topics, the main ideas, and the topic sentences. Requesting them to write the main ideas in their own words can be particularly revealing. An examination of their responses will indicate which students need work on particular skills. Also their outlines, or summaries, of text material will furnish clues to the strengths and weaknesses in main idea skills.

Suggestions for Teaching Main Idea Skills

To locate the topic of a sentence the student must be able to distinguish the subject of a sentence; not the structural subject or the specific substantive, but the topical or notional subject. They are often the same. But because students' minds often close at the mention of anything which smacks of grammar it is probably wise not to use the term *subject* at all. The bright students will note the parallel on their own. Often, however, the topic or notional subject is more inclusive than the simple subject, as in the following example:

There are no billboards or other advertising on the Blue Ridge Parkway.

The structural subjects are the nouns "billboards" and "advertising." The topic is simply "advertising on the Blue Ridge Parkway." That is what the sentence is about.

Perhaps the simplest way to begin teaching this concept is to put several sentences on the board:

The present goal of our space program is to land a man on the moon.

Bluntly stated, Jackson's thesis arouses some skepticism, but as Jackson states it, explaining his basis, it becomes convincing.

It was just twenty years ago that the Supreme Court handed down its famous decision in the *Esquire Case*.

As he presents each example, the teacher should demonstrate the process of identifying the general topic of each. He might reason aloud, considering alternatives and explaining why he rejects some and concludes with topics like these: (1) goal of the space program, (2) Jackson's thesis, or (3) Supreme Court decision in the *Esquire Case*. The problem of terminology will become immediately apparent to the teacher. What else can you call these but topics? It is probably not as important what the teacher calls them so long as he gives adequate illustration of what he seeks and students are led to understand that he has isolated the notional subject.

Bright students may react to such an exercise with the question "Why bother?" After all, the notional subject or topic apart from its predication is a meaningless phrase. Students should be led to understand that this stage is a stage of preparation similar to the initial stages in programmed instruction. Its usefulness may become apparent only after more complex problems are confronted.

Next, students might be provided with sample sentences followed by two or three options from which to choose the topic:

There is hardly an area of modern life—education, industry, agriculture, medicine, etc.—in which computers do not perform some important function.

The topic is:
1. The complexity of modern living.
2. Areas of modern life.
3. Complexity of computers.
4. Computers in modern life.

The teacher should keep in mind that such exercises are teaching tools and not tests. They should be gone over carefully and students who make errors should be aided to see why they were wrong.

After students have demonstrated proficiency with this exercise, direct them to appropriate sentences in any of their textbooks to locate the sentence topics. If they can identify—without assistance—the topics of the sentences selected they are ready for the next phase. If they are still having difficulty more demonstrations are probably in order.

The development of the next stages might proceed in much the same manner. The teacher may present sample paragraphs first, demonstrating how he identifies the topic of the paragraph by examining the sentence topics and details. After his demonstrations he may present the students' paragraphs with several options from which to choose the appropriate one. The following example paragraph from Emerson's "Beauty" illustrates a typical exercise:

Beauty is the quality which makes to endure. In a house that I know, I have noticed a block of spermaceti lying about closets and mantelpieces, for twenty years together, simply because the tallow-man gave it the form of a rabbit; and, I suppose, it may continue to be lugged about unchanged for a century. Let an artist scrawl a few lines or figures on the back of a letter, and that scrap of paper is rescued from danger, is put in portfolio, is framed and glazed, and, in proportion to the beauty of the lines drawn, will be kept for centuries. Burns writes a copy of verses, and sends them to a newspaper, and the human race takes charge of them that they shall not perish.

This paragraph is about:
1. A spermaceti rabbit.
2. Beauty.
3. An artist's scrawls.
4. A Burns poem.

By first examining the details with the students and having them search for the most general and inclusive of the topics which can relate to all of the details, the students can be led to choose the correct topic. Following this exercise almost any paragraphs from their texts will provide a challenge to their independent efforts.

The same sample paragraphs will also be suitable for practice in locating the topic sentence. After successfully locating the topic they should have little difficulty locating the topic sentence. Some care may be necessary at this point to help students see the difference between the topic of a paragraph and the topic or thesis sentence. After several exercises they should be led to see that although the topic of a paragraph identifies the subject matter of the paragraph, the topic sentence makes some assertion about that subject.

This will be facilitated by using the same paragraphs for teaching both elements. With the previous example paragraph, for instance, after the students have identified "beauty" as its topic, they should have little difficulty noting the sentence that makes the most general statement about "beauty"—the first sentence.

In the following paragraph, students should be able to determine that the topic is grammar, and that the topic sentence specifies the author's attitude toward that topic:

The teacher who considers the traditional grammatical rules of English to be sacred and inviolable must be unaware of the true nature of language. The English language is not static. It has never been, despite the attempts of numerous grammarians to make it so. It changes as our technology changes, as new things and new concepts come into being. The fact is that our dictionaries and our grammars are out of date from the moment they come off the press.

The first sentence, the topic sentence, immediately gives us the author's focus and direction but even after identifying it we have not adequately captured the author's main idea. The second and third sentences contribute vital clarification for the first. For this reason it is often appropriate to have students express a paragraph's main idea in their own words.

It is important to be consistent in the types of paragraphs presented for instruction in the early stages. It would be confusing, for example, to present descriptive paragraphs which do not contain topic sentences or inductively organized paragraphs in which the topic sentence is last until students can deal efficiently with the typical expository paragraph. It is advisable also to explain with examples the various types of paragraph structures before requiring students to analyze them. This may require some research on the part of the history or science teacher for adequate material, but if he recognizes the value of guided learning he will see its merit.

It will be also helpful, after students' work with paragraphs choosing options provided by the teacher, to present them with paragraphs from which topic sentences have been removed. Allow them to write topic sentences and compare them with the original. The final test of the effectiveness of this instruction is given when students attempt to identify topic sentences and main ideas unaided in their textbooks.

An expository paragraph is an essay in miniature and, if the skill of identifying the main ideas in paragraphs has been adequately developed, instruction with longer selections should be relatively easy. The teacher need only continue with the same inductive approach. One simple way to begin might be to locate a well-unified selection of several paragraphs in a chapter or essay and have students extract the main idea from each paragraph. Present them with several choices of topics and main ideas from which to choose the ones appropriate for the selection.

After a few experiences of this kind, students can generally be led to identify the main ideas and thesis statements when guided by proper questions: Do the topic sentences of the paragraphs deal with similar or related ideas or elements? How are they related? What new information does each contribute? Is there one statement which is general enough to include the topics of all the paragraphs?

Through such an analysis students can usually be led to see not only the relationships between the paragraphs but the thesis idea to which each paragraph is related. It is vital that students have guided practice of this kind before they attempt to analyze longer selections on their own.

Some of the following exercises may also be useful in teaching topic sentences and main ideas:

1. Students construct topic sentences for possible paragraphs on subjects suggested by the teacher.
2. Students provide major headings for outlines after being provided with subheadings.
3. Students write headlines for hypothetical articles about school events.
4. From a list of relevant and irrelevant details, students select details related to main ideas provided by the teacher.
5. Students do research to locate facts to support conclusions provided by the teacher.
6. Students locate main ideas in the body of a textbook chapter which parallel ideas restated in the chapter summary.
7. Students synthesize portions of assigned reading into main ideas.
8. Students formulate main ideas for teacher's lecture which provides significant details.

Responsibility of All Teachers

It has become almost trite to proclaim to every high-school teacher that he must teach reading. Nevertheless, past pleas for an acceptance of this notion have fallen largely on deaf ears; so the pleas must continue. Until the teachers in every field accept some responsibiltiy for teaching basic reading skills when students need them to achieve in their areas, many gross weaknesses in the study-meaning skills will continue. It is almost a gleeful irony to the reading teacher that one hears the subject matter teachers complaining the loudest about students' inability to study their material effectively.

Granted that the history teacher should not be expected to deal with serious reading problems, there is still much that he can do to contribute to students' study skills. And there are too many fine articles and textbooks available to the teacher today to make any excuse of ignorance about teaching reading an acceptable one.

It seems particularly vital that the subject matter teacher concern himself with main idea skills. Authorities agree that the most effective learning of any skill occurs when the skill is taught as the need for it arises and when students can recognize that need. It is in this regard that the subject matter teacher has a distinct psychological advantage, for his students—particularly those who are in difficulty—are quite aware of their needs. The subject matter teacher has an additional advantage in that his students can be learning significant facts in the area in conjunction with the skill instruction. Also the experience of proving instruction and testing on the skills will give the teacher new insights into the strengths and weaknesses of each student and into the problems each has comprehending the reading material in his subject.

CONCLUSION

A remedy for any reading skill weakness is likely to be regarded like any suggested remedy for a bad cold. As a prescriptive cure, it is likely to be viewed with doubt and its advocate branded as asinine for not being aware that there are a great variety of cures which might be just as effective, particularly when combined—a sort of eclectic cure. Well, this writer is aware of the danger. And he is aware that any creative teacher who recognizes the need for instruction on main idea skills can certainly add many other suggestions for improving instruction in this skill or create an entirely different approach that might be just as effective. He has hoped to accomplish two ends: to make teachers aware of the vital need for instruction in this skill and, following accepted principles of learning, to provide a prescription—regimented though it appear—that might be used where *no* remedy has been used in the past. Hopefully, if more teachers become aware of the vast need for remedying this ill, they will experiment with prescriptions of their own.

REFERENCES

1. Perry, William G., Jr. "Students' Use and Misuse of Reading Skills: A Report to the Faculty," *Harvard Educational Review*, 29 (Summer 1959), 193–200.

2. Karlin, Robert. *Teaching Reading in High School.* Indianapolis: Bobbs-Merrill Company, Inc., 1964, pp. 138–48.
3. Smith, Nila B. *Reading Instruction for Today's Children.* Englewood Cliffs, N.J.: Prentice-Hall, Inc., 1963, pp. 305–51.

Reading Deficiencies Among Able Pupils*

Iver L. Moe and Frank Nania

Some teachers select for special help in reading those individuals whose reading skills are below the class or national average. However, a basic question is, "Which individuals should profit most from instruction?" The answer is: those who show the greatest discrepancy between achievement and capacity. Now selection is put on a psychologically sounder basis and individuals selected will be reading below, at, and above average; but they are the ones who need and should be able to *profit* from instruction.

In this article Moe and Nania prove that able pupils do have reading deficiencies and that these pupils can be helped to overcome such deficiencies.

1. What are the problems in this study?

2. Note the difficulties that are encountered in using standardized tests. How are these difficulties overcome?

3. What, basically, does the corrective program attempt to do?

4. Why do the authors advocate selective underlining?

5. What are the implications of this statement: "Probably few people can read difficult material for both general concepts and detail simultaneously"?

6. Is the practice in this book of having you read the questions before you read the selection substantiated by the authors of this article?

7. How can you apply the conclusions of the study to your reading and to the reading of your able students?

Pupils whose standard reading scores place them well above national norms and whose academic records are exemplary can be, and often are, retarded in reading. "Retardation," as used in this article, describes a situation in which the pupil's development in reading is significantly below a readily accessible potential. In this study, twelve high-achieving junior high school pupils were selected to receive special help in an effort to further develop reading skills. Weaknesses found among these students were concealed

---

* FROM the *Journal of Developmental Reading* (Autumn 1959), pp. 11–26. Reprinted with permission of Iver L. Moe and the International Reading Association.

from perfunctory view by a smokescreen of exceeded norms and excellent report-card marks. However, an analysis of their performances on standardized and informal tests revealed correctable deficiencies. Two deficiencies, common to all students, were identified: (1) deficiency in study approaches to chapter-length materials, and (2) inflexibility in reading rate. The general inadequacy in their approach to chapter-length materials was established by interviews with the students, and inflexibility of reading rate was identified when the students were given an informal test especially devised for this study. Accordingly, this article will focus upon selection of students, analysis of reading development, the corrective program, and the results observed. Technical clinical procedures, complicated statistics, mechanical reading aids, and formal research design were not used. Therefore, the procedures of this study, including the devising of a Rate Flexibility Test, can be duplicated in any junior high school where teachers recognize that all pupils—including high achievers—need a continuous, carefully planned, skills program to accompany efforts to provide enrichment of reading experience. This article is intentionally limited to skill development. Growth "in" reading (skill development) is coessential with growth "through" reading.

SELECTION OF PUPILS

Four criteria were used for selection of pupils: (1) excellent report-card marks, (2) high scores on two different standardized reading tests, (3) an intelligence quotient of 110 or better, and (4) parental and pupil consent. A testing program was administered after which twelve pupils were selected, six boys and six girls. Equal distribution of boys and girls was coincidental.

First, the *Gates Reading Survey,* Form I, was administered (1). This test purports to measure speed and accuracy, reading vocabulary, and level of comprehension. The complete *Iowa Every-Pupil Tests of Basic Skills,* Form O, was also administered (2). Only subsections "A" and "B" were used for selecting pupils. These subsections purport to measure reading comprehension, vocabulary, map reading, use of references, use of index, use of dictionary, alphabetizing skill, and ability to read graphs. Form G of the *Kuhlmann-Anderson Test* was used to obtain psychological data (3).

After the standardized testing program was completed, high scorers were tentatively selected. At a group meeting, the students were informed that data accumulated were generally favorable. It was pointed out that an analysis of standard scores, administration of informal tests, and interviews, would be used to identify deficiencies, if any. The students were then invited to participate in the experiment. All concurred. The next step, therefore, was designed to identify possible deficiencies through the use of procedures described earlier in this paragraph. When the analysis was complete, weaknesses identified, and a tentative corrective program planned, the parents were invited to attend a group meeting at which time a report was given describing the findings to date and the plan of work. All students were represented by at least one parent, all of whom indicated their support. Final selection of twelve eighth-grade pupils from the Campus School at the State University of New York, Teachers College, Cortland, New York, was then made. It was decided that twenty-four forty-minute sessions over a six-week period would be arranged.

PRESENTATION OF STANDARD TEST DATA

Following are the data from the tests, in turn, with an analysis for each:

DATA FROM GATES READING SURVEY AND KUHLMANN-ANDERSON TEST. The Gates test was administered during the first month of the eighth-grade term. Accordingly, the norm for the test was 8-1 (eighth-grade, first-month). For convenience the results of the Gates and Kuhlmann-Anderson tests are shown in Figure 1.

FIGURE 1

Scores on Part II of the Gates Reading Survey of the Kuhlmann-Anderson Intelligence Test

| CASE NUMBER | GATES READING SURVEY* | | | | KUHLMANN-ANDERSON† | | |
	SPEED	VOCAB-ULARY	COMPRE-HENSION	AVERAGE	C.A.	M.A.	I.Q.
1	11–8	12–6	12–0	12–1	13–5	17–0	127
2	12–1	11–7	10–6	11–5	13–5	14–1	117
3	11–9	11–2	10–3	11–1	13–0	15–0	115
4	11–3	11–5	11–1	11–3	12–10	16–5	128
5	11–3	11–3	8–8	9–1	13–3	14–7	110
6	10–6	10–0	10–6	10–4	13–6	15–4	114
7	7–1	10–6	11–1	9–6	12–2	14–2	116
8	7–8	10–4	8–2	8–8	13–6	14–11	111
9	7–8	10–3	10–3	9–5	13–7	17–3	127
10	11–0	10–8	9–5	10–4	13–5	15–0	112
11	11–3	10–8	10–6	10–9	13–5	15–6	116
12	10–6	9–6	11–1	10–4	13–0	14–7	112

* Gates Reading Survey data are expressed in grade equivalents.
† Chronological age (C.A.) and mental age (M.A.) are expressed in years and months.

It can be noted in Figure 1, that the high grade-equivalent score in speed was 12–1 (Case No. 2) and the low score was 7–1 (Case No. 7). The median score was 11–1, thirty months above the norm. Case Nos. 7, 8, and 9 were the only students below the norm in speed of reading. It becomes apparent, superficially, that the standard scores in speed were favorable. However, after closer analysis to be described later, evidence will be presented to indicate that the selected pupils read materials at an inflexible, habituated, rate irrespective of purpose for reading or the relative difficulty of materials being read.

In the vocabulary subsection of the Gates test, all pupils were above the norm. The high score was 12–6 (Case No. 1 and the low score 9–6 (Case No. 12). The median was 10–8, twenty-seven months above the norm. Favorable scores also accumulated from the comprehension subsection of the test, the high score being 12–0 (Case No. 1) and the low score 8–2 (Case No. 8). The median score in comprehension was 10–6, twenty-five months above the norm. In average reading, the high pupil (Case No. 1) was thirty-nine months above the norm and the low pupil (Case No. 8) was one month above. The median score in average reading was 10–4, twenty-three months above the norm.

THE KUHLMANN–ANDERSON TEST. Results, in Figure 1, show that intelligence quotients were 110 or better. The high quotient (Case No. 4) was 128 and the low score (Case No. 5) was 110. The median intelligence quotient was 116.

ANALYSIS OF DATA: GATES READING SURVEY

The form of the Gates test used in the experiment is advocated for upper third grade through grade ten. The first subsection purports to be a test of reading speed and accuracy. The experimental pupils scored high as previously indicated. Since the writers believe that standard scores can be misleading unless carefully examined in an effort to determine what the test measures, the structure of the speed subtest was studied. The speed subsection is comprised of thirty-six short, simple paragraphs written at about third-grade level. The paragraphs presented no conceptual or ideational challenge to the experimental students. However, if the speed subsection was given to third-grade pupils, the concept load represented in the thirty-six paragraphs may well represent a different problem. Third-grade children may score low on such a subsection for a variety of reasons. Some younger children may score low because of poor word-recognition skill, or poor comprehenion, or low reading rate. However, the speed and accuracy subsection presented only one problem to the selected eighth-grade—speed of reading. The time limit of four minutes was the only obstacle to their reading the thirty-six paragraphs containing approximately 1000 words. It was estimated that if the experimental pupils had read third-grade material at 350 words per minute, ample time would have been provided for reading and answering questions and all would have reached the ceiling for that subsection. However, as shown in Figure 2, no student was able to finish the test. The "number attempted" column in Figure 2 shows the number of paragraphs attempted. The highest number of paragraphs at-

tempted was thirty-four (Case No. 2) and the fewest number of paragraphs read was seventeen (Case No. 7). A further study of Figure 2
indicates that only one student failed to score perfect comprehension on
paragraphs read. Case No. 5 attempted twenty-seven paragraphs and
scored correct responses in twenty-six paragraphs.

This analysis led to the conclusion that while these students were characteristically above norms (median score 11–1) the speed subsection did
not measure practical speed and accuracy well enough to justify generalizing. Some questions remained. Is it reasonable to expect able eighth-
grade pupils to read third-grade materials at the rate of 350 words per
minute and answer simple multiple-choice questions? If all students had
been able to do so, they would have reached the extreme upper limits of
the speed subsection. Another question remained. Is it reasonable to expect that competent eighth-grade pupils should be able to vary reading
rate according to purpose and content? An attempt to answer these questions will be discussed later.

FIGURE 2

Scores on the Speed and Accuracy Subtest of the Gates
Reading Survey

CASE NUMBER	NUMBER ATTEMPTED	RAW SCORE (NUMBER RIGHT)	PERCENT ACCURATE
1	31	31	100
2	34	34	100
3	32	32	100
4	26	26	100
5	27	26	96
6	24	24	100
7	17	17	100
8	19	19	100
9	19	19	100
10	25	25	100
11	26	26	100
12	24	24	100

Examination of the results in the vocabulary section of the Gates test
revealed no particular need for further testing. However, the comprehension test was considered to be limited in scope. It is comprised of twenty-
one short paragraphs which gradually increase in reading difficulty. The
high scores on this subsection seemed to be justified. However, an informal
analysis of reading chapter-length materials was considered necessary and
later administered.

PRESENTATION OF DATA: IOWA EVERY-PUPIL TESTS OF BASIC SKILLS

As indicated earlier, the *Iowa Every-Pupil Tests of Basic Skills* was also administered in September. Only results of subtests "A" and "B" are shown in Figure 3. It was decided by the writers that these data were sufficient to establish high achievement levels for the twelve pupils selected. As can be observed in Figure 3, scores in comprehension and vocabulary essentially support the findings of the *Gates Reading Survey*. The median score in comprehension was 10–6 while the median score in vocabulary was 9–5. All pupils were substantially above norms on the comprehension and vocabulary subsections of the Iowa. There were, however, some relatively low scores in map reading (see Case Nos. 2, 3, 4, and 12). Case Nos. 3, 4, 5, 6, 8, 10, and 12 were comparatively weak in the "use of reference" subtest. Scores on index, dictionary, alphabetizing, and graphs were characteristically substantial.

FIGURE 3

*Scores on the Iowa Every-Pupil Tests of Basic Skills**

CASE NO.	COMPRE-HENSION	VOCAB-ULARY	MAP READING	USE OF REFER-ENCES	USE OF INDEX	USE OF DIC-TIONARY	ALPHA-BETIZING AND GRAPHS
1	11–3	10–7	10–6	9–0	9–7	10–8	10–3
2	10–9	10–1	7–5	9–0	8–8	9–6	8–8
3	11–0	10–4	8–0	8–0	8–0	10–8	9–8
4	10–0	9–4	7–2	8–0	9–7	10–1	10–0
5	10–1	9–7	8–5	5–5	8–4	8–9	8–3
6	9–8	9–2	11–2	6–5	9–5	10–1	9–8
7	11–3	8–6	9–5	8–5	9–5	10–1	10–3
8	10–5	8–6	10–0	6–5	8–4	8–9	9–3
9	10–0	8–7	10–3	8–5	10–1	9–6	9–8
10	10–0	10–4	10–6	7–0	9–5	8–4	9–8
11	10–8	10–7	10–3	9–5	9–7	8–9	10–7
12	10–9	8–9	8–0	7–5	8–4	10–8	8–3

* Scores are expressed in grade equivalents.

Space here does not permit recounting the analysis of standard scores on the Iowa test. Weaknesses were noted, as mentioned above, in map reading and use of reference materials. Appropriate notations were made to guide the instructors in formulation of a corrective program.

INFORMAL TESTING

COMPREHENSION. It is recognized that standard tests of comprehension are necessarily designed to be easily administered and scored. This precludes the possibility of testing comprehension in chapter-length selections in various types of materials. Therefore, a series of individual interviews was arranged in an attempt to assess the students' ability to approach chapter-length materials. All pupils were vague with regard to reading for general ideas, reading for details, and specific study approaches. *Reading was just reading.* It was believed that special work in reading chapter-length materials was indicated.

FLEXIBILITY TEST. In order to augment and clarify the speed subtests of the *Gates Reading Survey,* an informal test of rate flexibility was devised. Materials for the test were selected from the *Reading Laboratory* published by Science Research Associates (4). The authors, Don H. Parker et al. have accumulated a great deal of interesting reading material designed for practice in speed and comprehension. The materials are graded as to readability by the Lorge and Dale–Chall formulas. The materials are divided into speed and comprehension exercises. There are fifteen speed selections and fifteen comprehension selections on each grade level from grade three through twelve. Selections vary in subject matter and include, among others, materials relating to science, biography, literature, music, art, and history. By experimenting with the graded materials, it was found that all twelve pupils could read and comprehend materials at tenth-grade level or above. With this information, a rate flexibility test was devised.

FIGURE 4
Flexibility Test

CASE NUMBER	RATE ON EASY MATERIAL	RATE ON DIFFICULT MATERIAL	FLEXIBILITY INDEX
1	510	330	180
2	520	408	112
3	360	330	30
4	360	282	78
5	228	210	18
6	282	216	66
7	252	234	18
8	204	200	4
9	276	240	36
10	310	282	28
11	390	288	102
12	240	198	42

* All rates are expressed in words per minute.
  Flexibility Index represents the difference in reading rate between easy and difficult materials.

Reading selections were chosen from third-grade, fifth-grade, seventh-grade, and tenth-grade levels. Each pupil, individually, was then given a rate flexibility test. Each was asked to read silently the graded paragraphs, in turn, from simple to difficult. The reading of each selection was timed with a stop watch and the percent of comprehension recorded when the student responded to the multiple-choice question accompanying each selection. In the interest of simplicity only the rates on easy material (grade three) and difficult material (grade ten to twelve) was placed in Figure 4.

It was noted that Case Nos. 1, 2, and 11 demonstrated superior flexibility as compared with other students. For example, Case No. 1 read and comprehended easy materials at 510 w.p.m. By subtracting the rate in difficult material from the rate in easy material, the flexibility index of Case No. 1 was found to be 180 w.p.m. (see Figure 4). Case No. 2 had a flexibility index of 112 w.p.m. A sharp contrast can be noted by inspecting the flexibility index of Case No. 8. This student read simple material only four w.p.m. faster than difficult material. The median flexibility index for the group was found to be thirty-nine w.p.m. The low flexibility index was four w.p.m., the high 180 w.p.m. The range in flexibility index was 176 w.p.m. which indicates a highly variable characteristic.

After the testing period—both informal and standardized—was completed, it was decided to devise an improvement program designed to develop study skills in chapter-length materials using textbook selections with which the students were currently engaged in their regular school program. In addition, the corrective program was directed toward improving the flexibility index in relationship to difficulty of materials read. To put it more concretely, we hoped that the twelve students could be taught to shift gears to the end that easy materials would be read faster than difficult materials. It was further hoped that reading rate could be improved at all levels of difficulty.

THE CORRECTIVE PROGRAM

STUDY SKILLS. The standard test results revealed comparatively high grade-equivalent scores in comprehension. However, it is not feasible, in a standard test, to use chapter-length selections for testing purposes. As indicated previously, pupils were vague concerning study approaches in regular school work. Accordingly, a program was devised to improve study approaches.

The pupils were taught how to survey a chapter to discover: (1) the general content of the chapter, (2) the author's plan for presenting material, (3) the location of introductions and summaries, (4) significance of illustrative materials such as maps, charts, pictures, and the like, (5) relationship of the chapter to the book, (6) careful examination of headings and subheadings, and (7) location of glossary, index, and other printed parts of the book. Several types of books were used to familiarize pupils with a variety of organizational patterns and content.

After the survey of the chapter, pupils were asked to read carefully the introduction (if one was included). After reading the introduction, the chapter summary was read where applicable. The survey and the reading of introduction and summary are believed to contribute materially to a reader's general awareness of the content of the entire chapter. The next step is that of changing headings of chapter subsections into question form. This can be done by writing questions or by simply keeping them in mind.

The first reading of the material begins at the first subsection and continues to the end of the subsection. At the end of the subsection the pupil either recites to himself or reflects upon whether his question or questions have been answered. In the first reading pupils were discouraged from underlining, or reading for detail. Each subsection is read in turn as quickly as possible consistent with good comprehension of general ideas.

During the second reading, pupils were encouraged to selectively underline where they believed necessary. Only key words were underlined. An example of selective underlining follows:

What Rights Did the English Colonies Bring to the New World?

The last stop in our journey is at the little home of Jonathan Blake in Massachusetts Bay Colony. Jonathan was a free man when he came from England to make a better living, and his life in America is much freer than that of Fernando or Pierre. He owns his house and farm, which he is free to manage as he wishes. He has a right to share in the government of the colony. He may vote for representatives who become members of the assembly for the whole colony. This assembly decides many important questions, including the taxes which each colonist must pay. Jonathan also has certain other rights. For example, he cannot be punished for a crime unless he has been found guilty by a group of his fellow men called a jury.

It is believed by the writers that selective underlining requires more thinking on the part of the reader as compared with solid underlining of material. Moreover, many pupils have found that, in review reading, it is possible to grasp general concepts through reading only the underlined words.

It should be noted that "key" words are underlined, not "big" words. The little word "but" is often a key word. Other short but important words may be among others, "before," "after," "first," "second," "however," "if," etc. Good selective underlining will vary from pupil to pupil. Each is encouraged to underline as much or as little as necessary to highlight the concept.

Three weeks, four 40-minute periods per week, were given to practice in this technique. Regular textbooks were used for practice material and pupils were encouraged to use the approach while doing homework. It was pointed out to pupils that the approach was to be modified according to pupil purpose and relative difficulty of material.

Details in the chapter were handled differently. After general concepts were familiar, pupils then read for detail. Names, dates, places, events, and the like were thus associated with the general concepts. Some pupils preferred to underline details in a different color. It is believed by the writers that details can often be memorized while concepts need to be understood. Probably few people can read difficult material for both general concepts and detail simultaneously.

FLEXIBILITY TRAINING. After three weeks of work designed to increase efficiency and comprehension in chapter reading, it was decided to begin work to increase flexibility of rate.

Research regarding the relationship between rate and comprehension is confused. Some are willing to assume that fast readers are always good readers. Therefore, these people assume that a desirable way to improve comprehension is to teach pupils to read faster. Unfortunate consequences may result from assuming that speed and comprehension are so closely correlated. Indiscriminate rate training may often result in teaching the pupil to *miscomprehend more rapidly*. Part of the confusion is due to the fact that results of a speed test cannot be very useful unless the results are coextensive with a test of comprehension. It is very difficult, if not impossible, to devise a standardized test of speed and one of comprehension in such a way that neither score is dependent upon the other. We know that speed without comprehension is useless. Low comprehension scores on tests received by bright pupils can be a result of overcautious procedures probably caused by an unnecessarily slow, inflexible, habituated, rate. While it is not easy to devise and standardize mutually exclusive measures of speed and comprehension, research indicates that efficient readers adjust their rate according to the difficulty of the material and the purpose for which they are reading.

As shown in Figure 4, only three pupils (Case Nos. 1, 2, and 11) demonstrated considerable flexibility in rate between third-grade material and material rated between tenth and twelfth-grade.

All pupils began rate training in third-grade material selected from *Science Research Associates Reading Laboratory*. After a warm-up period, pupils were timed on each exercise. Timing was done with a stopwatch. The instructor placed time in seconds on the blackboard. When a student finished reading, he copied the last number written on the board. Then, without rereading, he answered the questions, scored them by using the key provided, and recorded his comprehension score and rate on his personal data card.

Since pupils had learned earlier in the experiment to formulate questions to guide their reading of chapter-length materials, it was decided to adapt this question-first technique to rate work. Accordingly, pupils were given ample opportunity to study the questions before reading the selection.

The procedure of reading the questions first is considered to be sensible even in rate work. Mature readers rarely, by choice, read and then answer questions. It is unfortunate, in the opinion of the writers, that school assignments are often given as follows: "Read the chapter, then answer the questions at the end of the chapter." Inquisitive, participating readers wish to read to answer questions or bring information to bear upon a problem. The reader in this situation is not passive, he makes demands upon the writer as he seeks information. Moreover, it is believed that where pupils read to get answers to questions, rate is increased without loss of comprehension. The procedure of reading questions first seemed to encourage confidence. All of the pupils preferred the question-first technique.

No machines, eye-span exercises, phrase-reading exercises, and the like were used. Pupils were asked to read as quickly as they could and still maintain adequate comprehension. Since the S.R.A. materials are graded as to readability, the twelve pupils were practicing speed reading at many different levels. When they were able to read quickly and effectively at a given level, they asked to try more difficult selections. Pupils exercised good judgment. Careful examinations of the individual data cards were made each day in order to furnish the instructors with information necessary to guide the pupil. From time to time, some were helped to reduce excessive head movement while reading. Early in rate training experience some pupils were helped to overcome lip movement.

All pupils began at third-grade level. They progressed to increasingly difficult material at their own discretion. At the end of the rate training, all were practicing in materials of tenth-grade level, or above. Four pupils were reading at twelfth-grade level.

The final results are shown in Figure 5. By subtracting the rate in column 2 from the rate in column 3, one arrives at the gain (in words per minute). This difference was placed in column 4. As can be seen in column 4, the gain varied from 66 to 630 words per minute. All pupils except Case Nos. 6 and 7, column 4, made substantial rate gains in simple material. The median gain in rate in simple materials was found to be 279 words per minute.

Rates in difficult material are shown in columns 5 and 6. The difference between columns 5 and 6 represents gain in rate and these data are shown in column 7. The smallest gain was 42 words per minute and the largest gain was 270 words per minute in difficult materials. The median gain was 139 words per minute.

Flexibility data were placed in columns 8 and 9. In column 8 are the flexibility data recorded October 12, the beginning of the six-week experiment. Flexibility scores represent the rate differential, in words per minute in simple material as compared with rate in difficult material. Case No. 8, column 8, read simple material only 4 words per minute faster than diffi-

FIGURE 5

Gains in Rate on Easy and Difficult Material and Flexibility*

COL. 1	COL. 2	COL. 3	COL. 4	COL. 5	COL. 6	COL. 7	COL. 8	COL. 9
CASE NO.	RATE ON EASY MATERIAL (NOV. 21)	RATE ON EASY MATERIAL (NOV. 3)	GAIN	RATE ON DIFFICULT MATERIAL (NOV. 21)	RATE ON DIFFICULT MATERIAL (NOV. 3)	GAIN	FLEXI-BILITY (OCT. 12)	FLEXI-BILITY (NOV. 21)
1	816	510	306	600	330	270	180	216
2	960	520	440	660	408	252	112	300
3	510	360	150	396	330	66	30	114
4	540	360	220	396	282	114	78	144
5	600	210	390	390	228	162	18	210
6	360	282	78	330	216	114	66	30
7	318	252	66	276	234	42	18	42
8	642	200	242	396	204	204	4	246
9	480	276	104	300	240	60	36	180
10	900	310	590	390	282	114	28	510
11	1020	390	630	500	288	212	102	520
12	630	240	390	396	198	198	42	234

* All figures are expressed in words per minute.
"Easy Material" refers to third-grade level.
"Difficult Material" refers to tenth- to twelfth-grade materials.

cult material. In contradistinction, Case No. 1, column 8, read simple materials 180 words per minute faster than difficult materials.

In column 9 are the final flexibility data. Case No. 11 established a flexibility of 520 words per minute between simple and difficult materials. For Case No. 6, flexibility was only 30 words per minute. Median flexibility in October was 39 words per minute. Median flexibility in November was 213 words per minute.

Actual rate training *per se* was begun November 3 and completed November 21, during which time twelve 40-minute periods were scheduled. However, it is believed by the writers that preliminary work in chapter reading with practice given in reading for general ideas served as a good foundation for rate work.

INTERVIEWS AND TESTING AFTER THREE MONTHS

Three months after the special teaching had been finished, the pupils were interviewed individually. Each was asked to comment concerning the value of the practice work in chapter-length materials. In general, selective underlining was considered to be the most helpful. Four pupils felt that little value was received from the attempt to improve study approaches as described in this article. All but three pupils reported that the procedures learned during the experiment were currently being used. At least eight of the twelve pupils were enthusiastic concerning their progress.

Finally, each pupil was given a rate flexibility test to determine whether gains made were maintained after the three-months' lapse. Rate of reading in both simple and difficult materials dropped for all but two pupils; however, all pupils maintained a substantial net gain. The highest net gain in difficult materials was 396 w.p.m. The lowest net gain was only 12 w.p.m. Flexibility (difference between w.p.m. in simple and difficult materials) was enhanced as compared with the initial test results. All but three pupils showed a net increase in flexibility. Perhaps the most important gain can be stated thus: *All but three pupils read difficult materials faster (even after three months' elapsed time) than they did simple materials at the beginning of the experiment.*

Conclusions

1. Correctable deficiencies in reading may exist among pupils whose achievement is high.
2. Skill in paragraph reading, as measured by standardized tests, is not a good measure of whether a pupil can effectively manage chapter-length materials in practical situations.
3. All standard tests results should be carefully analyzed to determine what is being measured and how it is measured.
4. Rate Flexibility Tests are useful diagnostic devices.
5. Pupils tend to read at a given speed regardless of materials or purpose.
6. Rate training should begin with simple materials. Adjustment in rate or difficulty of materials should be made when comprehension consistently drops below 80 per cent.
7. Pupils should take an active part in deciding when they are ready to increase rate.
8. No particular rate can represent the goal for all pupils. The characteristic is highly variable even among able pupils.
9. The goal of rate training is not directed toward set norms but rather toward individual flexibility. Pupils can learn to "shift gears" as materials and purpose change.
10. The typical practice of saving only standard test profiles (outside covers) while destroying the test itself is contraindicated. The whole test is needed if full benefit is to be derived.
11. Skill development in reading should be taught at all grade levels and include all pupils.
12. Improvement in rate and flexibility were substantially present after three months had elapsed from the end of the teaching cycle.

While this experiment was limited in scope, it presented some evidence that reading problems of able pupils are often unnoticed. Many able pupils are retarded in reading regardless of high achievement established by standard norms. If Johnny is really to grow in reading at a rate commensurate with his potential, teachers on all levels from kindergarten through college have a significant responsibility. The early struggle of the first-grader to build a sight vocabulary and the task of the graduate student in handling an extensive bibliography are all part of the complicated reading process.

REFERENCES

1. *Gates Reading Survey*, Form I. New York: Bureau of Publications, Teachers College, Columbia University.
2. *Iowa Every-Pupil Tests of Basic Skills*, Form O. Boston: Houghton Mifflin Company.
3. *Kuhlmann-Anderson Test*, Form G. Princeton, New Jersey: Personnel Press, Incorporated.
4. *Science Research Associates Reading Laboratory*. Chicago, Illinois: Science Research Associates.

STUDY SKILLS FOR SUPERIOR STUDENTS IN SECONDARY SCHOOL*

Francis P. Robinson

When Robinson points out in this article that even Phi Beta Kappas study quite inefficiently and that their study skills can be improved, he whets our appetite for more information: what research says about developing effective reading-study skills, how academic skills are like athletic skills, and how a special technique is best used to improve comprehension and retention of material.

1. Why is it often difficult to interest superior students in learning better reading skills?

2. What evidence exists for the contention that many students, including superior ones, are inefficient readers?

3. What do authors, publishers, and teachers do to help readers take advantage of what is known about the writing and organizing of textbooks?

4. How would you impress upon your students the value of each of the steps in the SQ3R study approach?

5. Give illustrative examples for the brief points the author lists in his summary.

* FROM *The Reading Teacher* (September 1961), pp. 29–33; 37, reprinted with permission of Francis P. Robinson and the International Reading Association.

Reading instruction is a regular part of most college programs (4, 8). It deals not only with remediation of reading disabilities but also with instruction in higher levels of reading skill needed for collegiate study. This article will emphasize the value of giving instruction in higher level reading skills to superior high school students, particularly those who may be taking collegiate courses early, or those who want to learn these reading skills in preparation for later college work. It is also obvious that these reading skills can be of value in doing high school work.

Because high schools give much emphasis to remedial work for poor readers and because superior students read so much better than their peers, it is usually difficult to interest these students in learning better reading skills. However, the fact that these higher level skills are needed in college, and are a part there of the regular instructional program, should increase interest of superior students in maximizing their reading skills. In addition, the use of instructional materials specifically written for the college level will help indicate that higher levels of skill are being emphasized rather than remediation.

It will be necessary to show students that their reading skills are actually quite inefficient. Some data obtained from outstanding students in college will be useful here. Studies of Phi Beta Kappa and other honor roll candidates show that their rate of reading is typically little above that of other students and that they have quite inefficient study skills (6, 13). Other studies show that superior students given selections with headings in and headings omitted read the former no faster nor comprehend them any better, although evidence indicates that such headings can with training be used to increase speed and comprehension (16). A study made during World War II of superior college students referred for specialized training showed that these students had been making their A's and B's more by strength of intellect than by efficient study skills (14). When these students were asked to read and take notes their "work rate" was only ninety-three words per minute, and the quality of their notes was little better than average.

Other studies show that with a single reading the typical reader gets only about 60 per cent of the ideas asked on an immediate quiz, and with immediate rereadings is able to raise his comprehension score only to about 65 per cent (7). Another study of several thousand high school students showed that there is rapid forgetting after reading: within two weeks after an initial reading only 20 per cent is remembered of what was known immediately after reading (17).

In brief, the average and superior student in high school and college is inefficient in his reading and study skills; he tends to excel other students in grades mostly because of differences in intellectual ability and not because of better reading and study methods.

Before turning to the nature of some of these higher level reading skills and how they may be taught, two preliminary points need to be made:

(a) textbooks should be even better organized to facilitate learning and (b) when students are given better books they will not do much better unless they are taught the necessary reading skills to use the facilitative cues. While modern textbooks are written in many ways to facilitate learning, e.g., use of headings, final summaries, illustrations, etc., there is good evidence that school textbook writers and publishers are still too much bound to the typographical style of ancient papyrus times, e.g., close printed, full line paragraphs in one type size. School textbooks make little use (except in footnotes) of paragraphs printed in different type sizes to indicate degree of importance. They do not use a style (found useful in governmental and industrial publications) of indenting the whole left side of subordinate paragraphs. Academic authors seem unprepared to use pictorial material as the main form of presentation, with prose added as explanation. Few help the reader by starting chapters with summary statements or by putting their headings into question form, etc. A great deal is known that could improve textbooks, and experiments such as trying the scramble order of the recent *Tutortexts* should be encouraged and evaluated.

The second preliminary point is that superior students may not be able to read better when they are given well organized and facilitative material *unless they are given special instruction.* Earlier it was stated that inserting headings into a text does not increase reading speed or comprehension of college students. A more extensive study by Christenson and Stordahl showed similar results and found in addition that adding such cues as underlinings, summary statements, etc., does not help uninstructed adult readers (5). Another study by Newman showed that when material is prepared which forces students to read in a manner which seems to better fit psychological knowledge of how learning takes place, the students actually do better using their own self-derived methods with which they are comfortable (12). Additional studies show that simple explanations of better techniques (either through reading about them or through oral explanation) are not sufficient to bring about better skill (2, 18). However, with supervised practice, as is necessary in learning any skill, there is a definite gain in skill to levels far beyond those attained with self-help methods (2). In brief, what has been discovered in developing optimum athletic and industrial skills applies to learning scholastic skills as well. Research can be used to design new higher levels of skill, and these must be taught in a coaching and practice situation.

What are some of the higher level reading and study skills? One of them is the SQ3R method—a technique devised from research findings for use in studying college textbooks (15). Some of the research will be summarized and the method then described. McClusky divided 118 college students into two equated groups; one group was shown how to skim over headings and summaries and the other was not shown. When these two groups were then given a selection to read, the trained group read 24 per cent faster than, and just as accurately as, the control group (11). Holmes also set up two large equated groups of college students and had them read selections about science and history (9). One group was given twenty questions *before* reading. As might be expected, the group given the questions did better in answering them, but they also did as well or better on additional questions. The advantage was particularly great on tests given two weeks after reading. Still another study by Washburne indicates the best placement for such questions (19). In this study 1,456 high school students were divided into several groups of equal ability. Questions were given to the different groups as follows: at the beginning of reading, at the end of reading, each question just before the material answering it, each question just after the material answering it, and no questions. The test contained questions already provided as well as other questions. Of these different placements two proved most effective: all questions at the beginning of the reading and each question just before it was answered in the material.

These findings, plus the fact that textbook writers regularly use headings, numberings, and summaries, provide a basis for designing the first three steps of the SQ3R methods: (1) *survey*, (2) ask a *question* before reading a section, and (3) *read* to answer that question. The reader is taught to quickly survey the headings and read the summaries before he starts to read the text. This gives him an orientation as to what the chapter will present, helps him recall what he already knows about these topics, and facilitates his subsequent readings.

We have already noted that students tend to forget much of what they learn from reading within a very short time, e.g., 80 per cent within two weeks (17). This same study also showed that a testing-type review immediately after reading was very helpful in reducing forgetting, e.g., instead of 80 per cent there was only a 20 per cent loss. Other studies show that readers often do not clearly comprehend ideas as they read along, and the rapid succession of ideas in reading tends to interfere with what is comprehended because of retroactive inhibition. So there is need for a system to check on comprehension while reading and also to help in fixing ideas better in memory. Notetaking can be used for this purpose, but the manner in which most students take notes is of little help. That is, studies show that students do as well with straight reading as they do with trying to read and take notes (1, 18). One reason for this is that students tend to copy down phrases as soon as they find an important idea, and if the phrase is in italics they may write it down without understanding the point. Many students do not like to take notes because they write in complete sentences, which markedly slows down their reading speed.

Thus, a method must be worked out which helps the student check his comprehension as he reads, helps fix the ideas in memory, does not take too long, and is useful for later review. The fourth and fifth steps of the SQ3R method are designed to take care of these needs: (4) after completing a headed section, *recite* by writing a brief phrase from memory, and (5) immediately after reading the whole lesson *review* it by looking over the notes taken and reciting on them from memory. Notes are not taken until *after* a headed section has been read. This enables the student to read to answer his question (step 3) and then check on his comprehension and help fix the material in memory by reciting a brief answer. Waiting until the end of the section means that all of the ideas in that section can be seen in relation to each other and the most important selected; writing the note from memory means that the student has to organize his answer, and if he has trouble he can recall the material as needed; using phrases means that much time is saved in writing, and these cues will be sufficient later on for reminders in review.

The SQ3R method then consists of five steps: (1) *Survey* the headings and summaries quickly to get the general ideas which will be developed in the assignment, (2) turn the first heading into a *Question*, (3) *Read* the whole section through to answer that question, (4) at the end of the headed section stop to *Recite* from memory on the question and jot the answer down in phrases (Steps 2, 3, and 4 are repeated on each succeeding headed section), and (5) at the end of reading the assignment in this manner then immediately *Review* the lesson to organize the ideas and recite on the various points to fix them in mind. This higher-level study skill cannot be learned simply by reading about it; it must be practiced under supervision just as with learning any skill. Modifications of this skill have also been worked out for studying collateral readings, English literature, and charts and tables (15).

While particular attention has been given to the explanation of one particular higher-level study skill, there are many other specialized skills which the superior secondary school student needs in college as well as in high school. Much use is made of specialized graphs, charts, maps, dictionaries, encyclopedias, resource books, etc., in college. A surprising number of college students tend to skip graphs and tables, refuse to use dictionaries and indices, or handle such material in an inefficient manner. Studies of college students' ability to use the library to find assigned books or to use easy short cuts in writing research papers show ignorance of fundamental and simple devices (10). Studies of the manner in which college students go about reading examination questions show that rather than use systematic skills in analysis they usually use a self-taught "jump and guess" system (3). In brief, superior students in high school need to learn many higher-level skills if they are to be highly effective in college work.

Since students going to college move away from their usual surroundings and conditions for study, they also need help with study habits and planning. Irregular class schedules and the need for self-planning of study time leave many students floundering. Both the home and high school usually provide study conditions with a minimum of distraction, but in college there are many places to study, and students often try to combine studying with social possibilities. Finally, many students—even superior ones—go through high school with only vaguely understood adult goals, and go on to college mostly because "everyone in school does." Such motivation is insufficient to help students direct study efforts when so many fascinating things are possible in college. Youngsters need help in thinking about why they want to go to college so that their college efforts can be more effectively self directed.

Our points, in brief, have been: Superior students in high school are typically inefficient in study methods; they have kept ahead of others through brilliance of intellect. College work will offer them particular difficulties because of greater demands and competition and because of many distractions for poorly controlled individuals. Furthermore, superior students are interested in making outstanding records of achievement and discovery and not simply in excelling others; this demands that they learn research-designed higher-level study skills.

REFERENCES

1. Arnold, H. F. "The Comparative Efficiency of Certain Study Techniques in Fields of History," *Journal of Educational Psychology*, 33 (1942), 449–57.
2. Barton, W. A. "Outlining as a Study Procedure," *Teachers College Contributions to Education*, No. 411 (1930).
3. Bloom, B. S., and L. J. Broder. *Problem Solving Processes of College Students.* Chicago: University of Chicago Press, 1950.
4. Causey, O. S., and W. Eller, eds. "Starting and Improving College Reading Programs," *Eighth Yearbook of the National Reading Conference.* Fort Worth: Texas Christian University Press, 1959.
5. Christenson, C. M., and K. E. Stordahl. "The Effect of Organizational Aids on Comprehension and Retention," *Journal of Educational Psychology*, 46 (1955), 65–74.
6. Danskin, D. G., and C. W. Burnett. "Study Techniques of Those Superior Students." *Personnel and Guidance Journal*, 31 (1952), 181–86.
7. English, H. B., E. L. Welborn, and C. D. Killian. "Studies in Substance Memorization," *Journal of General Psychology*, 11 (1934), 233–259.
8. Entwisle, D. R. "Evaluations of Study-Skills Courses: A Review," *Journal of Educational Research*, 53 (1960), 243–51.
9. Holmes, E. "Reading Guided by Questions Versus Careful Reading and Rereading Without Questions," *School Review*, 39 (1931), 361–71.
10. Loutitt, C. M., and J. R. Patrick. "A Study of Students' Knowledge in the Use of the Library," *Journal of Applied Psychology*, 16 (1932), 475–84.
11. McClusky, H. Y. "An Experiment on the Influence of Preliminary Skimming on Reading," *Journal of Educational Psychology*, 25 (1934), 521–29.
12. Newman, S. E. "Student Versus Instructor Design of Study Method," *Journal of Educational Psychology*, 48 (1957), 328–33.

13. Preston, R. C., and N. E. Tufts. "The Reading Habits of Superior College Students," *Journal of Experimental Education,* 16 (1948), 196–202.
14. Robinson, F. P. "Study Skills of Soldiers in ASTP," *School and Society,* 58 (1943), 398–99.
15. ———. *Effective Study,* revised edition. New York: Harper and Brothers, 1961.
16. ———, and Prudence Hall. "Studies of Higher Level Reading Abilities," *Journal of Educational Psychology,* 32 (1941), 241–52.
17. Spitzer, H. F. "Studies in Retention," *Journal of Educational Psychology,* 30 (1939), 641–56.
18. Stordahl, K. E., and C. M. Christenson. "The Effect of Study Techniques on Comprehension and Retention," *Journal of Educational Research,* 46 (1956), 561–70.
19. Washburne, J. N. "The Use of Questions in Social Science Material," *Journal of Educational Psychology,* 20 (1929), 321–59.

TEACHING MAP READING SKILLS IN GRADE 9

Peter L. Sanders

An axiom of education is "Clarify concepts through discussion." Sanders conducted an action research project to compare the effectiveness of methods of teaching a unit on map-reading skills in ninth-grade world geography classes. His experimental method utilized inductive teaching which featured guided reading and small-group discussions.

1. What was the purpose of the study?
2. Why was the social studies textbook not appropriate for the students?
3. Which procedures were used in the inductive approach?
4. Try to account for the larger—ten points or more—differences between the traditional-method group (A) results and the new-method group (B) results.
5. State the article's key ideas.
6. Discuss in class the implications of these findings for teaching content (reading) skills.

Students vary in ability to handle the textbooks assigned to them. Some experience little or no difficulty; others are frustrated to the point of antagonism. They find the task of unassisted reading impossible and eventually may rebel against the school. Much has been written about this situation, but the problem remains very real. There is a consequent need

* FROM *The Journal of Reading,* 12 (January 1969), pp. 283–286, 337, reprinted with permission of Peter L. Sanders and the International Reading Association.

for the classroom teacher, regardless of subject area, to individualize instruction. The teacher must do more than *assign* textbook readings. He must anticipate his students' difficulties and organize his instruction to provide for individual needs. *This paper reports the results of an attempt to adjust instruction to the reading needs of the members of a ninth grade lower-track social studies program.*

THE PROBLEM

The world geography textbook assigned to the students in question had been selected after careful review as the most appropriate text available for the grade and ability level. Serious problems were nevertheless encountered by the students in their reading. Examination of the text by the teacher and the reading consultant revealed that it exhibited all those characteristics of social studies reading matter identified by the National Council for the Social Studies[1] as contributing to difficulties in comprehension. The situation was further aggravated by the extensive use of figurative language and a tendency toward vagueness and loose organization. The students who were to use this text suffered almost without exception from serious reading disabilities. Most were achieving considerably below grade level as measured by standardized reading tests; a few were unable to read. Several had taken the course before and had failed.

Aware of her students' disabilities, the social studies teacher had resorted most often to a lecture method accompanied by assigned readings and careful review. The method had been only partially successful. Searching for an alternative, she had requested the assistance of the reading consultant in preparing to teach a map-reading unit, one of the most difficult of the year. The complexity of the concepts in this unit and the factual density of the textbook presentation were impressive. A new approach was needed which would simultaneously develop the essential concepts of the subject matter and teach the skills necessary to the reading.

A COMPARISON OF TEACHING METHODS

The availability of two classes of apparently equal ability and achievement suggested that a comparison of the new approach vis-à-vis the old might be made. Both groups were tested to determine the extent of their familiarity with the subject matter of the map-reading unit. This same test was later used for a final evaluation. The test measured both map-reading skills and vocabulary; its several parts reflected the unit objectives which the teacher had decided upon.

[1] Ralph C. Preston, J. Wesley Schneyer and Franc T. Thying. "Guiding the Social Studies Reading of High School Students," Bulletin No. 34, National Council for the Social Studies, 1963.

Group A followed the procedures of previous years: a lecture was given, readings were assigned, and there was a careful follow-up or review. Group B was taught more inductively. No lectures were given; reading assignments were carefully planned. Prereading activities included the establishment of pertinent background and purposes for reading and the pre-teaching of vocabulary. Assigned readings were accompanied by study guides designed to assist students in the process of reading by causing them to manipulate the components of essential concepts and skills. Small group activities were employed extensively in an effort to promote maximum student participation and an exchange of views.

Two kinds of evaluation were made: (1) a comparison of the results of pre- and post-testing, (2) assessment by the teacher of pupil understanding and reaction.

THE EFFECTIVENESS OF GUIDED READING

Pre-test scores revealed an approximately equal familiarity with the subject matter in the two groups. Post-testing revealed a substantial difference in favor of Group B (the new method), as indicated by Figure 1. Without exception, the students of Group B participated enthusiastically in class activities, previously non-contributing members in several in-

FIGURE 1. *Comparison of mean group performance on subskills and vocabulary. (Graph indicates percent right of total possible correct answers.)*

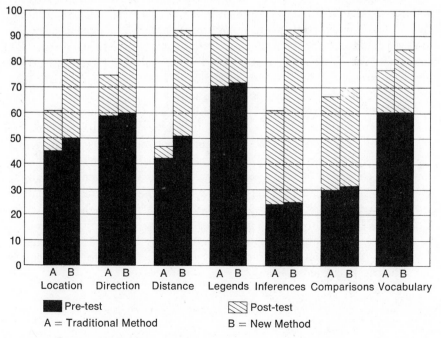

stances assuming leadership in small group discussions. By way of contrast, the participation of the members of Group A remained at the pre-study level. In the judgment of the teacher, the students in Group B reached a depth of understanding not attained by the students taught by the lecture-assigned reading method.

The two programs took about the same amount of time.

Some Reflections on the Differences Obtained

Identical instructional objectives had been adopted for both groups in this comparison; the test was an attempt to measure the degree to which they had been achieved. Examination of subscores of the test reveals the superiority of Group B in all areas but the reading of map legends and drawing inferences based on map-reading skills. Both programs were apparently successful in the former of these. A review of the materials and techniques employed suggests that little difference existed between the approach of Group A and that of Group B. Limitations of the test device may have been responsible for the similarity of inference scores. A follow-up examination of the ability to apply map-reading skills to other units of study might have proved more revealing.

The mean vocabulary score on the post-test of Group B was 84.3 percent as compared to a mean score of 78.0 percent by Group A. Mean scores for post-tests in skills (cumulative over all areas) were 83.55 percent and 65.86 percent respectively for Groups B and A. No students in Group B failed either part of the post-test; though the percentage of failures in Group A was reduced substantially, several students did fail one or both parts of the concluding examination. The teacher's evaluation of group performance is no doubt influenced by her enthusiasm for the new methodology. The test data would nevertheless appear to support her contention that the students of Group B had achieved a deeper level of understanding than had those of Group A.

Of particular interest was the performance of those students who had failed the ninth grade social studies course before. The limited number of repeaters in Group A makes a generalization about their performance impossible. There were several repeaters, however, in Group B; and they had revealed no greater familiarity with the subject matter prior to the study than did students taking the course for the first time. In marked contrast to their performance on units studied earlier in the year, these repeaters achieved final test scores equal to those of the other members of the class. This unusual degree of success suggests a higher level of interest and motivation than before and perhaps reflects the improvement in participation cited above.

Summary

The students of a ninth grade lower-track social studies program had experienced little success with the lecture-reading-review method employed by their teacher. The teacher sought the assistance of the reading consultant in preparing a revised approach to one of the more difficult units of study of the year. A comparison of old and new techniques was made. The teacher's evaluation and the results of the tests employed suggest that the new, more inductive approach was superior. By structuring the reading assignments and more actively involving the students in the process of learning, the teacher improved the students' chances for success, as well as their motivation. The individual needs of a group of poor readers were successfully met through the cooperation of content teacher and reading specialist.

Measurement and Evaluation in Reading

Introduction

The teacher who wants to teach well and effectively must discover both the reading instruction needs of his students, and their capacity for profiting from such instruction. These needs and capacities can be determined through the use of appropriate diagnostic and survey instruments. A careful analysis by the teacher of the information provided by such instruments helps him to select materials and methods which, when wisely and assiduously used, will help his students grow in reading and through reading.

But the teacher faces a problem in the selection of reading tests. The type of test he selects depends upon such factors as the purposes for testing; the validity of a test

197

for those purposes; the number of students to be tested; the time and facilities for testing; and how the test results are to be used.

The problems presented by the contemplation of these factors are discussed by the authors of the selections in this unit. These problems are focused in the debate between those who favor informal tests, which require the students to produce a correct answer, and those who favor standardized tests, which generally require the students to recognize a correct answer.

Dulin, with convincing logic and data, shows the fallacy in "teaching" to the "middle half" of the class. Smith, Guice, and Cheek explain how to construct informal reading inventories for mathematics and science and then provide inventories which are useful in gathering diagnostic data on individuals with reading problems.

Tuinman and Blanton present a masterful discussion of problem areas in the measurement of reading skills. Their article clarifies many theoretical issues and practical issues confronting educators interested in competency-based education.

THE MIDDLE HALF: HOW ALIKE ARE THEY, REALLY?*

Kenneth L. Dulin

Eleventh-graders in the middle half of the reading achievement spectrum vary from those who find *harass*, *idolize*, and *predominate* to be the most difficult words they know to those who know such words as *mutable*, *satiate*, and *feign*. Quite a difference! Dulin shows the exact grade equivalents (in difficulty of material) of eleventh-graders reading at the 25th, 50th, and 75th percentiles. Finally, he raises some questions that teachers must face.

1. What is the "middle-half" philosophy? Is it tenable? State your reasons.

2. What is the self-fulfilling prophecy?

3. How is the "middle-half" philosophy wrong? Peruse the entire article to develop your argument.

4. What are the article's key ideas?

The setting could be the faculty room of almost any high school in America. The speaker is conscientious, dedicated, and sincere. He probably teaches science or social studies.

---

* FROM *Journal of Reading*, 13 (May 1970), pp. 603–609, reprinted with permission of Kenneth L. Dulin and the International Reading Association.

"I'm a content-man, myself. Sure, I sympathize with the problems of my poor readers. Most of them shouldn't have ever been passed on with their poor mastery of the basic skills. And I know I've got a few bright kids I don't challenge very much. But with the time I've got, and with the material I've got to cover, I can only do so much. That's why *I* teach to the 'middle half.' And that's why I don't have to be too concerned about individual differences in reading ability!"

Does this sound familiar? To most reading consultants this "middle-half" philosophy is old stuff, one of the toughest arguments he ever comes up against. And the reason it's such an important argument to counter is that its proponents generally *aren't* selfish, lazy, or basically unprofessional. On the contrary, they're often the very people he'd most like to win over—the young, intellectually vigorous, sure-to-get-ahead professionals who take their teaching responsibilities seriously and try their very best to do a good job.

But just how sound is their argument? *Is* the middle half the group teachers should be most concerned with? And if so, are these students really all that much alike? The final question, of course, is esssentially a philosophical one; each teacher must answer it for himself in terms of his own beliefs, attitudes, and values. The second question, however, can be answered, and it was to this end that this study was directed.

Defining and Measuring the Middle Half

To many who use the term, what this expression really means is simply "those who get along all right with my present methods." As such, it contributes to a self-fulfilling prophecy: those who are successful are those with whom I succeed. Statistically, of course, the middle half of any group consists of those who fall between the 25th and 75th percentiles in whatever performance is being measured. Let's see what this means in terms of reading ability.

It was in this manner that the study proceeded. The norm tables of the Nelson–Denny Reading Test (1960) were examined, raw scores coinciding with the 25th and 75th percentile points for tenth, eleventh, and twelfth graders were located, and these raw scores were then converted to grade equivalents.

As reported in Table 1, reading abilities within the true middle half of a typical high school class are actually far from uniform. In comprehension, for example, the range derived was to have approximately four grades at all three grade levels. Differences in vocabulary ability were somewhat less, but still extended well beyond three grades. In rate of reading, readers within the middle half varied well over 100 words per minute at each grade level. The "middle-half" philosophy embraced by many content teachers overlooks a great deal of diversity. Even the usual "C" students within a class differ strikingly in how well and how fast they can read.

TABLE 1

"Middle-Half" (25th to 75th Percentiles) Ranges in Reading Performance*
at the 10th, 11th, and 12th Grades

READING SCORES		GRADES		
		10TH	11TH	12TH
Vocabulary	Raw scores	14.2 to 27.0	16.5 to 32.3	19.2 to 36.5
	Grade-levels	8.8 to 12.2	9.3 to 12.8	9.9 to 13.3
	Ranges	3.4	3.5	3.4
Comprehension	Raw scores	22.0 to 37.3	25.2 to 43.0	28.0 to 46.5
	Grade-levels	8.4 to 12.2	9.1 to 13.3	9.8 to 14.0
	Ranges	3.8	4.2	4.2
Total reading	Raw scores	37.0 to 63.0	43.0 to 74.5	48.0 to 82.0
	Grade-levels	8.6 to 12.0	9.3 to 13.1	9.9 to 13.6
	Ranges	3.4	3.8	3.7
Rate of reading	Raw scores	164 to 291	185 to 301	197 to 315
	Grade-levels	7.6 to 16.0	8.4 to 16.1	8.9 to 16.5
	Ranges	8.4 (127 wpm)	7.7 (116 wpm)	7.6 (118 wpm)

* As measured by the Nelson–Denny Reading Test Form A (1960 Edition)
Note: Numerical data in most cases are interpolated and/or extrapolated.

DISCUSSION

But how can this best be illustrated to the classroom teacher? And what does it mean in terms of the reading materials he uses? Perhaps the following examples will help. They were all adapted from a United States history text currently in use. They represent three levels of presentation of a topic commonly encountered at the eleventh grade level: the development of political parties in early America. Their reading difficulty levels, as measured by the Fog Index[1], a readability formula for material at this level, are 9.1, 11.0, and 13.3—the exact grade-level equivalents of eleventh graders reading at the 25th, 50th, and 75th percentiles.

VERSION ONE

Sometimes people who share the same ideas about government unite to form political parties. This happened during Washington's term in office. Two parties were started then by Jefferson and Hamilton. Jefferson's people, who were called the Democratic-Republicans, wanted everyone to vote and participate in government.

[1] Gunning, Robert. *The Technique of Clear Writing.* New York: McGraw-Hill, 1952.

They felt that the states should have more power than the central government, and they were against a bank run by the government. Hamilton's party, called the Federalists, wanted a strong central government, and felt that a bank run by the government would be good.

90 words   9.1 Grade Level

VERSION TWO

In America, people sharing the same views on government have often united to form political parties. Our first two were Jefferson's Democratic-Republicans—often cited as the ancestors of today's Democrats—and Hamilton's Federalists, who represented the pro-English business interests of that time. Jefferson was a staunch advocate of states' rights, and felt that all levels of society should be drawn into government. Hamilton, however, believed in a strong central government controlled by "the rich, well-born, and able." On the issue of a national bank, too, the two groups differed, with the Federalists for it and the Democratic-Republicans against. Though he never did join either party, Washington usually supported the Federalists.

110 words   11.0 Grade Level

VERSION THREE

When persons who share like political ideologies unite in hopes of influencing the policies pursued by government we say they have formed a political party. This phenomenon first occurred in America during Washington's administration. Jefferson's people, who advocated strong states' rights, rule by the common people, a tightly structured constitutional framework, and no national bank, became known as the Democratic-Republican Party. Though their name was subsequently shortened to "Republican," they were really the ancestors of our modern-day Democrats. The other political party of the day—the one Washington himself favored, though never officially joined—was led by Hamilton and called the Federalist Party. The Federalists favored a strong federal government, rule by "the well-born and able," a loosely constructed constitution, and a national bank. Roughly speaking, this party was the ancestor of today's Republicans.

135 words   13.3 Grade Level

While a 50th percentile reader is reading Version Two, a 75th percentile reader could equally easily be reading Version Three, and a 25th percentile reader ought to be reading Version One. And while these three levels of readers are reading these versions, here are what the 10th and 90th percentile readers would be encountering if they, too, were to read at their own appropriate levels:

VERSION FOUR

In America we have political parties. They are made up of people who want to get the same things from the government. Jefferson and Hamilton started our first two political parties. Jefferson's party was called the Democratic-Republican Party and wanted strong states for the common people. Hamilton's party was called the Federalist Party and wanted a strong central government for the rich people.

63 words   7.6 Grade Level

VERSION FIVE

An abundance of diversity of opinion within the colonial body politics made the evolution of partisan political alliances an inevitability. During the administration of Washington, this resulted in the formation of our first two parties: Jefferson's Democratic-Republicans and Hamilton's Federalists. Jefferson's support came primarily from the rural areas, where Hamilton's hopes of a national bank and a strong centralized government presided over by the "rich, well-born, and able" were dual anathemas. Hamilton, of course, drew a great deal of his support from the affluent metropolitan communities, which tended generally to be pro-British and anti-egalitarian. Rather than hearkening in camaraderie towards the revolutionary French, these men hoped for the reestablishment of ties—both economic and quasi-political—with the recently ousted mother nation. Though Washington never officially affiliated with either party, his sympathies were quite openly with the Federalists. Whenever possible without any breach of ethics, he supported their policies in every way he could. This undoubtedly helped them win their first campaign.

161 words   17.0 Grade Level

At this point, the reader could very easily quarrel with my treatment of the basic facts presented, particularly in Version Four, rewritten to fit the reading ability of the 10th percentile reader. Haven't I overgeneralized badly, and haven't I left out many important, even necessary qualifications and explanations? The answer, of course, is an unqualified "yes." But within the reading power of a 7.6 reader, not much more can be said beyond defining—simplistically—the two political parties. Unless, of course, I were to go on and on, using many, many short, easy words to say what can only be said briefly and succinctly with a few well-chosen long, difficult words. And this, of course, leads us to a second part of the problem: the extreme differences in *rate* of reading that are found at different levels of reading ability.

A 10th percentile eleventh grader reads at approximately 140 wpm, a 25th percentile reader at 185 wpm, a 50th at 236, a 75th at 301, and a 90th at 359. Thus, all five versions of the material presented above will take their respective readers almost exactly the same length of time to complete (in this case, about 27 seconds). When extrapolated to chapter-size chunks of reading material, this presents a whole new problem.

A typical chapter in an eleventh grade history text, for example, runs about 10,000 words in length. Table 2 shows what this means in terms of time expended by readers within the middle half and at the 10th and 90th percentiles.

Thus, when assigning a chapter of reading to a class, a teacher is demanding strikingly different amounts of time to be expended by the various levels of readers within the group. While the 50th percentile reader is being asked to spend 42 minutes to read the chapter, the 25th percentile reader must spend 54 minutes, and the 75th percentile reader will be finished in only 33 minutes. In the cases of the 10th and 90th percentile

TABLE 2

*Relative Average Number of Minutes Needed for 11th Grade Readers
to Read 10,000 Words*

LEVEL OF READER	AVERAGE RATE OF READING*	AVERAGE TIME NEEDED
90th percentile	359 words per minute	$\dfrac{10{,}000 \text{ words}}{359 \text{ w.p.m.}} = 28$ minutes
75th percentile	301 words per minute	$\dfrac{10{,}000 \text{ words}}{301 \text{ w.p.m.}} = 33$ minutes
50th percentile	236 words per minute	$\dfrac{10{,}000 \text{ words}}{236 \text{ w.p.m.}} = 42$ minutes
25th percentile	185 words per minute	$\dfrac{10{,}000 \text{ words}}{185 \text{ w.p.m.}} = 54$ minutes
10th percentile	140 words per minute	$\dfrac{10{,}000 \text{ words}}{140 \text{ w.p.m.}} = 71$ minutes

* As measured by the Nelson–Denny Reading Test Form A (1960 Edition).

people, the differences are even more dramatic. The 90th percentile reader
will be finished in only 28 minutes, while the 10th percentile reader must
plow on for a full 71 minutes. Can any teacher, then, be truly uncon-
cerned about individual differences in reading?

A final question might be raised here. Haven't I, in bringing in the
90th and 10th percentile people—certainly not part of the middle-half
group—beclouded the issue? Aren't these rather extreme examples for a
"normal" or regular classroom? On the familiar Gaussian Curve—not
infallible, but still "the curve" on which many teachers claim to grade
and to which they are implicitly alluding when they use the expression
"middle half"—the 25th, 50th, 75th percentile points represent low C to
high C. The 10th and 90th percentiles fall within the D and B ranges
respectively. Neither the A students nor the E's (nor even, truly, the high
B's or the low D's) fall within the 10th to 90th percentiles. If differences
extending into these *truly* extreme cases were to be considered, even the
differences presented here would appear small by comparison.

No, the examples presented here have *not* been extreme ones. What
we've looked at have been the differences in reading ability ordinarily
present within *average* classes at the high school level—first, the true middle half of a typical eleventh-grade group of readers, and then, for additional insight, the middle eighty percent. Gross differences *do* exist, and
no content teacher can ethically ignore them.

Informal Reading Inventories for the Content Areas: Science and Mathematics*

Edwin H. Smith,
Billy M. Guice,
and Martha C. Cheek

Any teacher or parent who as a student missed two days of a mathematics class or a foreign language class should understand the difficulties students face in a class when required to read material containing a number of words or phrases that present decoding and/or meaning difficulties. The authors show how to determine students' instructional reading levels in the areas of science and mathematics and provide informal reading inventories for accomplishing this purpose.

1. What is the major self-study tool used in learning in middle and secondary school years?

2. What is the significance of the studies by Janz and Cox?

3. How may an orally administered informal reading inventory give a false picture of a student's comprehension ability?

4. List the criteria for each of three reading levels.

5. Determine the percentage of interpretation questions at each level.

6. What would be the advantage of having four choices in the answer section?

7. In class or with colleagues discuss the meaning of the terms listed under each of the following headings: Science Reading Deficiencies; Mathematics Reading Deficiencies.

8. Use the inventories with some students and report your findings.

9. Extend the inventories several grade levels.

From the intermediate grades through the secondary school, students spend more time reading or trying to read in the subject matter areas than they spend in formal reading groups or sessions designed to develop their reading skills. From fourth grade through the university years, reading is the major self-study tool used in learning. If the assignments are correct, students learn through reading and at the same time develop their reading skills. If the assignments are incorrect, students are frustrated and tend to develop both learning problems and personality problems and THEY are held accountable for the mismanagement of their education.

* FROM *Elementary English*, 49 (May 1972), pp. 659–666, reprinted with permission of Edwin H. Smith and the National Council of Teachers of English.

One aid in the prevention of such educational mismanagement is the informal reading inventory.

Two of the major problems facing the content area teacher are: (1) How to determine the *readability levels* of the materials to be assigned her students and (2) How to determine the reading levels of her students in the content areas in which reading assignments will be made. The second of these problems will be dealt with here.

Recent research has disclosed that publishers' stated readability levels of textbooks and the readability levels disclosed by the application of readability formulas are often quite different. Janz (4) and Cox (2) found that publishers stated readability levels were often considerably under the readability levels determined by readability formulas. Thus, it is imperative that the teacher either apply readability formulas to the materials she is going to assign or, perhaps more validly, take samples from the materials to be used and informally test them with students whose reading levels have been determined and whose backgrounds are representative of the backgrounds of their classmates.

In the intermediate grades there tends to be a range in the reading levels of the students of five or more reading levels (1). At this stage of reading, a book that is one or more readability levels above the reading level of the student either cannot be used as a learning tool by such a student, or can be used by him *only* with extreme difficulty for short periods of time.

Informal reading inventories are of many types (3, 5, 6). Generally they consist of carefully graded reading passages arranged in order of increasing difficulty. The student being tested is asked to read the passages orally, beginning one or more readability levels below the readability level where the teacher thinks he might be. As he reads the teacher records his errors and when he finishes a passage she asks him questions about it. The kinds of errors noted include, *decoding errors* such as vowel, consonant, and syllabication difficulties; *perceptual errors* such as reversals, omissions, and transpositions, *rhythm errors* such as hesitancies, word by word reading, and regressions; and *processing errors* such as difficulties in structural analysis, detecting major details, and forming generalizations. However, the orally administered informal reading inventory may give a false picture of a student's comprehension ability; for oral reading is used primarily to send messages while silent reading is done to receive messages. Thus the student should do at least one silent re-reading of the test passages prior to the check. This is a normal process used in content area reading where two or more readings of the same material are often needed for effective processing, organizing, and memorizing.

In addition to noting decoding and processing difficulties, teachers using the informal reading inventory observe students for *signs of frustration*. These include damp palms, tense body, high voice, and finger pointing.

Generally several levels of reading are determined. One level is the *independent level*. At this level students make less than five errors per 100 running words and have little difficulty with word or passage comprehension. Another level is the *instructional level*. In the intermediate grades a student's instructional level is that readability level where he makes fewer than eight errors per 100 running words, and can answer seven out of ten questions (7). The third level the teacher seeks to determine is the *frustration level*. This is the level where the student may show signs of high anxiety, have difficulty with comprehension, and may make numerous word decoding errors.

For content area reading, the materials should be on the student's independent or instructional levels. Obviously, the less difficulty he has with the mechanics of reading the more efficiently he can process and remember what he reads. However, the standards given for the independent and instructional reading levels do not always hold up. Fast learners can often tolerate more errors than the upward limit while most slow learners cannot read effectively when they make six, seven, or eight errors per 100 running words. The standards are based on the middle group of learners and they should be so interpreted. As with most educational "tools" the teacher has to adjust them for use with individual students. The standards for the use of the informal inventory are guidelines, not absolute criteria. These guidelines may be used with any type of reading material and students should be given short informal inventories in materials they are assigned to read. Remember, in content area reading, to have the student do silent re-reading for the comprehension check.

The following Science and Mathematics informal reading inventories are abstracted from the Smith-Guice uncompleted manuscript *Teaching Development Reading*. They should be supplemented by an informal inventory in the material finally assigned.

Informal Science Reading Inventory

Name _____

Grade _____

Date _____

Readability Level 2.5

If you are like most people, you do many of the things a scientist does, but you do not do them as well. A scientist is trained to observe or look at things carefully. He *experiments*. He tries things out to see how well they work. He may have an idea for a new kind of airplane wing. He will read about airplanes. He will talk to people about airplanes. Then he may make a drawing of the wing he wants to build.

He may then make a model airplane using the new wing. After trying it out, he may then build a plane using his new wing and try it out.

A scientist keeps careful records of his work. In that way he can tell where he made mistakes. He can also use it to tell others about his work. Do you watch things closely? Do you make notes of your work? Do you try things out and change them after trying them out? If you do, who are you like?

Draw a line under the *best* answer.
1. When you try something out for the first time you are
   observing　experimenting　recording
2. Most scientists have been trained to

fly   record   build
3. A new airplane wing begins with
   a model   an idea   an experiment
4. A scientist's records tell him
   what he will do
   what his mistakes were
   what he should do

Readability Level 3.5

A scientist may work in a *laboratory*. That is a place where experiments take place. Some of these are controlled experiments or ones that are done in different ways. Both ways are almost the same, but there is one thing that is different. Suppose you want to know how light changes the growth of a certain kind of plant? Then you need two of the same kind of plants. They would have to be of the same age and size. The dirt they grow in would have to be the same. Both would have to have the same amount of water. The temperature of the room in which they grow should be the same for both. Then you would change one thing. One plant would get more light than the other plant. You would watch them carefully and keep notes to see what differences happen between the plants. You would find out how light changes the growth of that kind of plant.

Draw a line under the <u>best</u> answer.
1. How many things are different in a controlled experiment?
   one   two   three
2. The two plants in the experiment would not have the same amount of
   water   light   dirt
3. The experiment would work without
   notes   water   temperature control
4. The experiment would be best done with how many plants?
   two   four   eight

Readability Level 4.5

A tiny drop of water holds many little plants called *bacteria*. Bacteria are so small that they cannot be seen by the naked eye. Bacteria are not only found in water. They are found almost everywhere. They are in the ground, in the air, and on our bodies. You are housing millions of bacteria right now. Some are on your skin while others are inside your body. Most of the bacteria in your body are harmless and some of them are needed for good health, but bacteria can also be dangerous for they can cause disease.

There are three main kinds of bacteria. They are named for their shapes. Some are rod-shaped and these are called bacilli; some are circular and are called cocci. Still others are twisted and they are called spirilli. Bacteria may be seen through a *microscope* which is an instrument which magnifies or makes very small things look hundreds of times larger.

Draw a line under the *best* answer to each question.
1. Round bacteria are called
   bacilli   cocci   spirilli
2. Without bacteria we would be
   healthy   sickly   harmed
3. A microscope makes things appear
   small   tiny   larger
4. Most bacteria are
   harmless   good   bad

Readability Level 5.5

Trees that lose their leaves in the winter time are said to be *deciduous*. In contrast to the evergreens, their leaves change color and drop away because they are no longer getting enough sunlight.

Leaves get their green color from the *chlorophyll* in them. This chlorophyll, in combination with sunlight, manufactures food for a tree or other leafy plant. The process by which this is done is called *photosynthesis*. Chlorophyll, using water, carbon dioxide, and light, manufactures the tree's food. Lacking sufficient sunlight, the chlorophyll disappears and the leaves change color and drop off and the tree rests for the winter. Without its leaves, the tree can conserve enough water to last through the season. It can live on food it conserved in spring and summer.

Draw a line under the best answer to each question.
1. What is not needed for photosynthesis to take place?
   water   trees   sunlight
2. What manufactures the tree's food?
   photosynthesis   sunlight   chlorophyll
3. From where does the leaf get carbon dioxide?
   trees   water   air
4. Chlorophyll disappears because of a lack of
   water   carbon dioxide   sunlight

Readability Level 6.5

Three quarters of all of the animals in the world are *arthropods*. The arthropods are *invertebrates* or animals without backbones. They include insects such as spiders and ticks, and crustaceans such as shrimp and lobsters. All these arthropods have jointed legs and all of their bodies have a hard covering or shell.

Insects make up the largest group of arthropods and there are 900,000 different kinds of them. All of these species are the same in some general way and they are all different in some way. They all have bodies that are made up of three parts. These parts are the head, thorax, and abdomen. In addition to having those parts, all insects have six legs and most have one or two pairs of wings.

Draw a line under the best answer to each question.
1. Which of the following is not an arthropod?
   crab   squid   shrimp
2. All insects have
   six legs   jointed legs   wings
3. About what percentage of animals are arthropods?
   25   75   95
4. All arthropods have
   six legs   jointed legs   backbones

SCIENCE READING DEFICIENCIES RECORD

Sometimes it is useful to keep a record of specific science reading deficiencies. An example of one such record follows.

Science Reading Deficiencies

Name _____
Date _____
Grade _____

At his reading and science level the student has difficulty with the following:

1. Specialized science vocabulary _____
2. The classification pattern of writing _____
3. The explanation of a technical process _____
4. The problem-solution pattern _____
5. The instructions for an experiment pattern _____
6. Synthesizing _____
7. Drawing generalizations _____
8. Remembering abbreviations _____
9. Following the steps in an experiment _____
10. Shifting from word text to diagramatic text _____
11. Judging the soundness of hypotheses _____
12. Judging the soundness of conclusions _____
13. Applying generalizations to other problems _____
14. Visualizing relationships _____
15. Discerning time and/or space order _____
16. Using the glossary _____
17. Other _____
    _____

INFORMAL MATHEMETICS READING INVENTORY

Name _____
Grade _____
Date _____

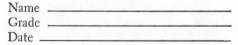

Readability Level 2.5

Three boys went fishing one day last week. Bill, the oldest boy, caught 3 fish. Tom, the youngest boy, caught 6 fish. Ed, the middle boy, caught 1 fish. Then they added the number of fish caught. It came to 10. The biggest fish weighed 2 pounds. The other 8 fish weighed 8 pounds. The boys had caught 10 pounds of fish in one morning. That was a lot of fish for them to catch. The boys took the fish to the store. There they sold them. The owner of the store gave them 1 dollar for the big fish and two dollars for the other fish. They thought that was a lot of money.

Draw a line under the best answer to each question.
1. The boy who caught the most fish was
   Tom   Ed   Bill
2. The biggest fish weighed
   1 pound   2 pounds   10 pounds
3. How much did the boys get for the fish?
   2 dollars   3 dollars   10 dollars
4. The boy who caught one fish was
   Ed   Bill   Tom

Readability Level 3.5

Bill knew how to add and subtract. He used these skills in counting change when buying things at the store. Bill knew that a quarter and a dime added up to 35 cents. Bill knew that a quarter, a dime, and a nickel added up to 40 cents. When Bill gave a storekeeper a dollar to pay an 85 cent bill, he expected to get 15 cents back. Today the teacher gave Bill some problems to do at home. She told him to get 5 pennies, 5 nickels, 5 dimes, 3 quarters, and 3 half-dollars.

Use in solving the problems shown below.

1. What 3 coins total 40 cents?
2. What 3 coins total 60 cents?
3. What 5 coins total 14 cents?

Bill divided his change into piles. After trying several different combinations he found that a quarter, a dime, and a nickel was the answer to the first problem. Two quarters and a dime was the answer to the second one. One dime and four pennies was the answer to the third problem. Bill was pretty good in arithmetic.

Draw a line under the best answer.
1. To do the problems Bill had to
   add   subtract   multiply
2. How many combinations did Bill try before he solved the first problem?
   one   two   three
3. Bill knew how to
   divide   subtract   multiply
4. How many piles of coin did Bill make?
   three   five   seven

Readability Level 4.5

Bill had to measure a table but he did not have a ruler, yardstick, or a tape measure. He thought about the problem. Then he remembered that his garage window is exactly 3 feet wide so he cut 2 sticks the width of the window. He put the two sticks on the table, but there was still some distance not covered. He then got a roadmap and found the scale of miles on it. On this scale one inch equals 10 miles. The scale was 6 inches long so he took a stick and marked it off in inches. He then measured the distance from the two yardsticks to the end of the table. He found that the table was 75 inches long or 6 feet 3 inches long. This afternoon Bill is going to town and buy a tape measure.

Draw a line under the best answer to each question.
1. How long was the table?
   2 yards 5 inches   3 feet 6 inches
   6 feet 3 inches
2. On the roadmap 6 inches equaled?
   6 miles   60 miles   5280 feet
3. Put together, the 3 sticks were how long?
   75 inches   72 inches   78 inches
4. The easiest way to have measured the table length would have been with a
   ruler   yardstick   tape measure

Readability Level 5.5

Bill and his father were planning a trip. Their cottage, near the river, was 240 miles away. They estimated that if they left home at 1:00 p.m. they could be at the house by 5:00 p.m. They could have the car unloaded by a quarter of 6:00 and walk the eighth of a mile to the river in 5 minutes. There they would fish until 8:30 and then go back to the house for, hopefully, a fish dinner.

The cottage lacked a water supply. They would take water with them. They estimated that they would need 30 gallons for 3 days. Since a pint of water weighs a pound, the water alone would weigh 240 pounds plus the weight of the containers. Bill and his father were careful planners.

Draw a line under the best answer to each question.
1. How many miles an hour did they plan to average for the trip?
   45   60   70
2. How much does a gallon of water weigh?
   10 lbs.   8 lbs.   5 lbs.
3. About how many feet was the house from the river?
   50   700   1000
4. Bill and his father's walking speed was
   slow   average   fast

Readability Level 6.5

With inflation hurting the family budget Mr. Jones decided to plant a family garden so he hired a man to plow up part of the back yard. It took the man two hours to plow a section 100 feet by 100 feet. The man was paid $3.00 an hour. Mr. Jones paid $5.00 for fertilizer and $3.00 for seeds and young plants. He also bought wire fence to go around the garden. The fence cost him 5¢ a foot. He took half a day off from work to put up the fence and that cost him $20.00. When he finally had the garden planted he asked his wife how much she spent on vegetables last summer. She told him that from June to September her vegetable bill was $185. Was Mr. Jones beating inflation by having a vegetable garden?

Draw a line under the best answer to each question.

1. When the fence was up it had cost Mr. Jones about
   $20.00 $40.00 $185.00
2. About how much will Mr. Jones save on vegetables if his garden supplies them for the summer?
   $10.00 $100.00 $200.00
3. How long did it take the man to plow 10,000 feet?
   2 hours   2 days   2 weeks
4. How much did Mr. Jones earn per hour?
   $1.00 $5.00 $10.00

Mathematics Reading Deficiencies Record

As the students are reading mathematics materials the teacher may want to observe them and record their mathematics reading difficulties. The check sheet that follows is one type of record that is useful in planning corrective work.

Mathematics Reading Deficiencies

Name _____
Date _____
Grade _____

At his reading and mathematics level the student has difficulties with the following:
1. Familiar words with specialized mathematics meaning   _____
2. Specialized mathematical terminology   _____
3. Terms that have multiple mathematical meanings   _____
4. Translating symbols into words   _____
5. Getting an overview of the problem   _____
6. Paraphrasing problems   _____
7. Visualizing relationships   _____

Reading combinations of words and symbols

1. Anticipating authors' wishes   _____
2. Translating generalized statements   _____
3. Phasing out information as it is not needed   _____

4. Recognizing the structure
   of problems _____
5. Listing the operations needed
   to solve problems _____
6. Ordering the elements of
   problems _____
7. Reading tables _____
8. Reading graphs _____
9. Deleting extraneous
   information _____
10. Estimating answers to
    problems _____
11. Inferring required processes _____
12. Other _____
   _____
   _____

3. Connotation _____
4. Adjusting Rate _____

Decoding
1. Grapheme-phoneme options _____
   _____
   _____
2. Syllabication _____
   _____
   _____
3. Dictionary pronunciations key _____
   _____
   _____
4. Other _____
   _____
   _____

This sample recording sheet for recording reading deficiencies can be elaborated or contracted according to teacher need.

Name _____
Date _____
Grade _____
Independent Level _____
Instructional Level _____

At his instructional reading level the student reveals the following deficiencies:

Perceptual
1. Reversals _____
2. Transpositions _____
3. Omissions _____
4. Other _____
   _____

Processing
1. Structural Analysis _____
2. Dictionary Meanings _____

Processing
1. Structural analysis _____
2. Dictionary meanings _____
3. Connotation _____
4. Adjusting rate _____
5. Typographical & other aids _____
6. Index _____
7. Main idea _____
8. Major details _____
9. Assumptions _____
10. Inferences _____
11. Generalizing _____
12. Evaluating _____
13. Other _____

Rhythm
1. Punctuation _____
2. Phrasing _____
3. Intonation _____
4. Syntax _____
5. Anticipation _____
6. Other _____
   _____

REFERENCES
1. Bond, Guy L., and Miles A. Tinker. *Reading Difficulties: Their Diagnosis and Correction,* second edition. New York: Appleton-Century-Crofts, Inc., 1967.
2. Cox, Juanita M. "An Investigation of the Reading Levels of Junior High School Students and the Readability Levels of Selected Modern Language Textbooks." Unpublished doctoral dissertation, College of Education, Florida State University, Tallahassee, Florida, 1970.

3. Deboer, John J., and Martha Dallman. *The Teaching of Reading,* revised edition. New York: Holt, Rinehart and Winston, Inc., 1964.
4. Janz, Margaret L. "An Investigation of the Reading Levels of Secondary School Students and the Readability Levels of Selected Modern Language Textbooks." Unpublished doctoral dissertation, College of Education, Florida State University, Tallahassee, Florida, 1969.
5. Johnson, Marjorie S., and Roy A. Kress. *Informal Reading Inventories.* Newark, Del.: International Reading Association, 1965.
6. McGinnis, Dorothy S. "Making Informal Inventories," in *Reading Diagnosis and Evaluation,* ed. by Dorothy L. DeBoer. Newark, Del.: International Reading Association, 1970, pp. 93–99.
7. Powell, William R., and Collin G. Dunkeld. "Validity of the IRI Reading Levels," *Elementary English,* 48 (October 1971), 637–42.

Problems in the Measurement of Reading Skills*

J. Jaap Tuinman
and B. Elgit Blanton

In this brilliant article Tuinman and Blanton explicate three problem areas in the measurement of reading skills: "the number of skills utilized during the act of reading, whether and how they should be taught, and whether they can be measured validly." Careful perusal of this article should help to clarify many issues confronting proponents and opponents of competency-based education.

1. Which kinds of skills have no psychological reality?

2. In discussing the number and kind of reading skills, what are the six points that must be considered?

3. How would you explain to someone why certain tests are not valid?

4. What kinds of problems exist related to test validity as determined by the test publisher and the eventual use of the test?

5. State key ideas in the article.

Reading is one of the more complex behaviors performed by man. As such it is comprised of a number of skills. Unfortunately gaps in our knowledge of the reading process and the acquisition of reading skill leave any discussion around the nature and number of reading skills an open issue. In fact, if Jeanne Chall had not already pre-empted the term, argument on this topic could justifiably be called The Great Debate. The urgency and importance of the issues focused on are magnified by the rapid rise of atom-

---

* Written especially for this volume.

ized competency tests for evaluating reading instruction based on instructional objectives emanating from seemingly infinite lists of reading skills.

Essentially, the debate focuses on three issues: the number of skills utilized during the act of reading, whether and how they should be taught, and whether they can be measured validly. This is of course an oversimplification, but nevertheless a realistic formulation. The purpose of this paper is to discuss the preceding issues as they relate to the debate over reading skills.

NUMBER OF READING SKILLS

Obviously there is no unique answer to the question regarding the number of skills requisite to or utilized during the act of reading. It is, however, necessary to demonstrate why this is the case in order to avoid the perennial confusion that seemingly surrounds the issue.

Under one interpretation, the term *reading skills* refers to a psychologically meaningful construct that is defined by inference rather than observation. Operationally, such skills are frequently defined as factors obtained from factor analyses of correlations among scores on a variety of reading tasks. The number of skills identified by this procedure, however, is necessarily a function of one's definition of reading and the measures employed. In addition, the correlations among particular measures may be unstable over time. Frequently these conditions are a function of time spent in instruction and the level of performance achieved. Consider, for instance, the correlation between speaking vocabulary and reading vocabulary of three-year-olds versus that correlation for nine-year-olds. Presumably that correlation is near zero for three-year-olds, because the reading scores for that group, being zero, show no variance. This, of course, is not true for the older subjects. On the other hand, such instability may follow from genuine changes in integration of abilities over time. The determination of factors underlying performance on a variety of reading tests, therefore, is not only a function of definition but of time in the learning sequence as well.

Reading skills can also be viewed from the perspective of basic literacy. More often then not, reading skills necessary for the individual to fulfill societal expectations are included under this topic. For example, behaviors such as the ability to complete an application form, ability to read traffic signs, ability to follow cooking directions, and so on, are listed. Skills in this sense are not defined by the statistical sediments of performances but rather by the intersection of specific reading material and, by implication, the demands these materials make upon the reader. However, in order to differentiate among these skills, one does not customarily make these demands explicit. There is no doubt that performance on such tasks could be explained by reference to a number of prerequisite skills and factors. On the other hand, there is some doubt as to whether the only justification for using the term *skills* here is the suspected independence among the skills requisite for basic literacy.

In the preceding discussion the term *skill* referred to terminal reading behavior rather than to performance on enabling reading skills. This is not true for the most hotly debated use of the term. By a process of subjective analysis, reading specialists have managed to produce almost inexhaustible lists of skills which by force of logical—but not necessarily psychological—argument "must" underlie the skill repertoire of the accomplished reader. Lately, such lists have been expressed in behavioral terms and have been referred to as behavioral objectives. Such skills lists usually imply some kind of hierarchy. Thus, one frequently encounters the argument that the teaching of reading should proceed in a sequence which reflects the hierarchy suggested by the behavioral objective lists. We might do well to point out, on the other hand, that the most frequently heard argument *against* the teaching of such skills is that they have no psychological reality, that performance on measures of these behaviors correlate so highly that their independent existence must be doubted. Regardless of the position one takes on this issue, the following points should be considered:

1. If we consider "reading a book" a terminal behavior, then there seems to be no doubt that the reader who has mastered this behavior can also show mastery of a set of less molar behaviors: turning a page, glancing from left to right, knowing the meaning of most words, and so on.

2. Enroute to a terminal reading behavior the set of component behaviors may grow and change in that some behaviors crucial at one point may become relatively less functional later in the reading process.

3. The fact that one can show mastery of a particular reading behavior, such as pausing after a comma when reading orally, does not reveal anything about how the behavior has been acquired. It may have been taught directly or indirectly or may have resulted from a student's instigated analysis of his or another reader's behavior.

4. To demand that reading behaviors or skills be independent in order to be considered for inclusion in the instructional process implies application of a nonrelevant criterion. If it can be shown that the teaching of skill A facilitates acquisition of skill B, justification for separate identification of A exists even if at the moment B is acquired A and B correlate perfectly, as they would if A were a necessary and sufficient condition for B.

5. The criterion needed for making decisions about the sensibility of discriminations among skills and about the justification of hierarchies must be one which relates to the efficiency of attainment of terminal reading behaviors. This means that one needs empirically established hierarchies in order to refute listings of skills that have been intuitively drawn up. It should be sufficient to refer to the work of Gagné (3) and to Bormuth's (2) discussion of this issue for elaboration of this comment.

6. The fact that empirical hierarchies can be established which show that mastery of skill B is contingent upon mastery of skill A still does not

imply that the teaching of reading must involve the direct teaching skills. Alternate routes, predicated on the assumption that such mastery will be indirectly acquired, are logically possible. Again, however, we have neither the evidence nor very good notions about how to acquire it, which would permit us to pronounce a particular detailed list of reading skills as either "good" or "bad."

A Test's Robustness Against Invalidating Factors

Leaving the issues related to the number and nature of reading skills, we would now like to consider some aspects of the validity of reading tests as measures of reading skills. A test may generally be a valid measure of reading behavior for some specific purpose and yet be invalid when it is applied for that purpose on some particular occasion. To illustrate this case, one must distinguish between a test's validity and its resistance to inadvertent or deliberate perversion of this validity. A simple illustration of the distinction can be formed by a short test of sight words. Let's call the short test of sight words the STSW. The test consists of twenty common words. It is used with a class of children who have not been taught to decode. No independent word-attack skills have been introduced to the students. The students in this class, however, have had instruction on a basic list of sight words. This list of sight words is sampled by the items of the STSW. It seems, therefore, fair to say that the STSW is a valid test of sight words in the situation described. Yet it is not very robust against invalidating factors. The teacher using this test would never discover that a number of her students responded not on the basis of memory for the word forms, but because they had a number of decoding skills as the result of activities they were exposed to out of the regular class.

The ease with which reading tests can be further invalidated is demonstrated by the fact that very few items in most tests are answerable exclusively by way of operations employed during the reading behavior sampled, although this is the basis on which the validity of items is assumed. The same point can be expressed differently: Though most members of a group respond to the items in the way the measurement operation was visualized, individuals may employ idiosyncratic strategies that tend to invalidate the testing. A concrete illustration of lack of robustness against such invalidating tendencies follows.

Consider for the moment that most tests of reading comprehension purport to measure how well a student understands what he is reading. Many of these tests employ questions to ascertain the degree of this understanding. At face value, these tests are very similar to any achievement test using the familiar multiple-choice format. In the case of reading comprehension tests, however, the tacit assumption exists that there is a direct relationship between the reading of the passage or the story and the ability to answer questions about it. In the case of a great many reading test items from standardized tests, this is a faulty assumption. It has been well demonstrated that probability of a correct answer to reading the paragraph exceeds chance in the case of most reading comprehension questions (6, 4, 1, 5, 7, 9). In short, the answers to items measuring comprehension on some tests may not depend directly on reading.

Test authors and publishers have given little attention to passage dependency. Its desirability has been only sporadically stressed by test reviewers. Tuinman (7) conducted a study exploring the effects of passage dependency on comprehension. The study had three purposes. First, attention was called to the degree of lack of passage dependency by obtaining data on six major reading tests. Secondly, an attempt was made to produce reliable item validity statistics (in particular, passage-dependency indexes) by using samples larger than those used in most of the research reviewed above. Thirdly, the shift in passage dependency of items and tests as a function of educational growth of the respondents was demonstrated by selecting subjects in three consecutive grade levels.

The final selection of tests used in the study was as follows:

Test 1. *Nelson Reading Test,* Form A (Number of items: 75).

Test 2. *California Achievement Tests,* Level 3, Form A (Number of items: 42).

Test 3. *SRA-Achievement Series, Reading,* Form E, Blue level (Number of items: 60).

Test 4. *Metropolitan Achievement Tests, Reading*—Elementary Battery Form F (Number of items: 45).

Test 5. *Metropolitan Achievement Tests, Reading*—Intermediate Battery, Form F (Number of items: 45).

Test 6. *Iowa Test of Basic Skills*—*Reading,* Multilevel, Form S (Number of items: 60).

Briefly, experimental versions of the tests were created by mimeographing the passages and the items separately. The tests were administered to fourth-, fifth-, and sixth-graders. Under one condition, part of the subjects read passages from the test followed by questions. Under the other condition, part of the subjects answered test questions without reading passages.

Table 1 details the extent to which the scores under the nonpassage condition exceeded chance scores. The entries in the cells can be contrasted directly with those in column 5, representing chance scores. In actuality, if a comprehension test item were passage dependent, subjects would not be able to answer test questions beyond the level of chance without reading the passages. As can be seen, Tests 4, 5, and 6, in particular, show a high degree of passage independency. The fourth-graders to whom Test 4 was administered managed to answer correctly 50 per cent of the items, even though they never read the passages upon which the items were based. Tests 5 and 6 fared little better, and even Tests 1, 2, and 3 resulted in "guessing" scores which are far above the level of statistical chance.

TABLE 1

Means Under the No Passage (NP) Expressed as (1) Percentages of the Number of Items in the Test and as (2) Percentages of the Means Obtained Under the Passage (P) Condition

TEST	x_P	x_{NP}	x_{NP} AS % OF NUMBER OF ITEMS	CHANCE SCORE (%)	x_{NP} AS % OF x_P
1	45.96	29.36	39	25	64
2	26.66	14.36	34	24	54
3	37.17	22.17	37	25	60
4	29.54	22.27	50	25	75
5	28.82	20.27	45	25	70
6	27.03	19.29	46	25	71

The entries in the last column are even more startling. Of the six tests, three allowed a student who did not have the passages to obtain a score as high as 70 per cent of what a student with the passages would have received. On the average, for these tests, not reading the passage resulted in a loss of performance of less than 30 per cent. Tests 1, 2, and 3 present only a slightly more reassuring picture. It may be noted that if one takes 60 per cent of the number of items as a typical mean score for multiple-choice tests, the expected chance score of 25 per cent represents approximately 40 per cent of the score obtained under the passage condition. Again, Test 2 shows up more favorably than the other tests.

It becomes obvious from the preceding data that none of the six tests approached passage dependency close to optimal limits. This is not so surprising in view of the fact that it is extremely difficult to construct highly passage-dependent items, even if the passages contain highly imaginary materials (1). In addition, as expected, the degree to which items are passage dependent is a function of the age, the I.Q. and educational sophistication of the child that takes the test. Tests in the preceding study, designed for grades 4–6, showed a consistent decrease in passage dependency from fourth-graders to sixth-graders. This fact should be kept in mind by the test user who decides to select a test with a wider grade range.

SUBSTANTIATING TEST VALIDITY

Up to this point our discussion has focused on the robustness of reading tests against certain invalidating factors, such as instruction and passage dependency. We would now like to discuss an additional problem area related to test validity. In particular, we would like to underline problems related to test validity as determined by the test publisher and the eventual use of the test.

First of all, let's consider the type of evidence publishers tend to provide as evidence of the validity of their products. Because validity is often defined in terms of the usage a test is put to, it seems logical to ask to what extent publishers can be expected to furnish validity data. One cannot expect that technical reports accompanying tests contain data which show that the test is valid per se. Neither can one demand that such reports present information which covers all possible usages of a test. The test user does have a right to request, however, that validity data are provided which make it possible for him to decide whether or not the test can be validly used for the purposes stated directly and implied indirectly by the publisher. If any statement by the author or the publisher appears in the manual or elsewhere which indicates the appropriateness of the test for some particular purpose, such statements should be backed up by adequate evidence. To this extent a test publisher *can* be held responsible.

The construction of most published tests involves procedures aimed at establishing content validity. To achieve content validity for a wide range of users is a difficult matter. Generally test publishers rely heavily on the input of qualified experts with regard to the selection of subject matter to be included in their tests. "Evidence" of content validity typically consists of listings of curricular materials from which items were drawn. Occasionally the familiar grid combining subject matter and taxonomy behavior categories is presented. The extent to which this kind of evidence is helpful to test users depends on the degree of detail in which it is presented. Presumably the user can always match the content of the test in terms of subject matter with the content of his curriculum. No such easy match is possible, however, in terms of the behavioral taxonomy underlying the items.

The remainder of our discussion of evidence of test validity will be restricted to the criterion-related validity of reading tests. One should logically assume that the criteria upon which the validity of a particular test is based are selected prior to the building of the test. The logic of test building seems to require that one builds the test in order to be valid for something definite, not that one builds a test in the hope that there will be some criterion in relationship to which it will be valid. Yet we are firmly convinced that the latter procedure is very common. There are hardly any technical data to be found in the descriptions of a number of tests we reviewed which do indicate that the validity obtained is the end product of a plan of systematic improvement during the test development phase.

The fact that some tests are published prior to any validity studies is in itself an indication of lack of systematic inquiry as to the validity of tests on the side of the test builder. Other evidence also exists. For one, the large discrepancy found to exist between the sample sizes used for norming and for validity studies seems to point to a certain casualness as far as ascertaining validity is concerned. Let us underline this point with the following examples. In the *Burnett Reading Series Survey Test*, 6,076 seventh-graders were used for norming the intermediate level test. Surprisingly, 1,456 of these were drawn for establishing reliability. The only validity data reported involved thirty-eight (sic) students. Similarly, the *Traxler Silent Reading Test*, 1969 revision, Level 7-10, reports criterion-related validity data involving only eighty ninth-graders for correlation of the test with school grades and fifty-four sixth-graders for correlation with a composite of four other reading tests.

The unsystematic nature of test builders' attempts to show validity for their tests is probably most clearly reflected in the choice of criteria used for establishing criterion-related validity. In addition to encountering a potpourri of tests with which the new test is being correlated, the student of test manuals is faced with the fact that the rationale for inclusion of particular tests for validity criteria is seldom given. Generally three classes of criteria are included in the more extensive technical reports: grades, intelligence test scores, and other reading test scores. High correlations with these criteria are thought of as desirable and quoted with a certain satisfaction. It seems, however, that a few questions may be asked in regard to the appropriateness of these criteria and that these questions justify the test user's expectation of a much more reasoned selection of criteria by the test developer. So far, the overriding reason for reporting the correlation with certain criteria seems to be the availability of the criteria rather than their appropriateness.

Let's take a look at teacher grades. Why should a reading test correlate highly with teacher grades? Or, a somewhat tougher question: If a reading test does not correlate highly with teacher grades, what does that mean in terms of the test's validity? Only if the major job the test is designed to do is predicting grades can an unequivocal answer be given to this question. The issue becomes even more complicated if one looks at the type of grades reading tests are often correlated with. In addition to grades in reading, grades in English, arithmetic, science, and so on, function as criteria. How to interpret high or low correlations in terms of the original purposes for which the reading tests were built is almost never made clear.

Many of the same questions can be asked when considering the correlation of reading test scores with intelligence tests. When one studies test manuals one gets the impression that the test authors hoped to maximize the correlation with such tests. Why? What *if* a reading test correlates .90 with an intelligence test? What does that tell us about the test as a test of reading? Moreover, why should we, other than in a tangential way, be very concerned with the predictive validity of reading tests in terms of forecasting I.Q. scores? As matters stand now, we have such I.Q. scores on our students anyway. Yet if any criterion-related validity data are reported at all, chances are that I.Q. scores make up for a large part of the criteria included. We are not suggesting that such information is totally worthless. We simply maintain that it is mostly so, unless a rationale for the inclusion of such data for a particular reading test is presented. As a general case, such validity data make the test very little more interpretable for the test user.

Then there are the other reading test scores. Often when correlations between a test and a number of criteria are reported, some reading scores are included among the criteria. Yet the actual number of such referents is often surprisingly small. A typical case is illustrated by examining the tables found in the manual of one of a number of widely used reading tests. Of the twenty-six correlations reported for the comprehension section of this test, only two are correlations between this test and another reading subtest. This is indeed a surprising finding; it is not, however, unique to this test.

Let's consider the possible rationales for inclusion of other reading tests as criteria somewhat closer. We do not expect to encounter much disagreement when we say that, for instance, most reading tests used in college and high school contain comprehension sections that are similar. Similarly, the stated purposes for inclusion of these tests in the battery don't differ very much. Builders of new tests basically can adopt one of the following positions:

1. They want to build a test which has the same purposes as existing tests and they are satisfied that existing tests achieve that purpose, i.e., are valid.
2. They want to build a test which has the same purposes as existing tests and they want to achieve superior validity.
3. They want to build a test notably different in purposes than any existing test.

Considering the preceding positions, what kind of validity data can we expect such a test constructer to present? In considering this question we will limit ourselves for the present to the issue of correlations with other reading tests.

CASE 1: SAME PURPOSES—SAME VALIDITY. This test builder simply has to identify which tests, or subtests, match his test or subtest in purpose. Because he accepts the validity of the other test as satisfactory and merely wants to produce a new product (less expensive, less time-consuming, or simply profitable), he then has to show that the correlation of his test(s) with these criterion tests is satisfactory. It is up to the test user to evaluate the purpose of the criterion tests, their evidence of validity, and the size of the correlation between the new test and the criterion tests.

CASE 2: SAME PURPOSES—SUPERIOR VALIDITY. Here the test builder's task is a more complex one. As in Case 1 he will have to identify the tests or subtests which basically purport to do the same thing his test is designed to do. A simple correlation coefficient between his test and the criterion test, however, is of no use in demonstrating superior validity. A perfect correlation would be damaging in terms of the premise of unsatisfactory validity of the criterion test. A less than perfect correlation could be due not only to obtaining superior validity but to a host of other, and probably more likely, factors as well. Various different approaches might be followed, depending on the particular purposes of the tests.

CASE 3: DIFFERENT PURPOSE. Here again, correlations with other tests are needed as part of the validity evidence. Yet such correlations do not necessarily have to be high. As a matter of fact, under specified circumstances they should not be. If a test author constructs a test different in purpose to any existing test, his first responsibility is to show validity independent of correlations with those other tests. If such correlations are included in the validity, a clear rationale and a careful interpretation for that action needs to be presented.

The preceding discussion of the meaning of correlations of reading tests with other reading tests can be summarized as follows: To present correlations indiscriminately of one's reading test with the other tests is meaningless, except for one narrow area of interpretation: prediction. As a general case, the prediction of scores on one reading test in terms of scores on another seems, however, a rather trivial preoccupation. From the discussion of the correlations among reading tests presented in current manuals one gets the definite impression that the intent is to show that the test under consideration does indeed do the job it was supposed to do or at least does not do that job worse than the other tests. The discussion of the three different cases pertaining to the construction of a new test is intended to illustrate that in many cases the mere presenting of correlations between a test and some other reading test constitutes insufficient and even uninterpretable evidence.

In summary, we have presented a discussion of a number of what we consider to be key issues related to reading skills and their measurement. First we have focused on alternate perspectives of the "number of reading skills" issue. Second, we have suggested that the validity of a reading test is in part an issue of the test's robustness with regard to invalidation factors which may operate in varying degrees any time the test meets a student. Finally, we have analyzed the rationale behind providing various kinds of criterion-related validity evidence. Admittedly, our discussion has been brief. Nevertheless, we feel that many of the points we have made will enable the reader to view the problems associated with reading skills and their measurement from a new perspective.

REFERENCES

1. Bickley, A. C., W. Weaver, and Fraughton Ford. Information removed from multiple-choice item responses by selected grammatical categories. *Psychological Reports*, 23 (1968), 613–14.

2. Bormuth, J. R. *On the Theory of Achievement Test Items.* Chicago: University of Chicago Press, 1970.

3. Gagné, R. M. *Conditions of Learning.* New York: Holt, Rinehart and Winston, Inc., 1968.

4. Farr, R., and C. B. Smith. "The Effects of Test Item Validity on Total Test Reliability and Validity," in *Reading: Process and Pedagogy. Nineteenth Yearbook of the National Reading Conference,* edited by G. Schick and M. M. May. Vol. 1, Milwaukee, Wis., 1970, 122–34.

5. Mitchell, R. W. "A Comparison of Children's Responses to an Original and Experimental Form of Subtests GS and ND of the *Gates Basic Reading Tests.*" Unpublished Doctoral Dissertation, University of Minnesota, *Dissertation Abstracts,* 1967, 9704A.

6. Preston, R. C. "Ability of Students to Identify Correct Responses Before Reading," *Journal of Educational Research,* 58 (1964), 181–83.

7. Tuinman, J. J. Selected Aspects of the Assessment of the Acquisition of Information from Reading Passages. Unpublished Doctoral Dissertation, University of Georgia, 1970.

8. ———. *Obtaining Indices of Passage Dependency of Comprehension Questions,* Indiana University, Final Report, USOE Project No. 2-E-005, 1972.

9. Weaver, W., and A. C. Bickley. Sources of Information for Responses to Reading Test Items, APA *Proceedings, 75th Annual Convention,* 1967, 293–94.

Section 8

Reading, Learning, and Human Development

Introduction

Man is a complex being. He is able to initiate ideas, to see how ideas are related, and to make decisions about these ideas. He is not an automaton that follows a predetermined sequence of instructions; on the contrary, he has some choice about what he is going to do and how he is going to do it. Yet the plans that he makes and is able to to carry out have a dimension of contingency; that is, these plans and their chances for successful execution are affected by such factors as his abilities, his interests, and his past decisions and accomplishments.

How a child will accomplish his many developmental and learning tasks depends, in part, on whether he is permitted to work on the tasks that suit his abilities, and his

223

needs and interests. He will have a chance (1) to complete tasks (such as reading) successfully; (2) to grow; and (3) to learn—if his teachers and parents utilize what the various disciplines tell us about how children develop and learn.

In this group of articles the authors draw upon the findings of research to explain how reading instruction can profit from what is known about the principles of human development and learning. The authors show how teachers can enhance the probabilities that children will learn and enjoy it. They show how the wise teacher arranges optimal conditions for learning, and then utilizes known principles of human development and learning in teaching pupils how to read well.

RECENT RESEARCH SOURCES FOR MIDDLE AND SECONDARY SCHOOL READING PROBLEM AREAS*,†

A. J. Lowe

Lowe has done a masterful and near-Herculean job in reviewing the research in key areas of reading that have applications especially for middle and secondary school reading instruction. These findings should be scrutinized carefully.

Freely translated, to *research* something means "to *take another look at* something." Before we lightly dismiss the efforts of those who have carefully taken another look at principles and practices in reading, let's see what they have found. Research isn't "just" theory, but it is a testing of theory; it is, so to speak, "taking

theory to task" by testing it out. For this research to mean anything to you, it will be necessary for you to "come to grips" with it, be active in analyzing and discussing it.

1. State the key ideas of each area of research.

2. To what extent do you agree or disagree with the findings as interpreted by Lowe? State your arguments. Discuss them in class.

3. Do you see the need for more research? Explain.

4. What implications for teaching do you see in these research findings?

Because of time and space limitations, this review was of a highly selective nature, a "writer's choice," with an emphasis on the basic causes and careful cures of reading problems in middle and secondary schools. In the main,

* Written especially for this volume.

† Acknowledgement is gratefully given to the EDR 635 students who allowed the use of their reviews in this paper and to Barbara Kelly who typed the original manuscript.

the reader is cautioned to peruse the original studies or reviews himself. There have been over 1,000 studies made in secondary reading in the past decade or so. As is usually the case, carefully designed and executed studies were relatively few in number. However, if a study or review was not mentioned here, the reader should not assume it was a poor one, as any reviewer will miss some sources. This review contains good news and bad news in that it was good that much attention was paid to secondary school reading problems but it was bad news to learn that the efforts were so unsuccessful.

LARGE-SCALE EFFORTS

Garner (24) reviewed the research on disadvantaged students reading in grades 7–9. She found that over $600 million had been spent on reading programs for disadvantaged students and the results of these programs (such as Compensatory Education, E.S.E.A., Performance Contracting OEO) were, when reported clearly, not fruitful. The review of independent studies showed few (only the well-designed and well-executed ones) as being worthwhile. Her overall conclusion was that "reading programs for Black and other disadvantaged students did not prove to be successful in significantly improving reading achievement" (24, p. 48).

The results of the $5.6 million OEO funding of six private contractors to teach reading and math to the disadvantaged in 1970–71 was reported in 1972 (44). Gains for students in grades 7–9 were negligible in all grades. It was concluded by OEO personnel that "performance contracting *was no more effective* than . . . traditional classroom methods . . . in working with culturally disadvantaged students" (44, p. 10).

BASIC THEORY

Holmes (32) studied 400 secondary students in testing his "Substrata-Factor Theory of Reading." Some fifty-six tests were given, and "Vocabulary" accounted for most of the variance, with "Reasoning" and "Range of Information" contributing much in support of "Vocabulary." The work of Holmes and his associates should be considered very important in studying problem readers. Again verbal intelligence and listening seemed to be the key to reading, i.e., reading to oneself suborally, as most people do.

Wiener and Cromer (71) wrote in 1967 one of the most thought-provoking and serious analyses of reading difficulties that this writer read. Numerous definitions of "reading" and the idea that reading is a part of language which is verbal intelligence in action were discussed. Four assumptions—relating to defect, deficiency, disruption, and difference—were elaborated upon and the authors restated their ideas that "poor readers have evolved different response patterns, i.e., they elaborate 'cues' in a manner different from that of good readers" (71, pp. 630–31). Various models for conceptualizing reading difficulty were given but one for true "silent" or "nonoral" reading was not. [As Puleo (55) has reviewed the research in this area, it will be discussed next.]

Puleo (55) reviewed the research on silent, nonoral, covert, internal, and inner-speech types of reading. She found that quite a number of studies have been made in class, clinic, and laboratory informally and formally since 1900. It is known that fluent readers don't necessarily have to "hear" when they read covertly and can "listen" to themselves as they wish to. It is indeed an enigma in reading that when people are taught to read they are not taught to see and comprehend *sans* vocalization. It is no mystery why listening or auditory perception and discrimination load up high next only to verbal intelligence when analyses are performed on the components of "reading." If we can help people to read truly silently, we may be able to "cure" a lot of reading ills.

Kling (39) and his associates have recently published a compendium of reading models which will be mentioned in this review. The reader is urged to study Wiener and Cromer's article carefully.

INTELLIGENCE, RACE, AND READING

Fishbein and Emans (17) have written on the intelligence and language bases for reading. The text is a combination of the authors' work and reading as well as that of selected scholars such as Carroll, Piaget, Chomsky, and Bruner. The authors stated that, "Both frustration and imitation may lead to failure (and it seems that each) child has an optimal rate of learning and an optimal environment" (21, p. 224). The one drawback of the book is that there is no subject index, but a name index is included.

Rohwer (59), in reviewing his research and that of others, discussed the areas of intelligence testing, learning, school success, and "race." His work is of a scholarly nature far above morbid racism or petty unprofessionalism. Rohwer has demonstrated that if Low SES blacks are given training and practice in *how* to "make it" in school before they are subjected to the school language and learning styles, they will often do as well as or better than whites. He feels that intelligence tests are reflective, *not* judgmental, and that tests of measuring learning style and proficiency are needed. He also recommended that low SES blacks have programs as early in life as possible which will help them to master learning skills (reading, computation, and so on). By actualizing children's capacity for imaginative conceptual activity through concrete explicit instruction programs, Rohwer feels that LSES blacks can succeed in school work.

Rystrom and Cowart (60) tested their hypothesis that the race of the tester has a significant influence upon testees' decoding scores. There were one black and white teacher in each of two grade 2 classes of thirty each (50 per cent white and black students used in the study). The first 110 words of the *Dolch Basic Sight Word Test* were used. Each teacher tested black and white students and an analysis of variance and Scheffe contrasts showed that the black students read fewer words correctly when evaluated by the white teacher and that this was the only significant (.01) contrast. The authors could have used a larger sample and a more suitable word list. But the results probably would have been the same as others have found, which, simply stated, is that as teachers we should appreciate patois, accent, dialect, or whatever and not assume that difference means deficit.

Shockley (62) responded to Light and Smith's (48) study with an analysis of their data and references to his own work and that of others. He has been criticized of late as being a "racist" of sorts, as was Garrett (25) a decade ago. If the reader is not versed in genetics and statistics, Shockley's article will be rough reading. However, and not to oversimplify or distort, we hope, the basic questions seemed to be these: (1) Are blacks genetically inferior to whites in some proportion? (2) Are blacks only inferior to whites on a social–cultural–educational basis? (3) Are both of these propositions in error and do we need to search for new ones? It is very difficult to perform basic research with humans, including orphans, adoptees, or whatever. The scholarship of *ex post facto* studies is suspect (though in some cases unfairly). The idea that "poorness" and "dumbness" are highly related phenomena is a questionable one, especially in a society which pays for talent but uses machines to replace nontalent labor. In sum, it seems evident that Shockley feels that eventually a genetic proof will be found for low-socioeconomic-status blacks' lack of success in such activities as reading.

Stodolsky and Lesser (67) discussed their research and that of others in the area of the disadvantaged's learning patterns. They approached the problem from an environmental stance and not from a child development point of view. The argument was given that because ethnic membership cannot be changed, the schools must provide equal educational opportunity to maximize development, even if the differences among groups increases. In sum, if all groups "get better," then the rank order may not change, but all may move up the scale.

PROGRAMS AND EVALUATION

As long ago as 1962, Bliesmer (4) published an article on the evaluation of gains in remedial reading programs. In the last few years, the span of this review, there have been countless numbers of such studies performed and, in many cases, reported in the literature. Few of these reports contained any mention of evaluation, especially comparing the experimental growth with usual, past, or expected growth. Thus, and also because of the delimitations of the review, these hundreds of studies are not reported here. Only an exceptionally good study or one which covered a longitudinal span (including follow-up) is reported.

Rankin (58) devised a residual gains technique which can be a great aid in evaluating reading programs. Again, most published reports of remedial programs did not use this available technique. By use of the formula, a check can be made to see if gains are real or superficial. Simply defined, *residual gain* is the derivation of the *observed* posttest score from the post-test score that is *predicted* from the pretest score. In this age of account-ability it may be wise to use such a technique and have any performance contractor use it also. However, one needs to be able to perform simple statistical analyses of data in order to use the technique.

Bliesmer (5), best known for his annual reviews of research in college–adult reading, discussed the problems involved in trying to do classroom (action) research. Realizing that "statistical overkill" can obscure favorable results, he presented an analysis of the practical problems. (More often published are *ex post facto* evaluation studies rather than research reports. If the reader is interested in doing *research* in a classroom setting, then he had best realize what he is about. A number of fine articles such as this one have appeared over the years, yet they go unheeded, probably because they are not read. It was quite obvious to this writer that the bulk of publica-tions in secondary reading were of little use to the classroom teacher.)

Gwaltney's (28) study is one of the better-designed evaluation studies of federally funded programs. He reported on a seven-week summer pro-gram for sixty tenth- and eleventh-grade Upward Bound students. Pre-, post-, and delayed (ten weeks) postdata were analyzed. No significant differ-ences were found on post- or delayed postdata. An analysis of variance showed (as it usually does) that intelligence and listening accounted for most (77.34 per cent) of the variance and each correlated over .80 as predictor variables with reading. Gwaltney felt that uncontrollable factors (optimum reading levels already reached before program started, lack of desire, inappropriate materials, and so on) may have caused a lack of progress.

Kimble and Davison (38) tested ninth- through twelfth-grade students at the Chilaco Indian Boarding School with the *Nelson Denny Reading Test* and the *San Diego Quick Word Test* and designed a program for the lowest 20 per cent's gross reading deficiencies. The plan included rein-forcement in the form of portable radios, cameras, and wrist watches for gains earned. Needs such as cultural bases of language, idiomatic confusion, auditory and visual discrimination, word meaning, linguistic cues, written English patterns, elements of style in literature, word-attack skills, and free readings were worked with. The size of classes ranged from ten to thirteen and the classes met daily for fifty-minute periods. The mean differences between February and May test scores were significant for grades 10 and 11 but not for grades 9 and 12 (almost) on the *NDRT*, but all grades made significant gains on the *SDQWT*. When the data were grouped, total mean gains were significant. Now, when it is considered that the first passage on the *NDRT* is written at the college level and the *SDQWT* is not composed of just common words, it is remarkable that such progress was made. However, the more difficult the words and passages, the more "reading needs" would be evidenced and the authors might then know that the students were not as deficient as indicated.

Kling (39) reported a special two-week summer reading and study program for sixty-one disadvantaged high school graduates held at Rutgers. The group was 84 per cent black and 16 per cent white, 53 per cent female and 47 per cent male. Math work was done in the morning period; the work from 1:00 to 4:15 P.M. consisted of reading and study with "core" reading for 90 minutes, vocabulary and study skills for 40 minutes, and an individualized reading class for 40 minutes. There was a total of 22 hours testing and instruction time. Only forty-three students showed up for posttesting but attendance was "high . . . even on Labor Day." Kling is quite aware of the problem involved in a quickie course, small N, statistical overkill, reading tests (NDRT), and disadvantaged black students. In any event, the subjects improved their scores on the NDRT significantly (.01), but as Rutgers freshmen average at the 75th percentile on the NDRT the students' postmeans in the 40th percentile would indicate they would have trouble competing at Rutgers. Kling concluded that despite the limitations of the study it was apparently possible to produce significant results in a short time. No mention was made of what happened to the students.

Jung (36) reported a comparison of 1960 and 1970 Project Talent high school juniors on an eight-passage, 30-minute reading comprehension scale which contained social studies, natural science, and literary content (in prose and poetry forms). Students were permitted to look back at the passages which had a vocabulary found in the first 15,000 entries of the 1944 Thorndike–Lorge List. Neither readability estimates nor passage reliabilities were given in the report. A fifth of the schools involved in the 1960 survey participated in the 1970 study. The various strata of the first group were kept proportionately the same for the later group. The results indicated that little or no gain in reading comprehension had been made. Jung felt that the study might be renamed "No Progress in Education." However, it may be that timed reading tests will yield consistent results year after year in normally distributed populations or perhaps attrition rates decreased in the schools so that "poorer" readers added to the regression toward the mean. But standard deviations were not that different in the groups so, no progress or not, it seemed that reading is not getting "better" or "worse."

Hill (31) reviewed twenty-five surveys of secondary reading activity with ten of the sixteen selected by Hill as pertinent being published between 1961 and 1969. He felt that some progress was being made but perhaps more because of "social-political pressures and Federal funds . . ." (31, p. 25). Hill commented that perhaps at least one half of the secondary schools in the United States made some planned provisions for reading improvement. However, if Lowe's (50) study is representative, probably most secondary schools are working with reading now. However, this writer knows of no national survey that has been published. Hill found that the most common program was junior high school classes taught by English teachers who lacked reading training.

Cole (10) reviewed Delacato's treatise on "dyslexics" and neural organization. Cole's credentials—physician on the staff of the Language Clinic of Massachusetts General—may lend credence to his statements. The review was included in this work because so many parents and teachers have been exploited by "Institutes for Achievement of Human Potential" and a host of other "dyslexia" clinics. The reader should see the original review in which Cole stated, "in a sense, this (Delacato's) is a dangerous book, because of the large amount of truth it contains, skillfully strung together in such a way as to mask a multitude of *post hoc ergo propter hoc* propositions which are quite unjustified in the light of modern neurophysiology" (10, p. 354). (This writer chose not to waste the reader's time reviewing Delacoto's and his supporter's studies.)

REINFORCEMENT

DeShayes (16) reviewed the research in reinforcement of secondary school students' reading behavior. She found that the social behavior of the subjects was improved by the reinforcement and that in all but one study, gains in reading were significant. A most interesting finding was that the work was done in regular classes with the regular teachers and/or paraprofessionals. DeShayes concluded that high-priced and highly educated people are not necessary for such programs to succeed.

Duggins (17) has compiled a most interesting collection of articles for a book of readings not about what reading is in terms of speed, comprehension, and so on, but about what the *human* aspects of reading are. Articles selected for the book range in publication date from 1948 to 1972, but the choices were quite appropriate. Chapter topics included bibliotherapy, language experience, and attitudinal effects on and of reading. The reader is referred to this text for help for problem readers.

Lipe and Jung (49) have presented an excellent review of the research on incentives to improve academic performance. Although not specifically directed at reading, the studies cited certainly have import for language development. The students' internal and external environments were delineated at focal points for research. The authors felt that cognitive mediation can be provided between present behaviors and future rewards. Standardized tests were listed as the primary criterion for large-scale incentive delivery. Criterion-referenced tests, with a parallel-item pool, were mentioned as the most promising development for developing and establishing criteria for incentive delivery systems. Types of stimulus incentive studies reviewed were material incentives, social incentives, knowledge of results, secondary reinforcement, vicarious reinforcement, and aversive incentives.

Response manipulation areas reviewed were high versus low probability responses and self-management of responses.

Maehr and Sjogren (52), in a review of some aspects of motivation theory, discussed Atkinson's model and those of others. If you would believe that $Ta = Ts + T - f +$ Test, then you will be happy to know that motivation is important to reading. However, extrinsic and intrinsic support for reading behaviors via motivation, behavior modification, reinforcement, or just plain good old teaching must carry over to when the student is "on his own." Unfortunately, little research has been reported on what the student does independently as a result or concomitant of the motivational scheme in class. If achievement orientation and threat of failure are incompatible, as some feel they are (but some think the terms may define the same thing), then reading, sadly thought of by many as a threat or failure area, has a problem to overcome. A number of attempts have been made to overcome the reading "hassle," and that is where the hope is, in trying. But "bribes" (as the kids call the candy, for example) are dangerous, and it may be that token reinforcement begets token reading, not to mention diabetes and cavities.

Vocabulary

Carroll and his associates (8) have published a research study of high importance to reading. One thousand six hundred and fifty-seven texts and other materials used in grades 3–9 (and ungraded schools) were sampled by use of a formula, with 10,000 samples of 500 words being used. The texts used had been recommended by the highest administrative officers in various school systems or someone delegated by them. No mention of readability checks was made. In the corpus, words were listed alphabetically, by grade level, and by subject matter. A list of the words by rank was compiled with *the* ranking first (followed by *of, and, a, to, is, in, you, that,* and *it*), with *trespasses* ranking last. Frequency distributions were given for all grades and subject matter areas. If the word lists are used in preparing materials, any school program should be enhanced, especially ones for problem readers.

D. D. Johnson (34) compared the "Dolch Basic Sight Word List" with the top 220 words of the Kucera–Francis (KF) corpus. He found that there were eighty-two words of the Dolch list not in the first 220 words of the corpus, and therefore eighty-two words among the first 220 of the corpus that were not on the Dolch list. Johnson provided lists of Dolch and corpus words. He felt that the Dolch list was outdated and that the KF corpus should be used instead for instruction and preparation of materials. The total KF corpus contained 50,406 words in rank order.

Knight and Bethune (41) tested 2,920 students in grades 7–12 on an author-devised, graded, science word list. Definitions for the words were constructed with words below grade 7 difficulty. If 75 per cent of the students at a grade level correctly identified that word, it was placed in that grade list. A number of words were not known by 75 per cent of the students at any grade level. Although the list was devised from "locally produced" (Broward County, Florida) materials, it would appear that the list would be useful anywhere.

Kucera and Francis (42) tabulated 50,406 words in rank order which were selected from fifteen different types of material that literate adults read. There were 500 samples of about 2,000 words each selected by a formula which resulted in a running word count of 1,014,232 terms and words. The Carroll (8) study was part of the same project but more useful to teachers because of the school material sources for the words. (However, the basic 220 words of both corpi do not seem greatly different.) Johnson (34) compared the Dolch list with this study but not with Carroll's.

Otto and Chester (53) have listed 500 words from the Carroll et al. corpus (8) third-grade rankings and titled it "The Great Atlantic and Pacific Sight Word List." It was claimed that such a list would be more relevant and useful than the Dolch (34), Kucera Francis (42), Johnson and Murphy (34) lists. Again, the Carroll lists were taken from texts in which the readability levels were mostly *above* the proposed grade level of the book (35). Thus, it would help students to learn the "GAP 500" as soon as possible, as the words will be in the difficult texts they will have to read. (The writer will prepare a "Vermont Tea and Butter List" to compare to the "GAP 500" as soon as he completes a "Sears and Roebuck" list based on rankings in ungraded schools.)

LINGUISTICS, SPELLING, AND PHONICS

The Minnesota Council of Teachers of English published an annotated bibliography of linguistic articles in 1968 (14). A section on reading was included which contained a few research reports on reading and linguistics. Many times a linguistics-based program is recommended for problem readers. There is no substantiated proof that such a plan would be highly successful.

Goodman and Goodman (26) edited an annotated bibliography on linguistics, psycholinguistics, and reading in 1971. Again, pertinent *research* studies were *not* listed in abundance. However, there were copious references to reviews of research in various areas. Suffice it to say that linguistics has not made any great inroads on the problem reader or illiteracy ranks, probably because it is based on an abstract concept of language which obscures the necessary prerequisite concrete learning needed for language development.

Hanna and his associates (29) studied over 17,000 words to see which words could be spelled solely on a phonological basis. They then determined the words, and phonemes in the words, which could be spelled only by taking into consideration factors of morphology and syntax in addition to the phonological factors. It was found that 49 per cent of the corpus words could be spelled solely on a phonological basis. The dialect used in the study was the same as in *Webster's New International Dictionary of the English Language* (second edition, unabridged). A spelling program was recommended, but it was felt that secondary teachers would need instruction in linguistics and structure of language. It is to be hoped that a language–experience–incidental approach would be devised by teachers utilizing the *visual–writing* aspects of spelling, for indeed it is in writing that one spells. Aural–oral spelling, despite phonological congruity, does not seem to do the job by itself. To a student, the English major students in this writer's reading class have found their linguistic and transformational grammar courses useless in helping problem readers and/or illiterates. Cahan and associates (7) have published a review of spelling research which is well worth reading. Classroom teachers will find the review most useful.

COMPREHENSION

Anderson (1) presented a well-researched review on the construction of achievement tests to assess comprehension. He defined achievement tests as "a set of questions asked to ascertain what a person has learned from exposure to instruction" (1, p. 145). Anderson felt that research workers have not yet learned how to develop "home-made" achievement tests. His review is important because students are bombarded with tests daily, especially tests they must read. An excellent point made by Anderson was that the proof of the worth of a test item is the wording of the test item in relation to the wording of the instruction. The Cloze procedure and programming were not studied as examples which could (and do in certain situations) meet the criterion of reproducibility. The usual tests students take are poorly constructed and often unfair.

Study skills are important for reading, so Butcofsky's (6) study is reported here. He studied 302 college freshmen in a learning skills center and concluded that four out of five were having problems because of inferior study habits. *The Preston–Botel Study Habits Checklist* was administered to 196 males and 133 females, with the males showing a mean of 11.1 and the females a mean of 8.1 inferior study practices. Note taking, rewriting, and reviewing were major shortcomings, along with not reading other sources than the text, not using table of contents or guide questions, not using SQ3R procedures, and reading word by word. Exam content was not anticipated by 54 per cent, 39 per cent didn't have a study schedule, and 31 per cent had cramming problems. Keep in mind these were college freshmen who somehow survived at a level high enough to get them into college. It seems apparent, however, that phenomenal feats of memory will not suffice for all college work. The question of who should prepare high school students for college work is still debatable.

Davis (15), in one of the best studies reviewed, calculated estimates of the per cent of nonchance variance of eight reading comprehension skills of 988 "mature" twelfth-grade readers. Vocabulary recognition, making inferences, and following the structure of a passage accounted for most of the percentage of unique variance in the nonerror variance of the eight skills. Davis recommended that teachers work with secondary students to develop these skills.

Lowe, Follman, and Burley (51) studied some tests of critical thinking and critical reading using fifty-seven subjects at the twelfth-grade level. A rather intricate statistical analysis was made of the data. It was found that critical reading and critical thinking did not strongly relate and had small overlap. Further analyses revealed that verbal ability probably accounted for any "critical" acumen and was represented by vocabulary knowledge and language ability. In sum, if you are reasonably bright and read reasonably well, you will do so "critically," whether you have been "taught critical reading skills" or not.

Quealy's (50) doctoral dissertation was concerned with context aid use of seventy-two tenth- through twelfth-grade male and female university high school students. He used the *Lorge-Thorndike Intelligence Test* (*LTIT*) scores to divide each group of twenty-four into high-, average-, and low-ability groups. The passages used were taken from *Readers Digest* and *Saturday Evening Post* material, presumably because of interest and feasibility value. Readability levels were not discussed, but both usually were written at a college level. In each of the twenty articles, every fiftieth word that met the criteria (adjective, verb, adverb, and noun) was deleted, with a simulated word substituted (for example, *lov* was substituted for *set*). The total group gave the desired word 42 per cent of the time. The higher the *CTIT* score, the better percentage of correct responses was found to be significant (.001) at all three levels. Again, verbal intelligence seems to predict reading acumen, all other factors being equal and/or accounted for. Only at the grade 10 level did significant (.05) sex differences occur; the females did better. No significant differences were found between grade levels on performance but as a group and by grades other significant differences were found. The author concluded that the study was useful in that the introspective technique was shown to be of value.

Smith's (65) study of fifteen "good" and fifteen "poor" readers involved asking the subjects to read "for details" and "for general impressions." Intensive structured interviews were conducted to determine the ways the readers handle the tasks regarding variability and/or adjustment of methods. It was found that the responses of "good" readers were significantly better than those of "poor" readers except when "poor" readers responded to detail questions when their purpose was to read for general impressions. This study was important because it showed how a careful check of the "how" of reading may be made and that "poor" readers were not necessarily deficient in all skills and the converse was so for "good" readers. However, the "good" readers were far more flexible in their reading, adjusted more, and kept the purpose for reading in mind much more than the "poor" readers.

READABILITY

Fry (23) described what is now called the "Fry-Graph" or readability formula, which was designed originally for an African reading series in Uganda. He felt that the formula was accurate within a grade level and found that it correlated highly with other formulas such as the Flesch which is used at the secondary level. This formula has been used extensively since its introduction and it has proved to be a great aid. This writer has found it useful in determining the difficulty of speech and writing samples. It is a tool that secondary teachers and students can learn to use with ease.

Dulin (18) presented a review of three other readability formulas useful at the secondary level. The Fog, Cloze, and Betts approaches were carefully described and models to follow were given. A good bibliography was provided, and the article should be of use to secondary people who wish to prepare materials or check the levels of materials at hand. One cannot believe all publishers grade designations, even in reading materials per se. This article will be useful to all teachers who have yet to discover readability.

Johnson (35) has determined that most of the secondary level social studies texts used in Florida schools were written at levels not commensurate with grade designation. He also found poorly written texts in the middle schools. Not only were sixth-grade texts poorly written, but some seventh-grade texts were written at the college–adult level. Johnson has made efforts to have the texts rewritten or not used. Many teachers do not use the texts for reading per se because of the high difficulty levels.

Simmons and Cox (64) applied the Flesch formula to three different sets of grades 7, 8, and 9 "modern language texts" and compared the results to students' standardized reading achievement test scores (texts and tests were not named, unfortunately). The grade 7 texts were all above grade level in difficulty and 74 per cent of the students tested as too low to read them; all grade 8 texts were written on a grade 9 and were judged too difficult for 59 per cent of the students. And at grade 9 there was one text each written at grades 8, 9, and 10 levels which would make them unreadable to 60 per cent of the students. The authors stated they didn't wish to remove English grammar (modern language?) from the curriculum and that reading was only one avenue to language insights, but because of the results of their study they asked that teachers be careful about using them with readers who might be frustrated by trying to read them. Again, because of the erratic readability of test and text passages, this study has more impact than the authors evidently realized. There have been quite a number of studies on the readability of content area texts (45, 46), and in most cases the books check out at very difficult levels.

INTERESTS

Artley (2) authored a very comprehensive research review concerning many areas of secondary reading. The section on reading interests was summarized with the following points: sex was a greater determiner of interests than I.Q.; same age and grade students, regardless of I.Q., read material of like thematic content; relevant material was desired by youth as opposed to "classics" (i.e., youth will create a new classic list); peer influence was greater than teacher influence; individual interests may vary drastically from group interests; students spent more time with TV than with books and the more the time spent with TV, the less the school achievement; a lot of "lower quality" magazines were read by adolescents, and newspaper reading is quite restricted to certain areas such as sports, comics, gossip, and "Dear Abby" type columnists; kids didn't like poetry (i.e., poetry of others); paperbacks were used by youth who found school libraries, in the main, a "drag." Violence, action, mystery, and sports stories were preferred by boys over all other areas.

Eron and associates (19) reported their longitudinal study of subjects when in grade 3 and ten years later. They were able to use 427 of the original 875 subjects; there were 211 males and 216 females in the group. The female subjects showed much less aggressive behavior than did the male subjects. It was shown that a preference for violent television in grade 3 was the major contributor to grade 13 aggression, exceeding the contributions of such factors at I.Q., ethnicity, social status, and parental disharmony.

Estes (20) developed a reading attitude scale which was "tried out" on 238 students in grades 3–12. Items for the scale were solicited from elementary and secondary teachers. The twenty items in the final version of the scale are included in the article. This scale would probably be as useful as the *Herber* and *Purdue* scales. It may be wise to check students' reading attitudes before one checks their skills or achievement. Problem readers need help more often in attitudes than in reading per se.

Squire (66) reported on interests and attitudes in reading as it related to English classes. He felt that some research had shown that it was quite important *how* reading was discussed in the classroom. Bibliotherapy—accidental or planned—can help youth to understand themselves and others better. Violence as a reading interest per se did not receive any direct attention in the review, but here in the United States and Britain *The Lord of the Flies* was the most significant reading experience named by high school graduates. Junior high students ranked physical action and conflict as top reading choices. Thus it would seem that themes of violence, aggression, and other conflict areas hold the attention of male readers more than any other topics.

AGGRESSION AND OTHER PROBLEMS

Cohen (9), in reviewing the development of aggression, stated, "there exists a paucity of information concerning the processes by which children organize experiences of those variables considered critical to the learning and performance of aggressive behavior" (9, p. 83). The question of a genetic cause of aggressive behavior is far from answered, as is the one dealing with it as a learned behavior. If failure to learn to read well is a cause of aggression, however manifested (aggression is not always violent as epitomized by the statement "kill them with kindness"), then perhaps reading needs to be less emphasized as *the* way to learn. We are a somewhat violent society, yet one would be hard pressed to find an unhappy, fluent reader. The contribution of TV alone was and is a fertile field of study, as Eron et al. (19) have recently shown.

Keldgard (37), in an issue of *Academic Therapy* devoted entirely to learning disabilities in teenagers, discussed the lack of research in the area of brain damage and delinquency. As a practicing criminologist, he felt that large percentages of "delinquents" are in reality brain-damaged youths who do not have control of their faculties. Males appeared to dominate, but keep in mind the typical "runaway" is a white, female, aged fourteen. Neurologists keep complaining that they wished they knew more about the brain, damaged or not. Diagnosing "brain damage" is no easy feat, yet many people seem to be doing so without neurological consultation. It may be wiser to use such terms as *shock, trauma,* or *mental illness* rather than *damage.*

Lane et al. (43) reported on a pilot study in which older eighth- and ninth-grade "disruptive adolescents" tutored third- and fourth-grade "learning and behavior problem" children. The adolescents were nontruants and reading "below grade level" and the youngsters were classed as "poor readers." During a seven-month period, the group met twice a week and the "oldsters" used Pollock's "Intersensory Reading Method," which was a programmed phonic-linguistic approach, and used reading, writing, and spelling all together. Admittedly, the study was not tightly designed or statistically "pure," but the results were quite positive. The oldsters' gained fourteen reading months and the youngsters gained nineteen reading months as measured by the *Metropolitan Achievement Test.* Behavior problems were reduced as viewed by teachers, counselors, and the students themselves. This study was a fine example of useful, profitable, and humane research.

Levin et al. (47) reviewed the research on school achievement and success after the end of formal schooling. They stated that educational attainment was related to opportunities in so many ways and the evidence was overwhelming in support of the proposition that the postschool opportunity and performance were related directly to educational attainment. However, the contributions of such areas as basic intelligence, drive, opportunity, success, and so forth, are still being researched. In short, what is the *real reason* for the low school achievement, including reading? When youth are told to "stay in school" the answer often is, "What for?" (Next time answer, "Money.")

The Silverbergs (63) reviewed the research on achievement, especially in reading, and delinquency. They stated, "in spite of all the years of intensive research by sociologists, criminologists, psychologists, and educators, the relationship between reading and delinquency remains an enigma . . . " (63, p. 24). Teachers usually rank behavior and reading problems as their main challenge and worry. They state that poor learning contributes to their ineffectiveness as teachers. The incidence of poor reading among delinquents is too high to be considered mere coincidence. But it has not been definitely determined that an inability to handle reading is a prime cause of behavior problems and resultant delinquency. It was recommended that reading become an *optional* method of learning, with other means, such as listening and looking, being used more. This suggestion has merit when basic learning research is considered; i.e., verbal intelligence and listening factors contribute more to variance than "reading" does (57).

Tomassi (70) reviewed some of the research on reading and dropouts and stated that the research was scarce and generally very poorly conducted. The cause–effect relationship is of interest here: Does reading disability directly cause some youths to drop out of school? The in-school "psychological" dropout was not studied much at all in this context. She concluded that no direct relationship had been conclusively proved but that the high correlations would lead one to suspect that there was more than met the eye in reading and the dropout. It was suggested that the family may have more to do with the drop-out rate than reading does.

DRUGS

Cowan (11, 12) has reported two studies on drug usage of secondary students as related to school factors. A total of 384 subjects from three upper-middle-class junior high schools were questioned as to their general background and specific experiences with pot, drugs, glue, and alcohol. Eighty per cent replied, "never used any of these substances," 10 per cent replied "hardly ever," 6 per cent said "once or twice a month," and 4 per cent replied "once a week or more." Experimenters and frequent users were mostly males whereas occasional users were evenly divided between males and females. Projecting these results to the total district, Cowan estimated 1,700 subjects had some contact with drugs, 4,600 with alcohol, and 1,260 with glue in grades 7–9. Lower grade point averages, less activity involvement, and higher suspension rates were correlated positively with drug usage. Pot led the list of drugs used most and morphine was least used.

In another study Cowan (12) surveyed three high schools of differing socioeconomic and urban characteristics. School A had a mean head of household salary of $12,000 and a 12–14-year education; school B had a $7,000 mean income and a 9–11-year educational level; school C had about the same as B but in a less populated and partly agricultural area. A three-page, twenty-seven-item questionnaire was administered to male and female subjects in grades 10–12. A sample of 150 was used in A, B had 120, and C had 114. It was found that school A had 34 per cent users, school B had 23 per cent, school C had 9 per cent. In order to check on the findings, Cowan compared school X with school A, with no significant differences being found. Pot led the list of most-used drugs; morphine placed last. The "users" tended not to live with both parents; they also "dated" more, were expelled more, were more often male, were older, had a lower grade point average, engaged in fewer co-curricular activities, and had a higher level of confidence. Cowan assumed that if the data were representative, 8 per cent, or 4800 students of the school district, were "pot heads" or worse.

Huddleston (33) reported one of the first studies involving a "psycho-energizer" ("Deanol", Riker Labs) and secondary students' reading. As part of an experiment involving matched pairs of subjects of elementary, secondary, and college groups, the experimental group received 75 mg. of "Deanol" daily for eight weeks and the control group received a placebo. The study was done by the blind technique and no subjects were to have any special help in reading but rather were to follow a regular educational schedule. The *Gates Reading Survey* and the *Differential Aptitude Test Battery* were the pre- and posttests. The only significant (.05) difference found was in the experimental group on the clerical speed and accuracy subtest of the DAT. An analysis of variance showed that the only significant (.01) source of variance was the Deanol. The findings were true for all levels of students.

Freeman (22) published a thirty-year review on drugs and learning in 1966. Although it was a most comprehensive review he cautioned that it was not complete. There were a number of drugs available and they were used to little or no avail. Dangerous side effects, placebo effects, and lack of controls (such as the double-blind technique) would lead one to be wary of using drugs to control behavior, affect learning, or prove a point. It would be interesting to attempt to find all the subjects in the studies and see how they are functioning today!

Schneyer (61) presented a brief review of drug therapy and reading. He felt that it would be best to involve parents, teachers, the psychotherapist, the students and anyone else concerned when drug therapy is used. It would seem that in a number of these studies, the children were relatively forgotten. As for reading, no drug has been shown to be the cause of permanent reading success.

An entire issue of the *Journal of Learning Disabilities* (69) was devoted to drugs and the "treatment of learning disabilities and related behavior disorders" (69, cover). Conner reviewed recent controlled studies in a number of areas relating to the "hyperkinetic child syndrome" and he mentioned that wherever comparisons of stimulants and tranquilizers have been made, the tranquilizers tended to yield, impairment of learning and cognitive functions. But he cautioned that cluster analysis must be refined in order to identify better the children who would be aided most. After rereading this journal issue, the writer had to wonder if there could not be a better way found to help children other than with drugs. (The drugs youths are taking on their own do not seem to help either.)

MIDDLE SCHOOL

There have been a number of texts and articles on the middle school but little hard research in reading. One text will be mentioned here which devoted nine pages to reading in a chapter on language arts. Although the book was published in 1971, no research reference later than 1966 in reading was cited. However, Hansen and Hearn (30) have presented a good book in general, as they tried to offer a broad text for every area. There have been some studies of middle school reading published recently that are worth reporting here.

Crawford and Conley (13) reported their two new reading labs at the Concord, Massachusetts, middle school grades (6–8) of 1,200 students. The pictures accompanying the brief article were more informative than the article. Of interest was the idea that a student could *choose* reading. No research was reported but those pictures are worth a turn of the pages. It was refreshing to see youngsters actually reading because they wanted to.

Lowe (50) surveyed the ninety-seven middle schools of Florida in February of 1972. There were sixty-two responses which represented sixty-four per cent of the schools. The predominant grade pattern (forty-one schools) was 6–9, and all but one middle school was desegregated. There were 105 reading teachers; of these, fifty-four had an M.A. in reading. Students were tested before grouping in most schools, with seventeen having a separate reading period. In forty-two schools content area teachers worked with reading, and in forty schools the librarians worked with reading guidance, readability analyses, and content area book selection. In forty schools the readability of the texts used was not known, but in twenty-one it was known. Reading was taught at all times during each day with a plethora of materials being used. Sixty schools reported the use of ten types of reading achievements tests and thirty-three different diagnostic tools, with the *California Test of Basic Skills* and informal reading inventories being used most. The most prevalent need stated was for teachers who could teach reading and for reading specialists. Lacking in most schools were liaison plans and parent involvement programs.

Petre (54) reported on the use of "reading breaks" in from fifty to seventy-five Maryland schools. Although we may never know the exact number, the first program was started in a middle school where a thirty-five minute reading break was held daily with everyone reading, including teachers and administrators. One school surveyed the students and only 2 per cent could remember seeing a teacher read, and only 10 per cent could remember anyone at home doing free or hobby reading! One school of 800 students read about 1,000 paperbacks a week, excluding periodicals. A middle school found that in five months, 43 per cent of their students grew one or more levels on a cloze reading test. This is research of a type that shows what you can do to foster reading if you go ahead and do it. In sum, you will not get reading going unless you *plan* and *make time for it*.

MISCELLANEOUS

Kling and Davis (40) and associates have compiled the most comprehensive review of research on models for reading to date. Many areas are covered quite completely and well. The reader is urged to get this volume and study it carefully if he is interested in the theoretical model and research bases for reading behavior.

Ramsey (57) sought to determine if school systems that obtained superior results in reading differed significantly from school systems whose results were less favorable" (57, p. 74). He obtained the *Stanford Reading Achievement Test* scores of 50,000 students in grades 4 and 8 from fifty-two Kentucky school districts (over one-half of the states' districts). Only the grade eight data will be discussed here. It was found that teachers' salaries, equalized assessment per child, local revenue ADA, and total revenue ADA were significantly correlated with reading test scores. The upper quartile schools and students and teachers had the following characteristics: The teachers had more college credits and less years experience, were paid 10 per cent more, spent more time teaching reading, innovated more, and worked in a larger school; the schools got greater local support for education and had more classroom and school libraries; the students median achievement was 9.3 (evidently end-of-year scores), with a range of 8.8 to 10.3. If these results are valid and reliable, the message seems clear; i.e., fact must replace myth in reading and education. For example, in this study class size was not a significant variable.

Summers (68) presented a review of research published from July 1963 to June 1966. The section on reading problems discussed ten studies, which were presumably the better ones found. The other areas reviewed were content areas, programs, reading achievement, reading skills, and interests, tastes, and attitudes. The review was written very well and as *RER* has changed its policy, it was the last three-year review in the series; however, other reviews are available.

Gunn (27) and others have presented research reviews on topics in reading for the secondary English "generalist." The articles were published in 1969 in four issues of the *English Journal* and is one special publication

(23). The publication is quite informative and is available at a nominal cost. The series of research reviews is well done and ought to be read by reading personnel and anyone else interested in reading. The topics discussed were The Teacher of English; High School Students; Attitudes Toward Reading; Successful Reading Programs; Practices in Teaching Reading; Reading in the Content Fields; Materials for Teaching Reading; and Evaluation in Reading. This is highly recommended reading.

Wysocki (72) in an eight-year review of secondary reading research, reported on about forty-five studies. The best section discussed the influences of the home and other environmental factors on reading. Again, parental influence was shown to be the most important factor in reading. Mobility in and by itself did not seem to be a direct cause of reading problems. Wysocki felt that upper-level high school teachers were unable to teach reading and that they needed to be prepared to do so.

Blanton (3) and his associates analyzed fourteen secondary reading tests which were all of a general achievement nature. No "diagnostic" or other special tests were reviewed. (Another well-used joke in reading is, "If you want 'retarded' readers, give a reading test.") *The Diagnostic Reading Tests* were politely laid to rest for good, one hopes), which may be the sole contribution of the authors. Nowhere could this writer find readability analyses of the reading passages, comparisons of vocabulary items to frequency counts such as the Carroll (8), Kucera–Francis (42), or the research on these tests as reported in Buros or in journals. For a number of years this writer has had his secondary reading students analyze the tests for readability, vocabulary, and so on. One widely used test for grades 7–9 contains as the first reading passage an article on the college level! However, the authors continually state or imply in careful terms that the tests really are not useful at all. What they might have said is that the *Chapman–Cook Tests* of 1920, the first secondary tests of reading, could be used today just as well despite the "vast resources and technical expertise of the test giants which have emerged in the field of reading" (3, p. 23).

Leeds (45, 46) discussed comment and research in the four major content areas and a few other subjects. Unfortunately there was more review and comment than description of the research studies. Programs based on research, but not limited by it, are probably going to be better than the usual box, workbook, or AV programs. However, Leeds reported a number of innovative programs which could help someone looking for ideas. The reviews would be very useful for in-service reading training of content teachers.

Summary and Conclusions

In summary, it would be safe to say that secondary reading has received a great deal of attention during the past few years. This fact, coupled with the fact that the United States has one of the highest *rates* of illiteracy in the world, should cause any professional to ask a resounding *why?* The reading hassle has pervaded the lives of millions of students, dropouts, delinquents, criminals, teachers, and just about anyone else one could think of. The Right to Read Project ("All will read by 1980"), however noble, cannot succeed in its present format, because, like most programs, it concentrates on reading something, *not on the human mind*, where, believe it or not, reading occurs. It seems ironic that the harder we try to teach "everybody" how to read, the more nonreading increases. We can do better than this, and we must do better.

Therefore, based on this writer's review of selected available research, it seemed reasonable to conclude that

1. The results of research dealing with the mind as it reads has either been ignored, been disbelieved, or gone unread.
2. Unless the overemphasis on reading as the main single avenue of learning is stopped, social problems will increase.
3. Reading is the most difficult, slowest, and most expensive way to learn for the human being.
4. The large number of reading organizations from international to local councils, journals and magazines containing research and commentaries on reading, reading teachers, specialists, consultants, supervisors and teacher trainees, federal, state, and local efforts, including performance contracting, and all kinds of special programs for people of all ages, have failed to stem the rise of illiteracy rates.
5. The efforts to help people to learn to read silently, i.e., without having to hear themselves read, should be revised, expanded, and researched exhaustively.
6. The family constellation, as the leading predictor of reading success or failure, should be utilized to a great extent.
7. Public education, never designed for all segments of society, needs to enter into a compact with private education so that all youth may have a chance to receive equitable instruction. It is a tragedy that the very students the public schools were designed for have been hurt so much by them.
8. Low social, economic, and attitudinal groups, such as blacks, need more than "equality." They need superior programs based on their needs and styles of learning.
9. Texts and materials used in reading programs and classrooms are written poorly and at unbelievably high levels. This includes materials said to be designed for LSES students.
10. The school, as the second leading cause of reading success or failure, must become a responsible partner with the family.
11. Drugs, legally or illegally used, have not helped readers or reading.
12. Better designed and executed studies in reading are sorely needed.

FINAL CAVEAT

After reading this article the reader may say,

Gee, the guy said there's no such thing as reading or critical reading, the reading tests are pretty inaccurate, more "poor" readers are graduating and/or dropping out than "good" readers, blacks need something unique for their learning style but we don't know what it is, hundreds of millions of dollars have been wasted, one has to learn to extend his intelligence to verbal activities, one of which is called "reading" (which cannot be taught), the texts are poorly written and are too difficult—often written at college levels, reading is the slowest and hardest way to learn, and in sum we have done more harm than good.

This writer didn't just *say* those things, he *found* them to be true in his own research and that of others. Check your own classes and school on these matters, do your own research, read the studies cited, and let me hear from you.

REFERENCES

1. Anderson, R. C. "How to Construct Achievement Test to Assess Comprehension," *Review of Educational Research*, 42 (Spring 1972), 145–70.
2. Artley, A. S. *Trends and Practices in Secondary Reading: A Review of the Literature*. Newark, Del.: International Reading Association, 1968. 131 pp.
3. Blanton, E., R. Farr, and J. J. Tuinman. *Reading Tests for the Secondary Grades: A Review and Evaluation*. Newark, Del.: International Reading Association, 1972. 55 pp.
4. Bliesmer, E. P. "Evaluating Progress in Remedial Reading Programs," *Reading Teacher*, 15 (March 1962), 344–50.
5. ———. "Problems of Research Design in Classroom Studies," *Journal of Reading Behavior*, 2 (Winter 1970), 3–18.
6. Butcofsky, D. "Any Learning Skills Taught in High School?" *Journal of Reading*, 15 (December 1971), 195–98.
7. Cahan, L. S., M. J. Craun, and S. K. Johnson. "Spelling Difficulty—A Review of the Research," *Review of Educational Research*, 41 (October 1971), 281–301.
8. Carroll, J. B., P. Davies, and B. Richman. *Word Frequency Book*. Boston: Houghton Mifflin Company, 1971. 856 pp.
9. Cohen, S. "The Development of Aggression," *Review of Educational Research*, 41 (February 1972), 71–85.
10. Cole, E. M. in "Book Reviews," *Harvard Educational Review*, 34 (Spring 1964), 351–54.
11. Cowan, R. A. "Drug Usage: Will the Pyramid Become Top Heavy?" *Occasional Papers*, 3, 1–8, Oakland Schools, Pontiac, Mich.
12. ———. "High School Pot Heads—How Do They Stack Up?" *Occasional Papers*, 2, 1–10, Oakland Schools, Pontiac, Mich.

13. Crawford, G., and R. L. Conley. "Meet You in the Reading Lab," *Journal of Reading*, 15 (October 1971), 16–21.

14. Curriculum Committee, *Linguistic Bibliography for the Teacher of English*, Minnesota Council of Teachers of English, University of Minnesota at Duluth, 1968. 86 pp.

15. Davis, F. B. "Research in Comprehension in Reading," *Reading Research Quarterly*, 3 (Summer 1968), 499–545.

16. Deshayes, J. "Effects of Positive Reinforcement on the Reading Achievement of Students Grades 5–12 Who Exhibited Deviant Behavior and Reading Problems." Unpublished review of research, University of South Florida, 1972. 36 pp.

17. Duggins, J. (ed.). *Teaching Reading for Human Value in High School.* Columbus, Ohio: Charles E. Merrill Co., 1972. 311 pp.

18. Dulin, K. L. "Measuring the Difficulty of Reading Materials," *Reading Improvement*, 8 (Spring 1971), 3–6.

19. Eron, L. D., et al. "Does Television (TV) Violence Cause Aggression?" *American Psychologist*, 27 (April 1970), 253–63.

20. Estes, T. H. "A Scale to Measure Attitudes Toward Reading," *Journal of Reading*, 15 (November 1971), 135–38.

21. Fishbein, J., and R. Emans. *A Question of Competence: Language, Intelligence, and Learning to Read.* Chicago: Science Research Associates, 1972. 231 pp.

22. Freeman, R. D. "Drug Effects on Learning in Children: A Selective Review of the Past Thirty Years," *Journal of Special Education*, 1 (Fall 1966), 17–44.

23. Fry, E. "A Readability Formula That Saves Time," *Journal of Reading*, 11 (April 1968).

24. Garner, J. H. "Black Students and Reading: Grades 7–9." Unpublished review of research, University of South Florida, 1972. 57 pp.

25. Garrett, H. E. (Personal conversations and correspondence with Dr. Garrett over a thirteen-year span have led this writer to believe that Dr. Garrett is sincere in his beliefs which will be proved or disproved someday by scientific research.)

26. Goodman, Y. M., and K. S. Goodman. *Linguistics, Psycholinguistics, and the Teaching of Reading.* Newark, Del.: International Reading Association, 1971. 35 pp.

27. Gunn, M. A. (ed.). *What We Know About High School Reading.* Champaign, Ill.: National Council of Teachers of English, 1969. 106 pp.

28. Gwaltney, W. K. "An Evaluation of a Summer Reading Improvement Course for Disadvantaged High School Seniors," *Journal of Reading Behavior*, 3 (Fall 1970–71), 14–21.

29. Hanna, P. R., J. S. Hanna, R. E. Hodges, and E. H. Rudorf, Jr. *Phoneme-Grapheme Correspondences as Cues to Spelling Improvement.* Washington, D.C.: U.S. Office of Education, 1966. 716 pp.

30. Hansen, J. H., and A. C. Hearn. *The Middle School Program.* Chicago: Rand McNally, 1971. 378 pp.

31. Hill, W. "Characteristics of Secondary Reading: 1940–1970," ed. by F. P. Greene. *Reading: The Right to Participate*, 20th yearbook. Boone, N.C.: National Reading Conference, 1971, pp. 20–29.

32. Holmes, J. A. "Speed, Comprehension and Power in Reading." Ed. by E. P. Bliesmer and R. C. Staiger. *Problems, Programs and Projects in College-Adult Reading*, 12th yearbook. Boone, N.C.: National Reading Conference, 1962, pp. 6–14.

33. Huddleston, W. O. "Deanol as (an) Aid in Overcoming Reading Retardation," *Clinical Medicine*, 8 (July 1961), 1340–42.

34. Johnson, D. D. "The Dolch List Reexamined," *Reading Teacher*, 24 (February 1971), 449–57.

35. Johnson, R. E. "Readability of Secondary Social Studies Textbooks Adopted by the State of Florida." 1972.

36. Jung, S. M. "Progress in Education 1960–1970: A Sample Survey." Paper read at AERA Annual Meeting, February 2, 1971. 16 pp.

37. Keldgard, R. E. "Brain Damage and Delinquency: A Question and a Challenge," *Academic Therapy Quarterly*, 4 (Winter 1968–1969), 93–99.

38. Kimble, R. L., and R. G. Davison. "Reading Improvement for Disadvantaged American Indian Youth," *Journal of Reading*, 15 (February 1972), 342–46.

39. Kling, M. "Summer Headstart for Disadvantaged College Freshmen," *Journal of Reading*, 15 (April 1972), 507–12.

40. ——— (Principal Investigator), and F. B. Davis (ed.). "The Literature of Research in Reading with Emphasis on Models." New Brunswick, N.J.: Rutgers University, 1971.

41. Knight, D. W., and P. Bethune. "Science Words Students Know," *Journal of Reading*, 15 (April 1972), 504–506.

42. Kucera, H., and W. N. Francis. *Computational Analysis of Present Day English*. Providence, R.I.: Brown University Press, 1967.

43. Lane, P., C. Pollock, and N. Sher. "Remotivation of Disruptive Adolescents," *Journal of Reading*, 15 (February 1972), 351–54.

44. Lee, B. C. (Ed.). "Performance Contracting–OEO Experiment." *NEA Research Bulletin*, 50 (March 1972), 9–10.

45. Leeds, D. S. "Summary of Research Related to Reading in the Content Areas: English and Social Studies," *Journal of the Reading Specialist*, 10 (March 1971), 175–86.

46. ———. "Summary of Research Related to Reading in the Content Areas: Science and Mathematics," *Journal of the Reading Specialist*, 10 (December 1970), 88–95.

47. Levin, H. M., J. W. Guthrie, G. B. Heindorfer, and R. T. Stout. "School Achievement and Post-School Success: A Review," *Review of Educational Research*, 41 (February 1971), 1–16.

48. Light, R. J., and P. V. Smith. "Social Allocation Models of Intelligence," *Harvard Educational Review*, 39 (Spring 1969), 484–510.

49. Lipe, D. H., and S. M. Jung. "Manipulating Incentives to Enhance School Learning," *Review of Educational Research*, 41 (October 1971), 249–80.

50. Lowe, A. J. "Reading in Florida's Middle Schools." 1972.

51. ———, J. Follman, and W. Burley. "Psychometric Analyses of Critical Reading and Critical Thinking—Twelfth Grade," ed. by F. P. Greene, *Reading: The Right to Participate*, 20th yearbook. Boone, N.C.: National Reading Conference, 1971, pp. 142–47.

52. Maehr, M. M., and D. O. Sjogren. "Atkinson's Theory of Motivation:

First Step Toward a Theory of Academic Motivation?" *Review of Educational Research,* 41 (April 1971), 143–61.

53. Otto, W., and R. Chester. "Sight Words for Beginning Readers," *Journal of Educational Research,* 65 (July, August 1972), 435–43.

54. Petre, R. M. "Reading Breaks Make It in Maryland," *Journal of Reading,* 15 (December 1971), 191–94.

55. Puleo, T. T. "Silent Reading." Unpublished review of research, University of South Florida, 1972. 27 pp.

56. Quealy, R. J. "Senior High School Students Use of Contextual Aids in Reading," *Reading Research Quarterly,* 4 (Summer 1969), 512–33.

57. Ramsey, W. "Which School System Gets the Best Results in Reading," *Journal of Reading Behavior,* 1 (Summer 1969), 74–80.

58. Rankin, E. A. "Residual Gain as a Measure of Individual Differences in Reading Improvement," *Journal of Reading,* 8 (March 1965), 224–33.

59. Rohwer, W. D. "Learning, Race, and School Success," *Review of Educational Research,* 41 (June 1971), 191–210.

60. Rystrom, R., and H. Cowart. "Black Reading 'Errors' or White Teacher Biases?" *Journal of Reading,* 15 (January 1972), 273–79.

61. Schneyer, J. W. "Drug Therapy and Learning in Children," *Reading Teacher,* 24 (March 1971), 561–63.

62. Shockley, W. "Negro I.Q. Deficit: Failure of a 'Malicious Coincidence' Model Warrants New Research Proposals," *Review of Educational Research,* 41 (June 1971), 227–48.

63. Silverberg, N. E., and M. C. Silverberg. "School Achievement and Delinquency," *Review of Educational Research,* 41 (February 1971), 17–34.

64. Simmons, J. S., and J. Cox. "New Grammar Texts for Secondary Schools: How Do They Read?" *Journal of Reading,* 15 (January 1973), 280–85.

65. Smith, H. K. "The Responses of Good and Poor Readers When Asked to Read for Different Purposes," *Reading Research Quarterly,* 3 (Fall 1967), 53–83.

66. Squire, J. R. "What Does Research in Reading Reveal About Attitudes Toward Reading?" *English Journal,* 58 (April 1969), 523–33.

67. Stodolsky, S. S., and G. Lesser. "Learning Patterns in the Disadvantaged," *Harvard Educational Review,* 37 (Fall 1967), 547–93.

68. Summers, E. G. "Reading in the Secondary School," *Review of Educational Research,* 37 (April 1967), 134–51.

69. Topaz, P. M. (ed.). *Journal of Learning Disabilities,* 4 (November 1971), 466–543. (Entire issue devoted to drugs and behavior, learning, etc.)

70. Tomassi, R. C. "Reading and the Dropout." Unpublished review of research, University of South Florida, 1972. 12 pp.

71. Wiener, M., and W. Cramer. "Reading and Reading Difficulty: A Conceptual Analysis," *Harvard Educational Review,* 37 (Fall 1967), 620–43.

72. Wysocki, M. R. "The Status of Secondary Reading Research," ed. by H. G. Shane, J. Walden, and R. Green. *Interpreting Language Arts for the Teacher.* Washington, D.C.: Association for Supervision and Curriculum Development, 1971, pp. 40–49.

Reading Readiness at the High-School and College Levels[*]
Ned D. Marksheffel

In any field of human endeavor, in any age, individuals have been able to arrange conditions which either facilitate or hinder further efforts.

Weaknesses in strategy, tactics, logistics, materials, or personnel reduce the chances of successful completion of a task whether the task be an attack on enemy troops, an attack on disease or slums, or an attack on the printed page. Leaders on the battlefield, in the scientific laboratory, and in city government insist on and help to develop conditions of readiness which facilitate successful completion of their respective tasks. Can the classroom leader, the teacher, do any less?

Marksheffel shows how classroom leaders train their charges to do battle successfully with the printed page.

1. Before reading this article, state in a column your ideas of reading readiness at the high school or college level.

2. In an adjacent column list the author's ideas on readiness. Compare and contrast your ideas with his.

High-school teachers and college professors are becoming alarmed at the "poor" reading skills of some of their otherwise more capable students. They are asking, "How can I get students to 'read between the lines'? Why don't they improve their vocabularies? Do students read for a purpose?"

There is no one answer to all of these questions. There is, however, an answer which is basic to all other answers—professors, teachers, and students must be ready for reading before any appreciable progress is made in learning through reading.

The secondary teacher or college professor can make an immediate and valuable contribution to student learning if he will do the following: (1) recognize that reading readiness is a prerequisite to learning in subject-matter areas; (2) provide for a reading readiness period.

ASSIGNMENT PERIOD

The much-abused assignment period is the key to reading readiness. Few teachers take advantage of this time to develop student interest in the reading, to introduce "new" vocabulary, to broaden concepts, or to set purposes for the reading.

---

[*] REPRINTED FROM *Education* (January 1961), pp. 269–272. Copyright, 1961, by The Bobbs-Merrill Company, Inc., Indianapolis, Indiana.

Inadequate use of the assignment period is not a new idea. Over twenty-five years ago, Yoakam (10) and others were criticizing the inadequacy of secondary-teacher lesson assignments. Betts (1), and Gray (6), and others give evidence that there was, and is, a lack of understanding of the value of the assignment period. Burton (2) condemns the "meager, vague, unanalyzed, wholly inadequate type of assignment which persists in the secondary schools." McKee (8) calls such practices "hide-and-seek education."

INADEQUATE ASSIGNMENTS

During the past year the writer questioned over one thousand experienced secondary teachers from the western states, Alaska, and Canada on how they assigned lessons in their subject-matter fields. With few exceptions they replied that they wrote the assignments on the board or told the students to "take the next chapter," or to "read pages 317–399 for tomorrow and be ready to answer questions." A few teachers used duplicate sheets of questions which the student was to answer, or had the students answer the author's questions at the end of the chapter. A "mere handful" of the teachers followed a method that could be termed sound and conducive to learning.

This "crude" sampling of teacher methods of assigning lessons does not lend itself to valid conclusions. It does, however, indicate that (1) many teachers receive little or no guidance as to the importance of the assignment period; (2) teachers need help in learning how to give assignments; and (3) some teachers are receiving such instruction, but they are relatively few in number.

When assigning a lesson, the teacher needs to keep in mind certain important factors which will be discussed in detail. They are as follows: (1) time for assigning lessons; (2) introducing "new" vocabulary; (3) purposes for reading; (4) concept development; (5) teacher use of questions.

TIME AND THE ASSIGNMENT PERIOD

It is suggested that assignments be given at the beginning of the class period. When this plan is followed, as much time as is needed may be taken so that the student is aware of his obligations and the intent of the assignment. When the teacher has completed the assignment, the student should know enough of what is expected from him so that he can ask intelligent questions pertaining to any vague portions. He must know the objectives of the assignment and be capable of setting additional purposes as he reads. He must know what he is expected to do, when he should do it, how he should do it, and some of the "why it should be done."

Introducing "New" Vocabulary

"New" vocabulary should be introduced orally and in context. The words need to be written on the chalkboard and pronounced clearly by the teacher. The pronunciation as well as the meaning behind the written symbol will be entirely new to some students. When two factors to be learned are introduced simultaneously, the student needs all the help he can get from the teacher.

The student must be taught that a previously accepted definition of a word may not apply in a different setting. It is no secret that high-school and even college students sometimes express amazement upon "discovering" that a word may imply many and varied meanings. Until a student understands that words shift in meaning according to context, his reading may be superficial and lacking in reality.

Setting Purposes for Reading

By asking specific as well as general questions, the teacher can direct student reading onto paths which lead toward definite and established goals. The successful achievement of goals in a sequential pattern tends to urge the student forward in his reading. He must, and can, be taught to set his own goals for reading. This, however, is a gradual process which calls for teacher guidance.

Once the student has learned to set his own goals for reading, he can adjust his rate of reading to the type of material being read and according to his own background of experience. When he can do this, the student has developed a skill which will take him far. It is a skill in which so many high-school and college students are lacking.

Concept Development

In a highly industrialized, atomic-age civilization, no one person can possibly be prepared for, nor engage in, all the direct experiences he will need for living in "tomorrow's" world. As the student progresses through the grades and into higher levels of learning, he gets farther and farther away from direct experiences. His learning becomes more dependent upon vicarious experiences such as reading, listening, and televiewing. He must consciously and continually improve his ability to deal with printed and spoken words lest his concepts become faulty, warped, or totally inadequate. The more complex the concept, the more abstract are the symbols for understanding. It is vital that each student recognize the necessity of, and the obligation for, learning and using spoken and printed symbols.

Concept development and vocabulary go hand in hand. Advanced learning is dependent upon one's ability to comprehend and use words. Precise use of words clarifies problems, saves time, and increases one's ability to think. Students can acquire new vocabulary and develop concepts when they participate in guided student-teacher-student discussions. Sufficient discussion of "new" words *before* reading will enhance the student's understanding of the material that he reads.

Types of Questions to Use

Teachers need to know and to use various types of questions. Too much emphasis has been placed upon fact-type questions. As a consequence, high-school students are quite adept at finding answers based upon facts. When confronted with inference-type questions based upon the same facts, they flounder and give up with a baffled, "The book didn't say." They need to be taught to "dig out" inferred meanings. Even the brilliant student develops the habits of seeking and remembering facts for but one purpose—to answer teacher questions.

Questions based upon vocabulary should not be slighted. Gray (6) said that "meaningful vocabulary correlates more closely with comprehension in reading than any other (factor), excepting intelligence."

During the assignment period, key vocabulary words should be introduced by the teacher. He cannot assume that the student will "look them up in the dictionary." In order to insure student understanding of new words, the teacher should use questions based upon knowledge of these new words. By providing for student use and review of the new vocabulary, the teacher is teaching reading and subject matter.

Every possible clue and device should be used to insure student mastery of vocabulary. Context clues, picture clues, charts and graphs, teacher-student discussion, explanation, structural clues, root words and affixes, and the use of the dictionary—all are means of helping the student to arrive at the meaning of words. This is teaching reading—this is teaching subject matter.

Summary

Teachers should not assume that all college and high-school students are ready to read assignment materials. Student readiness for reading at all grade levels is a prerequisite for optimum learning. Students can develop readiness for reading when teachers prepare them for it by introducing some of the difficult vocabulary, and by asking thought-provoking questions which lead students to read "deeply" rather than to "soak up" information or to "gather" facts.

References

1. Betts, Emmett A. *Foundations of Reading Instruction.* New York: American Book Co., 1957.
2. Burton, William H. "Implications for Organization of Instruction and Instructional Adjuncts." *Learning and Instruction,* Forty-ninth Yearbook,

Part I, of the National Society for the Study of Education. Chicago: University of Chicago Press, 1950, p. 227.

3. Burton, William H. *Reading in Child Development*. Indianapolis: Bobbs-Merrill Co., Inc., 1956.

4. Durrell, Donald D. "Learning Difficulties Among Children of Normal Intelligence," *Elementary School Journal*, 55 (December 1954), 201–208.

5. Gates, Arthur I. *Improvement of Reading*. New York: Macmillan Publishing Co., Inc., 1947.

6. Gray, William S. *Reading in the High School and College*, Forty-seventh Yearbook, Part II, of the National Society for the Study of Education. Chicago: University of Chicago Press, 1948, p. 98.

7. ———, and Nancy Larrick (eds.). *Better Readers for Our Times*, International Reading Association Conference Proceedings, Vol. I. New York: Scholastic Magazines, 1956.

8. McKee, Paul. *The Teaching of Reading in the Elementary School*. Boston: Houghton Mifflin Company, 1948, p. 548.

9. Strang, Ruth, Constance M. McCullough, and Arthur E. Traxler. *Problems in the Improvement of Reading*, second edition. New York: McGraw-Hill, Inc., 1955.

10. Yoakam, Gerald A. *The Improvement of the Assignment*. New York: Macmillan Publishing Co., Inc., 1934.

Developing Flexibility: The Ability to Read for Different Purposes

Introduction

Flexibility is a characteristic of the mature, healthy, creative personality. Rigidity is a characteristic of the immature, unhealthy, and imitative personality. Flexibility is characteristic of a Leonardo Da Vinci; rigidity is exemplified by an Adolf Hitler.

Just as there are behavioral differences within a species, there are also behavioral differences across the broad spectrum of species represented among living organisms. The flexibility-rigidity dimension is related to differences in personality characteristics among humans, and also to differences among behavioral characteristics between higher-level and lower-level organisms.

Generally speaking, the lower an organism is on a scale of complexity, the more limited the range of activities it is able to perform; the less complex are these activities, the more rigidly it performs the activities, and the shorter the time until the organism reaches developmental maturity. The progression is easy to see if we compare the behavior of organisms as we go up the complexity scale from earthworm to cat to chimpanzee to man. Flexibility is seen as a characteristic of the human personality and mentality; and within the species Homo sápiens, flexibility is a characteristic of the creative, effective personality, for example, the creative musician and architect, the creative writer, the creative reader!

Just as we shift gears and drive at different speeds to accomplish such varying purposes as threading our way through traffic, turning a corner, driving up a mountain road, or passing a car on a four-lane highway, so must we "shift gears" to accomplish our various purposes for reading. If a person uses a wrong speed and approach to accomplish a particular driving task, the result can be deleterious. In like manner, the individual who uses an incorrect speed and approach to accomplish a particular task or purpose in reading will reap disastrous results.

A key to creative, effective reading, then, is flexibility—adjusting the reading speed and approach to the difficulty of the material, and the purposes for which it is read. The authors of the articles in this section generally agree with this thesis. Adams discusses the known factors about speed and flexibility and explains procedures for developing speed and flexibility in reading. Lastly, he discusses strategies for improving several kinds of comprehension. Fisher shows the teacher how to overcome some of the limitations associated with the use of reading training machines.

Utilizing Known Factors to Increase Reading Speed and Flexibility[*]

W. Royce Adams

Those individuals making claims of being able to develop fabulous speed readers have a proclivity for demonstrating their success by utilizing highly intelligent young people who are extremely well informed and who know most of the concepts in the books used for demonstration purposes before they open the books, although they may not have seen

[*] REPRINTED FROM *Combined Proceedings of the First, Second, and Third Annual Conferences of the Western College Reading Association*, Frank L. Christ, editor (Los Angeles: WCRA, 1970), pp. 125–36, reprinted with permission of W. Royce Adams and the Western College Reading Association.

the particular books before. Actually, they could "lecture" as well on the topics of the books *without opening* the books. P. T. Barnum said it long ago.

Adams provides a corrective to the outlandish claims of the speed reading merchants, discusses the known factors about speed and flexibility, and provides exercises and techniques to improve the areas underlying reading speed and flexibility —word discrimination, word sense, and vocabulary. Finally, he provides strategies for improving literal, critical, and aesthetic comprehension.

1. According to the research by Holmes and Singer, what are the factors most important to gaining reading speed?

2. Design a word discrimination exercise utilizing synonyms, antonyms.

3. For your own vocabulary development overlearn five words each week for a three- to five-week period; utilize vocabulary cards that you make. Write a summary of this experience, including your reactions to the possible value of this method of vocabulary development.

4. Help another person to learn vocabulary using this method.

5. Differentiate literal, critical, and aesthetic comprehension.

6. What kinds of questions can a student legitimately ask an instructor before reading an assignment?

7. How can critical comprehension be improved?

8. How can one use fictional literature in a speed reading text.

The idea of reading thousands of words per minute is intriguing to us in an era of speed in which man is going to the moon, jets are flying several times faster than the speed of sound, and automobiles register 120 mph on the speedometer. Breaking speed records of any type always makes interesting news. Unfortunately, much of what we read about "speed reading" is misleading. The present confusion began about a decade ago.

Around 1960, newspapers and magazines began out-doing one another with sensational reports of people learning to read at fantastic rates of thousands of words per minute. Undoubtedly, the impact of the Evelyn Wood Reading Dynamics Institute has been as strong an influence on those of us teaching reading as Flesch's *Why Johnny Can't Read* (8) was in the 1950's. Influenced by Wood's claim that a "breakthrough" in reading had been found, industries instigated rapid reading courses for their executives. Politicians such as Senator Proxmire of Wisconsin and Senator Talmadge of Georgia claimed speed reading was equated with responsible citizenship. (They were authorities, having completed an Evelyn Wood course.) President Kennedy, who reportedly read 1200 words per minute, was linked with speed reading courses being offered. Books, articles, and gadgets purporting to develop speed flooded the market. In a 1962 article "Rapid Reading: Uses and Abuses," Arthur Heilman (10) claims there were two unusual phenomena during Kennedy's administration: fallout shelters and speed reading. The irony is that none of the fallout shelters Heilman examined had any space for books. The emphasis was being placed on *how fast* one could read, not on *what* one was reading or *how well*.

Professional educators were also impressed by Evelyn Wood's claims. A prime example is Russell Stauffer (16), Director of the Reading-Study Center at the University of Delaware, who was instrumental in appointing Evelyn Wood as assistant professor in the School of Education so that she could train teachers, graduates, and under-graduate students in her methods.

With this academic acceptance the reading camp was immediately divided. Disagreements began and still continue regarding the definition of speed reading, methods for evaluating comprehension, machines versus non-machines in teaching reading, adequacies of eye movement photography, eye movement and eye span training, and even the legality of the speed reading claims in advertising. Spache (16) and Ehrlich (7), among many others, took Stauffer and Wood to task for their claims. Liddle (12), in his doctoral dissertation on the Wood Reading Dynamics Method, found that the students who were taught the Woodian way did increase their rate but "an analysis of the data . . . does not substantiate the claim that exceptional rates are obtained without a loss in comprehension."

This paper is not going to discuss the history of the "speed reading" controversy but for those interested, a fairly thorough coverage of it can be found in Allen Berger's (4) "Speed Reading: Is the Present Emphasis Desirable?" and in Paul Witty's (18) "Rate of Reading—A Crucial Issue." Both articles cover the topic rather well, citing pro and con arguments. In addition, Berger's (3) *Speed Reading: An Annotated Bibliography* provides coverage of the topic up to 1967.

KNOWN FACTORS ABOUT SPEED AND FLEXIBILITY

Researchers do agree on at least one point: it is possible to increase reading rates. To what degree depends on the individual's intelligence, practice and type of training. The research of Jack Holmes and Harry Singer (6) (11) of the University of California reveals that while there are many unknown factors contributing to the development of reading speed and power, there are seven known factors. Of those, the factors most important to gaining speed are in order of importance: *word discrimination, word sense* and *eye span;* eye span contributing only five per cent. Those factors most important to gaining comprehension are in order of importance: *vocabulary in context, intelligence, perception of verbal relations,* and *eye fixations;* eye fixation factors contributing only four per cent. There are still unknown factors involved in reading speed development, but until research determines what they are, we can at least base our instruction on the known factors. The rest of this paper will direct itself to the application of these known factors to two major areas vital to developing speed and flexibility in reading: vocabulary and comprehension training.

Flexible Vocabulary-Type Training

Since word discrimination, word sense and vocabulary in context are contributing factors for developing reading flexibility, proper training in these areas seems appropriate. The importance of word discrimination drills are obvious. A sentence which reads "The pilot changed his residence," could seem to read "The plot charged his resistance." If such faulty discrimination occurs it obviously destroys comprehension and produces regression. Many students at the college level suffer from various levels of poor word discrimination. When they attempt to read faster their comprehension suffers not so much because they can't mentally comprehend at faster rates, but because they can't discriminate quickly enough for the correct perceptual images to be received.

There are several textbooks which provide helpful word discrimination drills. Miller's *Increasing Reading Efficiency* (14), Rausch and Weinstein's *Mastering Reading Skills* (15), and at the remedial level, Adams' *Increasing Reading Speed* (1) all contain assorted rapid word, phrase, and number recognition drills which develop the ability to discriminate more rapidly. Basically, drills of this type require that the student identify a designated word or number among several other words on a line which have the same basic shape or configuration such as the following example:

Directions: For each line, read the numbered word and then move your eyes swiftly across the page. Underline that word every time it appears on the line. Work rapidly. You will have only 25 seconds to finish all twenty items.

1. interest	interested	intern	interest	intrigue	interesting
2. piece	peace	price	prize	person	piece
3. believe	behave	believe	before	belongs	behave

Variations of this activity should involve drills in number recognition, synonym recognition and antonym recognition.

Other helpful drills are varied forms of rapid phrase recognition exercises that can be read both in a vertical column and from left to right as illustrated in the following examples.

Example 1

Directions: Mark the phrase which contains the approximate meaning of the key phrase by the number.

	the result of	too near it	
1. an opinion	on the top	a belief held	frankly speaking
	open to men	due to that	
2. to be exposed	to rise above	during old age	to increase

	physics book		
	powerful arm	even so	
3. sign of force	(etc.)	afraid to say	now and again

EXAMPLE 2

Directions: Mark the phrase *break of day* each time it appears in the fol- lowing column. Try to finish in 15 seconds or less.

break of pace	break of day
breaking bread	break of dawn
break a leg	(etc.)

Such drills are actually more sophisticated extenuations of readiness type exercises often used in primary level reading workbooks. Such drills are easily prepared on stencils or ditto masters. They should be made available for students to use as often as possible and should be practiced under the pressure of time.

In addition, the well publicized tachistoscopic machines such as EDL's TACH-X, AVR's Eye Span Trainers, Craig Readers and others are useful in word and phrase discrimination development. However, the use of machines in developing reading flexibility is not a necessity. Berger's (2) findings (among others) in "Are Machines Needed to Increase Reading Rate?" are that "what can be done with machines can be done as well, if not better, without." However, there are always a few students who are motivated by machines or who can better understand principles of eye movement through machine demonstration.

The factor *word sense* covers much and implies flexibility in vocabulary usage. One method for achieving this flexibility in word sense is the personalized vocabulary card. The student, using 3×5 cards, prints the word he wants to learn on one side of the card and on the other side the phonetic spelling, the definition, synonyms, antonyms, word roots, and a sentence using the word. The student, depending on his ability, should be required to make and over-learn at least five to ten cards per week. He accumulates these so that he mixes in the new cards for one week with the others he has already made. At least once every two weeks the instructor should check all the students' cards by flashing them at the student for quick visual discrimination, and should request that he pronounce the word and give its definition. The advantage to this method is that it allows the student to select words he personally doesn't know from any source and it requires that he meet with the instructor to correct his pronunciation, to check his responses and to reveal any other problems the student may have with the word.

Because not all students learn the same way or have the same problems, the instructor should also provide materials and drills in all five basic word attack skills: sight discrimination, structural clues, phonic clues, contextual clues, and dictionary usage. The student should be encouraged to work in any or all of these areas of vocabulary development he needs most, but the heaviest emphasis should be placed on vocabulary in context.

There are many excellent vocabulary textbooks available but it is highly doubtful that any one book would provide proper vocabulary training for every student in any given class. A book such as Brown's *Programmed Vocabulary* (5) requires the student to learn fourteen words which are said to contain prefix and root elements found in over 14,000 words from a desk dictionary. However, personal experience reveals many students cannot relate this knowledge very readily and that they often memorize for memory's sake and soon forget. Some books, such as Greene's *Word Clues* (9), are based on Latin and Greek roots. Many students can expand their word sense with these texts, but there are always some who find little relevance in memorizing words or word parts they never use. EDL's *Word Clues* (18) attempts to use context, roots, and dictionary entries on a programmed format. Again, for some students the appeal is great; for others, a different approach is needed. The personalized vocabulary cards help close this deficiency when a reading lab cannot provide numerous vocabulary texts for student use. But whatever the approach, quick word recognition and a flexible vocabulary are vital for increasing rate and should be an integral part of any speed reading course.

FLEXIBLE COMPREHENSION TRAINING

Despite the agreement of most educators that speed without comprehension is meaningless, there are many college reading courses paying lip-service to real comprehension. Some textbooks which claim to aid speed and comprehension are guilty of perpetrating the speed myth by providing the same type of comprehension exercises with each timed reading selection. Soon the student begins to read to answer certain expected questions and a spurious comprehension gain is felt. In too many of these books, reading comprehension tests are mostly objective-type exercises. In addition, the questions are often nothing but literal recall questions which students can correctly answer without having read the article.

In order to help a student develop flexibility in his reading speed he should be given a variety of comprehension quizzes which deal with literal, critical and aesthetic levels of comprehension. *Literal comprehension* involves the finding, understanding and recalling of main ideas, the ability to follow directions, and an awareness of a sequence of events. It is the most fundamental level of comprehension. *Critical comprehension* involves the ability to discriminate between fact and opinion, to recognize bias and propaganda, to recognize an author's inference and to make valid judgments. It requires using past experience to evaluate what is read. *Aesthetic comprehension* is the awareness of beauty, style, humor, satire, irony and quality in writing. It is a personal, affective comprehension. All too often, speed reading texts as well as many teachers operate mostly at the literal level with some training given to critical levels of understanding and virtually no training in aesthetic comprehension. However, all levels of comprehension should be treated equally if true reading flexibility is desired.

DEVELOPING LITERAL COMPREHENSION

To help the student develop his literal comprehension, instruction should be provided in finding the thesis of the material being read, in noting how the author proves or supports his ideas, and in an awareness of the variety of paragraph patterns used to develop his ideas such as: the use of illustration and example, comparison and contrast, definition of terms, division and classification, the use of factual details, and combinations of these methods. Helping the student to see patterns in writing can in turn speed up his reading comprehension and develop his appreciation of style and technique.

Skimming and scanning drills are essential and helpful to developing reading flexibility in the literal comprehension area. Maxwell (13) reports that the best technique for skimming and scanning practice is to reduce the amount of time the student is permitted to read the selection so that he is forced to try shortcuts. In addition, she reports that rapid scanning speeds among students produce fewer errors than among those who work slowly. Maxwell feels that instructors must do more than make suggestions and provide a few practice sessions to improve skimming and scanning techniques.

Frequent as well as a variety of drills are necessary to develop true flexible rates. There is no real need for special equipment or texts. Indexes, glossaries, and tables of content from the student's textbooks can be used for drill practices. Dictionaries and encyclopedias can be used. Xeroxed pages from the telephone directory, newspaper ads, television programming and various news stories make excellent drill material. Requiring the student to first read the questions which usually follow a timed reading selection and then to skim the article for the answers is also a helpful training device. Questions asked *before* students read help set purposes for reading. They direct students to relationships they should look for, thus *teaching* the student rather than just testing him. Still another method is to request that a student, after checking his answers to a comprehension quiz, always skim back through the article to locate the place where the correct answer appears to any question missed. All of these drills should be done under a severe time pressure.

In addition to skimming and scanning drills, students need to be taught to ask their instructors *how* to approach their reading assignments. For instance, when a student is told to read Chapter Six from his history text, the student should legitimately be able to ask his instructor questions such as these:

1. Should I read rapidly or carefully?
2. What is the main thing I should get from the chapter?
3. How does this chapter relate to what has been covered so far?
4. Will I be tested on reading? If so, what type of test?

When students begin asking such questions of their subject matter instructors, both student and instructor will be utilizing study techniques advocated in practically all how-to-read books.

Since good comprehension is based on the purpose for reading, the student should be shown how to preview, survey or focus his attention on an assigned reading in order to establish purposes for reading. There have been many SQ3R type mnemonic study devices developed (SQ4R, PQ3R, PQRST, OARWET, etc.) but they all basically advocate that the student preview the material to be read before attempting to read carefully. Practice sessions using previewing or focusing techniques on chapters from actual textbooks or essays are vital to developing flexibility. Since an author's thesis is usually expressed in the opening paragraphs, and since topic sentences are usually the first sentence in a paragraph, it is imperative to show students how a quick reading of these areas in a chapter or an essay can give a very clear picture of general content. In fact, such previewing is often all the reading a student may need, depending on the purpose of the assigned readings.

Developing Critical Comprehension

Once a student can understand clearly at the literal level, he then needs practice in critically evaluating the author's purposes and in challenging the validity of the author's statements. Drill work in discriminating fact as opposed to opinion is essential. The student should be asked the following questions about some materials he reads:

1. What is the thesis of the article just read?
2. Do you agree with the thesis? Why?
3. Is this the opinion you had on the subject before reading the article?
4. Where did you get your present opinion?
5. What would it take to change your opinion?
6. Was the article worth reading?
7. What is worth remembering?

Questions such as these do not lend themselves to answer keys and they are often omitted from reading texts. But they are vital questions if true meaning is to be gleaned from reading and such questions need to be incorporated in a reading program aimed at developing flexibility.

In addition, a student's critical comprehension can be enhanced when he is not just told but shown that everything that appears in print is not always accurate or true. Have students compare how two history texts deal with the same subject. Have students compare two different movie or television reviews from newspapers and magazines. Have students carefully examine certain advertising claims for their cleverness, accuracy, implication, and word selection. A good visual lesson on purpose in reading can be taught by showing two advertisements for the same brand automobile from magazines such as *Playboy* and *Time*. The use of bikini clad models draped around a super sports model Ford in a *Playboy* advertisement is a startling contrast to the use of a Ford station wagon loaded with children and dogs in a *Time* advertisement. The implications are obvious. Many students have an adequate background for such critical comprehension but they often fail to realize they have it or fail to use it if they have.

Developing Aesthetic Comprehension

Aesthetic comprehension is a natural outgrowth of literal and critical comprehension. It is a personal reaction to what has been read and reflects tastes and experiences. Unfortunately, students are seldom taught that their personal reactions and tastes are tied in with comprehension. They are more often taught that comprehension is "remembering what is read." But remembering what is read is often easier when it can be made personally meaningful and relevant—not always an easy task.

Aesthetic comprehension is usually left to the English teacher's domain. It is the English instructor who is supposed to be teaching appreciation of literature, awareness of style, an author's use of humor, irony, satire and so on. It is unfortunate that while these aspects of literature are being taught they are sometimes taught at the expense of expanding a student's aesthetic comprehension. Caught up in the terminology and their expertise, English instructors often discourage rather than encourage reading imaginative literature.

An example which reflects the lack in clarifying and developing thorough comprehension is taken from a college freshman English teacher's test on Shakespeare's *Othello*. Here are three typical questions:

1. In what folio edition does *Othello* first appear?
2. Who is Iago's mother?
3. How old is Othello?

There is nothing wrong with these questions. What *is* wrong is that those are the *only* kinds of questions on the test. They deal with only one level of comprehension. The student is not asked for his feelings about Othello, or if he has ever known someone like Iago, or even if he enjoyed reading the play. Thus, aesthetic or affective comprehension is stifled by tests which require a sponge-like absorption of every detail.

Training in reading imaginative literature (poetry, short stories, plays, novels) is just as vital as training in reading expository writing. Yet a gleaning of many contemporary speed reading texts shows an absence of such material. Most workbooks and texts restrict their reading selections to materials which lend themselves to multiple-choice or true-false questions, thus enabling the reader to check his answers in an answer key, plot his score on a chart and then start all over again doing the same thing. Inductively, these books teach a narrow view of comprehension.

Using fictional literature in a speed reading text would mean the following type questions would be necessary:

1. Did you enjoy the story? Why?
2. What do the characters represent?
3. Why do the characters act as they do?
4. What is the conflict between characters?
5. Discuss the writing techniques the author uses.
6. What images are particularly well done?

Incidentally, answering such questions after reading thousands of words per minute would indeed be worthy of a news article.

Oral discussion, both formal and informal, is another good means for developing student comprehension powers. Allowing students to exchange viewpoints regarding an assigned article or a timed reading selection from his text is recommended. Such activity enhances a reading assignment by taking its importance beyond a comprehension quiz. It allows a healthy interchange of ideas and permits students to actually use and become involved in what they read. It also shows students how differently other people react to the same reading material, an important lesson in comprehension.

SUMMARY AND RECOMMENDATIONS

Accepting the fact that reading rates can be increased, and accepting some known factors which research has shown to contribute most to increasing reading flexibility, the following recommendations are offered:

1. Flexible vocabulary-type training is essential to developing increased reading rates. Some valuable vocabulary activities are the use of:
   a. rapid word, phrase and number discrimination drills,
   b. personalized vocabulary card drills,
   c. word context drills,
   d. vocabulary textbooks designed to develop *all* word attack skills.
2. Flexible comprehension training which develops literal, critical and aesthetic levels of comprehension is also essential. Such training should include:
   a. exercises in developing literal comprehension or the ability to

identify main ideas, organizational patterns and pertinent facts;
b. extensive and varying exercises in skimming and scanning for literal comprehension as well as rate flexibility;
c. exercises in study-reading which would include methods for previewing, surveying or focusing to determine a purpose for reading;
d. exercises in developing critical comprehension so that the student recognizes bias and propaganda, recognizes the difference between fact and opinion, and learns not to believe everything he reads;
e. exercises in developing aesthetic comprehension or the student's sensitivity to levels of quality in writing and enjoyment in reading;
f. exercises in oral discussion of selected materials.

Until more valid research is done regarding man's ability to read thousands of words per minute, we can at least provide instruction based on the known factors.

To quote Bacon, "Some books are to be tasted, others to be swallowed, and some few to be chewed and digested." Our jobs as reading instructors are to help students learn to read and then help them to read to learn. We need to help them to know *when* and *how* to taste, *when* and *how* to swallow, and *when* and *how* to chew and digest what they read. If we can do this, we will be providing students with an awareness that there is no such thing as a reading rate but many reading rates of comprehension all based on the need and purpose for reading. But let us be careful that in our efforts for speed we do not, as did the old fisherman in Hemingway's *The Old Man and the Sea*, end by going too far out.

REFERENCES

1. Adams, W. Royce. *Increasing Reading Speed*. New York: Macmillan Publishing Co., Inc., 1969.
2. Berger, Allen. "Are Machines Needed to Increase Reading Rate?" *Educational Technology*, 59 (August 1960), 60.
3. ———. *Speed Reading, An Annotated Bibliography*. Newark, Del.: International Reading Association, 1967.
4. ———. "Speed Reading: Is the Present Emphasis Desirable?" *Current Issues in Reading*. Newark, Del.: International Reading Association, 1969, 45–70.
5. Brown, James I. *Programmed Vocabulary*. New York: Appleton-Century-Crofts, Inc., 1964.
6. ———. "The *Look* 20-Day Course in Quick Reading: Part II," *Look* (February 1970), 62–68.
7. Erhlich, Eugene. "Opinions Differ on Speed Reading." *NEA Journal*, 52 (April 1963), 44–46.
8. Flesch, Rudolph T. *Why Johnny Can't Read*. New York: Harper & Row, 1955.
9. Greene, Amsel. *Word Clues*. New York: Harper & Row, 1962.

10. Heilman, Arthur. "Rapid Reading: Uses and Abuses," *Journal of Developmental Reading,* 5 (Spring 1962), 157–63.
11. Holmes, Jack A. "The Substrata-Factor Theory of Reading: Some Experimental Evidence," in *New Frontiers in Reading,* ed. by J. Allen Figurel. New York: Scholastic Magazines, 1960, pp. 115–21.
12. Liddle, William. "An Initial Investigation of the Word Reading Dynamics Method," Unpublished doctoral dissertation, University of Delaware, 1965.
13. Maxwell, Martha J. "Assessing Skimming and Learning Skills Improvement," *The Psychology of Reading Behavior.* Eighteenth Yearbook of the National Reading Conference. Milwaukee: The National Reading Conference, Inc., 1969, pp. 229–33.
14. Miller, Lyle L. *Increasing Reading Efficiency,* Third Edition. New York: Holt, Rinehart and Winston, Inc., 1970.
15. Rausch, Sidney J., and Alfred B. Weinstein. *Mastering Reading Skills.* New York: American Book Company, 1968.
16. Spache, George D. "Is This a Breakthrough in Reading?" *Reading Teacher,* 15 (January 1962), 259–63.
17. Stauffer, Russell G. "Speed Reading at the University of Delaware," *Proceedings of the 44th Annual Education Conference,* University of Delaware, 10 (1962), 3–9.
18. Taylor, Stanford, et al. *Word Clues* (Books J, K, L, M), Huntington, N.Y.: Educational Development Laboratories, 1963.
19. Witty, Paul. "Rate of Reading—A Crucial Issue," *Journal of Reading* (November 1969), 102 ff.

TRANSFER TECHNIQUES IN READING IMPROVEMENT COURSES*

Joseph A. Fisher

There are many problems connected with the use of specialized equipment in reading improvement programs. In this article Fisher points to the need to re-evaluate both materials and teaching methods if federal monies available for materials, such as reading machines, are to be spent wisely. It is Fisher's view that certain limitations associated with the use of these machines can be attributed to the way they are used by the teacher rather than to the machines themselves. The basic purpose of this paper is to explain proven techniques whereby "transfer of the mechanically induced improvement of reading skills to the normal reading situation" can be effected.

1. What are some of the problems connected with the use of specialized equipment in reading improvement programs?

---

* Written especially for inclusion in this volume.

2. How can the two major problems associated with intensive pacer work be solved?

3. What is the "reading score"? What are the advantages of using the reading score?

4. How can the teacher "wean" students from the pacer?

5. How does one justify the use of the tachistoscope in reading improvement work?

6. How are progress charts used to best advantage?

7. What can be done legitimately to insure increases in comprehension scores?

The availability of federal monies for establishing and equipping reading improvement programs has done much to alleviate the age-old problem of finances that has traditionally plagued school systems considering such programs in the past. In order to insure that the money be wisely spent, it is reasonable to expect that it should also serve to stimulate considerable re-evaluation of teaching methods and materials as well. It is not surprising, then, to find many schools taking long hard looks at the specialized equipment being offered by various manufacturers as adjuncts to reading improvement programs in a serious effort to assess their true value.

In all likelihood, not all such reviews will be equally critical or motivated by the same needs. No doubt there will be found some newly appointed program development committees, composed of members largely ignorant of the more subtle aspects of remedial teaching, who will eagerly welcome the advice and guidance of equipment manufacturer salesmen in the selection and use of equipment and materials. Without questioning the sincerity of either party, this probably amounts to a delegation of the committee's responsibility in most cases. Others too, recognizing that it will probably be difficult—if not impossible—to employ a fully trained reading specialist to conduct the program will, unconsciously at least, expect the equipment and materials purchased to compensate for the lack of training in the teacher. For them the purchase of such equipment represents a kind of insurance against failure of the teacher to achieve the sort of minor miracle that the generous financing of such a program commonly envisions.

However the decision to purchase equipment is reached, and regardless of the motivation that originally prompted it, in most cases the sizeable capital investment such equipment represents will be justified ultimately on the grounds that it will make a positive contribution to the development of new and presumably better reading skills in those who use them. Although research findings have not yet quite justified blind confidence in all such equipment, it must be admitted that the machine approach can offer certain unique advantages.

Such devices do provide a welcome variety to the approaches open to the teacher; they regularly afford much needed motivation for students; they make it possible to effectively handle a larger group of students at one time; and they undoubtedly offer new hope for reading improvement in cases where reading is excessively slow because of bad habits, lack of confidence, or a certain compulsion to perfectionism on the part of the student. They proved effective where other methods have failed. Yet one must bear in mind that machines cannot be used successfully with all students and certainly should not be used indiscriminately with any students. These devices do not and cannot teach a child to read; they serve only as aids to the teacher in teaching the child by providing a special kind of control over certain facets of the reading process.

It will not be surprising, then, to find that many of the limitations associated with the use of such machines are not really inherent in the devices themselves but can be attributed to the manner in which they are used by the teacher. To be really effective, the training these devices afford must be transferred to the normal reading situations in which the student does his everyday reading. By using a pacer device it is quite possible to train a student to achieve quite high reading rates with good comprehension, only to learn that he is unable to read at even half that rate when unassisted. The unusually wide recognition spans which students learn to use effectively in tachistoscope work are almost impossible to find in use in the normal reading situation of those same students. There is, therefore, a valid basis for the criticism of reading improvement statistics based directly on skills employed while using various reading improvement devices. They are only measures of the student's success in learning to read with the device, and are not necessarily valid measures of the improvement that will be shown in normal reading situations. Teachers must not confuse learning to read *with* a machine with learning to read *from* a machine.

The procedures or techniques used to effect the transfer of the mechanically induced improvement of reading skills to the normal reading situation thus becomes the central problem in the effective use of equipment for improving reading skills. The purpose of the present discussion is to explain several proved techniques whereby such transfer can dependably be achieved for each of the more commonly used types of devices employed in machine-oriented reading improvement programs.

READING ACCELERATORS OR PACERS

Reading rate is perhaps the most readily measured phenomenon associated with reading and, because it appears to be dependent upon habit to a large extent, it has proved to be the most easily-improved reading skill. Devices which have been designed most specifically to improve rate of reading are generally referred to as reading accelerators or pacers. Regardless of type, whether driven by spring, gravity, or electricity, and whether the pressure to read faster is derived from a moving shutter, a bar, or a beam of light, all are designed to place the reader in a position in which he must read at a rate fast enough to outdistance a moving object or find it either impossible or inconvenient to see the reading material.

Student motivation for pacer work is usually quite high and is not noticeably affected by the usual factors of sex, age, or intelligence. Probably this motivation is founded on the feeling of accomplishment or success that one receives when beating the pressure mechanism to the bottom of the page. This page-end reward is immediate and recurrent, two characteristics of reinforcement having known validity in establishing new habits. Because of the unquestionably objective evidence the pacer affords that he is performing effectively at a given speed, the student is more willing to set new standards with confidence.

Two major problems are associated with intensive pacer work. First, there is danger that the student will become so fascinated with the challenge of beating the shutter to the bottom of the page that he will begin to neglect his comprehension. Younger children particularly seem to become satisfied with very superficial reading comprehension when they are allowed to work too long with pacers, but almost any student will give some evidence of this if he is not properly supervised. This problem is readily controlled, and may even be eliminated entirely by providing frequent comprehension checks over all material read with the pacer. Probably no more than twenty minutes should ever be devoted to pacer work in a given class period, but even during this twenty-minute period several comprehension tests should be taken. Students who achieve below the 70 per cent level on such tests should not be allowed to increase their reading speed further until their comprehension scores improve to at least this minimum level.

A second problem arising in connection with pacer work is not so easily avoided. The very interest and support such devices afford tend to make students dependent on them. After a few weeks of practice it is not unusual to find students who can read quite rapidly and with satisfactory comprehension while using the pacer and yet be unable to read at more than half that speed with comparable comprehension without it. Frequent comprehension checks and specific transfer exercises are essential prerequisites to intelligent and beneficial pacer usage, especially in these cases.

One very effective way to provide for this transfer is to have students, after only a few periods of training, shut off the drive mechanism when beginning the fourth page of pacer reading and require them to read the remainder of the page without external pressure. The pressure should be applied again at the beginning of the following page, and the same procedure repeated again with every fourth page thereafter.

The technique is easy to implement in the classroom, if all the students are required to read the same material at a rate set by the teacher. Because the pacers will control their reading rates and the teacher knows exactly where the group will be reading at all times, it is possible to signal the students to read without pressure when the proper page has been reached. Later, after students learn the technique themselves, they can be held responsible for reading every fourth page without pressure. Since this may entail a certain amount of distracting page counting by the students, it is recommended that students mark every fourth page of their pacer reading material before beginning work. The procedure is very effective in making students aware that they must be able to use the higher reading rates they are developing on the pacer, independently of the machine.

Another very effective procedure for achieving transfer of pacer speed is to require students to take a timed reading at the end of their pacer work period. A timed reading is an article of some fifteen hundred words which students read, keeping a record of their reading time. It is always followed by a comprehension check. The procedure can be simplified considerably if all students are required to begin reading on a signal from the teacher, and the time lapsed is recorded in five-second intervals on the blackboard by the teacher. To determine his reading rate, the student need only note the time on the board when he finishes reading and refer to a conversion table prepared by the teacher. By comparing his pacer scores with his timed reading scores, both teacher and student can see how much transfer has taken place.

In all evaluations of reading improvement mentioned thus far, two figures have been employed. When both of these vary in the same direction, it is a simple matter to interpret their meaning; unfortunately, there are frequent occasions in which one may rise and the other drop. When a student reads 200 wpm at 70 per cent on one occasion and on another reads 300 wpm with 80 per cent, he has undoubtedly improved. But when a student reads at 200 wpm with 80 per cent, and then finds that he reads 300 wpm with 70 per cent comprehension, he is less certain about his improvement. To eliminate such doubt it has been found useful to compute a single score that will make it easier to evaluate improvement by eliminating concern over whether increases in speed were justified by the loss of comprehension or vice versa. This figure is called a reading score, and it is computed by multiplying the reading rate in words per minute by the comprehension score in percentage form.

The reading score is easy to compute and provides a simple means of assessing overall growth of improvement, but it has other advantages which are not apparent until it has been used for some time. Reading rate and comprehension scores may vary widely from day to day, depending on a variety of circumstances; but the reading score, because it combines the two variables, is less affected by changes in either and tends to be more stable. Also, because it tends to weight comprehension more when speed rises and rate more when comprehension drops, it makes comparisons between easy and hard reading material more meaningful. By affording ready means of comparing pacer and independent reading, and difficult and easy materials, the reading score should be preferred as a measure of improvement over either rate or comprehension in most cases, especially where improvement graphs are employed to sustain motivation.

As work with the pacer progresses, the teacher should take active steps to wean students away from it entirely. This can be achieved by increasing the "off pacer" reading time systematically. When the student reaches the stage where he is able to read with the pacer about twice as fast as he reads without it and has adequate comprehension, or is found to be reading more than 500 wpm with the pacer with good comprehension, the weaning process should be initiated. This is accomplished in stages by requiring the student to read three pages with the pacer and the fourth without it for about one week; then the ratio is changed to three with and two without the pacer for another week or so. When this becomes comfortable, the student should begin reading two pages with the pacer and two without for another week. Then the off-pacer time is increased again so the student reads one page with it and three without it for a few sessions.

In the final stages of weaning the student uses the pacer only for a few minutes in the beginning of the period, and reads without it until the last few minutes of the practice period. Using and not using the pacer in the manner described develops a sense for speed in the student, because if his speed slackens between pacer usages the student immediately becomes aware of the change when he returns to the pacer. Used in this way the student literally learns to read from the pacer instead of learning to simply read with the pacer.

TACHISTOSCOPE

There is considerable controversy over how valid tachistoscopic training is in improving reading skills. But because of the close relationship between reading and perception, it is possible that it has more than motivational value. There is evidence that most poor readers spend much more time than is necessary to adequately perceive what is seen in a single fixation, and anything that can even motivate readers to reduce this fixation time would be accounted valuable in improving reading efficiency.

The tachistoscope is considered by many to be a means of developing word-grouping skills which can be applied to the printed page and result in rhythmical eye movements very conducive to accuracy of perception as well as speed. The increased visual span that such training is intended to develop is probably most readily transferred if the work is inserted between pacer practice sessions. During time allotted to pacer work, the students may be interrupted for a five-minute drill with the tachistoscope. After presenting five or ten 2-word phrases flashed at 1/25th of a second, a number of 3-word phrases may be presented at the same speed. It is important that the phrases increase in length as the exercise progresses. But extending phrases much beyond four words or about fifteen characters is probably unnecessary.

Toward the end of the training program phrases of different length may be intermixed. Time can be saved in this sort of drill if the student is not required to write out the phrases, but shown the phrase and immediately given the correct response. Then he need only check with a mark to see whether he was correct or not. To be correct, it must be entirely accurate.

His score is the per cent correct. The time exposure is often reduced to 1/100th of a second, but it is unlikely that reducing exposure rate below 1/10th of a second is ever actually transferred to normal reading conditions. Since it does not follow that a student who is able to read three words in 1/100th second using the t-scope will be able to read at a speed of 1,800 wpm—which is what this comes to in words per minute—it is difficult to imagine how such skill can be transferred to normal reading conditions. Hence there is little justification for developing it as a reading skill.

One feature of t-scope work deserves special attention, namely, the adaptability of this sort of drill to individual needs. The device is of considerable value in setting up a success pattern in students who have become discouraged about their progress or who possess a defeated attitude at the outset of their training program. In such cases number recognition drills seem to have a decided advantage over words or phrases, at least in the beginning. The student should be assigned to flash a series of 20 five-digit numbers only once at half-second speed. When he succeeds in correctly identifying 16 out of 20, he can reduce exposure time to one-fourth second. When necessary, in successive practice periods, higher speeds can be used to build the student's confidence even further. There is no real advantage in increasing the number of digits beyond about five because the drill is primarily designed to provide self-confidence. In working with numbers the student should write them before checking his work because of the danger of transposing digits.

When the student has overcome his defeated attitude, he may be given work with phrases instead of numbers and proceed much as the group work does. Since the value of such work lies in the tangible evidence it gives the student confidence that he can improve both in accuracy and speed of perception, there is no need to attempt a direct transfer of the skills so developed—except perhaps that with this conviction the student should be able to profit from the usual reading improvement program.

READING FILMS AND FILMSTRIPS

Reading films and filmstrips is essentially a mechanization of tachistoscopic exposure with the added dimension of rhythm and return sweep. Because of the pressure created by the sequential exposure of continuous material, these also share certain characteristics of the accelerator or pacer devices described earlier. The elimination of the time lag between successive exposures of phrases and the continuous character of the material makes the reading film much closer to a normal reading situation than is possible with the tachistoscope. This is an important attribute because it somewhat reduces the problem of transfer.

Because of common psychological foundations, transfer techniques suitable for pacer training will be suited to reading films or filmstrips as well. Just as the speed of reading developed with use of pacer devices often exceeds speed in reading without such pressure, so after using a film or film-strip there will very likely be a dropping off in reading speed and for identical reasons. Just as the reading speed developed under pacer pressure was transferred to normal reading by following pressure periods with short unassisted reading periods, so films and filmstrips may be employed before reading short articles to increase normal reading rate.

This can be achieved by having the class set up for a timed reading as described earlier, then turning off the lights and showing a part of a reading film. After the group has become accustomed to the reading rate imposed by the film, the lights may be turned on and work begun on the timed reading. Since it is advisable to avoid unnecessarily sharp contrast in lighting conditions, the room should not be entirely darkened when the film is shown.

PRINTED READING MATERIALS

Though it is possible to conduct a very effective reading improvement program by employing any of the mechanical adjuncts described earlier, it would be quite difficult to imagine an effective reading program that did not make considerable use of printed materials. Because they are such an essential part of the program, the teacher should be aware of techniques which will insure that these materials are used to the maximum advantage.

Because of the premium it seems necessary to place on rate and comprehension in the measurement of reading proficiency, extensive use is made of articles for which word counts have been made and conversion tables prepared which make it possible for the student to determine his reading rate at a glance if he knows how long it took him to read it. These articles are always followed by a comprehension test the student corrects himself and determines a percentage score. Although the primary purpose of such exercises is to measure reading efficiency, a careful record of performance in the form of a graph serves the additional purpose of motivation by providing the student with visual evidence of his improvement with each successive entry. These graphic records of performance, called progress charts, are excellent motivational devices. However, it is imperative that the charts indicate a general upward trend if they are to sustain student motivation, and therefore the teacher must be careful not to allow prolonged plateaus—or continuous drops—to develop in these graphs.

To convince the student of his potential, when these discouraging points develop, the teacher could use several variations of procedure. The student may be allowed to complete such a reading using only the even-numbered questions as a comprehension check. Then, after encouraging him to exert still greater efforts at speed, he may be allowed to read the same article a second time using the odd-numbered questions as his comprehension check. This approach is effective because it allows the student to concentrate on his speed feeling that he already knows the content of the selection. The true objective of such an exercise is to increase reading speed without resorting to mechanical aids. This constitutes a transfer of speed arising from the confidence built up by a previous reading.

Less dramatic, but perhaps more generally valid, increases in speed can be achieved by having students read two articles in succession. Care must be taken in this case that the two readings assigned are of equal difficulty, or that the second is somewhat easier that the first.

Increases in comprehension scores can also be highly motivating. These can often be insured by allowing the students to skim selections before reading them. Two approaches are available. In one, the students are allowed to read the first and last paragraphs of the article and the first sentence of each of the intervening paragraphs. Then the student is asked to pause and formulate questions for himself which he will keep in mind while reading the same article under timed conditions. This seems to enhance the student's power of concentration by providing him with a clear purpose for reading. The effect of the increased attention is revealed in proportionately higher comprehension scores for most students. An exercise of this kind is particularly valuable in cases where the student is discouraged by persistently low comprehension scores. A variation on this approach is to allow students a minute—more or less—depending on the length of the article, for skimming and having them read it under timed conditions.

Another method useful in raising comprehension scores is to allow students to read the comprehension questions before reading the article. The student should be urged to read only the questions, not the answer choices in this procedure. This type of exercise assists the student in the formulation of questions for which he should seek answers in his reading. It is particularly useful with students who find it difficult to frame valid questions prior to reading, or who have difficulty remembering them as they read. The exercise is really practice in directed reading.

As soon as the plateau or drop in the student's progress graph is improved these crutches can be eliminated. Meanwhile, the student has been occupied with developing useful supplementary reading skills.

Undoubtedly, other effective techniques of transfer will occur to the enterprising teacher who takes time to analyze the nature of the equipment with which he works. The degree to which the teacher succeeds in achieving such transfer determines the training value of the specialized equipment at his disposal. To this same degree he will succeed in improving the reading skills of his students.

Reading in the Content Areas

Introduction

The important goals of reading instruction are growth in reading and growth through reading. This growth does not stop, but it can be slowed down because of lack of adequate reading instruction at the time when it is needed—the high school years!

As the student advances through junior and senior high school, the reading materials increase in complexity and difficulty. In addition, new, higher-level purposes for reading place greater demands upon the reader. Because the subject-matter teacher has the responsibility of teaching his students to think more effectively about the ideas in his subject—and reading is a thinking process—it follows that the subject-mat-

ter teacher bears much responsibility for helping his students to improve their reading skills.

The nature of this help is two-fold. First, the teacher helps the students apply the basic reading skills to the reading task. (How these skills are taught initially was discussed in the first nine sections.*) Second, these teachers teach their students the specialized reading skills and modes of inquiry that are specific to their particular subjects. How the basic skills are applied in the content areas is discussed in some of the articles in Section 10. Most of the articles are devoted to explaining how to teach the specialized reading skills needed to master a subject.

* Certain basic topics such as teaching the nonreader to read are dealt with thoroughly in Section 12.

Vocational Arts

READING AND INDUSTRIAL ARTS; INTERVIEW*

Gordon Funk

Reading plays a vital role in developing competence in the industrial arts. Funk discusses the nature of this role and how industrial arts teachers can capitalize on what is known about helping students improve their reading skills. He shows how the ten basic reading skills can be applied specifically to industrial arts.

1. List in descending order of importance the ten most important concepts discussed in this article.

2. Evaluate, in terms of these ten concepts, the reading instruction aspects of an industrial arts class, or program, with which you are familiar.

3. What basic steps would you take to implement the initiation of reading instruction in industrial arts classes?

4. State the article's key ideas.

The belief that industrial arts—as a phase of general education—has a role in fostering improved ability in reading—as the basic facet of the three "R's"—indicates that I-A instructors should re-examine their teaching practices in this area.

The following report questions Gordon Funk, supervisor of industrial education for the Los Angeles, Calif., City Schools on: (1) the modern concepts of presenting reading and how they should be incorporated into industrial arts education; and (2) how, specifically, the ten basic skills of reading are presentable in the typical I-A program.

---

* REPRINTED FROM *Industrial Arts and Vocational Education*, L. (October 1961), pp. 24, 25; 45. Copyright, 1961, The Bruce Publishing Co.

Q. Mr. Funk, why would you say, first of all, that the reading program has special implications for industrial arts?

A.   The role of industrial arts in the total pattern of general education in the secondary school certainly implies an objective for our field of reinforcing and expanding the three "R" skills. And I believe there are two reasons why industrial arts educators should expand their practices in the methods used to teach and to develop the first "R," reading. First, many secondary students, who have a deeper interest in industrial arts than in academic subjects, have achieved reading levels no higher than the intermediate elementary grades and need additional reading practice which can be gained through this motivation. Secondly, methods used to develop basic reading skills have special applications to the development of reading ability in the highly technical subject matter of industrial arts.

Q. In illustrating this role, wouldn't the changing concepts in the modern reading program provide a basis for discussion?

A.   Very definitely. Before industrial arts instructors will acknowledge the point of view which involves their acceptance of an expanded responsibility for reading instruction, they must become aware of, and accept, the modern concept that there is no subject matter of reading; that all teachers in secondary education share in the responsibility for teaching reading; that the elementary school does not have the sole charge for teaching reading skills. And beyond that, the I-A instructor must accept the concept that a reading program conducted within his specialized field, is not only beneficial to the reading program but also to the subject field.

Q. What is the status of research in this area?

A.   To my knowledge there is no published research available with regard to the results of a reading program in industrial arts; however, research by Kathleen B. Rudolph[1] definitely established that a reading program in the social studies area helped the student master the subject more adequately, while improving in reading skills and increasing reader comprehension. As a result of this reading instruction, pupils improved in such reference skills as notetaking, outlining, and summarizing, as well as in the ability to comprehend written materials.

Q. And you would say that this has direct applications in industrial arts?

A.   It is reasonable to assume that a high degree of basic reading ability, supplemented by specific instruction in the reading skills pertinent to industrial arts, would find that there was growth in overall reading ability as well as a quickening of abilities in the mechanical areas. And Rudolph's study implied that such superiority in social studies content achievement can be accomplished in a similar manner in regular industrial arts instruction

[1] Kathleen B. Rudolph, *The Effect of Reading Instruction on Achievement in Eighth Grade Social Studies* (New York: Bureau of Publications, Teachers College, Columbia University, 1949).

patterns without additional class time or additional expenditure for reading instruction.

Q. How, then, can and should industrial arts contribute specifically to reading?
A. First, let's identify the reading skills most needed by learners. Then we can demonstrate how these skills can be developed in the I-A program. A widely accepted list is that organized by Simpson in her manual, *Helping High School Students Read Better:*[2] (1) developing reading readiness; (2) reading to get the main idea; (3) reading to get important details; (4) reading to answer a specific question; (5) reading to evaluate; (6) applying what is read; (7) developing vocabulary; (8) outlining and summarizing what is read; (9) reading for implications; and (10) increasing the reading rate.

Q. And industrial arts has responsibilities for the development and application of all ten of these reading skills?
A. In varying degrees, of course. This variance is in accord with the relationship of basic reading abilities to the content field, since all subject areas do not require the same reading abilities.

Q. How does industrial arts help develop the first skill, reading readiness?
A. As used in elementary school, readiness means the organization of the instructional program in reading to accommodate the individual pupil's physical, social, emotional, and mental development and to help this pupil acquire the understandings, skills, and attitudes necessary to master the reading material presented. Reading readiness, applied on the more mature secondary school level, promotes growth in basic reading abilities and develops skills in specialized reading areas.

Q. And what techniques in industrial arts will accomplish these reading readiness goals?
A. In *labeling*, tools are identified by labels at the beginning of the semester. In *identifying*, an orientation device, such as a floor plan of the shop with equipment located and numbered, is given to the student on his first day in class. Each piece of equipment in the shop has a printed identification sign conspicuously attached. Eager to become familiar with the equipment, the student completes a numbered sheet with the name of the piece of equipment listed opposite the number corresponding to that on the floor plan. In *demonstrating*, the teacher uses the technical names of all tools, material, and equipment during each demonstration. He writes the new name on the chalkboard and uses the name in context. In *technical illustration*, a pictorial representation of tools and equipment, parts are labeled.

[2] Elizabeth A. Simpson, *Helping High School Students Read Better* (Chicago: Science Research Associates, Inc., 1954).

In addition to these techniques, reading readiness is promoted in industrial arts by the very nature of the materials and tools used. When a teacher talks about a jack plane, for example, he has one in his hand and he points out and demonstrates its functions and how it differs from other planes. When the teacher discusses the wood used for building a shoeshine box, he shows samples of white oak, white pine, and mahogany. The student handles each piece and notes its color, weight, grain characteristics, strength, workability, etc. These examples for nurturing reader readiness are part of the fiber of the everyday teaching process in industrial arts. Let's go on to the second reading skill, reading to get the main idea.

Q. Does industrial arts contribute to this skill also?
A. To develop this ability, students are taught to vary their reading rates. The speed-up reading rates used to select the main ideas are known as skimming and speeded reading. This important skill is promoted in industrial arts through the use of a textbook and supplemental books.

Q. What are illustrations of this?
A. One example of this is a student in auto mechanics bringing his 1954 Plymouth into the shop. He reports to the instructor that he is getting poor mileage and has difficulty starting the car when it is cold. After trouble shooting, under the instructor's direction, the student determines that the carburetor needs to be overhauled. Before the student undertakes the job, he is questioned by the instructor as to his general knowledge about carburetion, and is referred to the section in his text which deals with this subject. His assignment is to skim the article, report back on the main idea—the function of the carburetor in the fuel system of an automobile. Thus, through individual questioning, the instructor builds the need for the skill of skimming for the main idea.

Another example of the development of this skill consists of the student who, under instruction, determines that a wood project ready for finishing, needs three coats of semi-gloss enamel, and wants the color to be mellow ivory. To select a can of paint to meet the two specifications of color and degree of gloss, the student must skim the information on the label of the paint can to obtain the pertinent information which indicates how closely the paint meets the above specifications.

Q. The third reading skill, reading to get important details, would seem to have a very direct application in industrial arts. How would you illustrate this?
A. By going back to the paint can label. I believe we can show how success in developing this skill is important in, and directly related to, industrial arts. This skill enables the student to follow specific directions, to organize work on an orderly step-by-step basis, and to be successful in using material according to directions. The paint can label supplies necessary directions which the student must understand in order to finish his project success-

fully. Outlined, according to the manufacturer's directions, are drying time, area of coverage (does he have enough paint to do the job?), preparation of surface to be painted, and safety instruction.

Again, this reading for specific information is handled by the teacher on an individual basis at the time of need; repeated questioning elicits the specific information and the student, in most cases, verifies the information he has read by inspection, measuring, and testing.

Q. The fourth skill, reading to answer a specific question, seems quite broad. How is this applied specifically to industrial arts?
A.   This skill involves a combination of the second and third basic reading abilities, I would say. Reading to answer a specific question is concerned with locating the information which requires skimming or speed reading, the use of an index, understanding a table of contents, the importance of footnotes, alphabetizing, etc. Through the use of textbooks and reference material, the I-A instructor reinforces and provides practice in the use of the standard means of locating information. After this first step, the second phase, finding the answer to a specific question, is identical to the third skill of reading for important details.

It is in the first part of this fourth skill that the instructor has specific responsibilities for reading instruction. The reference books used regularly in I-A classes have such an unusual organization that for their correct use students need specific instruction.

Q. What are some examples of these specialized reference materials which require the exercise of the reading skill—accomplished, of course, on an individual basis at the time of need and in answer to a specific question?
A.   Well, there is the *Machinery's Handbook*, which is organized in a typical reference manner, and *Chilton's Automobile Repair Manual*, which is an example of the complexity of organization of auto repair manuals. It has the table of contents arranged by topic of the separate car section and not by page number.

However, let's consider *The Radio-Electronic Master*,[3] the official buying guide of the industry. It is an example of a specialized I-A reference book which requires specific instruction in its use. The use of this specialized reference material is an example of one of the extensions of reading skills developed in Industrial Arts. As are many shop reference materials, this buying guide is not organized according to standard reference practices. It can be confusing, therefore, unless specific instruction for its use is given. Instead of an index at the back of the book, it has three separate indices: (1) alphabetical index of manufacturers, (2) general index, and (3) outlines index of display pages. These are in the front of the book and occupy the same

---

[3] *The Radio-Electronic Master*, 20th ed. (New York: The United Catalog Publishers, Inc., 1955).

place as the usual table of contents. The pages are not numbered consecutively, but are organized in sections A–U and numbered within each section.

In using such a reference work, students read to answer a specific question by locating the information and reading for important details. This area of reading instruction is one, perhaps, which many instructors have not recognized as a contribution to their students' reading skills. Students certainly are not aware that they are acquiring reading skills.

Q. *And the fifth skill, reading to evaluate; how does that gear with I-A instruction?*
A. This skill enables the student to differentiate between statements of fact and statements of opinion. They also check the basis of authority for making a statement. The time that a statement was made is important, since it might have been made prior to the discovery of some new data. Students learn to evaluate by comparing statements made by different authorities and then to check these authorities whenever possible by direct experience and research.

Q. *And how is this accomplished in industrial arts instruction?*
A. This is, perhaps, the least used reading skill in Industrial Arts, but on an advanced level, the student with experience and skill evaluates design information, construction procedure, etc. The reading of schematic dia-

---

HOW DO YOU COMMUNICATE?

In your teaching, do you help students learn through these experiences? Check those you develop.

__ Listening	__ Accuracy in reading	__ Schematic diagrams
__ Graphic and concrete experiences for understanding	__ Following directions	__ Graphs
__ Oral use of new words	__ Reasoning	__ Figures
__ Word recognition	__ Use new words in writing	__ Charts
__ Vocabulary Building	__ Fact recall	__ Maps
__ Comprehension	__ Evaluation	__ Pictures
__ Selecting main points	__ Critical analysis	__ Cartoons
__ Using textbook aids	__ Integration of new ideas	__ Symbols
__ Using supplementary books	__ Forming sensory images	__ Working drawings
__ Alphabetizing	__ Making comparisons	
__ Using the dictionary	__ Organizing ideas	
__ Selecting correct definitions	__ Making generalizations	
__ Adjustment of reading rate to purpose	__ Summarizing	
__ Enjoyment of reading	__ Recreational reading	

If, in your classes, students are learning some of the above,

YOU ARE TEACHING READING!

grams, working drawings, etc., needs to be evaluated, particularly those in some of the hobby magazines.

Q. *Let's go on to the sixth skill, applying what is read. This would seem to have a direct relation to I-A instruction.*
A. Absolutely. It's most important in our field and every instructor should include the teaching of this skill as a regular part of his program while using the three common methods of communication: (1) oral instruction, (2) working drawings which include some writing, and (3) written instructions. The good teacher balances, of course, these three methods of imparting information.

Q. *And what are examples of how these methods of instruction are utilized to help students apply what they read?*
A. First, in making a job card, a sequential list of operations in building a project, the student, from reading instructions, is required to write the operations in order. (This technique parallels development of reading charts in the elementary school.) This individual effort follows, of course, from the making of a job card as a class project.

Another operation which involves the application of information obtained from reading is that of planning a "routine bill" for a production job. This involves planning production stations for the step-by-step operations of cutting, fastening, assembling, finishing, packaging, and distributing.

The reading of dimensions, the selection of materials, the use of fasteners, the selection of drills and taps, and the setting of a form all involve reading followed by application. Of course, simpler examples consist of interpreting such safety signs as "place only rags here," "observe safety lines," "do not use this piece of equipment without the instructor's approval," etc.

I would say the important factor in the application of what is read in industrial arts is that the results of the interpretation of the written material is immediately apparent. It is the responsibility of the I-A instructor to have students use written material as directed, to help students develop abilities in this type of reading, and to challenge the able students with problems in applying what they read to complex situations.

Q. *Has the seventh skill, developing a vocabulary, a high degree of application in industrial arts?*
A. Instructors with industrial arts training have made, I would judge, more progress in the development of vocabulary than any of the other basic reading abilities.

Although there has been some recent literature published concerning the vocabulary needs for the different activities by grade level—as well as lists appearing in study guides—there is a need for basic research in the vocabulary of industrial art subjects. The principal areas which seem to need investigation are: (1) the level of vocabulary of secondary school textbooks; (2) basic vocabulary lists developed by activities and grade levels in oral and reading and writing functions; and (3) the words which have industrial arts meanings differing from their common usage, for example, "tolerance."

But, to go on, instructors promote the development of vocabulary by labeling, by the use of completion quizzes, by captions on bulletin boards and other displays. Instructors must realize that it is not enough for them to say a word. In order for students to learn a new word, they must hear it, see it, use it, and review it.

Q. And the eighth reading skill?
A. Before we go on to that, I would like to interject a few devices which the instructor must use to further the seventh skill. One commonly used practice is to have students develop a vocabulary list in a notebook. Another is to have a "word-of-the-week" sign in which the letters can be changed to follow a schedule to highlight important words. By including this series of words in shop demonstration and in "quickie" quizzes, the teacher helps underline the importance to students of adding technical words to their vocabulary.

The elementary school technique of using flash cards is highly adaptable here. Many teachers are using flip charts for instructional purposes with carefully prepared and labeled illustrative material; this labeling makes it easy for the teacher to coordinate oral and visual stimuli so necessary for vocabulary building.

In addition, I'm eager to learn the results of using a dictionary box. This has a series of 5 by 8 cards with an important word printed in the upper left-hand corner of each card. Immediately under this is the word divided by syllables with accent for pronunciation. Pictures and sentences illustrate the word. On the reverse side of the card will be a definition of the word. This dictionary box is essential when used by students writing job cards, bills of material, and other written reports; by amplifying dictionary information, it extends learning and increases student independence.

Q. And how does the eighth skill, outlining and summarizing what is read, apply to industrial arts?
A. Let's consider the last three skills together: the eighth; the ninth, reading for implications; and the tenth, increasing the reading rate.

Outlining and summarizing what is read facilitates organizing of important and valid information according to a purpose in mind—a study technique, according to research, which helps the learner retain more information than merely reading and rereading assigned material. This skill does have limited application in industrial arts. When we discussed the use of the job card for the sixth reading skill, we noted that this card is one form of an outline, or a step-by-step organization of doing activities.

Reading for implication, the ninth skill, is again, of relatively little importance in our field. In consumer education, though, students are taught to question material published in advertisements. Statements such as "brass finished" and "walnut finished hardwood" are analyzed.

And the tenth skill, increasing the reading rate, is approached when students are taught to adjust their reading rate from skimming to locate needed material to reading slowly to find important details.

Q. What would you say then, that the Industrial Arts teacher might do by way of furthering reading skills in his instruction?
A.   Well, on the secondary level in the Los Angeles City Schools, students are encouraged to do free reading in I-A classes. Each shop has a small library—approximately 50 books, plus magazines which apply to the area of instruction. Several magazines are supplied in classroom sets. Research has shown that there is a high interest factor, I might add, in mechanical and technical magazines and students are taught to read these for enjoyment. Above all, I-A teachers need to be aware of their role and responsibilities in reading instruction.

Q.   Finally, Mr. Funk, would you care to suggest what might be done on different levels by way of accelerating the role of industrial arts in teaching reading?
A.   Teacher training programs must include at least a survey course in principles and purposes of the reading program. School districts should establish in-service training programs to enlighten industrial arts instructors about their responsibilities.

The importance of the role of industrial arts in the development of basic reading abilities is clearly evident. It must be apparent also that there are specialized reading skills peculiar in industrial arts. Our instructors should be alerted to the contribution to, and responsibility for, developing this basic skill. An analysis of the more successful teachers' techniques reveals many areas where reading instruction is taking place—and it is taking place without the teacher designating the instruction as reading, in his own thought or in that of the students.

The most significant contribution that the discipline of industrial arts can make to reading is in the area of development of meaning! In the industrial society in which we live we need to understand the language of industry. In order to be an educated man in this civilization, one must have an understanding of the world of industry. Basic to this understanding is reading. And basic to all reading is meaning!

How to Provide Better Assignments for Improved Instruction[*]
John W. Struck

What do assignments have to do with reading? Practically everything! To a large extent the nature of the reading approaches employed reflect directly the nature of the assignment given. Struck discusses various aspects of assignment making, and relates them to reading in industrial arts. These ideas have applications in other fields, also.

1. How important is the assignment in teaching?

2. Evaluate the course assignments that you have made or that have been given to you during the last week in terms of the characteristics of good assignment making.

3. Write three examples of each type of question for some specific material and a specific class.

4. In view of the many suggestions for improving reading instruction in industrial arts, criticize the adage, "Teachers are born, not made."

As the "starting point in guiding learning," assignments can be an effective teaching technique; this discussion tells how to use them, with information on types, characteristics, and so on.

How many of us have fallen into the habit of making class or shop assignments in a matter-of-fact, perfunctory manner? Or worse yet, have we come to the point where assignments of homework, reports, and other in-school or out-of-school work has been relegated to such an unimportant role so as to be virtually nonexistent? In both our industrial arts and our vocational–industrial classes, are we *really* challenging our students? Are we really developing minds parallel to and equal with the development of manipulative skills? Certainly we must admit to overemphasis of the manipulative phases of training at times; we must also recognize that in this modern industrial and technical world, the mental development of students is not among the least important reasons for the very existence of industrial education.

SIGNIFICANCE OF ASSIGNMENTS

Educationally, assignments are of far greater importance than is commonly recognized. As far as organized school instruction is concerned, the assignment is the starting point in guiding learning. With increased emphasis

[*] REPRINTED FROM *Industrial Arts and Vocational Education*, LI (November 1962), pp. 24, 25. Copyright, 1962, The Bruce Publishing Co.

being placed upon attitudes in learning and upon the prime importance of interest, it can be seen that the assignment can, and should, become the means for a right start.

Though not intending to minimize teaching methods and organization, it has been held by many experienced teachers that (1) the desire to learn is more important than are methods of teaching, and (2) the student's attitude toward learning is more important than well-organized courses of instruction. It is precisely for these reasons that assignments are so educationally important. Through them, the teacher has many opportunities to so influence student attitudes that effective learning will result.

RELATION TO INDIVIDUAL DIFFERENCES

All teachers recognize the existence and extent of individual differences, and assignments provide an opportunity to do something about it. The teacher can modify the assignment in amount, quality, difficulty, sequence, and type. Such changes take into account personality traits, previous experience, capacity, and other factors that must be considered in fitting work to individual requirements.

Other differences may likewise serve as guideposts in making assignments. There are differences between individuals and also between schools and communities, such as differences in resources, equipment, facilities, public opinion, occupational opportunities, etc.

TYPES OF ASSIGNMENTS

So important are proper assignments to today's effective teaching and so different from yesterday's type, that brief mention should be made to illustrate this point. The "old-type" assignments were usually made on the basis of pages, paragraphs, topics, chapters or questions. Today's "new-type" form of assignments more often stresses the development of original thinking and of more carefully directed learning.

Weaver and Cenci list a variety of student assignments, such as "reports, observations, experiments, readings, investigations, shop work to be done, notebooks to be expanded, or problems to be solved."[1] Other assignments may be made on the basis of job sheets, units, projects, contracts, or work orders.

ESSENTIAL CHARACTERISTICS

While assignments differ greatly from class to class and individual to individual, most are characterized by a number of rather essential elements.

[1] Gilbert G. Weaver and Louis Cenci, *Applied Teaching Techniques* (New York: Pittman Publishing Corp., 1960), p. 50.

Check the various assignments you now make to see if they meet most of the following suggested characteristics:

1. *The Assignment Should Be Related to Previous Learning.* An old principle of starting with the known and proceeding to the unknown is involved here. An old, time-worn suggestion, but still excellent and worthwhile.

2. *The Assignment Should Be Clear and Definite.* Use some of the rules of a good, concise newspaper report by indicating *what* is to be done, *when* it is to be done, *how* it is to be done, and how *well* it is to be done. It is possible for poor assignments to be definite, yet not clear to the students. Don't use hazy phrases or unfamiliar technical terms, words, or expressions. Use concrete and specific examples where possible.

3. *Good Assignments Indicate Sources.* Save students time by mentioning specific references, materials to be used, tools and equipment needed. With more mature students, teachers may be justified in giving less detailed or specific sources in order to develop students' abilities in finding sources.

4. *Good Assignments Stimulate Interest.* Well made assignments call into play both emotional and intellectual responses so that the problem or job will be begun with zeal. In making assignments, interest may be destroyed by too much talking, whereas demonstrations and specific examples used to illustrate what is wanted and expected from an assignment are often very effective motivators. Show students what to look for, what parts to study. Use thought-provoking questions to stimulate curiosity and a desire. Interest is also developed by appealing to desirable forms of competition and rivalry and to the inherent urge of constructiveness and curiosity.

5. *Good Assignments Guide Learning.* Good assignments should give certain suggestions, should ask for certain information, and should lead to thought-provoking activity. They should not be so detailed that they require little more ability than to do as one is told. Neither may they be so general that students must guess as to what is expected. Good assignments should not do all the thinking for the student; neither should they lack suggestions for a good approach. Assignments can direct attention to possible points of difficulty and can make suggestions concerning them.

6. *Assignments Should Be Suited to Goals and Circumstances.* When assignments are made in industrial arts where tryouts, exploration, and guidance are important factors in the outcomes desired, they should definitely encourage student growth in these directions. But when assignments are given with specific trades or vocational objectives in mind, the procedure needs to be different.

All assignments should enable students to be successful in completing them with reasonable effort. Problems and tasks should increase in difficulty from week to week in order to challenge students. Success breeds interest, confidence, additional effort, and more success. Make each assignment appropriate to the individual concerned and the objectives desired.

QUESTIONS MOTIVATE AND GUIDE

Both oral and written questions serve as excellent guides to study and many a student has been motivated to do intensive reading and searching as a result of well-timed, pinpointing questions by his instructor. Several types of questions serve well to achieve this goal:

1. *Factual Questions.* These often call for facts secured through memorization or through more thoughtful learning.
2. *Recall Questions.* Should involve not only memory, but also selective thinking.
3. *Questions Requiring Reasoning and Selective Thinking.* This involves thought processes of a higher order than in the two preceding ones. Explanations of processes and principles are often called for in this type. Can be quite involved. Excellent practice and training.
4. *Questions Calling for Application or Interpretation.* One may know much and still lack appreciation. An assignment can be made more meaningful through questions that ask for evaluation or interpretation.

Many other types of questions also serve well. For purposes of motivating assignments, first one, then another, will serve best. A varying combination of types is also often helpful.

OTHER MOTIVATORS

TRADE LITERATURE. All alert teachers in the various phases of industrial education know of the interest and appeal to students that information concerning new tools, materials, and processes holds. A wide range of educationally valuable trade literature is readily available from manufacturers and magazines. Technical advances within recent years have been rapid, affecting particularly materials which are now available. Assignments of reports and readings can be most interesting and stimulating.

INDUSTRIAL, TRADE, AND TECHNICAL TERMS. New words and terms arouse interest, and many varied and interesting assignments involving this work can be made. Simply distributing a list of technical terms together with definitions for the students to learn can be quite deadening. To explain in a class discussion what various tools are called or parts are named, and having the *student* make up a definition *which he can best remember*, is much more stimulating from the student's point of view.

BLUEPRINT READING. Assignments asking questions concerning blueprints, shop drawings, or manufacturers' schematics is like challenging students with a game or puzzle. Judicial use of such assignments offers many advantages. By asking students to make shop sketches in connection with the blueprint reading, the teacher combines muscular participation together with practice in mastering blueprints. Skills thus developed through the use of several senses, together with high interest, are likely to be more permanent.

JOB SHEETS, WORK ORDERS. Assignments of this type should not provide all decisions, but should be designed so as to give the student practice in planning and making decisions. The objective must be stated clearly, but students (except rank beginners) should plan materials to be used, estimate costs, determine order of procedure, etc. Only through practice do people learn to plan and make good decisions. It is through interesting assignments that teachers can hope to achieve these aims of their teaching.

CONTRACT ASSIGNMENTS. Probably educators borrowed the term *contract* from the field of business or industry. Just as a contract is usually made for service of considerable extent, so the contract in educational work is a large-unit assignment. In form and content, the contract should vary greatly in order to be suited to its purpose. Outcomes sought may be either highly specialized or broad in scope. The contract must not be a standardized form of school work. Flexibility is the keynote here. Relatively long-time assignments such as these have the advantage of promoting the co-ordination of learning. Various areas of learning, such as mathematics, science, and drawing, may be needed. Completion of contract assignments often cuts across traditional, academically determined boundary lines just as do life experiences. While the term *contract* is not often heard in today's industrial education shops, laboratories, and classes, it is a teaching tool well worth using.

OPEN YOUR TOOLBOX

Good teachers, just as good mechanics, must have the best tools to do a good job. There are *many* fine tools in the creative teacher's tool kit— each with its own special or general purpose. Among these are the various types of assignments just mentioned. Each is used to help achieve a certain objective, to get a certain job done.

Let's open our tool kit of teaching tools, dust them off, oil them up a little, and start putting these specialized tools to work. A good mechanic would never try to use an adjustable crescent wrench for everything. Neither do good teachers rely upon only a few techniques of teaching to do the best job. With your next assignments, put some planning and thought into them—and good results will surely be yours.

Solving Reading Problems in Vocational Subjects*

Isidore N. Levine

In this extensive report Levine identifies very specific reading problems that occur in vocational subjects. He gives detailed suggestions for helping the student overcome these reading problems, and he expresses a definite attitude about who is responsible for giving this instruction.

1. Who should help solve reading problems in vocational subjects? Why?

2. Do you agree with the various assumptions of the author regarding experiential backgrounds of English teachers? (See also Point Two in the summary.)

3. How might "English" teachers and "vocational arts" teachers work together to solve the problem raised in this report?

4. State the article's key ideas.

Many teachers of trade subjects in the vocational high schools are convinced that their students can't read. The pupils show their inadequacies by being unable to cope with the texts provided for them. They indicate their limitations by their failures on the final written examinations. They are unable to read the job sheets that can be crucial in daily shop work. Every teacher would like to see some improvement in this deplorable situation.

Some shop teachers feel that reading is the job of the teacher of English. He teaches spelling, composition, vocabulary and literature—all the elements comprising the study of reading. Why doesn't the English teacher do his job well enough to solve the reading difficulties the students experience in other subjects? Perhaps the language arts teacher would assume such responsibility if he were certain he could do the work required. However, mere willingness to teach "reading" does not solve special problems to be met in instructing pupils in the art of getting meaning from a page of trade information.

---

* REPRINTED FROM *High Points*, 43 (April 1960), pp. 10–27, by permission of the publisher.

SPECIALIZED VOCABULARY

What are some of those problems? Suppose we take electric wiring as a possible trade subject for teaching reading. The class in English is taught to recognize the words "splice," "junction," "tap," "tee," "knotted," "pigtail," and "Western Union." The dictionary definitions of these words are as follows:

splice—joining of ropes or timbers by overlapping.
junction—joining or being joined, station.
tap—(1) strike lightly (2) a stopper or plug (3) tool for cutting internal screw threads.
tee—a mark from which a golf player starts, a little mound of sand and dirt.
knotted—(1) joined (2) tangled. (There are eight other definitions the teacher of English could rule out as being unrelated to electrical work.)
pigtail—braid of hair hanging from the head.
Western Union—a telegraph company.

The final electrical wiring examination includes this typical question:

To make a splice in a junction box where a number of wire leads are to be joined, the best splice to use is the (a) tap or tee (b) knotted tap (c) pigtail (d) Western Union.

No combination of definitions will yield a solution to the problem for the ambitious teacher of English. We can go farther and say that even accompanying illustrations for each of these splices would still leave the language arts instructor feeling that he was teaching an unfamiliar language.

Lest some teachers suppose that the electrical trades have the only occupational information the English teacher cannot read, we will have to take an example from the radio and television field. A recent final test in that subject carried this question:

In a 100% modulated AM transmitter the modulator varies the carrier (a) from zero to the strength of the carrier, (b) from zero to twice the strength of the carrier, (c) from zero to half the strength of the carrier, (d) does not vary.

As an English teacher, the writer cannot help admiring any pupil who has the knowledge and understanding to read the above intelligently—not as an academic studies teacher would read it, that is, with correct pronunciation, phrasing, inflection and emphasis, but with the meaning necessary to arrive at a correct answer and to be able to explain the reason for such selection.

As a matter of fact, the above passage takes the writer back to his high school Latin study days, when he could "read" the orotund phrases of Caesar's Commentaries with little inkling as to what that ancient was trying to communicate. In the case of radio and television, there is no Latin "pony" to help understand the above question. We can go farther here and state that no application of the thousand and one skills of reading so exhaustively described in the new Board of Education Curriculum Bulletin, "Reading Grades 7-8-9. A Teacher's Guide to Curriculum Planning," can be of any help here. Reading the above properly means studying the subject.

Perhaps other examples from the trade subjects will make this situation even clearer. In the pamphlet on "Machine Shop Practice for Vocational High Schools" (Curriculum Bulletin #10—1954–1955 Series) on page 82, we find the following in part:

Unit—How to Turn Tapers by the Offset Tailstock Method
Topic—Checking Offset with Dividers
1. Set the legs of the dividers to the required offset. Adjust set-over screws until the distance between the index line on the base and the index line on the tailstock body corresponds to the setting of the dividers.

Here the teacher of English is not too puzzled since the number of technical references is limited and there is an accompanying series of illustrations with the directions. But after calling out the words and studying the drawings we are still far from a complete understanding of this first step. These directions are not meant to be read and discussed. They are useless without the equipment to which they can be applied as far as instruction is concerned.

Another illustration from still another trade will throw light on still another facet of this problem. In the course of study called "Hairdressing and Cosmetology for Vocational High Schools" (Curriculum Bulletin #8—1952–1953 Series) we note the Instruction Sheet on page 85 includes this series of steps:

FACIAL MASSAGE

STEPS IN FACIAL

1. Apply cleansing cream
2. Give manipulation for cleansing
3. Remove cream
4. Apply massage cream
5. Give massage manipulation
6. Remove massage cream
7. Apply astringent
8. Apply powder base
9. Apply makeup

POINTS TO REMEMBER

Apply cream with an upward and outward movement.
To remove cream dab at it lightly with tissues.

As a male teacher of English it might be a little embarrassing to study this with a class of girls, but there would be little difficulty in interpreting and understanding the words. Here at last is a trade sheet we can read. But, would it be wise to take the time in the English classroom for this? Like Shakespeare's plays, these directions are not meant to be read aloud only.

They are supposed to be *acted* out and certainly not in an English room except in pantomime. And further, the trade of cosmetology has its own foreign language. Among the terms to be studied by a language-arts teacher determined to give proper reading guidance in this occupation are included:

free edge, keratin, lunula, nippers, oil glove, pledget, French twist, effilating, sebum, bias wave, reverse roll, cuticle of hair

and hundreds of others which take years to learn properly.

VOCATIONS AND THE LANGUAGE ARTS

We have not discussed some of the implications of the English teacher's efforts to teach the reading of vocational subjects in the language-arts class. The woodworking boy who wants to know why his English teacher is taking the time to have his students read the expressions below would be compelling us to reexamine our goals in vocational education:

Explain how to make a mortise on a leg.
List the first five steps in squaring a piece of wood to size.
Draw a marking gauge.
Name five different types of lines used in making a drawing.
Give three uses of the hack saw.
Draw a combination square.

Do we want our vocational students to have a restricted curriculum involving trade experiences exclusively? Would any teacher of English accept appointment to a vocational high school knowing that he would be expected to familiarize himself sufficiently with the trades taught in that school to be able to teach the reading matter of those shops?

In desperation some shop subjects chairmen might suggest that the English teacher should interest himself in the trades of the school. They may not be impressed with the argument that the teacher of English selected his subject just as the trade teacher did, that is, because of a personal interest or talent in that field of study. Nor may it be important that the language-arts instructor spent many years studying and preparing for the teaching of literature and composition. However, we may well ask such chairmen whether we have the right to deprive the vocational high student of his share of appreciation of the cultural products of writers in every field of literary expression.

The shop teacher presented with this situation might adopt one or both of the attitudes below:

1. The English teacher should teach pupils to recognize words, not teach the meaning of the words in a technical sense.
2. The English teacher should teach pupils the general skills of reading,

such as selecting main ideas in a paragraph, reading for details, skimming, reading in phrases, reading with a purpose, reading to understand and follow directions, and many others; in sum, to develop those skills which some experts claim can be transferred from one type of reading matter to another.

WORD RECOGNITION IN CONTEXT

In answer to the first view, teachers of English claim that they are doing their utmost to assist students to use the various skills of word recognition when these skills are needed in the reading of literature in the language arts classes. For example, in the study of O. Henry's short story, "Gift of the Magi," the pupil meets the phrase "imputation of parsimony" in the first paragraph. The teacher will help the students analyze the parts of each difficult word (*im-pu-ta-tion*) (*par-si-mony*) where such analysis is needed. Then he will go on to discuss with the class the meaning of this phrase in the complete picture of that first paragraph. He will select as many such word groups for study as he thinks are material for the appreciation of an O. Henry story, with the hope that the student will be stimulated to look up such phrases as, "instigates the moral reflection," "with sniffles predominating," "on the lookout for the mendicancy squad," and numerous others.

If the trade instructor were to suggest that the English teacher take the opportunity to teach such word recognition skills using the technical terms of the shops, the answer would be that this learning activity would be a waste of time for teacher and student. As we have seen above, the English teacher does not merely analyze the word elements in "imputation of parsimony." What is more important is that he spends valuable class time discussing the meaning of the words as used in *that paragraph* of the story. If the teacher of English were merely to attempt analysis of the oral elements of the technical terms, he would be giving little assistance to the shop teacher anxious to have his students read for understanding. The pupils could call out the words from the examination of radio as smoothly as the teacher and still be no farther into reading the question than when they first started the analysis of words like "modulating."

TRANSFER OF TRAINING

Going on to the suggestion that the English instructor train students in the general skills of reading other than word recognition, it can be said that such practice is given in most English classes in the vocational high schools. Most schools are equipped with reading workbooks which are used to develop the general reading skills used in informational reading. However, it has yet to be determined that any such training can be carried over into the other fields of study included in the vocational school curriculum.

Let us take an example from such workbooks to reveal the possibilities of transfer of training in reading. One of the many such used in the high schools is the Scott, Foresman text called "Basic Reading Skills for High School Use" (Revised Edition, 1958). Included in this text are 18 sections, each devoted to a different reading skill such as Main Idea, Summarizing and Organizing, Word Analysis, Phrase and Sentence Meaning, etc. Suppose we turn to the section called Relationships (cause-effect, sequence). Within this section are included twelve reading sections varying in length from 150 to 1,700 words. The titles of these passages indicate that two of them are stories (A Fish Story, Old Three Toes), nine are informational essays (The Dust Storm, The Flood, The First Basketball Game, Fire-Boats to the Rescue, It's the Ham in Them, The Giants of the Galapagos, Who Is Handicapped?, and Collecting Animal Tracks) and one is a biographical sketch (Thirteen). Students are asked to read these selections and answer questions specially prepared to develop the ability to see cause and effect relationship and sequence of ideas in stories.

It is doubtful that a student who has read all these selections and scored a high percentage of correct answers is any nearer to understanding his trade text or has become more skillful in seeing cause-effect relationships in his radio work. The thinking processes to be used in these selections are not the same reasoning skills to be applied to the trade subjects. To be specific, a reading of the most technical of these essays, "It's the Ham in Them," which is concerned with amateur radio operators, is followed by such nontechnical deductions as these:

1. Why might a shut-in enjoy operating a "ham" radio outfit as a hobby?
2. Why would "ham" radio operators be valuable in any community in an emergency?
3. Why might being a "ham" be valuable to you as an individual?

Compare these questions with the following appended to chapters from the text "Elements of Radio" by Abraham and William Marcus (Prentice-Hall, 1952):

1. Why cannot the magnetic field of an electromagnet be used to send wireless messages in a practical manner?
2. Why must a reproducer be used in a radio receiver?
3. Why must a receiver have a detector?

The first set of questions can be answered without reading the text if one knows, as is explained in the first sentence of the paragraph, that a "ham" is an amateur radio operator. The latter set of questions carries no clue to the answer without the reader's having some previous knowledge and information to be obtained only in a graded course of study such as a trade subject curriculum provides.

The writer believes that most authorities who assume transfer of training in reading skills fail to take account of the cumulative knowledge of technical words and phrases needed to draw meaning from a paragraph in a textbook.

To be specific, when an English teacher uses a workbook such as "Unit Drills for Reading Comprehension" by R. Goodman (Keystone Education Press, 1955) with its 45 paragraphs and accompanying thought test questions, he is supposing that the student brings to each selection only a general knowledge of things. In fact, the pupil is expected to confine his thinking to the items in the paragraph. Thus, in the paragraph below (Paragraph 2, page 27):

If you watch a lamp which is turned very rapidly on and off, and you keep your eyes open, persistence of vision will bridge the gaps of darkness between the flashes of light, and the lamp will seem to be continuously lit. This optical afterglow explains the magic produced by the stroboscope, a new instrument which seems to freeze the swiftest motions while they are still going on, and to stop time itself dead in its tracks. The magic is all in the eye of the beholder.

The thought questions bearing on this selection are:

The "magic" of the stroboscope is due to (1) continuous lighting, (2) intense cold, (3) slow motion, (4) behavior of the human eye, (5) a lapse of time.

"Persistence of vision" is explained by (1) darkness, (2) winking, (3) rapid flashes, (4) gaps, (5) afterimpression.

We will note two points here. First, the author has included no technical terms or phrases which he has not explained, or which could not be found in an ordinary dictionary. Second, there is no graded block of knowledge on which this paragraph depends for clarity of understanding.

Turning to a textbook in the trade, the above-mentioned text on elements of radio, let us study some typical paragraphs:

All the above methods of communication suffer from one common fault; they are useful only over comparatively short distances, a few miles at best. (p. 1)

Having mastered the theory of the crystal receiver, we are now ready to go ahead. If you have constructed the receiver described here and "listened in" on it, you must be aware that the crystal detector has shortcomings. First of all, it is difficult to manipulate. Not every spot will work. You must move the cat-whisker about for some time before you touch a spot which enables you to hear radio signals in your phones. (p. 100)

The problem, therefore, is to devise a system that will build up the signal before it reaches the detector. (p. 200)

But corresponding points on each vertical arm are struck simultaneously and, therefore, the electrons are set flowing in these arms in the same direction at the same time (*up* in Fig. 199) and with equal pressure. Since the electron streams in each of the vertical arms are equal and flow toward each other, these streams cancel themselves out; hence we have no electron flow into the receiver, and, therefore, nothing can be heard. (p. 300)

You will notice in Figure 281 that in both curves the electromotive force and current reach their maximum in the same direction at the same time and are likewise at zero at the same time. When the electromotive force and current have this relationship to each other, we say that they are in *phase*. (p. 400)

On the other hand, the further up we go, the rarer the air gets—that is, there are fewer molecules in any volume. Beyond a distance of 200 miles from the earth's surface, there probably are so few molecules that ionization is virtually nil. So we see that the ionosphere is a layer or region beginning at about 60 miles beyond the surface of the earth and extending about 200 miles beyond the surface of the earth. (p. 500)

If some of the voltage from the bottom end of the coil is fed through a small variable capacitor (Cn), called a neutralizing capacitor, onto the grid of the tube, neutralization is achieved. The neutralizing capacitor controls the amount of voltage so fed to insure that it is just enough to neutralize that arising from the capacitance of the electrodes. Since this neutralizing voltage comes from the plate circuit, this method is called *plate neutralization*. (p. 600)

This continues until a whole series of bright spots, corresponding to the outline of the shore, have appeared on the screen of the tube. Since the screen of the cathode-ray tube is of the high-persistence type, the bright spots will remain for some time after the sweep has moved on to other angular positions. The result then would be a picture of the area surrounding the ship, whose position is indicated by the center of the screen. (p. 689)

Certain points should be made with respect to these paragraphs. The first paragraph is a sentence which has meaning only when read with the previous related sentences. The second paragraph notes the existence of a body of knowledge which must be brought to bear on subsequent pages for proper understanding. The third paragraph is again a sentence which states a problem developed at some length in previous paragraphs. It has little meaning in isolation, but is necessary for summation. Paragraph four refers to an illustration and demands a special type of reading rarely found in workbooks used in the English class. Here, the pupil's eyes and thoughts must shift from print to picture, a skill developed by comicbook readers but not usable for this text even by the most avid devotee of this art form. The fifth paragraph develops a technical term which may be the key to future pages in the book. Unfortunately the authors do not include this item in the index. Paragraph six leads the reader to believe that the authors are no longer discussing elements of radio. It contains a number of concepts which are clear only to a student of previous pages. The seventh paragraph would probably be double talk to most students in their third year of science. The last paragraph appears easy to understand, but it has a few terms which may or may not be keys to proper understanding of the passage: *e.g.*, "cathode ray tube," "high persistence type," "sweep" and "angular positions." The writer is not sufficiently conversant with the ideas to decide whether those technical words are the solution to the meaning of the paragraph. He is in the same position as an individual who has read a paragraph in a novel and attempts to compare his understanding of it with that of a person who has read the complete narrative. A typical example of this would be the following:

Tom went to bed that night planning vengeance against Alfred Temple; for with shame and repentance Becky had told him all, not forgetting her own treachery; but even the longing for vengeance had to give way soon to pleasanter musings, and he fell asleep at last with Becky's latest words lingering dreamily in his ear—"Tom, how could you be so noble!"

A junior high school pupil who has read *Tom Sawyer* with understanding would be able to explain that paragraph more clearly than a college student who had never taken the opportunity to follow the adventures of that Mark Twain hero. There is little to indicate the true age, character, or motives of the individuals mentioned. The college student would not know what Becky's "treachery" encompassed, or what "planned vengeance" included.

GUIDED GROWTH IN READING

If then, we come to the conclusion that the English teacher cannot help teach reading in the trade subjects, what other solutions are there to our problem? Let us examine the conclusions of some authorities on the subject.

1. Mr. Herman Hall in his book, *Trade Training in School and Plant* (Century Company, 1930) has this to say about the problem:

As far as the writer knows there are few if any textbooks that are likely to be of service to the trade instructor in his teaching. There are many books which may be valuable if used as reference books for occasional use in connection with some definite job.

The academic instructor in the high school has all too often "gotten by" in his work with the help of a well-known textbook used as a sort of crutch to hold him up. Such instructors are prone to assign "pages so-and-so for tomorrow's lesson." If the instructor himself learns those pages, or even contrives to have them before him, he can sample his learner's ability to repeat the material contained in the pages. Such teaching will not meet the objectives of trade instruction.

. . . Textbooks as such have little place in trade education. . . .

2. "Guideposts in Vocational High School," a pamphlet issued by the Board of Education in 1946 states:

Teachers of all subjects, especially English, should guide the student's growth in reading. (As we have seen above, teachers of English in most vocational high schools have taken practical steps to follow that suggestion.)

3. *Methods of Teaching Industrial Subjects* (Gerald B. Leighbody, Delmar Publishers, 1946) decries this practice:

Some teachers follow the practice of assigning pages in text or reference books to be studied outside of regular school hours. The mere reading of material is no guarantee of comprehension or retention.

4. In the bulletin of June 1952 entitled, "Instruction in English and Speech," (page 57) it is stated that,

It is the opinion of the committee, however, that the problem of reading cannot be solved by the teacher of English in isolation. English is to a degree a tool subject; so to a degree are other subjects. It cannot be assumed that because teachers of English teach vocabulary, pupils will know the meaning of all words, or will understand the special vocabulary and concepts of other subjects. All departments must know the factors involved in the reading process and must take direct application of the skills which are taught in the English class.

5. The authors of "Machine Shop Practice for Vocational High Schools," Board of Education Curriculum Bulletin #10, 1954–55 Series, have this to say about the problem:

The systematic use of instruction sheets helps students learn to read and follow written directions. (page 71)

Mention of references is one means of stimulating curiosity about the subject matter and of leading pupils to subject matter that will supplement instruction. However, on the instruction sheet or otherwise, the teacher should suggest only reading that is available and within the student's comprehension. (page 81)

It is necessary to bear in mind that many pupils have difficulty in getting information and direction from the printed page; they prefer to depend on spoken language. However, the ability to follow written material is an important part of the equipment of the machine shop worker. . . .

Show the pupils exactly how to use the various instruction sheets. For example, if you are conducting a demonstration, have a pupil read aloud the steps of the operation while another pupil performs each step. (page 87)

The writer is of the opinion that we should reject the advice to use little or no reading in the shops. On the other hand, few trade instructors have the time or energy to become reading experts.

Shop Teacher and Reading

For the shop teacher, fundamental reading tasks are involved in the job sheets which guide the pupil's work from day to day. Such instruction sheets can be made the subject of reading instruction with profit to both teacher and student. As to when such instruction can take place, it seems wise for such purposes to use the shop information period when demonstrations, lectures and discussions are an important part of the procedure.

There cannot be a blueprint for every type of reading lesson in shop subjects, or academic studies, for that matter. However, it seems to the writer that a carefully thought out lesson should contain some or all of the following steps:

1. Motivation for reading.
2. Study of difficult words and concepts.
3. Oral reading of the selection.
4. Discussion and questioning for understanding.
5. Application of knowledge gained.

Let us apply these steps to the teaching of the job sheet on page 82 of the Board of Education Bulletin "Machine Shop Practice for Vocational High Schools." (The first paragraph of that job was quoted previously.)

After the teacher has explained and demonstrated the required processes orally with the use of appropriate equipment, the attention of the class is turned toward the blackboard where the teacher has written the key words of the job. Among these would be included such phrases as the following:

1. required offset
2. set-over screws
3. corresponds to the setting
4. tailstock body
5. index line
6. tailstock assembly
7. toward the headstock
8. adjust set-over screws
9. amount of offset
10. inside caliper
11. caliper setting
12. secure the tool post
13. compound rest
14. extends far enough
15. lighten spindle lock

The meaning of each of these phrases may be checked by student demonstration or verbalization. Thus in teaching set-over screws, the instructor might have the pupil point to the equipment part and give its function if that is an important part of the learning. This helps concentrate attention on the appearance and spelling of key words. The teacher can take one or two of these words for study of correct spelling by erasing them and having a student write them in again. The rest of the class can be ready for corrective work if necessary.

After these are studied, the teacher reads the sheet orally, or has a capable student read it while the rest of the class follows the reading on their own sheets. Despite the emphasis on silent reading in our schools today, there are immediate values to be derived from reading the job sheets aloud. Just as in the study of a poem the English teacher dwells on the oral reading of the verses for rhythm, color and expression, similarly the trade instructor can read for pronunciation, phrasing and emphasis.

The lesson can be closed with a series of questions designed to develop various reading skills. Many job sheets have such prepared questions, but the teacher may wish to use his knowledge of the needs and capacities of his students to formulate his own tests of understanding. The teacher might thus ask his students,

1. Where would the caliper setting be taken from?
2. How far should the set-over screws be adjusted?

It is possible that neither of those questions would be of concern to an instructor. The writer cannot claim a knowledge of the subject sufficient to decide the points of emphasis on this particular job.

The results of this learning period can be tested through the use of a short quiz given perhaps before the next job is begun. The quiz might include objective questions requiring one-word or one-phrase answers, and one or two essay questions to be answered in two or three sentences if possible. Such quizzes have value in preparing students for final or midterm examinations. In most cases they can be marked by pupils who are provided with key answers.

Developmental Lesson an Aid

Two things should be noted concerning this lesson. First, this training in reading skills closely parallels the developmental lesson which is the stock-in-trade of every teacher. Second, this procedure follows the steps taken in learning a language. We begin with listening and go on to speaking, reading and writing. If it is argued that the difficult words and phrases can be explained through the use of a technical dictionary, it should be understood that mere definition too often means substituting one set of unknown words for another set. For example, the definition of a set-screw as given in the glossary of W. L. Shaaf's *The Practical Outline of Mechanical Trades* reads, "A screw, usually hardened, which is used to lock a machine part in position by pressure on the point." However, when a set-screw is actually shown to a class and its function observed, its definition can be derived by the pupils themselves. In fact, preparing a clear definition of a term may be a test of knowledge in shop subjects. Such facility with trade language may not mean the making of a good workman, but all things being equal, a worker who can handle the language of his trade in reading and writing will probably be the more efficient mechanic.

Authorities on the subject of reading list a number of skills which should receive attention in developing the ability to following directions. Thus, in the bulletin "Reading—Grades 7-8-9" previously mentioned, such achievements as these are listed:

1. Recognizing need for preliminary reading.
2. Care for complicated or confusing statements.
3. Recognizing need for understanding the purpose of each step.
4. Recognizing need for second reading.

5. Visualizing steps during re-reading.
6. Need for final review before applying directions.

Most of these excellent skills will be acquired during the process of learning to read the job as outlined above.

After some success with the job sheet, the instructor might attempt to use the text or periodical for reading purposes. An arrangement might be made with the school librarian to borrow appropriate trade magazines from her files to be read, studied and discussed in class.

The writer attempted to stimulate an interest in trade periodicals through the procedure mentioned above when he taught English in a vocational high school. However, the report formulated below, one of many, to be used as a basis for oral discussion, lacked vitality because there was no authority present to evaluate the relevance of the facts or their significance to the trade.

Electrical Construction and Maintenance
Vol. 55 No. 5   May 1956

Questions on the Code – – – – – Page 295
by B. A. McDonald, G. Powell and B. Z. Segall

Wiring for a Service Station

If a device had to be 18 inches or more above the floor level in order to comply with the Code, is it OK to install sealing fittings as close to the floor as possible?

The Code answers this question by stating that it permits the sealing fitting to be located on either side of the boundary where the Conduit run passes from a more hazardous to a less hazardous location. The answer means that you can if the pipe or other material that you are using comes out from an ordinary run and has to pass through a room of high explosives. It must be completely sealed and as tight as the sealing fitting can go.

If we were installing lights at a baseball field, could we run No. 14 wire circuits for individual light outlets which will be lamped with 1500 watt light?

We can use No. 14 wire if we limit the load on a branch circuit to 80% at 12 amps. But if you don't want to limit the load you can use No. 12 wire, which is a safer investment.

The teacher of English never did get around to asking the electrical shop teachers whether that written report made by an eighth-term student was related to the work in the shop. However, it seems that this library lesson was profitable because many boys did testify that they learned something therefrom. The English teacher did not have time in his program to include many such periods.

What is accomplished by using the assistant to teaching afforded by a job sheet, text or trade periodical? A student who uses printed sheets or textbooks in school really has two teachers: the living instructor with his foibles and sympathies, and a silent teacher who has no psychological reactions to every-day student activities. The first implements the program of learning which the curriculum envisages for the years the student will remain in school. The second will ready our student to continue to learn long after he has left school. Neither teacher can be very effective without the other. The pupil who uses no printed matter in his shop is almost at the same disadvantage as the student who takes home study courses. If we wish to train our students to take their places in the social-economic world, we cannot deny them the reading skills and habits needed to progress with the movements in industrial development.

SUMMARY

To sum up we have tried to sketch the following points in this paper.

1. Vocational students need training in reading trade subjects.
2. The English teacher is willing but unable to provide such reading instruction.
3. The vocabulary, idioms and language of the trades demand special language arts instruction to be provided only by one who is familiar with that trade.
4. Even where language is not a barrier, reading the trade subjects requires application and activity appropriate only to a shop room.
5. The tendency to compel the English teacher to solve such problems will compel us to change our objectives in vocational education.
6. The reading skills taught in the English classroom cannot be used profitably in the trade subjects.
7. A trade text or series of job sheets accumulates a host of concepts which must be mastered to make further reading possible.
8. There are solutions to this problem which are not entirely realistic.
9. Shop teachers should attempt a sample reading lesson in their trade and make such changes in procedure as their experiences dictate.
10. Such reading lessons will have educational perquisites which will facilitate attainment of our vocational high school objectives.

James Joyce in his novel "Portrait of the Artist as a Young Man," illustrated one of the fundamental concepts of this essay in these words (Modern Library Edition—Page 221):

The language in which we are speaking is his before it is mine. How different are the words "home," "Christ," "ale," "master," on his lips and on mine! I cannot speak or write these words without unrest of spirit. His language, so familiar and so foreign, will always be for me an acquired speech. I have not made or accepted its words. My voice holds them at bay. My soul frets in the shadow of his language.

As long as students regard their trade texts with the same feeling as the person speaking above views his teacher's language, we as instructors have failed to prepare our boys and girls for vocational competency after their school days are over.

Science and Mathematics

SCIENCE WORDS STUDENTS KNOW*

David W. Knight
and Paul Bethune

Knight and Bethune provide information that will allow a science teacher to make more rational decisions about teaching science content requiring reading. They provide lists of selected science words known by 75 per cent of the students at each of the following grade levels: 7, 8, 9, 10, 11, and 12, plus a list of words *not* recognized at the 75 per cent level by grade 12 students. Finally, they discuss four possible applications for the lists.

1. What is the reason for developing a science word list?

2. How was the list developed?

3. Of what value is the 75 per cent criterion?

4. Expand on the possible applications of the list.

5. Make plans to supplement the list for grades 5 and 6 of the middle school.

6. Adapt the procedures to produce a list to be used in a school system of your choice.

Each of the content areas includes special technical vocabularies which must be known before the reader can comprehend the content material. Teachers may easily assume that students through previous experiences have learned the necessary vocabulary for understanding topics in science. In order for the teacher to adequately "teach" the specialized vocabulary peculiar to a given content area, it would be helpful if the teacher knew which words are probably known or understood by students at a given grade level. For instance, what percentage of the students in grade seven would know or be able to derive meaning from the word "vapor" should they encounter it in their reading?

Edgar Dale (2) has done an extensive study of the vocabulary of students in grades 4, 6, 8, 10, 12, 13, and 16. The final product of this study is a dictionary which states the word, its meaning and the percentage of stu-

---

* FROM the *Journal of Reading*, 15 (April 1972), pp. 504–506, reprinted with permission of David W. Knight and the International Reading Association.

GRADE 7

absorb	contagious	graph	image	reverse	speed
amphibian	expand	gravity	microscope	revolve	telescope
behavior	experiment	horsepower	rays	sanitary	temperature

GRADE 8

artery	diet	election	neutron	proton	structure
artificial	digestion	identity	organ	reproduction	tides
corpuscle	eclipse	meter	parallel	select	value

GRADE 9

activity	collision	electricity	humidity	planets	tactic
antibiotic	compass	flexible	lubricate	primary	triangle
atmosphere	diameter	fossil	nucleus	resistance	
barometer	disinfect	geological	period	series	

GRADE 10

accelerate	circuits	embryo	instantaneous	organism	techniques
adapt	circulation	environment	internal	ovum	theory
adhere	cohesive	equilibrium	involuntary	particle	trait
alpha particles	combustion	evaluation	irrigate	pollute	transform
analysis	conserve	evaporate	lateral	posterior	transmit
anatomy	contaminate	exoskeleton	luminescent	pressure	transparent
antenna	crests	extinguish	magnify	progressive	uncertainty
atom	density	fluoresce	marine	quadrant	uniform
buoyancy	diagnose	fluctuate	membrane	regenerate	vapor
capillary	displace	focus	metabolism	respiration	vegetative
carbohydrates	dissect	fragile	migrate	response	velocity
carnivorous	distill	frequency	minimum	rotate	ventricle
cartilage	distribute	friction	molecules	saturate	vibration
cavity	dorsal	function	mutation	secretion	
cell	ecliptic	glucose	observe	serum	
chlorine	elastic	gram	optic	solar	
chlorophyll	electron	hypothesis	orbit	soluble	
cilia	element	insoluble	organic	stability	

GRADE 11

ampere	bacteria	cycle	emit	generate	microbe
anterior	beta particles	desalinization	endothermic	heat	source
apparatus	centrifugal	duct	epidermis	liter	suspend
auditory	conic	efficiency	formulas	mass	symptom
					vitality

ABOVE GRADE 11 AT 75 PERCENT LEVEL

alternating	deviation	excavate	horizontal	momentum	radial
calorie	disintegrate	filament	hygiene	permeable	sterilize
celestial	equation	filter	inert	photosynthesis	symmetry
composition	equatorial	fusion	inertia	plane	torsion
condense	equinox	germinate	intensity	qualitative	transverse
crystal	evolve	herbivorous	micron	quantum	vacuum
					ventricle

WORDS NOT RECOGNIZED AT 75 PERCENT LEVEL

abstract	centripetal	homogenous	narcosis	replicate	variation
abyss	conduct	hybrid	oscillation	salinity	vestigial
acoustics	diffract	hypothesis	ovule	superpose	viscosity
amplitude	dipole	inhibit	oxidation	synthesis	volatile
anaerobic	dynamic	interval	pattern	taxonomy	zenith
apogee	ellipse	invariant	perennial	terrestrial	
aurora	energy	joule	propagate	trajectory	
biennial	exothermic	kinetic	quantitative	tropism	
biosphere	heterogeneous	latent	refract	turbidity	

dents who know the word at a given grade level. In this article, a word list of a similar nature, but limited to a specialized vocabulary related to science, is presented. This word list was developed to provide teachers evidence of the recognition of selected science words by students in grades 7, 8, 9, 10, 11, and 12. Though the list was developed for use by teachers in the Broward County (Florida) Schools, a subsequent study indicates its utility for other populations (Knight and Barry, in press).

Initially, some 450 science words were identified in locally produced materials. From these words a list of 277 scientific terms, which could be defined by use of common graded word lists, was selected. Definitions were provided that contained words with difficulty already established as below the seventh grade vocabulary (5, 6). Each word was tested with a significant sample of students (N = 2,920) in grades 7–12 from the twenty-nine junior and senior high schools in Broward County. The instruments were designed to test the ability of students to substitute meaningful words or phrases for the vocabulary words as they are used in sentences. The definition developed for each word was not designed to test depth of science knowledge but hopefully would provide a measure of the ability of students to read material that contained these words (1, 4).

In compiling the lists, if 75 percent of the students at a given grade level knew the word, it was included for that grade level. This is an arbitrary percentage. It is felt that, given proper contextual support, students at a given grade level would recognize a larger percentage of words. The words in the list could thus be used successfully in classes at that level. Since the trend was to higher percentages at higher grades any word appearing on the seventh grade list could be considered proper for eighth grade and above. Conversely any word on the eighth grade list but not on the seventh grade list should be clarified for the seventh grade students.

Some possible applications for this list are:

1. Teachers may use words that are already in the reading vocabulary of students as they prepare materials for classroom use. They will be able to omit words which are probably not understood by the intended reader thereby making their materials more readable.
2. Teachers may use the list as a guide in estimating the number of "new" vocabulary words introduced in commercially prepared materials.
3. Teachers may use the list as a guide in selecting supplementary materials.
4. Teachers may use the list as a guide toward the development of lists which meet more specifically the needs of their students or respective content areas.

The science word list and the suggested applications are not presented as being comprehensive in nature. They are intended to supplement similar information and word lists available to teachers. The fact that it is based on students' responses to words rather than word frequency counts of published materials and that the definitions are composed of graded words makes it somewhat unique.

REFERENCES

1. Bethune, Paul. *Science Vocabulary Inventory, A Guide for Science Materials Writers and Science Teachers*, 7–12. Fort Lauderdale, Florida: Broward County Board of Public Instruction, 1969.
2. Dale, Edgar. "Edgar Dale: The Future Tense," *Theory into Practice*, 9 (1970), 140–42.
3. Knight, David W., and Michale G. Barry. "A Partial Replication of a Science Vocabulary Inventory Administered to Seventh Grade Students," *The Southern Journal of Educational Research*. In press.
4. Knight, David W., and Paul Bethune. "An Inventory of 227 Science Words," *The Florida Reading Quarterly*, 6 (1970), 10–14.
5. Rinsland, Henry D. *A Basic Vocabulary of Elementary School Children*. New York: Macmillan Publishing Co., Inc., 1945.
6. Thorndike, Edward L., and Irving Lorge. *The Teacher's Wordbook of 30,000 Words*. New York: Teachers College, Columbia University, 1944.

VOCABULARY DEVELOPMENT TO IMPROVE READING AND ACHIEVEMENT IN SCIENCE*

Ray F. Deck

Vocabulary load is, of course, an important factor in determining the comprehensibility of reading material; and the technical vocabulary load in the sciences is almost overwhelming. It hardly seems practical to reduce the quantity of technical vocabulary; therefore, a sound and comprehensive approach that will enable teachers and students to learn systematically and well is needed. Deck offers such a rational approach, which is designed to stimulate an interest and desire in reading with comprehension and also with the ability to grasp the content of the science material.

1. Why do you think the division of science terms into different categories might help improve the effectiveness with which they are taught? Give your *own* reasons after examining characteristics of the words.

2. How does the author make use of learning principles in the development of his unit?

3. Do the outcomes of the unit seem logical? In what ways?

4. How would you overcome the difficulties of this plan?

* REPRINTED FROM *American Biology Teacher*, XIV (January 1952), pp. 13–15, by permission of the publisher.

Through experience as a teacher in science the writer has concluded that the inability to read with comprehension accounts for pupils who are interested in science but not interested in the reading of science. This difficulty is largely one caused by the vocabulary of science. Thus there is need for procedures which serve to help them develop an interest and desire to read with understanding and at the same time grasp the content of the science material.

It is all too easy to assume that students have learned through previous experiences the necessary vocabulary for topics in science. Instead we should realize that each field of science has its own technical vocabulary and that we must develop with pupils the terms necessary to understand the basic concepts which the particular unit of science is designed to develop. The nature of the problem is twofold; first, the teacher must identify the words or terms which may be new or difficult. Second, the teacher must discover and arrange learning activities which help pupils develop meanings and facility in the use of technical words.

This article presents procedures used by the writer. To make the procedures specific they are related to a particular unit in biology entitled, "Our Welfare Is Tied Up with That of Other Living Things."

Preliminary Planning

Before introducing the unit to the students the writer made a careful selection of words and terms on which pupil difficulty was anticipated. A list of one hundred thirty-eight words or terms was formed, and each word was studied to see in what way it could best be learned. In selecting the words the writer relied on his experiences with pupils, realizing that more techniques might be used. These words were then segregated into different categories as follows:

1. Those which were considered as key words of the unit, such as pollination, interdependence, nitrification, parasite, and symbiosis.
2. Words that serve as basic stems in the learning of related words; e.g., pollen as the base for pollination, self-pollination, cross-pollination; depend as the base for dependent, independent, interdependence.
3. Terms needed to identify the basic concepts of the unit; e.g., nitrate, nectar, lichen, modules, terracing, shelter belt, stomach poison, arsenate, public domain.
4. Words which present the possibility of mechanical difficulty; e.g., ichneumon fly, entomology, exploitation, inevitably, exquisite, insectivorous.
5. Words which are new to many pupils but not especially necessary to understand basic concepts; e.g., mongoose, symbionts, seine, lespedeza, plum curculio, cormorants.
6. Words which should be learned by associating them with objects,

typical of which are pollen, nectar, legumes, gypsy moth, lichen and termites.

7. Terms which should be learned by experiences or a background of associated activities; e.g., balanced aquarium, balance of nature, biological control, gullying, overgrazing, crop rotation, check dam, green manure.

8. Words to be learned because they are necessary in a world becoming more dependent upon science; e.g., inoculation, nitrification, shelter belt, contour cultivation, sanctuary, contact poison.

9. Technical scientific words—insectivorous, quarantine line, clean-cultivated crops, close-growing crops, migratory, denitrification.

10. Words demanded by exact biological terminology—pollination, parasites, symbiosis, biological control, limiting element, propagation.

Having segregated these words and terms into the various groups it was recognized that some of them fit into more than one group. This is as it should be and naturally means that the same word or term will be presented and used in its varied different groupings, and undoubtedly will be fixed and learned the better thereby.

Development of the Unit

The unit was introduced by relating an interesting account of an interdependence of living things.

The key words pertaining to the first division of the unit were written upon the blackboard and underlined with colored crayon. This list included pollinations, interdependence, and others of this type.

Another list of all the new words on which difficulty of comprehension by the pupils was anticipated was made. This list included pollen, nectar, depend, dependent, independent, and similar words, all of which have a direct relation to interpretation of the key words.

In order to familiarize pupils with these words the following activities were used.

1. Showing actual flowers with their pollen and nectar glands, and making microscopic examinations.

2. Showing pictures of bees and other pollinating insects on flowers.

3. Examining live bees in specimen jars or showing preserved bees and observing means of carrying pollen.

4. Mounting legs of bees and mouth parts on slides and showing on seoscope to pupils.

5. Projecting mounted specimens of lengthwise sections of pistils to observe stages of fertilization of ovules.

6. Asking pupils to read an account of the failure of raising clover seed in New Zealand until the introduction of the bumblebee. This serves to

create a stage for the understanding for the word *depend*. Using depend as a stem of a basic word, teach the meaning of *dependent, inde-
dependent*, and *interdependence*.

In order to clarify and enrich the meanings of the above words, questions
such as the following were suggested to stimulate purposeful reading.

1. Why do fruit growers wish for fair weather during the time their fruit
   trees blossom?
2. Why do apiarists desire to have fields of clover or buckwheat growing
   close by?
3. Why are night-blooming flowers frequently white?

Reading of certain books and magazines was suggested so that pupils
might do some research findings as to discovering some specific cases of
interdependence of insects and flowers.

The second division of the unit, namely, the nitrogen cycle, and all other
subsequent divisions of the unit were taken up in study in the same procedure. The list of key words of each subsequent division was added to
original list until eventually the whole list of key words for the unit was
completed and in view on the blackboard. However words from the other
classifications were only presented and written on the blackboard as they
appeared in the respective divisions and as they were being taught.

Words or terms newly learned can only be remembered and of value to
the learner if he has opportunities to use them again and again. In order to
gain more experiences with the new vocabulary and assist the pupils in remembering them, many of the following suggestions were done.

1. Pupils may collect specimens of insects and flowers illustrative of
   pollination and exhibit them.
2. Draw diagrammatic charts of the nitrogen cycle.
3. Model soil-conservation programs.
4. Exhibit models of wildlife preservation practices.
5. Perform experiments on water absorption, run-off, and erosion of soil.
6. Collect exhibits on parasitism.
7. Carry on simple experiments on soil-conservation in gardens or nearby
   fields and lots.
8. The class make field trips for observations on interdependence of
   living things.
9. Conduct an exhibit of pictures portraying examples of the key words
   learned.
10. Conduct forums on United States reclamation services.

Some of the above projects were carried out while the various divisions of
the unit were studied, others were used as summations of facts learned. A

few served as a splendid means of summarizing the whole unit on the interdependence of living things. The above list of suggestions is obviously incomplete; it may readily be augmented.

OUTCOMES OF THE UNIT

The procedures mentioned above result in varied outcomes. Some of the specific outcomes may be stated as follows:

1. It is a varied way of vocabulary development using objective and sensory experiences. Vocabulary development need not necessarily be a dull, uninteresting procedure of drill. In fact, if proper methods are followed in vocabulary building, interest will be increased rather than destroyed.
2. Reading the textbook and other reference literature becomes interesting, understandable and easier to the pupil because of a familiarity with the meanings of the difficult words.
3. The pupil is reading to learn while he is learning to read.
4. The concepts of science are learned as a unit of coherent and correlated facts as they are built up around the key words.
5. Studying and learning sciences is not a coverage of so many pages but a compilation of interrelated causes and their results.
6. Such a procedure may be academic but it will seem purposeful to the pupil and incidentally he is acquiring a proper habit of work which is one of learning through vocabulary building.

DIFFICULTIES TO OVERCOME

Naturally any conceived plan of instruction is not wholly applicable in any and all cases and therefore difficulties may develop. The number and kinds of difficulties arising would depend on local conditions in the school.

1. Forty-five or fifty-minute periods of class time are too short for some of the experimental and project work.
2. Where other classes meet in the same room as biology, inadequate blackboard space may be reserved for the biology classes.
3. If there is more than one section of biology, using different textbooks, the plan becomes inconvenient and cumbersome to administer.
4. If there is extreme variation of reading ability amongst the members of the class the plan is not equally effective for all students.

Inasmuch as this plan was used in the development of a unit in biology it does not mean that the procedure is thus limited. I feel certain that it can be equally adapted in any other field of the content studies.

SCIENCE INSTRUCTIONAL MATERIALS FOR THE LOW-ABILITY JUNIOR HIGH-SCHOOL STUDENT*

Arnold J. Moore

The upsurge of technological development has increased the demand for adequately trained personnel in many fields of science and technology. Not all of these personnel will be scientists and engineers; some will be technicians. These technicians are classified into several grades according to their knowledge and skills. Some of the lower-grade technicians can be drawn from the ranks of persons with less than average intelligence. Their training is facilitated by their ability to read scientific and technical materials.

Moore devotes this article to explaining the need for special science materials written for low-ability junior high school students and showing how to write such materials.

1. List the problems encountered by the teacher who selects science texts for his classes.

2. What guidelines for the construction of special materials for students with below-average ability does research provide?

3. List the psychological traits of low-ability students that authors should consider when writing special science materials.

4. Relate the suggestions given for writing special materials to the actual sample of specially written material provided.

INTRODUCTION

The recent accomplishments of Soviet Russia in man's efforts to overcome the obstacles of space have caused the American educational system to be subjected to increasing scrutiny. One of the adverse effects of this assessment, according to Tanzer, is that, in our eagerness to raise standards for the average and above-average student, we may lose sight of the needs of a large segment of our pupil population—the low-ability students (13). The increasing growth of the comprehensive high school with its heterogeneous population complicates the problem of providing equal learning opportunities for all youth. Concentrated efforts by professional educators and citizens of our communities to increase the holding power of our schools, to reduce the drop-outs, and to promote students on the basis of social and chronological growth have increased the complexity of the task of teaching

* REPRINTED FROM *School Science and Mathematics*, 62 (November 1962), pp. 556–563, by permission of the publisher.

secondary school pupils. Naturally, increased holding power and social promotion have extended the range of individual differences at the lower extreme and increased the number of pupils in this category. These and other factors have contributed to the problem of providing desirable instructions to students with widely diverse interests and capacities.

For the purposes of this article, the low-ability student is defined as a student whose measured intelligence quotient is ninety-five or below. Under normal conditions this type of student will continue to lag behind more intelligent youth in academic attainments. The more he advances in the typical secondary school, the greater will be the differences between his academic skills and knowledge and those of brighter pupils. Due to the fact that the student with limited ability has difficulty understanding and recalling the verbal concepts which are common in the academic curriculum, he requires careful guidance and a more concrete, and often individualized type of instruction which is time consuming both for the teacher and the student. Most of the instructional materials that have been produced by publishing companies, because of commercial factors, have been developed to meet the needs of students who have average or above average ability.

The problem of reading difficulty, with its related facets, long has been recognized as one of the most important problems in the field of education. In his extensive investigations of the vocabularies of science textbooks, Curtis found, among other things, that both the technical and non-technical vocabularies of general science textbooks were too difficult for the pupils for whom the books were written (3). Due to numerous requests and inquiries, a recent study of the reading difficulty of science textbooks was undertaken by Mallinson, Sturm and Mallinson (7). They state:

Recent textbooks do not seem to be easy. If the level of reading difficulty of a textbook should be one grade below that of the students for whom it is designed, few can be considered suitable. . . . It would seem that recent textbooks in science are as variable and are likely to cause as much difficulty as their predecessors which were analyzed in early studies. . . . It is obvious that no matter how well organized, a book is not likely to be of much value to students if they cannot read it with sufficient ease to understand it.

If our science textbooks are too difficult for the average students in the class, it is little wonder that our low-ability students become frustrated in their futile attempts to read the science textbook.

It is important that instructional materials provided for the low-ability junior high school students be written at their reading level so that they can understand them. However, it is equally imperative that such materials also be on their level of interest and maturity. Textbooks written for fifth or sixth grade pupils may be easy enough for low-ability junior high school students to read, but the subject matter or manner of presentation probably will be of such a nature as to cause these students to reject the books. Pittler found that most junior high school basic textbooks do not meet the needs of the reader whose ability is below the average of the group, nor do books written for the elementary school child, even though the readability of the book is appropriate (9).

Using as criteria the data obtained from research studies and the opinions of recognized educators, it would seem safe to conclude that low-ability junior high school students need specially prepared science instructional materials. Perhaps Flesch's contention that textbooks are written for teachers, not for students, has greater implications than textbook authors and educators are willing to admit (5).

In order to overcome the difficulty of reading encountered in many of the science text materials, several people have suggested that the same textbook be written at different levels of reading difficulty. Thus, the same basic areas and content would be included, but the manner of presentation and level of understanding required would be differentiated for the different levels of student abilities. Conant recommends that students in the ninth grade, who read at a level of the sixth grade or below be provided with special types of textbooks (2). Mallinson says that theoretically this is a fine plan, but publishing three versions of the basic textbook would triple the costs of publication and tend to raise the costs of textbooks to prohibitive levels (6). However, some publishing companies have accomplished this feat in subject matter areas other than science. Consequently, it would seem that the people in the science education field will need to increase the intensity and persistency of their demands if the needs of the low-ability junior high school student are to be met.

Most of the science instructional materials for schools are designed for average students and are found easily by examining catalogues, indexes, and book lists (6). Unfortunately germane materials for the low-ability student either have not been prepared in any quantity, or are not accessible, with the former premise probably being more true. Consequently, the burden of obtaining appropriate instructional materials falls on the teacher, who seldom has either the time or the facilities for such a task. These facts, however, do not suggest that nothing can be done about the plight of the low-ability student.

Is it possible to write suitable science text materials for the low-ability junior high school student? Using research evidence as a criterion, it would appear that the answer to the preceding question is yes. Prichard, when unable to locate any science instructional materials for the low-ability student, developed four units for students in the seventh grade (12). He was able to demonstrate that his units, written at the reading grade level of the experimental classes, with high interest, concrete and concise, were far better for the low-ability student than the traditional textbook materials. He also learned that the interests of the below average student were no different than those of the average student. In a similar study, another investigator prepared text-type units for low-ability ninth grade students (8). Data obtained from this study demonstrated that it was possible to compose instructional materials having a degree of readability commensurate with the capabilities of the low-ability student, as well as being equal to or superior to standard textbooks with respect to scope of science concepts. In addition, it was found that the special materials were more effective than standard textbooks in enhancing the low-ability student's achievement of science concepts.

PREPARING SPECIAL MATERIALS

In teaching the student with below average ability, several learning concepts are pertinent. Perhaps the one that is most important is to keep the language composition at a level that is not beyond the capacity of most of the students. Data from research studies indicate that the average low-ability junior high school student has a reading level at least two grades below that of his grade classification. Due to the fact that many experts maintain that text materials should have a level of reading difficulty one grade level below that of students for whom they are designed, congruous instructional materials for low-ability ninth grade students would have a sixth grade level of reading difficulty.

Since one of the incessant criticisms of science text materials has been the use of non-scientific vocabularies which are too difficult, it is important to use easier synonyms of difficult words. For example, one ninth grade textbook describes lightning as a spectacular exhibition of static electricity. If the words "spectacular exhibition" were replaced by "great display," the level of reading difficulty of the sentence would be greatly reduced without adversely affecting the validity of the concept or appeal to the ninth grade student. One wonders if the use of such words as incredible, permissible, innumerable, bleakest, brilliantly, injurious, severity, words which currently are being used, can be justified in a ninth grade science textbook when easier synonyms could readily be substituted. Such sources as *The Teacher's Word Book of 30,000 Words* (14), and the vocabulary lists compiled by Curtis (3), Powers (10), and Pressey (11) are extremely valuable in preparing instructional materials at an appropriate reading level. Other graded vocabulary lists are also quite helpful.

Authors of science instructional materials should be mindful of the fact that in addition to difficulty, diversity is an important part of vocabulary load. Data from most studies indicate that the fewer the different words, the easier the material is to read. Unfamiliar words, both scientific and non-scientific, should be defined when introduced. As an aid to comprehension these unfamiliar words should be redefined in a variety of contexts. It seems paramount that only those words that are absolutely essential in presenting a concept and are to be utilized in the presentation of subsequent information should be introduced.

Thorndike's recommendation that one difficult word in two hundred running words seems reasonable. Yet in many science textbooks unfamiliar words occur more frequently than one in fifty. Although the extension of the reader's vocabulary is important, it should be secondary to the acquisition of science concepts. Comprehension should not be jeopardized in an attempt to augment the vocabulary of the reader. Difficult science text materials usually can be simplified by substituting more concrete and familiar words for unfamiliar and abstract words.

According to Chall there is a significant relationship between sentence structure and comprehension difficulty, with the most popular method of estimating sentence structure being sentence length (1). For the most part, longer sentences make comprehension more difficult. However, it does not follow that all long sentences are hard to read and understand. In fact, there are some very short sentences which are more difficult to comprehend than longer ones. But, conversely, many of the instructional materials are difficult to comprehend because the words used are unnecessarily abstract and the sentence and paragraph structure needlessly complex.

What about sentence structure in frequently used ninth grade science textbooks? An examination of these texts reveals that, in general, the sentences are unduly long with the average sentence length in several books being about seventeen words. Many of the sentences vary in length from about thirty to forty-five words. Some even longer. For example, in ten random samples from selected textbooks, this writer discovered a sentence containing fifty-nine words. In writing text materials, the use of sentences whose average length is about ten to twelve words and whose structure is simple rather than complex would tend to make the materials easier to read. However, some concepts are difficult to describe because the ideas are intricate. It may be impossible to simplify the description of these kinds of ideas. These intricate concepts will need to be re-interpreted which may involve an extensive amplification of the concepts or a reduction in the total number of concepts presented.

Another trait of the low-ability student is a short attention span. It is possible to make provisions for this characteristic by varying the materials and learning activities as much as possible, and by making a concerted effort to relate the content and activities to previous experiences of the students. In order to enhance understanding, the concepts should be presented in several ways so that through repetition, comprehension might be increased. An effort should be made to make the explanations explicit and precise as well as including frequent summaries and self-evaluations.

Pupils characterized as low-ability students are often those who learn more readily from overt and direct experience than from reading. The student with below average mental ability also encounters considerable difficulty comprehending abstract concepts. However, such pupils often do well in science work which involves experimentation and laboratory-type experiences. Therefore, materials designed for this type of student should include activities which call for a modicum of reading. Student interest in and a need for reading as a means of gaining additional information can be developed and fostered by the project type activities just suggested.

The student who belongs in the category being discussed can write a little about what he has done, observed, and read, but he cannot project with much success. Instructional materials which establish a greater similarity between what the low-ability student does in the classroom and what he does or sees other people do outside the school are more meaningful to him. Activities should be made concrete by basing them on tangible features of the student's environment.

There is reason to believe that the low-ability students require more cues in the way of details to stimulate thought. Consequently, for these students the simplification of instructional materials will often necessitate their expansion to include much necessary detail and illustrative material. In writing special instructional materials, the teacher should be cognizant of the fact that the meagerness of treatment accorded many concepts makes them difficult to comprehend. For the low-ability student this means that the number of principles presented probably should be reduced with the depth of understanding remaining as nearly constant as possible.

According to Mallinson, the selection and utilization of reading materials in science for slow learners should be based on the premise that the level of social and cultural sophistication of these students is well above their levels of intelligence and/or reading ability (6). He says this premise is often ignored by educators. After having observed low-ability secondary school students using elementary school textbooks, Mallinson concluded that the students were not interested in such a naive approach and ultimately rebelled at being treated as juveniles. Tanzer also feels that the use of elementary school textbooks by junior high school students will often result in violent rejection because of the undesirable psychological effect (13). These opinions, and previously cited research data, provide cogent arguments for guidelines in the preparation of special materials.

Previous research has indicated that evaluations of the levels of reading difficulty of instructional materials should be accomplished by use of reading formulae rather than by inspection. Of the many formulae devised to measure the reading difficulty of materials, the one developed by Dale and Chall has been shown to be highly reliable and easily applied (4). This formula takes cognizance of the percentage of unfamiliar words and the average sentence length. Although this or similar readability formulae should be used to indicate the relative levels of reading difficulty, these formulae should not be used as rules in writing. Chall maintains that the more mechanically a readability formula or any readability factor is used in simplifying material, the smaller will be the effect on either comprehension or readership (1).

The following excerpt from special instructional materials is given to illustrate a type of textual material which has been used quite successfully with low-ability ninth grade students (8). Other examples of this kind of material can be found in the original source. Although the very nature of excerpts tends to destroy continuity and eliminates preliminary background information, it is hoped that some guidelines for writing special materials are demonstrated. Most of the factors previously given as important aspects in the simplification of instructional materials are included in this passage. The use of many personal references and "active" verbs as techniques in the simplification of instructional materials is also demonstrated in this excerpt. Using the Dale–Chall Readability Formula as the criterion, the grade-level classification of this excerpt is fifth–sixth grade. The grade-level classification indicates the grade at which the material can be read with understanding by average children in that grade.

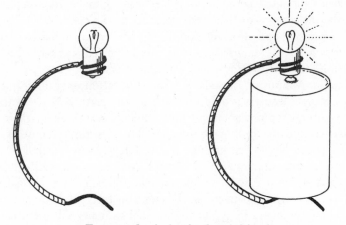

FIGURE 1. *A simple electric circuit.*

You can best understand electric circuits by working with some circuits. It will be easy for you to make the simple circuit shown in Fig. 1. Wrap the end of a short piece of bell wire around the screwlike base of a flashlight bulb. Be sure the wire is wrapped tightly around the base of the bulb. Bend the rest of the wire in the shape of the letter C. Next place the tip of the flashlight bulb on the flashlight cell as is shown in Fig. 1. Adjust the free end of wire so that it will be against the bottom of the cell. If the connections are tight, the bulb should light. Any flashlight bulb should operate when connected in this way. However, a bulb for a single cell flashlight will give a brighter light.

Turn the cell upside down and reverse the connections. The bulb will be pressed against the bottom of the cell. Does the lamp still operate? It should. The electrons move through the wire and the bulb in the opposite direction now. However, the electrons always move from the negative post to the positive post. An electric current always flows from the negative to the positive. Make a drawing showing the path and direction of the current. In the dry cell the zinc can is the negative post. The carbon or the center post is the positive post.

Let's see how a switch works. Bend the bell wire as shown in Fig. 2a. Now fasten it to the dry cell with a rubber band as shown in Fig. 2b. Adjust the wire so that the tip of the bulb touches the center post. Now use the free end of the wire as a switch. The bulb will not light unless the wire is pressed against the bottom of the cell. No current can flow through the circuit as it is shown in Fig. 2b. This is an open or incomplete circuit. Your switch makes a gap in the circuit. Electrons cannot move across this gap. Now complete the circuit by pressing the wire or switch against the cell. This closes the gap and provides ɑ bridge for the electrons to use.

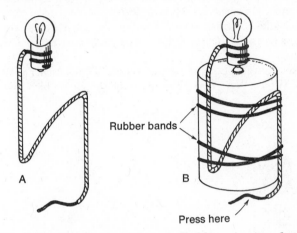

Rubber bands

A   B

Press here

FIGURE 2. *An electric current is controlled by a circuit and a switch.*

REFERENCES

1. Chall, Jeanne S. *Readability: An Appraisal of Research and Application,* Bureau of Educational Research Monographs, No. 34. Columbus, Ohio: Ohio State University, 1957.
2. Conant, James B. *The American High School Today.* New York: McGraw-Hill, Inc., 1957.
3. Curtis, Francis D. *Investigations of Vocabulary in Textbooks of Science for Secondary Schools.* Boston: Ginn and Co., Inc., 1938.
4. Dale, Edgar, and Jeanne S. Chall. A *Formula for Predicting Readability.* Columbus, Ohio: Bureau of Educational Research, Ohio State University, 1948.
5. Flesch, Rudolph. *The Art of Plain Talk.* New York: Harper & Row, 1946.
6. Mallinson, George G. "Science for Slow Learners and Retarded Readers," *Materials for Reading.* Annual Conference on Reading, University of Chicago, Supplementary Educational Monographs, No. 86, December 1957.
7. Mallinson, George G., Harold E. Sturm, and Lois M. Mallinson. "The Reading Difficulty of Some Recent Textbooks for Science," *School Science and Mathematics,* 57 (May 1957), 364–66.
8. Moore, Arnold J. *The Preparation and Evaluation of Unit Text Materials in Science for Low-Ability Junior High School Students.* Unpublished doctoral dissertation, State University of Iowa, Iowa City, 1961.

9. Pittler, Fannie. *An Analysis of the Relationship Between the Readability of Textbooks and the Abilities of Students in a Junior High School*. Unpublished doctoral dissertation, University of Pittsburgh, 1956.

10. Powers, S. R. "The Vocabulary of Scientific Terms for High School Students," *Teachers College Record*, 28 (November 1926), 220–45.

11. Pressey, Luella Cole. "The Determination of the Technical Vocabularies of the School Subjects," *School and Society*, 20 (July 1924), 91–96.

12. Prichard, L. Brenton. *Science for the Slow Learner*. Unpublished doctoral dissertation, University of Denver, 1957.

13. Tanzer, Charles. "Utilizing Our Total Educational Potential: Science for the Slow-Learner," *School Science and Mathematics*, 60 (March 1960), 181–86.

14. Thorndike, Edward L., and Irving Lorge. *The Teacher's Wordbook of 30,000 Words*. New York: Teachers College, Columbia University, 1952.

READING ANALYSIS IN MATHEMATICS*

Anthony C. Maffei

In this article Maffei applies an adaptation of the SQ3R paradigm to reading analysis of word problems in mathematics. PQ4R, the adaptation developed by reading scholars, is a fine technique which Maffei has put to good use. It should be assiduously applied.

1. Which learning principles are involved in PQ4R? (You must bring information from your study of psychology to bear on this question.)

2. Apply PQ4R to a classroom situation; report your findings.

3. State the article's key ideas.

Teachers of high school algebra know the difficulties involved when presenting word problems to a class of average or below average students. "Those dreaded problems again," you, the teacher, silently vocalize and they at times blatantly exclaim.

Fortunately, due to a study by Call and Wiggin (1), relief is in sight for the apathetic student and frustrated teacher. Through an experiment, they indicate that the teaching of word problems is basically an implementation of reading study skills rather than mathematical skills. In their article they explain how an English teacher, experienced in teaching reading comprehension, had more success in instructing word problems to students than did the experienced mathematics teacher.

From the personal experiences of this author, teachers of mathematics

* FROM the *Journal of Reading*, 16 (April 1973), pp. 546–549, reprinted with permission of Anthony C. Maffei and the International Reading Association.

TABLE 1

PQ4R Outline Sheet

---

1. Preview:
    a. First reading of problem
    b. List unknown words and phrases for possible discussion:
        (1) consecutive
        (2) even
        (3) integers
        (4)
2. Question:
    a. Second reading
    b. Write direct question of problem:
        Find 3 consecutive even
        integers
3. Read:
    a. Third reading
    b. List all word facts of problems in some logical order:
        (1) 4 times the first
        (2) decreased by the sec-
            ond
        (3) is 12 more than
        (4) twice the third
        (5)
4. Reflect:
    a. Fourth reading
    b. What is x, the unknown quantity, representing?
        Let $x = $ 1st consecutive even integer: $x, x + 2, x + 4$
    c. Translate word facts into algebraic facts with the use
        of x:
        (1) $4(x)$
        (2) $- (x + 2)$
        (3) $= 12 +$
        (4) $2(x + 4)$
        (5)
5. Rewrite:
    a. Rewrite algebraic facts in terms of a "balanced" equa-
        tion and then solve for x:
        $$4x - (x + 2) = 12 + 2(x + 4)$$
        $$=$$
        $$=$$
        $$x = 22$$
6. Review:
    a. Substitute value of x in equation to check for true sen-
        tence:
        Check: $4(22) - (22 + 2) = 12 + 2(22 + 4)$
    b. Does the problem make sense in terms of the question?
        22, 24, and 26 are 3 consecutive even integers such
        that . . .

need not worry about their lack of proficiency in implementing reading skills, helpful though it might be.

Success can be found by using a variation of a study skills device originally developed by Robinson (2) called SQ3R (Survey, Question, Read, Recite, and Review). This variation, developed by reading specialists Thomas and Robinson (3), is called PQ4R (Preview, Question, Read, Reflect, Recite, and Review). Essentially, the creators of PQ4R claim that it is a do-it-your-self method of reading/study attack that can be very useful in helping students study subjects in topic and paragraph forms, such as English, social studies, and the sciences.

Using different interpretations for each heading, this author applied PQ4R to word problems. From the needs of the situation it was also necessary to change the third "R" of "Recite" to "Rewrite." After doing several problems using PQ4R, students were asked on evaluation sheets if they found this approach more helpful than their previous study of word problems. Most of the average and below average students claimed they liked the method more because it gave them a system for doing something they had previously, at times, found impenetrable. PQ4R had, at least, provided them with the how and where to start, even if it did not give them the correct equation and answer.

The use of PQ4R on word problems stresses a careful reading and rereading of the problem with emphasis on mathematical word and phrase meanings and their relationship to the whole problem. Before doing the problem, students were told that this approach would not necessarily guarantee them the correct results. It was explained to them that the device would hopefully provide them with a way of setting up their problem in individual and comprehensive parts so that a solution could be more easily reached. In more cases than not, and after several problems, students began to understand them.

STEP-BY-STEP PROCESS

Before a class is ready for word problems, it would be beneficial if they are familiar with the solution of equations in terms of one variable, that they know to represent quantities in the term of x, and that they are acquainted with the very basic ideas of the various types of word problems, such as number, coin, and motion. The teacher should provide each student with a PQ4R Outline Sheet similar to the table. When applied to word problems, PQ4R involves these six steps.

1. PREVIEW. The student reads the problem obtaining a general idea of what it is about. He writes down next to his P-step on the outline all unfamiliar words and phrases. He then attempts to define them within the context of the problem, with the aid of a dictionary or in a discussion with the teacher. Word and phrase meaning is very essential in helping students understand these problems. It would be very helpful if the student kept a

notebook to record his new vocabulary since many of the words and phrases appear quite often in other problems.

2. QUESTION. The problem is reread. This time the student is looking for what the problem is specifically asking him to find. Usually this is in the form of a question and is at the end of the problem, such as "What is . . . ?" or "How many . . . ?" It should be explained to the student that synonymous phrases such as "Find the average speed . . . " are used instead of direct questions. He writes the actual question on the sheet so that he is always aware of his goal.

3. READ. In this third reading the student is looking for the specific phrases and sentences related to the question of step 2. The actual words and phrases should be written down in some type of sequential form. The student should be asked to think of the mathematical operations that such key words and phrases as "more than," "is," "at the same time," "as much as," and "less than" are representing.

4. REFLECT. The teacher now asks about what type of word problem they are handling. Is it a motion problem? If so, what relationships among distance, rate, and time do they remember? If it's a mixture problem, what are the relationships between the weight and cost of individual ingredients and the desired mixture? If it's a geometry problem, what do they recall about finding the perimeter and area? Students should also be thinking of the value of x, the unknown quantity that the problem is basically operating around. After finding the value of x, the student transforms the word phrases of step 3 into algebraic data in terms of x. Charts and diagrams made by the teacher can be helpful visual aids in making this transformation easier for the student.

5. REWRITE. After a final reading of the problem the student is now ready to rewrite the numerical information of step 4 into a balanced equation. The teacher should take time to explain with various examples the meaning behind a "balanced" equation, as in the example of a scale. The student then solves the equation for the value of x.

6. REVIEW. The known value of x should now be substituted into the equation and checked for a true sentence. The student should also review the whole problem with his known quantity to see if everything makes sense in terms of the question in step 2.

The table is an ideal implementation of PQ4R on a number problem commonly taught in an average high school algebra course.

Problem:

Find 3 consecutive even integers such that 4 times the first decreased by the second is 12 more than twice the third.

Teachers will find that PQ4R works best with average to below average students since the brighter students usually have their own way of doing the problem and should be rightfully encouraged to do so. After repeated practices with PQ4R the outline sheet could be abandoned for some since hopefully the skills would be implanted.

Word problems should represent to students the most meaningful part of mathematics since they show how useful mathematics can be. It is hoped that the approach of PQ4R on word problems would become more enjoyable for students to study and for teachers to teach, as well as for its other possible uses in elementary mathematics grades and up.

REFERENCES

1. Call, R., and N. Wiggin, "Reading and Mathematics." *The Mathematics Teacher*, 59 (February 1966), 149–57.
2. Robinson, F. *Effective Study*. New York: Harper & Row, Publishers, 1946.
3. Thomas, E., and H. Alan Robinson, *Improving Reading in Every Class*. Abridged edition. Boston: Allyn and Bacon, Inc., 1972.

IMPROVING READING IN THE LANGUAGE OF MATHEMATICS—GRADES 7–12*

Harold H. Lerch

The confidence of an individual to pursue the study of a subject is increased if he develops facility in using the language of the subject. This facility, in turn, is developed by meaningful, correctly paced exposure to this language. In this article Lerch explains how to teach students the distinct vocabulary for the language of mathematics and its unique form of symbolization. He discusses certain instructional procedures for increasing reading skills which can be used with the poor reader who suffers disabling difficulties as well as with better readers of the language of mathematics.

1. What are some factors that complicate the meaningful interpretation of the symbols used in writing the language of mathematics?

2. What are some of the major causes of reading difficulty cited by the author?

3. How does one ascertain the student's readiness to read mathematical materials?

4. List several principles to follow in developing mathematics concepts.

5. How can individuals be helped to read the language of mathematics in short form?

6. How can teachers encourage students to read mathematical materials?

7. State the article's key ideas.

---

* Written especially for inclusion in this volume.

MATHEMATICS AS A LANGUAGE

There is some validity to the argument that there is a distinct language of mathematics. This validity is built not upon the idea that many students have a great deal of difficulty in the area of mathematics and regard pages of mathematical materials as "Greek" to them, but upon the fact that there is a distinct vocabulary for the language of mathematics and a unique form of symbolization. Even though many of the terms of mathematical language are abbreviations for and have meanings similar to words and phrases in the regular vocabulary of the speaker or reader of the language, there are words and signs to the language of mathematics.

For those students and former students who have been somewhat unsuccessful in their study of mathematics, the language of mathematics is quite often thought of as cold, impersonal, too precise, inconsistent, and highly inflexible. To others, the language is much more meaningful because an understanding of the mathematical concepts described or used has been developed. In actuality, the language of mathematics has inconsistencies in its vocabulary and in its symbolization. To those who thoroughly understand the topic of mathematics under discussion, these inconsistencies do not really hinder communications or growth in the topic.

The means of communicating mathematical ideas or concepts are much the same as they are for communicating other ideas—speaking, listening, reading. It has been said that the process of reading the language of mathematics is the same as the process of reading English or any other language. However, it should be noted that the language of mathematics is actually written not only with words or verbal symbols but also with mathematical symbols. These symbols or signs are used to represent not only words, but also concepts or phrases with meanings much more complex than the meaning of a single word.

As the student studies mathematics he proceeds from the use of a simple sign used to represent a rather simple concept to the use of more complex symbolization, often involving combinations of signs representing concepts which are also more complex or difficult to understand. Consider, for example, quantitative symbols and the student's study and use of such signs as

3, $\frac{1}{2}$, $5\frac{1}{4}$, -4, $\sqrt{2}$, x, y^2, $3n$, and $\sum\limits_{x=2}^{n}$. In order to interpret the meaning of

these symbols the student must understand the meaning of each singular sign in its relationship to the total symbol, and combine the meanings into a mathematical concept. In addition to quantitative symbols, the student must also deal with symbols representing comparative ideas, operational ideas, descriptive or definitive ideas, and other mathematical abbreviations.

The meaningful interpretation of the symbols used in writing the language of mathematics is somewhat complicated by the fact that the reader must know the meaning of both words or verbal symbols and the meaning of the signs, both singularly and in combination. It is further complicated by the fact that a singular sign may have somewhat different meanings or interpretations in different situations. The symbols, both English words and mathematical signs, must be meaningfully interpreted for the reader to receive the ideas to be communicated. An analysis of the mathematical materials to be used in the junior and senior high schools will indicate that English words are used in explanations, giving directions, descriptions, and in word problems, and that mathematical signs are also used in much the same way in explanations, illustrations, examples, and descriptions.

The Mathematics Teacher as a Teacher of Reading

There is little doubt that the teacher of mathematics must also be a teacher of reading, insofar as the language of mathematics is concerned. Virtually every teacher of mathematics at every level wants his students to be able to read the language of mathematics and to use this reading skill as a self-learning tool. The problem then, for teachers of mathematics, is two-fold. They must help students learn to read mathematical materials, and they must help them read to learn mathematical concepts.

In helping students learn to read mathematical materials, teachers of mathematics must be concerned with developing mathematical concepts and comprehensive speaking and reading vocabularies of mathematical terms and mathematical signs. They must also be concerned with developing skills in identifying familiar words; developing speed and fluency in the reading process; helping students grasp the major idea of concept in sentences and paragraphs; helping students read to find details or facts; to follow a logical presentation or sequence of ideas; and to develop the ability to follow written directions.

In helping students to develop the ability to read to learn mathematical concepts, mathematics teachers must be concerned not only with developing the previously mentioned skills, but also in helping students to find and use such materials as may be appropriate or necessary. This would include the use of reference materials such as the dictionary, the encyclopedia, programmed instructional materials, and other discourses related to the topic or area of mathematics being considered. They must also be concerned with developing skills in the reading of problems, maps, charts, and graphs; with developing abilities to select the materials needed; and, with developing abilities to organize what is read.

Difficulties in Reading the Language of Mathematics

Before discussing suggestions for improving reading in the language of mathematics, perhaps it would be well to cite certain causes of reading difficulties in this area. In general, students having difficulties in reading other materials will also have difficulties with reading the language of mathematics. In addition, other mathematics students at the junior and senior high-school level will come to the mathematics class with a distinct lack of prerequisite learnings necessary to read and to understand the mathematical content presented.

They may be lacking in the necessary understandings or knowledge of mathematical concepts which would enable them to comprehend the materials being presented. They may not have the desirable speaking or reading vocabulary in terms of mathematical reference. They may also be somewhat confused as to the meaning of some of their vocabulary in regard to its mathematical reference and a different reference or meaning in its regular English usage. They might also lack the necessary reading vocabulary of the mathematical signs to be used in a particular program.

This is especially true of students who have moved from one mathematics program or school system to another mathematics program and, quite possibly, because of the fact that there are inconsistencies in the symbolism used by mathematicians preparing the material to be studied. Although the variations in notation may be minor, they could very well lead to frustration on the part of the student.

Another major cause of reading difficulty for students may be that they lack clarity of purpose in their reading. In the mathematical materials of the junior and senior high schools, students are often required to read to obtain a main idea. In other sections of these materials they may be asked to follow a logical presentation, assimilating ideas as they go or as they proceed in order to make an inference or to come to some conclusion. In any case, the nature of reading to accomplish one purpose is different from the type of reading required for other purposes.

Closely related to the causes of reading difficulties, and adding to the complexity of the problem, is the poor self-concept held by students who are unable to read adequately the language of mathematics and are unsuccessful in their mathematics classes. The poor attitudes they have developed toward their own abilities to read and to understand mathematical content are detrimental to the development of those skills. At the junior and senior high-school level these attitudes are rather firmly entrenched and no amount of telling such pupils that they can learn to read mathematical materials will bring about a noticeable change. Poor self-concepts in regard to achievement can be improved only through success on the part of the individual student.

INCREASING READING SKILLS

Whether the student is a poor reader suffering with some of the disabling difficulties previously cited, or whether he seems to be a good and able reader of the language of mathematics, there are certain instructional procedures which the teacher of mathematics can and should use to increase reading skills. The specific nature of these procedures is dependent upon the reading and mathematical ability levels of the students, but the general suggestions given are applicable to all levels.

Ascertaining Readiness

Asking a student to read mathematical materials which are beyond his ability will almost certainly cause him to fail in this endeavor and will probably contribute negatively to an already poor self-concept. The concept of readiness for reading is as applicable at the junior and senior high-school level in regard to reading the language of mathematics as it is for developing reading skills at the first grade. Ascertaining students' readiness to read mathematical materials dealing with a specific area of content should involve:

1. Checking the students' knowledge of the mathematical concepts which are prerequisites to understanding the new concepts to be introduced and developed. Teachers of mathematics cannot assume that students possess the necessary prelearnings, and attempts to develop new learnings upon poor or nonexistent previous learnings will be unsuccessful.

2. Checking the students' speaking and reading vocabulary that is to be used in developing the new concepts and to develop larger vocabularies. It is impossible to communicate effectively ideas or concepts in mathematics unless the teacher and students have common meanings and understandings for the terms being used. For example, in modern programs of mathematics a set approach is used to great advantage. The importance of the set concept in clarifying mathematical ideas is great, and it is therefore helpful to use the language of sets.[1] However, if students are unfamiliar with the language of sets, the teacher's attempts to utilize a set approach to clarify mathematical ideas will be unsuccessful.

3. Checking students' understanding and use of the mathematical signs to be employed in the study of the new concepts. This idea is closely related to that of checking the speaking and reading vocabulary. The mathematical signs used must be precise and correct and in common usage between teacher and students. Kenner, Small, and Williams[2] in a chapter on "Equations and Inequalities" list the following as important symbol conventions which students should know before beginning study of the unit: $x < y$; $2x$; mx; $\{2, 3, \ldots, n \ldots\}$; and $\{5, 6, \ldots, 105, 106\}$.

Ascertaining readiness to read the language of mathematics is not an activity to be conducted only once or twice during the academic year. Rather it is a continuing activity in which the teacher repeatedly checks and rechecks the use students make of concepts, vocabulary, and signs and in

[1] Mervin L. Keedy, *A Modern Introduction to Basic Mathematics*. (Reading, Massachusetts: Addison-Wesley Publishing Company, Inc., 1963), p. 84.

[2] Morton R. Kenner, Dwain E. Small, and Grace N. Williams, *Concepts of Modern Mathematics*, Book 1 (New York: American Book Company, 1963), p. 52.

which he attempts to determine the extent of their understandings. Activities used by the teacher to ascertain student readiness are quite varied. They may involve teacher-made-inventories or pretests, question-and-answer sessions, discussions, or some other review activity.

In any case, aspects of readiness are to be determined as objectively as possible, are to involve both good and poor students, and are to be directed toward ascertaining individual abilities and understanding rather than those of a group. If it is determined that certain students are not ready to study particular mathematical materials, the teacher must insert into his teaching plan those activities which will develop the necessary prerequisite concepts, vocabulary, and use of symbolism.

Developing Concepts

After student readiness to begin the study of certain mathematical materials has been established, the mathematics teacher's concern in increasing reading skills should be that of helping students develop clear and precise concepts which will be presented in the material to be used. The student's interpretation of the materials he reads will be a function of the concepts he possesses and his understanding of those concepts. In modern programs of mathematics these concepts are to be developed meaningfully, using instructional procedures which emphasize student participation in discovering or recognizing patterns and relationships upon which conclusions and generalizations can be based. In most instances, initial activities in the instructional procedures should involve practical situations and visual instructional aids such as models, mock-ups, diagrams, illustrations, and should be conducted without reference to textual materials.

Suppose, for example, that the objectives for a unit of work concern student acquisition of knowledge and understandings of certain relationships between the size of angles and the length of sides in right triangles. The teacher might initiate study with models of similar right triangles (having equal angles, unequal sides) on a pegboard using pegs and string, or with drawings or diagrams of similar right triangles. Pupil participation in the measurement of angles and sides of several similar right triangles, in establishing the desired ratios, in discussing the relationships of sides and angles in one triangle with the relationships of sides and angles in similar triangles, and in developing the desired generalizations will help to develop the conceptual foundations necessary for the meaningful interpretation of textual materials. The fact that the measurements are not exact and that the derived ratios will only be approximate should not hinder development of the general concept.

It should be noted that activities such as these would be appropriate whether the teacher was trying to develop concepts of the Pythagorean theorem, or whether he was trying to develop the concepts concerning sine, cosine, or tangent. Similar activities would be helpful in developing concepts of other geometric relationships or trigonometric functions. Conceptual foundations developed in this manner will contribute to the effectiveness of the students' reading of textual materials as resource or reference aids which will further develop and reinforce concepts in a formal approach and provide exercises and examples to strengthen the students' understandings of the concepts through practice.

Developing Speaking and Reading Vocabulary

An integral part of that aspect of the instructional program concerned with developing mathematical concepts through active participation is an emphasis upon further development of the students' speaking and reading vocabularies. As these learning experiences proceed, the teacher and students will be questioning and discussing the mathematical concepts being developed. The teacher will be able to interject orally new terms in context in such a way that meanings of the terms will be implied or intuitively understood. Students should be encouraged to use the new terms in their verbalization or participation in the learning activities. The term "hypotenuse" (the side of a right triangle opposite the right angle) may be introduced in this manner when students are studying the characteristics of right triangles. Many other mathematical terms could be similarly introduced and used.

At times it may be appropriate to try to incorporate terms into the students' speaking and reading vocabularies simultaneously. This should be done through procedures which will assist students in attacking new words encountered in materials to be read. After a new word has been introduced in the context of oral discussion, the word could be written on the chalkboard and an appropriate kind of word analysis used. Thus, contextual clues and structural analysis of the word combined to help students develop skills in pronunciation and recognition and to develop meanings and understandings. The form of structural analysis used to develop these skills is somewhat dependent upon the word being considered.

The most generally useful form of structural analysis is syllabication[3] which involves dividing a word into syllables and helping students pronounce the word syllable by syllable. This method seems very appropriate for helping students with such terms as "hy-pot-e-nuse," re-cip-ro-cal," and "pa-rab-o-la." Syllabication is also useful in combination with other forms of structural analysis and in helping students learn to spell. Another form of structural analysis that becomes important when polysyllabic words are met with some frequency is the technique of looking for familiar prefixes, root words, and suffixes.[4] In many instances the meaning of the part of the word being considered will have to be reviewed, and reference should be made to other words containing the same prefix, root word or suffix. For

[3] Albert J. Harris, *How to Increase Reading Ability,* Fourth Edition, revised (New York: David McKay Company, Inc., 1961), p. 340.
[4] Ibid.

example using a prefix in this manner, consider the terms *trihedron, trinominal, triangle, trilateral, trisect, trillion, tripod,* and *tricycle. The* root word "nominal" referring to a single name or term could be used in developing understanding of *monomial, binomial,* and *trinomial.*

If an approach utilizing the oral development of the language of mathematics is used with techniques of structural analysis, not only will students' speaking and reading vocabularies be increased but they will also be more likely to apply skills such as looking for contextual clues and structural analysis when they are reading to learn mathematical content and encounter unfamiliar terms.

In addition to developing speaking and reading vocabularies of words or terms, students must also learn to read the language of mathematics in its "short form" as it is written with signs. No amount of skill in reading word sentences or paragraphs will enable students to interpret meaningfully such expressions as $+3 < x < +8$ or $\overline{AB} \cong \overline{CD}$ or to distinguish between the meanings of the parentheses in the expression $x(x + 2)$, $f(x)$, and (a, b). In the language of mathematics certain symbols are deliberately allowed a wide variety of interpretations.[5] Skills in reading such symbolism must be developed sequentially and meaningfully. It cannot be assumed that students will assimilate skills in recognition, meaning, and use of the signs without direct efforts on the part of the teacher. New signs should be introduced; old signs should be reviewed; and the appropriateness of the symbolism should be discussed with students when concepts are being meaningfully developed.

Encouraging Students to Read Mathematical Materials

Persuading students to read mathematical materials is a difficult task for teachers. Students will not be encouraged to read if they have not developed the abilities which have been briefly discussed. Only the practice of reading and an appreciation for the materials being read will develop speed and fluency in the reading desired of students. It would be ideal if mathematics students wanted to read more mathematical materials than the textual materials specifically required of them in mathematics classes, and to read for purposes other than being able to solve problems and exercises for homework and for tests. Students may be more encouraged to read mathematical materials if teachers help them (1) to clarify their purposes in reading; (2) to understand that most mathematical materials cannot be read in the same manner as less concise materials; (3) to find mathematical materials that are enjoyable, interesting, and informative; and (4) to use their mathematical reading skills to study and organize content in other academic areas.

[5] M. Evans Munroe, *The Language of Mathematics* (Ann Arbor: The University of Michigan Press, 1963), p. 8.

The purposes for which a student reads mathematical materials may be as distinct as reading to (1) obtain or reinforce a major idea; (2) gather pertinent facts or details; (3) acquire general information; (4) collect data from which an inference or a conclusion is to be drawn; (5) logically follow directions until a task has been completed; and (6) derive satisfaction or enjoyment. Or, the objective may be a combination of these purposes. In any case the mathematics teacher can help students clarify the purpose of their reading by discussing with them the nature of the material and what they are supposed to achieve by reading it. He can also help students by making suggestions as to how they might read the material.

The conciseness of mathematical materials is such that most of it must be read at a slower and more exacting pace than materials in other academic areas. Skipping a symbol or word when rapidly reading some materials may not deter students from achieving their goals or obtaining precise meanings; but skipping a symbol or word in mathematical content may alter the derived meaning drastically. Students must be made to understand that they cannot be careless in reading mathematical materials and that they may have to slow their reading speed. In oher instances they may have to use special kinds of reading skills suitable to the presentation of the content such as in formulas, tables, and graphs. By using appropriate reading skills and reading speed in accordance with purpose, students will be more successful in their reading endeavors—and few things are as encouraging as success.

In too many instances the junior and senior high-school student's reading in the language of mathematics is limited to the basic textbook used in his mathematics class. This limitation could be very stifling to his growth in mathematical understandings and to his development of reading skills in the language. One way of broadening the scope of the mathematical content to be read is for the mathematics teacher to work co-operatively with teachers in other academic areas such as chemistry, physics, geography, history, and industrial arts to co-ordinate efforts in developing reading skills in the content of those areas which is presented in mathematical terminology. Another way of broadening the scope of materials in the language of mathematics is to provide either in the school library or in the mathematics classroom suitable supplementary materials of need or of interest to the students.

An encouraging trend in the field of mathematics is an increasing amount of resource, reference, programmed instruction, trade books, and other supplementary materials appearing on the market. These materials can be used both to stimulate interest in mathematics and to broaden mathematical understandings. Accompanying this trend is a willingness on the part of school systems to financially support the acquisition of such materials. The following references are only a few examples of the available materials that may stimulate interest and encourage students to read more in the language of mathematics.

REFERENCES

1. Adler, Irving. *Magic House of Numbers*. New York: The John Day Company, Inc., 1957.
2. Asimov, Isaac. *Quick and Easy Math*. Boston: Houghton Mifflin Company, 1964.
3. Barr, Stephen. *Experiments in Topology*. New York: New York: Thomas Y. Crowell Company, 1964.
4. Clark, Frank. *Contemporary Math*. New York: Franklin Watts, Inc., 1964.
5. Hafner, Lawrence E., and Hayden B. Jolly. *Patterns of Teaching Reading in the Elementary School*. New York: Macmillan Publishing Co., Inc., 1972. Chapter 7.
6. Juster, Norton. *The Dot and the Line: A Romance in Lower Mathematics*. New York: Random House, Inc., 1963.
7. Lerch, Harold H. *Numbers in the Land of Hand*. Carbondale, Ill.: Southern Illinois University Press, 1966.
8. Munroe, M. Evans. *The Language of Mathematics*. Ann Arbor: The University of Michigan Press, 1963.

READING AND MATHEMATICS*

Russell J. Call and Neal A. Wiggin

The contributions that reading skills can make to content-area achievement have long been recognized. There are even hard data to substantiate these beliefs. Call and Wiggin perform a valuable service by reporting their experimental study which shows the differential effect of a reading emphasis approach to second-year algebra compared to a conventional approach. The procedures, choice of teachers, and findings are very interesting.

1. What was the purpose of the experiment?
2. Discuss the interrelationships among words, concepts, and context.
3. Explain the design of the experiment.
4. What was the purpose of the experimental instruction?
5. What inferences did the authors make from the data?

The teaching of the general topic of solving word problems in mathematics is often a topic of discussion at meetings of mathematics teachers. In an effort to collect data which might suggest areas for curriculum revision and improvement, the study described in this article was conducted by Dr. Russell J. Call, Chairman of the Mathematics Department at

* FROM *The Mathematics Teacher* (February 1966), pp. 149–157. Copyright by The National Council for Teachers of Mathematics. Used by permission.

Winnacunnet High School, Hampton, New Hampshire, and Mr. Neal A. Wiggin, House Coordinator at Hampton.

The purpose of the experiment was to determine whether there is some correlation between a student's ability to solve word problems in second year algebra and the presence or absence of special reading instruction. In particular, the experiment hoped to show that the instruction in reading would contribute to the development of skills in solving word problems.

Before any experiment is carried out, there ought to be some clear understanding of the learning theory involved, in order to discover whether or not the instructional techniques and the inferences make sense psychologically. The premises upon which this study is based are not inconsistent with Gestalt psychology.

The first step was to define the problem which we hoped to solve. We noted that students who had a high degree of proficiency in performing mathematical operations were considerably less proficient in solving word problems. There is obviously some different factor or factors at work in such situations. To state unequivocally that the problem is one of reading is risky or highly suppositious; of particular interest is the fact that students who can read all the words still have difficulty in solving the problem. Thus, the source of trouble is not entirely vocabulary, since all could identify the words and define them. What, then, is the problem? It may be that lack of reading comprehension is involved, since we know that there can be considerable discrepancy between vocabulary scores and comprehension scores on standardized reading tests.

Words are linguistic signs which call up or reactivate a memory trace; they are symbols of concepts. In and of themselves, words are nothing; they derive their meanings from the context in which they are found. The mathematical context is, or may be, quite different from some other context. Thus, mathematics reading presents some special denotations—denotations which must call into play the proper traces if inhibition is to be minimized. The technique, then, must be such that conceptualization provoked by the words must be consonant with the mathematical context. It becomes a problem akin to translation, as the sample lesson plans will show.

We settled upon the following experimental method because of its practicality within our school. First of all, one of us, Dr. Call, is a teacher of mathematics. The other, Mr. Wiggin, is a teacher of English with some specialization in the field of reading. It might, then, be possible to select two classes of comparable abilities and use one group as a control and the other as an experimental group. The next question is to consider at what level the experiment should be conducted. We decided upon a course in second year algebra: (1) Students in second year algebra are usually among our better students, both in mathematics and in other subject areas; thus we might reasonably expect that there would be less likelihood of widespread reading deficiency or widespread deficiency in mathematics, as there would be in general mathematics classes, for instance. (2) Since one of us, Mr. Wiggin, had never studied second year algebra, even in high school, we concluded that this would be desirable for the reason that the instruction given in Mr. Wiggin's section would not benefit from any great familiarity with methods of teaching mathematics; thus any significant results would further emphasize the reading factor, rather than a difference in mathematical approach. (3) Lastly, as a matter of practicality, it would be easier to schedule classes on this basis, since the comparability was less likely in other mathematics courses in the school.

Certain information necessary in the development of the experiment was already available in guidance files. For example, we needed to know what factors in intelligence and aptitude, as well as in previous achievement, might have a bearing on our experiment, particularly as it applied to establishing comparability between the groups. After compiling the available data, we "paired off" a student in the control group with a student in the experimental group. In this way, we could establish individual, as well as group, comparability.

The instruction in both groups lasted for ten days. During that time neither teacher consulted with the other relative to methods used. This precaution may not have been necessary, but we had concluded that it might be possible for either of us to be influenced by what we knew was taking place in the other class.

There is one other factor which we wished to overcome as much as could be reasonably expected; that is what is known as the Hawthorne effect. In substance, what the Hawthorne effect means is that a noticeable difference is likely to occur in any experimental situation wherein the subjects are aware that they are involved in an experiment. To avoid this problem, we agreed that Dr. Call would inform the group which Mr. Wiggin was to teach that he (Dr. Call) had some important work to do in the next two weeks and that Mr. Wiggin would be standing in. Thus, neither group knew that an experiment was under way.

The instruction began, and during the period of the experiment we compiled the data. We had to be sure that we had a way to measure the results. No standardized test had been constructed which is designed to measure the results, or the kinds of instructional outcomes, which we were expecting. Thus, we had to resort to teacher-made tests. Both of us contributed items to the test, but neither was aware of what the other was including in the test. This was done to prevent any conscious, or unconscious, effort to "teach for the test."

The basic text in use was *Second Course in Algebra* by Arthur W. Weeks and Jackson B. Adkins, published by Ginn and Company in 1962. For the experiment, we taught Chapter 3, "Systems of Linear Equations, Word Problems." No new procedures were employed in the control group, and an effort was made to keep the instruction as much like that of the usual procedure as possible.

Following are two sample lesson plans from the experimental group. The principle is, in general, this: Words are just symbols with a variety of meanings until they appear in context. Thus, they derive their meaning from the whole of which they are a part. We need, then, to examine the whole first before we begin any analysis of the parts. Secondly, we should note that 5 is a symbol for a concept which may be represented by the fingers on a hand, the toes on a foot, by the tabulation sign /////, by the Roman numeral V, and by the word "five." Naturally, the same concept may be represented in other ways as well. The important factor to remember is that sounds, words, and mathematical symbols may represent the same concept. More specifically, the word "equal" and the mathematical symbol "=" are represented in problems in a variety of ways. We have to examine the whole problem, and then we have to study the parts to determine which words represent concepts that may be translated into mathematical signs. Note that in a rate-time-distance problem, "equal" is sometimes expressed as ". . . the same distance," ". . . the same speed," and so on. Also, the equal concept sometimes appears in many subtle ways. For example, we have a problem in which a man leaves his home at some given time and another man leaves his home at a later time. At some point, the second overtakes the first. Here we have to learn to observe relationships. The second man traveled less time (represented by a minus sign), but traveled the same distance (represented by an equals sign). Thus, we see that the expression "overtakes" is here equivalent to "equal," and the term "later" indicates "less" and is represented by "minus." We are not presuming in these paragraphs to present the step-by-step procedure used in the classroom. These explanations will give the reader some insight into the complex factors in reading which we believe influence the success or failure of the student attempting to solve word problems.

Lesson Plan 1

What is a mathematics problem? When most people think of mathematics, they think of numbers or numerals; they think of computations—of addition, subtraction, multiplication, square roots, and so forth. There is no question that these are parts of mathematics. These factors are operations. They are, in fact, pure mathematical concepts, which, in and of themselves, are useless.

Mathematics, to be of use, must be capable of application, and must be applied. Now, how do we apply mathematics in life? We are confronted with some kind of situation which must be resolved by the use of mathematics. It is not enough to know how to perform the operations. We must know which operations apply to a particular situation.

Suppose that I want to lay out a baseball diamond. I must know something of the standard measurements of baseball diamonds, and I must know how to construct 90 degree angles and how to find a point 60½ feet from the vertex of an angle and equidistant from two points located on the sides of the angle 90 feet from the vertex. In other words, I need to know what the situation requires and how to perform the operations in resolving it. It does me no good at all in this situation to know how to construct a square, if I don't know how long each baseline is and how far the pitcher's mound is located from home plate.

In any situation where mathematics is to be applied, we need first of all to acquire the data involved; it is necessary to find out such things as what the following are: 90 feet, 60½ feet, right angles, and so forth. Then we must perceive the relationships between items; then we must proceed with the operations. It is not possible for us in the classroom to set up sample situations for everyone to carry out. That is, the real application of mathematics cannot be taught in class because of physical limitations. Yet, if mathematics is to be of use, we must teach the practical application of it. If we can only perform the mathematical operations, we are a very poor substitute for a machine, because one machine can outperform many of us humans.

What I am saying, in other words, is this: If you think that the value of studying math lies in the ability to compute, you are wasting your time. Machines have already replaced you. You are training to do a job that doesn't exist. Thus, we must find a suitable substitute for practical situations in order to learn the principle involved in applying mathematics.

The best means we have at present is the word problem. Instead of confronting you with a real situation, we describe the situation to you. From our description of the problem, you must decide what computations to make; then you must make them.

My job in the next few days will be to see if I can help you learn to apply mathematics. I shall not de-emphasize accuracy in performing computations; but I shall place in the number one position the learning of "what" to do; how well you do it will take second place.

If industry can find a man who is poor at computation, but an expert at discovering what computations need to be made,

he'll never be without a job. A machine can do the computation. It can't do the first job.

Any subject or field has its special vocabulary. If you are able to solve word problems, you must know the terminology of the field. When I say "I know it," I don't mean "recognize it." I mean that you must be able to paraphrase it and give an example of it. This is the only way we can determine whether you understand the terminology you are using. Today's lesson will be partly devoted to some terminology. At the same time, we will learn to make the computations which we are about to study. *First Degree or Linear Equation:* Define "Linear" (having to do with a line). A solution is equal to a pair of values of x and y which make the statement true. The equation has an unlimited number of solutions. It is represented by a line on a graph. The conditions of a problem may be represented by two equations in two variables. Then the solution must satisfy the conditions of both equations.

$$y = 3x - 4$$
$$8x + 2y + 1 = 0$$

When they have one common solution the equations are referred to as a system. The process of finding the common solution is called "solving the system of equations." If the two equations are contradictory—if they do not have a common solution—we say the system is inconsistent. (*Illustrate*) If the two equations are equivalent, a solution of one is also a solution of the other. This kind of system is called "dependent." (*Illustrate*) At this point, let's practice a few solutions using two different methods. (*Assignment*)

Lesson Plan 2
Reading the Mathematics Problem

What often happens in a problem is that students supply an answer other than the one required. Look at the problems in Exercise A-2 on page 32. What does the problem ask for in numbers 18 and 19? (The authors are asking "how many pairs of values," and not "what are the values." The less discriminating reader may supply the actual values rather than the number of pairs.) In number 19, we are asked to express x in terms of u. This is analogous to expressing a given sum of money in terms of dimes or nickels. We are really asking: "How many u's make an x?" The second part of the problem asks us to find the value of u when x is given a definite value. When we give a value to x, we are applying a condition to x. We must then find the value of u which will satisfy this condition. (Students need to learn to recognize from the words the condition or conditions which apply to the situation.)

Number 22 has a strange wording. What is asked for? What must we supply for a correct answer? (Values of x and y which will satisfy the conditions expressed by all three equations.) What do we call these systems which have a common solution? (Dependent systems.)

Do Exercise B, problem 1, page 32. Note that a solution of the equation is an answer to the problem.

Note that in problem 2, solutions to the systems of equations are not answers to the problem.

In number 4, the wording is difficult. Restate the problem in your own words so that we know that you understand what is asked for. (Possible answer: We have to find some whole number value of y. There is probably more than one value of y. The one we select will have to give us a value of x that is less than 1.) What are the conditions which apply to y? (It must be the smallest whole number which will make x have a value less than 1.) What are the conditions which apply to x? (It must be smaller than 1.)

What is asked for in number 6, on page 33? (This problem is stated in a negative fashion: "Show that no pair of values of x and y satisfies the three equations . . ." We must show that this system of equations is inconsistent.)

What is the condition applied to the equation system in number 7? ("Find the value that a must have if the three equations are to have a common solution." The condition is that they all must have a common solution.)

What is asked for in number 10? Note that we ask how many solutions, not what is the solution. Restate each part of the problem in your own words. What is the mathematical sign indicated by "the sum of"? What word represents the minus sign? (Difference) What sign is indicated by the word equal? How many different conditions apply to a? to b? to c?

What conditions apply to x in number 11?

What conditions apply to y? Note that these are simultaneous conditions.

The foregoing may be of some help in understanding the nature of the instruction in the experimental group. In all cases, the purpose was to get the meaning from the context by seeing the relationship between the parts and the whole. Mathematical signs are symbols of relationships, as well as of operations. Thus, the meaning is not readily translated from words to mathematical symbols until the relationships between the parts are clear. So much for procedure! A seven-question test was administered at the end of the experiment. The first two items were systems of equations; the last five were word problems. The first three tables indicate some of the more useful data.

Table 2 shows the initial analysis figures. Since we are dealing with read-

TABLE 1

Analysis of a Frequency Distribution of Word Problem Test
Scores of 44 Students in Second Year Algebra Classes:
Arithmetic Mean and Standard Deviation

RAW SCORE	FREQUENCY (f)	DEVIATION (d)	fd	fd²
13	0	9	0	0
12	2	8	16	128
11	0	7	0	0
10	1	6	6	36
9	3	5	15	75
8	4	3	12	36
7	5	2	10	20
6	2	1	2	2
5	4	0	0	0
4	6	−1	− 6	6
3	4	−2	− 8	16
2	5	−3	−15	45
1	2	−4	− 8	32
0	6	−5	−30	150
	44		− 6	546

A.M.: 4.86
S.D.: 3.52
Median: 4
Approximate reliability coefficient of test, based on arithmetic mean,
    standard deviation, and number of items is .60.
The number of items used to compile these data is 18. Though there
    were only seven questions, there were 18 separate items which we
    scored.

TABLE 2

Data Analysis Sheet
(Figures based on 19-member control group and 25-member
experimental group)

	CONTROL GROUP	EXPERIMENTAL GROUP
Number of problems correct	12	46
Number of procedures correct	24	69
Average number of problems correct	.63	1.8
Average number of procedures correct	1.26	2.6

ing comprehension as well as with mathematics, we have taken into account both the number of problems correctly solved and the number in which the procedure was correct but computational errors led to a wrong solution. It is reasonable to assume that if the student translated the reading into the correct mathematical equation, he understood the problem. From that point on, if he made an error, we counted the procedure correct, but the answer wrong. For our purposes, it seems important to know some comparative data on what pupils did on the reading, as well as upon the computations. Thus we discover, in addition to the above data, that in the control group 63 percent were not able to solve any of the problems correctly, and 42 percent did not have any of the procedures correct; in the experimental group, however, only 20 percent got no correct solutions, and only 6 percent were unable to get any correct procedures.

The discriminative power of a test item is represented by the difference between the number of above-average and below-average pupils answering it correctly. These numbers are converted into percentages of the total group. Above-average and below-average are determined by the performance on the total test, and have nothing to do with external data. Thus, on item 3, eleven of those who scored in the upper half on the test also got item 3 correct, whereas only three of those who scored in the lower half got that item correct. According to J. Raymond Gerberich, in his book, *Measurement and Evaluation in the Modern School*, items are usually rated satisfactory individually when they have indices of discrimination of at least 10, but the average of such indices for all items in a test should probably be above 10, preferably around 15. The average here is 18.6.

Item difficulty is usually expressed as the percentage of pupils in the above-average and below-average groups combined who answer the item

TABLE 3

Difficulty and Discriminative Power of Test Items for 44-Pupil Distribution

ITEM NUMBER	NUMBER CORRECT			INDEX		
	UPPER HALF	LOWER HALF	SUM	UPPER-LOWER DIFFERENCE	DIFFICULTY	DISCRIMINA-TION
3	11	3	14	8	31	18
4	16	2	18	14	41	31
5	14	3	17	11	38	25
6	8	1	9	7	20	15
7	2	0	2	2	4	4

This table is listed for the purpose of determining whether the test items constructed by one teacher were any more difficult than those constructed by the other. There might be a possibility that the teacher of reading had made the items so that they were more readily understandable by the pupils. If this were so, both groups should have performed better on those items. The data do not seem to indicate this.

TABLE 4
Comparative Scores Using Reading Level as a Control

	CONTROL GROUP	EXPERIMENTAL GROUP
1.	0	1
2.	2	8
3.	9	4
4.	4	2
5.	4	9
6.	8	9
7.	0	8
8.	7	7
9.	4	12
10.	0	3
11.	5	10
12.	7	5
13.	2	7
14.	3	6
15.	7	5
	62	96
A.M.	4.14	6.4

These scores are paired on the basis of the Cooperative Reading Test "Level" score, with not more than three points variation between scores. The actual average variation is 1.3 percentile points. Only 40 percent of the control group scored above the 4.86 mean of the two groups combined; 73.3 percent of the experimental group scored above this mean.

correctly. Thus, the number of correct answers to each item is divided by the total number of pupils in the group to obtain the index of item difficulty. In general, items ranging from 30 to 90 percent of correct responses, with an average of 70 percent, are considered acceptable in difficulty for objective classroom tests. However, we should note that if a test is to measure effectively, there must be some items of very low discrimination power and/or difficulty in order to reach the poorest performer and the best performer. The average here is 27 percent. There is nothing here to indicate that the items constructed by one teacher were easier than those constructed by the other.

Additional data appear in the tables that follow. In order to be as objective as possible in all conclusions, we have exerted every effort to show that the results might have come from some source other than the type of instruction used. The evidence, however, seems to be overwhelmingly

TABLE 5
Comparative Scores Using Verbal Score of DAT as Control

	CONTROL GROUP	EXPERIMENTAL GROUP
1.	0	7
2.	2	4
3.	9	3
4.	0	8
5.	4	4
6.	4	2
7.	8	6
8.	0	3
9.	7	1
10.	4	9
11.	0	4
12.	5	3
13.	7	5
14.	3	9
15.	0	12
	53	80
A.M.	3.5	5.3

These scores are paired on the basis of the verbal score
from the DAT, with not more than three points variation between scores. The actual average variation is
1.8 percentile points. 33.3 percent of the control
group fall above the 4.86 mean; 46.6 percent of the
experimental group fall above the 4.86 mean.

in favor of the instructional techniques employed in the experimental group!

Since a number of variables are involved in this experiment, it was necessary to examine the results with the variables controlled. For example,
since this was an experiment in the teaching of reading to a mathematics
class, the reading ability of the subjects needed to be measured; then we
paired off the subjects, one from each group, on the basis of the level of
comprehension as measured by the Cooperative Reading Test. The pairs do
not vary more than three percentile points; in fact, the average variation
between pairs was 1.3 percentile points. Thus, for all practical purposes,
it can be assumed that the reading levels were the same. Table 4 shows
the results of this comparison. The two columns show the test scores on
the math achievement test when the reading level is controlled. The mean
score of the control group was 4.14, whereas the mean score for the ex-

TABLE 6

*Comparative Scores When DAT Quantitative Score
Is Controlled*

	CONTROL GROUP	EXPERIMENTAL GROUP
1.	0	3
2.	2	8
3.	9	7
4.	0	4
5.	4	1
6.	4	9
7.	8	6
8.	0	8
9.	7	9
10.	4	2
11.	5	6
12.	7	7
13.	2	12
14.	3	5
15.	0	2
16.	7	5
	62	94
A.M.	3.9	5.88

These scores are paired on the basis of the Quantitative
Score from the DAT, with not more than three points
variation between scores. The actual average variation
is .4 percentile points. 37.5 percent of the control
group fall above the 4.86 mean; 66.6 percent of the
experimental group fall above the 4.86 mean.

perimental group was 6.4. To further solidify the significance of these results, we made a similar comparison using the verbal score of the DAT.
This was done to discover whether those in one group had a greater aptitude for learning material presented in a verbal manner as opposed to a
mathematical manner. If the experimental group had had a greater aptitude
for verbal material, the results would have been inconclusive. Table 5
shows the comparison of the math achievement scores when this verbal
factor was controlled. The mean score of the control group was 3.5; the
mean score of the experimental group was 5.3. Since the pairing was done
with no more than three percentile points between any two subjects (actual average variation was 1.8 points), we can assume, for all practical
purposes, that there was no difference in verbal aptitude between the
groups.

TABLE 7

Comparative Scores When I.Q. Is Controlled

	CONTROL GROUP	EXPERIMENTAL GROUP
1.	0	4
2.	2	4
3.	9	8
4.	0	9
5.	4	2
6.	8	12
7.	0	3
8.	0	8
9.	0	7
10.	0	8
11.	5	10
12.	7	4
13.	3	3
14.	7	5
15.	1	7
	46	94
A.M.	3.1	6.2

These scores are paired on the basis of I.Q. scores on the Otis Gamma, with not more than three points variation between scores. Actual average variation is 1.6 points. 33.3 percent of the control group and 73.3 percent of the experimental group fall above the 4.86 mean.

Another factor which had to be examined under controlled conditions was the aptitude of each group for mathematical reasoning. Obviously, if one group was better than the other in this respect, the results could not then be attributed to the difference in instructional techniques. Table 6 shows the comparison when the pairs are controlled on the basis of the quantitative score from the DAT. Pairings were so nearly identical that the mean variation on the quantitative score between each set was .4 percentile points. We were able to match sixteen pairs of students in this manner. Note that the experimental group did considerably better, with a mean score on the mathematics test of 5.88, whereas the mean score of the control group was 3.9.

Finally, we made a similar pairing on the basis of I.Q. scores from the Otis Gamma. Here we are able to match fifteen pairs, with an average variation of 1.6 points. Insofar as measurable intelligence is concerned, this is considerably closer than we had hoped to get. Thus, for all practical purposes, the groups were identical in intelligence. Again, the control group scored lower that the experimental group. In fact, the mean score is doubled by the experimental group. No matter how you slice it, the results point to a better response by the group which was taught reading.

Let us summarize the experiment and see what tentative conclusions can be drawn. Two groups were taught the same unit in second year algebra, a unit involving linear equations and word problems. The control group was taught by an experienced mathematics teacher, chairman of the mathematics department at Winnacunnet High School. The experimental group was taught by an English teacher with a limited amount of training in the teaching of reading and with no training in the teaching of mathematics. In fact, he had never had a course in Algebra II. The major difference in instructional techniques was the fact that the experimental group was taught to get the meaning from the words and translate it into mathematical symbols. This was done more in the manner of the teaching of reading than that of the teaching of mathematics. The results seem to indicate that the experimental group did better, even when reading abilities and mathematical aptitude were controlled. We make the following inferences from the data acquired:

1. There is some merit in teaching special reading skills for the solution of mathematical problems
2. Even very good readers, as measured by the Cooperative Reading Test, have difficulty in the interpretation of the kind of reading found in word problems
3. Part of the difficulty which teachers encounter in the teaching of mathematics comes from a special kind of reading disability which does not appear on standard measuring instruments
4. Part of the difficulty which teachers encounter in the teaching of mathematics is that they are not equipped to teach reading
5. If by teaching reading, instead of mathematics, we can get better results, it seems reasonable to infer that the competent mathematics teacher might get considerably better results if he were trained to teach reading of the kind encountered in mathematics problems

We also suggest that this experiment has some cogent implications for further testing. An experiment done on a much larger scale might be of significant value in making recommendations for the improvement of teacher education and in-service training. It is time we took note of the necessity for studying relationships between disciplines where no relation has seemed apparent. The experiment further points up the need for a fundamental, but good, developmental reading program in which a trained reading specialist can help to prepare materials which will improve reading skills in all subject areas. All our classes have textbooks; all our students are expected to be able to read them; yet, in the vast majority of cases, not even the high school English teacher has had any training in the teaching of reading skills. How, then, may we expect the student to come from the elementary school and continue to improve his reading skills when he is offered no instruction for that purpose? This study has shown that mathematics is one such area where reading instruction may be enormously beneficial.

English

AN ENGLISH DEPARTMENT BUILDS A MEANINGFUL READING PROGRAM*

Judy Bazemore

When I read this article I became very jealous of the valuable experiences which the students in Burlington High School are having. What effect, I thought, would such an instructional program have had on me? What kinds of contributions could I have made in life had I been able to participate in a program of this quality? My hope now is that our three younger children will be fortunate enough to be involved in a similar program when they are in secondary school. How about your students and children?

1. What were two basic considerations that prompted the move toward a nongraded English program in Burlington High School?

2. Explain why you do or do not agree with the two basic assumptions relevant to this article?

3. What changes in the organization of English classes were made?

4. What advantages can you see in the American Studies course for Level A students?

5. The author listed six subconcepts for the third major concept area. Now list subconcepts for the first and second major concept areas.

The move toward a nongraded English program in Burlington High School, Burlington, Vermont, was promoted by a number of things; but the primary consideration was student need, not just the need for relevance, but the need for achievement in basic skills. What had been before was not so bad; actually the department was, comparatively speaking, better than most. Anthologies were on their way out; paperbacks lined the shelves of classrooms. Seniors had fourteen courses from which to choose; a reading

---

* Written especially for this volume.

teacher dealt with five to ten students for a class period daily. Teachers were aware, careful, and caring people; and because they were so, they found they could no longer ignore the discrepancies in ability which they encountered daily. They, under the direction of department chairman Lucile White, examined themselves and set to work with several basic assumptions, two of which are relevant to this article: (1) reading is an acute instructional problem in high school and (2) an English curriculum will make sense only when it is built upon skills and performances with specifically stated behavioral goals or learning objectives.

The results of their work can be summarized in this way: (1) the distinction among tenth-, eleventh-, and twelfth-grade students was abolished, thus repudiating the traditional assumption that all fifteen-, sixteen-, or seventeen-year-old students have attained the same level of achievement with respect to language arts and reading skills. (2) Course descriptions for twenty-one different courses, each of which was to be offered on two to five levels, a total of fifty-six placement possibilities, were written. (3) Five ability levels were designated, and all students were leveled according to their scores on the S.R.A. Achievement Test in Language, the S.R.A. Reading Record, and a composition written by each student and rated by a team of three teachers. (4) Behavioral objectives which concerned both cognitive and affective behaviors were written· for each course level. (5) A learning center which housed a variety of materials for individualized skill building was created. (6) A fourteen-session in-service workshop offering two semester hours of certification credit and concentrating on the techniques and materials involved in the teaching of reading was attended by eight of the sixteen department members.

The courses which dealt most directly with reading improvement are the particular concern of this article. In the curriculum listings, they were labeled "A" and "B," signifying the lowest and second lowest levels. There was a total of twelve A and B level courses; not many, it is true, but a start. The objectives, approaches, materials, and methods of evaluation of the B level course, Unfreed Man, are generally typical of B level courses.

1. Objectives.
   A. Given material which purports to be of ethnic value, the student will be able to analyze this material to determine its subjectivity or objectivity.
   B. The student will be able to recognize conditions which lead to inequity and can offer practical suggestions for their alleviation.
   C. The student will be able to evaluate his own knowledge of and attitude toward minority groups.
2. Approaches.
   A. Seminar, discussion.
   B. Films, work sheets.
   C. Role playing.

3. Books.

A. *Patch of Blue, Black Like Me, 1984, Nobody Knows My Name, Of Mice and Men, Escape from Coldity, Black Boy, Eighth Moon, West Side Story, The Outnumbered, Animal Farm, When the Legends Die.*

4. Methods of evaluation.

A. Pre- and posttests to determine existing knowledge of various minority groups, to examine existing prejudices, and to discover weaknesses in ability to manipulate specific concepts.

B. Class participation.

C. Self-evaluation.

A second, and somewhat different course in that it was more action–performance oriented, for the B level (and C and D levels also) was media of communications. The objective was stated in this way: The student will be able to use the mass media for knowledge, thought, judgment, and action. Perusal of the methods of evaluation will indicate many of the approaches used:

1. Indicates a discrimination in selecting films and television for viewing.
2. Indicates awareness of emotional appeals and other propaganda types in the mass media.
3. Indicates an ability to meet a deadline.
4. Indicates a degree of ability in script writing and story boarding.
5. Indicates a certain degree of proficiency in camera technique.
6. Indicates increasing poise and confidence before a microphone and a camera.
7. Indicates individuality of expression through the use of the mass media.
8. Indicates an ability to make a video tape and to make a film.
9. Indicates an increased understanding of himself and others through use of the mass media.
10. Indicates an increase in his own experience and creativity.
11. Indicates an ability to distinguish between mass-media form and the idea expressed within that form.
12. Indicates a knowledge of the history of the mass media.
13. Indicates an understanding of certain terminology of the mass media.

Level A students were those who needed the most help in basic reading skills. In order to give them aid in two areas and/or to lessen their frustration by dividing it, a course which provided both the social studies units and the English units necessary for graduation was created. Students were scheduled into this course, American Studies, for a total of ten modules a week, four to six of which modules were to be spent in the learning center where attention was given to specific reading problems and help was given with class assigned material if such was necessary.

American Studies had but one "social studies" objective: The student will develop an awareness and appreciation of his present environment and will understand his role as an effective member within this environment. This objective involved, however, a number of concepts: (1) community partic- ipation, (2) self-awareness, (3) responsibility, (4) awareness of others. These concepts were approached by means of small and large group dis- cussion, field trips, guest speakers, role playing, experimentation, and read- ing material not generally found in the typical classroom.

Books used were: *Are You Running With Me, Jesus?*; *Blackboard Jungle*; *Bulldozer*; *Catcher in the Rye*; *Cress Delahanty*; *The Cross and the Switch- blade*; *Drop-Out*; *God Is for Real, Man*; *Goodbye, Mr. Chips*; *Hot Rod*; *Mr. and Mrs. Bo Jo Jones*; *The Outsiders*; *Raisin in the Sun*; *Snow on Blue- berry Mountain*.

Help with basic reading skills, as mentioned earlier, was provided in the learning center. There a student was guided to individualized learning activities provided on graduated difficulty levels for every skill area. These materials had been "packaged" to follow major concept areas:

1. Skill in the recognition and use of words is vital to functional writing, reading, and speaking.
2. Comprehension is the major goal of reading and is a primary factor at every level of reading from simple pleasure to critical evaluation of sophisticated material.
3. The ability to function in the areas of communication requires knowl- edge of and ability to perform certain acts.

Each of these areas was subdivided into a number of subconcepts. For example, subconcepts for number 3 were these: (a) Knowledge of the various parts of a book enhances independent study; (b) use of the diction- ary provides help in spelling, defining, and pronouncing; (c) outlining a projected piece of work encourages logical development; (d) following an orderly study plan will improve learning; (e) the ability to read nonprose materials is essential to learning in many subject areas; (f) an appropriate response indicates the listener's ability to follow lecture, directions, discus- sions, and other material presented through the medium of sound.

Practice materials for all subconcepts were available in quantity. Those for subconcept f above, for example, were (1) EDL Tape 1, "How Well Do You Listen?" (2) a series of overhead masters, "Introduction to Listen- ing," available at the local A/V center; (3) exercises from the Bazemore manual made available to all teachers; (4) SRA Listening Skill Builder Series; (5) EDL Tapes G 1–15 for speeded listening.

This program has been in operation only two years and already changes are being made; more courses are being added. There are no statistics to cite proving that Burlington High students are better readers overnight. There is possibly some proof in the fact that some of these students are taking, by choice, two and three English courses per semester and that they are being successful in what they undertake. Perhaps most importantly, in an effort to increase the possible alternatives for their students when they finish school, these educators have given the students alternatives now.

Teaching Levels of Literary Understanding*

John S. Simmons

Do boys in high school develop a dislike for poetry because it is a "sissy activity" or because they do not understand poems? It is the latter reason, according to Simmons. Boys do develop a taste for poetry if they understand it. A teacher can be more successful in helping students understand poetry if he applies techniques to the reading of poetry, rather than techniques developed for reading an essay.

The main part of the paper is devoted to showing the English teacher how to help students differentiate their approaches to the reading of drama, poetry, and prose fiction. In addition, Simmons explains how certain specific sequential steps must be taken if the teacher is to succeed in establishing literature as a basis for good reading instruction.

1. What are the two responsibilities for the teaching of reading that secondary school teachers have?

2. What intellectual demands are made on students as they study literature?

3. What reading problems does one encounter when reading drama?

4. How can the teacher help students develop adequate meanings as they read poems?

5. How does the reading of modern prose fiction differ from reading fiction written in the traditional narrative patterns?

6. What steps should the teacher take to help students read literature skillfully?

7. State the article's key ideas.

A source of frustration to secondary school teachers imbued with the "reading point of view" may well be found in their unsuccessful attempts to promote developmental reading through the use of literary selections. Often it is not that the task cannot be done but that the wrong approach is taken with the materials used. That is, teachers are sometimes guilty of attempt-

---

* FROM *English Journal*, 54 (February 1965), pp. 101, 102; 107; 129, reprinted with permission of the National Council of Teachers of English and John S. Simmons.

ing to employ selections of imaginative literature as vehicles for certain reading exercises when in fact the forms of the selections do not fit the exercises in question.

My first premise in this matter is that all secondary school teachers, regardless of their field, have the dual function (among countless others, of course) of *extending* certain reading abilities among their students, and *developing* others. Those aspects of the reading act taught and reinforced in elementary school should be extended in the more mature and complex environs of high school reading material. Those reading abilities which are, relatively speaking, unique to high school should be developed. Literature study, it would seem, is largely the function of the secondary school English teacher. Within this study lie special kinds of reading approaches, those infrequently and (no malice intended) superficially handled in most elementary schools.

In the study of literature, students are taught and/or guided in the interpretation, analysis, and appreciation of a variety of selections. For many students such demands are largely unfamiliar; they must learn to perform a task which is new to them. Teachers require a series of reactions to the literature read, both in speaking and in writing. In this they are asking for *critical* reading, a task which should be central to reading assignments in all secondary content areas. Students must go beyond mere passive acceptance, or *comprehension*; they must do something with what they read. In evoking a critical response, English teachers are moving students toward more mature, sophisticated reading activities.

The teacher of literature could also hope for a degree of involvement by her students with the selections they read. Since most selections studied will present conflicts in human ideals, or desires, offer moral choices, or identify ways to the good life, it would be hoped that some works would have an effect on the *attitudes* of the great majority of students. Research gathered to date suggests that this goal is not achieved as frequently as we would like, but this does not make the desire to affect students' personal feelings through literature study less desirable or less popular with most teachers. Most important to this discussion, however, is that in the study of literature, secondary English teachers are asking students to deal with "new" kinds of materials.

From the point of view of most instructors of "general reading abilities," the essay and the biography, together with some conventional selections from prose fiction, represent the kind of material most suitable for certain reading exercises: developing rate, improving comprehension, increasing vocabulary, finding main ideas in paragraphs, identifying key facts and the relationship among sentences, and the like. Actually, it must be made clear that in the study of imaginative literature, the teacher *must depart from these kinds of activities*. The process of comprehending literature demands other approaches. One of the major reasons for this needed modification is that the nature of imaginative literature is quite different from the typical materials used to develop reading skills and is thus not suited for developing the kinds of reading skills indicated above. To amplify this assertion, I will call attention to some of the special considerations involved in reading drama, poetry, and prose fiction.

READING DRAMA

As a form to be read silently, drama takes about as big a structural departure from "regular developmental" reading materials as one could imagine. The play tells a story but not along familiar narrative lines. The main portion of the narrative is written in the form of speeches of one or more characters; thus, no one is really *telling* the story. Both action and setting are largely supplied by stage directions, usually italicized, which are vitally important to the understanding of the play but are often understated. These directions also serve to break up the dialogue, making the following of a sequence of events more difficult.

Another dimension of drama which causes reading problems is the "simultaneous action" within the play. Drama has been written chiefly to be acted, not read silently. Therefore, several things are meant to happen at once during a presentation. A character may be walking, gesturing, making facial expressions while he is speaking. At the same time, other characters may be doing the same things, and some of them may even be speaking as well. To perceive the total situation of the play, the student must be able to do more than *comprehend*; he must *visualize*. As reader, he must intuitively sense that certain things are happening or are about to happen that will cause certain inner reactions from various members of the cast. Such reading calls for imagination, guidance, and experience. It is not provided for in basic reading instruction and thus demands another kind of *readiness* on the part of the reader.

READING POETRY

Poetry offers at least as large a number of structural problems as does drama. Lines of poetry obviously do not conform to prose "reading" models. They are long, short, and have little to do with typical sentence structure. Syntax in poetry is highly irregular, with phrases, clauses, and unusually placed single modifiers jutting out all over the place. Students often have trouble finding not only the end of a sentence, but its subject and verb as well. The juxtaposition of words for intellectual, emotional, and aesthetic effect further complicates the issue. The poet is frequently working for audial effects of various kinds and does this by the conscious selection of certain words (often unusual) and certain constructions (often irregular) to effect the exact intonation or balance. The student who searches for even surface meaning in poetry must adjust to all of these manipulations.

Another kind of reading readiness of an extraordinary nature must be built by the teacher of poetic selections. Many poems, including a fair proportion of those often taught to high school students, either tell a story or relate a fact in the denotative sense. They may create an impression (Pound, "In a Station of the Metro"), a mood, an observation on the human situation. They may tell a story in a most oblique manner (Robinson, "Eros Turannos"), or they may reveal only the barest of details. Metaphor is a fundamental, vital ingredient, and the reader must be ready to pursue relationships among unusual entities to clarify and intensify his perception of meaning. In reading poetry, that is part of the game.

Finally, and obviously, in poetry much is compressed into a few words. The poet habitually speaks volumes in a few lines. Consider the first two and a half lines of the third stanza of Yeats' "Leda and the Swan":

> A shudder in the loins engenders there
> The broken wall, the burning roof and tower
> And Agamemnon dead.

A reader who has no more than a slight background in classical mythology misses the idea as well as the *sweep* of those lines.

I have suggested here only a few of the problems that poetry presents to the student who has not been taught to read in a "special" way. Certainly such problems are not met in basic reading instruction at any level. They must be dealt with by a teacher who is trained to read and to *teach the reading* of poetry. A contention which I have harbored for years is that many high school boys dislike poetry because it is effeminate. They do not like it, because they are not competent enough to *read* it.

READING PROSE FICTION

It would seem that prose fiction offers the most fertile ground in a literature class for the teacher who would develop the reading skills mentioned earlier. Although this is in part true, many fictional selections, important in the high school curriculum, offer reading problems of a most unusual nature.

I feel, or at least I *hope*, that it is safe to assume that there is a perceptible trend in the curriculum away from the *Silas Marner, Ivanhoe* preoccupation to an interest in considering works of more recent vintage. If this is true, some pitfalls await the unsuspecting reader. Novels and short stories, particularly those of the twentieth century, are replete with structural and stylistic involvements for which the typical high school reader is not necessarily prepared.

Modern prose fiction characteristically deviates from traditional narrative patterns. The more frequent uses of limited point of view, in which the reader views the situation through the eyes of one of its participants, brings about some unusual sequences. When, as in Faulkner, reality is viewed through the eyes of a Benjie Compson, some most irregular structures result; stream of consciousness, interior monologue, and abrupt shifts in the identity of the narrator demand flexibility on the part of the reader.

The ease of following the chronological sequence was once a big selling point of the novel or short story as a reading exercise. In much significant fiction, however, the writer has tampered with his clock, as E. M. Forster might say. Irregular placing of events, lengthy and unusually developed flash-backs, and rapidly shifting locales often make following the plot a chore. A reader not aware of such stylistic jockeying can soon become confused and frustrated.

The opening and closing of many significant works of prose fiction deserve careful attention. In *The Return of the Native*, the opening chapters develop a setting, Egdon Heath, slowly and painstakingly. This description must be read and fully perceived, because much of the characterization and plot structure that follows depends directly on such understanding. In the beginning passages of a large number of short stories, vital events, and propositions of human experience are developed with such a sparseness of detail as to demand minute analysis. In Poe's "Cask of Amontillado," it is virtually impossible to follow the narrative intelligently unless the personality of Montresor, self-described at the outset, is clear.

Restraint in use of detail in the presentation of key actions is characteristic of today's prose fiction, as are abrupt, anticlimactic conclusions. When the untrained reader is left up in the air, he tends to become confused. Such a reader must be taught to examine the text more carefully so that such endings will not be so obscure of intent. Throughout all subtle fiction, it must be realized that the paragraph, and even the sentence, are not the functional elements they are in conventional reading exercise materials. Teachers should not expect students to search for "main ideas" in structures where none in fact exists.

The forms of literature represent material for which special and mature reading abilities are required. Teachers who would teach students to read literature skillfully should first settle on specific areas of competence to be developed. They should next find selections appropriate to these purposes. Before assigning the selections, they should find and prepare devices that insure *honestly critical* responses from the students (and these do *not* include memorization, teacher's critical pronouncements, or long "background" lecture assignments). If we are to move adolescent readers toward *appreciation*, we must remember that they must perceive symbolic meaning in order to discriminate, that they must develop the ability to relate symbol to referent, within the structurally difficult, on their own with no heavy-handed prompting. Literature becomes the basis for good reading instruction when it becomes a vehicle for individual critical insight and true aesthetic revelation. This kind of instruction must be both mature and sophisticated. It cannot be done in the early stages of high school reading instruction.

TEACHING TO COMPREHEND LITERARY TEXTS—POETRY*

Morris Finder

My experience in teaching high school poetry to boys shows that cognitive clarity and understanding of poetry come through discussion of techniques for understanding poetry and application of the techniques to a number of poems. Also, there are always poems for which one student may have more experience than the teacher; for example, a boy who has lived in a coastal town may understand more terms and figures of speech in a poem about the sea or ships than does a "land-locked" teacher. I have found a direct relation between understanding and appreciation.

Finder suggests specific ways to help students attain five objectives for reading imaginative literature. Be sure to note Dewey's thesis on the relationship between the affective and the cognitive.

1. What are some differences between imaginative literature and expository prose?

2. By which two main principles is any given literary work constructed? Explain these principles.

3. Do you agree with Finder's and Dewey's point of view on the relationship of cognitive objectives and affective outcomes? Please explain.

4. Discuss in class the author's suggestions on teaching the plain sense of a poem. Try his suggestions by teaching a suitable poem to a group of students.

5. Try out the author's ideas on teaching to distinguish argument from imitation. Note the helping questions.

6. Do a task analysis for *argumentative* poetry.

7. Do a task analysis for comprehending imitative poems.

In earlier issues of this journal,[1,2] I present and explain a theory of comprehension and illustrate its application to the prose of exposition and argument. In this present article, I relate that theory mainly but not exclusively to poetry.

I begin by assuming, first, that for teaching, this study of literature follows

[1] Morris Finder. "Comprehension: An Analysis of the Task," *Journal of Reading*, 13 (3), 1969, pp. 199–202, 237–240.

[2] Morris Finder. "Teaching to Comprehend," *Journal of Reading*, 13 (8), 1970, pp. 581–586, 633–636.

---

* FROM *The Journal of Reading* (March 1971), pp. 353–358; 413–419, reprinted with permission of Morris Finder and the International Reading Association.

the study previously described, of exposition and argument. I assume, second, that poems are examples of communication in the sense that they produce effects upon readers. Effects are produced by causes, which are necessarily incorporated into literary works.

The comprehension of literature, I submit, consists of identifying the effects intended, their causes or analytic parts, and the relations between cause and effect.

This view of comprehension implies that a work of literature is a thing made to achieve purposes, which are the intended effects. As mentioned in the previous articles, the purpose of a thing is not part of the thing itself. That idea needs to be specifically taught. Suggestions for doing so appear in the May, 1970 article.

SOME DIFFERENCES BETWEEN IMAGINATIVE LITERATURE AND EXPOSITION AND ARGUMENT

Everyone knows that there is a difference between imaginative literature and expository prose. Conscious knowledge of the causes of that distinction is required for intelligent teaching and learning. I assume that one possesses this conscious knowledge if he can explain three points of difference between these two kinds of discourse. They differ in principle of construction, in intended audience, and in author's role. These three differences explain partly but importantly the causes of the distinction. Further explication follows.

Unlike exposition and argument in nonfiction prose, any given literary work is constructed by one of two main principles. One of these principles is argument. Arguments may be embodied in poems, plays, and works of fiction as well as in nonfiction prose.

The other principle is often called "imitation." An imitative poem, play, or work of fiction represents a human experience, an action within a situation. A work is imitative if such an action or reaction is a means not primarily of persuading to a point of view, but of arousing emotions of pleasure or pain. "Pleasure," here, refers to such emotions as amusement, joy, and exaltation; "pain," to pity, disgust, grief, and similar feelings. Emotions or feelings are aroused by opinions formed by reacting to certain kinds of situations, events, people, sights, sounds, and so on. One sees a villain doing villainous things, forms an opinion of disapproval, and feels angry or indignant. In general, people "smile at the good and frown at the bad." These smiles and frowns signify emotions formed by opinions of approval or disapproval of what is observed.

For works of literature, I use the term "argument" or "argumentative" to refer to works intended to inform as well as to persuade. The same set of parts is incorporated into works that serve those two purposes.

An obvious and familiar example of argument in literary form is Upton Sinclair's novel *The Jungle*, which reveals the horrendous conditions of employment and sanitation of the Chicago meat-packing industry early in this century. Its purpose was to arouse public opinion and to bring about reform. The human experiences depicted were not the main interest of the novel but were a means to achieving social amelioration.

Treasure Island exemplifies an imitative work. By depicting a swash-buckling tale of piracy and adventure, the novel arouses the kind of pleasure and excitement appropriate to its action.

The second difference between works of literature and those of exposition and argument is the perceived audience. As noted in the earlier articles, exposition and argument are typically aimed at a particular reader or group. Names of publications suggest the varying audiences to which expositions and arguments must be specifically adapted; for example, *Reader's Digest, Fortune,* and the *Monroe High School Record.*

But in an important sense, the audience for literary works is essentially a constant one. In our culture it consists not of everyone, but of those who have learned to comprehend literary discourse and who form typical, pre-dictable opinions toward generally accepted notions of good and bad, right and wrong, admirable and contemptible. For it is upon such predictable opinion that literary artists, consciously or unconsciously, base their strate-gies for eliciting responses.

The third difference concerns the author's role. I have in the previous articles explained and illustrated this proposition: Whether the writer knows it or not, his composition conveys a representation of himself; that repre-sentation is a means for producing desired effects.

In works of literature, the representation of the author requires further consideration. In the course of inquiring into the artistic effects and means of a literary work, the familiar practice of referring to the author's "voice" or "role" is dubious. Whether the words of "My Papa's Waltz" by Theo-dore Roethke are to be viewed as spoken by Roethke is not at all a literary question, but a biographical one. The literary issue is the appropriateness of the speaker, whoever he may be, to the purpose of the poem. That is why, despite common practice, it is a good idea to avoid reference to the author when discussing poetic effects and means.

OBJECTIVES FOR TEACHING TO COMPREHEND LITERATURE

From the foregoing discussion I infer five primary objectives for teaching to comprehend literary works: *First,* the student should be able to state the literal sense of what is going on in a poem, play, or piece of fiction. In works of literature, the uses of language sometimes cause difficulties in comprehension. That suggests the recovery of the literal sense as a skill to be acquired.

This skill, moreover, is fundamental to any and all learning that requires the comprehension of a literary text. Elementary and high school students as well as university graduate students have difficulties getting the literal sense, as do literary critics. The contention is amply documented by the everyday experience of those who read controversies among critics and authors. It is therefore hard to underestimate the importance of that skill, and it is usually naive to assume that a class has already acquired it.

As a *second* basic objective the student should be able to classify a work as an "argument" or as an "imitation" as these terms have been defined. The two kinds possess different sets of parts and require, therefore, corresponding differences in skills of comprehension.

The other three basic objectives are similar to those stated for the reading of exposition and argument. Thus, a *third* objective is that the reader identify intended effects; *fourth*, that he identify their causes or analytic parts; and *fifth*, that he relate part to effect.

My stating cognitive objectives for literary study is consistent with the assumption that affective or emotional outcomes are of first importance. The terms "appreciation," "interest," and "favorable attitudes" suggests these affective aims. A passage in one of Dewey's early writings suggests a relationship between the affective and the cognitive: "I believe that if we can only secure right habits of action and thought, with reference to the good, the true, and the beautiful, the emotions will for the most part take care of themselves."[3]

The objectives cited for the study of literature, I assume, are intended to lead to these "right habits of action and thought." In the discussion that follows, I exemplify procedures through which students may acquire these habits or skills.

TEACHING FOR PLAIN-SENSE MEANING

To illustrate the "plain-sense" objective, I use a familiar poem by Robert Herrick, which I have found appealing to students of varying abilities, grade levels, and social classes:

TO THE VIRGINS, TO MAKE MUCH OF TIME

Gather ye rose-buds while ye may,
  Old Time is still a-flying,
And this same flower that smiles today,
  Tomorrow will be dying.

The glorious lamp of heaven, the Sun,
  The higher he's a-getting,
The sooner will his race be run,
  And nearer he's to setting.

[3] John Dewey. "My Pedagogic Creed" (1897), as quoted in Daniel J. Boorstin (ed.), *An American Primer*, "A Mentor Book." New York: The New American Library, 1966, p. 639.

That age is best which is the first,
　　When youth and blood are warmer;
But being spent, the worse, and worst
　　Times still succeed the former.

Then be not coy, but use your time,
　　And while ye may, go marry;
For having lost but once your prime,
　　You may forever tarry.

A first step is to introduce students to the poem. That means relating what the poem says to their experience. There are an uncertain number of ways to do it. One is to ask them whether they have heard of unmarried young women being urged to get married. Next, tell them that we are going to consider how this urging is done in a good poem.

A second step is anticipating difficulties they are likely to have with vocabulary. A simple, straightforward explanation is all that is required. Write on the board the difficult words and their glosses. For this poem, the glosses are likely to be these:

> virgins—unmarried young ladies
> still 　—always
> tarry 　—wait

Explain that the poet lived in the seventeenth century ("the 1600's"), and the meanings of some English words have changed from the way he used them.

A third step is the oral reading of the poem. The students have a printed copy which they can follow silently. Before reading, however, ask them to answer a broad question pertinent to the poem. For example, "This poem urges young, unmarried women to seek husbands. What main reason does the poem give for doing that?" The poem is then read aloud. The oral reading should convey clearly the sense of the poem. Students should not be asked to read to the class orally unless they have already studied the poem and practiced reading it. No one should expect to listen to an inept oral reading.

With the oral reading completed, ask for replies to the questions posed earlier. During the discussion, insist upon replies that are justified by reference to the poem. It is impossible to predict just what miscomprehensions will be revealed by a given discussion. The guide for conducting the discussion is the desired achievement—the student's skill in getting the literal sense of what is going on in it. Ideally, the discussion should clear away whatever problems may be revealed and thus clarify the poem's literal sense. When the trend of the discussion suggests that the difficulties have been for the most part cleared away, read the poem orally once again for sheer enjoyment and then go on to other poems, following a similar procedure.

Do not "hold them responsible" for the poem by threatening them with a test or examination on it. My experience suggests that by holding enjoyable discussions on enjoyable poems, students become gradually but surely more adept at apprehending the literal sense, more responsible in their comments during discussion, and more interested in poetry.

The kind of procedure just outlined may profitably constitute the greater part of literary study, especially at its beginning. When the class seems to have progressed appreciably toward the desired proficiency, then evaluate more formally. Present the class with a poem within their experience but one that presumably they haven't seen before and ask them to state the literal sense of what is going on in it. The results will reveal strengths and weaknesses of the instruction and will identify those who are doing well, badly, and somewhere in between. Perhaps during a study period, some of those doing well can tutor, under guidance, those who seriously need help.

TEACHING TO DISTINGUISH ARGUMENT FROM IMITATION

If the class seems to be ready for something different, a good plan is to work toward the second objective: "Classify a work as argument or imitation." A discussion of whether a poem is organized by an argument or by a human experience almost always arouses differences of opinion and becomes a means for increased understanding of the poem. This classification of a poem determines which of two sets of parts it may be said to consist of. Although controversy usually characterizes the discussion, that fact denies neither the validity nor the usefulness of the distinction.

The discussion may well begin by presenting the class with two short poems, one of which is a rather clear example of argument and the other of imitation. An example of each follows:

TELL ALL THE TRUTH

Tell all the truth but tell it slant,
Success in circuit lies,
Too bright for our infirm delight
The truth's superb surprise;
As lightning to the children eased
With explanation kind,
The truth must dazzle gradually
Or every man be blind.

EMILY DICKINSON

DUST OF SNOW

The way a crow
Shook down on me
The dust of snow
From a hemlock tree

Has given my heart
A change of mood
And saved some part
Of a day I had rued.

ROBERT FROST

Simply present the two poems on the board, on duplicated handouts, or by overhead projection. Tell them that one presents an argument intended to persuade and the other, an experience for eliciting a particular kind of pleasure. Ask them to read the poems, decide which is the argument, and justify their responses. The discussion should arouse no great controversy. Having studied argument in prose, they should be able to see that "Tell All the Truth" urges upon the reader an opinion and that "Dust of Snow" depicts a human experience.

The poems just presented are clear examples of their kinds. This is as it should be at the beginning. Other poems, however, are less clearly one or the other. Therefore, the following discussion is offered as guidance to teachers in their conduct of what I have found to be a valuable kind of class discussion.

Probably most lyrics are imitations. Some imitative poetry may seem on the surface to be arguments. An example is a poem already discussed, "To the Virgins, to Make Much of Time." The poem does present an argument. But the proposition turns out to be a simple truism that is not addressed to the knowing reader, but to the unmarried young girls. They seem to the speaker to need the advice. Simply put, the experience or action depicted is this: The speaker, observing unmarried young ladies, forms an opinion and responds to the situation as he does. The effect upon the reader is not his being informed but rather his being light-heartedly amused by the admonition and pleased by the exquisite poetic expression and sound effects.

The poems just discussed suggest some further distinctions between argument and imitation. In "Tell All the Truth," the reader is addressed directly; the rhetorical point is probably more than a truism and probably needs to be made; and the poem provides no basis for inferring an underlying human experience or action. "Dust of Snow" presents directly an experience in the order in which it occurred.

Reference to the qualified audience is of some help in deciding whether a poem is argument or imitation. Arguments are offered to those who are believed to be in need of being informed or persuaded. This imitative work, on the other hand, implies a reader who possesses the desired knowledge or viewpoints expressed in the work, which then becomes means for producing within him particular pleasures or pains.

Imaginative works, then, represent directly or indirectly some overt or mental experience, action, or response to a situation. Experiences and actions occur in time-bound order; but they may be told in other sequences —the flashback is one example.

Poetry and fiction convey their effects through language. Unlike painting, language characteristically represents only one thing at a time. Therefore, in whatever sequence an experience may be related, that experience permits reconstruction in chronological order. If a poem seems to be an argument and provides no basis for a reader's inferring a main underlying sequence of human thought or action that can be chronologically ordered, and if the main effect is not pleasure or pain but persuasion, then the poem is probably an argument.

One may well ask: "Isn't any argument a sign that the speaker was concerned with some situation and then responded to it with the argument he presents? Therefore, aren't all arguments really depictions of experience?" In a sense, the answer to each of those questions is yes. The distinction between argument and imitation, however, rests on whether a main intended effect is on the one hand pleasure or pain aroused by an action or experience, or, on the other, persuasion through reason, logic, or other rhetorical device.

From the foregoing discussion, I derive the following two questions for helping learners classify a poem as argument or imitation:

1. Does this poem depict, directly or by clear implication, a human experience or action? If so, describe that action or experience.
2. Does this poem present, directly or by clear implication, an argument intended to inform or persuade? If so, state the main proposition.

In conducting discussion of these questions, insist that students justify their answers by explicit reference to the text of the poem. The most defensible classification of a poem is that which most completely and convincingly accounts for it.

So that students will learn how to carry on this kind of inquiry for themselves, conduct classroom discussions on several poems. Those cited in this article may be included. Use the two questions as main guides to discussion. Ask them to do individual work on particular poems only when the discussions suggest that they are ready. Small groups may be assigned poems to study and to report the results of their inquiries to the class.

A TASK ANALYSIS FOR ARGUMENTATIVE POETRY

As noted, I assume that the study of poetry follows the study of expository prose. It is convenient, then, to consider first the teaching of argumentative poems.

A list of skills unified by a principle of order guides the further inquiry. Whether an argument is in prose, poetry, fiction, or drama, the parts, skills, and procedures for teaching comprehension are essentially the same. The following task analysis is an adaption and reformulation of the one already presented for the comprehension of argument in prose.

1.0 TASKS OF EFFECT

(a) Describe the intended emotional and other effects on a continuum of serious—comic and pleasure—pain. (b) Justify the response to (a) by explicit reference to the text.

2.0 TASKS OF PARTS

For each part listed below (a) identify the part, (b) justify the response to (a) by explicit reference to the text and (c) state how the part functions toward producing the effect. Following is a list of the parts:

2.1 *Object of presentation.* Typically a main proposition about which the audience is to be informed, persuaded, delighted, and so on. State relation between effect upon the reader and the proposition that the poem presents.

2.2 *Manner of presentation.*

2.21 A selection of details

2.22 An organization of the details into a sequence

2.23 A scale or emphasis

2.24 Speaker(s) and point(s) of view

The results of applying the tasks listed under manner should be formulated so that the following is made explicit: what is presented (selection), in what sequence (order), in what light (speaker and point of view) and to what extent (scale).

2.3 *Means.* Explain the function of language in lending the poem the characteristics it possesses. If a particular poem arouses pleasure through sound effects, then identify the devices of language (rhyme, meter, or whatever) that arouse such responses. If a poem is a unified whole, explain how language contributes to that unity. If a poem depicts what it does succinctly, then identify the linguistic means through which such succinctness of expression is achieved. Guard against holding preconceived notions of what the language of poetry is supposed to be like. Instead, assume that the task of means directs readers to discover, without preconception, just what language actually does in particular poems, just how it functions to produce the effects.

As mentioned, the learner's apprehension of the plain, literal sense is prerequisite to his acquiring other skills of comprehension.

A Task Analysis for Comprehending Imitative Poems

Having classified a poem as an imitation, a student should first identify the effect of the entire work; second, state the experience depicted; and, finally, inquire into the representation of that experience and the language used to convey it. Following is a formulation of the task:

1.0 TASKS OF EFFECT

(same as for argumentative poems)

2.0 TASKS OF PARTS

2.1 *Object of imitation.* Describe the experience that the poem depicts. Formulate that description in such fashion that your reader or listener can see the experience as a time-bound synthesis of *thought*, which includes the situation as perceived by the speaker, *character*, and *action or reaction*, as these underlined terms have been defined. State relations between effect upon the reader and the experience that the poem depicts.

2.2 *Manner of imitation.* For each part (a) identify the part, (b) justify the response to (a) by explicit reference to the text, and (c) state how the part functions toward producing the effect.

(2.21–2.24 same as for argumentative poems)

2.3 *Means.* (same as for argumentative poems)

USING THE TASK ANALYSIS

Illustrate the use of the tasks of effect, object, and of manner with a brief poem.

WITH RUE MY HEART IS LADEN

With rue my heart is laden
For golden friends I had,
For many a rose-lipt maiden
And many a lightfoot lad.

By brooks too broad for leaping
The lightfoot boys are laid;
The rose-lipt girls are sleeping
In fields where roses fade.

A. E. HOUSMAN

A. TASK OF EFFECT

Q. What emotional effects is the poem intended to arouse?

A. Because the poem treats seriously life and death, youth and maturity, these produce serious responses. The speaker's perception and use of language excite our admiration. Because his feelings are sad and nostalgic, so are the readers'. There is, moreover, pleasure aroused through such means as meter, rhyme, and choice of words.

B. TASK OF OBJECT

Q. Describe the experience that the poem depicts. Show that experience is a synthesis of (1) thought, which includes the situation as perceived by the speaker; (2) character; and (3) action or reaction.

A. The following experience may be inferred from the poem: The speaker had many young, lively friends who died; he contemplates and responds to that with a feeling of regret which his words express. Of this inferrable experience, however, only the speaker's contemplation and response are directly represented. From the unrepresented part of the experience we infer that the speaker is mature because it is in the nature of things that mature people contemplate the death of many friends. The speaker refers to the mutability of life, to the value of friends and he draws a fitting comparison between the friends and certain aspects of nature. The speaker's thought is thus revealed as perceptive to such matters, and his character, to prefer these. His response is an expected result of his thought and character. The poem, then, depicts the experience directly.

C. TASKS OF MANNER

Q. State the details, the order in which they appear, and their uses.

A. The details and the order in which they appear may be briefly stated:

  1. The speaker's statement that he is sad because he has lost many of his "golden friends."

  2. His observation that the "lightfoot boys" are laid "By brooks too broad for leaping" and the rose-lipt girls "are sleeping / In fields where roses fade."

  This order proceeds from a statement of his sadness at the death of his friends to a comment on their places of burial. He suggests resemblances between the "lightfoot boys" and the broad brooks and between the "rose-lipt girls" and the fields where roses bloom and fade. An analogy between the blooming and fading of roses and that of the girls' lives seems clear. But there is not a similar analogy in the reference to the burial places of the boys. The reason for that lack of parallelism is not made plain.

  The order gives the reader first the knowledge of the speaker's feelings and attitude toward the deaths. With that knowledge in mind, the reader can then respond properly to the observations of the places of burial.

Q. Describe and justify the choice of speaker and his point of view.

A. The speaker has already been described. Briefly, he (or she) is serious, contemplative, and gifted in the use of language. Such qualities arouse our admiration and our sympathy. He speaks as he undergoes the experience which gives an effect of immediacy, spontaneity and perhaps sincerity.

Q. What in the poem is given more or less emphasis and why?

A. By far, the poem emphasizes such matters as sadness, regret, and places of burial. These are contrasted with the less emphasized youthful liveliness of these friends. This emphasis and contrast makes more poignant and nostalgic the speaker's memory and regret.

SUMMARY

Given the theory of comprehension being explained, the two task analyses presented probably comprise at its level of generality a complete inventory, and therefore provide guidance for teaching to comprehend all lyric poems.

The set of parts for all argumentative poems is the same. A somewhat different single set of parts is incorporated into all imitative poems. Therefore, the complicated argument or imitation possesses the same set of parts as the simple ones do. When the principal aim of teaching is knowledge of the parts and their uses in comprehension, then it is expedient to use simple poems.

No one can predict just what questions and explanations a group of learners will need so that they can perform the sets of tasks presented here. The teacher's best guidance is a clear understanding of poems as made things, of the ends and means of the poem under study, and of the achievements expected of learners. This and the preceding articles have attempted to explain and clarify such matters. Because of limitations of space, a discussion of language has been omitted.

PERFORMANCE OBJECTIVES IN READING AND RESPONDING TO LITERATURE*

Arnold Lazarus

Just as some students might be turned off by doing the kinds of activities involved in the six kinds of responses to reading, there are many who can do them, want to do them, and need to do them. It seems to me that a school system must work hard at identifying such people and providing the kinds of experience that Lazarus (and Bazemore, in a previous article) are delineating. Just be careful not to overlook the "diamond in the rough," the nascent scholar, or the diffident nugget. Although the spellings are somewhat similar, there is a

I am indebted to discussions with three colleagues at the State University of New York at Albany: Robert N. Andersen, James E. Cochrane and Mary Elizabeth Grenander. I am indebted, also, to numerous writers of "Chicago School" criticism. The faults, however, are mine alone.

* FROM *English Journal*, 49 (January 1972), pp. 52–58, reprinted with permission of Arnold Lazarus and the National Council of Teachers of English.

world of difference between *nugget* and *nugatory*.

1. How do valuing and evaluating differ?

2. How do you value the section on valuing?

3. After studying this article, write a statement of its controlling idea, along with some of its supporting arguments.

4. Try some of the activities suggested for "Discovering Relationships." Apply them to some literary work you are now reading.

5. Try activities from other sections and report your findings to a group.

6. How do you value the section on "Entering Performance"?

7. Evaluate this article, please.

The Sixtieth Annual Convention of the National Council of Teachers of English passed a Resolution urging caution against behavioral objectives in English. English teachers and professors are understandably hostile toward the whole idea of behavioralism, but all too many are innocent of the fact that behavioral objectives (or, as the Tri-U Project prefers to call them, performance objectives) need not be behavioristic in the sense of Orwell's 1984 conditioning. It is not the purpose of this article to reply point by point to the teachers who attacked the *Tri-University Catalog of Objectives in English, Grades 9–12*[1] in Atlanta. Rather, the directors have decided to release some representative excerpts from the Section on Reading and Responding to Literature,[2] chief target of the attack, so that persons interested can get a look at what the Project is actually up to and decide for themselves whether it is doing a disservice.

Although the Catalog contains an index of objectives by literary genres for the convenience of teachers who like to "teach a novel" (or a short story or a poem or a play), the Reading Section organizes student experiences as responses (what most students and other pleasure-loving people enjoy doing): Valuing, Describing, Discovering Relationships, Discriminating, Inferring, and Evaluating. Each of these spheres of response thus deliberately combines the affective (attitudes and feelings) with the cognitive (knowledge and skills)—segregating those two domains having hitherto tended only to accommodate, perhaps, the nicely theoretical taxonomies, especially the excellent models compiled by Benjamin Bloom and his associates.[3]

[1] A first draft of this Catalog, compiled by J. N. Hook and Paul Jacobs of the University of Illinois, Edward Jenkinson and Don Seybold of Indiana University, Arnold Lazarus and Thomas Pietras of Purdue, in consultation with scores of distinguished consultants, was recently field-tested by many teachers and students under the monitoring of Adrian Van Mondfrans in several key communities and inner cities, thanks to a grant from the Office of Education.

[2] The section on Responses to Literature was compiled by Arnold Lazarus. Other members of the team compiled such other sections as I. Non-Verbal Communication, II. Listening and Speaking, III. Language, V. Writing, and VI. Mass Media.

[3] Benjamin Bloom et al., *Taxonomy of Educational Objectives: Cognitive Domain;* David Krathwohl et al., *Taxonomy of Educational Objectives: Affective Domain* (David McKay, 1956 and 1964, respectively.)

Here, then, are some of the Tri-U performance objectives in Reading and Responding to Literature.

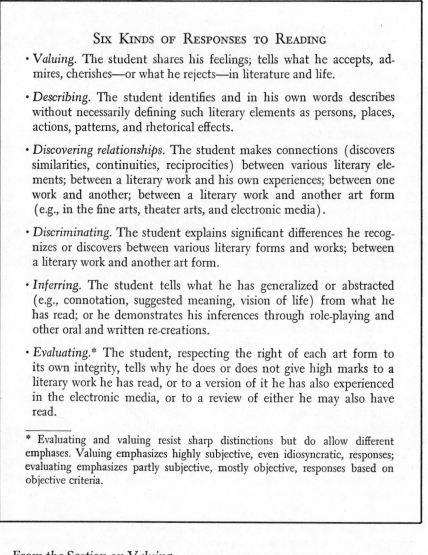

SIX KINDS OF RESPONSES TO READING

· *Valuing*. The student shares his feelings; tells what he accepts, admires, cherishes—or what he rejects—in literature and life.

· *Describing*. The student identifies and in his own words describes without necessarily defining such literary elements as persons, places, actions, patterns, and rhetorical effects.

· *Discovering relationships*. The student makes connections (discovers similarities, continuities, reciprocities) between various literary elements; between a literary work and his own experiences; between one work and another; between a literary work and another art form (e.g., in the fine arts, theater arts, and electronic media).

· *Discriminating*. The student explains significant differences he recognizes or discovers between various literary forms and works; between a literary work and another art form.

· *Inferring*. The student tells what he has generalized or abstracted (e.g., connotation, suggested meaning, vision of life) from what he has read; or he demonstrates his inferences through role-playing and other oral and written re-creations.

· *Evaluating.** The student, respecting the right of each art form to its own integrity, tells why he does or does not give high marks to a literary work he has read, or to a version of it he has also experienced in the electronic media, or to a review of either he may also have read.

---

* Evaluating and valuing resist sharp distinctions but do allow different emphases. Valuing emphasizes highly subjective, even idiosyncratic, responses; evaluating emphasizes partly subjective, mostly objective, responses based on objective criteria.

From the Section on Valuing

● Faced with an attractive variety of literature (e.g., periodicals on the classroom table; paperbacks, hobby books, anthologies, and encyclopedias on the shelves), the student gravitates toward rather than away from them; he browses and reads.

● The student becomes a card-carrying borrower from his school or public library.

- In an informal panel or a rap session, the student tells which kinds of periodicals and books he likes (e.g., sports, hobbies, science fiction, or any kinds of materials from anywhere on the spectrum) and defends his preferences.

- During oral interpretations of plays and the dialog of fiction, the student often volunteers and participates with animation.

- After reading a work that stimulates soul-searching (e.g., *Black Like Me, Notes of a Native Son, Death of a Salesman, The Prophet*), the student, participating in a symposium, tells how one or another of the episodes or issues is or is not compatible with his own values.

- Having read a work like *Hair, Catch 22,* or *Soul On Ice,* the student defends orally or in writing the right of other people to read it regardless of its potential offensiveness.

- In reading works that combine fantasy with humor and satire (e.g., *The Martian Chronicles, The Hobbit, Childhood's End, Cat's Cradle*), the student tells why he is willing, if he is, to suspend his disbelief—to accept imaginative distortions of the manifest or literal.

From the Section on Describing

- Having read a nonfictional work like *Silent Spring, Unsafe at Any Speed,* or *The Peter Principle,* the student writes a statement of the work's controlling idea along with some of its supporting arguments.

- After reading any work containing characters, the student describes one of them on the basis of what the character says and does, and what other characters feel about him.

- For a given poem or story, the student describes the speaker or the narrator.

- In any piece containing irony, the student identifies it or in his own words describes it without necessarily defining it.

- Having read a poem, story, or essay, or any other piece containing allusions, the student identifies one and explains how it contributes to the meaning of the work. (If evaluating, he also judges whether the allusion has contributed imaginatively and economically to the work's overall meaning and tone. The Catalog assumes that students will simultaneously combine two or more kinds of affective and cognitive responses.)

From the Section on Discovering Relationships

- Reading a work containing character foils (e.g., *Demian* or *A Separate Peace*), the student identifies the emphasized likenesses and differences that relate two particular characters.

- Having read two literary works (e.g., *Macbeth* and *Antigone*) with the same theme (i.e., the individual against fate), the student writes a brief paper on ways in which the two works are related.

- After reading several fictional works centering in such archetypal experiences as alienation, initiation, ritual sacrifice, and so on, the student discusses one of the ways in which one of the fictional episodes relates to a real-life episode that he has experienced or observed.

• In reading a work set in a different social, ethnic, or religious culture than his own (e.g., *Kim, Siddhartha, Persia Is My Heart, Exodus*), the student explains which feature, if any, is similar to a feature in his sub-culture or his own life style.

• After reading, or listening to a recording of, a contemporary poem or song (e.g., Paul Simon's version of "Richard Cory"), the student explains how the poet relates to the reader—e.g., how the imagery recreates in the reader the poet's mood or attitude.

• From a given literary work (e.g., *The Pump House Gang*), the student lists several frequently used expressions (e.g., *Me-dah!* and *jaysus*) and explains how they relate to the tone and meaning of the work.

• Given some narrative verse or prose selections (e.g., from *The Odyssey* or *The Oxbow Incident*) containing verbal phrases at ends rather than at beginnings of sentences, the student identifies the phrases that spell out concretely what is introduced only generally in the initial main clauses.[4]

• After reading, or listening to a recording of, a poem like Dylan Thomas' "Do Not Go Gentle," the student explains how the line-ends and the beginnings of subsequent lines are related (e.g., how they play with each other in such rhetorical games as echoing and punning).

• Having taped their choral reading of a poem or song (e.g., Burns' "Sweet Afton" or Lennon and McCartney's "In My Life"), and having played the tape for the class, a group of students or their spokesman explains at least one relationship between the choral reading and the musical version.

• The student discovers and re-creates relationships between a literary work and any other art form of his own making—for example, a collage, a photograph, a drawing, or even a film.

From the Section on Discriminating

• In reading editorials and advertisements, the student identifies and explains the difference between a legitimate and a fallacious dilemma.

• When he reads dialog in fiction, drama, and narrative verse, the student discriminates by means of pitch, stress, and pause, between alternative meanings dependent on intonation.

• After reading several poems by one poet (e.g., Frost's "Birches," "Departmental," "Canis Major"), the student distinguishes the speaking voice in each poem.

• Given such comparisons as "the boy looked like a man" and "the boy looked like a bulldozer," the student, without being rehearsed in

---

[4] From the *Purdue Project English Unit on The Odyssey* (Skokie, Illinois: National Textbook Co., 1971).

trivial distinctions between simile and metaphor, distinguishes between more prosaic and more imaginative comparisons.

- After reading some such nonfiction as *Growing Up Absurd* or *The Armies of the Night*, the student identifies and distinguishes between some of the documentary and some of the lyrical passages.
- After reading a tragedy (e.g., *A Man for All Seasons*) and a comedy (e.g., *Pygmalion*), the student explains some of the differences between tragedy and comedy; or he may identify some of the differences between either mode and its parody, (e.g., *Hamlet* vs *Rosencrantz and Guildenstern Are Dead*).

From the Section on Inferring

- Given a piece containing innuendo (e.g., a Volkswagen advertisement, a Bill Mauldin cartoon, a column by Art Buchwald, an excerpt from *Mad* Magazine), the student infers what was meant beyond what was said, then tells what may have been suggested.
- After reading any literary work, the student infers and states in his own words the work's main theme or thesis and if possible the reflected vision of life.
- Having read a play (e.g., *The Admirable Crichton* or *The Miracle Worker*), the student draws, or constructs a mockup of, a stage appropriate to the action.
- By means of oral interpretation, at first, the student demonstrates what he has inferred about a given character's convictions, prejudices, and life style. Then in a script-free, role-playing episode, the student, given a contemporary issue (e.g., pollution), orally reacts as he feels the character whose persona he now inhabits would react.
- Having read, or listened to a recording of, some such allegorical verse as E. E. Cummings' "Anyone Lived in a Pretty How Town," the student infers and explains (a) why the word *did* in "he danced his did" must have been used as a noun (b) what this noun may be naming, and (c) who is represented by such characters as Anyone, No-one, and the Somebodies.

From the Section on Evaluating

- Given a used-car advertisement that emphasizes a car's virtues without mentioning its shortcomings, the student lists on the chalkboard some possible shortcomings omitted from the ad.
- Before attending a movie, the student reads a review or two of it (e.g., in *Saturday Review, Life, Scholastic*). On the basis of what he reads he may decide not to attend. But if he does attend, he compares—in a brief oral or written critique—his own judgment with that of a reviewer.
- After reading a work like Shaw's *Pygmalion* or T. H. White's *The Once and Future King* and then experiencing a stage or screen version (e.g., *My Fair Lady* or *Camelot*), the student, respecting each medium's

right to its own integrity, writes a brief critical review in which he judges where each medium gained a little or lost a little.

• While reading a work of his own choice, the student informally tells of the work's effectiveness or lack of it in invoking his response. He may also wish to reveal whether or not his personal values stood in the way of the transaction, as Louise Rosenblatt puts it, between himself and the author.

• Having read, and on the screen witnessed, many stories in which boy meets girl, falls in love with her, and despite complications marries her, the student talks about any treatment of this formula that he believes failed or succeeded in rising above banality (e.g., Segal's *Love Story* vs Shakespeare's *Romeo and Juliet*).

• For a work of his own choice, the student writes a brief critique with examples, in which he judges how much the medium or manner of the work contributed, for him, to the work's message or impact.

• In an informal panel or a rap session, the student tells why he judges as successful or unsuccessful, serious or trivial, any artistic work that he has read, seen, or heard.

General Goals and Rationale Statements. So much for representative performance objectives. In the face of orthodox prescription against writing objectives in general terms[5] we have prefaced each group of performance objectives with a general goal. And wherever appropriate we interpolate statements of assumption. For example, bracketed after one of the general goals in *Valuing:* "The power of positive reinforcement along with the need for experiencing a variety of pleasures, including those in *printed* as well as electronic media, are here assumed as imperatives of the human condition, as Ray Bradbury warns in *Fahrenheit 451.*"

ENTERING PERFORMANCES.   Before a series of performance objectives we usually stipulate one or two prerequisites labeled *Entering Performance Objectives.* These experiences, or most of them, have engaged most youngsters long before Grade 9. Anyway, before a student can be expected to make inferences beyond literal levels (e.g., in allegory, parody, paradox, irony, satire, etc., which remain at bottom a kind of game-playing), before he could in fact transact many vibrations with stories and poems, he would presumably have been exposed to a number of the latter quite early in life. Thus from our section on *Inferring*, then, compare a couple of *Entering Performances:* "(A) The student, recalling how he participated during his childhood (whether in suburbia or the ghetto) in hop scotch and rope jumping and in playing such games as 'Simon Says' and 'Red Rover, Come Over,' talks about some of the sensations he enjoyed—

---

[5] See, for example, Robert F. Mager, *Preparing Instructional Objectives* (Fearon Publishers, 1962). Compare the more humanistic approaches in John Maxwell and Anthony Tovatt, eds., *On Writing Behavioral Objectives in English* (NCTE, 1970) and in Lazarus and Knudson, *Selected Objectives for the English Language Arts, Grades 7–12* (Houghton Mifflin, 1967).

rhythmical stepping, hopping, jumping, saying or singing the magical words, passwords, rhymes, incantations; relating ritually with members of his group. In a later discussion he may also talk about some of the ways in which game-playing and role-playing help recreate or interpret poems, plays, stories, and life itself. (B) The student has as a child listened to stories containing riddles and paradoxes, Biblical and other parables, Mother Goose rhymes, folktales, and songs from his own subculture."

ENABLING OBJECTIVES. Finally, under many a performance objective, we spell out even more specifically some possible responses to a given piece of reading. (Nominated titles of literary works are only intended to represent a wide pool of possibilities.) Under the performance objective on discriminating among intonations, for example, is the following "enabler": "Oraly reading the passage in *The Yearling,* in which Mr. Baxter asks Jody, 'How come you to take off such a fur *piece* down the road?' the student does not put more stress on *fur* than on *piece.*"[6] Under the performance objective on showing relationships between literary work and other art forms, there is this "enabler": "Having read a poem like Marianne Moore's 'The Steeple Jack,' the student compares the poem's colors, perspectives, and drollery with similar qualities in paintings by Dürer or by Chagall—perhaps brings to class a Chagall print (e.g., 'I and My Village') and points out similarities between such Chagallité and such Marianne Moore-ness in 'The Steeple Jack'." For the performance objective on describing a literary feature like "point of view" the following "enabler" typifies certain enabling objectives consisting of questions: "Having read *A Separate Peace,* the student demonstrates his understanding of 'point of view' by answering questions like these: Can you always tell whether Gene is relating how he felt at the time an event happened or how he feels about it fifteen years later? Why or why not? . . . Is Gene using these words to describe how he felt at the time or how he now knows that he felt?"[7] For the performance objective on sharing one's values after reading Baldwin's *Notes of a Native Son:* "Did this book (or passage) suggest answers to, or move you to raise, questions like Who am I? (Machine? Product? Person?) What does being a person mean? What does loving one's neighbor mean? Is the opposite of love, indifference? What did reading this book do for your conscience or your other feelings about values?"

The Tri-University objectives should not create robots, and in the field-testing so far do not seem to have generated either Frankensteins or

---

[6] From the *Purdue Project English Unit on The Yearling* (unpublished). Oral interpretation, as an art form in its own right, is to be distinguished of course from the dialectologist's science of field recording.

[7] From Edward Jenkinson and Donald Seybold, "An Approach to A *Separate Peace* and *Demian*" in William Evans (ed.), *New Ways to Teach Literature* (Bantam Books, in press).

monsters. Teachers who fear performance objectives as early warnings of operant conditioning should consider the crucial distinctions that Alan Purves ("Of Behaviors, Objectives, and English," *English Journal*, September 1970) and others have identified, especially the distinction that humanistic performances include thinking and feeling, which may or may not be measurable.

Activity-centered (or process- or student-centered) objectives are not novel; they weren't even novel in the 1930s when they appeared in the NCTE's *An Experience Curriculum*. Still, their *application* remains radical. Whether because of puritanic resistance to a hedonistic youth culture or for whatever reasons, few teachers implemented such objectives in the 1960s, as reflected in James Squire and Roger Applebee's report *High School English Instruction Today* (1968).

Under whatever labels, performance objectives, especially the nonmeasurable or delayed-measurable kinds sampled above, will no doubt disappoint the devotees of accountability, although not the teachers and students willing to look beyond the letter—beyond measuring, weighing, having, and holding. For in the end, Norman Brown's criterion in *Life Against Death* (Random House, 1959) strikes us as the more sacred accountability: achievement in the sense of just having demonstrates a love of death; achievement in the sense of doing demonstrates a love of life.

Social Studies

ANTIDOTE FOR APATHY—ACQUIRING READING SKILLS FOR SOCIAL STUDIES*
Helen Huus

The social studies are generally considered an important part of the school curriculum. Therefore any hint that these studies are not being taught as well as they might be taught is a cause for concern.

In this selection Huus comments on apathy in our social studies classrooms. There are students who approach social studies in a way that is not conducive to developing the concepts, skills, and attitudes they need to be adequate citizens. Huus explains her antidote for apathy and details the prescription under three categories.

* FROM *Challenge and Experiment in Reading*, J. Allen Figurel, editor International Reading Association Proceedings, 7 (New York: Scholastic Magazines, 1962), pp. 81–88, reprinted with permission of Helen Huus and the International Reading Association.

1. What is the apathy to which the author refers in the title of her article?

2. Pronunciation skills can be taught deductively or inductively. Does the author suggest which method to use?

3. Can you see any advantages or disadvantages in teaching some of these skills to individuals or small groups of students before attempting them with larger groups? Explain.

4. At your first opportunity, examine a social studies text and list particular examples under the headings listed under "Inference" in this article, for example, "cause-effect implications."

5. Develop and write out an argument for *not neglecting* the teachings of application skills in social studies. Subject it to the criticism of others.

While school keeps in thousands of classrooms throughout our country and while a generation of pupils grows up to take their turn at running the world, time does not stand still. Europe busies herself with the Common Market, Algeria has an uneasy truce, trouble crops up in Indonesia, Argentina, or Syria, and our children study school and community, state and nation, often in a half-hearted, mechanical way, and dull their senses by rote memory, a multitude of proper names (many unidentified), and a lack of zest for the whole idea. Why an apathy for social studies, when it is constantly teeming with action, people, adventure, and daring—all aspects that interest the elementary school child? Why, indeed?

The answer lies, perhaps, in three directives—the pupils' own skills, the materials available, and the teacher's enthusiasm and know-how. The antidote for apathy, as for any evil, lies in counteraction—in working against, and since the opposite of apathy is interest, feeling, activity, and excitement, the obvious way to counteract it is to promote these opposites.

While there are many and varied ways in which such skills might be analyzed, they have been organized into the three general categories of pronunciation, meaning, and application for purposes of this discussion. Each of these will be treated in turn.

PRONUNCIATION SKILLS

MULTISYLLABIC WORDS. Whenever a reader faces new material, his first responsibility is to decipher the symbols into meaningful units. In social studies, as in any subject area, the reader applies the skills of phonetic analysis, structural analysis, and context clues that help him arrive at the pronunciation and ultimate recognition of the words he must read. Since many of the words in social studies are multisyllabic words, the reader needs the ability to apply the generalizations dealing with words of this type. Following are five useful generalizations for this purpose:

1. When a word has a double consonant (or two consonants) following a vowel, divide the word between the consonants, such as: Hit-tite, Mis-sis-sip-pi, Ham-mer-fest, Col-lec-tive, Ap-pian, Bren-ner, and tun-dra, Mos-lem, mon-soon, or-bit, or Den-mark.

2. When a vowel is followed by a single consonant in a word of more than one syllable, the division is made *before* the consonant, as in: A-ra-bi-an, A-so-ka, as-tro-labe, co-lo-ni-al, Hai-fa, Rho-de-sia, So-viet, and ve-to.

3. When a word ends in "le," the preceding consonant belongs with the unaccented ending, as in: Bi-ble, mid-dle, Con-stan-ti-no-ple, and mar-ble.

4. When a word contains a consonant blend, the blend is usually not divided, as in: We*st*-min-*ster*, Rem-*br*andt, man-u-*scripts*, Liv-ing-*st*one, and Ca-sa-*bl*an-ca.

5. A word may be composed of a root plus a prefix and/or a suffix. Common prefixes that should be learned are: *un, ex, pre, ab, ad, com, en, in, re, de, sub, be, dis, pro*. Common suffixes include: *ment, tion, ly, less, ance, ness, ful, ship*.

Unless pupils are given practice in using syllabication skills, both in the regular developmental reading class and as applied in social studies and other classes, they do not acquire the needed ease of recognition that allows them to read material of difficulty with interest, and simply plodding along can become a deadly bore.

FOREIGN WORDS. Even a student who may have acceptable skills in word recognition will almost certainly encounter difficulty when he tries to apply those he knows with some of the words he finds in his social studies reading—words derived from foreign languages that have kept certain elements intact, and proper names that have retained the original pronunciation and have not been Anglicized.

In the first category are such words as: *plateau, saga, mesa, fief, kaiser, hotelier, veld, apartheid, fjord, atrium,* and *ballet,* while in the latter are the French Renaissance, Marseilles, Versailles, St. Chapelle, and Basque, but Paris (not Paree); the German Roentgen, Gutenberg, Bach, Beethoven, Wagner, Worms, and Frankfort am Main (not Maine); the Italian da Vinci, Verdi, Rossini; the Indian Brahman and Buddha; the African Leopoldville, Afrikaner, or Nkrumah; or other difficult pronunciations like Goteberg, the Louvre, and Popocatepetl or Port Said. At any rate, children who learn correct pronunciation of the many proper names in social studies have a small beginning toward becoming multilingual.

USE OF THE DICTIONARY. Knowing the basic generalizations for getting words independently will help, but there comes a point when even the mature reader needs the verification that can be found only in an authoritative source. Is it Himälaya or Himalaya? Hamburg or Hämburg? Istanbul or Istambul? Yucatan or Yucatän? Edinburg or Edinboro? The dictionary or glossary should tell, but the difficulty lies in checking the pronunciation initially so that incorrect forms are not practiced and thus become difficult to eradicate.

MEANING SKILLS

TECHNICAL WORDS. In addition to the pronunciation problems already described, the number of technical words used in social studies promote apathetic reaction. The technical words may be unique to the field or may be words for which the student already has one meaning. In the former category are words like *latitude, longitude, Constitution, Declaration of Independence, dictatorship, consumer, transportation,* and so on. In the latter are such words and phrases as *compass rose,* the *Gold Rush, world trade, the world market, diet* (as in Diet at Worms), *man power, raw materials, fixed salary,* and others equally obscure.

ABSTRACT WORDS. Social studies also abounds in abstract words like *democratic, loyalty, dignity, appreciation, interdependence, conservation, Dark Ages, industrial revolution, capital and labor,* the Iron or Bamboo Curtain, the Cold War, and the New Frontier.

The antidote for getting meaning into these technical and abstract words lies in tapping the pupils' own experiences by first relating the unknown word to some similar concept within his knowledge—location by latitude and longitude, for example, could be related to the location of buildings at a street intersection. Explanation is another way, and easy, or a study can be made of the word itself by first stripping off the prefix and suffix, as in the word *transportation,* leaving only the root word. Some pupils may already relate the root *port* to other words like *porter* or *portable* and make their own generalization about its meaning. When the prefix meaning of *across,* and the suffix meaning of *the act or state of* are added, pupils arrive at a meaning for *transportation* as "the act or state of carrying across." By substitution in the sentence, pupils clinch the idea and learn its use.

Of course, first-hand experience is the best teacher, and pupils who have been to Sutter's Mill have heard vivid tales of the Gold Rush; first-hand experience with maps will soon clarify what a compass rose is. Excursions are by far the most fruitful techniques for developing vocabulary easily, quickly, and permanently. Students learn new vocabulary naturally as they use the proper terminology for describing a place, an object, a method, or a product. A visit to a mill, for example, clarifies such words as *millwright, grist, rollway, undershot, mill race, vats, roving, carding, spinning jenny, sawyer, turbine, penstock,* or *sluicegate.*

The maps, diagrams, pictures, and other types of illustrations found in abundance in many social studies texts are there for a purpose—to help children visualize the scenes, to help them grasp relationships of rainfall, products, income, taxes, or time. Meaning is certainly enhanced when a diagram or photograph accompanies a description of locks on a canal, water wheels or ladders for fish, when a graph shows the distribution of rainfall for a certain area according to seasons or months, or when a time line puts the Age of Exploration into proper relationship with the Viking Era and the present. To make time really meaningful, let children put their own dates of birth on the line and let them see how short a span their life up to the present actually is.

For those pupils who simply cannot keep up, even with expert help, Fry recommends "glossing" as an aid to comprehension. This means "simply reading to students from the text, stopping frequently to explain concepts and terms."[1] At best, the teacher makes the page come alive by supplementing from his extensive background and, when coupled with enthusiasm, is guaranteed to capture the interest of even the most apathetic.

ORGANIZATION SKILLS.   Inherent in the total complex of skills in comprehension lies those related to the organization or structure of the material. The "cluster" of skills, as Robinson calls them, related to organization includes reading for details and main ideas, changing main ideas to topics and details to sub-topics, then labeling them in outline form. He presents three steps as a practical approach: (1) locating key words in sentences, (2) finding the key sentence in a paragraph, and (3) determining the main thought in a paragraph.[2]

While pupils may be able to see the structure of a sentence or a paragraph, they must be able also to obtain the larger view of a section or a chapter—yes, even of a total book—if they are to place historical events in proper perspective or obtain an international rather than a national or regional view alone. This means a constant shifting of position as additional information is obtained, and seeing these new relationships may require help. Modern textbooks provide useful aids in their varied type faces, side headings, and sectional titles, and teachers help pupils use outlines. One practical way is to have topics set down without numbers or letters, but using indentation instead to show relationship between main and subordinate levels. Then, as the story unfolds, these outline parts can be rearranged and literally lifted out and placed in the new frame of reference in its proper location.

Certain words act as "cue words" to help readers define organization and relationships, or shifts, and transitions. Such words include: *on the other hand, furthermore, nevertheless, in addition, moreover, since, because, for, but,* and the obvious *first, second, third,* and *finally.* These indicate transition, connection, and relation, and give warning that such will occur. Teachers can give added practice in heeding these signals by concocting exercises where pupils fill in missing connectives or change meaning by substituting

---

[1] Edward B. Fry, " 'Glossing,' An Ancient Method to Aid Social Studies Teachers with Reading Instruction." *California Journal of Secondary Education,* 32 (February 1957), 90–92.

[2] H. Alan Robinson, "A Cluster of Skills: Especially for Junior High School." *The Reading Teacher,* 15 (September 1961), 25–28.

other connectives. Another technique is to have pupils locate words clues in their textbook and other reading materials.

Besides the logical organization embodied in the main idea-detail structure of writing, other types encountered in social studies include chronological organization, with pertinent events related in the order they occurred, or the fictional approach sometimes used in the lower grades, where events lead up to the climax of the story. Time lines help give the proper chronological perspective, as do two-dimensional charts that place topics like "economics," "political history," "geography," "invention," and "trade" along the top of a chart and the names of various countries along the side. Each row then shows one country in relation to each topic, while each column shows the status of that topic in the various countries listed. Such charts can be made for a decade, a century, or even an era, but reducing organization to visual form has the added advantage of sensory appeal. Picture charts serve a similar purpose and catch the interest of some students who might not be enticed by the abstract approach.

Understanding the over-all pattern of a subject area, such as social studies, provides a background and a Gestalt for further learning. While this pattern is complicated by the staccato presentation of facts without expansion, by the introduction of many names and terms, and by the remoteness to pupil experience, it has the advantage of providing many new learnings and enough "top" for even the brightest, as well as a certain exotic flavor inherent in eras past and places distant.

SIMPLE COMPREHENSION. Anderson makes a plea for the constant use of the "unseen question" as a stimulus for students to read and comprehend. He emphasizes the importance of the reader's purpose, that he set his own, and that he then answer what he started out to find.[3] While it may not always be practical for pupils to set their own purposes, teachers can arouse interest and, together with their pupils, set the purposes for reading. The SQ3R technique (survey, question, read, recite, review) is a similar method couched in catchy terms, but useful nonetheless.

Once purpose is set, pupils need to choose a speed of reading commensurate with the job to be done. For the survey, skimming to locate key words and headings, to see the over-all job, and to obtain an overview will suffice. For the answering of questions, a more careful reading than before is needed. For the review following the recitation, a quick cursory reading will be sufficient. Being able to shift speed gears smoothly is a mark of the mature reader, and students need practice under supervision in order to accomplish this task.

INTERPRETATION SKILLS. The intricate "cluster" of skills comprising thoughtful interpretation cannot be discussed fully here; only two will be mentioned—inference and evaluation.

---

[3] A. W. Anderson, "Directing Reading Comprehension," *The Reading Teacher*, 13 (February 1960), 206–207, 211.

Inference refers to those ideas implied but not explicitly stated and which are acquired by reasoning or concluding. The contents of social studies texts are replete with cause-effect implications, time relationships, generalizations about exploration, the effect of terrain on development, the organization of governments, the influence of imperialism or a thousand other ideas. How to teach becomes a problem, for, of necessity, the making of inferences requires the use of higher mental abilities—to see two ideas, to note common elements and make a connection between the two, then adapt the new idea to the unknown—and slow learners will need explicit help in having the points of similarity and relationship specifically cited while fast learners are already applying the method to new content.

The first question that might well be asked in *evaluation* relates to the author and his purpose. "Who wrote this material? Is he qualified to do so?" In an article entitled "The Power and the Glory of the Word," Nance makes the following statement about authors in general:

> The writer is a human being and a citizen. The scope and content of his material will be conditioned by his major interests, his outlook on life, his responses to life, and his experience, knowledge, abilities, and opportunities. . . .[4]

The competency of the author becomes particularly important when facts disagree, or when different works place different interpretations on the same series of events, or when events are presented from different points of view. Finding pertinent information about living authors is sometimes difficult, but students can look at the book jackets, the comment column in a periodical, or the blurbs from the publisher. The reputation of a publishing house can lend dignity and prestige to an unknown author until he makes his mark. At any rate, readers must be taught to consider the source.

Related questions, "Why did the author write on this topic? Was it to advertise, to propagandize, to present information, to present a point of view?" must also be given attention. Nance comments on purposes for writing by saying:

> Writers throughout the centuries have had many different goals: To recover the past, to record and conserve for the future, to interpret, comment, report, arouse, condemn, defend, entertain, annoy or to obtain personal or institutional publicity.[5]

Certainly if there are hidden or ulterior motives, students should be able to locate the signals and analyze the material accordingly. The use of sweeping generalizations not backed by data or examples, the "snob appeal" so rampant in advertising, the pseudo-scientific surveys often quoted, the testimonial or "everyone believes" technique, or the use of emotionally tinged

[4] E. C. Nance, "The Power and the Glory of the Word," *Vital Speeches*, 23 (April 1, 1957), 381.
[5] *Ibid.*

words like *fellow traveler, anarchy, slave, imperialistic, dictatorial,* or *beneficent, philanthropic, generous, handsome, immense proportion,* or *gigantic, colossal, stupendous, magnificent* reach various people in different ways. It becomes important to create in readers a studied wariness that aids them in objective judgment: to paraphrase *caveat emptor,* "Let the reader beware!"

The second question in evaluation ought to be, "Is the information true?" In part, a reputable author's word is taken, but skeptical readers and careful scholars check to see if facts agree and decide if enough facts are presented. Here is where the student's knowledge and background come into play, for his incidental or systematic learning serves as a backboard against which to bounce the ideas of the author, as well as to raise questions about facts that seem somehow to ring not quite true. Checking against other references—encyclopedia, atlas, almanac, or any number of handbooks and general works—becomes necessary, and through practice and guidance students become proficient in locating the right source and finding within that source the material needed.

A third aspect of evaluation relates to the quality of writing exhibited by the author. For illustration, the following excerpt from an aricle entitled, "Hong Kong Has Many Faces," in a recent issue of *National Geographic* describes Hong Kong's rise as an industrial city:

> For decades . . . Hong Kong was the front door for the great China market. Sitting astride the world's trade lanes the city endlessly shuttled goods in and out of its busy warehouses, bound from China to the world, and from the world to China. Then came the Korean War. The United Nations voted an embargo on trade with China, and Hong Kong—the old Hong Kong—sickened.
>
> The city might have died if another "disaster" had not come along at almost the same time. The years of the refugee were 1949 to 1951, when men poured out of Red China in the hundreds of thousands.
>
> "Fortunately," he said, "that problem arrived with a built-in solution, for the refugees were not all poor men. . . .
>
> "Here, in one place, were capital and labor, eager to work together."[6]

Figures of speech like *the front door, sitting astride, sickened* . . . and *might have died, men poured out,* and *a built-in solution,* add meaning through the imagery and relationships implied. Certain of the words connote a tone that transcends the description. These words create a feeling of greatness and strength, as implied in the phrases *front door for the great China market, sitting astride the world's trade lanes,* and *endlessly shuttling.*

The style of writing—the figurative, picturesque, and connotative aspects—influences the reader's understanding and reaction to what he reads. A lack of awareness of the subtleties of style will result either in gullibility or lack of accurate perception.

[6] John Scofield, "Hong Kong Has Many Faces," *The National Geographic Magazine,* 121, No. 1 (January 1962), 9–10.

The acquisition of complete meaning, therefore, lies in the reader's ability to understand the technical and abstract vocabulary, to grasp the structure and organization of the whole, to interpret the ideas implied but not directly stated, and to evaluate not only the author's competency and the validity of his statements, but his style of writing as well.

APPLICATION SKILLS

PROBLEM SOLVING. The third reading skill to be emphasized here is reacting to and using the ideas and impressions gained through reading. The highest level of reaction and application is the actual integration of the concepts, attitudes, and appreciations into the reader's own life so that what he reads becomes a part of him forever. For each person, there could be compiled, perhaps, a list of "Reading that changed my life." And is not this, after all, the ultimate goal of education—social studies, too—to change people from illiterate to literate, from uncultured to cultured, from irrational to rational? When reading materials in the social studies serve this goal, they are powerful agents indeed.

Students may react to their reading about Hong Kong, for example, by changing or forming opinions about the city itself, the people who live there, or they may do further research in order better to understand this complex city.

EXTENDED READING. What other use can the student make of his new found skills in reading? Merely keeping up with textbook assignments keeps some students busy, but even they should have an opportunity to use some of the beautiful, interesting, up-to-date books about our own and other countries, about historical eras, geographical areas, and the function and operation of government. The hundreds of books for children published each year contain a wealth of information; teachers need but to make them available to the right children at the right time.

Teachers stimulate extended reading when they take time for current events, for even elementary school children are interested in weather, sports, space, royalty, and the President and his family. Keeping up to date with the news is a good way to establish the habit of news reading with young children.

But it is in books that many children find their identification with heroes of another age or of another culture. Serviss recommends that teachers "help children find books convincing in portrayal, vivid in sensory imagery, reasonable and alive in characterization, discerning in the revelation of universal traits."[7]

Library books contribute in various ways to make the social understandings meaningful and interesting to children. They paint images in depth and

[7] K. Trevor Serviss, "Reading in the Content Areas," *Elementary English*, 30 (October 1953), 359.

detail, for one paragraph in the text can be amplified by extended treatment. They clarify concepts and expand reasons only briefly mentioned in the text, and they put the breath of human life into historical characters and people who live in other countries.[8]

In choosing books to counteract the pallid fare or pulp material so easily available to children, first ask, "What do children of this age *like* to read?" If the group is young, they like stories of children their own age, animals, slapstick humor, pictures with clear colors and not too much detail, and simple plots with repetition and refrain. A book like *Nu Dang and His Kite* not only tells of Siam (Thailand) as Nu Dang paddles up the long river to look for his kite, but also contains the gloomy refrain, "But nobody had seen it. Nowhere. No kite at all." Fortunately the kite is at home when Nu Dang arrives, for the wind had carried it there; so the ending is most satisfying to young readers. Children sympathize with Ping, the duck who runs away rather than being last on the boat and getting the spank he knows will come, for they, too, know that "fair is fair." But they rejoice when he escapes, and they realize that after all, a spank is nothing much compared to what Ping has survived.

Children learn about the world of work through such books as Lois Lenski's *Farmer Small, Cowboy Small,* and *Pilot Small,* or through Burton's *Mike Mulligan and His Steam Shovel,* or Bate's *Who Built the Bridge?* While some of these books personify machines, nevertheless the power and importance of their work is clearly portrayed. Children get gentle nudgings about manners from Munro Leaf, and through the charming books of Tasha Tudor they follow the seasons and the calendar, learn to count, and recite the alphabet in order. Holidays give a chance for biography—the colorful picture books by the D'Aulaires of Lincoln and Washington, Franklin, and Columbus—or for stories like *The Thanksgiving Story* and *The Fourth of July Story,* by Alice Dalgliesh, or *The Egg Tree,* that won the Caldecott Award, and *Patrick and the Golden Slippers,* that tells about Philadelphia's annual New Year's Day Mummers' Parade. (Yes, there are many books that appeal to younger children.)

The middle-graders love adventure and mystery, exploration and invention, and girls begin to look for romance. All of these can be found in books that enhance the social studies. Biography is fun when there is *Ben and Me* to compare with the facts, or *Mr. Revere and I.* History becomes contemporary when *Adam of the Road* contains the story of a budding wandering minstrel, an eleven-year-old boy who has lost his beloved dog, even though the story begins in the year 1294. Geography is really people

[8] See Helen Huus, *Children's Books to Enrich the Social Studies: For the Elementary Grades,* Bulletin 32 (Washington, D.C.: The National Council for the Social Studies, 1961), p. 196.

The World History Bibliography Committee of NCSS, Alice W. Spieseke, chm., *World History List for High Schools: A Selection for Supplementary Reading,* Bulletin 31 (Washington, D.C.: National Council for the Social Studies, 1959), p. 119.

when preadolescents follow Big Tiger and Christian, who gets caught on a troop train just because they tried to fly their kites from an empty box car. Their adventures through Mongolia and Sinkiang include robbers, bandits, a lama, and soldiers, and the responsibility of carving a secret message. Geography is people when Young Fu has grown gradually into a capable coppersmith craftsman, and when Li Lun, Lad of Courage, plants seven grains of rice on the highest mountain, then tends the last grain so that it survives to bear rice heads. Thus he shows his people a new way to combat hunger. Geography is people, too, when Momo, a little Tibetan girl, follows the trail of her stolen golden Lhasa terrier, Pempa, from her home in the hills to the busy city of Calcutta. Even boys will thrill to the suspense in this story, and all who read it will learn about the people of the mountains and about their customs and country. Pearl Buck's story of Japan, *The Big Wave*, Armstrong Sperry's *Call It Courage*, and Elizabeth Lewis' *To Beat a Tiger* are other books that show the character, traditions, and problems of peoples of the Far East.

Older boys and girls can find in books stories that contain the drama and daring of yesterday and today—books like those of Roman Britain by Rosemary Sutcliffe or *The Byzantines* by Thomas Chubb, which begins during the Fourth Crusade in 1203 and describes the wealth and culture of this great empire at the crossroads of the world. *Engineers Did It!* contains interesting accounts of feats like Roman aqueducts and roads, the flying buttresses of the cathedral at Amiens, and the laying of the Atlantic cable, while modern adventures are depicted in books like *Kon Tiki*, or Quentin Reynolds' *The Battle of Britain*.

These are but a few of the exciting, well-written, vivid tales that transport the reader for a time into another era, another place, another culture, and allow him to identify himself with these heroes to obtain vicariously some of the emotions, the grandeur, the problems of a different age, a different sphere. When he returns to reality, he will be more knowledgeable, more insightful, more understanding, and more thoughtful than before his flight of fancy, and this, in itself, is reward enough.

SUMMARY

And so it becomes evident that pupils who have the skills of pronunciation and recognition, who can put meaning into words, see order in the content, delve beneath the written word and look at the total with a studied appraisal have acquired the reading skills that make social studies an enjoyable experience. Then when pupils have, in addition, books and books that let them rove through the world and down the centuries, vicariously experiencing the triumphs and disappointments of people who really lived or might have done so, then teachers can say, "We tried to teach them about people. We taught them to read and think." We gave them books and time to read. We helped them when they asked and prodded them when they would be complacent. It remains for the future to tell how well we have succeeded."

MATERIALS FOR THE UNIT PLAN IN SOCIAL STUDIES*

Jean Fair

It is a commonly accepted fact among educators that the unit plan of teaching is effective because the learner can set many of his own goals and work on problems that interest him. A second advantage of the plan is that it allows the learner to work with materials that interest him and are at his ability level. Finally, the unit plan permits experiences to be organized in a way that brings out meaningful generalizations, facilitates seeing interrelationships among the experiences, and allows the learner to see the wholeness or the unity of these experiences.

In this article Fair shows how materials are used to best advantage in teaching the social studies unit so that the purported values of the unit method can be experienced.

1. For what purposes are various types of social studies materials used?

2. What can you infer about the author's attitude toward the importance of developing mature readers?

3. The author is cognizant of psychologically sound teaching–learning principles. Can you infer what these principles are?

4. State the article's key ideas.

A unit plan implies that students are to organize some wholeness or unity out of many aspects of their experiences. A unit plan usually calls for the development of several kinds of behavior, understanding, beliefs and attitudes, interests, skills, and thinking, in content areas appropriate for individual students. The topic or problem on which the content is centered is frequently, although not necessarily, structured in some other fashion than that of the conventional subject field. Since a unit plan is usually expected to organize several weeks of student time, some careful decisions must be made about definitions of, and priorities among, objectives, with mere coverage for its own sake ruled out. Student purposes take on great importance, and materials and experiences need to have maximum meaning.

* REPRINTED FROM *Materials for Reading*, Helen M. Robinson, editor, Supplementary Educational Monographs, No. 86, pp. 158–162, by permission of The University of Chicago Press. Copyright, 1957, by The University of Chicago Press.

Learning activities must be chosen with an eye to what students are to learn, and these activities must be ordered to facilitate organization of experiences.

MATERIALS TO PROMOTE A VARIETY OF OBJECTIVES

Let us turn to the kinds of reading materials required in a unit plan of study. It is obvious that we shall need a wide variety; no one book is likely to permit the development of the several kinds of behavior appropriate for the purposes of a particular group of students. Textbooks are useful for giving information about, and understanding of, topics and problems. Many teachers and students limit what can be learned by relying almost exclusively on such books. Others go to the needless trouble of finding the necessary discussions in a cumbersome variety of sources, when equally useful, and sometimes more suitable, treatments could be found more efficiently in classroom textbooks. The helpfulness of textbooks is increased when several are available and when students free themselves of the mind-set that textbook information can be used only in the organizational structure of the textbook itself.

Still, textbooks alone are not likely to be sufficient. Students also need encyclopedias appropriate for their reading ability; reference books, from the common almanacs to the less often used, but frequently more efficient, *Statistical Abstracts* (U.S. Government Printing Office), maps, atlases, gazeteers, biographical dictionaries, and the like; pamphlets; magazines suitable for readers of different abilities (to be saved over a period of years to increase sources); and books. We are all aware of the variety of sources which promote understanding.

However valuable these may be, they are usually not the most useful materials for involving students' feelings and so developing meaningful understandings, attitudes, and interests. Novels can help here. Consider, by way of illustration, Lewis' *Young Fu of the Upper Yangtze* (Winston, 1937) and Pearl Buck's classic, *The Good Earth* (World Publishing Co., 1952), for a unit dealing with China. Short stories are helpful; how valuable in a study of civil rights is a story such as Shirley Jackson's "The Lottery."[1] Plays are useful, for example, Miller's *Death of a Salesman* (Viking, 1949), for showing the values of modern society. Titles from biography and poetry will occur to all of us. We sometimes forget, however, the non-fiction articles and books. Think of the power of "The Blast in Centralia No. 5"[2] in a problem unit on how to improve conditions of labor; John Hersey's *Hiroshima* (Knopf, 1946) in a topical unit on World War II or a problem unit on what to do about national defense; or James Michener's *The Bridge*

---

[1] Shirley Jackson, "The Lottery," *Fifty Great Short Stories*, pp. 175–185. Edited by Milton Crane. New York: Bantam Books, 1952.

[2] John Bartlow Martin, "The Blast in Centralia No. 5," *Harper's Magazine Reader*, pp. 38–89. New York: Bantam Books, 1953.

at Andau (Random, 1957) in a study of present American policy toward Europe. There are classic documents, too: Webster's "Reply to Hayne," Bryan's "Cross of Gold" speech, and many more. Such materials, while not sufficient in themselves, do represent a needed type.

Many of these can be used also for the development of abilities in critical and creative thinking. Textbooks should be used to obtain comparisons of authors' points of view and for documents, graphs, and tables for interpretation. However, students will frequently need materials, other than textbooks, specifically chosen to permit questions like these: "What is the problem discussed?" "To what kind of audience does the author intend to speak?" "What are his assumptions or conclusions?" "Is his argument consistent?" "Are his facts relevant, accurate, and adequate?" "How does this interpretation compare with that interpretation?" "What difference does it make whether we adopt one or the other interpretation?" "What other solutions are possible?"

For able students, several sets of materials are particularly useful in units on American history. The Amherst series of "Problems in American Civilization" (Heath), which range over many significant problems (for example, "Slavery as a Cause of the Civil War" and "Loyalty in a Democratic State"), help students define problems and analyze and compare arguments in both contemporary statements and interpretations by later historians. Similar remarks might be made about Leopold and Link's *Problems in American History* (Prentice-Hall, 1952) and other excellent collections. Somewhat less difficult are the three pamphlets dealing with American foreign policy toward China, Russia, and Germany, recently published under the auspices of the North Central Association of Colleges and Secondary Schools (Science Research Associates, 1957). The series in the yearly "Reference Shelf" (H. W. Wilson) on such problems as federal taxes and national defense can also be mentioned. Such materials as these, which offer help in defining problems and choosing among alternative solutions, are particularly valuable in unit plans where individuals or small groups are working on aspects of a problem independently.

Students will need what we often call "documents." Some of the classics ought not to be overlooked. The *Declaration of Independence* and Number Ten of *The Federalist Papers* are easily available arguments for some units. Analyses of contemporary materials, such as quotations from Churchill and Hitler, may be needed in a unit on the origins of modern war. Eye-witness accounts are helpful when properly criticized or skimmed for a point of view. While there are fewer such accounts suitable for world-history units, a wealth of such material is available to us in other areas. Moreover, accounts of current events are readily obtained from newspapers and magazines.

Controversy is inherent in almost any meaningful social-studies unit, whether the content comes from the past or the present. In a unit on problems of improving law and justice, the concepts of justice embodied in Hammurabi's Code can provoke controversy when applied to cases of modern wrongdoing. Contemporary materials from books, magazines, and newspapers will be needed both for units on recurring issues in human affairs and for those dealing with specific present-day problems. Articles in magazines of opinion and editorials will be integral parts of plans for a unit; they are to be criticized, evaluated, and compared, and used as statements of alternatives in decision-making.

Graphs and tables, too, are helpful, particularly when they encourage interpretation. Those of the National Industrial Conference Board, "Road Maps of Industry" (The Board, New York), a regular and easily obtained series, fit into many units dealing with recurring issues. They present enough data to compare trends, question predictions, and check the accuracy of many other materials.

Students will need, then, materials which allow the development of a range of behaviors in content flexibility structured to meet their particular purposes.

MEANING IN MATERIALS

Young people must also have meaningful materials, for they cannot organize what does not carry meaning. I will do little more here than call attention to the use of audio-visual materials and the study aids, pictures, and the like found in textbooks and pamphlets. We might help students by taking advantage of many excellent television programs which can contribute meaning to the reading material used. Picture magazines, both those current and those saved from past years, are useful at many ability levels.

Some special mention may well be made of the kind of pamphlet material which contains enough of what we may call "case material" to put meaning into often empty generalizations. The "Life Adjustment Series" (Science Research Associates), by way of example, includes more than fifty titles, some at two maturity levels, on such topics as *Relations with Parents, Leisure Time,* and *Unions,* which are of particular use in problem units dealing with the family, recreation, working, and the like.

Documents like the Magna Charta can often be rewritten by able students and used by the less able in units such as one centered on the growth of democratic government.

Life magazine has done some heavily illustrated series on general topics, such as "The World's Great Religions" (Time, 1957), which, by drawing matters together, promote meaning in topics of broad sweep. Cartoons like Burr Shafer's "Through History with J. Wesley Smith," which have appeared frequently in the *Saturday Review,* can clarify, in a memorable way, the meaning of many an important point.

Relationships Among Materials

Students also need materials selected with particular reference to the organization planned for in the unit. To develop, within a unit centered on the American West, the generalization that frontier life influenced the growth of American democracy, students might read a variety of novels for pictures of western life and compare them in group discussions. Just any novels set in the West will not do; students need those which actually present pictures of democratic living. Rölvaag's *Giants in the Earth* (Harper, 1927), for example, contains enough material for students to work from; Willa Cather's *Death Comes for the Archbishop* (Knopf, 1927) does not, even though this book has much merit in itself and may be useful in other kinds of units. To enable students to discuss the control of wealth, excerpts taken from the writings of Jefferson, Hamilton, Bryan, M. Dooley, Andrew Carnegie, and Franklin D. Roosevelt must be carefully selected; selections from just any of their writings and speeches will not do. Teachers and students are often bewildered about the use of a variety of reading materials in group learning activities, partly because the variety of materials gathered has only a tenuous connection with the hoped-for organization.

Moreover, students need enough materials to arrive at sound conclusions. Learning activities sometimes have not borne fruit because students have not read enough. Concretely, the weekly current-events paper or even two or three well-selected pieces of material may be insufficient to permit students to apply the concept of the balance of power, which has been developed, let us say, in an international relations unit in a panel discussion on "Should We Revise NATO?"

Reading materials must be capable of fitting into some sort of sequence within the unit. Some materials are first rate for the beginnings of units; think of the power of Irwin Shaw's short story "Preach on the Dusty Roads"[3] for raising questions about citizens' responsibilities in foreign affairs. We have already mentioned the value of materials which define problems. While controversial materials may also be used to raise questions and to define problems, students are not likely to be able to analyze and interpret the reading until they have had opportunities to read materials which give them information and understanding. The excellent chapter on the Constitution in Bragdon and McCutchen's *The History of a Free People* (Macmillan, 1954) is usually more suitable for developing understanding in a unit on the development of American government than for the beginning or the concluding activities. Materials to be interpreted or skimmed for a point of view very often fit best after students have some information and understanding. Maps are likely to be most useful, too, when students are developing understanding, although I can think of times when they might be used as summary materials. Teachers will be wise, also, to consider as

[3] Irwin Shaw, "Preach on the Dusty Roads," *Best American Short Stories of 1943.* Edited by Martha Foley. Boston: Houghton Mifflin Co., 1944.

reading materials the sources which enable students to locate the information they need. Forum discussions are useful for comparing points of view, generalizing, and summarizing.

Moreover, our unit plans need to permit sequence among units within a course and, for that matter, among courses. If students in a course on problems of democracy are to relate various concepts of democratic method, some collection of such materials as Stuart Chase's short article, "Zoning Comes to Town";[4] a more difficult article, "A New Attack on Delinquency";[5] and Vern Sneider's *Teahouse of the August Moon* (Putnam, 1951) will be useful. An article like Kouwenhoven's "What's American about America?"[6] is fine material for extracting common elements from several kinds of American-history units.

CONCLUDING STATEMENT

There is a wealth of reading material for the kinds of unit plans that high-school students need. Some clear ideas of what the students need materials for and some imaginative thinking help both teachers and students to find them.

[4] Stuart Chase, "Zoning Comes to Town," *Reader's Digest*, 70 (February 1957), 129–133.

[5] John Bartlow Martin, "A New Attack on Delinquency," *Harper's Magazine*, 201 (May 1944), 502–512.

[6] John Kouwenhoven, "What's American about America?" *Harper's Magazine*, 213 (July 1956), 25–33.

THE PROBLEM OF UNDERSTANDING HISTORY*

John R. Palmer

The citizens of a country are faced with the problem of making critical judgments about contemporary domestic and international social and political problems. Most teachers of history in the secondary schools feel that the insights one can gain from the reading of history can be applied to understanding these problems. However, the so-phistication with which teachers, as well as students, approach the reading of history varies widely. Palmer discusses factors which affect the individual's approach to history and the depth of understanding that he will be able to gain from it.

1. What does it mean to think historically?

2. Discuss the problem that

* REPRINTED FROM *The Educational Forum*, 30 (March 1966), pp. 287–294, by permission of Kappa Delta Pi, An Honor Society in Education, owners of the copyright.

readers face in making accurate inferences and generalizations on the basis of text materials of the type cited in the article.

3. What problems complicate the explanation process in teaching history?

4. Why is it difficult to establish generalizations in history and to apply the generalizations appropriately?

5. What are two major problems that must be considered if the teaching of history is to lead to an understanding of society? How can the teacher of history successfully cope with these problems?

The lay reader often approaches a history book as he would a novel. He expects to be carried along by the rapid succession of events, the drama of war, intrigue, the conquering hero, turning the rascals out, and so forth. Some historians are content with this view of history as an interesting story and nothing more. Most, however, are not. If history is merely a colorful story, then we should read a few selections from historical writing in English courses as one example of narrative form and be done with it.

Part of the historian's job, of course, is to tell a story and tell it as accurately as possible. W. B. Gallie recently defended again the history-is-a-story point of view and in so doing suggested an interesting analogy between following a story (the "story" of the past, for example) and following a game.[1] Consider the different perspectives brought to a game by the expert observer as compared to the youngster attending one of his first matches. In explaining the moves of the players, the expert brings them under certain relevant generalizations or principles. After assimilating and appreciating the expert's explanation, the younger spectators are in a position to follow more fully the progress of the game. The need of explanation in this sense shows that following a game always admits of degrees of fullness or depth of understanding. We naturally presume that the spectators, like the audience in a theater or those listening to a story, are able to follow in a sufficient degree. There is a question, of course, as to what are the minimum or basic qualifications for following a game at all; and arising from this is the question of how further experience and practice, and more particularly the comments and explanations we receive from others, can help us to improve that basic capacity.

Knowing the rules of the game (the commonly understood and accepted generalizations, if you will) is essential for following the game but not sufficient. Following a game also presupposes some sense of the point and purpose of the game, what makes it "go," what makes it move to a climax, what counts most from the point of view of the pleasure of playing it, and so on. What is required is a much-more-than-legal appreciation of such notions as winning or losing a game and playing a good or worthwhile game. In the study of history these are counterparts of the value

[1] W. B. Gallie. "The Historical Understanding." *History and Theory*, 3, No. 2 (1963), 149–202.

problem, the moral issues, the questions involving "ought," which, although frequently very difficult to get hold of, are so very important. To think historically, to exercise historical understanding, always includes the appreciation of human aims, choices, valuations, efforts, deeds—things that are to be attributed exclusively to individual men, whether acting on their own or in concert, whether on their own personal behalf or as representatives of their group or cause or nation.

Our concern here, of course, is not with games but the study of the past. While the analogy between the two breaks down at many points, the task of "following" (which I take to mean understanding or making sense of) an historical account and the peculiar situation of the novice with respect to this task raise some interesting problems.

What is required to "follow" this selection from Stavrianos' A *Global History of Man*, a recent and very carefully prepared world history textbook?

We come here to an important difference between Western Europe and Russia. In Western Europe, serfdom existed in the Middle Ages and disappeared in modern times. In Russia it was the other way around—serfdom did not exist in the Middle Ages but appeared in modern times. The explanation for this difference is that in the medieval period there was too much land and too few people in Russia to make serfdom possible. So long as there was plenty of land on all sides, no Russian peasant would stand for any abuse from his landowner. A peasant simply picked up his belongings and moved off to the empty lands of the nearby frontier.

However, a remarkable change took place in modern times with the coming of rulers such as Ivan the Terrible and Peter the Great. These men wanted to make Russia strong and to do this they needed a big army and plenty of money. But they could get neither so long as the peasants were free to run off to the frontier whenever they saw a recruiting officer or a tax collector. So the government cooperated with the nobles in forcibly tying the peasants to the land they tilled. Laws were passed which steadily took away the peasant's freedom of movement. . . .

This system of serfdom is very important because it helps us understand why Russia fell behind the West with the coming of the Industrial Revolution. . . . One of the main reasons for this lag is to be found in serfdom. After all, the Industrial Revolution was nothing more or less than the invention and use of machinery in order to save labor. But there was no need for labor-saving machines in Russia at this time because there were plenty of serfs who could be ordered to do any work. . . .

For these reasons Russia during the nineteenth century fell far behind the West in her economy and technology. This became clear when Russia fought the Crimean War against France and England in 1855–1856. . . .

Russia lost the war but learned a lesson. During the following years the government initiated a number of basic changes. The most important were the abolition of serfdom and the pushing of industrialization.[2]

---

[2] Leften S. Stavrianos, A *Global History of Man* (Boston: Allyn and Bacon, 1962), pp. 342–343.

We have little difficulty in following the rapid transitions that occur in this passage, but consider what we bring to the account that really isn't there. We are well acquainted with the situation of the serf in Western Europe during the Middle Ages. Our knowledge of the concept "serf" as well as the attributes and attitudes of the peasant in various societies contribute to our understanding. Probably the Turner thesis flashes across our mind for an instant, and we toy with the notion of possible comparisons between our own frontier and that of Russia. Is the author making use of some generalization in the first paragraph concerning availability of land and a sense of independence? If so, certainly the next paragraph suggests the need for qualifying the generalization, for it appears that strong rulers can overcome the desire for independence despite the availability of land. Are the actions of Ivan and Peter accountable on the grounds of nationalism, the lust for power, or was it a matter of balance of power and the threat of outside domination? The concert between the nobles and the government which served the self-interest of each raises interesting questions about the use of power, the organization of governments, and the exercise of power by various classes.

The next causal leap takes us into the area of economics—the relationships which exist among the availability of cheap labor, the need for more consumer goods, and the effect of technical advances. We feel certain the author knows that when one asserts that serfdom caused the lag in Russian industrial development a key factor is being considered but hardly the complete picture.

The narrative shifts quickly to the Crimean War. It is suggested that somehow technological advancement and success in war are closely related. A number of examples, perhaps the use of the cross-bow in the Hundred Years War or our own explosion of the atomic bomb in World War II, come to mind. The aftermath of the Crimean War brings the story full circle. Apparently the author feels that nations, like people, frequently learn from their mistakes, for after a miserable showing in the Crimean conflict the Russians abolished serfdom and promoted industrial growth. Perhaps the author has in mind here a situation of challenge and response in the manner of Arnold Toynbee. Now the story of Russian serfdom is before us from beginning to end.

It is impossible in a short time to suggest all the nuances of meaning and interpretation that one might develop from this passage. Indeed, they are almost endless. The reader can be said to have "followed," to have understood the narrative, however, without being aware of every possible referent. But it certainly is necessary, if one is to follow this account, to be somewhat of an expert, to know the rules of the game, to sense what the game is all about without having to be told at every turn, to have the knowledge and experience necessary to make sense out of the narrative.

The words written by the author constitute, to use Hempel's expression, a mere sketch of a succession of explanations that form a causal chain.[3] If the reader—and we are thinking particularly of the high school student—is to follow this very sparse narrative, a great deal of filling out is required. He will need an expert sitting at his elbow to interpret the plays for him. I have already suggested a number of aspects of the narrative that may need attention and will call for the exercise of the student's critical powers: examining the value problems, clarifying concepts, and establishing the pertinent ideological forces that may have been present. I shall discuss only one aspect crucial to the reader's understanding—the explanation process.

The essential elements in an explanation are (1) a description of the situation or circumstances which are relevant to the thing to be explained and (2) one or more generalizations or hypotheses asserting relationships among these prevailing factors that produced the occurrence in question. Obviously textbooks prepared for survey courses only begin to provide the context in which events have taken place. When more details are needed, we provide outside readings, use multiple texts, or prepare lectures. A number of critical thinking tasks accompany the building up of context: determination of relevancy, assessing the accuracy of the source, and so forth.

Establishing the pertinent generalizations or hypotheses appears to present great difficulties. Every characteristically human action involves a tacit reference to other actions, and not simply to such other actions as actually have taken place or will take place. To talk, to think, to promise, to trade, even to fight requires references to what *any* person subject to certain conditions or answering to a certain description would do or can be expected to do. In other words, characteristic human actions are performed and interpreted as expressions of generally accepted institutions, beliefs, routines, and norms. With land available, the peasants acted in a predictable manner. The Tsars and the nobles calculated moves in accordance with their own self-interest as we would expect them to do.

In order to construct a narrative and relate events sequentially the historian must draw on all manner of general knowledge about life in society, from traditional truisms to the theorems and abstract models of the social sciences. He presumes that the reader, like the spectator at the game, is well enough acquainted with these generalizations, hypotheses, and models to follow the narrative at a satisfactory level of understanding. My experience indicates that most elementary and high school students are unable to follow the typical history textbook in this sense without a great deal of assistance.

The Stavrianos material quoted earlier will serve as an example. Generalizations, both stated and implied, abound in this passage. We are not certain, of course, whether the author expects all or even any of these to be learned, but almost any reader will take note of some of them. But just how

[3] C. G. Hempel. "The Function of General Laws in History." *Journal of Philosophy*, 26 (1942), 33–48.

valid are they? Shouldn't they be pulled out of the passage and examined more closely? If not, there is a dual danger. The student may accept those he picks out by chance as truisms that apply in all times and places, or he may overlook many that provide genuine insight into the actions of men and nations. In any case, is it the teacher's place to call attention to such generalizations and provide a classroom situation such that they can be examined, clarified, qualified, rejected, accepted, or whatever?

The following is a slightly abbreviated version of an explanation used by Stavrianos:

> This system of serfdom is very important because it helps us understand why Russia fell behind the West with the coming of the Industrial Revolution. . . . One of the main reasons for this lag is to be found in serfdom. After all, the Industrial Revolution was nothing more or less than the invention and use of machinery in order to save labor. But there was no need for labor-saving machines in Russia at this time because there were plenty of serfs who could be ordered to do any work. So why should the nobles spend their money on machines and factories when all their needs were taken care of by the serfs? Why should anyone in Russia offer prizes for labor-saving inventions as was being done at this time in England? Not only were there plenty of workers, but also there was no need to turn out more and more goods because Russia did not have the world-wide markets that England did. . . . And the market in their own country was very small, since almost all Russians were serfs who could buy almost nothing.[4]

It was suggested earlier that the historian bases his explanations and assertions of causal relationships on commonly understood uniformities in social behavior. This is often true, but it is a dangerous assumption. It undoubtedly leads the student to think he is getting much more out of a history course than he really is. In the passage above the author has supplied more detail than for most of the explanations in the book. Perhaps he surmised that commonly understood generalizations were not enough to enable the reader to follow his narrative at this point. This attempt to account for variations among nations in economic development is much more complete than most such accounts one finds in high school textbooks, but it still assumes a great deal of economic understanding on the part of the reader. The Industrial Revolution is grossly over-simplified. What does the way the nobles spent their money have to do with economic development? How is economic growth related to the labor supply and the development of domestic and foreign markets? Is this example of lag purely an economic matter or are there ideological or value aspects that are crucial? In any case, a number of generalizations developed in the area of economics have been presumed by the author that may not be clear to the student or understood by him. If this is the case, he can read the passage, learn it in a relatively meaningless manner if that is required, but certainly he will not follow the explanation in the sense we have been using the term.

[4] Stavrianos, *loc. cit.*

In most explanations found in history textbooks some concepts, generalizations, or models are used from one or more of the social sciences. In the instance just cited, much of the knowledge required for the explanation came from economics. This reliance on the social sciences can be either a virtue or a vice in the education of the student. It is a virtue when the generalizations and concepts of the social sciences are brought into the history class, examined and related to historical situations, and are understood by the students. However, when the crucial role of the social sciences in historical explanation is not recognized, the student may learn to be content with superficial and vague explanations that tend to distort his understanding of social reality and the process of social change. This affects not only his understanding of the past but also his understanding of current and future happenings.

There is space to make only brief mention of a number of aspects of historical explanation that appear to have a bearing on the reader's ability to understand historical writing and thus need to be taken into account in the teaching of history.

There is little place at present in any area of knowledge, except possibly mathematics, for universal truths, the sort of generalizations that may be stated in the form "If and only if. . . ." We must recognize and learn to be emotionally content with probabilistic generalizations that are continually subject to revision and the possibility of exception.

It appears that the historian generalizes at a number of levels. Terms or concepts are grouping words and therefore a type of generalization. Nouns such as "serfdom," "nation," "freedom," and "industrialization" or verbs like "subdue," "revolutionize," and "cooperate" are examples. At another level there are groupings of statements about events. "So long as there was plenty of land on all sides, no Russian peasant would stand for any abuse from his landowner." This statement contains a number of assumptions about the Russian peasant, social psychology, history in general, and so forth. The sentence generalizes in a way that covers possibly thousands of individual cases over decades or even centuries. The historian, as historian, is not primarily interested in what he may be implying about the nature of history, or the peasant, or social psychology. It seems, however, that for purposes of general education these matters are more important than the statement of fact taken at face value.[5]

The historian also brings to his data one or more generalized schema which play a significant role in the shaping of his narrative. These may be dealt with in terms of structure and process. Process involves a coherent theory of change through time as implied by such terms as "urbanization," "adaptation," and "industrialization." Structure is concerned with an analysis of a slice of time with respect to the economic, sociological, political, ideologi-

[5] Ernest Nagel, The Structure of Science (New York: Harcourt, Brace and World, Inc., 1961), Chapter 15, and H. Stuart Hughes, "The Historian and the Social Scientist," American Historical Review, 66 (October 1960), 20–46.

cal, and other factors which existed in a given situation. Clearly this approach assumes a degree of regularity and orderliness in the social realm. It brings us again to the application of hypotheses, techniques, and models from the social sciences to historical events.[6]

One further matter should be mentioned. Some of the claims made for the study of history emphasize the value of students' knowing about the past, while other claims require that the student, through the study of the past, gain a better understanding of the present and the future. Hypotheses which are valid only if stated in the past tense may assist in the fulfillment of the first set of objectives but not the second.[7] "But there was no need for labor-saving machines in Russia at this time because there were plenty of serfs who could be ordered to do any work." This statement suggests the hypothesis: "There was an abundant supply of cheap and readily available labor in Russia during the first half of the Eighteenth Century so few labor-saving machines were introduced." This assertion is limited in application to one particular time and place. But change the tense of the verb and the hypothesis becomes: "If there is an abundant supply of cheap and readily available labor in a society, the introduction of labor-saving machines is relatively slow." Now the statement suggests that it is true at the present time and has wide applicability. It must be determined, of course, whether or not it is valid at present, if it is true only in societies at a certain level of technological development, and so forth. If we actually mean to use the study of history to increase the student's understanding of the present, it seems crucial to rephrase generalizations so they are stated in the present tense and then test their validity on this basis.

It is in the explanation process that the historian makes use of generalizations and hypotheses stating relatively stable societal relationships. Very often these are not stated directly but are implied in historical narrative. The narrative may make very interesting reading for the student even though he is unaware of these generalizations. However, if we are concerned for developing proficiency in following historical (as well as the contemporary) narrative, "knowing what the game is all about" and comprehending it as the expert does, it is necessary to expose these generalizations and hold them up for scrutiny. In so doing students will be called upon to exercise a wide variety of critical skills necessary in the analysis of historical situations. This poses serious obstacles to the teaching of history in the elementary and secondary schools, unless the objectives of such teaching are limited to entertainment and the inculcation of certain attitudes associated with love of country and adoration of national heroes.

There are at least two major problem areas with respect to the teaching of history that must be dealt with if it is to lead to an understanding

[6] *The Social Sciences in Historical Study*, Social Science Research Council, Bulletin 64 (New York: Social Science Research Council, 1954), Chapters 4 and 5.

[7] Lawrence E. Metcalf. "The Reflective Teacher." *Phi Delta Kappan*, 44 (October 1962), 17–21.

of society, whether it be past, present, or future society. An appreciation of human aims and values must be continually considered in the process of social education. The second broad area consists of the cognitive social understandings: the information, concepts, and generalizations that are used in the writing of history. Can the teacher of history systematically deal with both of these broad domains of content? To do so leads one into virtually an infinite regress which traverses much of the total human culture. This is obviously an impossible task. But how does the history teacher stop short of this? What reasonable and workable criteria establish the limits of historical study? The answers, of course, depend to a large extent on what one perceives as the purpose of studying history. If the history that is being taught in the schools is not to be "followed" or "understood" in the manner suggested earlier, then what is its purpose? And where in the curriculum are the very significant learnings essential to such understanding to be dealt with?

Business Education

The Reading Problem in Teaching Bookkeeping*

Vernon A. Musselman

How much of a problem is reading in bookkeeping? What are the three elements that combine to aggravate the reading problem in bookkeeping? After discussing the nature of these problems, the author gives some excellent suggestions for overcoming them.

1. How can you know your students as individuals?

2. What three factors complicate the reading problem in bookkeeping?

3. Can you infer from the discussion several principles regarding the teaching of bookkeeping vocabulary?

4. How would you use suggestions four, five, and six to make your bookkeeping class an instruction period?

5. State the article's key ideas.

It has become popular to remain in school and complete at least a high school education. As we have increased the percentage of those who stay

---

* REPRINTED FROM *Business Education Forum*, XIV (December 1959), pp. 5–7, by permission of the National Business Education Association, a department of the National Education Association.

and finish we have widened the range of individual differences in the student body. Any group of boys and girls which elects to study bookkeeping is anything but homogeneous. The students vary from one another in mental ability, family background, interests, hobbies, skill in reading, skill in computation, habits of workmanship, and attitudes. They even vary in reasons why they choose to study bookkeeping.

During recent years a great deal of attention has been focused on the problems of meeting individual differences adequately. Some students make good grades in all of their school subjects; others make low grades in all. Some like to study and have good study habits; others find studying difficult and have not yet really learned how to study. Some are good in reading comprehension or in arithmetical ability; others are poor. Each member of your bookkeeping class varies from all other members in many ways.

Know Students as Individuals

First of all we must learn to know our students as individuals and find out what the differences in students are. Some personal information may be obtained through informal class discussion and reports. Brief questionnaires may be used to gather additional data desired by the teacher. Many schools have records of the mental abilities of their students. Many schools also have indexes of student abilities in such skills as vocabulary, reading comprehension, spelling, and arithmetic. Where cumulative records are kept, all of this information is available in one place. In schools where cumulative records are not in use, it may be necessary to administer achievement tests to secure all of the data one needs. Valid and reliable tests are available at a very small cost per student. In addition to test results that are of interest to all high school teachers, the business teacher may wish to use some type of clerical ability test such as the *Detroit Clerical Aptitude Examination, Minnesota Vocational Test for Clerical Workers,* or the *Turse Clerical Aptitude Test.* These tests give a measure of abilities basic to successful performance in various types of clerical work.

The Reading Problem

Students who can read with understanding have less difficulty with bookkeeping than do those who are retarded in their ability to read with comprehension. Bookkeeping teachers have been aware for many years that many students have difficulty with their reading, but what to do about it has long been a question of utmost concern. In bookkeeping there very definitely is a reading problem, but there are also several things that can be done and that have been done about it.

How serious is this problem of reading high school bookkeeping? Wayne House, in his study of some of the factors that affect student achievement in bookkeeping, focused our attention on the seriousness of the problem: His conclusions as they pertain to reading are:[1]

The technical vocabulary load in beginning bookkeeping is extremely heavy, particularly in the early parts of the course.

Beginning bookkeeping students vary in reading ability from a level comparable to the *lowest* 5 percent of seventh-grade students to a level comparable to the highest 5 percent of twelfth-grade students.

When measured by standardized tests, there is a significant relationship between achievement in beginning bookkeeping and ready ability.

There is a significant relationship between achievement in beginning bookkeeping and reading ability examined by questionnaire responses and personal interviews.

There are three elements that combine to aggravate the reading problem in bookkeeping: (a) the extremely heavy "vocabulary load," (b) the high level of difficulty of textual materials, and (c) the wide range of reading abilities of the students in any class.

The Vocabulary Load

Because of its technical nature, bookkeeping carries an extremely heavy "vocabulary load." This load consists of two types of terms: technical bookkeeping terms and common terms that have a special bookkeeping connotation. Most high school bookkeeping textbooks contain well over 200 technical bookkeeping terms. House found that in one textbook there were 33 such terms in the first chapter alone. He also found that approximately 30 percent of the questions on tests covering the early parts of the bookkeeping course are specifically designed to test the student's knowledge of technical bookkeeping terms.[2]

COMMON WORDS WITH SPECIAL MEANINGS.   There are a number of common words that are already a part of the vocabulary of many students but that have a special bookkeeping meaning frequently quite different from the meaning the student normally associates with the word.

These common words may represent a greater learning barrier than the new technical terms. This results from the natural tendency on the part of both the teacher and the student to assume that an understanding of these terms exists. A partial list of such words includes:

abstract	credit	post	ruling
capital	extend	prove	statement
charge	footing	register	terms

[1] F. Wayne House, *Factors Affecting Student Achievement in Beginning Bookkeeping in the High School.* Oklahoma Agricultural and Mechanical College, Stillwater, Okla.: 1953, p. 89.

[2] F. Wayne House, "Are You Solving the Reading Problem in Bookkeeping?" *Business Education World*, 33: 291; February 1953.

If you will analyze the words in the list, you will observe that each word has more than one meaning. For example, "charge" has a meaning on the football field and quite another in the bookkeeping classroom. "Abstract," when used in the term, "abstract of accounts receivable," has a meaning different from its meaning when used to refer to the condensation of a story.

The vocabulary problem is further complicated in that a number of bookkeeping terms are used interchangeably. A few of these terms are given in the following list. Some of these terms have different precise meanings, but few teachers are aware of the difference and there is a tendency to interchange the terms freely in class discussion.

Analysis paper, work-sheet paper, working paper.

Bad debt, bad account, uncollectable account.

Cash on hand, cash balance, balance on hand.

Proprietorship, net worth, capital.

Minus asset, valuation account, reserve account.

Principal of note, face of note.

Profit and loss statement, operating statement, income statement, income and expense statement.

Liabilities, debts, obligations.

READING DIFFICULTY OF MATERIALS. Sentence length and syllabic intensity are two commonly used measures of reading difficulty. The longer the sentence and the higher the syllabic intensity, the more difficult the reading.

A common goal in business-letter writing is to have 70 percent of the words one-syllable words. Such magazines as *The Saturday Evening Post* and the *Ladies Home Journal*, which are written for a wide range of adult readers, strive to maintain an average sentence length of less than 12 words and a low syllabic intensity.

A study of two high school bookkeeping textbooks shows that the average sentence length was 21.6 words in one textbook and 16.9 words in the other. The syllabic intensity of both textbooks was found to be approximately 1.6. When these data are plotted on Flesch's "Reading Ease Chart," the textbook material scores as "Fairly Difficult." It is equivalent to the reading difficulty of such magazines as *Harper's*, *New Yorker*, and *Business Week*. The material is beyond the reading ability of over 50 percent of the high school students.

This reading difficulty is further verified by House who found from interviewing bookkeeping students that nearly one-half of the students reported they did not finish reading textbook assignments because they could not understand what they were reading.

RANGE OF READING LEVELS OF STUDENTS. The students in any bookkeeping class represent a wide range of reading levels. House found that 62 percent of the 357 students included in his study were below the average tenth-grade student in vocabulary proficiency as measured by the *Co-opera-*

tive Reading Comprehension Test and 60 percent were below the average tenth-grade student in reading comprehension. He states:[3]

Since a tenth-grade reading level is considered essential for comprehending material that is "Fairly Difficult," *only 40 percent of the students possessed enough reading ability to read and comprehend satisfactorily the subject matter in bookkeeping.*

Suggestions for Overcoming the Problem

1. APPLY SOUND PRINCIPLES OF LEARNING TO THE VOCABULARY BUILDING. Memorization of word lists and definitions has been rather generally discredited as a means of developing vocabulary. Memorization, devoid of association with real, purposeful experiences, is but temporary learning. Words become a permanent part of the vocabulary of an individual only when they are given meaning through experiences or association with experiences.

For example, the word "assets" and its definition, "things owned which have a money value," has little meaning to the student until it is associated with things that are real and meaningful, such as a bicycle, radio, wrist watch, and clothing. When the term is associated for the boy who works in the filling station with such things as tires, gasoline, oil, auto supplies, or delivery truck, it becomes meaningful.

The term "auditing the sales slips" becomes meaningful when the class makes a field trip to the office of a store and observes an office clerk checking the accuracy of the calculations on the sales slip. The term "dividends" takes on meaning when, through dramatization, the class has set up a corporation and has participated in the dramatized situation to determine the amount to be paid to stockholders from profits.

The answer to the vocabulary problem, therefore, is (a) to give the students as many direct and indirect experiences as possible through the in-school learning situation and (b) to assist them in associating terms with those experiences which they have had or are having outside the classroom.

2. PREPARE VOCABULARY LISTS. Analyze each chapter or unit before it is presented and prepare a list (a) of technical bookkeeping terms that are introduced for the first time in the chapter, and (b) of common words or phrases that have a special bookkeeping connotation. Such a list identifies the words that must be emphasized and considered in the lesson planning.

In planning for the lesson, each term should be studied by the teacher to determine what experiences the students have had that might be associated with the term. It is for this reason that, early in the course, the teacher

[3] F. Wayne House, "Are You Solving the Reading Problem in Bookkeeping?" *Business Education World*, 33, 292 (February 1953).

should obtain as complete an inventory as possible of the students' work and business experiences and of the occupation of the parents. It is possible through this information to associate the new bookkeeping terms with experiences the students already understand.

Common words or phrases that have a special bookkeeping connotation also should be emphasized in the planning. Care must be taken to point out the distinction and relationship between the meaning of the term as it applies to bookkeeping and its other meanings. For example, pointing out the relationship between the use of the word "overhead" when referring to the ceiling and then when referring to bookkeeping, helps the student to understand the term better.

3. AVOID CONFUSION, BY BEING CONSISTENT IN TERMINOLOGY. A number of terms that are used interchangeably in bookkeeping have been pointed out. Confusion can be avoided if the teacher is consistent in the terminology used in the introductory weeks of the course. Such interchangeable terms as "account period" and "fiscal period," or "account sales," "credit sales," "sales on credit," "charge sales," and "sales on account," should be explained and used interchangeably before the completion of the course. However, to use these multiple-terms when the student is first being introduced to the topic increases the learning problem.

4. MAKE THE BOOKKEEPING CLASS PERIOD AN INSTRUCTION PERIOD IN PLACE OF RECITATION AND TESTING PERIOD. Many teachers follow the practice of assigning new material to be read and studied from the textbook. The following day's class period is devoted primarily to questioning and testing the student's understanding of the assigned reading. Such a plan is certain to result in low class morale and a high dropout and failure rate, for this procedure completely ignores the vocabulary and reading problem.

After a topic has been explained, illustrated, and visualized in the classroom, after new bookkeeping terms have been carefully presented, students may then profitably turn to the textbook for further study and clarification. The textbook then becomes a valuable and intelligible reference source for the student.

5. TAKE TIME TO EXPLAIN TO THE STUDENTS HOW TO READ AND STUDY THE TEXTBOOK. Bookkeeping requires a different reading pattern from that to which most students are accustomed. Most bookkeeping textbooks are well illustrated. The illustrations are keyed to the reading and must be included as part of the reading pattern. Daily oral reading demonstrations, therefore, are an essential part of the lesson plans for the first few days of the bookkeeping course.

Those students who have the greatest difficulty in reading might be encouraged to use a blotter or a sheet of paper as a reading guide.

6. USE STUDY GUIDES AS A LEARNING AID AND NOT AS A CHAPTER TEST. The workbooks that accompany most bookkeeping textbooks provide study or learning guides for each unit or chapter. When these study

guides are used as chapter tests, which is frequently the case, the student is being denied a valuable learning aid.

When correctly used, the student completes the guide as he reads the textbook. The guide focuses the student's attention on the textbook material; thus, it aids the student in his reading. Again, class demonstration must be used to show the student how to use the study guides correctly.

The heavy vocabulary load, the reading difficulty of the textbook, and the low reading level of students represent barriers to the learning of book-keeping. These barriers become formidable to many students when the bookkeeping course is kept largely on the "verbalized level," as opposed to the "experience level." Reading drill and rote memorization of definitions are not enough.

The solution is to tie bookkeeping vocabulary to the direct experiences the students have had and to provide as part of the bookkeeping course, as many direct and indirect purposeful experiences as possible. This can be done through in-school and out-of-school work experience, through drama-tizations, through field trips, through effective demonstration, through vis-ual aids, and through well-organized practice materials.

TEACHING ACCOUNTING STUDENTS HOW TO READ*

L. J. Harrison

A subject-matter teacher does well to devote classroom time to overcoming reading deficiencies in order to increase the competence of his students in the subject. In this brief report Harrison explains the procedures he used to help students and reports on the success of those procedures.

1. Before reading the article, make a short outline of procedures that you would use to improve the reading of accounting students.

2. Compare your ideas with those of the author.

3. What basic reading principles did the author use with his class?

Based upon writings in the journals and panel discussions at professional meetings, there seems to be general agreement among business educators that one of the greatest hindrances to effective learning is the inability of a large number of students to read textbook material with comprehension.

* REPRINTED FROM the *Journal of Business Education*, XXXV (January 1960), pp. 169, 170, by permission of the publisher. Copyrighted by Robert C. Trethaway.

My experiences with teaching college courses in accounting lead me to agree that this is a problem which the teacher faces all too frequently.

Recently, my instructional efforts with a class of prospective teachers in a course in intermediate accounting seemed to be yielding unusually poor results. The students experienced great difficulty in completing their regular problem assignments, and their scores on examinations were much below acceptable standards.

ACTION WITHOUT THOUGHT

After nine weeks of very little progress, an analysis of the difficulties appeared to point toward weaknesses in reading abilities. It became apparent that quite a number of the students did not understand what information was given in a problem, the instructions relative to what was to be done, and the steps to take in solving the problem. One common fault was reading a problem hastily and carelessly. Without knowing what was required or what steps to take, students then took up paper and pencil and made a start. This tendency to spend very little time thinking about the problem but to hurry to get something down on paper was very noticeable. Needless to say, this resulted in many false starts and waste of time.

Even though aware that perhaps I was invading the domain of reading experts, I decided to see what an accounting teacher could do to help the students improve their ability to read and comprehend textual and problem material. At the same time, I was aware that to devote much of the class period to work on the reading deficiencies would mean that the class would not "cover" the material outlined for the course. Still, the sacrifice of "accounting time" to "reading time" might be beneficial in the long run.

Two principal procedures were adopted for the class reading sessions. One technique was to have the students read over an assigned problem in class. Then, individual students were called upon to express in their own words the general information given. Next, they were asked to tell in detail the instructions for solving the problem. Finally, students were asked to present a step-by-step procedure for solving the problem without using any figures at all. Thus, before attempting to solve a problem, students were encouraged to spend some time determining the information given, the requirements of the problem, and mentally outlining the steps to be used in solving it. The teacher tried to emphasize the thought that a problem which is well understood is half-solved, and that the more time spent on this "mental" phase means less time spent on the "activity" phase.

STUDENTS STUDY COMPREHENSION PROBLEMS

The idea for the second type of reading exercise came from an article in *The American Business Education Yearbook* which reported what Ball State Teachers' College had been doing for a number of years in order to sharpen the reading habits of its accounting students.[1] For every new unit of work students spend ten to twenty minutes in class reading a few significant paragraphs concerning the particular topic. Then, a short quiz is given on the material covered. For my class, the paragraphs to be read generally came from the textbook, and it did not matter whether the particular material had been previously assigned or not. After reading the material once, the students were given a quiz and the papers checked. Then, they were given an opportunity to study the paragraphs again and to make changes in their answers if found to be incorrect. The papers were graded again, a record of the two scores being kept for each of the reading exercises.

An example of the type of material read in class and the quiz given appears on this page.

NATURE OF TEMPORARY INVESTMENTS

A company with an excess of available cash may deposit such funds as a time deposit or under a certificate of deposit at a bank, or it may purchase securities. Income will thus be produced that would not be available if cash were left idle. Investments made during seasonal periods of low activity can be converted into cash in periods of expanding operations. Asset items arising from temporary conversions of cash are commonly reported in the current asset section of the balance sheet under the heading, Temporary Investments. Temporary investments are frequently limited to only marketable securities.

Securities that are purchased as temporary investments should actually be marketable on short notice. There should be a day-to-day market for them, and the volume of trading in the securities should be sufficient to absorb a company's holdings without considerably affecting the market price. While there may be no definite assurance that the securities will be disposed of without loss, it is essential that any possible loss resulting from such disposal be kept at a minimum. Securities that have a limited market and fluctuate widely in price are not suitable for temporary investments. The prices of United States government securities tend to be relatively stable and the market for these securities is quite broad. Because of these factors, short-term government securities are particularly favored despite their relatively low interest rates.

COMPOSITION OF TEMPORARY INVESTMENTS

Investments qualify for reporting as temporary investments as long as (1) they are readily available for conversion into cash and (2) it is management's intent to sell them to take care of cash requirements. Such investments may be converted into cash within a relatively short period after being acquired, or they may be carried for some time. In either case, however, since they represent a ready source of cash, they are properly shown under the current heading. The following types of investments do not qualify as marketable securities, and should not be included in the current section: (a) reacquired shares of the company's own stock, (b) securities held in subsidiary companies, (c) securities held for maintenance of business relations, and (d) other securities that cannot be used or are

---

[1] *The American Business Education Yearbook,* 8 (1951), pp. 30–33.

not intended to be used as a ready source of cash.[2]

INTERMEDIATE ACCOUNTING 311
READING COMPREHENSION EXERCISES

Chapter 5—Temporary Investments

Name ....

Score ....

1. Check the items below which may be included in temporary investments.
   _____ Idle Land
   _____ Time Deposit at a Bank
   _____ Marketable Securities
   _____ Treasury Stock
   _____ Investments in Subsidiary Companies
   _____ Certificate of Deposit
   _____ Mortgage Bonds

2. Short-term government securities are of doubtful value as temporary investments.   __ Yes __ No

3. All stocks and bonds should be classified as temporary investments.   __ Yes __ No

4. Temporary investments provide a means of putting idle funds to work.   __ Yes __ No

5. Temporary investments should be reported on the balance sheet under **current assets.**   __Yes __No

It would be good to report that all members of the class showed marked improvements and that the procedures were highly successful. With only nine weeks left in the semester such a possibility is highly improbable. However, there was sufficient evidence of improvement on the part of many of the students to justify a continuation of such experiments. Also, it appeared that once some of the students learned to be more careful in their reading habits they would continue to make an effort to further develop their reading ability and skill in problem solving.

From the teacher's standpoint, the greatest benefit derived was the stimulation of having tried to wrestle with a perennial problem and coming to the conclusion that through a systematic plan and a little special effort business students may be assisted in overcoming special weaknesses.

[2] *Intermediate Accounting* (Standard Volume), 3d Edition. Karrenbrock and Simons, South-Western Publishing Co., pp. 133–134.

Home Economics

NUTRITION, LOVE, AND LANGUAGE: KEYS TO READING*

Lawrence E. Hafner and Billy M. Guice

Some people are claiming that nature is the predominant factor contributing to intelligence and implying that nurture does not make a very important contribution. It is a good idea, therefore, to study several

---

* Written especially for this volume.

aspects that do contribute to functional intelligence and, consequently, to reading development. Prenatal nutrition of the mother and postnatal nutrition make contributions that some individuals may classify as nature. If so, something can be done about nature. I think the upshot of the argument in this article is that we do not have to relegate or consign certain people to an inferior place in society, claiming that, "Well, what can you do? You know, they inherit what they are. They're just naturally inferior." We can't buy that and we think you will see why as you read this article.

1. What is the basic argument advanced by the authors?

2. What meanings does the word *survival* have in the context of the article?

3. From the discussion of the importance to the development of her offspring of the mother's nutrition when she was an infant can you see how nature and nurture factors can be confused even by a Jensen or a Shockley? Discuss.

4. Explain the role of nutrition to brain growth and eventual measured intelligence.

5. Discuss ethical and moral problems connected with educating and aiding poor people.

6. Trace the development of malnutrition to irreparable brain damage.

7. How can poor people obtain adequate protein?

8. When should nutritional therapy take place?

9. How do you feel about Lewis and Dull's argument on the complexities involved in working out the problems of the poor, disadvantaged people? Discuss the problem raised in question 5. [Clue: Remember (1) Cain, who wasn't exactly a charmer, who said, "Am I my brother's keeper?" and (2) Bagdikian, who speaks of the need for a bridge of human beings.]

10. What are some of the results of a lack of love?

11. What kinds of language and cognitive stimulation can be provided for children?

In 1970 the senior author wrote for the *Journal of Reading Behavior* a brief article which voiced some of his concerns about the necessity of developing people who are good readers. In that article he pointed out that we should teach individuals to read skillfully, to interpret well, to react to ideas that they read, and to integrate the best ideas and apply them in various aspects of living. It was his contention that we must develop excellent readers who could bring superior skills, attitudes, and information to bear upon the multitudinous problems that face mankind. The article was titled "Reading for Survival."

It was about this time that the authors read articles and editorials in several journals regarding the increasing interest in and the importance of such things as nutrition and love for the development of children. Adequate development is not possible without proper food, and by proper food we mean *protein, language,* and *love.* Without adequate development a person will not be successful in academic skills such as reading, and without proper development of reading skills a person cannot use the ideas and information in print which can be useful for survival in the world.

There are other impediments to survival besides malnutrition and lack of love. Among these impediments are such things as hate, pollution, and war. The purpose of this presentation is to delineate some of these problems and to offer solutions.

NUTRITION

Adequate nutrition is basic to survival for reading and other nice things. Survival has several meanings in the context of this paper. It means to continue to live physically, as will be pointed out in the second part of the presentation, but it also means existing above a certain level of nutrition and health so that the individual can grow and develop in a way that, in addition to being able to enjoy living, he can make contributions to the lives of others.

Nutrition data were obtained from studies of animals and of human beings. Prenatal nutrition of mothers and postnatal nutrition of children are important; we recognize that fact. But the nutrition of the mother when she was an infant is also a matter of interest and concern. The animal studies by Novakova et al. (29) and by Platt (31, 32) have shown that poor nutrition of infant female rats can affect, in turn, the development of her offspring many months later. Because there are so many nutritional need similarities between rats and human beings, it is probably safe to assume that a nutritionally adequate diet for today's infant female human beings bodes well for their eventual progeny.

PRENATAL CARE

We are concerned with the effect of prenatal care upon the growth and development of the fetus and, subsequently, the infant and child. Various aspects of care are important—the effect of foods, drugs, exercise, rest, and so forth. Specifically, we are concerned with the effect on the child of nutrition or malnutrition. Because brain growth and development are acknowledged to be of importance for reading, it can be said that survival (actually maximal growth and development of the brain) for reading, both in the narrow and the broad sense, is a special concern of this report.

Dobbing (12) shows that the "maximum rate of brain growth occurs in the time period from five months prior to birth to about 25 months following birth. . . ." Furthermore, he says, and this fact is substantiated by Sinisterra (35), that if adequate nutrient "building" blocks are not provided the infant (or fetus) at the time of rapid brain cell formation, it is technically impossible to build an adequate (or superior) brain, and the brain cannot be rebuilt or improved later in life.

Too many pregnant mothers, particularly from low-income families, do not receive adequate nutrition. Ledesma, Lease, and Malphrus studied ninety-five pregnant mothers from low-income families in the Greenville,

S.C., area who had applied for maternal care and found them to be grossly below normal in intake of protein and a number of vitamin requirements. Percentages of subjects *below* normal intakes and blood values are: protein (intake), 74; iron (intake) and hemoglobin, 62; vitamin C, 58; riboflavin, 12. The investigators concluded that "not one of the 95 women had a diet that could be considered fully adequate." In a related study, Ledesma and Lease (23) found malnutrition to be widespread among lower-income expectant mothers in the Columbia, South Carolina, area. The nutrients most frequently inadequate in the diets were calcium, iron, niacin, and ascorbic acid.

PARTURITION

According to Caster and Burton (7), about 333,000 (8 per cent of all live births) infants are born prematurely in the United States each year. In this instance *prematurely* means "immaturely" and refers to low birth weight and not to gestation period. They reported further that the "incidence of immature birth weights—which factor is well correlated with malnutrition—has essentialy doubled in the last 15–20 years in the case of the non-white population in Georgia, while there has been no similar change in the data regarding the white population."

POSTNATAL CARE

Malnutrition, particularly during the first year of life, will curtail the usual rate of increase in head circumference, according to Stoch and Smythe (37, 38). This reduced head circumference reflects the reduced number of brain cells present in their life (42). By the time a child is six years of age his brain will have achieved 90 per cent of its growth, and lack of adequate nourishment during the first six years of life results in irreparable mental damage (35).

What are the eight indispensable building blocks for brain development? According to White et al. (39) they are the following amino acids: isoleucine, leucine, lysine, methionine, phenylalanine, threonine, tryptophan, and valine. White, furthermore, stated that arginine and histidine are probably necessary for the normal growth of children.

How does one obtain these indispensable amino acid building blocks? Can they be synthesized by the human organism from such common, relatively abundant foodstuffs as corn and rice? No, these building blocks are *not* derived in this manner, but must be provided by the protein a person eats, and only *animal* proteins provide all of the needed amino acids.

Protein deficiency, as stated previously, seriously retards mental development. Animal nutrition studies show how in a few cases very young animals that were placed on a deficient diet for a *brief* time and then raised to adulthood on rather normal diets showed a decrement in learning ability and decrease in exploratory behavior (29). Furthermore weaning animals "placed on certain nutritionally deficient diets . . . show deleterious neurological changes in as little as four to seven days" (31, 32, 36).

Adequate protein can be found in the diet of only a few countries in the world. Diets of slum dwellers in the richer nations consist mainly of foods of poor biological quality, including soft drinks, fried potatoes, and bread (35). "From 1955 to 1965 consumption increased for soft drinks, . . . potato chips, . . . ice cream, . . . lunch meats, and peanut butter. . . . Many of these foods replace others in the diet that contain more of needed nutrients" (9). Lack of adequate protein intake is, of course, a problem for low-income pregnant mothers. Ledesma and Lease (23) found 66 per cent of low-income pregnant mothers to have inadequate protein intake.

Studies in various parts of the world suggest that undernourished children have lower IQ's than do children on normal diets (7). A study done in South Africa by Stoch and Smythe (37) revealed that children who were malnourished early in life were as adults smaller in stature, had a reduced head circumference, and had lower IQ's than was the case with members of the control population. Caster and Burton (7) refer to several studies and conclude from them that "if the malnutrition develops before the age of six months the retardation may be very severe and there will be little or no chance of reversal at a later date." Prolonged rehabilitation in the case of children who suffer malnutrition after the age of two years, but not before, would probably result in significant increases in their IQ scores. We would not take this fact to imply either that much prolonged rehabilitation work is going on now or will in the future or that the children will be anywhere close to the ability they might have shown had no malnutrition occurred. The nature of gains is known to some extent as will be shown shortly, but the foregoing two points still seem valid.

Nutritional therapy, when given for a year or so to malnourished children ages two to nine, had a significant effect of raising the intelligence quotient by 10 to 18 points on standard tests (20). Do we want nutritional therapy? Yes, but as in so many areas of life, let us try to prevent these deficiencies in the first place. (We still prefer to fix curves in the road at the top of the cliff to expanding hospitals, staff, and training services at the bottom of the cliff.)

Do we find hungry children in American schools? In 1969 Linden and Guller could still say that "free (or reduced cost) school lunches are available in some schools, but according to some estimates another 100,000 school children in Georgia go hungry each noon because they lack the necessary money to buy food." It should be noted, too, that a supplemental food program designed to provide food for poor and malnourished pregnant women has been started recently (in Georgia). The diet quality of low-income families in the South is scandalously poor. Among low-income (under $3,000) Southern families 40 per cent had poor diets (9).

We also note that there is more to alleviating the problems than providing nutritionally adequate food.* The obstacles to putting poor, distraught families on the uphill road are overwhelming. The most ordinary and common home-making skills which middle-class and upper-lower-class people take for granted are unknown to many of these poor women. When workers go into these homes once a week to train such people, it is found that over a period of a year some advances can be made. Chapter 3 of Caster's (7) book is the log of a nutrition aide who made weekly visits to an extremely poor (less than $2,000 per year income) family over a period of six months. Reading this log gives one a tremendous jolt. Lewis and Dull (24) point out how the log revealed two recurring characteristic themes found in the logs of many other poor families:

1. The poor live in a chronic, multiproblem situation in which they lack the economic and human resources of their own to cope with the problems of being poor.
2. Problems relating to food habits are only part of a larger syndrome of human problems.

Lewis and Dull continue by pointing out that in order to alleviate the hunger which this family endures, a number of problems will have to be worked out concurrently and gradually at the same time. They show that, among other things, there is a need to encourage self-confidence and pride in the homemaker, increase knowledge of nutrition, improve homemaking skills, use present income more efficiently, expand available income, raise total income, and make food assistance programs available.

This calls for a large task force of people who are concerned for the poor and who are dedicated to alleviating their dilemmas. These concerned people would "define the problems, direct the necessary research, carry out educational programs, and plan and implement constructive social programs that are flexible to meet effectively the needs of the poor." Also, the need to understand poverty culture is great. Bagdikian, in his book *In the Midst of Plenty*, stated that the "greatest gap between the poor and the affluent in the United States . . . is the lack of human beings to bridge the two worlds. It is . . . pertinent to be well-versed in the world of poverty and to understand the needs and feelings of its victims."

* We find, for example, that it isn't enough to provide adequate diet, although adequate diet is a desirable goal. Lease and others point out that "nutritional status studies, dietary intake studies, prescription food demonstrations, and even school feeding programs lose their meaningful impact when the subjects harbor heavy burdens of intestinal parasites." The investigators reported that among 884 Head Start Day Care Center and elementary school Negro children studied in the central area of the state of South Carolina, 194 (or 29.2 per cent) of the children harbored intestinal large round worms (*Ascaris*).

LOVE

Defining *love* is not terribly difficult, but loving is, for the better definitions of *love* imply that one might have to inconvenience himself at times really to love another person. At one extreme the word *love* means willingness to lay down one's life for another; at the other extreme it means people touching, caring for, and helping one another. The latter idea is what Montagu (28) evidently had in mind when he defined *love* as the "relationship between persons in which they confer mutual benefits upon each other." Yet, lest we try to operate on a 50–50 basis, parrying for favors and requital on a contingency sort of basis, he says—and this is in keeping with theological definitions of love—that love is unconditional and supportive.

Love is necessary for survival, and the lack of love has immediate and long-term effects. An immediate effect in infants is that if they are not loved, they waste away and die (33). Montagu (28) points to two long-term effects of a lack of love: (1) emotional deprivation during childhood may result in a person being severely retarded in growth and development, and (2) a child who is not loved adequately during the first six years of life, may not be able to love himself or his neighbor. In fact, "criminal, delinquent, neurotic, psychopathic, asocial, and similar forms of unfortunate behavior can, in the majority of cases, be traced to a childhood history of inadequate love and emotional stability." What a fantastic price we pay for not loving.

Emotional deprivation knows no socioeconomic bounds. In the Binning (5) study of 800 children it was concluded that the detrimental effect of separation from one or more parents, plus the feeling that normal affection and love were lacking did much more damage to growth than did disease. Can anyone be so callous and obtuse as to think that malnourishment and emotional deprivation can in any way (except in a neurotic way) be propaedeutic to learning to read?

WAR AND POLLUTION

Our land, except for assorted Indian wars and World War II, in which Hawaii was bombed, has not been ravaged directly to any great extent since 1865. We have lost millions of young men since that time who did not survive for reading and other nice things, but we probably have not lost many very young children. The children lost something to the extent that they were deprived of their fathers during crucial developmental periods or deprived of them permanently through death.

Besides war—which is debilitating in so many ways—there exists a slower but just as sure means of decimating the population. There is the pollution of air and water and earth and the pollution of noise and drugs and hatred. These all lead to shortened lives. We see that young children are suffering from the pollutants, even from drug addiction; and we can trace the difficulty of drug addiction to the other social and emotional problems that we have been discussing. Not only is survival for nice things becoming increasingly difficult, but keeping and developing nice things is a rough task too.

LANGUAGE DEVELOPMENT

Neither Martin (27), Strickland [reported in Chall (8)], or Loban (26) found a significant relationship between complexity of oral language and reading ability in grades 1 and 2. Both Strickland and Loban found that this relationship increased so that by sixth grade oral language use was a very significant predictor of reading success and reading failure. Language development is important for reading success.

Language development is facilitated by having an adequately developed brain, a stimulating environment, and the chance to explore that environment; furthermore, language development is enhanced by having conversations with people.

Durkin's (13) studies of early readers show that as a group they

1. Have a high IQ (facilitated by adequate protein [as we have shown] for optimal brain development as well as by appropriate experiences).
2. Have books in the home (it is helpful to have a decent income).
3. Have parents who read to them (helpful to have parents who can read; see points one and two).
4. Are surrounded by people who constantly communicate and read.

What kinds of experiences lead to a state of readiness to read? Krech, Rozenzweig, and Bennett (19) have indirect answers, that is, information based on rat experiments:

1. Rats which lived eighty days in an enriched physical and social environment were found to have larger brain cells, a better blood supply, more glia cells, heavier and thicker cortex, and greater activity of two brain enzymes than their deprived counterparts.
2. The only really effective experience was the freedom to roam around in large object-filled space which presented continuous and varied maze-solving problems.

These findings jibe with certain other studies reported in this paper. We are all familiar with the studies of J. McV. Hunt (15), M. Deutsch (10), Johns and Goldstein (18), and others which show the importance of early, enriched language experiences for the language and cognitive development of children.

Yet Hunt and Kirk (17), after reviewing several studies, conclude that the evidence tends to "support the social pathology perspective, or the hypothesis that children accidentally born to parents of poverty commonly lack in their earliest years within the family the opportunities to acquire the cognitive, linguistic, and motivational skills more commonly provided by families of the middle class."

Painter (30) studied the effects of a tutorial language program for disadvantaged Negro and Caucasian infants ranging in chronological age from eight to twenty-four months. Medical examination showed no evidence of physical limitation and measured intelligence on the *Cattell Infant Intelligence Scale* was within the 80 to 120 I.Q. range. Each experimental subject was tutored one hour a day, five days a week for a period of one year by a female tutor. Each program was designed to ameliorate the development lags of the specific child. Following is a general outline of training procedures:

A. Language Training.
  1. Initiation of training, imitation of actions of others (10 months).
  2. Training the infant to imitate sounds (12 months).
  3. Training in identifying and naming objects (14 months).
  4. Teaching the child to verbalize needs and wants (16 months).
  5. Introducing picture books (18 to 24 months).
  6. Teaching the child to use elaborative language (18 months).
  7. Encouraging internal dialogue (24 months).
B. Concept Training.
  1. Body image (14 months).
  2. Space (10 months).
    a. More activities involving space (16 months).
    b. Introduce jigsaw puzzles.
    c. Introduce matching activities.
    d. Introduce seriatim.
    e. Teach child to copy designs.
  3. Teaching number concepts.
  4. Time.
  5. Classification.

When the program was begun, the infants were of average intelligence and motor development but below average in language development, in interpretation of symbolic representation, and in conceptual development.

Posttest data showed that (1) the experimental group now had a significantly (.05 level) higher IQ than the control group on the Stanford Binet, 108.1 and 98.8, respectively; (2) the experimental group exceeded the control group on the *Illinois Test of Psycholinguistic Abilities* and the *Merrill Palmer Scale of Mental Tests*, except for one subtest of the ITPA. On two of the subtests the .05 level of significance was reached; (3) the experimental group exceeded the control group on all eight conceptual developmental tests, five at the .05 level of significance; the experimental group only slightly exceeded the control group on six of the sensory–motor development tests. On one of the tests there was a statistically significant difference. It is safe to say that what is good for early childhood education is good for reading development.

Reading is a cognitive activity, and the child who has the well-developed, active brain, and is curious about many things, is the one who will perceive reading as a tool to further his own goals of acquiring and communicating information. We can lay the groundwork for this perception by developing language competency alongside cognitive competency.

Let us hope we can use our resources to improve nutrition, God's resources to improve love, decrease wars, and all available resources to eliminate any obstacles that work against survival for reading and other nice things.

Conclusions

The academic and social skills that allow a person to make particular contributions to the lives of others can be learned if certain conditions obtained during a person's early development. These skills can be learned by a person only if his pre-natal as well as post-natal growth and development were adequate. Such growth and development require adequate nutrition, loving care, and language stimulation.

Adequate intellectual functioning is based on proper brain growth. The fetus and infant must receive nutrient building blocks in the form of essential amino acids. Only *animal* protein provides the eight essential building blocks that must be provided by outside sources.

Low birth weight is correlated with malnutrition and low I.Q.'s. Nutrition affects the development of the brain, head circumference, and birth weight. Malnutrition developing before the age of six months renders little or no chance of reversal at a later time. Five months prior to birth to 25 months after birth is the critical period for adequate protein supply. If malnutrition develops after age two, but not prior to that time, prolonged rehabilitation will result in some significant increases in I.Q.

Protein intake that is much below normal is a problem that plagues too many mothers from low income families. One study of low income mothers revealed 95 mothers with a sub-par protein intake. Adequate protein is to be found in only a few countries. Even in the better countries the diets of slum dwellers is comprised of foods of poor biological quality.

The poor live in a continuing chain of circumstances which deprive them of the human and economic resources which might allow them to cope with the myriad problems of being poor. Such problems must be worked out concurrently and gradually. These poor people need to be trained in work skills, homemaking skills, economic skills, and other coping skills. The many workers needed to train these poor people in such skills also need to provide understanding of the needs and feelings of these unfortunate victims of poverty.

Infants must be loved or they may die. Emotional deprivation is a latter-day plague that knows no socio-economic bounds. The child who is not loved adequately in the formative first six years of life cannot love either himself or his neighbor, that is, anyone who needs his love and help. Psychopathic and sociopathic forms of behavior can usually be traced to a lack of both love and emotional stability during the formative years of a child's development.

War—one of our more stupid pastimes—makes survival difficult. It is an unequalled method of population control rivalled perhaps only by the proclivity of man for propelling himself—sans mind—through earth space in a weird assortment of motor vehicles. Pollution is an equally effective, albeit slower, means of winding down our population. War, pollution, and assorted methods of homicide must be drastically reduced and finally eliminated.

There is no significant relationship between complexity of oral language and reading achievement in the primary grades, but by grade six oral language is a quite significant predictor of reading success. Experiments with animals show that living in an enriched social and physical environment during the formative period results in increased brain development. Furthermore, enriched early experiences—beginning as early as eight months of age or earlier—aid the language and cognitive development of children. Whatever aids early childhood development and education, then, is good for reading development.

Reading is a cognitive activity that proceeds better for the child with the well-developed active brain who is curious about many things. It is this kind of child who will see reading as a tool to further his goals of obtaining and communicating information. The groundwork for this perception can be laid as we develop language competency alongside cognitive competency.

All resources of God and man should be aimed at improving nutrition, developing love, and decreasing the animosity, greed, and envy that lead to wars and that work against full development for reading and other pleasurable aspects of living.

REFERENCES

1. Allen, V. L. (ed.). *Psychological Factors in Poverty*. Chicago: Markham, 1970.
2. Bagdikian, B. H. *In the Midst of Plenty: A New Poor in America*. New York: Signet Books, 1964.
3. Bakan, R. "Malnutrition and Learning," *Phi Delta Kappan*, 51 (1970), 527–30.
4. Barnes, R. H., A. U. Moore, I. M. Reid, and W. G. Pond. "Effect of Food Deprivation on Behavioral Patterns," in *Malnutrition, Learning and Behavior*, ed. by W. S. Scrimshaw and J. E. Gordon. Cambridge, Mass.: M.I.T. Press, 1968.

5. Binning, G. "Peace on Thy House," *Health* (1948), 6, 7, 28, 30.
6. Birch, H. G., and J. D. Gussow. *Disadvantaged Children: Health, Nutrition, and School Failure.* New York: Grune and Stratton, 1970.
7. Caster, W. O., and T. Burton. "Maternal and Infant Malnutrition as It Relates to Mental Retardation," in *Hunger and Malnutrition in Georgia, 1969,* ed. by W. O. Caster. Athens, Georgia: University of Georgia, 1969.
8. Chall, J. *Learning to Read: The Great Debate.* New York: McGraw-Hill, Inc., 1967.
9. Clark, F. "Trends in Food Consumption in the South," in *The Food Problem in Georgia,* ed. by Gerald G. Dull. Athens, Georgia: University of Georgia, 1970.
10. Deutsch, M. "The Role of Social Class in Language Development and Cognition," *American Journal of Orthopsychiatry,* 35 (1965), 78–88.
11. Dinnan, J. A., and H. Cowart. *Key to Learning Series, Kit O: Oral Language Readiness.* Athens, Georgia: Jaddy Enterprises, 1973.
12. Dobbing, J. *Science Journal,* 3 (May 1967), 81–86.
13. Durkin, D. "Children Who Read Before Grade One: A Second Study," *Elementary School Journal,* 64 (1963), 143–48.
14. Hafner, L. E., W. Weaver, and K. Powell. "Psychological and Perceptual Correlates of Reading Achievement at the Fourth Grade Level," *Journal of Reading Behavior,* 2(4) (1970), 281–90.
15. Hunt, J. McV. *Intelligence and Experience.* New York: The Ronald Press Company, 1961.
16. ———. "The Psychological Basis for Using Pre-School Enrichment as an Antidote for Cultural Deprivation," *Merrill-Palmer Quarterly,* 10 (1964), 209–45.
17. ———, and G. E. Kirk. "Social Aspects of Intelligence: Evidence and Issues," in *Intelligence: Genetic and Environmental Influences,* ed. by R. Cancro. New York: Grune and Stratton, 1971.
18. Johns, V. P., and L. S. Goldstein. "The Social Context of Language Acquisition," *Merrill-Palmer Quarterly of Behavior and Development,* 10 (1964), 265–74.
19. Krech, D., M. R. Rozenzweig, and E. L. Bennett. "Effects of Early Environmental Complexity and Training on Brain Chemistry," *Journal of Comparative Physiological Psychology,* 53 (1960), 509–519.
20. Kugelmass, I. N., L. E. Poull, and I. Samuel. "Nutritional Improvement of Child Mentality," *American Journal of Medical Science,* 208 (1944), 631ff.
21. Lease, E. J., B. W. Dudley, and M. F. Ziegler. "Intestinal Parasites and Nutritional Status: II. Parasitic Infection in Children in South Carolina," *The Journal of the South Carolina Medical Association,* 66 (1970), 42–45.
22. Ledesma, R. E., E. J. Lease, and Malphrus. "Nutritional Deficiencies of Low Income Mothers in the Greenville, S.C., Area," *The Journal of the South Carolina Medical Association,* 62 (1966), 287–89.
23. ———, and E. J. Lease. "Nutritional Deficiencies of Low Income Mothers in the Columbia, S.C., Area," *The Journal of the South Carolina Medical Association,* 63 (1967), 80–83.
24. Lewis, K. J., and G. G. Dull. "An Epilogue to a Log," in *The Food Prob-*

lem in Georgia, ed. by G. G. Dull. Athens, Georgia: University of Georgia, 1970.

25. Linden, L. L., and W. H. Guller. "Data Related to Hunger and Malnutrition in Georgia," in *Hunger and Malnutrition in Georgia, 1969,* ed. by W. O. Caster. Athens, Georgia: University of Georgia, 1969.

26. Loban, W. D. *The Language of Elementary School Children, Research Report No. 1.* Champaign, Ill.: National Council of Teachers of English, 1963.

27. Martin, C. "Developmental Relationships Among Language Variables in the First Grade," *Elementary English,* 32 (1955), 167–71.

28. Montagu, A. "A Scientist Looks at Love," *Phi Delta Kappan,* 51 (1970), 463–67.

29. Novakova, V., J. Faltin, V. Flandera, V. Hahn, and O. Koldovsky. "Effects of Early and Late Weaning on Learning in Adult Rats," *Nature,* 193 (1962), 280.

30. Painter, G. "A Tutorial Language Program for Disadvantaged Infants," in *Language Training in Early Childhood Education,* ed. by C. S. Lavetelli. Champaign, Ill.: University of Illinois Press, 1971.

31. Platt, B. S. "Protein in Nutrition." *Proceedings of the Royal Society of London, Series B.* 156 (1962), 337–44.

32. ———, D. R. C. Heard, and R. J. C. Stewart. "Experimental Protein-Calorie Deficiency," in *Mammalian Protein Metabolism,* Vol. 2, ed. by H. N. Munro and J. B. Allison. New York: Academic Press, 1964.

33. Ribble, M. A. "Infantile Experience in Relation to Personality Development," in *Personality and the Behavior Disorders,* Vol. 2, ed. by J. McV. Hunt. New York: The Ronald Press Company, 1944.

34. Scrimshaw, W. S., and J. E. Gordon (eds.). *Malnutrition, Learning and Behavior.* Cambridge, Mass.: M.I.T. Press, 1968.

35. Sinisterra, L. "Nutrition and Early Mental Development," *The Journal of Educational Research,* 64 (1970), i.

36. Stewart, R. J. C. Paper Presented at the Symposium on Malnutrition, Learning and Behavior, Massachusetts Institute of Technology, 1966.

37. Stoch, M. B., and P. M. Smythe. "Does Undernutrition During Infancy Inhibit Brain Growth and Subsequent Intellectual Development?" *Archives of Diseases in Childhood,* 38 (1963), 546–52.

38. ———. "Undernutrition During Infancy, and Subsequent Brain Growth and Intellectual Development," in *Malnutrition, Learning and Behavior,* ed. by W. S. Scrimshaw and J. E. Gordon. Cambridge, Mass.: M.I.T. Press, 1968.

39. White, A., P. Handler, and E. L. Smith. *Principles of Biochemistry,* third edition. New York: McGraw-Hill, Inc., 1959.

40. Wiley, R. C. "Children's Estimates of Their Schoolwork Ability as a Function of Sex, Race, and Socio-Economic Level," *Journal of Personality,* 31 (1963), 203–24.

41. Williams, F. *Language and Poverty.* Chicago: Markham, 1970.

42. Winick, M. "Nutrition and Cell Growth," *Nutrition Review,* 26 (1968), 195–97.

Foreign Language

GIVE THE STUDENT TIPS ON HOW TO GET THE MOST FROM FOREIGN LANGUAGE BOOKS*

Ralph C. Preston

The foreign language student gets bogged down quickly in his reading if he is required to read materials that are too difficult for him. As in reading one's native language, there are many (if not more) problems in reading a foreign language. If one is to make progress in reading a foreign language, specific obstacles to progress must be identified and dealt with systematically.

Preston gives general and specific suggestions for helping a student increase his proficiency in reading foreign language materials.

1. What are the three basic steps for overcoming problems in foreign language reading?

2. Which teaching of reading principles has the author applied to the area of building a more substantial vocabulary?

3. Do the injunctions regarding the mastering of the grammar of a language seem plausible to you?

4. What does "syntax" mean?

5. How can the foreign language notebook-dictionary be used as an auto-instructional device?

6. What can the student do to help himself read in terms of ideas and phrases?

7. State the article's key ideas.

A student who studies a foreign language or who must read extensively in foreign language references in connection with his courses often spends unduly large amounts of time in extracting the meaning from a comparatively short passage. Most of his woes in this task can be overcome through (1) building a more substantial vocabulary in the language, (2) mastering the grammar, and (3) acquiring the ability to think in the language. Correct study procedures in learning a foreign language are of especial importance.

1. BUILDING A MORE SUBSTANTIAL VOCABULARY. The student should be persuaded to test his basic sight vocabulary by examining the vocabulary list in the back of his first-year foreign language textbook to see

---

* REPRINTED FROM *Teaching Habits and Skills* (New York: Rinehart and Company, Inc., 1959), pp. 34–37, by permission of the publisher.

if he can instantaneously and accurately identify the meanings of at least a hundred of the words. If he cannot do this, he may assume that his stock of sight words is deficient. Using the same book, he may read aloud its simple sentences and stories—repeatedly if necessary—until he knows them well. This method is more effective than trying to memorize word lists.

However, this is a mere beginning. It is doubtful if he will be able to read the language with fluency and adequate understanding unless he knows over 95 per cent of the running words at sight. This means he must set about to expand his vocabulary vastly. Systematic reading of interesting material—stories, newspapers, and the like—should be carried on apart from regular class assignments. In fact, language teachers often make such reading a part of the regular assignment to ensure its being done. In this recreational reading, it is not essential that all unknown words be looked up in a dictionary. The student should be encouraged to utilize as fully as possible the clues offered by the context. New words supplied by the clues will be gradually added to the student's vocabulary. Where context is insufficient, examination of the unfamiliar word may help through recognition of cognates (e.g., Spanish "concerto," French "concert," German "Konzert") or through structural analysis (e.g., in German, "Strassenbahnhaltestelle" = Strasse (street) + Bahn (railway) + Halt (stop) + Stelle (place) = "streetcar stop"). There are always those words, of course, which have to be looked up.

Important words, or words that the student finds he is looking up more than once, he should be advised to keep in his own notebook-dictionary for recording words and idioms, and perhaps he should also make flash cards. To clinch the difficult words and idioms, the student should be instructed how to recite them to himself through using them orally and in writing sentences, through repeating them from memory, and through reading them aloud.

2. MASTERING THE GRAMMAR OF THE LANGUAGE. Although much grammar is learned through a program emphasizing wide reading and vocabulary building, many constructions in a student's reading continue to have a fuzzy meaning for him if he has no firm understanding of the language's structure. Each language has its peculiar syntax, which is described in beginning textbooks and in grammars. They are sufficiently different from English to cause trouble in reading comprehension until they are thoroughly grasped. The rules of sentence structure are not numerous and can be briefly summarized. The best test of having mastered them is the student's ability to give his own examples of sentences representing each type of sentence order. Aside from syntax, each language has its peculiar conjugations. Each student seems to have his own particular difficulties with grammar. He can be helped to identify them and to focus his study upon them.

The nomenclature of foreign grammars often constitutes a hurdle for the student. He should be provided with a book of English grammar and helped to see parallels between English forms and those of the language he is learning. Through making such comparisons he will inevitably identify many distinctive and important features of the foreign language. For example, he will discover the French use of the comparative form of adjectives in connection with superlative expressions as in *mon meilleur*

WORD	PHRASE IN WHICH IT OCCURRED	TRANSLATION	OTHER MEANINGS	A
anstellen	Wenn ich mich gut anstelle...	set about a thing	pretend make a fuss	B
Abschnitt	...im ersten Abschnitt.	paragraph	section era segment	
beobachten	...den Flug eines Adlers zu beobachten.	observe	examine execute obey an order	
Ankunst	...die Ankunst des Zugs.	arrival	advent	

From a student's foreign language notebook-dictionary.

ami (my dearest friend); and the German use of adjectives as adverbs as in *sie singt schön* (she sings beautifully). Incidentally, it is advisable that the student be told that translating English sentences into the new language in connection with each grammatical concept will be more helpful than the learning of rules and conjugations, although that has its value, too.

3. ACQUIRING THE ABILITY TO THINK IN THE LANGUAGE. As long as the student's reading comprehension depends upon literal translations from the foreign word to the English word before forming the image for which the word stands, reading in the foreign language will be a tedious experience for him. Furthermore, such a word-by-word approach, whether in his native tongue or in the foreign language he is learning, interferes with fluent, accurate comprehension. The teacher can assist him in drawing parallels between his successful reading in English and his lumbering reading of the foreign language in order that he may pattern the latter after the former, orienting himself to the author and trying to anticipate the author's plan and thoughts. When the student succeeds in doing this, he will find himself reading in terms of phrases and ideas as he reads, and thinking ahead. It will take abundant practice before such reading becomes habitual. Unfortunately, instructors who emphasize literal translation in class inhibit this growth toward truly participating and thinking in a foreign language. Students should never be permitted to be satisfied with literal translations in their reading, but should be urged to get an image directly from the foreign words and phrases without the intermediary of the corresponding English words and phrases.

TEACHING CODE-BREAKING SKILLS IN FOREIGN LANGUAGE READING *

Alfred N. Smith

Anyone who has worked at learning a foreign language or at teaching it is familiar with the problem of learning the code. Smith utilizes a number of procedures for teaching the codes of several languages. If these techniques are applied assiduously, they should prove quite helpful to the student.

1. What are the basic techniques used in identifying a word?

2. Study the model lesson in French. Try to apply these techniques to learning a different grapheme–phoneme association.

3. Under what conditions would you utilize drill procedures for teaching sight words? Sound–symbol correspondences?

4. What are the advantages of using context-clued procedures?

5. When will structural analysis skills likely be used?

6. Discuss the pros and cons of any of these procedures.

In reading jargon, "breaking the code" means to identify words in sentence patterns by deciphering in some way the written characters which represent them. An efficient reader will use a number of techniques in the code-breaking process: (1) He may simply learn to recognize a word by sight. He sees a series of letters, and without analyzing the sounds that the letters represent he assigns to that particular graphic configuration the spoken word it represents. This is frequently the way a student will attack a word in which there is poor fit. For example, with the French word *est*, the student may simply see the word as a whole and identify it immediately as /E/. (2) He may identify a word through phonics, i.e., assigning to the written symbol the sound it represents. (3) He may recognize a word because it appears in a familiar context. For example, the beginning Spanish student has heard and spoken many times the expression, ¿Como se llama? Having identified the first two words in the sentence, he quickly recognizes the last word with little or no analysis because of the context. As an isolated reading word, the student might very well mispronounce or not even recognize the word *llama*, which he identified readily in its familiar context. (4) He may identify a word by analyzing its structure. A knowledge of certain inflections, affixes, and basic root forms will enable a student to recognize a word. It is the consensus among reading authorities that all or a combination of these techniques should be used in helping the student "break the code."

* REPRINTED FROM *American Foreign Language Teacher* 2(3) (February 1972), pp. 4–8, 43, by permission of the publisher.

1. Model Lesson in French: /S/ – ch

The approach described in the following lesson is an eclectic one, since it makes use of nearly all the techniques described above.

a. The teacher elicits from the students the following dialogue sentences by showing pictures or asking questions. The teacher writes the sentences on the board, on a transparency or wall chart. These sentences are read in chorus and individually.

Je n'ai pas de chance.   Tu vas chez Michel.
Il mange du chocolat.   Il fait chaud.

b. The words *chance, chocolat, chez*, and *chaud* are underlined. The teacher may drill these words on flash cards. Students are asked to identify the word on the card and then to read the sentence in which it appears.

c. This short generalization is the next step:

TEACHER: Read the underlined words. (Pointing to *chance, chez*, etc.)

STUDENT: *Chance, chocolat, chez*, etc.

TEACHER: With what letters do these words begin?

STUDENT: With *ch*.

TEACHER: What sound do these letters represent?

STUDENT: The sound /ʃ/.

TEACHER: What are some other words you know that have the sound /ʃ/?

STUDENT: (Dictate the words as the teacher writes them on the board) *chose, dimanche, marche, chic, chambre, chemise, chat, chaise.*

d. The teacher conducts drills to fix the sound-symbol correspondence and to develop rapid word recognition. (See 3 a-e). These exercises may include substitution and contrast drills to help students distinguish this sound-symbol problem from other problems they have already studied. For example, in German, reading drills to help students distinguish long and short vowel sounds will be needed.

e. To see if students have fixed the relationship, the teacher will now present unfamiliar words containing *ch*. These words must present no new problems to the student; i.e., even though the words are unfamiliar, all of the sound-symbol problems have been studied. A list of words suitable for practice in this lesson might be *cliche, fiche, cache, chasse, chape, chaine*, etc.

f. Familiar *ch* words are combined to form new sentences. These are placed on the board and read. The individual words which make up these sentences may be placed on cards to be arranged on a felt board or magnetic board by the student as he makes up his own sentences.

Charles n'a pas de *ch*ance.   Je *ch*erche ma *ch*emise.
Allons *ch*ez Michel.   Le *ch*at est sous la *ch*aise.

g. Finally, the students read a recombined dialogue or narrative containing the newly learned sound-symbol relationship. The purpose of this activity is to test the recognition of *ch* words in a completely new situation. The student must grasp the meaning of an unfamiliar context while using various "code-breaking" skills. Students can be asked to read the material aloud or silently. The teacher follows the reading with questions to check comprehension.

Charles cherche ses disques. Ils ne sont pas dans sa chambre. Ils ne sont pas sous la chaise. Charles ne les trouve pas. Il n'a pas de chance. Où sont-ils? **Chez** Michel, son meilleur ami.

2. Drilling Whole Words by Sight

As a prelude to phonics instruction, many teachers like to begin by grouping familiar words which contain the same sound. These words can be drilled in various ways to train students in whole word recognition by sight.

a. Presenting words for drill. A familiar sentence is shown with a blank representing the word to be practiced. The teacher repeats the whole sentence. A student is asked to supply the missing word. After he repeats it, the word is immediately shown on a flash card, or it is written on the board.

T: (Showing on flash card) ¿ como se llama usted? ¿Cómo se llama? What is the missing word?
S: Cómo.

T: (Showing *Cómo* on a flash card) **Lean** Vds.
S: (Several students repeat the word) *Cómo.*

Many words containing the same sound can be isolated in this way. This numbered list of Spanish words will be used to illustrate other exercises:

1. Ocho	5. pronto	9. ojo
2. cómo	6. tomo	10. foto
3. profesor	7. gorro	11. todo
4. domingo	8. nosotros	12. otoño

b. Naming and pointing. The teacher asks the students to name the words to which he points or to give the numbers of words which he names.

T: (Pointing to 8) Lea.
S: *Nosotros.*

T: (Reading: *pronto*) Qué número es?
S: Número cinco, etc.

c. A student is asked to go to the board and erase one of the words in the list (or the teacher may erase a word). Another student is asked to say the word. A variation on this exercise is to send a student to the board and have him erase words as they are read to him by other students.

d. When many sight words on flash cards have been drilled, the cards may be placed face down on the desk. Students are asked to draw them, read the word to the class, and then supply the familiar context from which the word was taken.

e. Using the list of words on the board, the students read the words that best answer a question:

¿ Cuántos son cuatro más cuatro? (ocho)   ¿ Qué día va a la iglesia? (domingo)
¿ Quién es delante de la clase? (profesor)   ¿ Con qué ve usted? (ojo)

f. For younger students in the elementary and junior high grades, these activities are effective:

(1) Wheel of chance—Students spin the hands of a clock. On the board appears a list of 12 words as the one above. They read the word which corresponds to the number where the hand stops.

(2) Guessing game—A student goes out of the room while others pick out a word from the list which he is to guess. When he returns, he is to read the words until he says the one that was selected.

(3) Bingo—This popular game can be played with words instead of numbers.

(4) Simon Says—This game can be used with the reading of words, phrases or whole sentences. The teacher points to words or phrases that he will read. If the reading does not correspond to what is written, the students remain silent. Otherwise they repeat.

3. Drilling Sound-Symbol Correspondences

To fix sound-letter relationships, the teacher may use a variety of recognition, substitution, addition, rhyming and contrast drills.

a. Recognition drills.

(1) Words with colored letters representing the same sound are drilled on flash cards. In the following German words the underlined letter might be printed in yellow to represent the sound /I/.

bitten	stimmen
mich	mit
bis	immer

(2) Sentences containing a certain sound-symbol problem are placed on the board or printed on mimeographed sheets. As the students read the sentences, they underline the letters that represent the sound in question. In the following French sentences, it is the sound /k/.

1. Il n'y a que quatre questions.   3. Deux et trois font cinq.
2. D'accord. Je ne suis pas occupé.   4. Nous allons au cours avec nos copains.

(3) The student is asked to choose the letter or letters that represent the sound common to a list of words he hears.

Student hears: Student sees:
1. Фжа,   Факт,   Фунт   А.   в   В.   ф   С.   б

Correct response: B

(4) The students read a list of words as the teacher repeats them. They are to circle only the word containing the sound under study. In the Spanish words below the sound is /j/ represented by the letters *ll* or *y*.

1.	a. calle	b. calor	c. caja	d. cara
2.	a. juego	b. lejos	c. llego	d. genero
3.	a. aire	b. algo	c. alto	d. ayer

Correct responses: A, C, D

(5) Single letters representing initial consonant sounds are written on the board. As the teacher reads each word, a student is asked to circle the letter on the board with which the word begins. The whole word is then written on the board and read by the student.

Student hears:		Student sees:	
цирк	ваза	з	п
шить	роза	р	ц
за	баба	в	ш
суп	папа	б	с

(6) The teacher says two words in a row that start with the same consonant. The students read a list of words silently, then pick the one that begins the same way. This exercise may be done with final consonants as well. Here is an example in German:

Student hears:	Student sees:		
ja, je	1. A. ich	B. jeder	C. heute
zu, Zeit	2. A. Zahn	B. schön	C. sagen

Correct responses: B, A

(7) The students are asked to underline every word in the sentence that ends or begins with the same sound as the word given. Here is an example in French:

Teacher says:	Students read and underline:
blond	1. Il ne *sont* pas de *Dijon*.
deux	2. *Mathieu* a les *yeux bleus*.
joli	3. Les *jeunes gens jouent* au tennis.

(8) Silent-letters—Words with silent letters are placed on flash cards for drilling. Strike out marks are placed over the silent letters to help students understand that the letters are not pronounced. This is a problem in French.

Pari*s*	ver*t*
*H*abit*e*	*H*eur*e*

b. Substitution drills

(1) To practice consonants, students are given a model word followed by letter substitutions. As the students pronounce the changed words, the teacher writes in the missing letters and they are reread. Here is an example in Spanish:

Model:

Student sees and reads:	Student sees: _ _ j _ , _ _ s _
c a r a	Students says: *caja, casa*
	The teacher writes in the missing letters and the students read.

1. g a t o	r _ _ _ p _ _ _
	(rato) (pato)
2. o r o	_ j _ _ ch _
	(ojo) (ocho)

(2) Students are given directions to make new words which they pronounce and use in sentences. Here is an example in French:

Student sees:	Directions:
sont	Changez *s à f*
mon	Changez *m à t*
bien	Changez *b à r*
Student changes:	Student reads:
font	Deux et deux (*font*) quatre.
ton	Tu as (*ton*) cahier?
rien	Ça ne fait (*rien*).

(3) Students substitute certain letters for underlined portions in given words and read. Here is an example in French:

T: We will change the underlined letters in the following expressions to either	*oi* or *ois* and pronounce these letters as /wa/.
Student sees and reads:	Student says, teacher writes, and student reads:
Que faire?	(Quoi faire?)
Pas m*al*.	(Pas moi.)
C'est t*out*.	(C'est toi.)
V*eux*-tu?	(Vois-tu?)

c. Addition drills

(1) In Spanish, adding endings can sometimes cause a change in stress. In the following exercise, the teacher repeats two words. The students listen, repeat and then read the sentence:

Teacher says, Student repeats:	Student reads:
habla – hablamos	Hablamos inglés.
llega – llegamos	Llegamos a la clase.
entra – entramos	Entramos con las chicas.

(2) In this Russian example, students are asked to add the soft sign which makes the final consonant soft. Both words may be printed on flash cards for drill.

стол	столб
брат	братб
стал	сталб

(3) Students can change words by adding initial or end consonant sounds. In this exercise the teacher repeats a pair of words. Final sounds are added to the second words. As the teacher repeats the second word, he fills in the letters that represent the added sounds. In this way students can see that sometimes there are several letters for a single sound, and that sometimes there are silent letters. The students then read the word in context.

Student hears:	Teacher fills in letters:
/ku/ – /kur/	c o u r s̸
/di/ – /disk/	d i s q u ¢̸ s̸
/ʃo/ – /ʃoz/	c h o s ¢̸
/ʃɛɪ/ – /ʃɛɪʃ/	c h e r c h ¢̸

Student reads:
Au cours de français.
Ecouter ses disques.
Pas grand'chose.
Je cherche le livre.

d. Rhyming drills

(1) Students underline the word in a list that has the same vowel sound as the word the teacher pronounces. Here are two items in German:

Teacher says:	Student sees:		
die	A. bei	B. wie	C. frei
Hut	A. tut	B. müde	C. Hüte

(2) The teacher supplies a single syllable word with which there are many possible rhymes. As the students give the rhyming words, they are written on the board and read. Here are some rhymes in French.

feu	peu	jeu
mur	sur	dur
bras	pas	bas

(3) Students underline the words in each sentence that rhyme with the word given. Here is an example in German:

Given:	Sentence:
acht	Sie macht die Tür auf.
Maus	Sie stehen vor unserem Haus, etc.

e. Contrast drills—After several associations have been established, contrasting exercises are necessary to check the student's ability to distinguish them.

(1) The teacher lists columns of words on the board or on mimeographed sheets. He reads only one word after each number. The student circles the word. Here is a sample in French.

I	II	III	IV
1. pont	peau	pois	peu
2. font	faut	fois	feu
3. sont	seau	soi	ceux
4. vont	veau	vois	veux

(2) In this exercise which contrasts long and short vowels in German, the students underline the word after each number read by the teacher.

1. Lied	litt
2. Hütte	Hüte
3. Bett	Beet
4. Staat	Stadt

(3) Students are asked to categorize words in a mixed list into certain sound-letter groups. The students tell the teacher under which group to put the words. When the lists are complete, the words are reread. Here are two lists that might be used in French:

écoute	courent	crie	ici	merci	Alice
incendie	garçon	court	contre	courage	descent

c – /k/	c – /s/
écoute	incendie
_____	_____
_____	_____

4. Context Clued

Skill in the use of context for word recognition at the beginning level can be developed with these activities:

a. Fill-in sentences—Familiar sentences are listed with blanks to be filled by words given in a lexicon. The teacher asks for the word which fills the blank appropriately. A student reads the words. The word is written in the blank and the sentence is reread. Here is an example in Spanish:

pizarra	hermana	ser	está

1. Pedro tiene una _____ muy gorda.

2. Aquí _____ mi radio.

3. Escribo en la _____ .

4. Quiere _____ un torero famoso.

b. Matching the beginnings and endings of sentences gives students practice in word recognition through context. This exercise also encourages reading in word groups. Students are asked to peruse the second column to find the appropriate ending. As soon as a student finds a match he reads it. Here is a series of items in French:

1. Attends-moi	de l'église.
2. J'aime mieux	à la porte.
3. Il a envie	le poulet.
4. C'est en face	de déjeuner.

c. Finishing sentences—Students are asked to complete the sentences with the most obvious words suggested by the context. The teacher writes in the word and the whole sentence is read. Here are several sentences in French:

1. J'aime la glace au   (chocolat).
2. Le drapeau français est bleu, blanc et   (rouge).

3. Avez-vous chaud? Au contraire, j'ai   (froid).

5. Structural Analysis

Because of the very limited vocabulary of the first year student, he will seldom use structural analysis as a means for recognizing words in his initial reading pursuits. The study of prefixes, suffixes, syllabication, compound words and word families is reserved for more advanced levels. Such study is designed primarily to help the student clarify meanings and enlarge his vocabulary. However, the elementary student can profit from reading drills which focus on important inflectional information. These inflections provide significant cues which the reader must identify rapidly if the reading act is to progress with ease and accuracy. The following exercises are samples of what can be used effectively.

a. Singular-plural contrast

(1) Students choose a singular or plural subject to fill the blank according to the inflectional clues given. The Spanish words are listed above the sentences:

muchacho   sopa   libros   alumnos

1. ¿ Qué hacen los _____?
2. ¿ Dondé está el _____?

3. ¿ Cuánto cuestan los _____?
4. ¿ Te gusta la _____?

(2) Students of French fill in the blanks with *est* or *sont* according to the inflectional information in the rest of the sentence. This is an oral reading drill, not a written assignment.

est   sont

1. Où _____ les livres?
2. Où _____ la juene fille?

3. Où _____ l'ami de Robert?
4. Où _____ les cahiers?

b. Formal vs. familiar forms

In this exercise in French, the student underlines the person he would address in the question. He then reads the question.

(Pierre, M. Dupont), *tu restes ici?*
(Mme Mercier, Maman), *vous dinez chez nous ce soir?*

(Luc et Jean, Marie), *tu ne viens pas tout de suite?*

c. Affirmative vs. negative

The teacher prepares a transparency with varied sentences. As the fourth sentence is produced orally by the student, the teacher writes it down. It is then read. Clues and inflectional changes in the second sentence of the first pair can be underlined to point out the pattern. These paired sentences in French deal with the negative partitive:

Nous avons des enfants.
Nous *n'*avons *pas d'*enfants.
Nous avons des amis.
_____ .

Prenez-vous des frites?
Non, je *ne* prends *pas de* frites.

Prenez-vous des fraises?
_____ .

Vous n'avez pas de légumes?
Si, nous avons *des* légumes.
Vous n'avez pas de tomates?
_____ .

d. Case endings

In this German example, the three columns of sentences may be placed on a transparency. The first two columns have sentences identical in meaning, but the difference in word order requires careful notice of case endings. One sentence is missing in each row. The missing form alternates from column to column as we read down the rows. Choral reading of the presented forms is suggested while the missing sentence is supplied by an individual student. The teacher writes in the response which is then read by all.

Fritz sieht den Mann.
    Den Mann sieht Fritz.
        Der Mann sieht Fritz.
Fritz sieht den Studenten.
    Den Studenten sieht Fritz.
        _____ .
_____ .
    Den Professor sieht Fritz.
        Der Professor sieht Fritz.

Fritz sieht den Lehrer.
    _____ .
        Der Lehrer sieht Fritz.
    _____ .
        Den Vater sieht Fritz.
            Der Vater sieht Fritz.
Fritz sieht den Bruder.
    Den Bruder sieht Fritz.
        _____ .

Practice on the part of teacher and students in the presentation and performance of these drills leads to improvement in all four skills of language learning. While it is apparent that most of the preceding exercises are designed for aural-oral practice at the beginning level of language study, the drills can be subsequently used for practice in reading and writing at all levels of study. Drills modeled after these examples may prove to be of great value in teaching students to "break the code."

Encouraging Reading
Interests and Tastes

Introduction

Reading interests and tastes are important topics. It is probably an overstatement to say that they are the key topics in education, but they are matters of great import, to be sure. Evidence of the concern educators and parents have for interests and tastes is found in the educational aphorisms we widely quote: "Success breeds interest." "Give a child a book that interests him." "You need to get the right book together with the right child at the right time." "Tastes are caught, not taught." If interests in general and reading interests in particular are such important facets of education, it might be well to ask which factors seem to condition or determine what a person will read. The following factors singly or in combination seem to condition what a person will read and the avidity with which he will read it:

1. *The availability of the material.*
2. *The difficulty of the material.*
3. *The style in which the material is written.*
4. *What he has read previously.*
5. *How much he depends on others (or allows others) to solve his problem of reading choice.*
6. *The feeling of hope or fear or satisfaction that he experiences when reading a given type of material.*
7. *What he has done before when confronted with the choice of reading versus not-reading.*
8. *His self-concept as a reader.*

In reading the articles in this section, the reader should check to see which of the eight points listed as determining factors are borne out by the experiences and contentions of the authors. Above all, the reader should take advantage of the insights the authors offer regarding the discovery, development, and utilization of reading interests and tastes.

WHAT DO TEEN-AGERS READ?*

Lorraine Kirkland, Wilda Clowers, and Betsy Wood

What are teenagers reading in the 1970's? People from all parts of the country live in the city in which this study was conducted; therefore the sample to some extent represents much more than a local area or region. The authors have replicated an earlier study and applied their findings by making a number of curriculum recommendations.

1. How would you account for the sustained popularity of the nine magazines that appeared in the earlier study and the present study?

2. Why do you think students of today are interested in current events?

3. What suggestions do the authors make for utilizing contemporary magazines?

4. How might science texts be improved?

5. Expand on and/or add to the other curriculum suggestions of the authors.

6. Speculate on the reading materials and interests of teenagers in the near future.

---

* Written especially for this volume.

In the first edition of this text we found an article entitled "What Do Teen-agers Read?" written by Richard H. Rice and James E. Sellers. The authors were searching for an answer to this question: "What does the teen-ager want to read and go to the trouble to read when there is no adult standing over him with an assignment?" Their questionnaire was given in March, 1960 to a tenth-grade class of six students and a senior class of eight students at Belmont Methodist Church, Nashville, Tennessee. Their findings would, they hoped, shed some light on the type of material which appeals to teen-agers. This knowledge could then be applied to the development of curriculum materials which teen-agers would actually read. Their specific concern was curricular material in religious education.

We duplicated the Sellers and Rice questionnaire and passed them out to sixty-six students, mostly from Leon High School, some from Lively VO-Tech Night School in Tallahassee, Florida. These students ranged in age from fourteen to eighteen. We have treated the separate ages and also the composite group and have derived the following information.

Life magazine placed first on an overall basis, having received twenty votes. *Seventeen* magazine took second place, receiving nineteen votes, followed by *Time* magazine, with twelve votes; *Newsweek* was fourth, with eleven votes. Four of the five age groups, all but the eighteen-year-olds, chose *Seventeen* as one of their three top choices, whereas *Life* was not chosen as one of the top three by the fifteen and eighteen age groups. *Playboy*, which had been mentioned only once in the Rice–Sellers study, was the top choice of the eighteen-year-olds; it was also mentioned in the sixteen- and seventeen-year-old categories. *Mad*, one of the favorites in the Rice–Sellers study, was mentioned by only one of the sixty-six teen-agers, an eighteen-year-old boy.

Other magazines mentioned were *Sports Illustrated, Ebony, Scope, Jet, Popular Mechanics, Popular Science, Good Housekeeping, McCall's, Teen, Ingenue, National Geographic, National Review, Ladies Home Journal, Cosmopolitan, Field and Stream, U.S. News and World Report, Readers Digest, Surfing, Hot Rod, Earth, National Lampoon, Women's Day, Co-ed, Vogue, Sing Out,* a folk magazine, and *Changing Times.* A degree of sophistication was evident in such choices as *Psychology Today* and *The New Yorker.* Only one romance magazine was cited, and that only once, *True Story.*

Some of the magazines cited above appeared on the Rice–Sellers list: *Life, Readers Digest, Sports Illustrated, Time, Seventeen, The New Yorker, Hot Rod, Playboy,* and the *Ladies Home Journal.* Seven of the sixteen magazines mentioned by the Rice–Sellers study did not appear in the present study; some of the magazines are no longer in print. A much broader array of magazines was presented in our study. This could be in part attributed to the greater number of subjects involved: 66 as opposed to 14. In addition, the proliferation of new magazines in our culture must also be taken into consideration. Both studies indicate that magazines are the stronger contender in the teen-age reading market. Only a very few subjects listed no magazines read, whereas over half the subjects left the book category blank.

The thirty books that were listed in response to item 5—"What was the last book, other than books assigned at school, you remember reading?"—reflect an awareness of current books absent in the Rice–Sellers study. Included in the current category were *The Naked Ape, The Godfather, Love Story, Valley of the Dolls, Portnoy's Complaint, Little Big Man, Beneath the Planet of the Apes,* and *The Electric Kool-aid Acid Test.*

Significant fiction included *Grapes of Wrath, Wuthering Heights, To Kill a Mockingbird, Billy Budd,* and *Bridge on the River Kwai.* One teen-ager listed the Hardy Boys mysteries read in the fifth grade as his last book read. Previously typical teen-age books were mentioned only by one girl—*Seventeenth Summer* and *Karen.* It is interesting to note that the *Silver Chalice* was read by the only girl to mention two religious magazines as her choices: *Decision* and *Presbyterian Journal.* Two books focusing on blacks were also listed—*Manchild in the Promised Land* and *In White America.*

CONCLUSIONS AND RECOMMENDATIONS

Conclusions reached in our study regarding teen-age reading interests and curriculum materials are as follows:

1. Students are interested in current events. This is evidenced by the addition to the 1960 study of *Newsweek* (number 4 in preference) and *U.S. News and World Report* (in addition to *Time,* which was in second place). The students indicated on the questionnaire that they had read of Nixon's trip to China, of pollution and the environment, and of the political candidates for president. If the class had access to an attractive magazine (perhaps put out for classroom use for various subjects), they could work current events into their classes, particularly in English, social studies, science, and the humanities.

2. Classes could include units, perhaps one each semester, that are worked up by the students utilizing contemporary magazines. The class could be divided into groups of four or five and each group could be assigned a specific magazine and a specific subject upon which to report. Records could be kept to see that students get exposed to as many different magazines as possible. Variations could include student-selected topics and enough interest could be generated in a certain subject to investigate what the community they live in is doing regarding a specific subject. Many exciting activities could be pursued using contemporary magazines.

4. New areas of contemporary thought could be investigated via new magazines. The new women's lib magazine *Ms.* could be the subject of a unit on the place of women in the past, the present, and the future.

5. Pictures obviously appeal to teen-agers, because the magazine listed by almost one third of the group was *Life*. Yet most curriculum materials do not rely on pictorial layouts. Television and movie films in combination with popular magazines should provide some insight into what interests teen-agers.

6. Perhaps textbook publishers could learn from the popular magazine and emulate the format of the magazine. *Time-Life* booklets are generally highly successful with teen-agers. For example, science could get rid of its bulky textbook and provide eight or ten attractively designed books with a maximum number of pages. Each booklet could contain pictorial lay-outs and Op Art covers.

    Note: English classes have been doing this for years with a gratifying return. English teachers use inexpensive paperbacks. The fact that they deteriorate more rapidly can be advantageous because it forces a more frequent evaluation of course content.

7. Social studies curriculum designers could use *National Geographic* as a model for some of its subjects—one sixth of the sixty-six teen-agers polled listed *National Geographic* as one of its magazine selections.

8. It might prove valuable to capitalize on the diverse interests of boys and girls. The girls in the class could present material from the magazines listed most frequently by girls: *Seventeen, Co-ed, Ingenue, Glamor, Vogue, Women's Day, Good Housekeeping, McCall's, Ebony*, and *Ladies Home Journal*. Boys could in turn present their magazines: *Popular Mechanics, Popular Science, Hot Rod, Cycle World, Field and Stream, Sports Illustrated*, and *Outdoor Life*. In this way both groups could re-examine their one-sex-oriented magazines in a new, critical light. This sharing could enlighten both groups. Exercises could ensue in which girls used traditionally male magazines to report from. The boys could critically assess their efforts. Boys, in turn, could report from magazines traditionally favored by girls and could be scrutinized by the girls.

    Note: The magazines in item 8 are all taken from the questionnaire. In no case did a girl mention a magazine preferred by boys, and likewise, no boy listed a magazine preferred by girls.

Because the Kirkland–Clowers–Wood study was not to be applied to a religious setting, the conclusions reached are somewhat different from the Rice–Sellers survey. They had to think in terms of applying the magazine format to a format to convey messages of the Protestant faith. We, having no such restriction, were able to utilize the popular magazines directly in classroom work. Of course, we also suggested using the contemporary magazines as a model from which to design curriculum materials as suggested in the Rice–Sellers survey.

The differences in the magazine and book selections in our study and the Rice–Sellers Study are due in part to a growing sophistication among teen-agers. Able to vote for the first time in a presidential election at eighteen places a responsibility upon them which the majority of teen-agers will take seriously. Now assuming some heretofore "adult" responsibilities and privileges, these teen-agers are becoming more concerned with the world around them. Their higher-quality selection of magazines reflects this.

Games, Games, Games—and Reading Class*

Linda Jones

There is no doubt that motivation is a key factor in learning. In this article Linda Jones points out some of the basic uses of games that can be used with existing materials such as newspapers, magazines, and commercial materials. These games are designed to improve reading vocabulary and comprehension. The games can be used in middle school and secondary school classes.

1. What are the three judicious uses of games that add interest and enthusiasm to the reading program?

2. Locate one or more of the books suggested and prepare several games for use in your methods class or a class in the schools.

3. Prepare the comprehension quiz game and play it in class.

4. Develop the materials and play the news comprehension game.

5. Select current magazine articles on a variety of topics, prepare one or more versions of the games, and play them in class.

6. Design an action study to evaluate the effects of these games on interest, comprehension, and so forth.

If the motivation and attitude of the learner is an important factor in learning, if what is learned in pleasure is remembered, and because students of all ages seem to enjoy games and game-type activities, it behooves reading teachers to incorporate a game approach to the teaching of reading, especially "remedial" reading.

In Adams County School District No. 12, Northglenn, a suburb of Denver, Colorado, junior high teachers working in the Title I Reading Program have assembled, over a period of several years, a useful collection of

---

* FROM the *Journal of Reading*, 15 (October 1971), pp. 41–46, reprinted with permission of Linda Jones and the International Reading Association.

commercial and teacher-constructed games designed to capture the interest of even the most reluctant secondary student. The teachers have discovered that the judicious use of games for (1) reinforcement of skills, (2) optional activities for students who finish assignments early, and (3) as rewards in reading contracts has added interest and enthusiasm to the reading program. By means of these games and game-type activities, reading and enjoyment become associated, with a concomitant increase in reading ability and interest in reading. The games themselves may not produce significant differences in learning, but they do generate enthusiasm and a positive attitude, which are essential to growth in reading.

COMMERCIAL GAMES

One of the easiest ways to incorporate games into the reading program is to begin by acquiring a collection of commercial games, such as those suggested below. Several shelves filled with games, including an assortment of attractive and appealing department-store word games which do not remind students of school, will add to any reading laboratory.

In addition, teachers and students get ideas on how to construct or adapt games from the principles and patterns of commercial games. For example, teachers may construct word rummy or Bingo games based on commercial prototypes. One teacher, who had used Dolch's Word Sounding Game, an educational game based on Bingo, creates vocabulary games using the Bingo idea. Her students use a piece of paper to make a Bingo card with twenty-five spaces. From a large group of words being studied in class, each student chooses twenty-five words and randomly writes one in each of the spaces. The teacher or student leader gives a definition and students locate the word, which corresponds to the definition, on their "cards." Students also like to invent original games or adapt existing games to their particular interests. A very popular game with ninth-grade students is Word Power. The students enjoyed this game so much that they not only added many new words and cards to the original game but also created a new version of the game for seventh-grade students.

GAMES FOR GRADE LEVELS 7–8, READING LEVELS 2–5. The following games, most of which aid in the teaching of phonics, are easy enough for students who have serious difficulties in reading. Numbers in parentheses refer to manufacturers listed at end of this article.

Group Word Teaching Game. 220 basic sight words. Played like Bingo. (3)

Phonetic Quizmo. Auditory discrimination of individual letters and groups of letters. Played like Bingo. (8)

Uno, A Phonics Game. Sets of flash cards which progress in difficulty. (5)

Build It. 1, 2, 3, 4. Phonetic games. Four different decks of cards. (11)

Take. Sound-matching card game. Players take tricks by pairing the sounds of beginning, middle, or ending of words. (3)

Phonic Rummy. A, B, C, D. Collecting three-of-a-kind sounds. Four boxes of cards with two decks per box. Each deck stresses different sounds. (5)

Doghouse. Phonic combinations. Students are given an envelope of consonants to combine with phonic families printed on cards. (5)

Group Sounding Game. Complete phonics course. Thirteen steps in sounding are used to play this Bingo-type listening game. (3)

Affixo. Word-building card game using roots, prefixes, and suffixes. (11)

The Syllable Game. Sight syllable solitaire. Contains three decks of cards progressing in difficulty. (3)

Educational Password. Synonym game. Differs from regular Password in that the vocabulary is controlled and clue words are given. (8)

Play 'n Talk. Phonics and vocabulary building. Uses game board, spinners, and box of letters. (9)

Spe-lingo. Word rummy. Each player competes for high score by composing words from letters dealt him. Triple letter combination cards are furnished for optional use. For more challenging competition, play may be restricted to words of not less than five letters. (4)

Phonoflip. Phonics, word structure, and vocabulary. Word cards are grouped in three colors for levels of difficulty. (12)

GAMES FOR GRADE LEVELS 7–10, READING LEVELS 5–9. Most of the following games may be played by students of differing abilities, since the variable of game-difficulty is a function of the sophistication and vocabulary brought to the games by the players themselves, rather than a function of the structural characteristics of the game; crossword games, for example, share a common structure, but may vary widely as to sophistication of content.

Password. From synonym game on television. Several volumes of the game provide more difficult words. (8)

Swap. Vocabulary game. Utilizes master cards with key words, synonyms, and antonyms. (16)

Crossword Cubes. A word-forming game using fourteen cubes which are tossed from a cup. Players compete for high score while forming words in crossword fashion, using a timer. (13)

Spill and Spell. Fifteen-cube crossword game with timer. (9)

Royalty. Cards with letters for word building. (7)

Scrabble for Juniors, Scrabble, and RSVP. Word-building crossword games. (13)

Perquackey. Word-building crossword game using dice with letters and an hourglass timer. Each player throws the dice, and then moves them to form as many words as possible. This game, if played using the rule book and complicated scoring procedures, can be quite challenging for older students. (6)

4 CYTE (Foresight). More difficult word game. Two players, using a limited number of letters, compete, each trying to out-score his opponent by making three to six letter words in a Word Square. (8)

Foil. Using a card tray, cards, and timer, the object of the game is to arrange letter cards to form words, then scramble each of the words so that opponents will not be able to unscramble them in the allotted time. (18)

Tuf'abet. Vocabulary and spelling. A competitive game based on the construction of interlocking words similar to those formed in a crossword puzzle. Instead of the play rotating from one player to the next, all of the students form words simultaneously. The use of three timers (Tuf-3 minutes, Tuffer-2 minutes, Tuffest-1 minute) makes it a fast game requiring continuous effort and concentration. (1)

Probe. Challenging, provocative game of words. Using card trays and cards, players conceal secret words, which their opponents try to guess. Since simple words are often hard to guess, it is not necessary to hide obscure words. (9)

Word Power. Word-definition game. Three different decks of cards list words ranging from everyday usage to infrequent usage. The object is to "publish books" by matching synonyms and antonyms that appear on the word cards. The game has its own dictionary. (1)

RESOURCE BOOKS FOR TEACHERS. There are two types of resource books which may be used in teacher-planned games. The first type consists of word game books for students and the second type might be called "how-to-do-it" books for teachers.

In the first category are included numerous books from Scholastic Book Services (14), ranging in difficulty from fifth to tenth grade vocabulary levels: *Arrow Book of Crossword Puzzles, Arrow Book of Word Games, Provocative Puzzler, Can You Solve It, Tab Crossword Puzzles, Crosswords for Teen-agers, Word Games and Puzzles, Fun with Puzzles, X-Word Fun, All-American Crosswords, Campus Crossword Puzzles, Word-A-Day* and the Scope/Skills books, *Across and Down* and *Word Puzzles and Mysteries.*

The word games in these books may be used in a variety of ways to build verbal skills. For example, transparencies or multiple copies of games similar to "Word Hunt in a Square" or "Odd Starts" and "Congested Centers" from *Word Games and Puzzles* (14) may be used in flexible grouping situations. In other words, students may work individually, in teams, or in small groups on this type of activity

Several teachers have made activity packets using individual games from these books combined with other short reading activities. Each game, word power exercise, or mini-mystery from *Scope Magazine,* and others like it, is glued on a separate sheet of colored construction paper. About ten activities make a packet. Students may work on the activities in the packet when other assignments are completed. A large envelope tacked on the bulletin board may be used to collect papers when students complete a packet. The packets should be constructed on varying levels of difficulty.

Another group of books for secondary students in the word games category is *Word Games, Book I,* third to fifth grade reading level, *Word Games, Book II,* sixth to eighth grade reading level, and *Word Games, Book III,* tenth to twelfth grade reading level (19). Each book consists of about fifty games, similar to the type found in Scholastic's *Word Games and Puzzles* mentioned previously.

The second group, or how-to-do-it books for teachers, are few in number. *Spice* (2), a language arts activity book for the elementary school, has several games in the back for grades 7–8. *Language Games, Listening Games,* and *Reading Games* (17), all for grades k–8, will give the teacher many ideas. *Reading Games* contains games to develop a wide range of skills, including vocabulary, dictionary, syllabication, comprehension, etc. After playing some of the games in this book, students often devise their own adaptations or originate completely new games.

IMPROVISED COMPREHENSION AND VOCABULARY GAMES

A comprehension quiz game may be made out of any material in the reading room. For example, *Help Yourself to Improve Your Reading* (10), An American Album kit (15), or any other kits or multi-level books which have comprehension questions may be used. Divide the class into groups or two teams and give them the multi-level reading assignments; individual students might want to be responsible for different cards or stories. A student leads the game by choosing a question from one participant's reading assignment; after the participant answers the question, the leader moves to the opposing team and the same procedure is repeated. To make it even more interesting, use various methods of keeping score, which might include the following:

1. Connect the dots to make a square on the board.
2. Play tic-tac-toe. Each team would be "O" or "X."
3. Baseball: Divide the room into teams and let each team choose a name. When a question is answered correctly, the team at bat advances a base, just as in regular baseball.
4. Football: Divide the class into teams and draw the yard-lines on the board. The ball is moved ten yards for each correct answer. The first team to reach the opponent's goal line has made a touch-down and receives six points.

NEWS COMPREHENSION GAME. For several weeks, read the newspaper and cut out short, interesting articles; students may bring articles too. Glue each article on a sheet of paper. Underneath the article, write and number a question pertinent to understanding the article. When twenty-five articles with questions have been collected, the game is ready to be played.

Divide the class into two teams, boys against girls or whatever students decide. Divide the articles in two groups and seat the students in two circles. Let each circle have half the articles for half the period. Then trade the articles. Students number a blank piece of paper for recording answers. Each paper is scored, and individual scores are added to get a team score. The team with the most correct answers wins.

HOMONYM, SYNONYM, AND ANTONYM CONCENTRATION GAMES.
After synonyms (or homonyms or antonyms) have been presented, print
each word on a piece of construction paper about the size of a playing card.
A set or game might be comprised of from fifteen to forty pairs of synonyms,
depending on the students. Two to four students may play with each set.
The "cards" are shuffled and each card is placed face down on a table. Each
student turns two cards over. He keeps the cards if he locates the pair of
synonyms, but he replaces them face down in the same position if he
doesn't, as in the game Concentration. It is helpful to have the contents of
each game, or set of cards, typed on a guide sheet so that students may
consult the list to see if they have chosen the two words that go together.

MAGAZINE COMPREHENSION GAMES. If magazines are not available
to cut up, read articles that appeal to students and write questions for them.
For instance, use six issues of *Life* and devise fifty questions. Duplicate
them with enough space for the answer. Either give one group of students
the period to work on the questions, or, if two copies of each magazine are
available, divide the class into two teams racing against the clock. The questions may also be stapled to the outside of the magazine.

Variations might include the following:

1. Cut the articles out and write the questions on the article.
2. Cut articles into sections, and place the sections in envelopes, using a
   separate envelope for each article. Have the students put the sections
   of each article into proper sequence.
3. Cut three or four different articles from the same newspaper or magazine. Cut them into sections, writing an identifying number or letter
   on the back sections of each and put them into an envelope. Make up
   several envelopes. The students place the headlines side by side and
   arrange the paragraphs under the appropriate headline.
4. Read an article or paragraph aloud to the students and ask a question
   over what was read. Then, let each student find part of a magazine
   article to read aloud; following the reading, he asks the class a question
   over his paragraph. After ten paragraphs have been read and ten questions answered, score the papers. Students enjoy inventing questions
   and "testing" classmates.
5. Cut off the headlines from a large number of short articles and place
   both the headlines and articles in an envelope. Students quickly skim
   to match the articles and the headlines. Some students like to time
   themselves with a stopwatch.
6. Ask the students to sort and identify articles in an envelope according
   to (a) how much interest the articles would hold for a housewife,
   athlete, mechanic, etc., (b) according to the particular section of newspaper to which it belongs, e.g., sports, editorials, etc., or (c) some content classification such as nature, foreign affairs, etc.

GAME MANUFACTURERS

1. Avalon-Hill Company, 4517 Harford Road, Baltimore, Maryland, 21214.
2. Educational Service, Inc., P.O. Box 219, Stevensville, Michigan, 49127.
3. Garrard Press, 1607 N. Market, Champaign, Illinois, 61820.
4. Holt, Rinehart, and Winston, 383 Madison Avenue, New York, New York, 10017.
5. Kenworthy, Box 3031, Buffalo, New York, 14205.
6. Lakeside Toys, 4400 W. 78th Street, Minneapolis, Minnesota, 55435.
7. S. J. Miller Co., Inc., Box 130, Coney Island Station, Brooklyn, New York, 11224.
8. Milton-Bradley Company, 43 Cross Street, Springfield, Massachusetts, 01103.
9. Parker & Sons Publishing Co., 241 E. Fourth Street, Los Angeles, California, 90013.
10. Reader's Digest Services, Inc., Educational Division, Pleasantville, New York, 10570.
11. Remedial Education Press, Kingsbury Center, 2138 Bancroft Place N.W., Washington, D.C., 20008.
12. Rocky Mountain Reading Clinic, P.O. Box 10071, Denver, Colorado, 80210.
13. Selchow & Righter Company, 200 Fifth Avenue, New York, New York, 10010.
14. Scholastic Book Services, 904 Sylvan Avenue, Englewood Cliffs, N.J., 07632.
15. Science Research Associates, Inc., 259 East Erie Street, Chicago, Illinois, 60611.
16. Steck-Vaughn Company, P.O. Box 2028, Austin, Texas, 78767.
17. Teachers Publishing Corporation, 23 Leroy Avenue, Darien, Connecticut, 06820.
18. 3M Business Press, 3M Center, St. Paul, Minnesota, 51101.
19. Word Games, P.O. Box 305, Healdsburg, California, 95448.

"SURF'S UP"—AND SO IS READING INTEREST*

Sister William Paul, O.P.

Can reading compete with surfing? In this article Sister William Paul explains how the English Department of her school, located near a good surfing area, convinced students that "reading is as important as surfing—and in its own way, just as exciting."

---

* FROM English Journal, 55 (January 1966), pp. 93, 94, reprinted with permission of the National Council of Teachers of English and Sister William Paul, O.P.

1. What problems faced the teachers in the English Department of this high school?

2. What steps did they take to solve these problems?

3. Why, in your opinion, was the "Reading in Depth" program successful? How might you adapt the program to your teaching situation?

It is a wonderful experience to teach in a high school located near the Atlantic Ocean, especially when the local beach happens to be one of the best surfing areas along the coast. The only difficulty is that frequently the teacher is in competition with six-foot waves! The problem that confronted us in the English Department was just that: how does one convince students who are needlessly retarded readers that reading is as important as surfing—and, in its own way, just as exciting.

Last September, when we surveyed the reading situation in our school, we found that approximately one-fourth of the student body was below grade. As a beginning step, four basic reading classes were included in the daily curriculum. Interested and enthusiastic teachers held several impromptu meetings to select appropriate remedial reading material. It was decided that they would begin by using the Globe series of graded readers, the SRA diagnostic kits and the *Reader's Digest* selections. Strong emphasis was to be placed on individualized reading. Standardized tests were to be used to check student progress throughout the year.

Slowly the groundwork was laid. A Language Arts Assembly was held in late September. The theme of the convocation was "Read Today—for a Better Tomorrow." Junior and senior students' Chamber Drama presentations of *John Brown's Body* and *Our Town* were enthusiastically received by the entire student body. The highlight of the assembly was the inauguration of a "Reading in Depth" program for all students who wished to participate. In essence this meant that anyone interested would meet once a month at night to discuss the book of his choice. (This plan of allowing students to choose the book for discussion was modified as the year went along. A better plan replaced it: to have the teacher present three or four choices and ask the students to select one.) Afterwards refreshments were to be served.

The response to the "Reading in Depth" series was astonishing. Seventy-nine teen-agers in Grades 9–12 agreed to come back to school at night to discuss books which interested them. The meetings were usually held from 7:00–8:00 p.m. Students were divided into three groups: freshmen in one; sophomores in another; and juniors and seniors in a joint session. Some of the topics covered in the junior-senior division were as follows: Hemingway's use of irony in his sketch, "On the Quai at Smyrna"; the satire in George Orwell's *Animal Farm;* Hardy's philosophy of determinism as evidenced in *The Return of the Native*. At the January meeting the choral director explained impressionism in the works of Debussy and Ravel; then students were introduced to the paintings of the French Impressionists.

This session demonstrated how music and art are related to literary impressionism. At another session, the symbolism in Golding's *Lord of the Flies* was studied and compared with Conrad's use of symbolism in *Heart of Darkness*.

Sophomore selections included Mark Twain's *Adventures of Huckleberry Finn*, Homer's *Iliad*, Stephen Crane's *The Red Badge of Courage*, Nathaniel Hawthorne's *Scarlet Letter*, George Eliot's *Silas Marner*, and John Steinbeck's *The Pearl*. Freshmen completed the study of Jules Verne's *Journey to the Center of the Earth*, Jack London's *Call of the Wild*, Harper Lee's *To Kill a Mockingbird*, and others.

Interest in the "Reading in Depth" program grew. Allusions were made in English classes to material which had been discussed at the evening sessions. Our daily paper, *The News Tribune*, heard of the project and printed a full page story, giving a detailed description of the venture. In early spring one senior girl was awarded first prize in *The News Tribune*'s Liberal Arts Contest, open to high school and junior college students and judged by author Philip Wylie, for her essay on the problem of evil in *Lord of the Flies*. The idea for her essay grew out of the February session, at which time Golding's book was discussed. In all, the program was judged to be so effective that a similar plan was introduced in the junior high school.

The English teachers who volunteered their time to the "Reading in Depth" program experienced moments of deep satisfaction when students, who formerly had never enjoyed reading, stopped to say how much they were benefiting from the series. And several senior students, who will be attending nearby Indian River Junior College in the fall, asked if they could be allowed to return in September for another year's session of "Reading in Depth."

At the Honors Convocation, as a natural outgrowth of their participation in the reading program, students enacted scenes from three novels they had studied during the year: freshmen presented excerpts from *To Kill a Mockingbird*; sophomores portrayed sections from *The Pearl*; juniors depicted significant passages of *Animal Farm*. At this assembly certificates were awarded to those who had participated in the "Reading in Depth" series. Then a summer reading program was introduced, and the students learned that those involved in the summer program would receive recognition at the September Arts Assembly.

Encouraged by the enthusiastic response to this year's reading program, the English department has future plans to include not only English teachers, but also those teaching in other content fields. A Developmental Program, which will include remedial and individualized reading, will be offered to all students during seventh period. In the face of such wholehearted cooperation from students, faculty, and community, the teacher trying to interest students in reading no longer has to cast a reproachful eye at the surf board jutting out of the junior boy's car window. After all, the "surf's up"—but so is reading interest!

Helping Disadvantaged and Reluctant Readers

Introduction

There is today no reason for students in middle and secondary schools not knowing how to read; however, many forces militate against students learning how to read. These are the forces of apathy, ignorance, incompetence, and improper support of the schools.

Students Can Be Taught to Read. *We have the materials and the methods, as will be shown in the article by Hafner. Now only the forces previously mentioned stand between the student and literacy. No longer can one find reasons for students not becoming literate, only excuses. For example, a federal budget reflecting more interest in armament expenditure than in education is a powerful force against education and sur-*

vival of real democracy; armament expenditure in the name of "preserving democracy"—while basic issues are neglected—is a poor excuse.

Stine shows how to teach secondary content to low reading achievers in the secondary schools; the ideas can be adapted for use in middle schools.

Rist's excellent study demonstrates that his prescription for ailing reading programs in urban black schools is effective. He also clarifies the role of deprivation and expectancy theories in the development of reading programs.

Smith suggests that paying attention to curriculum is not only wise and prudent but necessary. He discusses what happened in adult basic education programs that looked carefully at curriculum. The key practices exemplifying the successful ABE programs can be adapted in order to improve middle and secondary school reading programs.

Teaching the Nonreader to Read[*]

Lawrence E. Hafner

The author explores several reasons that some students cannot read, including the existence of a number of misplaced emphases in many school systems. Students' reading needs are discovered through careful diagnosis. When students have been stumbling around and failing to learn to read it is time to use sure-fire methods. Four such methods are discussed in the article: the *Language Experience Approach*, which is good for building initial interest and confidence; the *Sound Reading Program*, which is a superior, programmed linguistic approach to teaching the nonreader and poor reader; the *Acoustifone RAP Series*, which begins at the second reading level; and *Develop-*

ing Sound Reading Skills, which begins at the fourth level. Finally, the author presents several techniques for "nailing down" high resistance words so that they can be recognized instantly.

1. Whose needs are uppermost?
2. How can capacity be diagnosed?
3. How can reading achievement and needs be ascertained?
4. What are the advantages of a *Language Experience Approach*?
5. What are the advantages of the *Sound Reading Program*? of the *RAP Series*?
6. How do you "nail down" words?

---

[*] Written especially for this volume.

Whose Needs Are Uppermost?

The Teacher's?

Observation and experiment yield decisive proof that many teachers mismanage their classes in a number of ways. One way is typified by the tenth-grade teacher who orders thirty biology texts of college-level readability for his tenth-grade biology class, whose average reading grade placement is 9.1. Several errors have been committed by this teacher: (1) he does not allow for a different point of view in text materials when he uses one text, (2) the textbook is much too difficult for his students, (3) if he is aware of the discrepancies and is not doing anything about them, he is morally culpable, and (4) if he is not aware of the basic principle of matching students to materials they can read, he is abysmally ignorant. Do we just not rock the boat and, consequently, meet the teacher's need to be ignorant or mean, or do we meet somebody else's need?

Joseph's?

Poor Joseph! He had so many strikes against him, and the teachers weren't content to throw him a curve; they "beaned" him. Joseph was sixteen years old, lived in an orphanage, went to public school, was sent to a reading class for help. On a reading vocabulary test he got items 1–4 right and also items 6–9. What happened on item 5? The word was *father*. He selected *paper* as the synonym instead of selecting the word *man*.

Joseph's comprehension grade placement was 4.2. He could understand a brief story on Salmon:

Salmon are fish that live in the ocean. Once every year they leave the ocean and travel up a river to lay their eggs. Summer is a good time to _____ salmon in the river because thousands of them go up the _____ then.

On a passage typical of the kind he was required to *try* to read in his regular classes in school he failed miserably. The passage in question reads:

No matter what the present success in straightening out ___A___ and harmonizing conflicts, it is certain that difficulties will recur in the future. . . .

A. extremes
B. sanctions
C. hair
D. problems

Jim's?

Jim is thirteen years old, black, not stupid, a good basketball player. I was asked to use him to demonstrate the use of the Informal Reading Inventory. (His teachers said he could read a little. When a boy is thirteen and his teachers don't know he can't even read at the first grade level, it is pretty sad.) I gave him a passage of 1.1 readability level. He failed it in front of all those teachers. What to do?

On the spot we developed a story about his basketball prowess. We couched it in the form of a letter to his favorite uncle. We went over it until he could read it, and then we nailed down individual words. He was elated and the teachers were nonplussed. Can you imagine a school so backward that the reading teachers hadn't even tried a Language Experience Approach with the lad! Then we put him into the *Sound Reading Program* (E. H. Smith, et al., 7), and he is doing fine.

Herman's?

Here is another one that is hard to believe. Herman is sixteen, black, good-looking, diffident, intelligent, and a member of the football team. On the *Hafner Quick Reading Test* he scored at the first grade level, 18, pronouncing *catch* as /church/, *could* as /call/, *enough* as /again/, *lady* as /hippy/, and *rather* as /right/. Would he like to improve his reading? Yes! We worked through several lessons of Book I of the *Sound Reading Program*, and then he did several on his own. He is making rapid strides in reading now and is able to participate in previously forbidden activities such as reading and singing songs during music period and reading simple stories. He smiles more now. As he progresses through the reading program his ability will increase and he will be reading more and more difficult stories.

The principal's?

All too typical of principals is the ex-coach who couldn't keep the local businessmen happy because he had two losing seasons in a row. He didn't seem to know much about football anymore, so they fired him. He knew a lot less about being an educational leader, so they hired him to be the principal. (And man is purported to be a rational being? No way, baby!) Well, this coach would not set the high jump bar at 6 feet for Joseph and Jim when the best they had ever jumped was 5 feet, 2 inches, but he saw nothing wrong with Mr. Jones' order for thirty grade 10 (actually college level) texts for the class when the reading achievement level ranged from 1.0 to 15.2 in the class, with a median reading level of 9.0.

How Do We Meet the Students' Needs?

Make a Careful, Intelligent Diagnosis

The teacher who does not ascertain a student's strengths and weaknesses of capacity and reading achievement is not able to design a reading program to meet the student's needs. Three basic pieces of information useful to the teacher in planning a program are (1) the student's *capacity to learn*, (2) his *reading instruction level*, and (3) his *knowledge of phonemic options*.

DETERMINING CAPACITY LEVEL. I like to administer one or two verbal comprehension tests, such as a general information test and a vocabulary test, convert the scores to grade placement scores, and average them to determine the capacity level. If you have a third score, say from a listening test, take the median of the three scores as the capacity level. You expect a person eventually to achieve at his capacity level after receiving firstclass reading instruction. Closing the gap between present reading achievement and his capacity level may take a few months or a few years, depending upon such factors as how big the gap is and the quality and quantity of instruction.

If you know how to administer and interpret the WISC (Wechsler Intelligence Scale for Children) or the WAIS (Wechsler Adult Intelligence Scale), I suggest you give your students the General Information, Arithmetic Reasoning, Vocabulary, and Block Design subtests and then utilize the Hafner Reading Grade Level Capacity Formula to determine the capacity or expectancy level. This will give you a more accurate estimate of the student's capacity.

$$H.R.G.L.C. = \frac{2I + 2A + .6V + .6BD}{6} + X$$

where scaled scores of the WISC or WAIS are used.

Value of X for a given chronological age (CA) follows:

CA	X	CA	X	CA	X	CA	X	CA	X
9–9	−3.2	11–0	−2.0	12–0	−1.0	13–0	0.0	14–0 to 14–5	0.6
9–10 & 9–11	−3.1	11–1	−1.9	12–1	−0.9	13–1	0.0	14–6 to 14–11	0.7
10–0	−3.0	11–2	−1.8	12–2	−0.8	13–2	0.1	15 and above	0.8
10–1	−2.9	11–3	−1.7	12–3	−0.7	13–3	0.1		
10–2	−2.8	11–4	−1.6	12–4	−0.6	13–4	0.2		
10–3	−2.7	11–5	−1.5	12–5	−0.5	13–5	0.2		
10–4	−2.6	11–6	−1.5	12–6	−0.5	13–6	0.3		
10–5 & 10–6	−2.5	11–7	−1.4	12–7	−0.4	13–7	0.3		
10–7	−2.4	11–8	−1.3	12–8	−0.3	13–8	0.4		
10–8	−2.3	11–9	−1.2	12–9	−0.2	13–9	0.4		
10–9	−2.2	11–10	−1.1	12–10	−0.1	13–10	0.5		
10–10 & 10–11	−2.1	11–11	−1.1	12–11	−0.1	13–11	0.5		

Following are the chronological age, Wechsler Scaled Scores, and the computed Hafner Reading Grade Level Capacity. Below these data are the calculations for the data for Joe and Maria.

Maria has the mental capacity to read at 8.6 grade level.

An excellent group test for determining the capacity level is the *Durrell Listening–Reading Series: Listening* test.* Capacity for learning to read is measured by the vocabulary listening test and the sentence listening test.

---

* Donald T. Durrell and Mary T. Hayes (New York: Harcourt Brace Jovanovich, Inc., 1968–1970). Grade levels: Primary, Intermediate (grades 3.5–6) and Advanced (grades 7–9).

Wechsler Scaled Scores

	CA	I	A	V	BD	H.R.G.L.C.
Joe	10–0	8	8	9	12	4.43
Ed	10–0	9	10	10	13	5.63
Maria	10–0	14	13	15	11	8.60
Nan	12–4	7	5	8	10	5.20
Fred	12–4	10	12	9	8	8.43
Kim	12–4	16	14	13	13	12.00
Sam	16–0	6	4	7	9	5.73
Sarah	16–0	11	9	12	10	9.67
George	16–0	18	16	19	16	14.10

Calculations:

$$\text{H.R.G.L.C.} = \frac{2I + 2A + .6V + .6BD}{6} + X$$

Joe:

$$\text{H.R.G.L.C.} = \frac{2(8) + 2(8) + .6(9) + .6(12)}{6} + (-3.0)$$

$$= \frac{16 + 16 + 5.4 + 7.2}{6} - 3.0$$

$$= 7.43 - 3.0$$

$$= 4.43$$

Joe has the mental ability to read at 4.43 grade level.

Maria:

$$\text{H.R.G.L.C.} = \frac{2(14) + 2(13) + .6(15) + .6(11).}{6} + (-3.0)$$

$$= 8.6$$

The rationale for the test appears to be quite sound. Also, the manual lists suggested methods for helping low achieving readers.

DETERMINING READING ACHIEVEMENT LEVEL. If you want a very quick, fairly accurate estimate of a person's reading level, administer the *Hafner Quick Reading Test*. (See Appendix A at the end of this article.) Use in the Florida State University Reading Clinic and in several school situations shows it to give results comparable to the *Slosson Oral Reading Test* (6), the *Gates–McGinitie Reading Test* (3), and the informal reading inventory—and much more rapidly. If you want to do further testing with an informal reading inventory, the *Hafner Quick Reading Test* provides results that can be used to determine where to begin testing with the IRI (5).

The IRI is a series of short, graded reading passages for which literal comprehension and interpretation questions are developed. The student reads the passage and then answers the questions which are asked by the examiner. He then reads the same passage aloud as the examiner records any errors that he makes.

At the instructional level the oral reading criterion should vary from 84 per cent correct for level 1 to 95 per cent correct for level 3 and above. The comprehension criterion for the instructional level is 75 per cent. Let's look at the results of testing Sue, a seventh-grade student. At what level can she be instructed in reading?

	PERCENTAGE CORRECT	
INVENTORY LEVEL	PRONUNCIATION	COMPREHENSION
4.8	97	85
5.3	95	77
5.8	93	63
6.3	87	55
6.8	80	40

Yes, Sue can be instructed at the 5.3 level.

To determine Sue's *capacity* level using the IRI, read the 7.3 level to her and ask her the questions. If she fails to meet the 75 per cent comprehension criterion, drop to the 6.8 level. If she had missed the criterion rather badly, you might have dropped to the 6.3 level. If she passes at the 7.3 level, continue upward until the criterion is reached.

If you develop an IRI, be sure to determine the readability of the materials you use in the inventory; you cannot trust the publisher's estimate. Choosing 2.3, 2.8, and so on, was purely arbitrary, but the successive inventory levels should be about .5 grade level apart.

DETERMINING KNOWLEDGE OF PHONEMIC OPTIONS. There are two sides to this coin; we may also determine the knowledge of graphemic options. If a person looks at a grapheme such as (ough) and says it can be used to represent /ō/, /ȯ/, /au̇/, and /ü/ (as in *dough, thought, bough,* and *through*), he shows a sophisticated appreciation of *phonemic options* for a given grapheme. If he demonstrates his knowledge that /ā/ can be encoded in a number of ways including <ay>, <a-e>, <eigh>, <ai>, (as in *stay, name, weight,* and *train*), he shows good understanding of the *graphemic options* for a given phoneme.

The *Hafner Quick Phonics Test* (see Appendix B at the end of this article), is a phonemic option test in which a person gives the phonemic options for a representative group of graphemic elements. After administering the test, scoring it, and profiling the results, one can see which grapheme–phoneme relationships need to be developed.

OTHER CONSIDERATIONS. Students who have trouble in concentrating on academic tasks often do poorly on the *Digit Span Test;* this is a measure of auditory memory. You should teach to your students' strengths and try to remedy their weaknesses, if possible. If a student has visual modality strengths and auditory modality weaknesses—and this situation is quite common—avoid methods that rely heavily on auditory abilities.

Students with visual strengths and auditory weaknesses who speak a dialect other than standard English can be expected to profit from (1) a language experience approach or (2) a programmed linguistic method that features visual, contextual, and pictorial cues and written responses. (*The Sound Reading Program* by E. H. Smith et al. is illustrative of such an approach.) The latter is a better approach because it is self-instructional and more practical.

Teach the Students to Read

THE LANGUAGE EXPERIENCE APPROACH. The student who (1) is weak in auditory skills or (2) cannot identify with prosaic reading instruction materials generally responds well to the Language Experience Approach (LEA). In the LEA the teacher elicits from the student a sentence, a description, or a story about an experience which the student has had, whether a real experience or a vicarious one. Then the teacher either reads the story to him often enough so he can memorize it or he puts it on tape for the student to play. Then the teacher helps him to associate the spoken sentence with the written sentence, next the spoken phrases with the written phrases, and finally the spoken words with the written words.

When this approach to the LEA is used, the following steps can be used:

1. Establish rapport.
2. Student tells story and teacher records it.
3. Rehearse story so student can memorize it in sequence (may use a cassette tape).
4. Point to words as student "reads" them.
5. Make two charts of the story.
6. Cut one of the charts into sentences.
7. Scramble the order of the sentences and have student match sentences to story on the intact chart. Student reads each sentence of the chart.
8. Continue to scramble and rearrange sentences; read them.
9. Cut sentences into phrases; match phrases to intact phrases and read them. Reassemble phrases into sentences. Read the assembled sentences.
10. Continue to scramble and rearrange phrases.
11. Cut phrases into word cards; reassemble and read as necessary.
12. Read chart and segments of the chart and note problem words.
13. Make a card for each word taught; scramble order of cards and test words in isolation. Note problem words.

14. Teach problem words by procedures explained in the section of this article titled "Procedures for 'Nailing Down' Sight Words."

Other Types of Language Experience Approaches

PHOTOGRAPH ILLUSTRATED. Take pictures with Polaroid Land camera of, for example, various activities the student is engaged in at school or home. Let the student tell a story or give a caption for each picture, and put the pictures and stories (or captions) into a little book or display them in some other way agreeable to you and the student.

MAGAZINE ILLUSTRATED. Stories can be thought up on the basis of pictures or the story can be told and pictures sought in magazines. This procedure is especially good for minority groups if you get pictures of these groups from magazines which contain a lot of appropriate pictures.

CARTOON ILLUSTRATED. Use original cartoons by students and/or teachers. Get comic strips from the newspapers and develop different dialogues which are pasted over the original dialogue "balloons" or printed in white space above the cartoon frames. (Black out the original dialogue.)

STICK FIGURE ILLUSTRATED. Use either a sequence of pictures or a single picture. Much fun.

FURTHER SOURCES OF MATERIAL. Couplets, poems, interviews, known songs or poems, events or stories from other subject matter areas all provide a variety of interesting reading material. Once again, use cassette tapes for help on the audio and don't be afraid to make colorful illustrations.

The Sound Reading Program*

Developed by Smith, Rowell, and Hafner (7), the Sound Reading Program (SRP) is a programmed linguistic reading series designed to teach the very beginning stages of reading and carrying on through to the equivalent of the first part of level 4. It emphasizes the learning of phoneme options and grapheme options, career awareness, and character development while teaching comprehension skills. The decoding options are taught in books 1, 3, 5, and 7 through picture cues and written context which utilizes a programmed format. The picture cues are direct and specific rather than the vague cues of the basal readers.

Book 1, page 1, shows the picture of a bed with the word *bed* written under it. In the word box to the right is this visual array <_ed>. The student's task is to fill in the blank with the correct letter. On turning the page he sees the correct answer, <bed>. His next task is to fill in the next letter and in the third frame he fills in the letter *d*. This method teaches him to see and understand how the word is constructed from left to right. Simul-

* This material is based in part on my article titled "Word Identification in Beginning Reading," which was delivered at the Third Annual Clemson University Reading Conference.

taneously he learns (1) the pronunciation of the meaningful word, (2) the word's construction, and (3) the graphemic option <e> for the phoneme /e/. The student does not have to be bored by learning a number of words that rhyme with *bed* as he would in some other programmed "linguistic" materials. Rather, he next learns another graphemic option, <ea>, for the same phoneme /e/. What is the advantage of learning the graphemic options? The advantage is flexibility, so conducive to transfer. Furthermore, it permits him to read in a more interesting context. In like manner, he works through the decoding books until he has learned the most important options for all the easily discernible phonemes.

The *Sound Reading Program* features the "new phonics" or "phonemics," a more natural syntax, the principles of discovery learning, and a programmed format. (It should be noted that the discovery learning is guided. The students don't stumble around.) The program does present graphemic options as they occur in normal written prose; in this manner the trap of letter–sound constancy generally found in programmed linguistic reading programs is avoided.

Books 2, 4, 6, and 8 utilize related stories. Using a modified cloze procedure, selected words are deleted from the text—only a few per story—although the first letter of the word remains. The student then is encouraged to think, for he can use his understanding of the context plus the initial letter cue to determine which word belongs in the blank. The spelling will present little problem because the intact word will also be nearby in the context. To stimulate comprehension development further, there is a small group of questions at the end of each selection. Feedback is provided by having the correct answers on the next page.

The *Sound Reading Program* utilizes related stories in which the personal and social development of the chief characters is unfolded. For example, Ed, at first an irresponsible youth, changes to a responsible businessman who is quite concerned with social problems. The characters, with intermeshed careers, range in age from young children to adults.

Objectives tests which can be used for entry into and exit from the decoding books are provided in the teacher's manual. At each level there is a test of formally presented words and a test of graphemic options. These tests can be used for diagnosis, prescription, and placement.

The *SRP* has been tested by Briggs (1). Within a three-month period an experimental group of three second-grade classes made a statistically significant greater achievement in reading over a control group of comparable second-grade students. In the experimental groups the average gain for black and white students was about the same. Read-along tapes in cassettes are now available so that instruction is truly self-instructional and individualized.

Presently the *Sound Reading Program* is being used in elementary, middle, secondary, and adult reading programs throughout the country. It has been my privilege to visit many of these programs and to note the outstanding success of the *SRP* with students. I have never seen it fail to produce excellent results.

Reading Achievement Program (RAP)

Acoustifone's *RAP* series, developed by Stoyanoff (9), is written in adult style and is designed to meet the reading needs of middle school and secondary school students who are reading at the second, third, fourth, and fifth levels. The five interrelated types of exercises are (1) key words, (2) essay, (3) comprehension questions, (4) word clue test, and (5) key word test.

The five *key words* that reoccur in the essay are presented, pronounced, and used in sentences taken from the essay. A simple spelling test follows. Immediate feedback on correctness of response is given. Meaning and spelling are emphasized in this procedure.

Nonfiction *essays* geared to the interests of upper elementary and junior high students are presented next. Subjects treated come from the natural, social, and physical sciences. Pictorial and print frames utilizing the Acoustifone (AV equipment) are synchronized with the narration. The goal is to give the students a learning experience.

Comprehension questions then stimulate students to listen critically in order to develop correct answers. Immediate feedback is provided.

The *word clue test* utilizes advanced words from the essay which are different from the five key words. They are given in the same sentences used in the essay.

The *key word test* is a comprehension and spelling test highlighting the five key words, their pronunciation, and meaning. Questions that the student may have answered incorrectly in the first sequence are now answered correctly.

Each RAP unit is comprised of ten filmstrips, printed materials, and audio. The audio is available in a choice of open reel tapes, records, or cassettes. The materials are color coded for quick identification. These Acoustifone materials supposedly fit all standard film strip projector and audio playing devices.

Developing Sound Reading Skills: From Context to Concepts

The *Context to Concepts* program is a reading series designed to aid students to satisfy the performance objectives associated with word and context processing. Developed by Edwin H. Smith and C. Glennon Rowell, *Context to Concepts* is a semiprogrammed reading series based on the performance objectives for word and context processing. The program is designed for those who have attained a fourth-grade readability level or higher.

This program is comprised of eight books. In the odd-numbered books two behavioral objectives are implemented in each of the lessons. In these books, the skills needed to satisfy the objectives are further reviewed.

The lessons in the odd-numbered books are broken down into eight parts. At the end of each part, questions testing the attainment of easily determined objectives are asked and the student immediately checks his answers by going to the next page. He then does the part of the lesson that follows and repeats the process.

The even-numbered books are designed for recreational reading to reinforce skills and concepts taught in their preceding odd-numbered books. Through printing cues the reader is made aware of skills that are being reinforced.

Furthermore, *Context to Concepts* is designed *to teach career education* skills such as goal setting, decision making, and leadership techniques as the context in which the reading skills are learned. The program emphasizes the attitudes, social awareness, and social responsibilities associated with the work ethic.

Procedures for "Nailing Down" Sight Words

Some reading approaches, such as the Language Experience Approach and certain basal reader approaches, teach words as whole words. In these instances one would need some good means of teaching pupils to identify words. Some activities used to develop associations between the graphemes of a printed word and the corresponding phonemes in the spoken word are given by Hafner and Jolly (5):

ASSOCIATION OF THE PRINTED WORD WITH A PICTURE. Display to the student a card which contains a printed word and a picture depicting the word *ball*— [*ball* ⊘]. After several paired presentations of (ball) and ⊘ , just (ball) should elicit /ball/. Pavlov's conditioned response paradigm is the rationale for this activity.

LANGUAGE MASTER. Any time after the student is taught to read through a word from left to right the *Language Master* device, or other suitable card reader, can be helpful in identifying the word and can provide as many repeated practices as necessary in order to help the student to pronounce the word at sight. The *Language Master* card contains both the visual and the auditory stimuli. The student can see the printed form of the word as he hears it played on the device's speaker. A teacher may develop his own cards or use commercially prepared cards. Phrases and sentences can be reproduced.

VISUAL SCRUTINY. Instruction emphasizing very careful inspection of the component parts of words helps a student identify a word and remember it. The procedure involves the teacher writing a word on the chalkboard, calling attention to the visual parts of the words as he writes them, and noting the beginning, the middle, and the ending parts of the word. It is not necessary to sound out the parts separately. The teacher names the word, of course. Then another word is written on the board. Finally parts of the two words are written and the students asked to state to which word a designated part belongs. The various parts of the words are examined.

TRACING A WORD WHILE SAYING IT. Here I refer to an adaption of the Fernald VAKT (Visual–Auditory–Kinesthetic–Tactile) approach. Have the student trace over the word as he says it. When he thinks he can write the word without looking at a model of the word, let him try. Actually, he does not have to write the word out without looking at it if he can recognize it any time it is shown to him, but in remedial work, with tough cases the procedure of having the person write the word without looking at the model is used. In addition to the forced visual inspection involved in this procedure, there is the kinesthetic and tactile reinforcement that the procedure provides. The basic point is to get the student to associate the written word with the spoken word.

ILLUSTRATED RHYME PHRASES. Use illustrated rhyme phrases to teach concrete words and abstract (function) words, such as *of, in, the,* and so on: <clown of the town>, <fox in a box> are examples of rhymed phrases.

MAGNETIC LETTERS. It is fun to build words, phrases, and sentences with magnetic letters. Forming new words by changing letters around is also an interesting and educational experience. The imaginative teacher and student can use these letters to excellent advantage.

KNOWN TO THE UNKNOWN. A fine technique for learning words is to pair a known word containing a given phonic element with a new word containing the element and underlining the common element. Let's say the new word is *chop*. The words should be aligned vertically so the common elements are contiguous:

<u>ch</u>erry
<u>ch</u><u>op</u>
<u>top</u>

In sum, there are many young people who have not learned to read. Because good self-instructional materials that actually teach are now available, there is *no excuse* for having nonreaders or poor readers in the middle schools or the secondary schools.

REFERENCES

1. Briggs, Barbara. "An Investigation of the Effectiveness of a Programmed Graphemic Option Approach to Teaching Reading to Disadvantaged Children," *Journal of Reading Behavior,* 5(1) (Winter 1972–1973), 35–46.
2. Durrell, Donald T., and Mary T. Hayes. *Durrell Listening-Reading Series: Listening.* New York: Harcourt Brace Jovanovich, Inc., 1968–1970.
3. Gates, Arthur L., and Walter H. MacGinitie. *Gates-MacGinitie Reading Tests.* Survey E. grades 7–9; Survey F for Grades 10 through 12. New York: Teachers College Press.
4. Gwaltney, Wayne. "Reading in Upward Bound: An Evaluation of a Reading Improvement Course and an Analysis of Some Correlates of Reading

Achievement." Unpublished Doctoral Dissertation, University of Georgia, 1971, p. 64.

5. Hafner, Lawrence E., and Hayden B. Jolly. *Patterns of Teaching Reading in the Elementary School.* New York: Macmillan Publishing Co., Inc., 1972.

6. Slosson, Richard. *Slosson Oral Reading Test.* East Aurora, N.Y.: Slosson Educational Publications, 1963.

7. Smith, Edwin H., C. Glennon Rowell, and Lawrence E. Hafner. *The Sound Reading Program.* Books 1–8; read-along tapes in cassettes with books 1–4. Waco, Texas: Education Achievement Corporation, 1972.

8. Smith, Edwin H., and C. Glennon Rowell. *Developing Sound Reading Skills: From Context to Concepts.* Waco, Texas: Education Achievement Corporation, 1973.

9. Stoyanoff, Louis. *Reading Achievement Program* (RAP). Chatsworth, Calif.: Acoustifone Corporation, 1970.

Appendix A. Hafner Quick Reading Test*

READING
GRADE _____
SCHOOL
GRADE _____

NAME _____   DATE _____
    Last   First   Middle   SCHOOL _____

SCORE

1. catch	name	in	she	could	_____
2. thank	enough	anyone	happen	lady	_____
3. rather	weight	easily	alive	certain	_____
4. orchard	quiver	improve	range	trumpet	_____
5. warmth	mosquito	ravine	neglect	ceiling	_____
6. possess	scroll	monstrous	forfeit	orphanage	_____
7. geology	chivalry	plague	unique	monotonous	_____
8. occupant	mythology	calamity	juror	reinforce	_____
9. idolize	encore	judicial	stealthy	physique	_____
10. deteriorate	linear	anonymous	suave	feign	_____
11. indict	boudoir	glower	cuisine	meander	_____
12. quiescent	liaison	pedagogy	iridescent	myriad	_____
13. satiate	avarice	matrix	cynosure	hyperbole	_____

Total Score _____

$$\text{Reading Score} = \frac{\text{T. S.}}{5} + 1$$

= _____

To the Teacher

1. Have the student read horizontally across the page. Circle mispronounced words.
2. Do *not* cue or teach the student these words under any circumstances before, during, or after the test.

3. Coaching invalidates the test.
4. Stop when the student misses four in a row.
5. This can be a valuable tool if used correctly.
6. Don't guess at the pronunciations. Look them up in a dictionary. If a pupil accents the word incorrectly, count it incorrect!

Appendix B. Hafner Quick Phonics Test

Name _____
Grade _____

Directions: Have the subject read across the rows. Encode his response (according to the Merriam-Webster key) directly to the right of the stimulus. In tests CD and VC he may give the phonemic options in any order. Encourage, but don't push. Count as correct any acceptable phonemic options which he may give. After the test is complete, circle incorrect responses, count number correct and compute the percentages.

SCORE

LN: *Letter Name.* Directions: "Please tell me the names of these letters."

_____%   g   s   v   n   b   x   a   j   d   q   /10

CB: *Consonant Blend.* (or Digraph: Consonant Diphone)

_____%   tr   sm   fr   gl   br   cl   pl   st   cr   pr   /10
(alternate)   troo   smoo   froo   gloo   broo
                    cloo   ploo   stoo   croo   proo

CD: *Consonant Digraph.* (or Digraph: Consonant Uniphone)
(Phonemic Options)

_____%   kn   wh   sh   th   ph   gn   ch   /10
                        th   ch
                        ch

VC: *Vowel Clusters.* (or Vowel Phoneme Options)

Group one   ea   ou   ow   ai   oa   oo   /10
_____%   ea   ou   ow   oo

Group two   oy   ue   aw   oe   au   ie   oi   /10
_____%   ue   au   ie

Group three   ough   ough   eigh   ei   ew   ay   /10
_____%   ough   ough   eigh   ew

OC: *Other Combinations.*

_____%   wr   ___ing   or   ur   ar   ___tion   er   /10
                    ir   alt   cil

		LN	CB	CD	VC-1	VC-2	VC-3	OC
	100	....
	90	....
	80	....
	70	....
PUPIL	60	....
%	50	....
PROFILE	40	....

	LN	CB	CD	VC-1	VC-2	VC-3	OC
30	....
20	....
10	....
00	....

TENTH GRADE CONTENT—FOURTH GRADE READING LEVEL*

Doris E. Stine

Competence, adaptability, responsibility, and energy yield the acronym CARE. Teachers who care will do as Stine did and then students will have a fighting chance. What she has done is a prime example of exemplary teaching. Try it, adapt it, watch the transformations among your students.

1. What was the situation that the author faced?
2. What do you like about the procedures?
3. Discuss each finding and the reasons for the findings.
4. How could you adapt the author's procedures to a situation with which you are familiar?

THE SITUATION

The problem of how to teach secondary content to low reading achievers was periodically rearing its ugly head. To the reading coordinator, with a social studies background, and a reading "foreground," the problem offered a challenge.

The subject was tenth grade World Cultures. The 24 students were at the low end of the achievement scale. The class met five days a week just as did all other World Cultures classes. The word "reading" was not attached to their instruction and their teacher denied any suggestion of being anything other than a World Cultures teacher.

THE MATERIALS

The only materials used were those readily available to all other teachers. There were two texts available. The readability of one was about eighth grade and the other about ninth grade. Paperbacks on various countries, published by Scholastic Book Services, were available. Their readability was about sixth to seventh grade. Films, filmstrips, historical records, and tapes were used frequently.

* FROM the *Journal of Reading*, 14 (May 1971), pp. 599–561, reprinted with permission of Doris E. Stine and the International Reading Association.

PROCEDURE

We studied one country at a time. Our study of China serves as an example.

First, each student was asked to write down what he already knew about China, and then what he would like to know about China. We made several maps of China showing physical characteristics, land usage, industrial development, and population.

Most of the things they wanted to know were in the Scholastic books. I read them the information and taught them how to keep a brief outline of the chapters. At first I told them exactly what to write down—but I didn't fuss if they did not do it just right. Absence was high and I encouraged them to share their papers with the absentees. They were permitted to work together so that the faster ones could help the slower ones. All the work was done in class—no homework.

The librarian selected materials on China and sent them to us for several class periods—during which time reports were written. The reports were given to the class orally and tape recorded. The atmosphere was lax and sometimes noisy.

At the end of six weeks I tested with one item—"Write down everything you know about China." One student gave me seventy-five facts about China. No one gave me less than twenty. For every completed outline I gave an A. For every completed map I gave an A. The test grades ranged from C to A. Everybody got C or above on his report card—the only passing grade for many students during the marking period.

Students worked hard and seemed to learn much more than the facts they wrote down. I helped them with their problems and kicked them out when they prevented others from working. I invited them to my home to ride horses and a year later some of them still visit us.

FINDINGS

1. These students can and will learn many things about World Cultures.
2. They do not learn the same quantity or at the same depth that more able students learn.
3. They thrive on success since they have had very little of it.
4. Motivation and attendance is more of a problem than the reading level of materials.

SUGGESTIONS TO AID THE READING PROBLEM

1. Make questions very specific and tell them where to find the answers. (In the beginning tell them the chapter, the paragraph and the page.) Poor readers feel it is an impossible task when confronted with a whole chapter in which to find an answer.

2. Teach the vocabulary pertinent to your subject and any other vocabulary you discover they do not know; never be shocked at what they do not know.

3. Feed them some success—even if you consider it elementary—lowering standards, etc. You would quit too if you were fed constant dissatisfaction with your teaching.

4. Poor readers often have poor memories so just telling them won't do. They should *write down* what you expect them to remember and *they* should talk about it. I teach them to outline and by the *end* of the year they do a fair job.

5. Poor readers have difficulty thinking coherently. I require them to write down their thoughts in sentence form, to organize their thinking.

6. Tests often tell us what pupils do not know but often they do not tell us what they do know. I like to give a test like this: Write down in sentence form everything you have learned in the last six weeks—(I sometimes tell them in advance that this will be the test). Open-book tests are good for poor readers since they reinforce what they have been doing in class. These students do poorly on true-false questions.

7. This particular class did their best when given a dittoed outline of the chapter with questions to fill in (sentence answers). In the beginning of the year I read the chapter to them. That convinced them the answers were there and not too difficult to find. Later we had volunteer readers from the group. By the end of the year they did it well completely on their own reading. (If I had six classes to teach I would tape the chapter so my voice wouldn't play out.)

8. By the end of the year I could say, "Outline Chapter 6" and expect a fair job. But if I said, "Read Chapter 6 and we'll discuss it tomorrow," they knew nothing.

9. To keep the class from being dull, we used various media: tape recording the class in a general discussion; tape recording reports; listening to records; watching film-slides.

10. Students were permitted to work together and quiet talking was allowed. There was no seating arrangement.

11. All of these students passed World Cultures. Maybe you think I lowered the standards. I think my students learned something.

Black Studies and Paraprofessionals —A Prescription for Ailing Reading Programs in Urban Black Schools*

Ray C. Rist

There is no doubt that black children can learn to read and to make steady progress in reading. Heretofore, we have not always provided the kinds of learning milieus, methods, and materials that would foster this learning, although they are *now* available. In this excellent study Rist has demonstrated that his prescription for ailing reading programs in urban black schools does work. He has shown also that both deprivation and expectancy theories have a bearing on reading programs.

1. Explain the seriousness of the findings of the Coleman Report.

2. What is Deutsch's theoretical perspective? Explain it, please.

3. Explain the theoretical perspective of Kenneth Clark. What name is given to this theory?

4. Explain the methodology and curriculum of Rist's study.

5. How can the findings be explained?

For whatever the multiple of reasons, the majority of black youth attending urban schools are experiencing serious difficulty in mastering the traditional reading curriculum offered them. As has been dramatically documented by the Coleman Report (3), the black child progressively falls behind the white student in reading ability as well as in verbal and mathematical ability with each grade completed. The seriousness of the findings from the Coleman Report are evident in data collected on students who were in the twelfth grade at the time of the study. Black students in the northeast in non-metropolitan schools, for example, were found to be 5.2 years behind their white counterparts in verbal ability, 4.9 years behind in reading comprehension and 6.2 years behind in mathematical achievement. It should be noted that the gap between the two groups of students may have been even greater had all those students who had quit school also been included.

A number of social scientists have attempted to explain why it is the case that black children (and minority group children in general) fare so poorly in the present system of public education. A variety of theories has emerged. Though it is not the purpose of this paper to seek to substantiate any of the theories, it would be beneficial to examine two currently held

* from the *Journal of Reading*, 14 (May 1971), pp. 525–530; 583, reprinted with permission of Ray C. Rist and the International Reading Association.

theories as a backdrop against which to evaluate the research findings to be presented later in this paper.

The first of the two major theoretical perspectives finds its clearest expression in the works of Deutsch (4, 5), who argues that the nexus of the problem of the non-achievement of black children in urban schools is derived from their early years before formal education. This theoretical perspective is best known as "Deprivation Theory." Succinctly, Deutsch contends that because of insufficient stimulation in the early years of life ("input experiences"), there is a thwarting of normal development and a restriction in "output experiences." The lack of early intellectual and cultural stimulation, according to Deutsch, restricts the child's normal development, including the skills necessary for academic performance. From this theoretical position the rationale emerged for the development of Headstart programs. It must be noted that selective pre-school programs have reported an appreciable impact upon IQ scores, but such findings are not universal. The theory fails to point out specifically what experiences are crucial to the development of IQ; moreover, Headstart programs have not sustained long-term growth in the child. This effect, however, may be due less to the early approach than to the children's later experiences in school.

The second of the theoretical approaches had one of its earliest formulations in the writings of Kenneth Clark. Data from the HARYOU study (1) which Clark directed in Harlem indicate that the longer the black child remains in public schools in Harlem the lower his IQ score becomes. In a discussion of these findings, Clark (2) suggests the decrease is due to neither genetic nor environmental factors, but to teachers' expectations that the children will produce inferior work, resulting in the confirmation of a "self-fulfilling prophecy." Clark contends that educational achievement for the black child rests with the teacher's developing a strong expectation of high performance. The findings of Rosenthal and Jacobson (9) also indicate support for what may be termed the "Expectation Theory." Most recently, the findings of Rist (8) in a three-year longitudinal study of black children in an elementary school tend to substantiate the importance of teacher expectations. This study also indicates that student social class position is the most crucial variable in the teacher's development of differential expectations as to academic performance.

These theoretical approaches do not readily provide guidelines for the adequate transformation of theory into practice in innercity classrooms. The following data are presented as one attempt at the formulation of a method of teaching reading to black youngsters in junior high school, drawing strongly from both deprivation and expectation theory.

METHODOLOGY

During the 1968–69 academic year, two seventh grade classes were chosen at random in each of two East St. Louis, Illinois, junior high schools. The total number of students in these four classes numbered 127. During the entire academic year, the language arts period devoted to a "traditional" reading curriculum was suspended and the students were involved in the project reported in this paper. During the same period, a comparable control group randomly selected at the same two junior high schools engaged in the regular reading curriculum. All students in both groups, with one exception, were black. At the beginning and again at the end of the program, all students were administered the Stanford Diagnostic Reading Test.

THE CURRICULUM: BLACK STUDIES AND PARAPROFESSIONALS

The curriculum offered to the 127 students in the four experimental classes was based on two crucial factors: black studies and black paraprofessionals in the classroom at all times during the year. In this study, the concept of deprivation was applied to the academic curriculum of the junior high schools. An examination of the textbooks offered in the regular curriculum showed that black students were in fact being "deprived" of an adequate knowledge of their history and cultural development as these related to the United States and to developing nations. The black students were being offered a culture and history which ignored them at best and demeaned them at worst. So the regular textbooks were discarded and approximately 250 paperbacks (often four or five copies of each title) became the core of the curriculum, supplemented by records, newspapers from the black community, and frequent readings from black poetry and literature.

From an understanding of expectation theory, it was decided that performance expectations would have to be reinforced frequently and for a long duration. Thus, for the entire school year, thirty freshman and sophomore black students at Southern Illinois University's Experiment in Higher Education were hired under the federal Work-Study Program to serve the four classrooms as paraprofessionals. The university students constantly showed the seventh grade students that they held high expectations for their reading performance. Each of the university students was assigned to two seventh grade students in two different classrooms. The university students were deliberately "non-directive," allowing the seventh graders to make decisions on what material to read and at what pace. The only requirement placed on the students was to write three pages per week in their "diary." (6) All grades during the year were decided upon jointly by the university student and seventh grader with the director mediating "deadlocked negotiations."

FINDINGS

The Stanford Diagnostic Reading Test was administered to all students in both experimental and control groups during the last week in September, 1968, and again at the end of school in June, 1969. This test was used as the principal measure of reading skills improvement. The students were evaluated in the following three areas:

1. Inferential meaning, which assesses the ability of the student to understand the general meaning of the paragraph.
2. Literal word meaning, which tests the ability of the student to use words in varying contexts.
3. Vocabulary, which measures the scope of the student's recognition of words.

Two types of statistical analysis were conducted. In the first (Tables 1 and 2), each group was compared internally with itself over time to determine if there had been improvement during the nine months of the program. The second set of statistical measures (Table 3) sought to compare differences in achievement between the experimental and control groups.

A test for significant difference between pre-, and post-test administrations within the experimental group showed the following results.

TABLE 1
Difference Between Pre- and Post-test
Administrations Experimental Group

	t VALUE	SIGNIFICANCE
Inferential	28.65	p < .001
Literal	27.50	p < .001
Vocabulary	12.20	p < .001

All significant differences reflect greater skills at the end of the program than at the beginning.

Testing for significant differences between the pre- and post-test administration within the control group revealed the following:

TABLE 2
Difference Between Pre- and Post-test
Administrations Control Group

	t VALUE	SIGNIFICANCE
Inferential	3.7	p < .05
Literal	2.2	not significant
Vocabulary	3.7	p < .05

Two of these tests show improvement, but the level of significance is much lower than is the case with the experimental group.

The tests for significant differences in improvement between the experimental group and the control group all favored the experimental group:

TABLE 3
*Differences in Improvement Between the
Experimental Group and the Control
Group*

	t VALUE	SIGNIFICANCE
Inferential	24.7	$p < .001$
Literal	21.9	$p < .001$
Vocabulary	42.2	$p < .001$

The Stanford also provided the average reading levels for the two groups. The average grade score of the experimental group in September, 1968, was 4.3. For the seventh graders in the control group, the average grade score was 4.8. When the students in the two groups were again measured in June, the average reading level of the experimental group was 7.7, an increase of 3.4 years within nine months. For the control group, the average grade score increased to 5.4, an increase of six months within the nine-month period. The control group experienced what may be termed a "regress phenomenon," actually falling behind what would have been expected of them during the period. This regression supports the findings of the Coleman Report where a nation-wide slippage by black students through the various grades is documented. The students in the experimental group, on the other hand, not only overcame the seemingly inevitable regression of reading level but in fact made substantial gains toward their expected reading skill development (8.0) by the end of the school year.

A New Formula for Success?

The findings from this study must, of course, be considered tentative for they are based on one study done in one city during one school year. Nevertheless, they do offer the basis for further research and study, not on merely pragmatic grounds but also within a theoretical framework. The findings suggest that both the deprivation and expectation theories provide important insights that can be transmitted into practice within urban black classrooms.

It has not been possible within this study to document the effects of the two major variables independently; that is of black studies material and paraprofessionals. Both were simultaneously in use throughout the length of the program. The literature to date appears quite scanty as to empirical verification of the benefits of black studies material with black children. It can only at this point be assumed that such material has a "high interest" saliency for the students which appears to be necessary for the success of any reading program. As for the utilization of paraprofessionals within the classrooms, Riessman and Gartner (7) surveyed the bulk of the literature of this topic and concluded, ". . . the illustrations presented here, representative of many others, indicate that aides can have an impact upon pupil learning and that their continued use and further training may have an even more powerful effect." The data from the present study suggest that the combination of black studies material with the continual use of paraprofessionals may provide the necessary ingredients for the formulation of a successful reading program with black studies in urban schools. As is often the case with social science research, one seldom finds significant findings which support one theoretical position to the exclusion of another, but rather what emerges is an eclectic position drawing strength from both.

REFERENCES

1. Clark, K. *Youth in the Ghetto: A Study of the Consequences of Powerlessness and a Blueprint for Change.* New York: Harlem Youth Opportunities Unlimited, Inc., 1964.
2. ———. *Dark Ghetto.* New York: Harper & Row, 1965.
3. Coleman, J. *Equality of Educational Opportunity.* U.S. Department of Health, Education and Welfare. U.S. Government Printing Office, Washington, D.C., 1966.
4. Deutsch, M. "The Disadvantaged Child and the Learning Process." In *Education in Depressed Areas,* ed. by A. H. Passow. New York: Teachers College Press, 1963.
5. ———. *The Disadvantaged Child.* New York: Basic Books, Inc., 1967.
6. Fader, D., and E. McNeil. *Hooked on Books: Program and Proof.* New York: Berkley, 1968.
7. Riessman, F., and A. Gartner. "Paraprofessionals: The Effect on Children's Learning," *The Urban Review,* 4(2) (1969), 21–22.
8. Rist, R. "Student Social Class and Teacher Expectations: The Self-Fulfilling Prophecy in Ghetto Education." *Harvard Educational Review,* 40(3) (1970), 411–51.
9. Rosenthal, R., and L. Jacobson. *Pygmalion in the Classroom.* New York: Holt, Rinehart and Winston, 1968.

Adult Basic Education: Some Spin-Off for Culturally Deprived Youth Education*
Edwin H. Smith

Pay attention to curriculum. Some of the better Adult Basic Education (ABE) programs have done just that. The results of attending to curriculum are so positive that middle schools and secondary schools would do well to study successful ABE programs. Then they should modify their own programs in terms of the key practices that exemplify these better ABE programs. In this article Smith carefully delineates these key practices.

1. What has been wrong with many of the poverty schools?
2. What are some of the basic assumptions in the modern ABE curriculum?
3. How can one characterize ABE programs that fail?
4. What are the characteristics of successful ABE programs?
5. Why did the Camilla program succeed?
6. Why did the Tallahassee program succeed?
7. How did the Okeechobee program adapt to the students' needs?

The term "inner city schools" in many Northern and border cities is synonomous with black, segregated, poverty schools. In much of the South it is likely to be associated with a poverty mixture of black and white. In both sections abundant funds for curriculum development and innovation have been available from Federal funding. However, the total educational impact of Federal funding may be questioned.

In many, if not most, of the poverty schools the children, with their special needs ignored, are presented with the traditional program. Such programs are for teachers and not for learners with the special problems associated with poverty. For a time the children tend to suffer cooperatively with their teachers as the teachers pretend to teach and the students pretend to learn. After the first three years both groups tend to give up the pretense with the students sweating out time and the teachers sweating out pay checks. The students, particularly the boys, tend to be unable to read the textbooks assigned to them and the teachers tend to be unable to teach the students to read at a level near the students' potential. Many of the children become school discipline problems. Frustrated, and operat-

* from *Adult Leadership*, 19 (February 1971), pp. 269–270, 275, reprinted with permission of Edwin H. Smith and the Adult Education Association of the U.S.A.

ing several years below their capacities in the basic skills, they go on to junior and senior high schools where they are faced with a curriculum that is ridiculous and impossible for them. Many drop out while others "play the game" for four years and then graduate as functional illiterates. Some are exposed to further teacher programs in correctional institutions where another educational facet of society often gives them more of the same. In the whole process the student alone is held accountable. The student is punished for not learning, but the administrators and teachers are rewarded for "keeping school." And still the special funding goes on without sufficient attention to curriculum. Perhaps a look at the adult basic education curriculum will provide some ideas about what a remedial curriculum should be for those that the elementary schools failed to teach and for those who are punished in the secondary schools because the teachers did not know how to teach them.

Evolution of ABE

Adult Basic Education, as a curriculum, evolved from the old literacy and Americanization Education during the 1960's (4). During the period America became concerned with its own sick, disabled, and underprivileged. Poverty was recognized as a fault of the social system rather than as a form of punishment for those unable to adequately cope with the system (6). The old literacy education was predicated on the assumption that if a person learned to read and do arithmetic he could advance himself. The fallacy of this assumption in a period of rapid social and technological change became more and more apparent. It was recognized that in order to cope on a minimal level with the present social and employment conditions a person needed literacy education plus a basic core of concepts and information necessary for upward mobility. This core includes orientation to the world of work, health practices, consumer education, fundamental social science concepts, fundamental science concepts, citizen rights and responsibilities, and personal-social development. The curriculum is designed to meet as much as possible the students' immediate needs and it recognizes that attitude change is vital to their success.

While ABE is still not properly implemented in most systems, it is apparent that ABE programs are more appropriate than the old literacy programs and it is the trend in adult education today.

The ABE curriculum assumes that most of the information which has been learned in the first seven years of school has been forgotten and that which is important and useful has been retained. Much of the retained is appropriate content for the ABE program if it is modified and presented in the light of adult needs and responsibilities. It is also assumed that learning the adult relevant skills and content can be done in a far shorter space than seven years. If this is true then why wait until the students are adults to offer them remediation?

Disadvantaged black children differ considerably from middle class black and white children. They often speak a dialect which interferes with the decoding and processing of written words (1). They lack readiness for the initial reading tasks and as a group they fall further and further behind as they go through the typical elementary grade program. By the middle grades their failure to develop such learning tools as reading, their confusion about the meaningfulness of the subject matter curriculum, and their often increasing need to fend for themselves in their neighborhood has turned them off. If they were adults and free to do so, many would, as Adult Education students often do, walk out on the whole set up and the poverty schools would close down. Perhaps we can learn from the Adult Basic Education programs which succeed.

PROGRAMS: SUCCESSES AND FAILURES

Adult Basic Education programs that fail tend to be: textbook oriented, time block centered, formal, future oriented, group centered, and negative behavioral modification oriented. Adult Basic Education programs that succeed tend to use the learning laboratory concept (5), utilize flexible time blocks, are informal, attempt to capitalize on students' perceived needs, utilize different approaches for different students, and utilize positive behavioral modification techniques to build feelings of self worth. Since most ABE students have been manufactured by the types of programs that made them, and since they reject those same programs as adults it might be well to consider taking the aspects of successful ABE programs and incorporating them into the curriculum for underachieving, disadvantaged middle grade and secondary students.

For many years educators have been saying that classrooms should be laboratories for learning and that much of the learning should take place in an individualized situation. In some few elementary schools the learning laboratory concept is applied. But it is reported as the principal approach to skills and information instruction in the best ABE programs in Florida, New York, Georgia, and other states according to the state supervisors of adult basic education. If such an approach works with such school systems' second attempts then perhaps it would work on the first attempt in the upper elementary grades. With this in mind, pilot programs were tried out in Camilla, Georgia, and Tallahassee, Florida. In grades four, five, and six time modules were discarded. The classes were stocked with selected materials developed for adult basic education and Job Corps materials. Instruction was individualized and subject matter was selected for its interest and immediate utility to the students. Discipline was largely student controlled and the teacher's role became that of diagnostician, prescriber, and leader. The children became interested in the world of work, real health problems, real social problems, and the practical world beyond Camilla and Tallahassee. The use of the ABE materials was ego-supporting and of great interest to most of the children who had already failed (by sixth grade the average reading ability was 3.0) in children's materials. By the end of the first year in Camilla the children had more than doubled their rate of reading growth in grades four and five and had increased it by fifty percent in grade six. Among the things that most of the children didn't learn that year were the capitals of the fifty states, the counties of Georgia, and the life style of the Eskimos.

The Tallahassee program was put into effect last September in the Lincoln Elementary School. The new principal, Mr. Murphy, recognized the disastrous results of the traditional program where the average sixth grade "graduate" had a reading level of grade 3.2. He asked for aid in changing the curriculum. Again as in Camilla, but making even more sweeping changes, a modified ABE program was instituted in grades four, five, and six. The traditional program was thrown out (the children never learned about LaSalle or the importance of the Tigris and Euphrates!), and the classes were organized as learning laboratories. Strong supervision was given and the teachers, a couple reluctantly, had to cooperate. Attendance went up. The number of lunches supplied went up, and many of the children's heads went up. At the end of two months two sixth grade classes had gained an average of over a year in reading ability and six non-readers were reading on a third grade level. Three fifth grade classes gained two-thirds of a year in reading, and two fourth grade classes gained a year and a quarter. One sixth grade class made little progress and one fourth grade class made little progress. In both cases the teachers opposed the program. In December the courts ordered a teacher transfer and with it came the collapse of the program.

Encouraged by the results with the elementary schools the program, again modified, was put into effect in the boys' correctional institution in Okeechobee, Florida. At approximately the same time a Guided Group Interaction therapy program was also begun. Under the plan used, the adolescents were formed into groups which lived in the same cottages, worked together, went to school together, attempted to solve personal and social problems together, and acted as self-disciplinary units (3).

The educational program in the correctional institutions had been a gross failure for many years. It consisted of more of the same curriculum that had failed with these adolescents in the public schools. Interviews with the students indicated that they thought the schooling was a waste of time. Very few students had earned high school credits and the program was set up as though the students came into the institutions in September and left in June. Most students were retarded in reading three or more years.

The programs were reorganized into what was essentially an adult basic education curriculum program and into a program designed to meet the competencies demanded for a high school equivalency diploma.

Several learning laboratories were devised and individually prescribed instruction, utilizing flexible time modules, was utilized for skills and information learning. Heterogeneous groupings was used for facilitating attitude change, concept and information application, oral language development, and expansion of experiential backgrounds.

The philosophy behind the communicative skills aspect of the program was that the learning of content should accompany the development of the communicative skills. Much of the content was already incorporated in materials designed for adult basic education. It included such areas as occupational orientation, law for the layman, government services, consumer education, basic health practices, basic social studies concepts, personal and social development, and basic communication skills training. Within a month after the installation of the program there was a noticeable change in attitude of both students and teachers. Runaway incidents declined and self discipline improved.

The academic effectiveness of the institutional program has not as yet been formally tested but runaways have dropped from 80 a month to five, vandalism decreased drastically, and the teachers report a great increase in interest and efforts to learn in school. How much of this is due to the new educational program or due to the guided interaction program or to the relating of the two programs has not been determined.

These pilot programs indicate that successful educational programs for disadvantaged adults should be examined for spin-off value to intermediate and secondary level disadvantaged students. A study is needed to determine similarities and differences in the psychological and social needs of disadvantaged adults with whom the educational system has failed and with older children with whom the educational system has failed.

REFERENCES

1. Baratz, Joan C., and Shuy, Roger W. (Eds.) *Teaching Black Children to Read.* Washington, D.C.: Center for Applied Linguistics, 1969.
2. Bloom, Benjamin S., Davis, Allison, and Hess, Robert. *Compensatory Education for Cultural Deprivation.* New York: Holt, Rinehart, and Winston, Inc., 1965.
3. Pohill, Leon. *A Model for Rehabilitative Education for Children in Juvenile Correctional Institutions.* Tallahassee, Florida, Division of Youth Services, 1970.
4. Smith, Edwin H. *Literacy Education for Adolescents and Adults.* San Francisco: Boyd and Fraser Publishing Co., 1970.
5. Sourifan, Vivian (Ed.) *Guidelines for ABE Learning Centers.* Trenton, New Jersey: State Department of Education, 1970.
6. Ulmer, Curtis. *Teaching the Disadvantaged Adult.* Atlanta, Georgia: State Department of Education, 1968.